U.S. Foreign Policy

U.S. Foreign Policy

Steven W. Hook
Kent State University

THE PARADOX OF WORLD POWER

Policy

Third Edition

CQ PRESS

A Division of SAGE
Washington, D.C.

CQ Press
2300 N Street, NW, Suite 800
Washington, DC 20037

Phone: 202-729-1900; toll-free, 1-866-4CQ-PRESS (1-866-427-7737)

Web: www.cqpress.com

Cover design: designfarm
Typesetting: C&M Digitals (P) Ltd.

♾ The paper used in this publication exceeds the requirements of the American National
Standard for Information Sciences—Permanence of Paper for Printed Library Materials,
ANSI Z39.48-1992.

Printed and bound in the United States of America

14 13 12 11 10   1 2 3 4 5

Library of Congress Cataloging-in-Publication Data

Hook, Steven W.
    U.S. foreign policy : the paradox of world power / Steven W. Hook. — 3rd ed.
        p. cm.
    Includes bibliographical references and index.
    ISBN 978-1-60426-609-2 (pbk. : alk. paper) 1. United States—Foreign relations.
2. United States—Foreign relations—21st century. 3. United States—Foreign relations—
Decision making. 4. Balance of power. I. Title. II. Title: United States foreign policy.

    E183.7.H66 2010
    327.73—dc22   2010019834

*To Debra-Lynn, Benjamin,
Emily, and Christopher*

Brief Contents

Contents

PART I   The Setting of U.S. Foreign Policy

PART III Outside-In: External Sources of Foreign Policy

PART IV Policy Domains

Figures and Tables

Figures

Tables

Boxes

In Their Own Words

Point/Counterpoint

Maps

(See color map insert following the preface)

Preface

The United States stands today as the preeminent world power. It is also an embattled and increasingly exhausted power, confronting both the limits of its domestic resources and mounting external challenges. How U.S. foreign policy makers respond to the many challenges facing them will dictate the course of the twenty-first century—not just for the United States but for all states and societies.

The first decade of the millennium proved withering for American leaders, who endured the terrorist attacks of September 11, 2001, launched protracted wars in Afghanistan and Iraq, and ended the decade engulfed in a financial crisis that fractured the global economy. When George W. Bush turned over the presidency to Barack Obama in January 2009, the federal government was preoccupied with damage control, its options narrowing daily in the face of spiraling budget deficits, rising unemployment, and gravely weakened financial institutions. The nation's global primacy, a centerpiece of its post–Cold War grand strategy, could no longer be assumed.

The Bush years, defined by the 9/11 attacks and subsequent foreign policy responses, witnessed a steady erosion of American power and prestige. The war in Iraq revealed gaping holes in U.S. intelligence, military doctrine, and defense planning. The overthrow of Saddam Hussein, without the sanction of the UN Security Council, strained U.S. diplomatic relations with key allies and the world body. This resentment was compounded by U.S. opposition, virtually alone among major powers, to global treaties on climate change, biodiversity, the testing of nuclear weapons, arms trafficking, land mines, and the International Criminal Court. The global spillover effect of the 2008 financial crisis further fueled anti-American sentiments.

The estrangement of the United States from the international community did not begin with Bush's arrival in the White House in January 2001. Rather, it began a decade earlier, with the collapse of the Soviet Union. After the United States became the world's lone superpower, its leaders could not agree on what purpose the nation's hard-won primacy should serve. Although President Bill Clinton adopted global "engagement" as a grand strategy, the Republican-controlled Congress slashed international programs and rejected a variety of treaties and commitments. This impasse prevented the restructuring of U.S. foreign policy institutions to reflect the changes of the post–Cold War era. Liberals and conservatives in Congress, rather than seeking common ground at this epochal moment in world history, turned against each other in pursuit of partisan advantage.

In the divisive political climate of the 1990s, many Americans felt cynical toward their own government and were uninterested in world affairs. They registered little concern as ethnic conflicts erupted around the world, scientific evidence revealed the extent of global warming, and the AIDS epidemic swept across developing nations. Media coverage and the public's attention were fixed not on the upheavals overseas, but on the O.J. Simpson murder trial. Meanwhile, Congress shut down the federal government twice in 1995 after failing to resolve a budget standoff with the White House, and then it consumed itself with the 1998 impeachment of Clinton over issues stemming from his affair with a White House intern.

The United States, in short, lost its way at the very time its self-proclaimed mission to re-create the global order in its image appeared within reach. Amid the domestic upheavals just noted, the forces of democratization, multilateral cooperation, and economic globalization—promoted so vigorously by U.S. leaders at the dawn of the "American century"—suddenly seemed threatening to the nation's sovereignty and vitality. Government officials felt trapped by UN peacekeeping missions, a proposed international criminal court, and global treaties to restrict fossil fuel emissions and ban the testing of nuclear weapons. Washington's hostility extended to the growing array of nongovernmental organizations (NGOs) around the world, many of them empowered by U.S.-style political reforms and mobilized through the Internet. At the same time, many foreign firms and governments reaped the benefits of globalization at America's expense, a predictable if not inevitable consequence of market-based economic development along the lines long promoted by the United States.

These developments reveal a paradox in the U.S. experience as a world power: the very sources of strength for the United States during its steady growth—a deeply ingrained sense of national exceptionalism, the diffusion of foreign policy powers, the free rein granted to civil society, and the promotion of free markets domestically and globally—have increasingly become sources of vulnerability as well. The decentralized and highly constrained federal government, deeply penetrated by civil society and largely unchanged since its creation more than two centuries ago, cannot effectively manage the dynamic world order that, to a considerable extent, is of its making. In this sense, the United States is a victim, as well as a beneficiary, of its own success.

This lesson is clearly evident in recent events. The near collapse of the U.S. financial system could be seen as a logical extension of the nation's *laissez-faire* economic system that discouraged regulation while encouraging (and rewarding) reckless speculation and lending practices. The deep recession that greeted President Obama upon his arrival to the White House forced him to focus on domestic recovery. Though essential for national recovery, this effort stymied Obama's ability to exploit his stature as a global leader and to establish a clear new direction for U.S. foreign policy. Beyond expanding the U.S. troop presence in Afghanistan, the president launched no major foreign policy initiatives in his first year. He also faced a toxic political climate at home, with a highly polarized Congress entrenched in bitter and disabling partisan conflict. Obama's second year was also plagued by a domestic crisis, this time involving a protracted oil spill in the Gulf of Mexico that devastated the coastal region. As with the financial meltdown, this tragedy was largely self-inflicted, the result of lax environmental standards and undue corporate influence over offshore drilling policies.

The paradox also applies to fateful decisions on war and peace. American leaders have maintained a "separate peace" with other industrialized democracies, while engaging in recurring conflicts against authoritarian regimes. As international relations theorist Michael Doyle observed more than a quarter of a century ago, *"The very constitutional restraint, shared commercial interests, and international respect for individual rights that promote peace among liberal societies can exacerbate conflicts in relations between liberal and nonliberal societies."*[1] This problem is compounded by the double standards commonly adopted by U.S. leaders, who preach the gospel of democratic reform while tolerating repression in strategically vital countries such as Saudi Arabia and China.

My primary objective in writing and revising this book is to explore this paradox of U.S. world power, to identify its key sources and manifestations, and to consider its future implications. Because of the sheer magnitude of U.S. military might, economic wealth, and political and cultural influence, the choices of U.S. foreign policy makers resonate in all corners of the world. Those choices, however, are made within a domestic institutional setting that is purposefully fragmented and conflicted. The coherence of U.S. policy choices is impaired further by transnational civil society—including corporations, nonprofit interest groups, the news media, and global public opinion—that are part of the U.S. foreign policy process as never before.

Because the contradictions and dilemmas inherent to U.S. foreign policy are woven into the nation's culture and institutional structure, they are unlikely to be overcome anytime soon. The stakes in the policy process, however, will remain enormous. If this book helps its readers make sense of these cascading developments, and if readers are better able to grasp the link between the process and the conduct of U.S. foreign policy, then the book will have achieved its main purpose.

My secondary goal for this book is to present a clear, concise, yet comprehensive overview of the U.S. foreign policy process to students at all levels. Instructors deserve a text that meets their pedagogical needs. Their students deserve a text that is tightly organized, limited in its use of jargon, visually appealing, and even pleasurable to read. No account of U.S. foreign policy will have its intended effect if its readers are lost in translation.

To this end, the twelve chapters that follow are organized into four parts— each with three chapters and each of roughly equal length—that cover distinct

---

1. Michael Doyle, "Kant, Liberal Legacies, and Foreign Affairs, Part 2," *Philosophy and Public Affairs* 12 (autumn 1983): 324–325 (emphasis in original).

aspects of U.S. foreign policy. Part I introduces the book's theme, briefly reviews key historical developments and milestones, and identifies theories of foreign policy analysis that shed light on the decision-making process. This latter material, found in Chapter 3, forms the analytic core of the book. Parts II and III identify the roles played in this process by state and nonstate actors, respectively. In this edition, greater attention is paid to the impact of domestic and international law, intelligence breakdowns and reforms, the "new media," and the demographics of public opinion. Part IV highlights the three primary domains of foreign policy: national security and defense, economic relations, and the management of transnational problems. The timing of this new edition permits final assessments of the Bush presidency and its foreign policies that are detailed in these chapters. The last chapter, after reviewing transnational policy issues, also considers the prospects for continued U.S. primacy and world power in the Obama era. All the chapters have been updated thoroughly in terms of both the scholarly literature and coverage of recent developments on U.S. foreign policy.

This analytic framework was designed to facilitate instruction in several ways. The symmetrical structure of the volume lends itself to break points and examinations at regular intervals. Visual aids—full-color maps, photographs, figures, and tables—enliven the text and reinforce its key lessons. The boxed features—Point/Counterpoint and In Their Own Words—summarize ongoing debates and provide insightful perspectives on the policy process. The comprehensive list of references not only identifies scholarly works in areas covered by the text, but also directs readers to the vast supporting literature on U.S. foreign policy, which is useful in informing research papers and subsequent study. The selected Internet references (links) that appear at the end of each chapter are another useful resource for students. Finally, the glossary at the back of the book defines the key concepts introduced in bold type throughout the text. It is preceded by two appendixes that list U.S. administrations since World War II and provide the text of the War Powers Resolution of 1973, respectively.

Students and instructors also benefit from a variety of ancillary resources. A companion Web site, available at **www.cqpress.com/cs/hook**, provides chapter summaries, interactive practice quizzes, exercises to promote active learning, and annotated hyperlinks to a wealth of online resources. I invite instructors to use the PowerPoint slides, the electronic versions of the graphics appearing in the book, and the test banks covering each of the chapters. These materials can be downloaded by adopters from the CQ Press Web site (http://college.cqpress.com/instructors-resources/hook).

As noted earlier, the paradox outlined in this book is ultimately based on the strengths that enabled the United States to gain predominance in world politics and serve so often as a catalyst for democratic reforms and improved living standards beyond its shores. For all its faults, the United States is a resilient world power whose checks and balances hold decision makers accountable—however sluggishly—for their policy excesses and setbacks. This resilience is also demonstrated by recent survey evidence that the United States, despite its many difficulties during the past decade, maintains a deep reservoir of goodwill overseas.

According to an April 2010 BBC poll, "Views of the USA are now positive in most countries around the world for the first time since tracking began" in 2005.[2]

Much of this goodwill could be attributed to President Obama, who received the Nobel Peace Prize in December 2009 on the basis of widespread optimism that he would renew U.S. membership in the global community. In this sense the award, along with the U.S. government's rising approval ratings overseas, was prospective in nature, looking forward to future U.S. foreign policies informed as much by moral principles and a sense of shared purpose as by considerations of power and primacy. This revived stature, however, will impose constant demands on U.S. leaders, who must reconcile America's many strengths with the limitations of its world power as described in the chapters to follow. Grasping these conflicting influences, and the balance between them, is the challenge posed to the readers of this book.

Acknowledgments

This third edition, like the first two, draws on the talents and hard work of a large supporting cast. I am grateful to the entire editorial team at CQ Press for making this revision not only manageable, but also highly enjoyable. As always, Brenda Carter, head of CQ's college division, fully supported the project. Charisse Kiino again provided the necessary leadership and resources to see the revision through, Elise Frasier kept the project and its many moving parts on schedule, and Gwenda Larsen skillfully guided the manuscript through production. Amy Marks, my copy editor, made sense of my often tortured prose, called out contradictions within and across chapters, and offered valuable suggestions for updates in response to developments within the Washington Beltway and overseas. In Kent, my research assistant Franklin Lebo proved indispensable as he guided my literature review, gathered the data featured in the tables and figures, proofread early chapter drafts, revised ancillary materials, and tamed "the Beast," our affectionate term for the lengthy references that follow the main text. And, I thank Tameaka Morris, who also provided research assistance.

Many reviewers provided much-needed criticism at various stages of the project. They include Clair Apodaca, Florida International University; William David Frost; Lionel Ingram, University of New Hampshire; John Masker, Temple University; John Quintus, University of Delaware; Steven Rothman, Ritsumeikan Asia Pacific University; Donald Schaefer, Lane College; Yohanes Sulaiman, Indonesia Defense University, and one anonymous reviewer. Their suggestions, some of which called for substantial restructuring and streamlining, were consistently on target. I am also grateful to my students, near and far, who have freely offered their comments about the text either in the classroom or via shook@kent.edu. Any deficiencies in the volume stem from my own inability to heed their collective guidance.

---

2. BBC World Service, "Global Views of United States Improve while Other Countries Decline," April 18, 2010, http://news.bbc.co.uk/2/shared/bsp/hi/pdfs/160410bbcwspoll.pdf.

Map 1 Nineteenth-Century European Empires and U.S. Continental Expansion

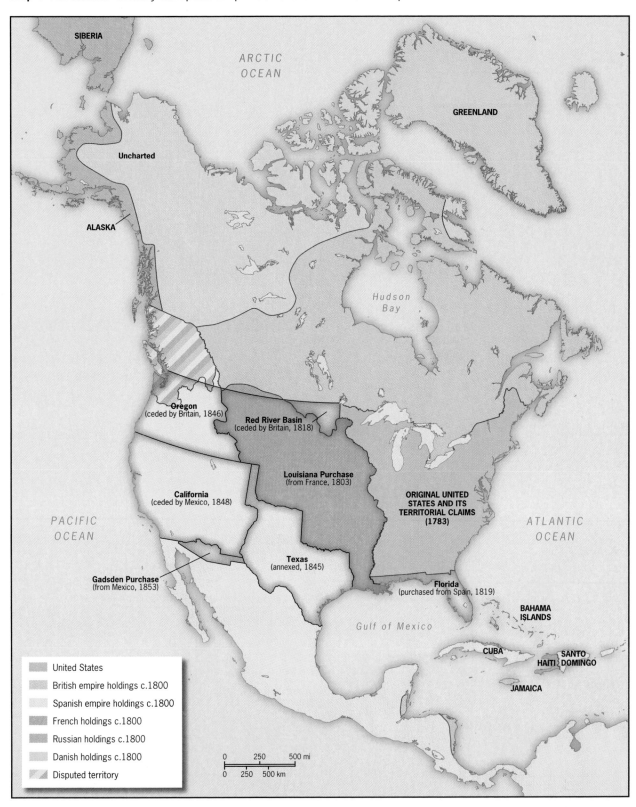

SIBERIA

ARCTIC
OCEAN

GREENLAND

Uncharted

ALASKA

*Hudson
Bay*

Oregon
(ceded by Britain, 1846)

Red River Basin
(ceded by Britain, 1818)

Louisiana Purchase
(from France, 1803)

California
(ceded by Mexico, 1848)

ORIGINAL UNITED
STATES AND ITS
TERRITORIAL CLAIMS
(1783)

PACIFIC
OCEAN

ATLANTIC
OCEAN

Gadsden Purchase
(from Mexico, 1853)

Texas
(annexed, 1845)

Florida
(purchased from Spain, 1819)

BAHAMA
ISLANDS

Gulf of Mexico

CUBA

SANTO
DOMINGO

HAITI

JAMAICA

United States

British empire holdings c.1800

Spanish empire holdings c.1800

French holdings c.1800

Russian holdings c.1800

Danish holdings c.1800

Disputed territory

| 0 | 250 | 500 mi |
| 0 | 250 | 500 km |

Map 2 Cold War Division of Europe

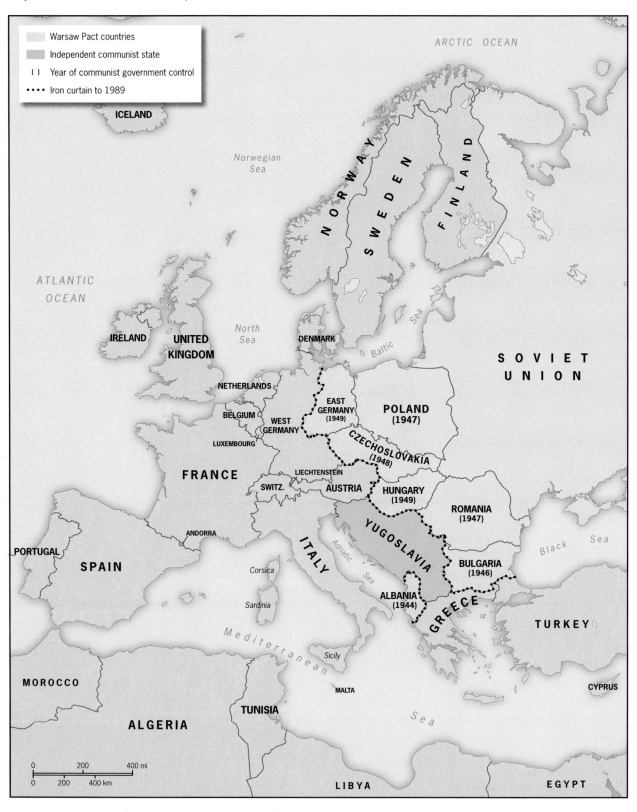

Legend:
- Warsaw Pact countries
- Independent communist state
- ( ) Year of communist government control
- •••• Iron curtain to 1989

ARCTIC OCEAN

ICELAND

Norwegian Sea

N O R W A Y

S W E D E N

F I N L A N D

ATLANTIC OCEAN

IRELAND

UNITED KINGDOM

North Sea

DENMARK

Baltic Sea

S O V I E T U N I O N

NETHERLANDS

BELGIUM

WEST GERMANY

EAST GERMANY (1949)

POLAND (1947)

LUXEMBOURG

CZECHOSLOVAKIA (1948)

FRANCE

LIECHTENSTEIN

SWITZ.

AUSTRIA

HUNGARY (1949)

ROMANIA (1947)

ANDORRA

ITALY

Adriatic Sea

YUGOSLAVIA

BULGARIA (1946)

Black Sea

PORTUGAL

SPAIN

Corsica

Sardinia

ALBANIA (1944)

GREECE

TURKEY

Mediterranean

Sicily

MALTA

CYPRUS

MOROCCO

TUNISIA

Sea

ALGERIA

LIBYA

EGYPT

0 200 400 mi

0 200 400 km

Map 3 Cold War Alliances with the United States

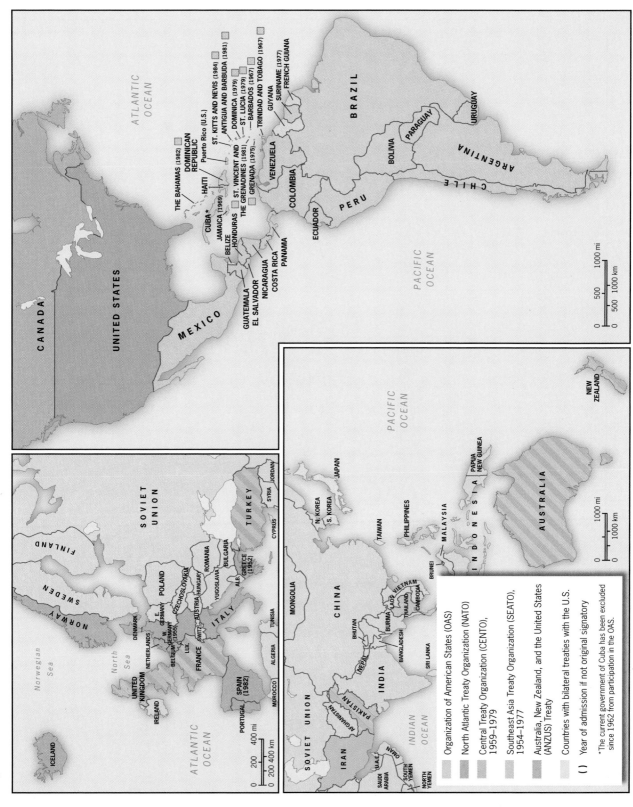

Organization of American States (OAS)

North Atlantic Treaty Organization (NATO)

Central Treaty Organization (CENTO), 1959–1979

Southeast Asia Treaty Organization (SEATO), 1954–1977

Australia, New Zealand, and the United States (ANZUS) Treaty

Countries with bilateral treaties with the U.S.

( ) Year of admission if not original signatory

*The current government of Cuba has been excluded since 1962 from participation in the OAS.

Map 4 Post–Cold War U.S. Military Operations

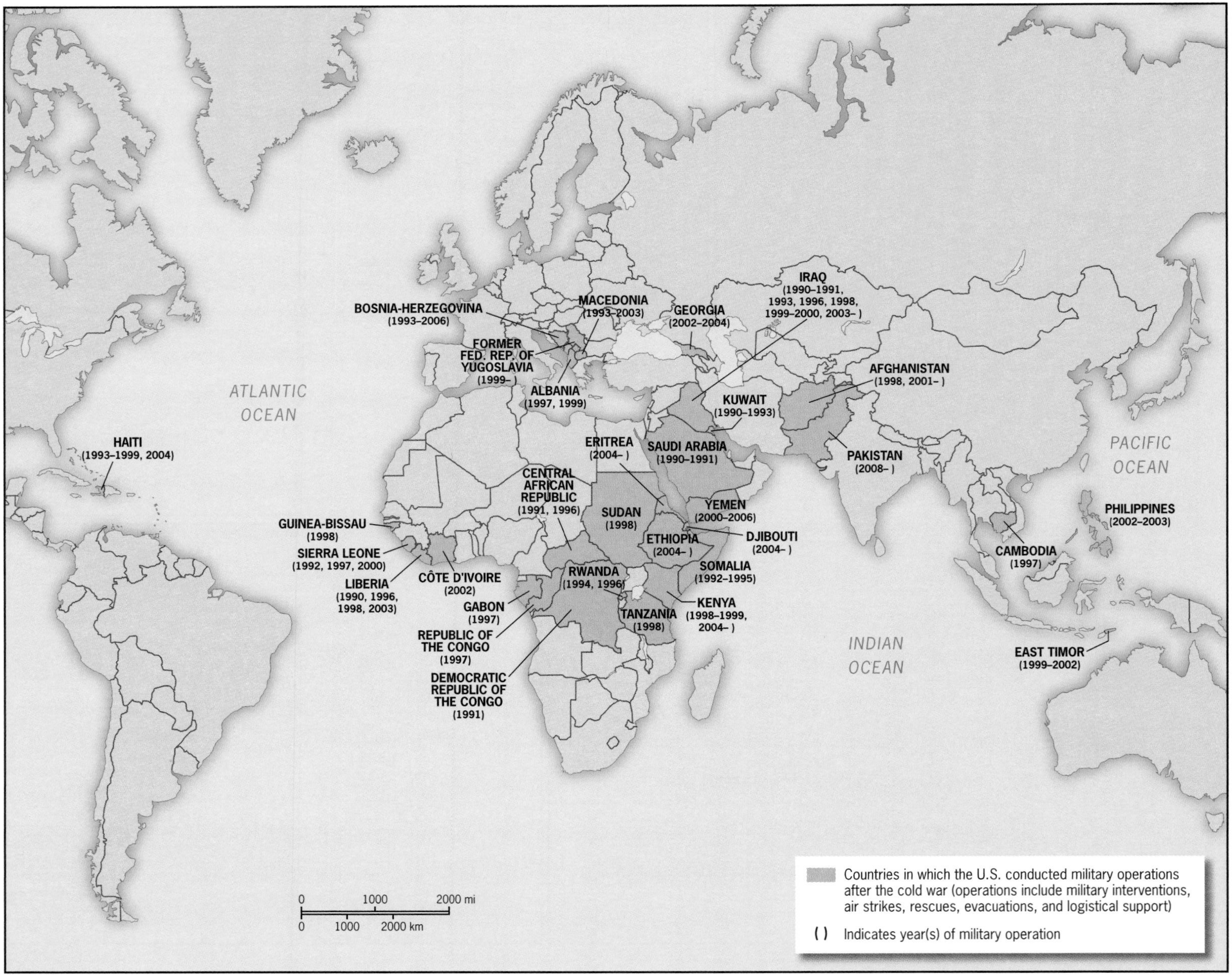

ATLANTIC OCEAN

PACIFIC OCEAN

INDIAN OCEAN

HAITI (1993–1999, 2004)

BOSNIA–HERZEGOVINA (1993–2006)

FORMER FED. REP. OF YUGOSLAVIA (1999–)

MACEDONIA (1993–2003)

ALBANIA (1997, 1999)

GEORGIA (2002–2004)

IRAQ (1990–1991, 1993, 1996, 1998, 1999–2000, 2003–)

AFGHANISTAN (1998, 2001–)

PAKISTAN (2008–)

KUWAIT (1990–1993)

SAUDI ARABIA (1990–1991)

YEMEN (2000–2006)

DJIBOUTI (2004–)

ETHIOPIA (2004–)

SOMALIA (1992–1995)

KENYA (1998–1999, 2004–)

TANZANIA (1998)

ERITREA (2004–)

SUDAN (1998)

RWANDA (1994, 1996)

CENTRAL AFRICAN REPUBLIC (1991, 1996)

GUINEA-BISSAU (1998)

SIERRA LEONE (1992, 1997, 2000)

LIBERIA (1990, 1996, 1998, 2003)

CÔTE D'IVOIRE (2002)

GABON (1997)

REPUBLIC OF THE CONGO (1997)

DEMOCRATIC REPUBLIC OF THE CONGO (1991)

CAMBODIA (1997)

PHILIPPINES (2002–2003)

EAST TIMOR (1999–2002)

Countries in which the U.S. conducted military operations after the cold war (operations include military interventions, air strikes, rescues, evacuations, and logistical support)

( ) Indicates year(s) of military operation

0   1000   2000 mi

0   1000   2000 km

Map 5 Major Ongoing Conflicts in the Middle East and South Asia

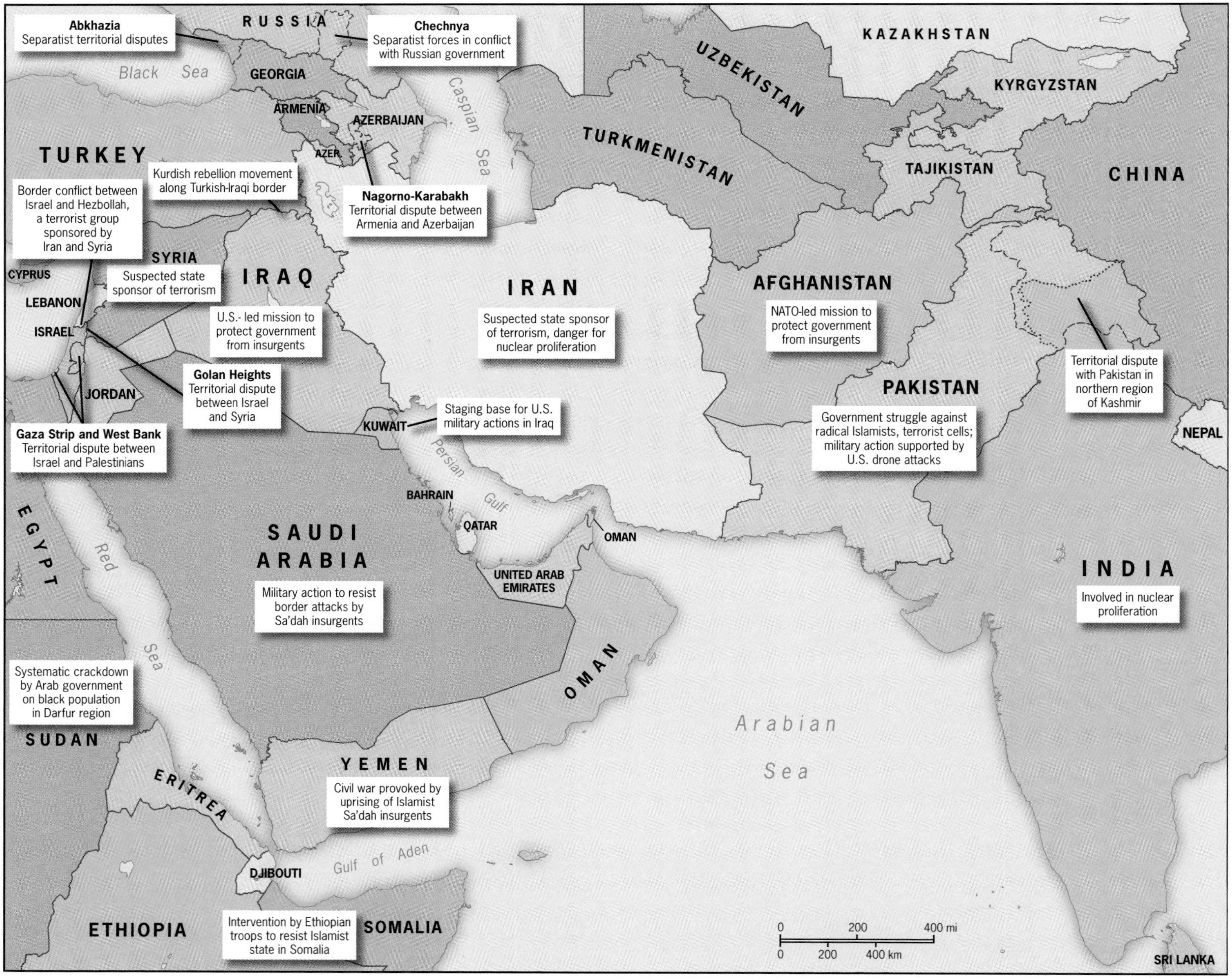

Abkhazia
Separatist territorial disputes

Chechnya
Separatist forces in conflict with Russian government

Nagorno-Karabakh
Territorial dispute between Armenia and Azerbaijan

Kurdish rebellion movement along Turkish-Iraqi border

Border conflict between Israel and Hezbollah, a terrorist group sponsored by Iran and Syria

Suspected state sponsor of terrorism

U.S.-led mission to protect government from insurgents

Golan Heights
Territorial dispute between Israel and Syria

Gaza Strip and West Bank
Territorial dispute between Israel and Palestinians

Suspected state sponsor of terrorism, danger for nuclear proliferation

Staging base for U.S. military actions in Iraq

NATO-led mission to protect government from insurgents

Government struggle against radical Islamists, terrorist cells; military action supported by U.S. drone attacks

Territorial dispute with Pakistan in northern region of Kashmir

Involved in nuclear proliferation

Military action to resist border attacks by Sa'dah insurgents

Civil war provoked by uprising of Islamist Sa'dah insurgents

Intervention by Ethiopian troops to resist Islamist state in Somalia

Systematic crackdown by Arab government on black population in Darfur region

RUSSIA
GEORGIA
ARMENIA
AZERBAIJAN
AZER.
TURKEY
CYPRUS
LEBANON
ISRAEL
JORDAN
SYRIA
IRAQ
IRAN
KUWAIT
BAHRAIN
QATAR
UNITED ARAB EMIRATES
OMAN
OMAN
SAUDI ARABIA
YEMEN
EGYPT
SUDAN
ERITREA
DJIBOUTI
SOMALIA
ETHIOPIA

KAZAKHSTAN
KYRGYZSTAN
UZBEKISTAN
TAJIKISTAN
TURKMENISTAN
CHINA
AFGHANISTAN
PAKISTAN
NEPAL
INDIA
SRI LANKA

Black Sea
Caspian Sea
Persian Gulf
Red Sea
Gulf of Aden
Arabian Sea

0   200   400 km
0   200   400 mi

Map 6 The World

ARCTIC OCEAN

Beaufort Sea

Baffin
Bay

GREENLAND
(DENMARK)

RUSSIA

UNITED STATES

Bering
Sea

Gulf of Alaska

CANADA

Hudson Bay

Labrador Sea

NORTH
PACIFIC
OCEAN

NORTH
ATLANTIC
OCEAN

UNITED STATES

ST. PIERRE-MQ. (FR)

UNITED STATES

BERMUDA
(UK)

MEXICO

Gulf of Mexico

THE BAHAMAS

CUBA

PUERTO RICO (US)
BRITISH VIRGIN ISLANDS
U.S. VIRGIN ISLANDS
ANGUILLA (UK)
ST. KITTS-NEVIS
ANTIGUA & BARBUDA
MONTSERRAT (UK)
GUADELOUPE (FR)
DOMINICA
MARTINIQUE (FR)
ST. LUCIA
BARBADOS
ST. VINCENT & THE GRENADINES
TRINIDAD & TOBAGO

DOM. REP.

JAMAICA

HAITI

BELIZE

HONDURAS

NE. ANTILLES (NE)

GUATEMALA

ARUBA

EL SALVADOR

NICARAGUA

GRENADA

COSTA RICA

VENEZUELA

GUYANA

PANAMA

SURINAME

COLOMBIA

FRENCH GUIANA (FR)

NAURU

Equator

ECUADOR

KIRIBATI

SOLOMON
ISLANDS

PERU

BRAZIL

TUVALU

TOKELAU (NZ)

AMERICAN
SAMOA
(US)

WALLIS & FUTUNA
ISLANDS (FR)

SAMOA

BOLIVIA

Coral Sea

FIJI

VANUATU

FRENCH
POLYNESIA (FR)

PARAGUAY

NEW CALEDONIA (FR)

TONGA

COOK ISLANDS (NZ)

CHILE

URUGUAY

NORFOLK ISLAND
(AUSTRALIA)

PITCAIRN ISLANDS (UK)

RAPANUI / EASTER ISLAND
(CHILE)

ARGENTINA

Tasman Sea

SOUTH
ATLANTIC
OCEAN

NEW ZEALAND

SOUTH
PACIFIC
OCEAN

FALKLAND
ISLANDS
(UK)

SOUTH
GEORGIA
ISLAND
(UK)

ARCTIC OCEAN

Greenland Sea

SVALBARD
(NORWAY)

Norwegian
Sea

ICELAND

RUSSIA

Sea
of
Okhotsk

SWEDEN
NORWAY
FINLAND

NORTHERN
IRELAND (UK)
UNITED
KINGDOM
IRELAND

North
Sea

ESTONIA
LATVIA
LITHUANIA

DENMARK

NETH.
BELGIUM
LUX.
GERMANY
POLAND
BELARUS

CZECH REP.
SLOVAKIA
AUSTRIA
SWITZ.
SLOVENIA
CROATIA
BOS. & HER.
MONT.
ITALY

HUNGARY
ROMANIA
MOLDOVA

UKRAINE

KAZAKHSTAN

MONGOLIA

NORTH
KOREA
SOUTH
KOREA

JAPAN

English Channel

FRANCE

Bay of
Biscay

MAD.
BULGARIA
ALBANIA
GREECE

Black Sea

GEORGIA
ARMENIA
AZERBAIJAN

Caspian
Sea

UZBEKISTAN

KYRGYZSTAN

TAJIKISTAN

CHINA

East
China
Sea

Sea
of
Japan

PORTUGAL
SPAIN

TURKEY

TURKMENISTAN

KOSOVO
SERB.

TAIWAN

MADEIRA (PORT)
CANARY ISLANDS
(SP)

MOROCCO

TUNISIA

Mediterranean
Sea

CYPRUS (T)
CYPRUS (G)
LEBANON
ISRAEL

SYRIA

IRAQ

JORDAN

IRAN

AFGHANISTAN

KASHMIR
(INDIA)

PAKISTAN

NEPAL

BHUTAN

WESTERN
SAHARA
(MOR)

ALGERIA

LIBYA

EGYPT

KUWAIT

SAUDI
ARABIA

BAHRAIN
QATAR
U.A.E.

OMAN

INDIA

BANGLADESH

MYANMAR

LAOS

NORTHERN
MARIANAS
(US)

MAURITANIA

MALI

NIGER

CHAD

SUDAN

Red Sea

ERITREA

YEMEN

Gulf of Oman

Arabian
Sea

Gulf of Aden

THAILAND
CAMBODIA

VIETNAM

South
China
Sea

Philippine
Sea

PHILIPPINES

GUAM (US)

MARSHALL
ISLAND

SENEGAL
GAMBIA
GUINEA-
BISSAU
GUINEA
SIERRA
LEONE
LIBERIA

BURKINA
FASO
CÔTE
D'IVOIRE
GHANA
BENIN
TOGO

NIGERIA

CENTRAL AFRICAN
REPUBLIC

ETHIOPIA

DJIBOUTI

SOMALIA

MALDIVES

SRI LANKA

BRUNEI

MALAYSIA

PALAU

MICRONESIA

SAÕ TOMÉ
& PRINCIPE

CAMEROON

EQUATORIAL GUINEA
GABON

DEMOCRATIC
REPUBLIC
OF THE CONGO

UGANDA

RWANDA
BURUNDI

KENYA

Equator

SINGAPORE

INDONESIA

PAPUA
NEW GUINEA

ASCENCION (UK)

REPUBLIC
OF THE CONGO

TANZANIA

SEYCHELLES

INDIAN OCEAN

0°

COCOS
(KEELING ISLANDS)
(AUSTRALIA)

CHRISTMAS ISLAND
(AUSTRALIA)

Timor Sea

TIMOR-
LESTE

Coral
Sea

ST. HELENA AND
DEPENDENCIES (UK)

ANGOLA

ZAMBIA

MALAWI

COMOROS

MAYOTTE
(FR)

SOUTH

ATLANTIC

OCEAN

NAMIBIA

ZIMBABWE

BOTSWANA

MOZAMBIQUE

MADAGASCAR

MAURITIUS

RÉUNION (FR)

AUSTRALIA

SWAZILAND

TRISTAN DA CUNHA (UK)

SOUTH
AFRICA

LESOTHO

Tasma
Sea

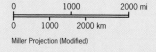

| 0 | 1000 | 2000 mi |

| 0 | 1000 | 2000 km |

Miller Projection (Modified)

Map 7 Department of Defense Regional Commands

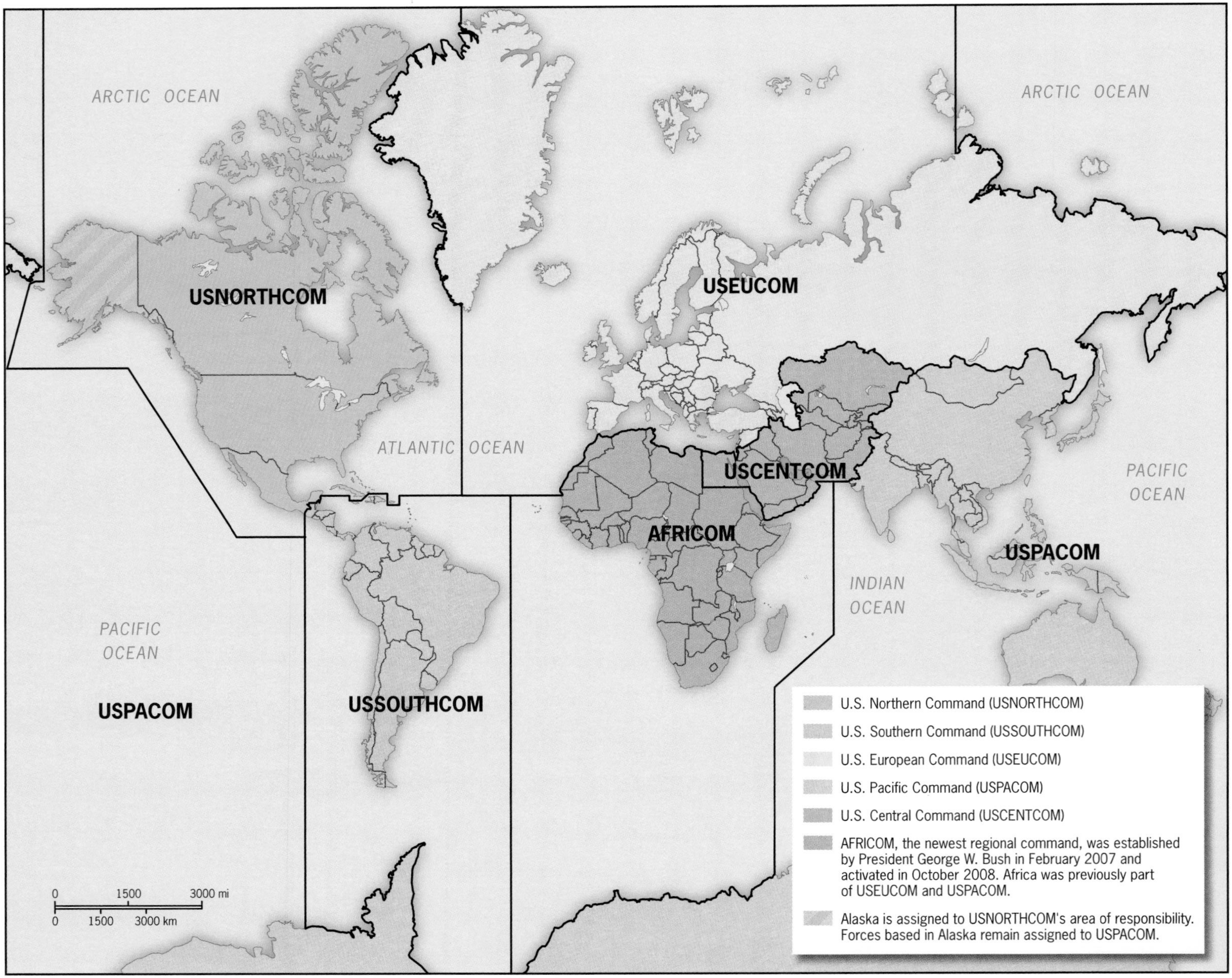

ARCTIC OCEAN

PACIFIC OCEAN

USPACOM

INDIAN OCEAN

USEUCOM

USCENTCOM

AFRICOM

ATLANTIC OCEAN

USSOUTHCOM

USNORTHCOM

ARCTIC OCEAN

PACIFIC OCEAN

USPACOM

U.S. Northern Command (USNORTHCOM)
U.S. Southern Command (USSOUTHCOM)
U.S. European Command (USEUCOM)
U.S. Pacific Command (USPACOM)
U.S. Central Command (USCENTCOM)

AFRICOM, the newest regional command, was established by President George W. Bush in February 2007 and activated in October 2008. Africa was previously part of USEUCOM and USPACOM.

Alaska is assigned to USNORTHCOM's area of responsibility. Forces based in Alaska remain assigned to USPACOM.

0   1500   3000 mi
0   1500   3000 km

Map 8 NATO Expansion

Greenland
(DENMARK)

ARCTIC OCEAN

ICELAND

Norwegian
Sea

ATLANTIC
OCEAN

N O R W A Y

S W E D E N

F I N L A N D

RUSSIA

ESTONIA

LATVIA

LITHUANIA

IRELAND

UNITED
KINGDOM

North
Sea

Baltic
Sea

DENMARK

RUSSIA

BELARUS

NETHERLANDS

BELGIUM

GERMANY

POLAND

LUXEMBOURG

CZECH
REPUBLIC

UKRAINE

FRANCE

LIECHTENSTEIN

SLOVAKIA

SWITZ.

AUSTRIA

HUNGARY

MOLDOVA

ANDORRA

SLOVENIA

CROATIA

ROMANIA

Black   Sea

GEORGIA

PORTUGAL

SPAIN

Corsica

ITALY

Adriatic

Sea

BOSNIA &
HERZEGOVINA

SERBIA

MONTENEGRO

KOSOVO

BULGARIA

ARMENIA

Sardinia

ALBANIA

MACEDONIA

GREECE

T U R K E Y

MOROCCO

ALGERIA

Mediterranean

Sicily

MALTA

Sea

SYRIA

CYPRUS

IRAQ

LEBANON

ISRAEL

JORDAN

LIBYA

EGYPT

SAUDI
ARABIA

Original signatories, 1949 (includes United States
and Canada, not pictured)

Joined in 1952

Joined in 1955 (unified Germany in 1990)

Joined in 1982

Joined in 1999

Joined in 2004

Joined in 2009

Application to join pending

0   200   400 mi

0   200   400 km

Map 9 Nuclear Threats and U.S. Defense Installations

ARCTIC OCEAN

PACIFIC OCEAN

NEW ZEALAND

Kwajalein Atoll (MARSHALL ISLANDS)

Guam/Marianas

JAPAN

N. KOREA

S. KOREA

Hong Kong

CHINA

RUSSIA

INDONESIA

SINGAPORE

AUSTRALIA

INDIAN OCEAN

INDIA

PAKISTAN

British Indian Ocean Territories (UK)

Diego Garcia (UK)

IRAN

KUWAIT

U.A.E.

OMAN

DJIBOUTI

ISRAEL

BAHRAIN

KENYA

TURKEY

BOSNIA & HERZE.

KOSOVO

GREECE

EGYPT

LIBYA

SOUTH AFRICA

NORWAY

DEN.

GER.

AUST.

ITALY

FRANCE

NETH.

BELG.

LUX.

SPAIN

PORTUGAL

UNITED KINGDOM

ICELAND

St. Helena (UK)

ATLANTIC OCEAN

Greenland (DENMARK)

ARCTIC OCEAN

CANADA

UNITED STATES

Alaska (U.S.)

PACIFIC OCEAN

THE BAHAMAS

CUBA

HONDURAS

ANTIGUA AND BARBUDA

ARUBA

VENEZUELA

COLOMBIA

ECUADOR

PERU

BRAZIL

ARGENTINA

ANTARCTICA

3000 mi

3000 km

1500

1500

0

0

Countries with nuclear weapons capabilities

Countries with unacknowledged nuclear weapons capabilities

Countries with U.S. Department of Defense installations

Countries with active nuclear proliferation programs

Countries with abandoned nuclear weapons programs

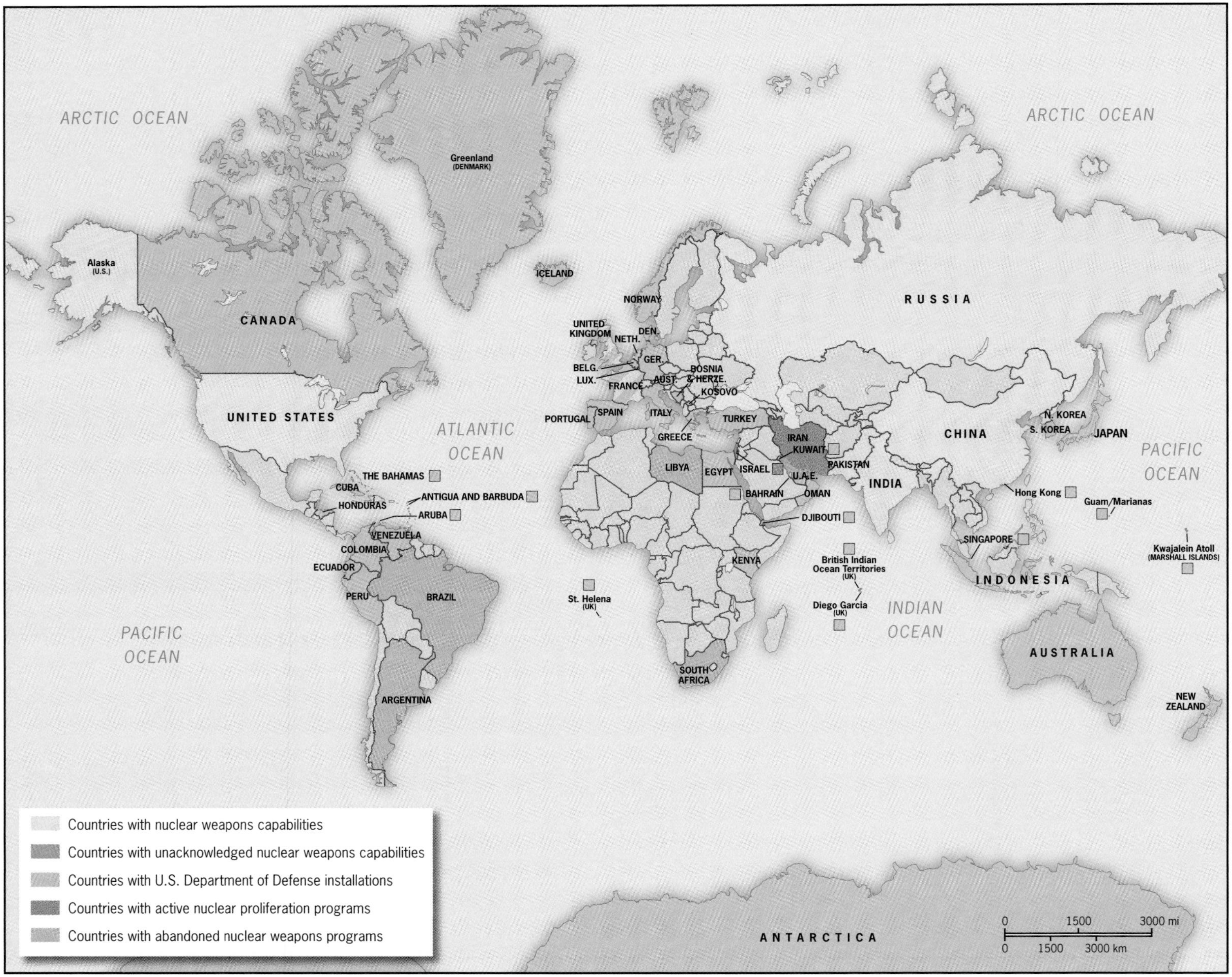

Map 10 U.S. Foreign Economic Relations

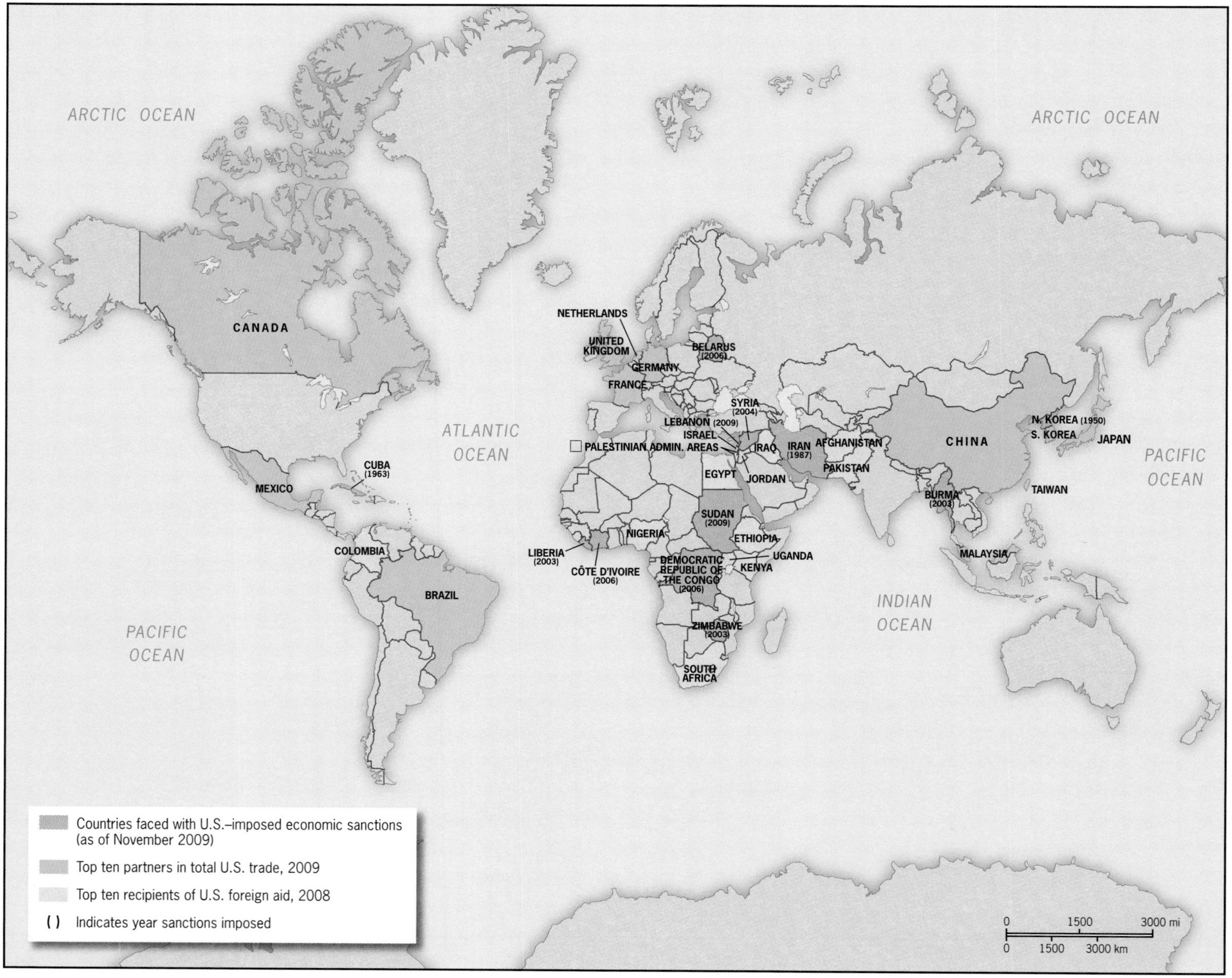

ARCTIC OCEAN

PACIFIC OCEAN

N. KOREA (1950)
S. KOREA
JAPAN
TAIWAN
CHINA
MALAYSIA
BURMA (2003)

INDIAN OCEAN

AFGHANISTAN
PAKISTAN
IRAN (1987)
IRAQ
JORDAN
SYRIA (2004)
LEBANON (2009)
ISRAEL
UGANDA
KENYA
ETHIOPIA
EGYPT
SUDAN (2009)
DEMOCRATIC REPUBLIC OF THE CONGO (2006)
ZIMBABWE (2003)
SOUTH AFRICA
BELARUS (2006)
PALESTINIAN ADMIN. AREAS
NIGERIA
CÔTE D'IVOIRE (2006)
LIBERIA (2003)
NETHERLANDS
UNITED KINGDOM
GERMANY
FRANCE

ARCTIC OCEAN

CANADA

MEXICO
CUBA (1963)
COLOMBIA
BRAZIL

ATLANTIC OCEAN

PACIFIC OCEAN

Countries faced with U.S.–imposed economic sanctions (as of November 2009)

Top ten partners in total U.S. trade, 2009

Top ten recipients of U.S. foreign aid, 2008

( ) Indicates year sanctions imposed

3000 mi
3000 km
1500
1500
0
0

Map 11 Freedom in the World, 2009

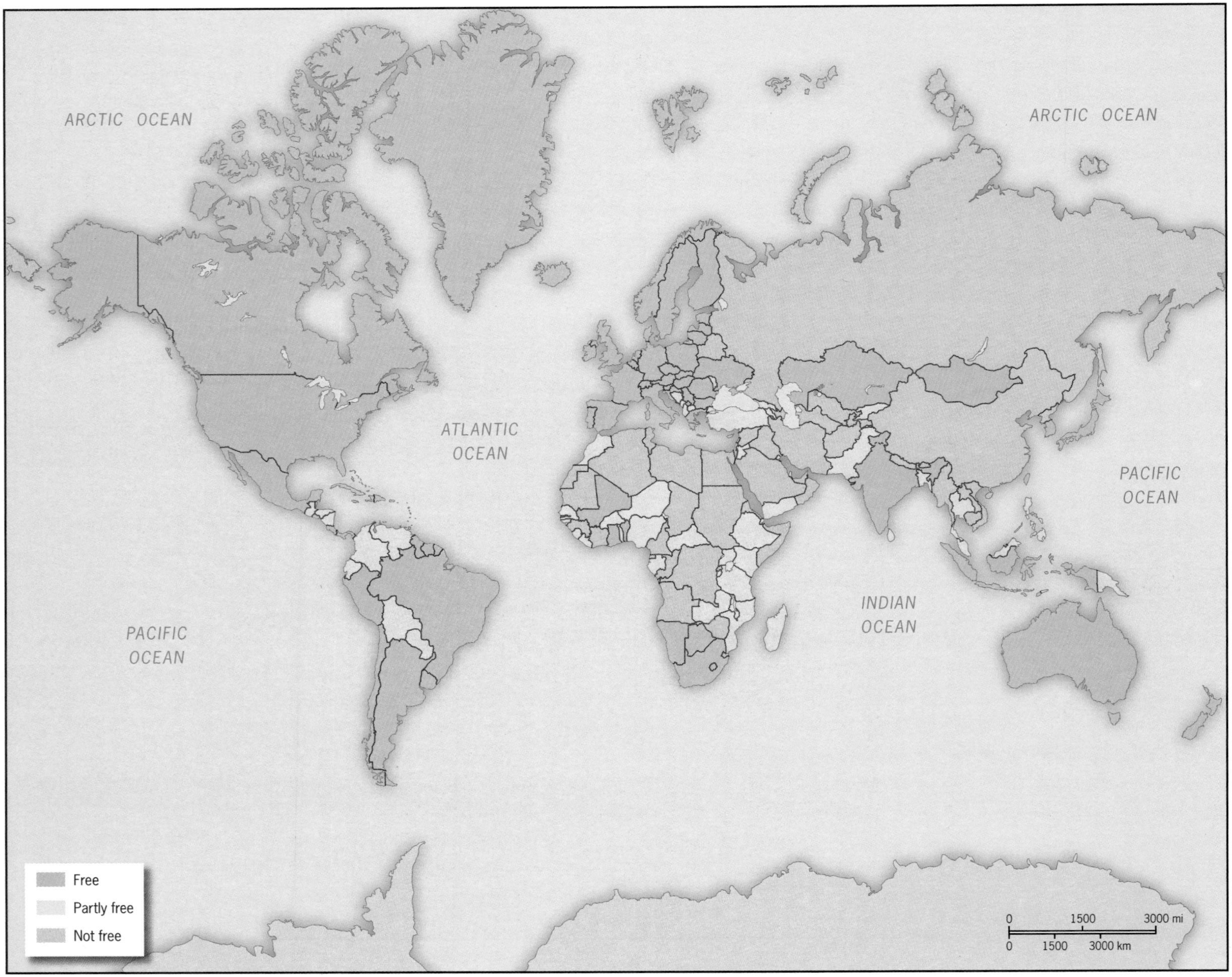

ARCTIC OCEAN

PACIFIC OCEAN

INDIAN OCEAN

ATLANTIC OCEAN

ARCTIC OCEAN

PACIFIC OCEAN

Free

Partly free

Not free

3000 mi

3000 km

1500

1500

0

0

CHAPTER 1

The United States in a Turbulent World

President Barack Obama addresses world leaders during the opening session of the United Nations on September 23, 2009. Obama used this opportunity to acknowledge growing anti-Americanism around the world and to pledge greater cooperation in U.S. foreign policy.

On September 23, 2009, President Barack Obama stood before the United Nations General Assembly and pledged to nearly 200 world leaders that America would provide the global leadership that was expected of the richest and strongest power. "We have reached a pivotal moment," Obama said. "The United States stands ready to begin a new chapter of international cooperation—one that recognizes the rights and responsibilities of all nations. And so, with confidence in our cause, and with a commitment to our values, we call on all nations to join us in building the future that our people so richly deserve" (White House 2009).

His audience applauded repeatedly as Obama described his plans to stop the spread of nuclear weapons, mediate regional conflicts, curb global warming, and revive "a global economy that advances opportunity for all people." The president, who took office just eight months earlier, had already gained widespread approval in global public opinion. A June survey of nearly 20,000 citizens in countries with 62 percent of the world's population found Obama was "inspiring far more confidence than any other world political leader" (World Public Opinion 2009). Even UN secretary-general Ban Ki-moon, with a 40-percent confidence level, did not enjoy the U.S. president's global appeal.

The promising tone of Obama's speech, however, soon clashed with the bloody realities of world politics. On October 5, a suicide bomber walked into the UN World Food Program office in Islamabad, Pakistan, and detonated enough explosives to kill five people and injure dozens of others. The UN, fearing more attacks, closed the mission indefinitely, a move that left an estimated 10 million dislocated Pakistani citizens without relief from hunger. Six days later, in Iraq, a meeting for national reconciliation was shattered by coordinated bombings that left twenty-three people dead and sixty-five wounded. The Islamic militants who planned and conducted both attacks identified their domestic rivals as targets, but their broader goal was to eject the United States from the countries it had earlier invaded and occupied.

At home, Obama was forced to devote his attention to reviving the U.S. economy, which virtually collapsed in 2008 as the result of reckless lending and speculation by major banks and mortgage brokers. The crash sent stock markets tumbling and the nation's unemployment rate soaring above 10 percent. Washington responded by spending massively on relief for paralyzed financial firms and on public projects to jumpstart the economy. These actions prevented an even greater calamity but boosted the U.S. budget deficit from $459 billion in fiscal year 2008 to nearly $1.6 trillion in 2009. The nation's debt, which ballooned from $5.8 trillion to $7.6 trillion, exceeded 11 percent of U.S. economic output in 2009—the highest rate since World War II (Congressional Budget Office 2009).

When Obama could spare time for foreign policy, he faced equally daunting problems, all lacking clear solutions. American forces nearly lost control of Afghanistan, where Taliban insurgents held most provinces by the end of 2009. The insurgents renewed their ties with al Qaeda, the terrorist group that planned the September 2001 attacks on the United States from safe havens in Afghanistan. The turmoil, which spread to neighboring Pakistan, forced Obama to deploy 30,000 additional troops to Afghanistan late in 2009. The winding down of the Iraq war, which began in March 2003, was expected to make possible this shift in U.S. military action. North Korea and Iran, meanwhile, continued to gain global stature by threatening to develop nuclear arsenals and upset regional power balances.

It did not help that, by the time Obama took office, the United States had become isolated in the international community. The White House and Congress took a "unilateral turn" during George W. Bush's administrations, rejecting major global treaties, international laws, and the authority of the UN. The **Bush Doctrine**, which called for preventive attacks on state sponsors of terrorism, raised fears of open-ended military operations around the world. The invasion of Iraq, which lacked support from the UN Security Council, left the United States and Great Britain virtually alone in the "coalition of the willing." According to a January 2007 survey undertaken in twenty-four countries, most citizens viewed U.S. influence in the world as "mostly negative" (BBC 2007). Anti-Americanism took many forms around the world during this period, ranging from general discontent over the U.S. government's violations of its own democratic principles to "radical" efforts to transform the U.S.-led international system (Katzenstein and Keohane 2007).

Despite all its troubles at home and abroad, the United States still faces no country or rival bloc that can credibly challenge U.S. primacy. "The United States alone retains the wherewithal to organize major politico-military action anywhere in the system," security analysts Stephen Brooks and William Wohlforth (2008, 13–14) concluded in a major study. "No other country will match its combination of wealth, size, technological capacity, and productivity in the foreseeable future." The soft-power advantages of the United States also survived the downturn of the Bush years, as reflected in October 2009 when Obama received the Nobel Peace Prize after just nine months in office. His actions to coordinate a global relief effort in Haiti after a devastating earthquake in January 2010 typified the president's more cooperative approach to foreign policy.

Americans today find themselves front and center on a volatile, rapidly changing world stage. The decisions made by their leaders, for better *and* for worse, have direct consequences for other countries and the world order generally. A clear grasp of U.S. foreign policy, therefore, is more vital than ever. This book seeks to strengthen this understanding by exploring the process by which U.S. leaders, faced with unending pressures at home and overseas, make these policies. As we will find, the United States has gained and maintained an unprecedented degree of global influence while confronting many obstacles—many of which are "made in the USA"—that make the coherent use of this power exceedingly difficult. Coming to grips with this paradox of U.S. world power is the primary task of this book.

Snapshot: The United States in the World

It is helpful to begin this inquiry by reviewing some basic economic and other indicators of the global balance of power. Taken together, these figures reveal a **unipolar balance of power** in which one country—at present, the United States—maintains a predominant share of the economic, military, and other resources needed to advance its interests in the interstate system. Indeed, foreign policy debates today take U.S. **primacy** as a starting point. Attention then focuses on the extent, consequences, and likely future of unipolar world power. Is the United States an **empire** that "exerts formal political control over the internal and external policy" of another sovereign territory (Doyle 1986a, 12)? If so, is an American empire desirable for other countries and the interstate system?[1] Or is the United States a **hegemon** that, while not imposing sovereign control over a colonial empire, still incorporates much of the world within its sphere of influence?

---

1. Most analysts—ranging from Williams (1959) and LaFeber (1963) during the Cold War to Chomsky (2003), Johnson (2004), Smith (2007), and Hoff (2008) in more recent discourse—are highly critical of *pax Americana*. Others, such as Boot (2002) and Ferguson (2004), welcome this state of affairs and only wish the United States would wield its power more effectively. For a recent summary of these debates, along with a historical review, see the various essays in Calhoun, Cooper, and Moore (2006).

Figure 1.1 World Economic Output: Seven Largest Producers, 2009

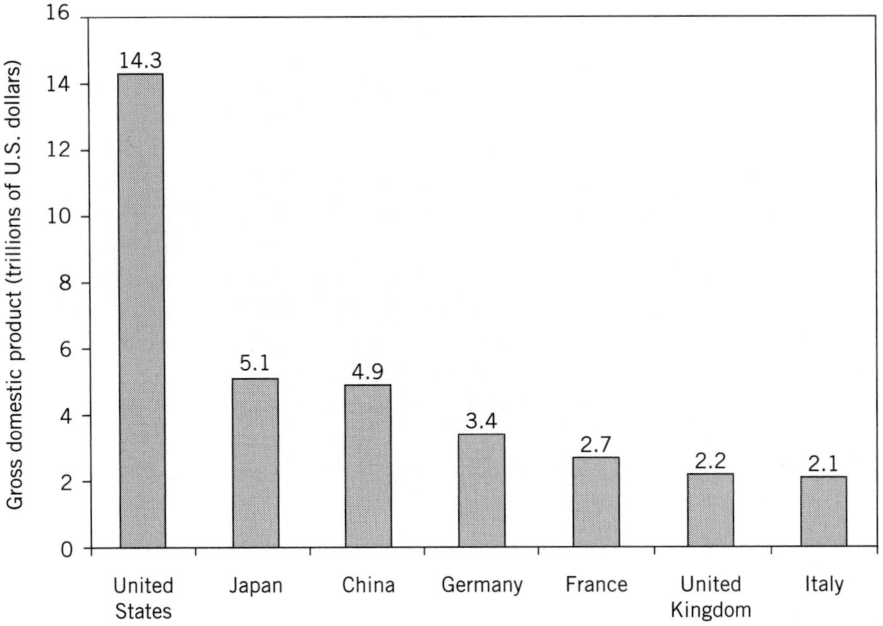

SOURCE: International Monetary Fund, World Economic Outlook Database (May 20, 2010), www.imf.org/external/pubs/ft/weo/2010/01/weodata/index.aspx.

Whatever label is applied, U.S. primacy is the central fact of life in world politics today: "Whether they like it or not, developing a strategy for dealing with American power has become an essential element of statecraft for every country in the world" (Walt 2005, 17). Like a stone that sends out ripples in every direction as it plunges into a pool of water, U.S. foreign policies have immediate and long-term impacts on the grand strategies, policy agendas, and even routine choices of other governments. "Leaders in much of the world believe they cannot avoid being affected by U.S. acts of commission or omission" (Bobrow 2008, 3).

The concentration of power resources detailed in this section is particularly notable in view of the fact that the United States is home to less than 5 percent of the world's population of 6.8 billion. Much of the nation's power advantage derives from the vast size and global scale of its economy, which produced $14.3 trillion in goods and services, or about one fifth of the world's total in 2009 (see Figure 1.1).[2] The world's second-largest economy, Japan, recorded $5.1 trillion in gross domestic product (GDP), about one third the U.S. total.[3] America's GDP

---

2. Unless otherwise noted, the other figures in this section are drawn from the World Bank's *World Development Indicators* database (World Bank 2009).

3. A country's gross domestic product includes the total market value of all the goods and services produced within its borders during a given year.

Figure 1.2   U.S. and World Military Spending (as percentage of world total), 2008

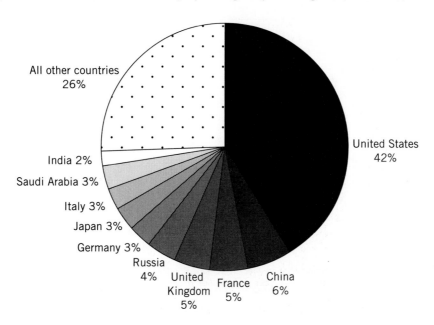

SOURCE: Petter Stalenheim, Noel Kelly, Catalina Perdomo, Sam Perlo-Freeman, and Elizabeth Skons, "Appendix 5A, Military Expenditure Data, 1999–2008: The Top 10 Military Spenders, 2008," *Stockholm International Peace Research Institute Yearbook 2009*, www.sipri.org/yearbook/2009/05/05A.

NOTE: Total exceeds 100% due to rounding of the percentages. The figures for China and Russia are estimates.

exceeded that of Europe's monetary union and was nearly three times the GDP of China, whose economy has grown rapidly in recent years. Russia, once the primary U.S. rival in a bipolar balance of power, recorded a 2009 GDP of $1.2 trillion, less than 10 percent of the economic output generated by the United States.

The United States holds the additional distinction of being the world's foremost trading state, exporting more than all other nations since World War II while displaying a voracious appetite for overseas goods and services (WTO 2009). American firms exported more than $1.2 trillion in merchandise in 2007, about 8 percent of the global total. The nation's imports were even larger in absolute terms (more than $2 trillion in 2007) and as a share of world imports (14 percent). The United States has also served as the world's leading source and destination of foreign direct investment in recent years (OECD 2009).

The degree of U.S. predominance is even greater in the military realm (see Figure 1.2). The United States, the only country that has divided the world into regional military commands, also maintains "command of the commons—command of the sea, space, and air" (Posen 2003, 7). This is a major geopolitical asset in an age in which holding physical territory, while vital, does not ensure national security. The U.S. government spent more than $600 billion on

Figure 1.3   The World's Seven Largest Energy Consumers, 2006

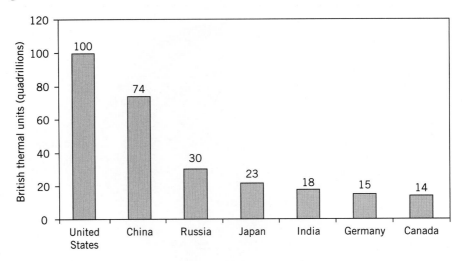

SOURCE: Energy Information Administration, "Table F.1, World Primary Energy Production (Btu), 1980–2006," *International Energy Annual 2006,* www.eia.doe.gov/emeu/iea/overview.html.

military defense in 2008, almost half of the global total (SIPRI 2009). This edge in military spending is compounded by the superior technology of U.S. weapons systems and the dominant position of the United States in its military alliances. In addition to its unrivaled defense forces, the United States provides the largest volume of weaponry to other countries; its approval of nearly $40 billion in foreign arms deals in 2008 was more than ten times the level of its closest competitor, Italy (Grimmett 2009).[4] At the same time, the United States provided more than one hundred foreign governments with military training and education, further solidifying its projection of world power (U.S. Department of State 2006b).

Energy and environmental statistics also reveal the long shadow cast by the United States (see Figure 1.3). Americans consumed nearly one-quarter of the electricity used worldwide in 2006 and the same share of oil, coal, and natural gas. Among other environmental impacts, this energy consumption produces annually more than 6 billion metric tons of carbon dioxide emissions, a major source of air pollution and global warming—about 20 percent of the total worldwide. In addition, the United States serves as the world's primary source of nuclear and hazardous wastes.

Finally, throughout its history, the U.S. government's influence has also taken the form of **soft power**—the expression of its political and cultural values that

---

4. See U.S. Defense Security Cooperation Agency (2009) for more timely data on the country's arms transfers, along with information provided by the Federation of American Scientists (2009).

Table 1.1 Top Twenty Universities, by Country, 2009

Institution	Country
Harvard University	USA
Yale University	USA
University of Chicago	USA
Princeton University	USA
Massachusetts Institute of Technology	USA
California Institute of Technology	USA
Columbia University	USA
University of Pennsylvania	USA
Johns Hopkins University	USA
Duke University	USA
Cornell University	USA
Stanford University	USA
University of Michigan	USA
Cambridge University	UK
University College London	UK
Imperial College London	UK
Oxford University	UK
University of Edinburgh	UK
Australian National University	Australia
McGill University	Canada

SOURCE: Adapted from U.S. News and World Report, "World's Best Universities," www.usnews.com/articles/education/worlds-best-universities/2009/10/20/worlds-best-universities-top-200.html.

other societies and governments may find appealing (see Nye 2004). Indeed, the United States is often known as an "idea" rather than an ordinary nation-state defined by physical boundaries, common ethnic or religious identities, and material interests. This "idea" combines several features of U.S. government and society: limited government, individual liberties, free markets, and vibrant forms of cultural expression, among others.

The soft power of the United States is reflected in many ways. For example, a recent study found that thirteen of the world's top twenty universities—ideal centers for the sharing of ideas, knowledge, and culture—are located in the United States (see Table 1.1). Foreign tourists spend more money in the United States than in any other country, an amount that reached $103 billion in 2006 (Euromonitor International 2007). American fashions, popular music, movies, and television programs are so pervasive overseas that they provoke charges of "cultural imperialism." More than one-third of global Internet communications originated or terminated in the United States at the turn of the century (Dizard 2001, 4). Finally, the United States consistently ranks first in the number of radios, television sets, and personal computers owned by its citizens (World Bank 2009).

American primacy is not unique to the current period. Indeed, after World War II the U.S. government sought, above all, to maintain its "predominance of power" (Leffler 1992). The Cold War strategy of communist containment was designed to accomplish the broader objective of sustaining U.S. primacy (see Chapter 2). The same motivations prompted U.S. leaders to favor creating the UN and other multilateral bodies such as the World Bank that "locked in" U.S. advantages after World War II (Ikenberry 2001; see also Skidmore 2005). After the collapse of the Soviet Union in 1991, the George H. W. Bush administration devised a strategy to "establish and protect a new order that holds the promise of convincing potential competitors that they need not aspire to a greater role." George W. Bush's election in November 2000 and the terrorist attacks in September 2001 elevated the doctrine of U.S. sustained primacy to a new level. His national security strategy, adopted in September 2002, vowed that U.S. military forces "will be strong enough to dissuade potential adversaries from pursuing a military build-up in hopes of surpassing, or equaling, the power of the United States" (White House 2002, 30).

Challenges to U.S. Primacy

Despite its strength, the United States today confronts a variety of challenges to its global primacy. These challenges can be grouped into four general categories. The first relates to the experience of past great powers and the difficulties they faced in preserving their advantages. The second group of challenges stems from the U.S. government's own historical experience and past foreign policy actions, many of which violated its proclaimed moral principles and created widespread animosity toward Washington. The third set of challenges to U.S. primacy stems from the nation's close association with economic globalization, which "aggravates anti-Americanism and appears to further isolate the United States in the world" (Kohut and Stokes 2006, 143). Finally, the United States faces the more immediate threat posed by international terrorism, which has preoccupied war planners since September 2001.

These challenges, along with the global responsibilities that naturally descend upon the world's most powerful country, are inescapable. How U.S. leaders manage the challenges and responsibilities will profoundly affect the course of the twenty-first century for American citizens and those beyond U.S. shores.

Cycles in the Balance of Power

Some political analysts see a U.S.-dominated world order as advantageous not only for the United States, but also for the international system as a whole. A preponderant yet benign world power, they argue, maintains stability in the international system, discouraging conflicts among regional powers and reassuring them that a peaceful and prosperous global order can be achieved and preserved. Under these circumstances, less powerful states will **band-wagon** with the dominant power rather than challenge it by forming rival blocs. The United States can serve this constructive role because it claims that it seeks to promote democracy and economic prosperity instead of its own selfish interests.

This optimistic view, however, is hardly universal. Many informed observers fear the concentration of power in one country and believe that "unbalanced power, whoever wields it, is a potential danger to others" (Waltz 1997, 915). Historian Timothy Garton Ash (2002, A4) finds that "the problem with American power is not that it is American. The problem is simply the power. It would be dangerous even for an archangel to wield so much power." A related argument identifies historical cycles in the global balance of power. Historian Paul Kennedy traced *The Rise and Fall of the Great Powers* (1987) to a pattern of "imperial overstretch" by which the Roman, Dutch, Ottoman, Spanish, British, and Russian empires bit off more than they could chew, and then succumbed to uprisings in their far-flung provinces and to political infighting at home. World history has revealed the "increasing costs of dominance" that accompany global primacy (Gilpin 1981). According to this view, the dominant power's strength in relation to others inevitably peaks, and then it erodes as smaller powers benefit from the leader's technological advances, economic aid, and military protection. Major wars and a restructuring of the global power balance result from this cycle of hegemonic boom and bust.

Equally ominous lessons can be drawn from the tendency of major powers to inflate their capabilities and minimize the costs and risks of militarism. "Napoleon and Hitler marched to Moscow, only to be engulfed in the Russian winter," Jack Snyder (2003, 30) recalled. "Imperial Japan, facing a quagmire in China and a U.S. oil embargo, tried to break what it saw as impending encirclement by seizing the Indonesian oil fields and preventively attacking Pearl Harbor. All sought security through expansion, and all ended in imperial collapse."

Similar dangers have become evident in the United States since it assumed the pivotal position in a unipolar world. As noted earlier, the nation's budget deficits soared as it became embroiled in the Afghanistan and Iraq wars following the September 2001 terrorist attacks. These deficits, along with the national debt, grew even larger in 2008 and 2009 in response to the financial crisis. The wars, meanwhile, sapped the strength of U.S. military forces in those conflicts and weakened the Pentagon's overall capacity to project force elsewhere. Sustained American primacy, in this view, is likely to give way to national decline and a new, multipolar balance of world power in the years to come (see Walton 2007). To journalist Fareed Zakaria (2008), this marks the third fundamental shift in world power in five centuries. The first, around 1500, featured the rise of Europe. The second, around 1900, witnessed the arrival of U.S. hegemony. Today's power shift, he concluded, can be labeled "the rise of the rest."

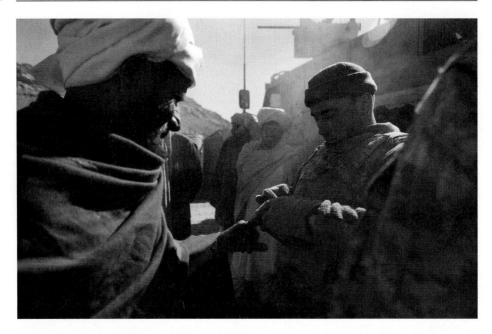

U.S. soldiers photograph and take fingerprints of Afghan villagers as part of a December 2009 mission to improve security in the impoverished and war-torn country. President Obama ordered a "surge" of 30,000 additional troops to Afghanistan, where Taliban insurgents reclaimed most provinces after being ousted from power by the United States eight years earlier.

The Shadow of the Past

The foreign policy record of the United States is known intimately to foreign governments, many of which were engaged, either as allies or adversaries, in the expansion of U.S. power (see Chapter 2). This record, which features burgeoning territorial growth and trade alongside the extension of domestic political rights and a vibrant, multinational civil society, is admired widely overseas. At the same time, many past actions of U.S. foreign policy makers provoked anger and resentment abroad that linger today and inspire anti-American social movements, hostile regimes, and potential threats to the nation's citizens or government (Sweig 2006).

Three episodes in early U.S. foreign policy—the importation of slaves before the Civil War, the wars against native American tribes during the period of western expansion, and frequent interventions in Latin America—revealed that for all its rhetoric about freedom and justice, the U.S. government frequently observed the Darwinian logic of the survival of the fittest. Slavery, of course, has long been condemned as an ultimate denial of human rights, and the U.S. treatment of native Americans fits the commonly accepted definition of genocide.[5] As for

5. Genocide constitutes acts that are "committed with intent to destroy, in whole or in part, a national, ethnic, racial, or religious group," according to Article II of the 1948 Convention on the Prevention and Punishment of Genocide, to which the United States is a signatory.

Latin America, U.S. forces seized northern Mexico in the late 1840s, and then intervened more than sixty times across the Latin America–Caribbean region prior to World War II (Grimmett 2004).[6] This pattern continued during the Cold War, when U.S. leaders turned to the Central Intelligence Agency (CIA) to overthrow elected regimes in Guatemala (1954) and Chile (1973). Elsewhere, the United States supported dictators such as Ferdinand Marcos of the Philippines and Mobutu Sese Seko of Zaire. American leaders aligned with Saddam Hussein's Iraq during its war against Iran in the 1980s even after Saddam used chemical weapons to massacre Iranian forces and ethnic minorities in his own country.

These actions cast doubts on the virtues of U.S. foreign policy even as the nation fought successfully against fascism and communism in the twentieth century. In the eyes of much of the world, these foreign policy feats were offset by the moral cost of American expansion—glaring gaps between words and deeds that revealed hypocrisy at the highest levels of government. More recently, the gap appeared graphically in the photographs of prisoner abuses by U.S. guards at Iraq's Abu Ghraib prison. Claims of U.S. double standards also extend to other areas, as critics question how the world's foremost nuclear power can demand nonproliferation elsewhere, and how the world's primary source of greenhouse gases can call for "sustainable development" in the world's poorest regions.

The shadow of past actions not only damages U.S. credibility abroad but also has provoked direct challenges to its world power. Iran's 1979 revolution, for example, was fueled by popular antagonism toward the United States, which had propped up its despotic shah for more than twenty-five years. In this context, the theocratic regime that still rules Iran can be seen as an antagonistic response to U.S. policies, or **blowback** (Johnson 2000). The same can be said for Nicaragua's revolution in the same year that toppled a former military general, Anastasio Somoza, who maintained his rule largely on the basis of his close ties to Washington. More recently, the terrorists who struck the United States in September 2001 explicitly cited U.S. support for the repressive monarchy in Saudi Arabia as a justification for their attacks. While such a rationale is hardly defensible for mass killings, one cannot deny that U.S. actions that violate a foreign country's proclaimed moral and ethical principles commonly spark anti-American movements and acts of vengeance.

Resistance to Globalization

Yet another challenge to the United States stems from the process of **globalization**, which is the linking of national and regional markets into a single world economy (see Stiglitz 2002). Advances in transportation and communications technology, intellectual developments, and public policy shifts in the eighteenth

---

6. These military interventions, which protected U.S. economic interests in Central America and the Caribbean, led to long-term occupations in Panama (1903–1914), Nicaragua (1912–1933), Haiti (1915–1934), the Dominican Republic (1916–1924), and Cuba (1917–1922).

century first spurred this historic trend. The Internet revolution late in the twentieth century accelerated the pace of globalization. In today's world economy, goods, services, and financial investments cross national borders at a record pace. This commerce is increasingly conducted by multinational corporations with headquarters, research centers, production facilities, stockholders, and customers in many countries.

Although Great Britain was at the vanguard of the globalization process through the nineteenth century, the primary catalyst since then has been the United States. Globalization conforms to a national consensus that private enterprise, unfettered by government interference, provides the surest path to prosperity as well as to individual liberty. According to this consensus, a prosperous world economy would resemble that of the United States, with few internal barriers to the movement of goods, services, labor, and capital. Trade, not political or military competition, would be the primary arena of foreign policy. Furthermore, "trading states" would have strong interests in a stable international system and would be reluctant to wage wars against each other. Globalization, then, would be a harbinger of world peace.

When the Cold War ended in 1991, it appeared that this model of political economy had triumphed. Former communist governments hurriedly instituted market-based reforms, and the United States subsidized the reformers with foreign aid to shut down government enterprises, create private companies, improve financial services and accounting, and open domestic markets to foreign competition. Through the World Bank and the International Monetary Fund, both based in Washington, D.C., the United States and other wealthy nations also assisted poor countries that agreed to follow the market-friendly script.

The quickening pace of economic globalization brought improved living standards to many nations, but others fell behind, unable to attract foreign investment or find new markets for their goods. The growing gap between the world's rich and poor then placed new strains on the international system. Critics believed globalization produced a variety of other problems: the triumph of consumerism over cultural diversity, heightened pollution and deforestation, and the exploitation of "sweatshop" laborers by multinational corporations. Because the largest share of these corporations were based in the United States and its government had played such a vital role in the globalization boom, the United States bore the brunt of these protests.

The most dramatic example of this backlash occurred at the 1999 annual meeting of the World Trade Organization in Seattle, when antiglobalization protesters blocked streets, smashed storefronts, and otherwise prevented the delegates from achieving their goal of furthering free trade. This outburst caught many Americans by surprise, as did the subsequent protests that revealed the depths of anti-Americanism in other countries. Managing this resistance to globalization will be difficult for the United States, however, given the many forces that propel the trend. "Today's globalization is the Pandora's Box we opened long ago," Thomas Barnett (2009, 37) observed. "It's past the point where we—or really anybody—can claim to be in charge."

Terrorism and Asymmetric Warfare

The challenge posed by antiglobalization protesters is linked directly to another challenge facing the United States—global terrorism. Among other motives for the September 11 attacks, a primary grievance of al Qaeda terrorists was the pervasive influence of the United States in the Middle East. The region and its vast oil fields have long been considered a vital interest of the U.S. government, which has used whatever means necessary to gain and retain access to them. Because the Middle East lies in the heart of Islam, many Muslims view encroachments by the United States and its Western allies as desecrations of holy lands. These dissidents, who also condemn the U.S. government's support for Israel, generally lack political power as well as substantial economic resources. As a result, they frequently turn to terrorism to force political change.

Terrorism, with a history that long precedes the rise of militant Islam, is a tactic that seeks to gain the upper hand in a political struggle through psychological means (see Pillar 2001). Terrorists do not seek to overpower the enemy in one swift blow—an approach that is not feasible because of their small numbers and lack of resources—but to gain attention and political concessions by instilling mass fear in the population that their enemy controls. In this regard, terrorism is a form of **asymmetric warfare** that "exploits vulnerabilities . . . by using weapons and tactics that are unplanned or unexpected" (de Wijk 2002, 79). Terrorists choose the time and place of their attacks, leaving an adversary perpetually on the defensive. They operate in the shadows, beyond enemy reach, and they meld into the civilian communities from which they may receive moral and material support. Terrorists' use of unconventional tactics (for example, car bombings, kidnappings, and airplane hijackings) further confounds their enemies.[7]

The United States faces three problems in confronting terrorism, which was deemed the primary threat to its national security after the September 11 attacks. First, the United States is seen widely as the primary target of global terrorists groups because of its visible role in the Middle East and its more general association with economic globalization. Second, U.S. military strategy has historically been based on fighting conventional wars, defeating foreign enemies on the battlefield through the use of overwhelming force, rather than confronting small groups of enemies who thrive in the shadows. Third, the United States has traditionally viewed warfare as an exception to the general rule of peaceful coexistence among countries. Fighting terrorism, however, is an ongoing struggle with no clear end, as was made clear in December 2009, when a terrorist came close to igniting an explosive on a commercial jet headed for Detroit. Furthermore, the enemy is not typically a nation-state, such as Nazi Germany or even Saddam Hussein's Iraq, but an invisible foe often impossible to engage through diplomacy.

---

7. Problems involving asymmetric warfare are not limited to fighting terrorism. The United States confronted the same tactics in the Vietnamese "guerilla war" and faces similar challenges today in trying to resolve civil and regional conflicts whose antagonists comprise ethnic or political groups rather than nation-states (see Smith 2005).

These difficulties plagued U.S. efforts to combat terrorism in the years following the September 2001 attacks. Fearing an attack by weapons of mass destruction (WMD), the Bush White House adopted a "one-percent doctrine" that called for preventive action even with slim evidence of impending danger (Suskind 2006). The invasion of Iraq, justified by the WMD threat, stemmed from this doctrine. But no such weapons were found by U.S. troops, not only proving these fears unfounded, but also placing U.S. troops in the midst of a growing insurgency that prevented their immediate withdrawal and the creation of a new government to replace Saddam Hussein's regime. Indeed, far from helping the United States gain the upper hand in the Middle East, the conflict in Iraq made victory in the war on terrorism more elusive (National Intelligence Council 2006).

Other major powers, as well as emerging powers such as India and Brazil, have multiple ways to "evade, modify, or resist" U.S. primacy (Bobrow 2008). The German government, for example, turned to the UN and other intergovernmental organizations to resist U.S. plans to invade Iraq (Schmidt 2008). Members of the European Union, meanwhile, reached out to developing countries for support on their environmental policies that conflicted with those of the United States (Ochs and Sprinz 2008). Chinese leaders, recognizing their growing global world power relative to that of Washington, chose not to "instigate a premature confrontation with the still-dominant hegemon" and instead simply "played for time" (Chan 2008, 67). These leaders also knew they could create economic havoc in the United States at any time by threatening to liquidate their massive holdings of treasury bills.

The United States faces other challenges, as well, as it seeks to maintain its global primacy. China's rapid economic growth has allowed its leaders to modernize their armed forces. In the meantime, they have signed a friendship agreement with Russia and appealed publicly for an end to American primacy (see Friedberg 2005). The steps being taken toward nuclear proliferation in North Korea and Iran, both declared enemies of the United States, raise the more ominous prospect of a worldwide nuclear arms race. Bilateral relations with other countries—Cuba, for example—have been hardened by decades of mutual suspicion and hostility, hindering the chances for diplomatic breakthroughs. Finally, an array of "intermestic" issues such as illegal immigration, drug smuggling, and energy dependence are proving equally difficult for the U.S. government to resolve, even with its immense power.

Military setbacks, rising anti-Americanism, and a severe economic crisis have damaged U.S. world power in recent years. Among those who stood to benefit from these problems were Russian president Dmitry Medvedev (left) and Chinese president Hu Jintao (right), who met in Beijing in May 2008 to resolve their political differences and to discuss closer military and economic cooperation.

The Paradox of America's World Power

These challenges to the United States raise profound questions about the nation's capacity to sustain its dominant position in a unipolar world. As noted earlier, this objective has long been pursued by the U.S. government, but recently it has been embraced explicitly as a top national security priority. Today, achieving this objective appears to be well within reach in view of the vast and unprecedented lead the country maintains in the essential categories of national power.

Such an outcome, however, will not be as easy to bring about as the hard numbers suggest. It is a central paradox of America's world power that, in seeking to sustain its global primacy, the United States is increasingly constrained by the very forces that propelled its rise to global predominance. These strengths—a culturally embedded sense of national **exceptionalism** (see Hodgson 2009), the diffusion of domestic foreign policy powers, and the free rein granted to civil society in the policy process—also create vulnerabilities for the U.S. government. Derived from an eighteenth-century model, the nation's governing structures remain remarkably unchanged in the twenty-first century. Yet the world order that the United States played a lead role in creating has changed in profound ways, along with the country's role in that order.

This book explores this paradox by examining its presence in the process of making U.S. foreign policy. Of particular interest are the institutions of power inside and outside the U.S. government that define the roles of public and private actors; create and reinforce common values, norms, and codes of conduct; and define what is possible among contending foreign policy choices. These institutions of power become more complex as the scope of U.S. foreign policy broadens, as the lines between domestic and foreign policy concerns are increasingly blurred, as the number and magnitude of problems crossing national borders increase, and as more individuals and groups become stakeholders and participants in the foreign policy process.

This paradox and its damaging consequences for the United States are visible in several recent examples:

- Domestic divisions over the U.S. grand strategy in the 1990s prevented the United States from adopting a coherent world role, despite its resounding victory in the Cold War and unprecedented global power. Instead, the Clinton administration pursued four contradictory strategies, often all at once: retrenchment, primacy, liberal internationalism, and selective engagement (Posen and Ross 1996/1997). This ambivalence was shared by the general public. When participants in a national survey were asked in 1999 to identify the biggest foreign policy problem facing the United States, they most often replied, "Don't know" (Rielly 1999, 11).

- Several members of Congress sued President Bill Clinton in 1999, without success, to force a withdrawal of U.S. forces from Kosovo. Legislators later charged that Clinton intervened in the renegade Yugoslav province to divert the public's attention from his impeachment by the House of

Representatives for lying about an affair with a White House intern. Well aware of domestic opposition to the Kosovo intervention, Clinton limited U.S. military action to high-altitude bombing raids, many of which missed their targets and produced large civilian casualties.

■ President George W. Bush's intelligence brief on August 6, 2001, featured the headline "Bin Laden Determined to Strike in U.S." and warned the White House of "suspicious activity in this country consistent with preparations for hijackings or other types of attacks, including recent surveillance of federal buildings in New York." No one acted on the warning, however, because of the many conflicting reports by the more than one dozen U.S. intelligence agencies that "lacked the incentives to cooperate, collaborate, and share information," according to the National Commission on Terrorist Attacks upon the United States (2004, 12). An October 2005 follow-up study by the commission reported "minimal progress" in sharing information among these agencies (9/11 Public Discourse Project 2005b).

■ Many top foreign policy positions in the Obama administration had yet to be filled by the end of its first year. These included many diplomatic positions in the State Department, a key Pentagon military post, and key jobs in the Treasury Department needed to manage the nation's economic recovery. This paralysis also afflicted the U.S. Agency for International Development, which is responsible for managing the nation's far-flung foreign aid programs. As one analyst (Rothkopf 2009b) observed, "It is now almost November and the new administration has failed to arrive at a candidate for the job everyone can agree on and who can pass the muster of the absurd vetting processes that dog would-be senior officials and impede this government's ability to function."

The costs of this paradox—in the loss of America's world power and prestige—can be enormous, as became painfully clear in Iraq. Late in 2002, the State Department gathered Iraqi engineers, financial managers, teachers, doctors, and public administrators to devise plans for reconstructing postwar Iraq. The Future of Iraq Project, as it was known, produced more than 1,200 pages, in thirteen volumes, of expert advice designed to "keep the lights on" and reassure a beleaguered population in the first days of foreign occupation. Seventeen working groups, including officials from several U.S. agencies, joined in the effort prior to the invasion of Iraq in March 2003.[8]

Secretary of Defense Donald Rumsfeld refused to consult these volumes, however. After he convinced President George W. Bush to grant exclusive powers of reconstruction to the Pentagon—historically, that task had been reserved for the State Department—"all references to the State Department disappeared from the organizational chart" (Gordon and Trainor 2006, 141). In its place, Iraq was managed by a U.S. administrator, Paul Bremer, who had little firsthand experience

---

8. See National Security Archive (2006) for a transcript of the report and more details on the project.

in Iraq. Among his first acts in office, Bremer disbanded the Iraqi security forces and Ministry of the Interior, thereby putting nearly 700,000 angry, unemployed Iraqis on the streets. The displaced forces, along with their weapons and ammunition, fueled an insurgency that turned on the American occupiers, paralyzed the new Iraqi government, and created regional instability that outlasted the Bush presidency.

In these and countless other cases, tensions among the White House, the foreign policy bureaucracy, and Congress produced negative consequences for U.S. foreign policy. Driven also by public opinion polls and partisan politics, government leaders made decisions on foreign policy that sapped rather than bolstered the nation's world power. The failure of the United States to steer a coherent course—a failure clearly visible to a global audience—reinforced the nation's image as a potent but dysfunctional superpower.

Cultural Roots of the Paradox

The roots of this paradox can be found in the U.S. **national style**—that is, the cultural influences that historically have shaped the country's approach to international relations (Dallek 1989). Although national style is an ambiguous concept and cultural influences are difficult to identify with precision, the conduct of every country's foreign policy reflects its distinctive sense of place within the international system. This sense of place, in turn, is shaped by tangible factors such as geographic location, the availability of natural resources, and the size and characteristics of the population. Other factors, such as a country's historical experience, also influence its national style.

When it became the first independent country in the Western Hemisphere, the United States was geographically far removed from the great powers of the time. This distance, combined with the ample territory and natural resources available within the thirteen original colonies, enabled the new nation to develop its political and economic systems with little outside assistance. The United States was distinctive in that its civil society, compared with those of most other countries, did not feature sharp divisions between a small but powerful aristocracy and a large but powerless feudal peasantry. As the French political thinker Alexis de Tocqueville ([1835] 1988, 56) observed after his tour of the young United States, "One finds a vast multitude of people with roughly the same ideas about religion, history, science, political economy, legislation, and government."

This consensus encouraged a sense of national exceptionalism, by which citizens felt the United States was destined not simply to survive as a nation-state but also to achieve the status of a superior world power. Long before the nation's independence, the first European settlers to North America proclaimed the founding of a "city upon a hill" that would inspire societies far from its shores. Colonial leaders later believed that independence from Great Britain would create "a more perfect union" based on limited, representative government.

This sense of moral righteousness, reducing world politics to a contest between good and evil, has persisted as a defining trait of U.S. foreign policy. In the early 1980s, President Ronald Reagan condemned the Soviet Union as an "evil empire." Bill Clinton adapted this view to the post–Cold War world by identifying "rogue states" as the principal threat to the United States. After the terrorist attacks of September 2001, George W. Bush described the struggle in starkly biblical terms: "Freedom and fear, justice and cruelty, have always been at war, and we know that God is not neutral between them." A year later, Bush declared the nation's enemies to be part of an "axis of evil" that must be destroyed for the United States to be truly secure. His call struck a chord among millions of evangelical Christians, who formed the core of Bush's voting bloc and favored the global promotion of U.S. moral values, by force if necessary (see Phillips 2006).

Such views have profound, but contradictory, implications for the conduct of U.S. foreign policy (see Brands 1998 and Monten 2005). One school of thought believes the United States should lead primarily by example, fearing that an activist foreign policy would only dirty the hands of U.S. leaders in "power politics." A second school of thought contends that U.S. leaders should engage in a global crusade against injustice, aggression, and war itself. Lacking consensus between **"exemplarists"** and **"vindicators"** in times of peace, the United States has pursued both strategies, detaching itself from the outside world during certain periods and immersing itself in foreign affairs during others. Most often, U.S. foreign policy exhibits the two tendencies at once, confounding observers at home and abroad (see Hook and Spanier 2010).

The public's ambivalent approach toward foreign affairs is most acute when the United States is at peace. Americans tend to focus on more immediate domestic concerns during these times, and elected officials respond in kind. Only when foreign problems reach crisis proportions do they spark the public's interest. As a result, the public makes a hasty demand for action by the U.S. government, which responds impulsively, frequently with little knowledge of the underlying problems that provoked the crisis. George Kennan (1951, 59), the architect of U.S. Cold War strategy, found this aspect of democratic foreign policy making particularly troublesome:

> I sometimes wonder whether in this respect a democracy is not uncomfortably similar to one of those prehistoric monsters with a body as long as this room and a brain the size of a pin. He lies there in his comfortable primeval mud and pays little attention to his environment; he is slow to wrath—in fact, you practically have to whack his tail off to make him aware that his interests are being disturbed. But, once he grasps this, he lays about with such blind determination that he not only destroys his adversary but largely wrecks his native habitat.

Institutional Branches

Every nation's political culture has a direct impact on the structures of governance that regulate public affairs, define the relationships between the rulers and the ruled, and carry out public policies. The prevalent ideas about the proper role of the government at home and abroad express themselves in the creation of legislatures, courts, and government agencies. These institutional "branches" of a nation's political culture determine what is possible in the policy-making process, constraining the options of policy makers. In addition, political institutions commonly multiply and produce new agencies and governing structures that further shape the policy process.

The links among prevalent cultural norms, political institutions, and government behavior can be clearly seen in the United States. Under the prevailing theory of the Enlightenment era, governments often do not simply regulate society, but also deny or suppress basic freedoms and, in the economic sphere, threaten private property and the profitability of firms through excessive taxes and regulations. Thus, governments must be actively restrained to protect individual liberties.

The architects of the U.S. government restrained its power in several ways. First, they established political liberties in the Bill of Rights that limited the sphere of governmental authority. Second, they dispersed power among the federal, state, and local governments. Finally, they provided for the sharing of federal powers among Congress, the president, and the judiciary. This institutional blueprint, devised more than two centuries ago, endures today. "The central feature of American politics is the fragmentation and dispersion of power and authority. It is not clear in the United States where sovereignty rests, if indeed it rests anywhere at all" (Krasner 1978, 61–62).

Yet for all its virtues in restraining centralized power, this fragmentation creates problems in the conduct of U.S. foreign policy, which requires a unified statement of national purpose, clear chains of command, consistency, and timely presidential action. Democratic norms "undermine and weaken the power and authority of government and detract, at times seriously, from its ability to compete internationally" (Huntington 1982, 18). This problem was illustrated in Obama's first year in office as he could not overcome bitter conflicts between the two political parties. Foreign powers can exploit such internal divisions and try to divide and conquer their more fragmented rivals. At home, a weak state is likely to be "captured" by interest groups that cater to their own needs rather than national interests. In this respect, Tocqueville considered democracies "decidedly inferior" to other governments (see In Their Own Words box).

In dispersing foreign policy powers across the legislative and executive branches, the architects of the U.S. government extended an "invitation to struggle for the privilege of directing American foreign policy" (Corwin 1957, 171). The institutional reality of divided powers leads to chronic friction between Congress and the White House over the ends and means of foreign policy. Unless the nation faces an unambiguous foreign challenge, the federal government rarely speaks with one voice. As a result, much of U.S. foreign policy is made, in the words of Supreme Court justice Robert Jackson in his concurring opinion in *Youngstown Co. v. Sawyer* (343 U.S. 579 [1952]), in a "zone of twilight in which [the president] and Congress may have concurrent authority, or in which its distribution is uncertain."

In wartime, however, presidents are generally granted far more power and freedom of action. As commander in chief, President George W. Bush seized on

IN THEIR OWN WORDS: ALEXIS DE TOCQUEVILLE

Alexis de Tocqueville, an aristocratic Frenchman, traveled through the United States in 1831–1832 to chronicle the social, political, public, religious, and intellectual life of the emerging democratic nation. His account of these travels, Democracy in America, *long considered one of the most astute observations of American life ever written, is still widely read and studied by historians and political scientists alike.*

I have no hesitation in saying that in the control of society's foreign affairs democratic governments do appear decidedly inferior to others. . . . Foreign policy does not require the use of any of the good qualities peculiar to democracy but does demand the cultivation of almost all those which it lacks. . . .

Democracy favors the growth of the state's internal resources; it extends comfort and develops public spirit, strengthens respect for law in the various classes of society, all of which things have no more than an indirect influence on the standing of one nation in respect to another. But a democracy finds it difficult to coordinate the details of a great undertaking and to fix on some plan and carry it through with determination in spite of obstacles. It has little capacity for combining measures in secret and waiting patiently for the result.

SOURCE: Alexis de Tocqueville, *Democracy in America*, ed. J. P. Mayer (New York: Perennial Library, [1835] 1988), 228–230.

this heightened authority after the September 2001 terrorist attacks. His decision to declare an open-ended war on terrorism and to redefine the laws of war in this conflict stemmed directly from this constitutional power. When Bush took office in January 2001, he filled his White House staff with lawyers and advisers who felt strongly that presidential powers had eroded over time and needed to be strengthened. The terrorist attacks in September silenced any differences between the White House and Congress (see Mayer 2008). Prior to the attacks, President Bush's domestic rivals had openly challenged his plans for nuclear missile defense, his rejection of global environmental accords, and his shift toward a unilateral foreign policy. After the attacks, Congress put these differences aside and gave Bush full discretion in pursuing and punishing the attackers (see Margulies 2006). Thus, the pendulum swung radically in the U.S. political system from legislative-executive gridlock to a virtual blank check for the president to prosecute the war on terrorism.

Still, Bush's efforts raised concerns heard earlier during the Vietnam War, when historian Arthur Schlesinger Jr. (1973) argued that an **imperial presidency** had taken hold in the United States. John Yoo, a legal adviser to the president, instructed Bush that Congress cannot "place any limits on the president's determinations as to any terrorist threat, the amount of military force to be used in response, or the method, timing, and nature of the response" (quoted in Shane 2005a). This view was rejected strongly by constitutional scholar Louis Fisher

(2007, 59), who observed that "the rule of law, the Constitution, and the 'sharing of power' cannot coexist with one-branch government."

An imperial presidency in the United States is of particular concern because of the lack of foreign policy experience most recent presidents have brought to the White House. Only three presidents since World War II—Dwight Eisenhower, Richard Nixon, and George H. W. Bush—had substantial backgrounds in foreign policy. Post–Cold War presidents Clinton and George W. Bush, elected in 1992 and 2000, respectively, had served only as governors. Bush reasoned that his very infrequent overseas travel during the many years his father was immersed in foreign affairs merely reflected his preference for the American way of life. Such a stance may seem paradoxical in view of the chief executive's immense world power. Yet, it is entirely consistent with the nation's ambivalent view of the "outside world"—a cultural perspective that looks to foreign peoples, places, and events with a mixture of intrigue and indifference, fascination and suspicion.

Institutional struggles within the U.S. government are not limited to legislative-executive relations. The executive branch itself is highly fragmented and prone to fierce internal competition over foreign policy. Officials in the Defense and State Departments routinely disagree over policy issues and compete for White House attention, larger budgets, and greater authority. These officials must also share power with their counterparts in the National Security Council, the intelligence community, and the other government agencies. Understandably, presidents often become frustrated by their inability to rein in the bureaucratic actors presumably under their control. President Harry Truman famously expressed this feeling in 1952 when he warned his successor, Dwight Eisenhower, not to expect the kind of discipline he enjoyed as commander of U.S. armed forces during World War II. "He'll sit here and he'll say 'Do this! Do that!' And nothing will happen. Poor Ike—it won't be a bit like the Army. He'll find it very frustrating" (quoted in Neustadt 1960, 9).

Pervasive Civil Society

In addition to these domestic political institutions, forces outside the government, and increasingly beyond the United States altogether, further complicate the American foreign policy process. These external forces, which include public opinion, the news media, interest groups, and intergovernmental organizations, collectively form a transnational civil society. Private groups, including business interests as well as religious institutions and think tanks, exert pressure continually on the United States to accommodate their policy preferences. Because U.S. elected officials must also heed domestic public opinion for electoral reasons, so must they be sensitive to public opinion overseas, particularly in democratic countries whose support for American foreign policy is needed. In addition, the financial ownership of major news outlets has become increasingly transnational, and the impact of their news coverage is felt immediately in the White House.

Presidents choose which private groups, as well as government agencies, they will invite into the foreign policy process. A primary source of input for all recent administrations has been the multinational corporations that share close connections with many top foreign policy officials. These firms actively seek benefits from the U.S. government in the form of contracts, tax breaks, favorable regulations, and access to foreign markets.[9] The greater influence wielded by multinational corporations than by nonprofit groups such as Amnesty International and Greenpeace demonstrates clearly that not all interest groups are created equal. "If there is government intervention in the corporate economy, so there is corporate intervention in the governmental process," sociologist C. Wright Mills (1956, 8) observed. This pattern, to be expected in any society that emphasizes market-driven economic growth, raises questions about the "democratic" conduct of foreign policy.

Public opinion plays an important role in the policy process of any democratic nation. The first scientific polling, conducted shortly after World War II, found Americans to be largely ignorant of events taking place overseas (Bailey 1948; Almond 1950). Although more recent surveys suggest greater coherence in public preferences (see Jentleson 1992), surveys and nationwide tests of U.S. school students reveal a lack of in-depth knowledge of world history, geography, and international problems. Several examples demonstrate this "knowledge gap" (Iyengar and Morin 2006). A 1999 survey found the historical knowledge of American college students to warrant grades of "D" or "F" (American Council of Trustees and Alumni 2000). Americans ranked next to last among sixteen countries whose citizens were tested in 2002 for their knowledge of world geography. More recently, American adults reported having little or no knowledge of the Middle East (Council on American-Islamic Relations 2006). Yet another survey, conducted by National Geographic (2006), found more than 60 percent of young adults (18–24 years old) unable to find Iraq on a map, and nearly 90 percent unable to locate Afghanistan, even as the United States waged war in both countries (see Figure 1.4).

Still, elected leaders must follow public preferences if they wish to remain in power, a fact of political life that plagued the White House in 2005 and 2006 as it confronted growing doubts about the war in Iraq and the overall direction of U.S. foreign policy. "Actively creating democracies in other countries" came in last among eleven foreign policy priorities identified in a national survey conducted in 2006 (Public Agenda 2006). The most popular item—helping the citizens of other countries recover from natural disasters—suggested that the public wished to see the United States as the "world's firefighter" rather than its policeman (Yankelovich 2006).

Trends in public opinion are closely related to coverage of international affairs by the news media. Such coverage decreased dramatically after the Cold War as news organizations closed overseas bureaus and reduced the proportion of international news to about 10 percent of total news coverage in the print and broadcast media (Graber 2006). National surveys consistently reveal that U.S.

9. A useful guide to these corporate contracts is provided by the Center for Responsive Politics, a nonprofit nongovernmental organization (www.opensecrets.org).

Figure 1.4   Young Americans and World Geography (percentage able to locate selected countries)

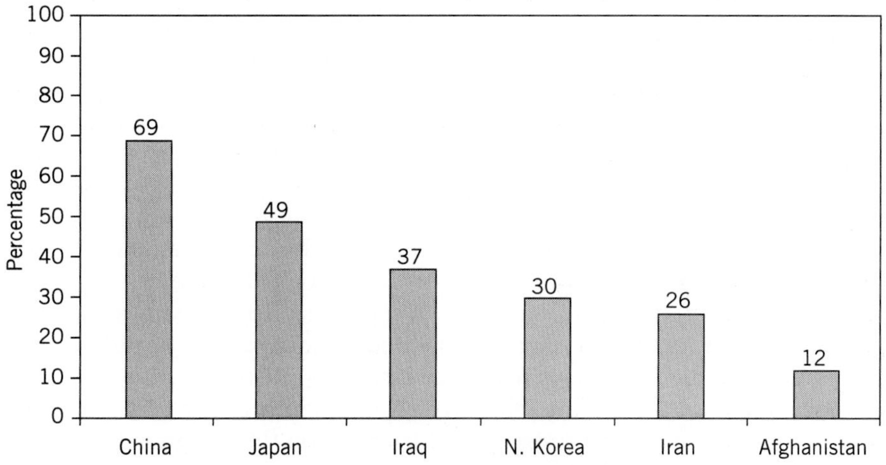

SOURCE: National Geographic, "2006 National Geographic–Roper Public Affairs 2006 Geographic Literacy Study" (May 2006), www.nationalgeographic.com/roper2006/findings.html.

newspaper readers find foreign news of the least concern (see, for example, Rielly 2003). But this indifference changes when the United States faces an international crisis. At that point, media outlets shift to saturation coverage, "parachuting" into war zones correspondents who have little knowledge of the regions or conflicts they will be covering. During the invasion of Iraq, ratings for U.S. news networks skyrocketed as news reporters "embedded" in U.S. battalions provided instant and dramatic images of Operation Iraqi Freedom. The same ratings then fell as the occupation dragged on and as global crises such as the Asian tsunami in 2004 and the genocide that began in 2003 in Sudan received little sustained attention by the American news media.

Conclusion

A central question examined in this book is how well the United States can provide the international leadership it espouses in the face of the domestic and global constraints that are essential features of its political and social system. Of particular concern is whether a political culture either indifferent to foreign affairs or obsessed with events overseas is compatible with this type of dominant world role. The institutions of power raise further concerns about the U.S. government's ability to overcome domestic divisions as well as pressures from transnational civil society, particularly economic pressures. How the government manages the paradox of its world power will determine how long U.S. primacy endures in the turbulent new millennium.

This paradox, which can be seen throughout the nation's history, has direct consequences for the course of U.S. foreign policy, which has vacillated for more than two centuries between policies of engagement with and detachment from the "outside world." Most recently, this pendulum swung from the administrations of Bill Clinton (engagement) and George W. Bush (detachment), then back to Obama's newest venture in global engagement. These divergent courses, reflecting a wider ambivalence in America's political culture, make the United States a curious and unpredictable world power. While this may be frustrating for leaders overseas, they have little choice but to manage the ongoing identity crisis in U.S. foreign policy.

The mutual love-hate relationship between the United States and the world beyond its borders may be inevitable given the nation's unprecedented primacy. There is little doubt, however, that the country's successes and failures also stem from the peculiarities of the U.S. government and social structures and the growing pressures imposed by transnational civil society. Historical patterns suggest that the U.S. political system is self-corrective; previous bursts of "creedal passion" have been followed by restraint and moderation (Huntington 1981). Halfway through George W. Bush's second term, observers proclaimed the "end of cowboy diplomacy" and noted the president's greater emphasis on diplomacy and allied cooperation (Allen and Ratnesar 2006).

It remains to be seen, however, how effectively the U.S. government will adapt to long-term trends in the global balance of power that confront the Obama administration. In his first year in office, the president could barely break away from the nation's economic crisis long enough to manage the array of foreign policy problems churning overseas. His use of many of Bush's war policies also provoked criticism: the continued use of the Guantánamo Bay detention center; the escalation of U.S. war efforts in Afghanistan; the rendition of prisoners to third countries for prosecution; and the CIA's use of unmanned "drones" to bomb and assassinate political enemies—not just in Iraq and Afghanistan but Pakistan as well (Mayer 2009). Most troubling, the president had failed to inspire consensus on national priorities within Congress, whose bitter rivalries left Americans disillusioned and highly skeptical of "politics as usual."

These issues make the study of U.S. foreign policy a challenging yet rewarding enterprise at this critical period in the history of the nation and the world. The chapters ahead examine more closely the impact of domestic and transnational institutions on the process of U.S. foreign policy making. The book's second and third sections analyze the structure of these institutions, and the final section illustrates their role in the primary domains of foreign policy: security and defense, economic affairs, and global problems such as environmental decay and weapons proliferation. First, however, Chapter 2 reviews the origins and evolution of U.S. foreign policy, and Chapter 3 introduces the contending theories of foreign policy decision making.

Point/Counterpoint
UNILATERALISM VS. MULTILATERALISM

A central point of contention in recent U.S. foreign policy involves the degree to which the United States works with other governments or "goes it alone" in pursuing its perceived national interests. Upon taking office in 2001, President George W. Bush embraced widespread public and congressional concerns that the multilateral foreign policy adopted by his predecessors since World War II was threatening the country's sovereignty and weakening its capacity to use its vast power and influence abroad. His shift toward a more unilateral foreign policy predictably angered foreign leaders, particularly those with whom the U.S. government had previously established close alliances and other means of collaboration.

Among Bush's primary critics was Jacques Chirac, the president of France, who openly complained about the U.S. government's turn away from multilateral engagement. "Any community with only one dominant power is always a dangerous one and provokes reactions," Chirac told *Time* magazine in an interview posted on its Web site on February 16, 2003. "That's why I favor a multipolar world in which Europe obviously has its place." He was especially upset with Bush's decision to launch a preventive invasion of Iraq in 2003 without support from the United Nations, an action he claimed was "a violation of international law and a threat to the current global balance of power." In 2007 Russian president Vladimir Putin joined the diplomatic assault on U.S. unilateralism, complaining that "this is the world of one master, one sovereign."

This burst of global opposition came, ironically, at the very time the United States had fulfilled its historic ambition of global leadership. Since the nation's founding at the height of the Enlightenment era, its leaders considered American political and social values to be universal and pledged to remake the world in the nation's image. Today, even under heavy strains, the U.S. constitutional government remains a model for emerging democracies, and its robust economy provides opportunities for millions of immigrants, foreign investors, and global exporters. The nation's universities, whose scientists swept the 2006 Nobel Prizes for physics, chemistry, and medicine, continue to attract top students from overseas.

President Obama's latest attempt to revive the nation's multilateral foreign policies was widely embraced overseas. But many Americans remained convinced that U.S. security is best assured by going it alone. The debate typifies the paradox of America's world power.

Key Terms

asymmetric warfare, p. 13	exemplarists, p. 18	primacy, p. 3
bandwagon, p. 9	globalization, p. 11	soft power, p. 6
blowback, p. 11	hegemon, p. 3	terrorism, p. 13
Bush Doctrine, p. 2	imperial presidency, p. 20	unipolar balance of power, p. 3
empire, p. 3		
exceptionalism, p. 15	national style, p. 17	vindicators, p. 18

Internet References

The **American Foreign Policy Council** (www.afpc.org) is a nonprofit organization whose research is devoted to democratization and bilateral and regional relationships between the United States and other countries. The organization's programs in Russia, China, and Asia address trade, defense, and other policy issues.

The **Brookings Institution** (www.brookings.edu) is a nonprofit, nonpartisan think tank in Washington, D.C. Its scholars, fellows, and academics produce policy reports, briefs, and books related to U.S. foreign policy. Areas of interest are trade, defense, diplomacy, international institutions, and bilateral relations with foreign countries.

The **Carnegie Council: The Voice for Ethics in International Affairs** (www.cceia.org/index.html) focuses on human rights, conflict, environmental issues, economic disparities, and political reconciliation in the world. Scholars produce research briefs and books on current topics that analyze the ethics of international relations with a specific focus on the U.S. role in these policy issues. Carnegie Council publications include the journal *Ethics and International Affairs,* much of which is available online via the "publications" link on the council's home page.

The **Carnegie Endowment for International Peace** (www.carnegieendowment.org) is a nonprofit, nonpartisan organization that concentrates on global change by examining international organizations, bilateral relations, and political-economic forces in the world. Special attention is devoted to the U.S.-Russia relationship as well as geopolitics involving the United States and other countries. The organization publishes *Foreign Policy,* one of the leading magazines on world politics and foreign policy with an emphasis on the United States (www.foreignpolicy.com).

The **Center for Strategic and International Studies** (www.csis.org) is a nonprofit, nonpartisan organization that addresses international defense and security issues, with an emphasis on policy analysis, policy recommendations, and geographic analysis. The center publishes the *Washington Quarterly,* which analyzes global changes and foreign policies, looking especially at the U.S. role in the world, defense procurement, terrorism and counterterrorism, and regional issues (www.twq.com).

The **Council on Foreign Relations** (www.cfr.org) studies international affairs, foreign policy, and the role of the United States in the world. The council examines an array of

(continued)

issues as they pertain to the United States, such as trade, defense, security, globalization, terrorism, specific regions, energy resources and the environment, and political systems. The council also publishes *Foreign Affairs,* a leading journal that features scholarly analysis of these issues (www.foreignaffairs.org).

The **Foreign Policy Association** (www.fpa.org) is a nonprofit organization dedicated to educating legislators and the American public on U.S. foreign policy issues. Its mission includes all aspects of U.S. foreign policy, especially current events and global issues. The FPA provides reports, videos, and books on regional and specific policy issues.

Foreign Policy in Focus (www.fpif.org) is a think tank that produces policy reports on the United States and its role in the world. Specific policy briefs and reports include, but are not limited to, human rights, regional relationships, bilateral relationships, defense funding and procurement, terrorism, trade, energy, and environmental issues.

Part of Johns Hopkins University, the **Foreign Policy Institute** (www.sais-jhu.edu/centers/fpi) provides training and research on the global role of the United States. The institute brings together all disciplines interested in U.S. foreign policy. It also publishes the *SAIS Review of International Affairs,* which analyzes current international policies.

The **Foreign Policy Research Institute** (www.fpri.org) studies U.S. national interests, the war on terrorism, security relationships, and long-term policy planning. The research is based on a multidisciplinary approach that includes scholars and advisers from economics, politics, law, the media, and history. *Orbis,* a quarterly journal published by the institute, consists of reports from conferences and scholars on U.S. and world national interests (www.fpri.org/orbis).

The **Hoover Institution on War, Revolution, and Peace** (www.hoover.org) is devoted to policy analysis and both domestic and international affairs research within the ideological framework of an emphasis on a free society. The Hoover Institution researches trade, markets, postcommunist transition, international law, and democratic growth. Fellows at the Hoover Institution produce policy briefs, the *Hoover Digest* (www.hoover.org/publications/digest), and books through the Hoover Press.

The **Institute for Foreign Policy Analysis** (www.ifpa.org) provides briefings for foreign policy students who are interested in the costs, benefits, and planning of U.S. foreign policy. The institute covers a variety of issues but focuses on globalization, missile defense, international institutions, and grand strategies.

The **RAND Corporation** (www.rand.org) is a private research group that concentrates on international affairs, homeland security, terrorism, and U.S. national security issues. It also produces reports on individual countries that have close ties to the United States, as well as the *RAND Review,* a magazine about current security and defense issues (www.rand.org/publications/randreview).

The **U.S. Department of State** (www.state.gov) manages many aspects of U.S. diplomacy and the U.S. foreign policy process, including foreign aid, peace building, democratization, and disease and poverty prevention. The Web site provides speeches, policy descriptions, and issue explanations for those studying American foreign policy.

2 CHAPTER

The Expansion of U.S. Power

U.S. president Theodore Roosevelt tests a steam shovel during construction of the Panama Canal in November 1906. Roosevelt had supported earlier efforts by Panamanian rebels to seize control of the future canal zone, declare independence from Colombia, and seek diplomatic recognition by the United States. Congress promptly approved a treaty with the new government that granted the United States "power and authority" over the canal "in perpetuity." Under President Jimmy Carter, the U.S. government agreed in 1977 to turn control of the canal over to Panama in 2000.

The central goal of this book is to help readers understand U.S. foreign policy today. This understanding is impossible, however, without reference to the nation's past experience, first as a regional power and then as the predominant world power. This chapter reviews these developments, evaluating their relevance to the current policy process. A single chapter cannot provide an exhaustive survey of U.S. diplomatic history, but it can highlight the pivotal events that shaped the nation's relations with the world beyond its shores.[1]

Such a historical perspective reveals the origins and development of the paradox of America's world power. As the United States grew from a regional power to the holder of global primacy, it continued to maintain the political arrangements, along with the social and cultural traditions, that prevailed in a time of diplomatic detachment. Early American leaders advanced claims of moral, political, and social exceptionalism, while seeking to protect the nation from global entanglements. Their ongoing promotion of democratic reforms in foreign countries contributed to a "constitutional" order after World War II that, by the twenty-first century, was seen widely as threatening to the nation's own sovereignty and an unacceptable constraint on its freedom of action. Meanwhile, the nation's record as a

1. Among the many sources of more extensive information on U.S. diplomatic history, see H. Jones (2002) and Paterson, Clifford, and Hagan (2000) for informative histories of the nation's early foreign policy; Hook and Spanier (2010) for a detailed review of U.S. foreign policy after World War II; and LaFeber (2004) and McCormick (1995) for more critical views of the Cold War.

catalyst for economic globalization affirmed one of its founding ambitions but fueled the rise of economic competitors, particularly in the area of industrial production.

This historical review covers two distinct time periods. The first involves the gradual expansion of U.S. territory, wealth, and influence from the nation's founding to the First World War. As we will find, early American leaders charted a course of unilateral action, avoiding diplomatic ties to the great powers of Europe while building an industrial economy that would make the United States a major force in global trade markets. As for territorial expansion, the western frontier offered a seemingly limitless opportunity to create, in the words of Thomas Jefferson, an "empire of liberty" from the Atlantic to the Pacific oceans. Jefferson and his successors acquired vast territories through a variety means, from negotiated agreements and sales to forced relocations of indigenous peoples and outright military conquest. This pattern of territorial expansion, typical of past imperial powers, was viewed widely as evidence of national exceptionalism. "Such claims are dangerous," observed Godfrey Hodgson (2009, 16), "because they are the soil in which unreal and hubristic assumptions of American destiny have grown" (for a similar critique, see Smith 2007).

The second period covers the conduct of U.S. foreign policy once the country became a great power in the twentieth century. The United States began the century in the midst of a struggle to colonize the Philippines, and then asserted hegemonic control over Central America. Emerging from the world wars with unprecedented military strength and economic clout, U.S. leaders then became engulfed in a struggle against the Soviet Union and other communist states. The Soviet Union's collapse in 1991 left the United States in the position of unprecedented global primacy. But maintaining this status proved more difficult than expected as regional conflicts and civil wars ignited in many parts of the world. The terrorist attacks on the United States in September 2001 literally brought these conflicts home, shattering the nation's historic sense of invulnerability, and ushering in a protracted "war on terrorism" that continues to this day. As journalist Michael Hirsh (2003, 25) observed, "We are in this world with both feet now. We have achieved our Founding Fathers' fondest dream, and, at the same time, their worst nightmare. We are a shining success, the supreme power on earth. And we are entangled everywhere."

Aside from the cultural roots of U.S. foreign policy, the nation's behavior must be viewed in the context of institutional arrangements, domestic and global, that were created by political leaders over the nation's history, under very different circumstances. Managing global primacy in such a complex environment has been just as difficult for U.S. leaders as for the nation's earlier "rise to globalism" (Ambrose 1988). This combination of cultural and institutional forces contributed to the successes of the United States as well as to its frequent failures, domestic struggles, and erratic changes of course—in short, the paradox of America's world power.

Economic and Territorial Expansion

America's earliest leaders were concerned first and foremost with building political institutions that could preserve the nation's independence. The Articles of Confederation, which in 1781 established the framework of the first American political system, featured a very weak central government. Under the articles, the original thirteen states conducted their own trade policies while the cash-starved Congress largely dismantled the nation's military forces, thereby making the United States vulnerable to intimidation from the more unified powers overseas. The country cried out for a stronger national government.

Under the U.S. Constitution, drafted in 1787 and ratified in 1788, states maintained primary control over their internal affairs while ceding sovereignty to the federal government. The president and Congress shared responsibilities for American foreign policy (see Chapters 4 and 5). James Madison, the primary architect of the Constitution, recognized that such power sharing was crucial for the democratic control of government. On the one hand, the president, who would serve as commander in chief of U.S. armed forces while conducting the day-to-day business of foreign policy, would be able to act more quickly and decisively than Congress. On the other hand, Congress, with its powers to declare war and control spending, among other powers, would restrain the president. Together, they would provide a unified front for the advancement of the nation's foreign policy goals.

The new framework was not meant to encourage U.S. activism in diplomacy, which many Americans saw as an artifact of the Old World, long dominated by monarchs, church leaders, and feudal despots. Thomas Jefferson, the first secretary of state and third president, observed in a note to his personal secretary, William Short, that diplomacy was "the pest of the peace of the world, as the workshop in which nearly all the wars of Europe are manufactured." Although the State Department was the first federal agency created under the Constitution, it received few resources, and for more than a century it maintained only a tiny staff.[2]

Architects of U.S. foreign policy institutions made an exception, however, for foreign *economic* relations, which they considered more suitable than diplomacy in advancing the nation's interests. Early in the nineteenth century, the government hired hundreds of consular officers to secure markets overseas and ensure the protection of U.S. merchant ships and crews. By 1820, the United States had become the fourth-richest country in the world as measured by per capita income (Prestowitz 2003, 84). A leading exporter of agricultural products, especially cotton and tobacco, the nation would soon become a major producer of industrial goods as well.

Although early American leaders disagreed about the means of attaining foreign policy goals, they shared an expansive view of the nation's future. Alexander Hamilton, the first Treasury secretary, believed the country should "erect one

---

2. The State Department had just eight employees in 1790, twenty-three in 1830, and forty-two in 1860. The U.S. government did not create a full-scale foreign service until 1924, long after the United States had emerged as a major world power (see www.state.gov for a chronology of the department's budget and personnel).

Table 2.1 U.S. Foreign Policy Chronology, 1783–1945

1783	United States gains independence from Great Britain.
1788	Constitution establishes stronger American government.
1793	United States proclaims neutrality in European wars.
1803	France sells Louisiana Territory to United States.
1812	Territorial and trade disputes provoke U.S. war with Great Britain.
1823	Monroe Doctrine proclaims U.S. sphere of influence throughout Western Hemisphere.
1845	United States annexes Texas.
1846–1848	Mexican-American War.
1853	United States forcefully "opens" Japan to American trade.
1867	Russia sells Alaska to the United States.
1898	United States annexes Hawaii.
1898	Spanish-American War.
1899	United States calls for "Open Door policy" toward China.
1902	U.S. troops overcome insurrection in the Philippines.
1903	United States signs treaty to build Panama Canal.
1904	Roosevelt Corollary to Monroe Doctrine proclaims United States "international police power."
1914	World War I begins in Europe.
1917	United States declares war against Germany.
1918	German surrender ends World War I.
1919	U.S. Senate rejects Treaty of Versailles and League of Nations.
1928	Pact of Paris, also known as the Kellogg-Briand Pact, renounces war as an "instrument of national policy."
1935, 1936	Congress passes Neutrality Acts barring American intervention in Europe.
1939	German territorial conquests lead to World War II.
1941	Japanese attack on Pearl Harbor naval base in Hawaii provokes U.S. entry into World War II.
1944	Bretton Woods system, including World Bank and International Monetary Fund, is created to manage world economy.
1945	Defeat of Axis powers ends World War II. United Nations is established.

great American system superior to the control of all trans-Atlantic force or influence and able to dictate the terms of the connection between the old and the new world" (quoted in Earle 1937, 69). Jefferson, too, envisioned U.S. dominance extending beyond the nation's borders. He foresaw an "empire of liberty" in which "our rapid multiplication will . . . cover the whole northern if not southern continent, with a people speaking the same language, governed in similar forms, and by similar laws" (quoted in McDougall 1997, 78).

Contrary to conventional wisdom, the United States was hardly an isolationist country in its formative years (see Table 2.1). The government pursued an

Point/Counterpoint
HAMILTON VS. JEFFERSON

Differences over the direction U.S. foreign policy should take were epitomized in the nation's early years by Alexander Hamilton and Thomas Jefferson. Although both political leaders believed the United States was destined to join the ranks of the great powers, they disagreed about how this feat should be accomplished.

An admirer of Great Britain's political and economic system, Hamilton thought the United States should establish itself as a major industrial power with a strong navy and close financial ties to foreign capitals, including London. Jefferson believed the United States should adopt a more modest course, refining its democracy at home and creating a nation of small farmers rather than industrialists. He worried that building the stronger national government favored by Hamilton

would inevitably lead to a standing military force and a tyrannical head of state.

The two men never resolved their ideological differences. However, after taking office in 1801, Jefferson, in the types of actions he undertook, displayed much of Hamilton's penchant for wielding power. The new president moderated his staunch support for France, where he had previously served as ambassador. As France descended into the Napoleonic Wars, Jefferson proclaimed that U.S. security should be maintained by "peace, commerce, and honest friendship with all nations—entangling alliances with none." Jefferson also exploited his presidential powers in negotiating the Louisiana Purchase and pursuing other measures that would enhance the nation's territorial and military strength.

---

expansionist foreign policy, westward and *away* from the great powers of Europe, while also aggressively seeking foreign trade. The nation's growing territory, detailed below, served as both a blessing and a curse. "Attaining even minimal security," Robert Kagan (2006, 12) observed, "required an ever-enlarging sphere of control and dominance, for whenever one boundary was established, other threats always existed beyond it."

The expansion of American power featured a consistent pattern of **unilateralism.** Rather than collaborating and pooling resources with like-minded states, leaders adopted a unilateral foreign policy favoring autonomy and self-sufficiency. For President George Washington, who severed an alliance with France in 1793 despite that nation's earlier role in securing U.S. independence, the benefits of going it alone were paramount. In his view, peacetime alliances presented unacceptable risks of surrendering the nation's control over its overseas commitments.[3]

---

3. The ill-fated pact between the United States and France was the last peacetime alliance signed by the U.S. government until the mid-twentieth century. See Gaddis (2005) for a detailed review of unilateralism as a centerpiece of U.S. foreign policy before the world wars.

Upon leaving office three years later, Washington summarized his view in his Farewell Address:

> The great rule of conduct for us in regard to foreign nations is, in extending our commercial relations to have with them as little political connection as possible. . . . Europe has a set of primary interests which to us have none or a very remote relation. Hence she must be engaged in frequent controversies, the causes of which are essentially foreign to our concerns. . . . Our detached and distant situation invites and enables us to pursue a different course. . . . It is our true policy to steer clear of permanent alliances with any portion of the foreign world.

Manifest Destiny on the Western Frontier

The United States, driven by a "cult of nationalism" that provided a moral basis for expansion, came to dominate the Western Hemisphere by default (Van Alstyne 1965). The nation's emergence as a regional power coincided with the demise of the British, French, Russian, and Spanish outposts in North America. Globally, a **multipolar balance of power** existed that was anchored by the European powers, which maintained relatively peaceful relations with each other in the century separating the Napoleonic and world wars. The United States, which along with Japan emerged as formidable "offshore powers" in the nineteenth century (see Figure 2.1), filled this geopolitical vacuum in a variety of ways: by buying vast territories at bargain prices, negotiating settlements, and forcefully seizing territories when other measures failed. Through these actions, the United States became the hemisphere's economic and military giant, and a global superpower in the making.

In expanding westward, settlers and government forces violently subdued the American Indian population, whose relatively small numbers, internal divisions, and lack of modern weaponry left them incapable of successfully resisting

Figure 2.1   Multipolar Balance of World Power (mid-nineteenth century)

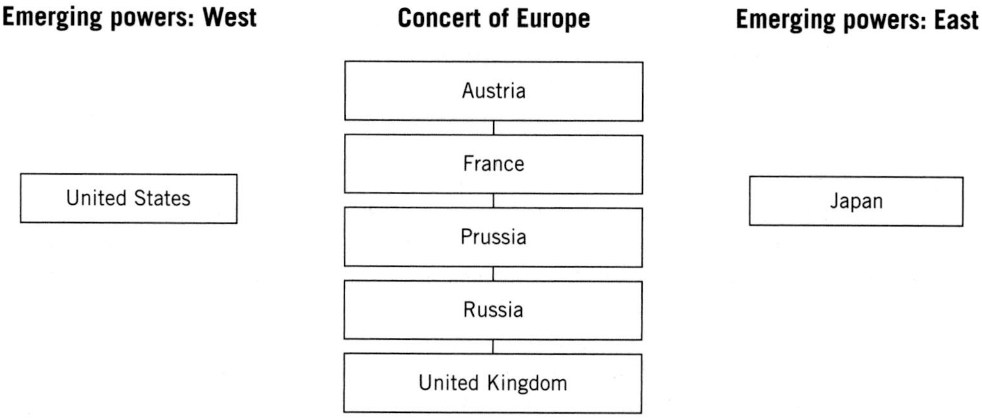

Emerging powers: West   **Concert of Europe**   **Emerging powers: East**

United States

Austria

France

Prussia

Russia

United Kingdom

Japan

encroachments on their lands. Early government leaders sought to assimilate the American Indians into the general population and society (Steele 1994). But their successors abandoned such notions and made the displacement or elimination of native Americans an object of government policy. Although this aspect of U.S. expansion falls outside the conventional bounds of foreign policy, it is neverthe- less "a central theme of American diplomatic history" (LaFeber 1989, 10).

The first major territorial gain occurred in 1803, when Jefferson acquired the vast Louisiana Territory, which stretched westward from the Mississippi River to the Rocky Mountains and northward from the Gulf of Mexico to the Oregon Ter- ritory. French ruler Napoleon Bonaparte, who had regained the territory from Spain two years earlier, was unable to govern, let alone defend, such a massive amount of land in North America while pursuing his ambitions in Europe. He made the most of his plight by offering Louisiana to the United States for $15 mil- lion (or about three cents an acre). Jefferson, though suspecting that his role in the Louisiana Purchase was "an act beyond the Constitution," eagerly accepted the offer (see Kukla 2003).

The acquisition of the Louisiana Territory, followed by the displacement of Spain from Florida, left the United States free to focus on state building, economic development, and further continental expansion (see Map 1, Nineteenth-Century European Empires and U.S. Continental Expansion, in map section). After the War of 1812, in which they struggled over unresolved trade and territorial differ- ences, the United States and Great Britain established close economic ties. The demise of the Spanish empire in Latin America, which led to the liberation of its colonies, paved the way for U.S. regional hegemony—that is, external dominance without formal political authority. In 1823 President James Monroe, seeking to discourage renewed European intrusions into Latin America as well as Russian ambitions along the Pacific coast, proclaimed the **Monroe Doctrine,** which fur- ther separated the United States from the European powers: "In the wars of the European powers in matters relating to themselves we have never taken any part, nor does it comport with our policy to do so. . . . With the movements in this hemisphere we are of necessity more immediately connected. . . . The political system of the [European] powers is essentially different in this respect from that of America. . . . [W]e should consider any attempt on their part to extend their system to any portion of this hemisphere as dangerous to our peace and safety."

Mexico's independence from Spain in 1821 paved the way for the next sig- nificant act of U.S. expansion. Many Americans had purchased land in the north- ern Mexican province of Texas, and in 1835 this growing population launched an independence movement of its own. Within a year, Texan rebels had defeated the Mexican army and declared Texas an independent country. The U.S. government's annexation of Texas in 1845 was viewed widely as further evidence that the United States had God's blessing to continue its westward expansion. In the *Democratic Review,* editor John O'Sullivan proclaimed the **manifest destiny** of the United States "to overspread the continent allotted by Providence for the free development of our yearly multiplying millions" (quoted in Pratt 1927, 797–798). Such claims were applied to the weakly defended Mexican territories west and north of Texas, for which President James K. Polk initiated a series of border skirmishes that escalated into a full-scale war. The United States quickly defeated the Mexican army and then signed a peace treaty in 1848 requiring Mexico to cede nearly 1 million square miles of land.

Opening the Door to Asia

The conquest of northern Mexico, along with the acquisition of the Oregon Territory from Great Britain in 1846, effectively closed the western frontier, which had been a symbol of virtually endless opportunity for American expansion. Advocates of continued expansion turned to the Pacific Ocean as the new frontier. "He would be a rash prophet who should assert that the expansive character of America has now entirely ceased," wrote historian Frederick Jackson Turner in 1920 (37). "Movement has been its dominant fact, and, unless this training has no effect upon a people, the American energy will continually demand a wider field for its exercise."

The United States had much to gain economically by tapping into the enormous markets of East Asia. Expansionists downplayed this economic rationale, however, emphasizing nobler motivations instead. An appeal to economic interests would cast the country in the same light as the traditional great powers, which supposedly lacked the "manifest destiny" uniquely bestowed upon the Americans. Even as it fought the Mexican army for control of the western frontier, the United States was making overtures to Japan for commercial relations. When these efforts failed, President Millard Fillmore, in 1853, deployed naval vessels to Tokyo. Faced with this early example of **gunboat diplomacy,** Japan's emperor accepted a "treaty of friendship" in 1854 that provided for U.S. access to the Japanese market.

American interests in the Pacific Ocean extended well beyond Japan. In addition to the several islands it occupied to serve as coaling stations for U.S. ships and to prevent other countries from taking the islands, the United States was especially interested in the Hawaiian Islands, located midway between North America and Asia. American officials first sought favorable commercial treatment from the Hawaiian monarchy. Unable to achieve a treaty on its own terms, the U.S. government, in 1893, recruited a rebel army that staged a successful coup against the monarchy. Within days, the new government of Hawaii signed a treaty of annexation with the United States. The United States also gained control of Alaska during this period, purchasing the remote territory from Russia's czar for $7 million.[4]

Critics accused the United States of behaving like the European empires it had long condemned. But such protests proved futile as illustrated by the Spanish-American War, in which the United States clashed with Spain over its colony in Cuba. As American forces were ousting Spain from Cuba, a U.S. fleet on the other side of the world was defeating Spanish forces in the Philippines, another Spanish

---

4. Alaska and Hawaii remained U.S. territories until 1959, when they became the forty-ninth and fiftieth states of the Union, respectively.

colony. The United States gained control of the Philippines only after waging a lengthy war that left thousands of casualties, largely Filipino, in its wake. President William McKinley chose not to annex Cuba, preferring to control the island indirectly, but he adopted a different approach to the Philippines. The United States recognized the commercial potential of the Southeast Asian islands, particularly when linked to the rapidly expanding markets of China. Advocates of American occupation seized on the prospect of bringing Christianity and "civilization" to the Philippines. These factors contributed to McKinley's decision to rule the Philippines as a U.S. colony, marking an exception to the U.S. government's general rule of opposing colonization.

The United States entered the twentieth century as the only major regional superpower, a hegemon, with foreign policy interests of global proportions. The nation's territory extended across North America and the Pacific Ocean. Between 1865 and 1900, its population had doubled to 71 million, in large part from European immigration. Meanwhile, U.S. economic output matched, and then exceeded, that of the major European powers. More Americans lived in cities than in rural areas, and industrial production contributed more than agriculture to national output. Securing overseas markets, therefore, became a national priority. In 1899 the United States proclaimed an **Open Door policy** that was designed to prevent China from being carved up among European trading interests. Historian William Appleman Williams (1959, 43), a critic of the policy, found it to be "derived from the proposition that America's overwhelming economic power would cast the economy and the politics of the weaker, under-developed countries in a pro-American mold."

A Big Stick in Latin America

President Theodore Roosevelt, a former naval commander, a veteran of the Spanish-American War, and a strong advocate of U.S. expansion, proved to be the central American figure in foreign policy as the new century began (see Morris 2001). He eagerly sought to become a world leader. In 1905 Roosevelt received the Nobel Peace Prize for negotiating the end of the Russo-Japanese War. Two years later, Roosevelt deployed a U.S. naval armada around the world, a symbol of the nation's arrival as a global power. The president believed in a version of social Darwinism that viewed wars as both inevitable and noble, with the victors assigned a "mandate from civilization" to look after less-powerful nations. Citing a favorite aphorism from his safaris in Africa, Roosevelt pledged that the United States would "speak softly, but carry a big stick."

The Roosevelt administration concerned itself in particular with Latin America, a U.S. sphere of influence since the proclamation of the Monroe Doctrine. The president engineered a domestic uprising in northern Colombia in 1903, after which the United States recognized the new Republic of Panama and signed a treaty to build and lease the Panama Canal. Concerned now not only with European meddling in the region, but also with internal power struggles that threatened friendly governments, the president issued the **Roosevelt Corollary** to the

Monroe Doctrine. Such unrest, it stated, "may ultimately require intervention by some civilized nation" and "may force the United States, however reluctantly . . . to the exercise of an international police power." The United States intervened militarily in Haiti, Honduras, Nicaragua, and other countries where internal unrest threatened U.S. foreign investments.

Fighting Two World Wars

The Roosevelt Corollary may have affirmed U.S. dominance of the Western Hemisphere, but developments elsewhere created new challenges for the United States. In Europe, a century of relative calm was quickly coming to an end. The creation of a unified German state in 1871 started this downward spiral. Germany's rise coincided with the decline of the Ottoman, Russian, and Austro-Hungarian empires, all of which had contributed to a crude, but durable, balance of power in Europe. These major shifts in the global balance of power, with the United States and Japan rising in stature beyond Europe, would lead to two world wars in the first half of the twentieth century.

The First World War

For Americans, Europe's plunge into war in 1914 affirmed the prudence of their country's historic aversion to foreign entanglements (see Tuchman 1962). Austria-Hungary's war declaration against Serbia, for example, was made possible by Germany's support for the Austro-Hungarian empire. Alliance commitments also came into play as Germany went to war against Russia, an ally of Serbia, and against France, an ally of Russia. Great Britain justified its entry into the war with its security guarantees to Belgium, through which German troops passed on their way to France.

As order unraveled in Europe, President Woodrow Wilson sought to keep the United States "neutral in fact as well as name." But the country could not maintain its detached posture once the conflict in Europe extended into the Atlantic Ocean. The German navy began attacking merchant ships, many of them owned and operated by Americans. Any hopes for U.S. noninvolvement ended in May 1915, when a German submarine destroyed the British ocean liner *Lusitania*, whose passengers had included 128 American citizens. Although the United States managed to stay out of combat for another two years, Germany's prosecution of submarine warfare had angered the American public, inclining it toward war. Russia's withdrawal from the conflict in November 1917 secured Germany's position in the east and allowed its forces to concentrate along the western front. The prospect of German control over all Europe and the implications this control would have for U.S. security prompted Congress to declare war against Germany in 1917.

The United States contributed to the war effort in two ways. First, Wilson drew on the nation's immense industrial capacity by shipping massive volumes of weapons, munitions, and medical supplies to its allies, who were mired in a defensive stalemate against Germany. Troops on both sides were dug into long lines of mud-filled trenches, unable to advance against the new generation of armored tanks, long-range artillery, and automatic weapons. Second, Wilson deployed U.S. troops to the western front to reinforce the exhausted French and British forces and begin the slow counteroffensive. The arrival and strength of the U.S. forces ultimately tipped the balance, leading to Germany's surrender in November 1918.

Failed Efforts to Keep the Peace

As noted earlier, neither the U.S. government nor the general public was eager for the United States to become engaged in the First World War. The "entangling alliances" of the European powers, which transformed a regional crisis into a world war, were precisely what U.S. diplomats had long avoided. However, Germany's early success in the war raised the prospect of an even greater threat: the emergence of a single European state that would overturn the balance of power. Such a scenario had struck fear into American leaders since the day in 1814 when Thomas Jefferson declared in a letter to Thomas Leiper, "It cannot be to our interest that all Europe should be reduced to a single monarchy" (quoted in Graebner 1964, 122).

The U.S. government, however, was also uncomfortable with a security policy based entirely on **geopolitics,** the distribution of global power. For Wilson, who was the son of a Presbyterian minister and had a strong sense of moral mission, the nation had to have a moral rationale for intervention (see George and George 1956). In his view, the United States should not fight simply for its survival or that of its allies. The nation should defend a more general principle: the right of citizens of any country to determine their own destinies. World War I, then, became a war to "make the world safe for democracy." When the war ended, Wilson felt duty-bound to seek a world order that would put these principles into practice and ensure that the recent conflict had been "the war to end all wars." To the president, the United States was uniquely able, and divinely ordained, to lead this effort: "America has said to mankind at her birth: 'We have come to redeem the world by giving it liberty and justice.' Now we are called upon before the tribunal of mankind to redeem that immortal pledge" (Wilson 1927, 645).

Wilson believed that a long-term solution was needed to overcome the anarchic world order, whose lack of global governance allowed such horrific wars to take place. His proposed solution was a new system based on the concept of **collective security.** In such a system, leaders would renounce war as an instrument of statecraft, and then pledge to defend each other in the event of outside aggression. If every government agreed to such a scheme and backed up its words with concrete action, any aggression would be doomed. Expansionist states would be deterred, and world peace would be assured. Wilson outlined his plan to Congress in early 1918, when he identified "fourteen points" that all countries should respect. Among them were worldwide disarmament, decolonization, freedom of the seas, open markets, and the prohibition of secret diplomacy. Most important, the president proposed the formation of a League of Nations that would provide the institutional foundation for collective security. Through the League, conflicting states would have a forum in which to discuss and resolve their differences peacefully. If any government violated the rules and invaded another country, League members would collectively repel the aggression.

Wilson's proposal, which presumably would deter nations from foreign aggression in the first place, was generally well received by other governments. In seeking to transform world politics, however, Wilson forgot about U.S. politics. Specifically, he neglected the constitutional sharing of powers that provided Congress with a vital role in foreign, as well as domestic, policy. Legislators resented their exclusion from the peace conference held in Paris in 1919 to conclude the war and complained that the Treaty of Versailles, in requiring military interventions when necessary to uphold collective security, deprived Congress of its authority to declare war. This combination of animosity toward Wilson and constitutional concerns led Congress to exercise another of its foreign policy powers by voting down the treaty. Thus, the United States, whose leader had been the primary architect of the organization, never joined the League of Nations.

Wilson also underestimated the powerful grip that national sovereignty held on the calculations of political leaders. In seeking to remake the interstate system, the League sought to weaken national sovereignty in its most vital area: military self-defense. The enduring hold of sovereignty on collective security was revealed in 1931, when Japanese troops invaded the province of Manchuria in northern China. This clear case of aggression presumably should have triggered the League's collective security mechanism, yet most members displayed no interest in deploying their troops to a remote region of little concern to them. League members denounced the Japanese invasion and voted to impose economic sanctions, but they took no military action. Italy's 1935 invasion of Ethiopia, in the horn of Africa, brought the same responses. In both instances, the League revealed itself to be a paper tiger that, far from rendering war obsolete, seemed to encourage and reward aggression by creating a false sense of security among nations that did not have aggressive designs.

Its nonparticipation in the League of Nations did not deter the United States from seeking ways to prevent another world war. To the contrary, during the 1920s the government actively pursued this goal in two ways. First, President Warren G. Harding called for disarmament among the major powers. Many people at this time believed the military buildups that preceded World War I were driven by arms manufacturers, or "merchants of death," and that the proliferation of weapons fueled distrust among the major powers and brought on a more destructive and protracted war than would otherwise have been possible. At the Washington Naval Conference in 1921 and 1922, the foreign ministers of Great Britain, France, Italy, and Japan agreed on a balance of naval power by which the size of the five navies would be fixed and strictly regulated.

Second, the United States cosponsored an international treaty to "outlaw" war. Two assumptions underlay the Pact of Paris, also know as the **Kellogg-Briand**

Pact (named for the U.S. and French foreign ministers): first, military force was an unacceptable tool of statecraft, and, second, the destructive power of modern military weapons, clearly demonstrated in the First World War, made the future use of such weapons suicidal to all parties. In 1928, representatives from fifteen countries signed the pact, which condemned "recourse to war for the solution of international controversies, and . . . as an instrument of national policy." Eventually, sixty-two governments, including those of Germany, Italy, Japan, and the Soviet Union, signed the agreement.

These heralded reforms, however, did not prevent the major powers from playing the same old game of power politics. After Japan seized control of Manchuria in 1931, Prime Minister Tojo Hideki ordered his forces to gain control of the entire Chinese coastline. Two years later, Adolf Hitler became chancellor of Germany and then repudiated the Treaty of Versailles and vowed to obtain the *lebensraum* (living space) required by the German people. Taking its cue from Hitler, Italy's fascist government, led by Benito Mussolini, launched its invasion of Ethiopia in 1935. In the United States, foreign policy makers reverted to their traditional posture of detachment.

President Franklin Roosevelt, elected in 1932, was most concerned with rescuing the American economy from the Great Depression. The crash of the U.S. stock market in 1929 had sent unemployment soaring. Another black cloud on the horizon was the global trade war that had culminated in the Smoot-Hawley Tariff Act of 1930, boosting U.S. tariffs to their highest levels ever and greatly worsening the economic slump. Meanwhile, Roosevelt initially sought to aid the victims of Italy's aggression, but Congress rejected his efforts and instead passed Neutrality Acts in 1935 and 1936 that barred the United States from aiding any of the belligerents.[5]

The Second World War

Once again, however, events in Europe made the U.S. hands-off policy impossible to maintain. After repudiating the Versailles treaty and rebuilding his armed forces, Hitler annexed Austria and eastern Czechoslovakia. He assured other European leaders afterward that these actions satisfied his territorial needs, but his pledges soon proved empty. In 1939 Germany invaded Poland and then divided the defeated country with the Soviet Union, with whom Hitler earlier had signed a nonaggression pact. That pact, though, proved just as worthless as the German leader's earlier promises. In 1941 Hitler launched a massive blitzkrieg against the Soviet Union. Having "neutralized" the eastern front, German forces then overran most of western Europe. Only Great Britain remained free of German domination.

By this time, American political leaders generally favored U.S. intervention, but the public remained unconvinced that the escalating conflict in Europe threatened the United States. Publicly, Roosevelt bowed to the popular view. During the

---

5. Isolationist sentiment was fueled by the publication of a best-selling book, *Merchants of Death* (Engelbrecht 1934), which charged that the U.S. entry into World War I had been the result of political pressure imposed by profit-hungry arms manufacturers.

1940 presidential campaign, he declared, "I have said this before and I shall say it again and again and again: Your boys are not going to be sent into any foreign wars" (quoted in Schulzinger 1994, 172). Nevertheless, Roosevelt brought the nation's considerable resources to bear in support of its allies. As German forces advanced toward the English Channel, the president, through the **lend-lease program,** provided Great Britain with U.S. military hardware and ships in exchange for American access to British bases in the Caribbean.

The first direct assault on the United States occurred half a world away. With French and Dutch colonies in East Asia up for grabs, Japanese leaders knew that only the United States stood in the way of their plan to create a Japanese-led "Greater East Asia Co-Prosperity Sphere" throughout the region. On December 7, 1941, Japanese warplanes attacked the large American naval base at Pearl Harbor, Hawaii. The raid killed some 2,500 Americans and devastated the U.S. fleet. Roosevelt declared December 7 a "date which will live in infamy." Three days later, Germany, which had formed an "axis" with Japan and Italy, declared war against the United States. Domestic debates on American intervention ended.

Roosevelt chose to avoid the moralistic rationales that Wilson had employed in World War I. Instead, he identified clear threats to national security and focused on military measures to overcome them. The United States would be engaged militarily on two fronts, thousands of miles apart. In the Pacific, the United States restored its naval forces and reversed Japan's advances, which by 1943 included the Philippines (still a U.S. colony) as well as Malaya, Singapore, and Vietnam. In the European struggle, U.S. and British forces expelled the Axis powers from North Africa and then drove northward through Italy. In 1944, Allied forces landed on the coast of France and began their eastward push against German troops. These forces joined Soviet troops, who had been equally successful on the eastern front. Germany's surrender, along with Hitler's suicide, came in May 1945. The Japanese emperor, however, remained defiant, despite the retreat of his forces to the mainland.

A month before Germany's surrender, Roosevelt had suffered a fatal stroke, and Vice President Harry Truman had succeeded to the presidency. The new president would face the most fateful decision of the war, and possibly the most ominous decision in human history. Unbeknownst to Truman, U.S. military scientists had been experimenting with nuclear energy, which, if ignited through atomic fusion, could yield an explosive force of unprecedented magnitude. The scientists involved in the secret Manhattan Project, based in Los Alamos, New Mexico, detonated the first nuclear bomb there on July 16, 1945. Only then did government officials notify Truman of this awesome new weapon, which could soon be made available for use against Japan. The president understood that defeating Japan through conventional means would require a massive assault on the Japanese mainland, leading to an incalculable loss of life on both sides. With this in mind, he approved the August 6 nuclear bombing of Hiroshima and the August 9 bombing of Nagasaki, which together killed nearly 150,000 Japanese citizens. Faced with the prospect of additional U.S. nuclear attacks, Japan surrendered to the United States and brought World War II to a merciful close.

Global Primacy and the Cold War

Immediately after World War II, the United States entered the third global conflict of the twentieth century. This conflict was labeled the **Cold War** because it never led to direct military combat between its principal antagonists, the United States and the Soviet Union. The basis of this conflict was ideological, pitting the capitalist countries, led by the United States, against the communist countries, led by the Soviet Union. Whereas capitalism respected private property and glorified free enterprise, communism sought to improve living standards by erecting a powerful state that owned and operated the means of economic production. A military showdown between the two superpowers would have produced death and destruction of unknowable proportions. The Cold War, while it avoided such an outcome, produced an endless series of "hot" wars in other parts of the world, mainly among developing countries caught in the crossfire (see Table 2.2).

Table 2.2 U.S. Foreign Policy Chronology: The Cold War

1945	Yalta Conference of victorious powers seeks to organize the postwar world.
1946	George Kennan devises containment strategy as the Cold War sets in.
1947	Marshall Plan and Truman Doctrine call for U.S. aid to allies; National Security Act creates new structures of U.S. foreign policy.
1949	NATO is formed by United States and eleven other nations.
1950	North Korea attacks South Korea, prompting UN military intervention.
1953	Korean War ends; CIA aids overthrow of Iran's government.
1954	CIA aids overthrow of Guatemala's government.
1959	Cuban rebels overthrow U.S.-backed Batista regime.
1962	Cuban missile crisis forces military and diplomatic showdown between Soviet Union and United States.
1964	Congress authorizes U.S. military intervention in Vietnam.
1968	Tet offensive in Vietnam prompts birth of antiwar movement in United States.
1970	Nixon orders bombing and invasion of Cambodia; four student protestors killed at Kent State University, Ohio.
1972	Nixon launches détente strategy, visits Soviet Union and China, and signs Antiballistic Missile (ABM) Treaty with Soviet Union.
1979	Iranian militants seize U.S. embassy in Teheran, leading to a 444-day hostage crisis; Sandinista revolution erupts in Nicaragua; Soviet Union invades Afghanistan.
1981	Reagan begins major military buildup as the Cold War heats up.
1986	Reagan and Gorbachev agree to sweeping cuts in nuclear arms, later ratified in first Strategic Arms Reduction Treaty (START); U.S. covert support for Nicaraguan contras leads to the Iran-contra scandal.
1989	Hungary opens borders with Austria, signaling the beginning of the end of the Cold War.
1990	Russia and Ukraine declare independence from Soviet Union; Germany reunified.
1991	Soviet Union dissolves, ending the Cold War.

Figure 2.2 Bipolar Balance of Power in Early Cold War

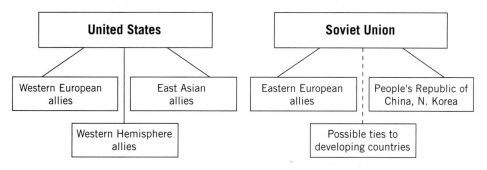

The United States emerged from World War II as the predominant world power, maintaining a nuclear monopoly for a time and producing as much economic output as the rest of the world combined. However, the Soviet Union, exploiting its considerable resources, both real and potential, soon shifted the global balance of power to a **bipolar** one, with the United States and the Soviet Union representing the contesting "poles" (see Figure 2.2). With a sphere of influence that spanned from East Germany to the Alaskan border, the Soviet Union possessed the world's largest conventional forces and gradually caught up with the United States in the nuclear arms race. In addition to the arms race, the worldwide competition for allies became a defining element of the Cold War. Each superpower hoped to tip the balance in its favor by recruiting allies beyond its borders.

Strains between the United States and the Soviet Union, allies against the Axis powers in World War II, became insurmountable shortly after the war. Joseph Stalin, the Soviet leader, imposed firm control over the countries of Eastern Europe that his armies had liberated from Nazi Germany. Stalin had no interest in withdrawing from the region that twice in his lifetime had served as a staging area for German invasions. In February 1946, he predicted an inevitable clash between the communist and capitalist countries and the eventual triumph of communism. A month later, Winston Churchill, the former British prime minister who had left office just before the war ended, announced the division of Europe that would last throughout the Cold War. He declared, "An **iron curtain** has descended across the Continent" (see Map 2, Cold War Division of Europe, in map section).

The task of formulating a Cold War strategy was assigned to George Kennan, a Soviet specialist in the State Department. Kennan first laid out his plan in a February 1946 "long telegram" that circulated within the government. It was reprinted a year later in the journal *Foreign Affairs* (see In Their Own Words box). Kennan's call for the **containment** of communism struck a middle ground between two alternatives: U.S. detachment from the emerging conflict and an all-out invasion and "liberation" of the Soviet Union. Under the containment strategy, the United States would accept the existing sphere of Soviet influence, but it would prevent further Soviet expansion by any means, including military force. In doing so, the United States would wait out the Soviet Union, looking

IN THEIR OWN WORDS: GEORGE KENNAN

George Kennan spent years studying the Soviet Union before devising the containment policy that became a pillar of U.S. foreign policy during the Cold War. Kennan's knowledge of Russian history and his contact with Soviet leaders during World War II reinforced his sense that though the coming struggle would be long, the United States would ultimately win it.

The political personality of Soviet power as we know it today is the product of ideology and circumstances: ideology inherited by the present Soviet leaders from the movement in which they had their political origin, and circumstances of the power which they now have exercised for nearly three decades. . . .

The maintenance of this pattern of Soviet power, namely, the pursuit of unlimited authority domestically, accompanied by the cultivation of the semi-myth of implacable foreign hostility, has gone far to shape the actual machinery of Soviet power as we know it today. . . . This means that we are going to continue for a long time to find the Russians difficult to deal with. It does not mean that they should be considered as embarked upon a do-or-die program to overthrow our society by a given date. The theory of the inevitability of the eventual fall of capitalism has the fortunate connotation that there is no hurry about it. . . .

In these circumstances it is clear that the main element of any United States policy toward the Soviet Union must be that of a long-term, patient but firm and vigilant containment of Russian expansive tendencies. . . . Soviet pressure against the free institutions of the Western world is something that can be contained by the adroit and vigilant application of counter-force at a series of constantly shifting geographical and political points, corresponding to the shifts and maneuvers of Soviet policy. . . .

The future of Soviet power may not be by any means as secure as Russian capacity for self-delusion would make it appear. . . . The possibility remains (and in the opinion of this writer it is a strong one) that Soviet power, like the capitalist world of its conception, bears within it the seeds of its own decay, and that the sprouting of these seeds is well advanced.

SOURCE: George F. Kennan, "The Sources of Soviet Conduct," *Foreign Affairs* 25 (July 1947): 566–582. © by the Council on Foreign Relations, Inc. Reprinted by permission.

forward to the day when its internal flaws—the denial of individual rights, the lack of a market economy, the high costs of foreign occupation—would cause the communist system to collapse from within.

Beyond waging the Cold War, the United States sought to create a stable world order that reflected its own political and economic principles. The behavior of the fascist governments had provided a strong case for democratic rule as a means of organizing political life at home and managing foreign relations. Meanwhile, economic prosperity based on private property and free markets would do more than simply prevent communist movements from forming and gaining political power. The U.S. economy would naturally thrive in a market-friendly global trading system that provided outlets for American goods and services. In addition,

U.S. banks, multinational corporations, and private investors would benefit enormously if they had free access to foreign markets. In this respect, the American grand strategy during the Cold War pursued objectives that extended well beyond the East-West struggle.

New Structures of Foreign Policy

The challenges and opportunities facing the United States after World War II, combined with the lessons of the interwar years, deterred U.S. foreign policy makers from retreating again into their hemispheric shell. It was clear that the country had to engage in world politics. Less clear, however, was *how* the United States would engage in politics at that level. Would the U.S. government pursue its own interests or those of the international community? Would it choose military or nonmilitary instruments to achieve its goals? Would it act alone or in collaboration with other governments? The answers came in the late 1940s. U.S. leaders found the nation's interests intimately tied to global stability, political reform, and economic growth. A world of governments and economies resembling those of the United States, they believed, would be more peaceful, democratic, and prosperous than the present one.

The United States would promote such a world order through a variety of means, working, when possible, with other governments. Historian Daniel Yergin (1977, 196) found that the new strategy left nowhere in the world outside the U.S. sphere of influence: "It postulates the interrelatedness of so many different political, economic, and military factors that developments halfway around the globe are seen to have automatic and direct impact on America's core interests. Virtually every development in the world is perceived to be potentially crucial. An adverse turn of events anywhere endangers the United States. Problems in foreign relations are viewed as urgent and immediate threats. Thus, desirable foreign policy goals are translated into issues of national survival, and the range of threats becomes limitless."

A common element of all postwar American foreign policies was the creation of new institutions to put the nation's principles into practice. The institutions of the **national security state** overshadowed the nonmilitary agencies of the government and rendered the foreign policy process far more complex than at any other time in the nation's history. Global pressures compelled the United States to centralize national security structures and increase the president's direct control over military policy—steps viewed as vital in the nuclear age. The National Security Act of 1947, the most sweeping reorganization of U.S. foreign policy in the nation's history, had three primary components:

- The Department of Defense (DoD) was designed to bring the army, navy, and air force under centralized control. In replacing the Department of War, U.S. leaders chose the word *defense* to signify that military affairs were now a permanent concern, not one reserved for wartime. James Forrestal, the first secretary of defense, believed the United States had to "maintain such overwhelming military power as to make it abundantly clear that future aggressors will eventually suffer the ruinous fate of Germany" (quoted in Yergin 1977, 299).

- The National Security Council (NSC) was created to coordinate the foreign policy process from the White House. The president's national security adviser, whose office would be close to the Oval Office, became a primary source of guidance and a gatekeeper controlling the flow of foreign policy advice from other government officials. A small NSC staff would specialize in various areas of foreign policy, and the most crucial decisions would be made at NSC meetings (see Chapter 6).

- The Central Intelligence Agency (CIA) came into being to oversee the collection, analysis, and distribution of foreign intelligence. Analysts widely agreed that intelligence failures virtually invited the Pearl Harbor attacks in 1941 and that the Office of Strategic Services, hastily established early in World War II and disbanded afterward, was not in a position to gather global intelligence on a permanent basis.

The creation of these agencies produced new tensions within the U.S. government and foreign policy process. Rivalries between the armed services, primarily the navy and air force, turned the DoD into its own kind of battle zone. Struggles over budget resources and, more important, missions in the emerging Cold War led the service chiefs to place their organizational self-interests above those of the nation. Meanwhile, the NSC soon found itself competing against the State Department for control of the foreign policy agenda, and the huge budget outlays required by the DoD left the foreign service chronically short-changed (see Hook 2003). The CIA proved incapable of serving as a "central" source of intelligence; more than a dozen other intelligence agencies came into being within various federal departments. In preserving and even encouraging internal power struggles, the new system was "flawed by design" (Zegart 1999).

Transnational institutions also took shape during these hectic transition years from World War II to the Cold War. The United States led the way in creating a worldwide intergovernmental organization that adopted many goals sought by the League of Nations, while recognizing that organization's limitations. Toward this end, officials from fifty governments came to San Francisco in early 1945 to create the United Nations (UN). Under the approved plan, the UN would be open to all countries and would provide a forum for resolving conflicts among them, solving problems that crossed national borders, and proclaiming shared principles about human rights and other issues. The last of these UN roles particularly interested the United States, which expected the world body to serve as an extension of its own values and principles. Maintaining collective security, the primary objective of the League of Nations, was conspicuously absent from the UN's mandate.

Along with the other great powers—China, France, Great Britain, and the Soviet Union—the United States protected its interests by means of a permanent seat and veto power on the UN Security Council. Key votes in the UN General

Assembly, in which all countries had one vote, could also be nullified by the Security Council's permanent members. Under Article 51 of the UN Charter, the United States and other countries kept their military options open by reserving "the inherent right of individual or collective self-defense" if they were attacked.[6] The newly formed International Court of Justice, meanwhile, had the power to resolve interstate disputes, but only if the governments involved accepted the court's jurisdiction.

Meanwhile, the U.S. government departed from its traditional practice of avoiding peacetime military alliances. The creation of the North Atlantic Treaty Organization (NATO) in 1949 resulted from several troubling developments in Europe. In 1947 Great Britain had withdrawn its military support for Greece and Turkey, whose governments faced internal revolts by communists and other groups. Under the **Truman Doctrine,** the United States provided military aid to both states and, more broadly, pledged support for "free peoples who are resisting attempted subjugation by armed minorities or by outside pressures." In February 1948, the Soviet Union gained control of Czechoslovakia by supporting a coup against its elected leader and imposing a communist regime in its place. Several months later, Stalin erected a blockade around the German city of Berlin, which was split into two zones by then, one open to the Western powers (West Berlin), the other controlled by the Soviets (East Berlin). Truman responded with a massive airlift to supply the citizens of West Berlin with food, coal, and other necessities. After nearly a year, Stalin finally gave up the blockade and reopened the Western zones of occupation.

These developments led to the formation of NATO, which comprised the United States, nine Western European countries, Canada, and Iceland. Under the terms of the North Atlantic Treaty, signed in April 1949, an armed attack against one or more of the members "shall be considered an attack against them all." By assuming the lead role in NATO, the United States committed itself to the security of Western Europe for the duration of the Cold War and long after its conclusion.

On the economic front, the U.S. government also engaged in a flurry of institution building. The nation's economy had grown rapidly in the years before and during the war (see Figure 2.3), and by 1945 U.S. output matched that of the rest of the world combined. In the summer of 1944, officials from forty-four governments met in Bretton Woods, New Hampshire, to discuss postwar financial arrangements. The **Bretton Woods agreements** created a system of fixed currency exchange rates based on the U.S. dollar, which because of American economic clout would be considered "good as gold." The Bretton Woods system included two international financial institutions designed to stabilize the world economy further (see Chapter 9). The World Bank would lend money to member states to rebuild their industries, and the International Monetary Fund (IMF) would manage currency exchanges and provide relief to member states facing short-term currency crises. Another multilateral pact, the General Agreement on Tariffs and

---

6. This provision allowed the United States and other governments in the Western Hemisphere to form the Organization of American States in 1947, based in Washington, D.C. Its primary mission was to preserve regional security.

Figure 2.3 U.S. Economic Growth, 1885–1945

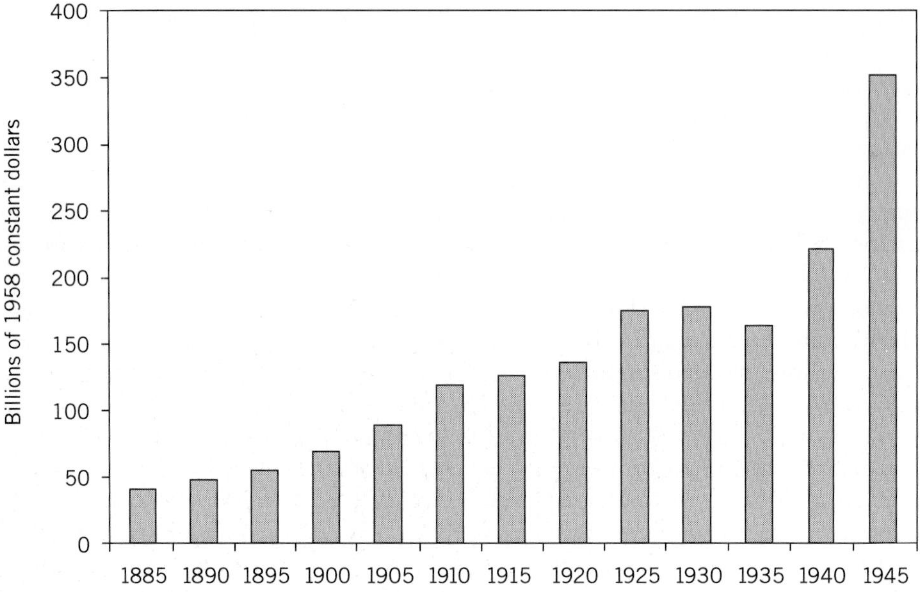

SOURCE: U.S. Bureau of the Census, *The Statistical History of the United States: From Colonial Times to the Present* (New York: Basic Books, 1976).

Trade (GATT), was signed in 1947 to create rules for keeping national markets open to global commerce.

The **Marshall Plan,** named after Secretary of State George Marshall, paved the way for Western Europe's economic recovery and its eventual political alignment within the European Union (EU). Truman agreed with Marshall that Europe urgently needed U.S. help to revive its slumping economies. Congress then authorized the transfer of $13 billion (about $50 billion in current dollars) in low-interest loans to these countries, which were required to coordinate their plans for recovery. They did so in 1948 by creating the Organization for European Economic Cooperation (OEEC). By 1950, with political stability returning to the region, the Europeans had regained their prewar economic growth. The success of the OEEC led to the creation in 1957 of the European Economic Community (EEC), which later became the European Community (EC) and is now the EU. In this respect, the Soviet Union was instrumental not simply in rallying a unified Western response to a perceived external threat, but also in forcing the Western European states to overcome their deep historical animosities toward each other.

Regional Conflicts and the Vietnam Syndrome

These measures laid the institutional foundations for postwar U.S. foreign policy. Such wide-ranging initiatives seemed essential in view of the opportunities available to the United States (the only major power to emerge stronger from the war) for achieving its historic mission of creating a world order in its own image. The new architecture also countered the threat posed by the Soviet Union, which detonated a nuclear device in September 1949 and neutralized the U.S. advantage in this area of military power. Of concern to U.S. leaders as well was the victory of communist forces in China after more than three decades of civil war. The People's Republic of China (PRC) came into being in October 1949 under the leadership of Mao Zedong. Among its first actions, the PRC signed a treaty of cooperation in 1950 with the Soviet Union, which deepened fears in Washington that the balance of global power was shifting against the United States and toward communism.

The PRC was particularly troubling because, unlike the Soviet Union, China represented a potential role model for other developing countries, located largely in the Southern Hemisphere, whose populations greatly outnumbered those in the industrialized nations. Colonial rule was yielding to the creation of new Asian and African countries, which quickly gained a voting majority in the UN General Assembly. The crushing poverty in these new states, and the lack of political institutions in place to satisfy their citizens' rising expectations, raised additional U.S. fears that these countries would turn to communism. The *third world*, a term used to distinguish the region from the *first world* (the capitalist bloc) and the *second world* (the communist bloc), figured prominently in U.S. foreign policy and attracted military intervention by both superpowers in three areas: Korea, Cuba, and Vietnam.

Korea. After World War II, the Korean peninsula in Northeast Asia was divided along the thirty-eighth parallel until the creation of a unified national government. Such a prospect became unlikely, however, and in 1948 two separate states, North Korea and South Korea (Republic of Korea), were created. Any hopes for reunification vanished in June 1950 when communist forces from North Korea attacked their counterparts in South Korea, prompting Truman to seek relief from the UN Security Council. A multinational force led by the United States pushed North Korean troops back across the thirty-eighth parallel.[7] Then North Korea struck again and seized Seoul, the South Korean capital, and the conflict dragged on. Truman failed to negotiate an end to the war in 1951 and 1952. His successor, Dwight Eisenhower, threatened North Korea with a new offensive if a peace treaty could not be signed. The two sides finally reached an agreement in July 1953 that effectively restored the prewar status quo. With no clear victor, North Korea and South Korea remained divided for the rest of the Cold War and into the twenty-first century, and a large contingent of U.S. troops continued to patrol the border to keep the peace.

The Korean War demonstrated the importance of developing countries to U.S. foreign policy in the Cold War. Recognizing this, Eisenhower turned the CIA into a tool for influencing weaker governments, and occasionally toppling regimes

---

7. The Soviet Union, which would have vetoed the resolution, was boycotting the UN at the time to protest its refusal to recognize the new communist regime in China.

disfavored in Washington. In Iran, the CIA backed the 1953 overthrow of Prime Minister Mohammed Mossedegh after he nationalized the country's oil fields. Once he returned to power, Shah (King) Mohammed Reza Pahlavi reopened the oil fields to British and U.S. oil companies. In 1954 the CIA staged another coup in Guatemala, whose elected president, Jacobo Arbenz Guzmán, had launched sweeping land reform and was suspected of being a communist with allegiance to Moscow.[8] Arbenz was replaced by a military general who aligned with the United States and reversed the land reforms.

Nuclear weapons also played an important role in Eisenhower's foreign policy, which he labeled the **New Look.** The president believed nuclear weapons provided more "bang for the buck" than did conventional forces. The New Look also featured new military alliances that created a "containment belt" around the Soviet Union and China (see Map 3, Cold War Alliances with the United States, in map section).[9] Each ally found a place under the U.S. "nuclear umbrella," and each became eligible for large volumes of U.S. foreign aid.

Cuba. The gravest challenge to U.S. foreign policy during the Cold War was posed by the nearby island of Cuba, less than a hundred miles from Florida. In 1959 the U.S.-backed military regime of Fulgencio Batista was overthrown and replaced by a Marxist regime led by Fidel Castro, who openly declared the United States to be an enemy of the Cuban people. Eisenhower's successor to the presidency, John Kennedy, turned to the CIA in 1961 to get rid of Castro. But the agency's covert operation failed when the invading force of Cuban exiles was repelled at the Bay of Pigs. Later efforts by the CIA to assassinate Castro, through the use of exploding cigars and other bizarre tactics, served only to elevate the Cuban leader's stature among other developing nations.

The standoff between the United States and Cuba took a perilous turn in November 1962. During routine aerial reconnaissance overflights, American officials discovered that the Cuban government, at the behest of the Soviet Union, had begun installing medium-range nuclear missiles on the island. The missiles had been secretly shipped to Cuba from the Soviet Union, and U.S. cities were their intended targets. Kennedy, well aware of the source of the nuclear missiles, insisted that Castro remove the missiles or face swift military action. After nearly two weeks of tense negotiations between the U.S. and Soviet governments, which came to be called the **Cuban missile crisis,** Soviet leader Nikita Khrushchev ordered the missiles removed. A direct, and possibly apocalyptic, clash between the superpowers was narrowly averted.

---

8. At the time, the richest 2 percent of Guatemala's population owned nearly three-fourths of its land. The U.S.-based United Fruit Company was the largest landholder in the country.

9. The United States pledged under the 1945 Inter-American Treaty of Reciprocal Assistance to protect the Western Hemisphere. The alliance wave accelerated with the creation of the ANZUS alliance (with Australia and New Zealand) in 1951, the Southeast Asia Treaty Organization (SEATO) in 1954, and the Central Treaty Organization (CENTO) in 1959. In addition, the United States formed bilateral alliances with Japan, the Philippines, South Korea, and Taiwan (Republic of China).

North Vietnamese troops celebrate their victory over the United States atop a tank in front of the presidential palace in Saigon on April 30, 1975. Thousands of Vietnamese citizens joined this celebration in Saigon, later renamed Ho Chi Minh City in honor of the leader of the revolutionary movement.

Vietnam. As the events in Cuba unfolded, the United States also was becoming more deeply immersed in a more distant conflict. Its outcome would reveal the limits of U.S. military power, raise doubts about the country's moral posture in the Cold War, and shatter the domestic consensus favoring the containment strategy. The conflict had erupted after World War II in Indochina, a tropical region in Southeast Asia long dominated by foreign powers. After Japan's defeat in 1945, France had insisted on reclaiming its colony in Vietnam rather than granting independence to the people. But the French could not subdue an independence movement in Vietnam and withdrew in 1954. The U.S. government, which feared the rise to power of a communist regime, stepped into the quagmire. Eisenhower had viewed Vietnam through the lens of the **domino theory,** which held that a communist victory in one country would lead to a succession of additional victories in neighboring states (see Kattenburg 1980, ch. 2).

The U.S. military presence in Vietnam grew slowly in the early 1960s and then soared to half a million by 1968. Like Korea, Vietnam was split into northern and southern regions, with the north allied with communism and the south receiving support from the United States and its allies. Despite the superior fire-power of the United States, Kennedy and his successor in office, Lyndon Johnson, could not defeat the north's Viet Cong forces, led by Ho Chi Minh. Back in the United States, growing U.S. deployments, followed by ongoing defeats and casualties, prompted the birth of an antiwar movement. As television networks broadcast graphic images of the carnage on a daily basis, the Vietnam War engulfed President Richard Nixon and his administration upon taking office in January 1969. Despite Nixon's promises to end the war, the conflict continued into the mid-1970s, when Vietnam at last gained its independence under a communist government. Nearly 59,000 U.S. troops had died in the conflict, and another 153,000 had been wounded. More than 1 million Vietnamese had been killed or wounded.

The Vietnam War proved disastrous for the United States in several ways. For one thing, U.S. leaders had wrongly viewed it as an ideological struggle rather than a war of independence and self-determination. As a result, their goal of winning the hearts and minds of the Vietnamese people had been doomed from the start. Militarily, the U.S. forces had failed to adapt to the demands of guerilla warfare, ground forces had been left without clear orders, and the daily aerial assaults by American bombers had merely strengthened the will of the Vietnamese.[10] All of these pitfalls offended the moral sensibilities of many Americans, who had long believed in the righteousness of their country's actions overseas. As the national soul-searching associated with the **Vietnam Syndrome** took hold across the country after the war, the moral superiority of the United States could no longer be taken for granted—nor could the virtues and open-ended military commitments of the containment doctrine.

The End of the Cold War

By the early 1970s, the Soviet Union had caught up with the United States in the most potent category of military power, nuclear weapons. At the same time, the U.S. economy was showing serious signs of distress. The costs of the Vietnam War and other burdens had prevented the country from maintaining its role as the "lender of last resort." Domestic unrest and new regional crises, particularly in the Middle East, forced Nixon to change the course of U.S. foreign policy.

Nixon assigned his national security adviser, Henry Kissinger, the task of designing a strategy that recognized these new realities. Kissinger, a Jewish refugee from Nazi Germany and a political scientist, soon settled on **détente,** a French term meaning an easing of tensions. Under the détente policy, U.S. and Soviet leaders established a closer working relationship so that regional crises could be resolved without threatening a direct confrontation. In addition, in return for Soviet restraint, the United States offered the Soviet Union material benefits, including American agricultural exports badly needed in Moscow. The two

---

10. For a reassessment of the Vietnam ordeal by the secretary of defense under Kennedy and Johnson, see McNamara (1995).

governments also negotiated a series of arms control treaties that first limited, and later reduced, the stockpiles of nuclear weapons on both sides.

Nixon also sought improved relations with the People's Republic of China, whose communist government the United States had not yet recognized. The PRC, still ruled by Mao Zedong, was struggling, and so it stood to benefit greatly from the economic opportunities U.S. recognition would bring. The breakthrough between the countries came in a May 1972 visit by Nixon to China, during which the United States officially recognized the PRC as the legitimate government of China. In return, Mao agreed to cooperate with the United States rather than the Soviet Union. By securing this commitment, Nixon and Kissinger achieved the upper hand in the now triangular superpower rivalry.

Despite these gains, the memories of Vietnam and the Watergate scandal that drove Nixon from office in 1974 compelled Americans to seek yet another shift in U.S. foreign policy. President Jimmy Carter, a former peanut farmer and born-again Christian from Georgia, turned the nation's attention away from the confrontation of the Cold War and toward a more cooperative posture emphasizing human rights, improved living conditions in the developing world, and a stronger role for the United Nations. Carter's policy of **liberal internationalism** offered a new route to global stability, and the president achieved a major foreign policy goal by brokering the 1978 Camp David Accords between Israel and Egypt. In his final years in office, however, Carter suffered a series of setbacks. First, a 1979 revolution in Nicaragua brought a Marxist regime to power. Second, the U.S.-backed shah of Iran was replaced in 1979 by a new government based on Islamic law and harshly critical of the United States. The final blow came in December 1979, when the Soviet Union sent 80,000 troops into Afghanistan to bolster a new puppet government. Carter could not overcome these challenges and lost his 1980 bid for reelection to Ronald Reagan, a Republican "hawk" who launched a more forceful approach to foreign policy.

Upon taking office in January 1981, Reagan called the Soviet Union "the focus of evil in the modern world." His rhetorical offensive was accompanied by an expansion of U.S. armed forces, which the president believed had been neglected during the détente and Carter years. Reagan also raised the stakes of the arms race by proposing a U.S. "missile shield" in outer space that would shoot down Soviet missiles headed for the United States. By the mid-1980s, annual U.S. defense spending had nearly doubled, thanks to a Congress that supported Reagan's proposals. As the buildup continued, many Americans became anxious about an impending nuclear war. Their fears were strengthened by scientific evidence suggesting that even a "limited" nuclear war would produce a "nuclear winter," leading to the extinction of most plant and animal life (Sagan 1983/1984).

Amid these fears appeared new signs of hope for improved superpower relations. The deaths of three aged Soviet leaders—Leonid Brezhnev, Yuri Andropov, and Konstantin Chernenko—between 1982 and 1985 brought to power a new generation of power brokers, most notably Mikhail Gorbachev, who openly acknowledged his nation's problems. The economy had succumbed to centralized control, a demoralized labor force, and a crumbling infrastructure, while the rigid political system had discouraged public participation and new ideas. Gorbachev proposed two reforms to rectify these problems: *perestroika,* the restructuring of the Soviet economy to spur innovation and efficiency, and *glasnost,* greater openness in the political system. Soviet citizens and foreign leaders, including Reagan, welcomed both reforms.

By the time George H. W. Bush took office in January 1989, the only question remaining about the Soviet Union was whether its decay was irreversible. Efforts by Gorbachev to salvage his nation merely compounded the problem. The Soviet leader first sought to ease the strains on the Soviet periphery in Eastern Europe by permitting client states to launch their own reforms. Citizens seized on the opportunity—not to restructure their communist systems, but to get rid of them altogether. The critical turning point came in September 1989, when Hungary's government opened its borders with Austria, permitting thousands of East Europeans to cross the iron curtain. The Berlin Wall fell two months later, and in quick succession democratic regimes were established across the region. Their leaders rushed to create market economies and attract foreign investment.

As the Soviet bloc crumbled around him, Gorbachev confronted an uprising among the fifteen republics that comprised the Soviet Union. In Russia, the largest republic, former Moscow mayor Boris Yeltsin won free elections held in May 1990. President Yeltsin, whose election provided him with the legitimacy the communist leaders had never had, moved quickly to assert authority over Russia's government, economy, and foreign relations. His actions prompted a similar independence movement in neighboring Ukraine, the second-largest Soviet republic. Belarus and the other twelve republics then issued their own declarations of independence. In the United States, the Bush administration adopted a cautious strategy of supporting Gorbachev and a "soft landing" for the Soviet Union. In the end, the United States won the Cold War in the most favorable manner possible—through the peaceful and orderly dismantling of its longtime rival in Moscow.

New Challenges after the Cold War

The end of the Cold War caught the world by surprise. The East-West conflict had become a deeply entrenched fact of life on both sides of the iron curtain. The ideological competition between communism and capitalism had seemed to defy resolution. The nuclear doctrine of mutual assured destruction (MAD) had locked the Soviet Union and the United States into a strategic stalemate, and the logic of bipolarity had established a manageable framework for superpower relations while constraining the ambitions of regional powers. Few analysts anticipated the dissolution of the Soviet bloc, an outcome that seemed beyond the realm of possibility because of the firm grip in which the Kremlin held its citizens and the Warsaw Pact states. The Kremlin's massive nuclear stockpile appeared to provide Moscow with indefinite status as a military superpower.

Even so, the Soviet monopoly on power could not be sustained amid poor living conditions and drained government budgets. The communications revolution of the early 1990s broke down the walls between the Soviet bloc and the outside world. Advances in satellite technology extended the reach of televised coverage into areas that were previously isolated. The arrival of personal computers in the Soviet bloc, including Internet access and e-mail capabilities, permitted contacts across national borders that could not be controlled by government officials. As a result, citizens gained new exposure to the world around them. What they learned not only contradicted the images and messages they had been fed by the government, but also revealed the profound gaps between their living standards and those of their Western neighbors.

Elements of the New World Order

The victory of the United States in the Cold War represented more than the defeat of one international coalition by another. The Soviet Union's collapse marked the triumph of liberalism over the two competing ideologies of the twentieth century: fascism and communism. The challenge of fascism was subdued with the military defeat of Germany, Italy, and Japan during World War II. Communism died a slower death with the demise of the Soviet bloc and the transition of Chinese communism into an economic system based largely on market forces. The United States, now the centerpiece of a unipolar balance of power, had achieved its two-century objective of transforming world politics (see Figure 2.4). In his 1989 article "The End of History," Francis Fukuyama captured the exuberant spirit of the time: "What we may be witnessing is not just the end of the Cold War, or the passing of a particular period of history, but the end of history as such, that is, the end point of mankind's ideological evolution and the universalization of Western liberal democracy as the final form of government" (4).

Nine months before the collapse of the Soviet Union, President George H. W. Bush had expressed this sense of triumphalism in an address to a joint session of Congress: "We can see a new world coming into view, a world in which there is the very real prospect of a **new world order,** a world where the United States—freed from Cold War stalemate—is poised to fulfill the historic vision of its

Figure 2.4   Unipolar Balance of World Power, 2010

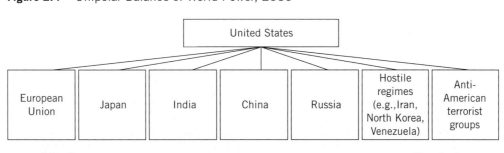

founders; a world in which freedom and respect for human rights finds a home among all nations." The president did not fully detail what this order would look like, but in his public statements he repeatedly emphasized three overlapping elements: democratization, economic globalization, and multilateral cooperation.

Democratization. The dismantling of communist regimes advanced the trend toward global democratization under way since the 1970s. During that decade, many Latin American countries overcame long histories of military rule and installed new political systems based on constitutionalism, free multiparty elections, and the protection of basic civil and political rights. Many African and Asian countries adopted similar reforms in the 1980s, as did the postcommunist countries in Europe in the early 1990s. Democratic freedoms and human rights, Americans widely believed, should be adopted and protected on a universal basis. According to the theory of **democratic peace,** a world of democracies would be more cooperative and less prone to civil and interstate violence (see Russett 1993).[11]

Economic globalization. A second central aspect of the new world order was the trend toward market-based economic commerce both within and among states, a trend that gained momentum in the latter stages of the Cold War. In short, international commerce in the world economy would resemble interstate commerce within the U.S. economy, which occurs with limited government intervention. Free trade in this model would be accompanied by foreign investments on a massive scale, enriching multinational corporations and effectively creating a single global economy.

Multilateral cooperation. Economic globalization was also fueled by multilateral institutions such as the World Bank and the IMF, which undertook new missions after the Cold War. Meanwhile, the World Trade Organization, created in 1995, enforced the market-friendly trade reforms written into the most recent global trade pact. Multilateralism extended further to environmental efforts, culminating in the 1992 Earth Summit in Brazil. On the security front, the U.S. government welcomed greater security cooperation and expected the UN to assume the stronger peacekeeping role unattainable during the Cold War. The United States also led the effort to maintain, and expand, NATO, even though its adversary, the Soviet Union, had disappeared.

President Bill Clinton embraced all three elements of this new world order when he took office in January 1993. Clinton, whose primary interest was domestic rather than foreign policy, believed the United States would be more secure and prosperous in a more tightly knit world whose nations shared common values, interests, and political institutions. His national security policy of **engagement and enlargement** presumed that closer interactions between countries, primarily on

---

11. This connection between democracy and world peace was made two centuries earlier by Enlightenment theorists Immanuel Kant and Jeremy Bentham, who anticipated a "pacific federation" of democratic states (see Doyle 1986b).

economic matters, would provide collective benefits to them while discouraging defections or challenges to the status quo. Along these lines, Anthony Lake (1993, 659), Clinton's national security adviser, observed that "the successor to a doctrine of containment must be a strategy of enlargement of the world's free community."

Overseas Unrest and Domestic Unease

Despite their great expectations for the new world order, U.S. leaders confronted a variety of armed conflicts overseas, which revealed that history had not "ended" with the demise of the Soviet Union. Instead, regional conflicts and internal power struggles suppressed during the Cold War resurfaced, producing large-scale violence and attracting the attention and military intervention of outside forces, including the United States. Conflicts in three regions—the Persian Gulf, Northeast Africa, and Yugoslavia—dampened the enthusiasm of American leaders for "engagement" and provoked a turn away from multilateral cooperation, which would intensify in the new millennium under Clinton's successor, George W. Bush (see Table 2.3).

The first regional conflict erupted in the Persian Gulf before the Soviet Union collapsed. Iraq's invasion of neighboring Kuwait on August 2, 1990, directly challenged the new world order and prompted the United States to deploy a military force to protect Saudi Arabia, and later, to oust Iraq from Kuwait. The international response to the invasion included a series of UN resolutions demanding Iraq's withdrawal. When Iraqi leader Saddam Hussein ignored these resolutions, the UN authorized a military assault (**Operation Desert Storm**) on Iraqi troops in the Kuwaiti desert. The U.S.-led assault quickly crushed the Iraqi military. Saddam remained in power, however, and he defied resolutions that he comply with UN inspectors in ridding his country of weapons of mass destruction. The imposition of economic sanctions and a "no-fly zone" across much of the country did not produce compliance from Saddam, whose control over Iraq only deepened in the years to come.

The UN also struggled to resolve upheavals in **failed states**—those countries incapable of maintaining order or providing even minimal services to their citizens (see Map 4, Post–Cold War U.S. Military Operations, in map section). Primary among these failed states was Somalia, where nearly fifty thousand citizens died in a civil war before a UN-sponsored ceasefire could be arranged in March 1992. By this time, a drought had led to widespread famine, and no government was in place to provide relief to the starving population. The humanitarian crisis compelled the United States to intervene militarily and provide relief to the Somalis. Meanwhile, a more ambitious UN effort to find a long-term solution failed, leading to more unrest and American casualties, which prompted Clinton to withdraw from Somalia. When a much bloodier ethnic conflict broke out in nearby Rwanda and Burundi in 1994, leaving nearly 1 million dead in a matter of months, the United States, fearing a repeat of the Somalia disaster, let the carnage run its course. With no other major powers willing to step in, the UN stood by as the genocide unfolded.

Table 2.3   U.S. Foreign Policy Chronology: Post–Cold War

1991	Iraq is forced out of Kuwait by a UN coalition led by the United States.
1992	Civil war escalates across former Yugoslavia; United States reluctantly attends Earth Summit in Brazil.
1993	U.S. forces killed in Somalia, forcing U.S. withdrawal; Congress ratifies North American Free Trade Agreement (NAFTA).
1994	Plan for World Trade Organization is approved.
1994	Remembering failure in Somalia, United States does not intervene in Rwandan genocide until over 800,000 Tutsis are slaughtered in ethnic cleansing by Hutus.
1995	United States brokers Dayton Peace Accords, ending ethnic warfare in Bosnia-Herzegovina.
1996	Clinton signs Comprehensive Test Ban Treaty (CTBT).
1997	Czech Republic, Hungary, and Poland are invited to join NATO.
1998	Al Qaeda terrorists bomb U.S. embassies in Kenya and Tanzania; global economic crisis spreads from East Asia to Russia and Latin America.
1999	NATO forces intervene in Kosovo to stop ethnic cleansing by Yugoslav government; Congress rejects CTBT.
2000	Terrorist bombing of USS *Cole* kills seventeen and injures thirty-seven Americans.
2001	George W. Bush renounces Kyoto Protocol on global warming; Islamic terrorists crash commercial airplanes into World Trade Center and Pentagon; United States invades Afghanistan and overthrows Taliban regime linked to September 11 attacks; United States withdraws from 1972 ABM Treaty with Russia.
2002	Bush declares Iran, Iraq, and North Korea an "axis of evil" that encourages terrorism; Bush Doctrine threatens preemptive strikes against U.S. adversaries.
2003	A "coalition of the willing" led by the United States invades Iraq and overthrows Saddam Hussein's regime; U.S. occupation fails to uncover weapons of mass destruction that prompted invasion.
2004	U.S. government transfers control of Iraq to interim government. Reconstruction of Iraq stalls as insurgency grows and U.S. personnel found to be abusing prisoners at Abu Ghraib; powerful earthquake beneath Indian Ocean triggers tsunami that destroys communities across southern Asia and Oceania.
2005	Summit meeting of Western Hemisphere leaders fails to produce agreement on Free Trade of the Americas; Iraqi voters elect parliament and approve a constitution amid ongoing political violence.
2006	Midterm elections return control of Congress to Democratic Party, reflecting widespread public concerns about the war in Iraq; Defense Secretary Donald Rumsfeld resigns a day after the election.
2007	Bush announces "surge" of U.S. troops in Iraq to suppress sectarian violence.
2008	Barack Obama, elected as U.S. president in the midst of a major economic crisis, calls for shifts in foreign policy that would restore the nation's stature and credibility.
2009	Obama wins Nobel Peace Prize based on his pledges to change the course of U.S. foreign policy; the president later deploys 30,000 additional troops to Afghanistan in order to reverse gains by insurgents and Taliban forces.
2010	United States assumes lead role in organizing relief effort following devastating earthquake in Haiti.

A family of Bosnian Muslims rests after being transported in July 1995 to a UN relief base in Tuzla, Yugoslavia. The refugees were displaced from the city of Srebrenica, where thousands of Muslims were massacred by the Orthodox Christian–led Serb government. Its "ethnic cleansing" of Yugoslavia, which eventually splintered into several smaller countries, symbolized the turbulent era in world politics following the Cold War.

The end of the Cold War also revived hostilities in the crumbling European state of Yugoslavia. Religious differences among Catholics, Orthodox Christians, and Muslims had been suppressed for decades by a communist government led by Marshal Josip Tito. But the end of the Cold War quickly unearthed these differences, producing a new cycle of violence, territorial conquest, and foreign intervention. Neither the UN nor the European Union could organize an effective response to the "ethnic cleansing" in Yugoslavia. In response, the United States finally ended the bloodshed in the provinces of Bosnia-Herzegovina (in 1995) and Kosovo (in 1999). In doing so, Clinton overrode domestic opposition to both interventions, limited the exposure of U.S. troops to enemy fire, and, once the fighting stopped, turned the reconstruction efforts over to multilateral institutions. By the end of the decade, Yugoslavia had broken up into several republics.

These foreign entanglements occurred at a time when the United States was experiencing unprecedented economic growth and prosperity. As stock markets reached record highs, inflation and unemployment fell to negligible levels. Enjoying a heyday in the first post–Cold War decade, Americans thus had little patience for conflicts overseas. This turn inward, historically common when the United States is at peace, was stimulated in large measure by the failure of the U.S. and UN missions in Somalia. Clinton responded by restricting U.S. involvement in future peacekeeping missions and by refusing to intervene in other failed states.

The shift in U.S. foreign policy gained further momentum in November 1994, when the Republican Party won control of both houses of Congress for the first time in four decades. Republican legislators resisted the trend toward multilateralism and used their "power of the purse" (see Chapter 5) to reduce U.S. foreign aid commitments and other international operations.

The Senate's refusal to sign the Comprehensive Test Ban Treaty (CTBT) in October 1999 epitomized the **new unilateralism** in U.S. foreign policy. As during the Reagan administration, the United States adopted a hostile stance toward the UN and its agencies, refusing to pay past dues owed them. Clinton, despite his support for global engagement, then found himself succumbing to the political realities at home. Vice President Al Gore's failure to win the 2000 election and the presidency of George W. Bush guaranteed that the new unilateralism would endure. Shortly after taking office, Bush renounced the Kyoto Protocol on Climate Change, the International Criminal Court, and the Antiballistic Missile (ABM) Treaty Nixon had signed with the Soviet Union. His primary concern upon taking office involved domestic issues, particularly lowering taxes and improving the nation's educational system. But the shock of the terrorist attacks of September 11, 2001, forced foreign policy back to the top of Bush's agenda and convinced the president to announce a national security strategy based on U.S. primacy and preemptive action against foreign adversaries that threatened the United States (see In Their Own Words box).

September 11 and the War on Terrorism

As the United States entered the new millennium, it seemed secure from foreign threats, and most Americans agreed with President Bush's emphasis on domestic problems. But all this changed on the morning of September 11, 2001, when al Qaeda terrorists hijacked four U.S. commercial jets and flew three of them into highly visible, well-known symbols of American power—the World Trade Center in New York City and the Pentagon near Washington, D.C. The fourth jet, apparently headed for the U.S. Capitol, crashed in rural Pennsylvania after the hijackers and several passengers struggled for control of the cockpit.

The attacks forced the grounding of all air traffic in the United States and the indefinite closing of the New York Stock Exchange and many public attractions, including Disney World and the arch in St. Louis. After returning to the White House from Florida and conferring with his advisers, the president made two decisions that formed the core of the Bush Doctrine. First, the U.S. government would treat the attacks not as crimes, but as acts of war. Second, the U.S. response would target not only the terrorist groups, but also the countries that harbored them. The subsequent "global war on terrorism" then became the centerpiece of U.S. foreign policy and the defining feature of Bush's presidency. The war took on global proportions because al Qaeda and other groups maintained cells in many countries. Therefore, defeating this foe and other terrorist groups would require sharing intelligence and other forms of international cooperation with other countries.

IN THEIR OWN WORDS: GEORGE W. BUSH

Each presidential administration is required by law to outline its national security strategy in a report to Congress and the public. The terrorist attacks of September 11, 2001, prompted President George W. Bush to focus his strategy, highlighted here, on fighting terrorism and striking preemptively, where and when necessary, against U.S. enemies abroad.

The United States possesses unprecedented—and unequaled—strength and influence in the world. Sustained by faith in the principles of liberty, and the value of a free society, this position comes with unparalleled responsibilities, obligations, and opportunity. The great strength of this nation must be used to promote a balance of power that favors freedom. . . .

The United States of America is fighting a war against terrorists of global reach. The enemy is not a single political regime or person or religion or ideology. The enemy is terrorism—premeditated, politically motivated violence perpetrated against innocents. . . . The United States will make no concessions to terrorist demands and strike no deals with them. We make no distinction between terrorists and those who knowingly harbor or provide aid to them. . . . In the war against global terrorism, we will never forget that we are ultimately fighting for our democratic values and way of life. Freedom and fear are at war, and there will be no quick or easy end to this conflict. . . .

The United States has long maintained the option of preemptive actions to counter a sufficient threat to our national security. The greater the threat, the greater is the risk of inaction—and the more compelling the case for taking anticipatory action to defend ourselves, even if uncertainty remains as to the time and place of the enemy's attack.

SOURCE: White House, "The National Security Strategy of the United States of America" (September 2002), www.whitehouse.gov/nsc/nss.pdf.

American officials immediately traced the terrorists to Afghanistan, whose Taliban government had provided Osama bin Laden, al Qaeda's leader, with political cover and sites for training camps on the country's remote mountainsides.[12] The U.S. retaliation, which began in late September, unfolded in two stages. First, American forces would help antigovernment Afghan militias overthrow the Taliban and round up the al Qaeda terrorists responsible for the attacks. Second, the United States would create a new, democratic regime that would not threaten its neighbors or serve as a sanctuary for Islamic terrorists. Although the first phase of the plan met with initial success (the capital of Kabul fell on November 12), bin Laden evaded his would-be captors and remained at large in the rugged terrain along Afghanistan's 1,500-mile border with Pakistan. But even

---

12. This was not the first time bin Laden had supervised paramilitary forces in Afghanistan. He had also served during the 1980s in the Afghan *mujahidin,* or resistance fighters, against the occupying Soviet army, with generous support from the CIA (see Coll 2004).

without bin Laden's capture, the effort to replace the Taliban regime proceeded on schedule; Afghans elected a new leader, Hamid Karzai, in 2004 and a new parliament in 2005.

After routing the Taliban from power in Afghanistan, Bush made the fateful decision to make Iraq the second front in the war on terrorism. Saddam Hussein's cat-and-mouse game with UN weapons inspectors had outlasted the Clinton administration, and many of Bush's top advisers—who had been labeled neoconservatives or "Vulcans"—had long argued that Saddam must be removed from power. It remained unclear whether Iraq possessed weapons of mass destruction, and the White House feared that Saddam's shared hatred of the United States with Islamic terrorists might tempt him to supply the terrorists with offerings from his stockpiles. Information provided by Iraqi exiles became part of the National Intelligence Estimate issued in October 2002, whose opening line summarized the case against Saddam: "Baghdad has chemical and biological weapons as well as missiles with ranges in excess of UN restrictions; if left unchecked, it probably will have a nuclear weapon during this decade."

This report convinced Bush that the time was right to settle matters with Saddam. Although the president faced a skeptical UN Security Council, he secured support from Congress in October 2002 to organize a "coalition of the willing" for an invasion. The invasion, code-named **Operation Iraqi Freedom,** began on March 20, 2003. As in the Afghanistan campaign, the initial "shock and awe" bombing campaign allowed coalition forces to advance rapidly and seize control of the capital and government. Although Saddam initially evaded capture, he was apprehended in December 2003 and placed on trial before an Iraqi war crimes tribunal.

Despite their initial military victory, the U.S.-led occupying forces faced unexpected resistance as they sought to bring Iraq under control. Far from being "greeted as liberators," as Vice President Dick Cheney had predicted before the invasion, the coalition forces were subjected to daily attacks that intensified after Pentagon officials dissolved Iraq's police and security forces. Secretary of Defense Donald Rumsfeld's decision to limit the size of the invading force to less than 200,000 troops left Iraq's border open to other insurgents. But the chaos in Iraq extended far beyond attacks on the coalition forces. The Iraqi militias, representing rival Sunni and Shiite Islamic groups, also turned their guns and missiles on each other in an effort to gain control of postwar Iraq. A third group, the ethnic Kurds in the north, saw an opportunity to realize their historic goal of seceding from Iraq and forming their own government.

The Bush administration found that its stymied mission in Iraq was imperiling its war on terrorism (see Gordon and Trainor 2006, and Ricks 2006). The United States was spending an estimated $8 billion a month on the war while receiving little in return. Yet the president remained determined to convert Iraq, whose citizens had also participated in unprecedented national elections, into a democratic and peaceful state. The nation's slide toward civil war not only threatened this transition, but also raised the prospect of regional sectarian struggles extending into neighboring Iran and across the Muslim world. At home, Bush faced turmoil within his own national security team. Colin Powell, his secretary of state, left the administration after Bush was reelected in November 2004, and Defense Secretary Donald Rumsfeld resigned late in 2006 amid continuing failures in Iraq (see Woodward 2006).

Bush approved a **surge strategy** in January 2007 that added five military brigades to conflict zones in Baghdad and other cities. The strategy included a heightened effort to train Iraqi security forces and to reassure Iraqi citizens that the United States supported their aspirations for peace and freedom. Although the level of violence eased along with the pace of American casualties after the surge, Bush left office in January 2009 with the U.S. mission in Iraq—and his global war on terrorism—far from over.

Even as the violence in Iraq subsided, insurgents and Taliban forces regained control of much of Afghanistan, leaving Bush's successor, Barack Obama, with the difficult choice of withdrawing from the war-torn nation or escalating U.S. military activities there. In December 2009, Obama chose to replicate Bush's surge strategy by ordering the deployment of 30,000 additional troops to Afghanistan. He assured Americans that this would be a temporary measure to regain the upper hand in the power struggle, which had spread into neighboring Pakistan and threatened a regional conflagration. Obama pledged to remove most U.S. forces from Afghanistan in 2011, when government security forces would presumably be self-sufficient.

As noted elsewhere, Obama came into office struggling to overcome the severe economic crisis that began while he campaigned for president. These domestic troubles prevented the new president from proclaiming a new grand strategy despite the many challenges facing the United States (see Leffler and Legro 2008). Obama's response to the economic crisis, the worst since the Great Depression, restored stability in financial markets. His effort to reform the nation's health care system also consumed much of his early presidency and faced strong resistance in Congress. Once again, the paradox of America's world power came into view as the world's preeminent nation turned inward, leaving a variety of global problems waiting for the leadership and inspiration that was expected of the United States.

Conclusion

As described in this chapter, U.S. foreign policy today is a product of the nation's history of global expansion, as measured by territorial control as well as by economic wealth, military might, and political and cultural influence. With these strengths have come equally formidable commitments overseas and a vast array of stakeholders in the foreign policy process. Each branch of government, each federal agency, and each intergovernmental organization stands to win or lose in this process, along with individual citizens, interest groups, corporations, the news media, and other agents of civil society.

American leaders must still overcome the widely perceived gap between the nation's past actions and proclaimed moral principles. Over the years, the rapid pace of U.S. expansion took many forms, including episodes of military conquest and colonialism that resembled the behavior of Old World empires (see Anderson and Cayton 2005). Although such actions were justified as essential in creating an "empire of liberty," they produced a legacy of distrust and anti-American sentiment in many countries that is evident today. As Daryl Glaser (2006, 267) has observed, "Even supposing a particular intervention is worthy of support, the intervening power's hypocritical record justifies a wariness about its actions. ... A power's historical hypocrisy is a reason for contemporary vigilance in monitoring its conduct."

In short, the United States must make the most of a world order it had a large hand in creating. Its success in balancing its commitments and capabilities, overcoming threats, and reconciling U.S. power and principles depends largely on its ability to manage these far-flung, and often conflicting, actors in the policy process. The role of these actors and their impact on American behavior beyond U.S. borders are the primary concern of the chapters that follow.

Key Terms

bipolar balance of power, p. 43

Bretton Woods agreements, p. 47

Cold War, p. 42

collective security, p. 38

containment, p. 43

Cuban missile crisis, p. 50

democratic peace, p. 56

détente, p. 52

domino theory, p. 51

engagement and enlargement, p. 56

failed states, p. 57

geopolitics, p. 38

glasnost, p. 54

gunboat diplomacy, p. 35

iron curtain, p. 43

Kellogg-Briand Pact, p. 39

lend-lease program, p. 41

liberal internationalism, p. 53

manifest destiny, p. 34

Marshall Plan, p. 48

Monroe Doctrine, p. 34

multipolar balance of power, p. 33

national security state, p. 45

New Look, p. 50

new unilateralism, p. 60

new world order, p. 55

Open Door policy, p. 36

Operation Desert Storm, p. 57

Operation Iraqi Freedom, p. 62

perestroika, p. 54

Roosevelt Corollary, p. 36

surge strategy, p. 63

Truman Doctrine, p. 47

unilateralism, p. 32

Vietnam Syndrome, p. 52

Internet References

The **BBC's history section** (www.bbc.co.uk/history) is "dedicated to bringing history to life" by providing animations, movies, and virtual tours, as well as a collection of articles by noted writers on historical subjects, figures, wars, and time periods.

The **Best of History Web Sites** (http://besthistorysites.net) provides more than one thousand links to American and world history sites. American sites are categorized further by historical period and topic, including Native Americans, African Americans, women, government, immigration, and other general resources.

The site informally called **a chronology of U.S. historical documents** (www.law.ou.edu/hist) is maintained and updated by the University of Oklahoma College of Law. The college provides links to the full text and printable versions of U.S. historical documents, such as speeches, charters, major laws, and agreements, from the precolonial era through the twenty-first century.

CNN Special Reports (www.cnn.com/specials) provides in-depth articles, reports, maps, and interviews on U.S. current events and foreign relations. "Special Reports" such as "Kosovo Conflict" and "Yugoslavia in Transition" are archived by year and date. Interactive media features include moving maps, live coverage of the events, and photographs.

In conjunction with the Smithsonian Institution, the **Cold War Museum** (www.coldwar.org) chronicles the half-century struggle between the United States and the Soviet Union, from early developments in the 1940s to the demise of the Soviet Union in the early 1990s. The site includes links to specific texts, chronologies, videos, congressional testimony, and relevant books and Web sites for specific aspects of the Cold War, and it highlights presidential doctrines, strategies, and Cold War military conflicts.

The Government Printing Office's **Core Documents of U.S. Democracy** site (www.gpoaccess.gov/coredocs.html) provides full-text links to documents considered most relevant to educating citizens on U.S. democracy. Categories range from early historical addresses to bills and laws from all congressional sessions. In addition to these documents, this site provides access to demographic and economic indicators and statistics relevant to the United States.

Developed and maintained by the University of Houston, the **Digital History** project (www.digitalhistory.uh.edu) uses Web technology to present chronologies, images, and sound bites from U.S. history. A full U.S. history and development textbook is included on the site, as well as suggested readings on specific time periods relevant to U.S. foreign relations, such as colonial expansion, military history, and relations with Europe.

Organized, researched, and published by the U.S. Department of State, the **Foreign Relations Series** (www.state.gov/www/about_state/history/frus.html) covers U.S. diplomacy and foreign policy decisions since the early 1800s. Included are presidential documents, treaties, intelligence reports, government conversations, and other relevant activities. The series has more than 350 individual volumes, including the most recent additions on the Kennedy and Johnson presidential administrations.

(continued)

History Matters (http://historymatters.gmu.edu) is developed and maintained by George Mason University. This site provides links and sources to help students and researchers understand crucial events in U.S. history. The site also provides advice and methods for analyzing historical works.

The **History News Network** (http://hnn.us) is a nonprofit, independent group of historians and journalists who post articles and editorial writings on U.S. foreign relations. Critical reactions to historical events, quotes, polls, and multimedia links for understanding history are included on this site.

The **Library of Congress** (http://lcweb.loc.gov) provides up-to-date access to legislation, historical documents, memorials, maps, and virtual and digital collections of historic time periods. For researchers with a specific focus, the library provides bibliographic and citation lists for topics such as the Cuban missile crisis or the war on terrorism. The library also has an interactive feature for communicating with a researcher and a librarian for in-depth questioning and help on research activities.

PBS (www.pbs.org) provides detailed access to historical events and biographies of leaders relevant to U.S. foreign relations. In addition to original Web text, PBS incorporates its television programs by posting interviews and the full text of its programs (with sound bites) on this site. Photos, maps, chronologies, and links to relevant sources are part of each series. *American Experience, Frontline,* and *People's Century* are the three primary programs relevant to U.S. foreign relations. *Frontline* features in-depth coverage of the Bush Doctrine and the ongoing war on terrorism.

The **Smithsonian Institution** (www.si.edu) is committed to helping researchers and citizens understand American identity, history, and culture. Exhibitions such as "American Expansion" as well as biographies of key leaders are useful to those wishing to understand the development of American history and politics.

3

Dynamics of Decision Making

Secretary of State Colin Powell (left) engages in a heated exchange with Donald Rumsfeld, the secretary of defense, prior to a White House cabinet meeting in January 2003. Despite Powell's popularity and stature, Rumsfeld's closer relationship with the president and vice president gave him greater influence over U.S. foreign policy.

The paradox of world power outlined in Chapter 1 became increasingly evident as the United States prevailed over the Soviet Union in the Cold War and assumed unchallenged primacy in the 1990s. But even before this seismic shift in world politics, the U.S. foreign policy process had grown steadily more complex. This trend was driven by transnational forces, including economic globalization, technological advances, and the empowerment of citizens and private groups generated by democratic reforms in many countries. All these forces were actively encouraged by the United States, the primary architect of the "constitutional" world order that emerged after World War II (see Ikenberry 2001).

The same trends, however, imposed constraints on the U.S. government's effective use of its power, adding to the constraints already built into the Constitution. The creation of new centers of power in the executive branch invited bureaucratic rivalries, sparked miscommunications, and sent mixed messages to allies and adversaries abroad. Growing trade, investment, and technology transfers brought "geoeconomics" to the top of the foreign policy agenda, although the primary agents of globalization worked in the private sector and maintained multinational allegiances. Connected by the Internet, thousands of nongovernmental organizations (NGOs) imposed new demands on U.S. and foreign leaders in areas such as the protection of human rights and poverty relief and called for new structures of global governance such as the International Criminal Court. At home, partisan manipulation of congressional districts virtually assured "safe seats" for each political party and unprecedented polarization in Congress. In fact, long before the current tumultuous era, domestic upheavals had reached such an extent that the nation's government and society experienced "a systematic breakdown when attempting to fashion a coherent and consistent approach to the world" (Destler, Gelb, and Lake 1984, 11).

As we will find, several factors influence the decision-making process in U.S. foreign policy (see Figure 3.1). The interstate system provides the setting of U.S. foreign relations, imposing a variety of *external* demands on the United States. Policy makers must also accommodate *internal* factors—rooted in civil society and the government itself—that further complicate decision making. Finally, presidents and their top advisers are also guided by psychological forces—preexisting beliefs, cognitive limitations, and diverse personality traits, among others—that are unique to each individual.

This chapter explores these challenges to America's exercise of world power by considering theories of foreign policy decision making. Theories are useful in identifying the causes of foreign policy behavior in order to anticipate, explain, and possibly influence government action. As we will find, theories make very different claims regarding the international system, the role of states and societies within that system, and the capacity of human beings—the vital but often "irrational" policy makers—to formulate and conduct coherent foreign policies.

Figure 3.1   Converging Factors in the Foreign Policy Process

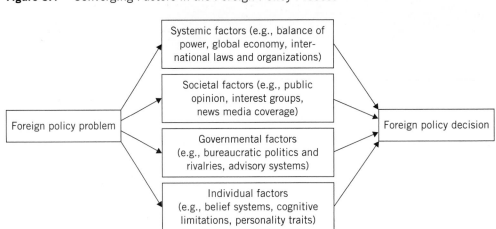

A theoretical perspective goes beyond questions of what happens in the foreign policy process, who makes key decisions, and when or where decisions are made. It also offers insight into *why* policy makers act the way they do. According to the authors of a classic study of foreign policy, "We would go so far as to say *that the 'why' questions cannot be answered without analysis of decision-making*" (Snyder, Bruck, and Sapin 2002, 35; emphasis in original).

Many Americans, for example, asked why President Barack Obama in 2009 chose to send more U.S. troops to Afghanistan while calling for a U.S. withdrawal from the country in 2011. Was this a rational decision based on sound intelligence, or was Obama hopelessly naive? Was he swayed by interest groups that stood to gain from the latest troop surge? Did he need to reconcile the conflicting needs of the State and Defense Departments and find a middle ground that would appease both political parties in Congress? Answers to these questions could not be found with confidence, as the variety of explanations reflected, above all, the theoretical lenses through which policy analysts viewed the decision.

The dynamics of decision making in U.S. foreign policy are best understood by examining policy behavior at the various **levels of analysis** noted above: the interstate system, civil society, government actors, and individuals or groups (see Table 3.1). Each of these levels sheds light on different actors in the policy process and the behaviors that are common to them in the day-to-day world of foreign affairs. The lack of world government, for example, compels states to pursue national interests as a top priority. Pressures from civil society—interest groups, corporations, and the news media, to name a few—alter the calculus of foreign policy in ways that may not serve national priorities. The U.S. government itself, a remarkably far-flung institution with multiple centers of decision making, virtually guarantees bureaucratic rivalries and breakdowns in communications.

Finally, foreign policy decisions are ultimately made by individuals and groups that operate under severe time constraints, lack complete information,

Table 3.1 Levels of Analysis in U.S. Foreign Policy

Level	Key actors	Common behavior
Interstate system	Nation-states, intergovernmental organizations (UN, NATO)	Pursuit of national interests
Civil society	Interest groups, social movements, multinational corporations, news media	Bargaining between U.S. government and private groups; government efforts to satisfy groups and public opinion
Government actors	White House, federal agencies, Congress, courts	Conflict between executive and legislative branches, bureaucratic conflict and bargaining, occasional judicial intervention
Individuals and groups	Policy makers and groups	Reliance on cognitive "shortcuts" to ease decision making; "groupthink"

and engage in group dynamics that are often dysfunctional. This convergence of external and domestic influences in the decision-making process greatly restricts the "rational" pursuit of U.S. foreign policy goals. Such a disorderly outcome, anticipated with favor by the architects of the U.S. government in the name of restricting state power, places heavy burdens on the capacity of the nation to manage its primacy in the international system.

The Global Context: Rival Perspectives

Analysts and practitioners of U.S. foreign policy maintain very different views of the international system in which policy problems arise. To some, this system is a treacherous jungle in which the states must respect the "survival of the fittest." To others, the system is far more orderly than this bleak image conveys, rewarding cooperation rather than conflict in most areas of foreign policy. Still others believe the international system—whether anarchic or orderly—is "constructed" in the minds of political leaders along with their sense of national identity and definition of friends and enemies. In all three cases, which are detailed below, the global context is crucial to grasping the dynamics of U.S. foreign policy.

Assumptions of Structural Realism

Our point of departure is the theory of **structural realism,** which is based on the lack of a world government to regulate the behavior of countries, a condition commonly referred to as **anarchy.**[1] A modern variant of realist theory that has dominated world politics for centuries, structural realism offers a bleak vision of chronic power struggles that are inevitable given the lack of a world government. A common reference point is the **Treaty of Westphalia** of 1648, which ended the Thirty Years' War in Europe and created the modern nation-state system that exists today. This treaty granted secular governments, not religious leaders, **sovereignty** over their territories and populations.[2]

Although the Treaty of Westphalia created a more orderly system for interstate relations, it left the anarchic world order intact. Political leaders remained burdened by a **security dilemma** that results from uncertainty about the motives of neighboring states, whose steps toward greater military power cannot be assumed to be defensive and nonthreatening. In this void, the primary objective of foreign policy must be self-preservation. Niccolò Machiavelli ([1532] 1985, 71), an adviser to an Italian prince, believed state survival itself was a moral end, justifying actions that may be considered cruel or immoral. This self-justifying rationale of *raison d'état* (reason of state) commonly appears today in the identification

---

1. This approach to foreign policy draws from realist theory, which has long dominated the study of world politics (see Gilpin 1986, Haslam 2002, and Wohlforth 2008).

2. Sovereignty was both *internal*, relating to domestic control, and *external*, relating to the right of all states to be free from attack.

of **national interest** as a rationale for foreign policy decisions. "We assume that statesmen think and act in terms of interest defined as power, and the evidence of history bears that assumption out," observed Hans Morgenthau (1967, 5), a well-known American realist of the Cold War. Peace can be maintained only by a **balance of power** among the strongest nation-states to create the global stability that would otherwise be required by a world government.

Another offshoot of realist theory, geopolitics, examines the impact of a nation's geographic position and resources relative to those of other powers, a perspective that is useful in understanding the historic conduct of U.S. foreign policy (see Brzezinski 1997; Cohen 2003; and Turchin 2003).[3] The territorial expansion of the United States was due in large part to the nation's advantageous position in North America and the fading presence of other great powers in the Western Hemisphere (Sicker 2002). In keeping with geopolitics as well, U.S. policy makers assumed that the nation would be threatened if either Europe or Asia became controlled by a single state, a concern that spurred U.S. action against Germany and Japan in the Second World War and the Soviet Union in the Cold War.

In confronting the world as a great power, American leaders have consistently turned to the standard instruments of structural realism, such as arms buildups and military alliances, to maintain security (Yergin 1977, ch. 8; see also Wolfers 1962). The George W. Bush administration explicitly based its emphasis on U.S. primacy in its "National Security Strategy" on structural realist assumptions (White House 2002). In particular, the strategy claimed that a unipolar balance of power led by the United States could enhance global stability by discouraging challenges from weaker states.

Liberal Theory and Global Governance

In contrast to realists, liberals acknowledge the anarchic structure of the interstate system but believe the absence of a world government does not inevitably lead to conflict (see Doyle 2008). To the contrary, problems such as global warming and nuclear proliferation, which do not respect national boundaries, create a growing sense of **interdependence** that rewards cooperation among governments out of "enlightened" self-interest (see Keohane and Nye 2001). The historical record speaks for itself, liberals point out: most countries have been at peace most of the time.

Because many global problems do not respect state sovereignty, they must be solved beyond the narrow bounds of the Westphalian interstate system. In this view, the UN, World Trade Organization (WTO), and other intergovernmental organizations are needed to confront collective problems that individual countries cannot resolve on their own. NGOs such as Greenpeace also play a crucial role in mobilizing citizens around these causes, pressuring governments to cooperate

---

3. See Spykman (1942) and Mackinder (1942) for earlier analyses of geopolitics that emphasized the importance of Europe to the global balance of power—and to U.S. security.

with each other, and, at times, lending their own resources and expertise to the resolution of transnational problems (see Chapter 9). By taking these actions, these nonstate actors have created a network of **global governance** that fills the "sovereignty gap" in world politics (see Weiss 2009).

Liberals find that global cooperation reflects and strengthens informal **norms** of behavior (see Kratochwil 1989). Such norms—that treaties and alliance obligations should be honored, for example—have been widely observed over time. The U.S. government's recognition of global poverty as a major foreign policy problem, for example, produced the creation in 2004 of a new foreign aid agency, the Millennium Challenge Corporation (Hook 2008). These changing norms reflect the capacity of citizens and governments to learn from past experience, and in many cases to suspend discredited practices such as dueling, slavery, and, perhaps, the recourse to world war (Mueller 1989).

One historical pattern stands out in this learning process: whereas democratic governments often wage wars against repressive or autocratic states, they have maintained a democratic peace with each other (see Russett 1993; Ray 1995; Rosato 2003; and Macmillan 2004). Whatever the cause, this connection between democracy and peace is hardly new. Immanual Kant ([1795] 1914), an Enlightenment philosopher, pointed out that only democracies joining together in a pacific federation could maintain a "perpetual peace." This concept was refined during the Cold War with the emergence of a **security community** in North America and Western Europe, an informal system of economic, political, and military cooperation that rendered war among these democratic states largely unthinkable (Deutsch et al. 1957). More recently, President George W. Bush frequently justified the U.S. invasion of Iraq as an effort to bring democracy—and peace—to the Middle East.

This moralistic impulse has characterized a long tradition of liberal internationalism in U.S. foreign policy. "In this view," theorist G. John Ikenberry (2009, 2) observed, "it is America's commitment to promote democracy worldwide—a sort of liberal imperial ambition—that is at the core of Wilsonianism, and it was at the core of the Bush Doctrine." American leaders following this tradition have justified U.S. military interventions on humanitarian grounds, collaborated with the UN and other multilateral institutions, and launched "state-building" projects in such countries as Haiti, Somalia and postwar Iraq. The presumed benevolence underlying such ventures, this approach contends, is what sets the United States apart from the "power politics" of Old World diplomacy.

Liberal theory has another variation, **neoliberal institutionalism,** which adopts a systemic view and is often supported by rational choice and game theory (see Oye 1986). In this view, political leaders repeatedly interact with their counterparts in other governments, and a common outcome of these repeated interactions is greater cooperation. Friendly gestures, in short, are reciprocated by gestures of trust and goodwill. Such a pattern, reinforced by

President Woodrow Wilson throws the ceremonial first pitch of the 1916 baseball season in Washington, D.C. Wilson, known for his liberal views regarding U.S. foreign policy, later justified the nation's 1917 entry into World War I on the grounds that "the world must be made safe for democracy."

societal and governmental institutions that benefit from stability, rewards both sides in a foreign policy negotiation while discouraging future acts of coercion or aggression. In some areas of foreign policy, this cooperation takes the form of **regimes,** or institutionalized cooperation based on common norms and objectives. The development aid regime, for example, has rendered large annual transfers of economic assistance from rich to poor countries a moral obligation (Hook and Lebo 2010).

Foreign Policy in a "Constructed" World

Still another theory of world politics with clear applications to U.S. foreign policy hails from the more contemporary tradition of social **constructivism** (see Onuf 1989, Katzenstein 1996, and Checkel 2008). Advocates of this approach argue that world politics, along with domestic politics and other aspects of public life, do not have fixed properties—they are "socially constructed" by people, primarily through public discourse. Thus the global balance of power is threatening only if political leaders *create* threats by making arbitrary distinctions between "friends" and "enemies." From this perspective, interstate anarchy—the absence

Point/Counterpoint

REALISTS VS. LIBERALS ON CAUSES OF WAR

A central question posed by theorists of world politics is what causes war? Classical realists believe wars break out whenever there is no central power to restrain human passions or competition for limited resources. "During the time men live without a common Power to keep them all in awe, they are in that condition which is called war, and such a war as is of every man against every man," wrote English philosopher Thomas Hobbes. Contemporary neorealists believe this linkage between anarchy and war, which Hobbes applied to civil conflicts, also applies to foreign affairs. "Among states the state of nature is a state of war," wrote political analyst Kenneth Waltz. "Among men as among states, anarchy, or the absence of government, is associated with the occurrence of violence."

President Theodore Roosevelt adopted another realist rationale for war: the advancement of national character. "There are higher things in life than the soft and easy enjoyment of material comfort," he observed. "A rich nation which is slothful, timid, or unwieldy is an easy prey for any people which still retains those most valuable of all qualities, the soldierly virtues." As a senior naval officer and later as president, Roosevelt pursued this vision by advocating U.S. military expansion in Asia and Latin America.

Liberals reject these rationales for war. For John Locke, an English theorist of the Enlightenment era, state tyranny over individual freedoms was a more common cause of war than anarchy in a "state of nature." Immanuel Kant, a like-minded German philosopher, argued that wars squander private liberty as well as public energies. As a result, "the full development of the capacities of mankind are undoubtedly retarded in their progress."

The U.S. leader most closely associated with liberal theory, Woodrow Wilson, rejected the "martial virtues" highlighted by Roosevelt and sought instead to direct U.S. foreign policy toward the transnational cause of peace. "I am proposing that all nations henceforth avoid entangling alliances which would draw them into competitions of power, catch them in a net of intrigue and selfish rivalry, and disturb their own affairs with influences intruded from without. There is no entangling alliance in a concert of power." Wilson's failure to achieve his goals through the League of Nations has not prevented contemporary liberals from promoting world peace through the Wilsonian means of international law, cooperation through the UN, and democratic governments that protect individual rights.

SOURCES: Thomas Hobbes, *Leviathan* (Indianapolis: Bobbs-Merrill, [1651] 1983), 64; Kenneth N. Waltz, *Theory of International Politics* (Reading, Mass.: Addison-Wesley, 1979), 83; Keith L. Nelson and Spencer C. Olin Jr., *Why War? Ideology, Theory, and History* (Berkeley: University of California Press, 1979), 27, 40.

of world government—is not necessarily a recipe for conflict but is instead "what states make of it" (Wendt 1992, 1999). There are no inherent national interests, only interests constructed by political leaders and then transformed into public policy through the creative use of language and images of domestic ideals and global threats.

A central aspect of constructivist theory relates to **identity,** or the definition of an individual or a group as considered apart from others. Political identities, which are socially constructed (that is, they have no objective material basis), define relations among governments and stipulate whether they will be allies or adversaries. From this perspective, the shared identities of the United States and Western Europe after World War II had more to do with the creation of NATO than the threat posed by the Soviet Union. "If material capabilities are all that count in world politics, one would have expected Western Europe to align with the Soviet Union rather than with the United States" (Risse-Kappen 1996, 359). Those same identities kept NATO members within the alliance after the Cold War, despite the absence of their stated enemy in Moscow, an outcome that also contradicts realist theory.

Constructivists view the nineteenth-century discourse of "manifest destiny" in the United States as a moral justification for westward expansion and territorial conquest. The same can be said for President Theodore Roosevelt's 1903 "corollary" to the Monroe Doctrine that granted the United States "international police power" over the Western Hemisphere. More recent historical cases further illustrate the impact of discourse in "creating" the world of U.S. foreign policy:

- In rallying the public during World War II, the U.S. government and major media outlets bolstered national morale by spreading stereotyped images of German soldiers as monsters and Japanese soldiers as rats, insects, and apes (Dower 1986, Hunt 1987).

- Harry Truman's 1947 call for U.S. action to protect the Greek and Turkish governments from communist takeovers failed to name this target of the Truman Doctrine (see Chapter 2), but instead cast the first major escalation of the Cold War as a struggle between global "liberty" and "tyranny" (Sjöstedt 2007).

- In vilifying nations such as Fidel Castro's Cuba at the height of the Cold War, American leaders fomented global tensions that brought the world close to nuclear holocaust (Weldes 1999).

- Bill Clinton's concerns about "rogue states" after the Cold War and George W. Bush's more recent statements about an "axis of evil" involving Iran, Iraq, and North Korea served the purpose of constructing a perilous world of U.S. foreign policy that required aggressive action by the government to maintain primacy.

Table 3.2 Theory in Practice: Perspectives on the Bush Administration's Global War on Terrorism

Theory	Cause of the war	Policy preferences
Structural realism	Challenge to U.S. unipolarity in global balance of power	Retaliate with maximum force against state sponsors of terrorism
Liberalism	Emergence of key nonstate actors and the growing impact of norms in world politics	Manage grievances of terrorist groups and respond through networks of global governance
Constructivism	Rigid state identities and definitions of friends and enemies; conflicts inflamed by hostile discourse	Redefine identities to emphasize shared problems and cooperative solutions; avoid hostile discourse

■ President George W. Bush "constructed" the terrorist attacks of September 2001 as the beginning a "global war on terror" rather than, for example, a mass homicide that should be investigated by law enforcement agencies and punished by courts. Bush's speeches, designed to spark a large-scale U.S. military response, described "a break with everything that went before and after in world history" (Nabers 2009, 204).

These examples demonstrate how U.S. foreign policy makers characterize problems overseas in ways that advance their priorities in global politics. Even in the absence of this manipulative use of discourse, however, studies of political psychology, described later in this chapter, reveal how the "construction" of reality is a natural process by which individuals—private citizens as well as public figures—make sense of the complex world around them. Foreign policy analysts, therefore, have much to offer by examining the manner in which national identities, perceptions of friends and foes, and policy initiatives originate within the minds of individuals rather than from the objective or brute "facts" of world politics (see Houghton, 2007).

In sum, the theories of structural realism, liberalism, and constructivism maintain very different conceptions of the global context. In so doing, the theories offer divergent perspectives regarding the formulation and conduct of U.S. foreign policy. This may be illustrated by applying the three theories to the Bush administration's global war on terrorism (see Table 3.2). This comparison reveals the link among theories, their conceptions of problems overseas, and the foreign policy solutions deemed most appropriate.

Opening the "Black Box": Foreign Policy as Rational Action?

Given the foothold that structural realism has in the field of international relations, it may seem surprising that the theory is widely rejected by foreign policy analysts who wish to open the "black box" of domestic politics—that is, the internal competition and bargaining among societal interest groups, government agencies, and individual policy makers with a stake in policy outcomes (see Gourevitch 2002). Indeed, much of the research conducted in the field of foreign policy analysis shares an interest in exposing the domestic rather than systemic sources of foreign policy (see Neack 2008 for an elaboration).[4]

Opening this black box is a daunting task. Press reports that the United States "made" a particular decision may be technically accurate and easy to digest, but lurking behind such a decision is a struggle for power and influence among competing government agencies, intergovernmental organizations, and private interest groups. Decisions about each foreign policy issue produce winners and losers in the policy process; the success or failure of the United States in world politics follows directly from the compromises and bargains the government makes at home.

Structural realism again provides a point of departure for considering the domestic sources of U.S. foreign policy. Structural realists assume political leaders to be **rational actors** who weigh their options based on common understandings of national interests, tangible measures of global power, and the ends and means of foreign policy. In this view, foreign policy goals are self-evident, or "given," as are the relative merits of alternative means to achieve those goals (see Verba 1961). Structural realists also see governments as **unitary actors,** speaking with one voice. Even though in all modern governments multiple bureaucratic agencies are involved in foreign policy making, the most crucial decisions are made by the top government officials in the name of the national interest. These officials can override the institutional self-interests of their subordinates and fend off pressure from individuals and interest groups outside the government. Based on these assumptions, structural realists believe it is possible to understand foreign policy without reference to the internal debates or trade-offs that led to those policies. In this sense, these assumptions support the view that foreign and domestic policies result from **rational choice** (see Bueno de Mesquita 2009, chs. 2 and 3).

Foreign policy analysts in this tradition often use **game theory** to test their claims. Game theorists, using the research methods of economics and mathematics, apply the assumptions of rational choice to negotiations and bargaining on a variety of foreign policy issues, including nuclear deterrence (George 1974) and arms control (Axelrod 1984). These theorists first establish the preferences of all decision makers in foreign policy negotiations and determine which bargaining positions and tactics would best achieve those objectives. Their analyses have two primary objectives: to *explain* the outcome of past foreign policy decisions, and to *prescribe* future policy-making strategies that would be most likely to produce "optimal" outcomes for the United States and other governments. Another key question is whether a **zero-sum game** exists in which the gains of one side will be matched by equivalent losses by the other, as in the case of a

---

4. This research figures prominently in a specialized academic journal, *Foreign Policy Analysis,* which began publishing in 2005.

Table 3.3 Rational Action and the Real World

Policy area	Rational action	The real world
Key actors in foreign policy process	Small group of like-minded decision makers	Multiple and conflicting centers of power in the White House, federal agencies, and Congress; constant pressure from private groups
State preferences	Determined objectively by national interests	Disputed by rival government and societal actors
Nature of decision-making environment	Centralized, consensual	Fragmented, chaotic
Degree of certainty regarding foreign policy problems	High	Low
Magnitude of varying foreign policy problems and merits of possible solutions	Discernible by objective cost-benefit analysis	Impossible to calculate given personal and institutional biases
Implementation of new policies	Efficient	Prone to bureaucratic delays, procedural conflicts, communication breakdowns
Outcome for U.S. foreign policy	Optimal	Suboptimal; often ineffective and self-defeating

territorial dispute, for example. Alternatively, the case being considered may represent a **positive-sum game** in which both sides enjoy net benefits (environmental issues often fit this model), or a **negative-sum game** in which both sides are likely to face net losses (as often happens in negotiations among foreign aid donors).

Liberals and constructivists strongly disagree with the rational-choice approach, which reduces foreign policy decisions to objective calculations of relative costs and benefits. In their view, opening the black box reveals fragmented centers of decision making that contradict the image of rational action (see Table 3.3). In practice, decision makers routinely disagree about the content of national interests, about the severity of threats to those interests, and about the implications of both for the day-to-day conduct of foreign policy. Even if all decision makers agree about the nature of a problem, information about the problem is likely to be incomplete or inaccurate. The other extreme exists as well, however, when information pours in at such high volumes that decision makers cannot hope to manage it. Making sound policy choices proves even more difficult in this situation because the costs and benefits of each option cannot be calculated with precision.

As for "unitary" action, the actual conduct of U.S. foreign policy is highly fragmented, with multiple actors involved within and outside the government.

Foreign policy in this view represents a **two-level game** in which government officials simultaneously negotiate with their counterparts overseas and with domestic actors who have stakes in the policy process (Putnam 1988). The internal bargaining includes interest groups outside of government who apply pressure on policy makers through several channels. In addition, the White House must accommodate members of Congress and stakeholders in various federal agencies. The trade-offs produced by these two-level games may lead to less-than-optimal outcomes on either level, but they are unavoidable in democratic states that welcome private interests in the process.

For our purposes, it is useful to view the policy arena of U.S. foreign policy as one located at the intersection of three spheres of political activity: transnational civil society, the interstate system, and domestic governing institutions (see Figure 3.2). The degree to which different actors engage in the foreign policy process varies across issue areas, as is demonstrated throughout this book. Nevertheless, the effective management of foreign policy requires that the needs and policy preferences of actors in all three spheres be taken into account, if not ultimately reconciled. Although external problems and opportunities create the foundation of foreign policy, one must recognize that, ultimately, foreign policy begins at home.

This central reality requires that we explore these domestic sources of U.S. foreign policy in greater detail. The following sections review the dynamics of decision making at the societal, governmental, and individual/group levels of analysis, respectively. Understanding all three levels is a vital analytic task, but one must avoid the temptation to view the levels as mutually exclusive. To the contrary, the success or failure of U.S. foreign policy often involves all three domestic forces. Analysis of President Bush's decision to invade Iraq in 2003, for example, finds that defects in the administration's foreign policy bureaucracy, combined with the president's distinctive world view and management style,

Figure 3.2   The Matrix of U.S. Foreign Policy

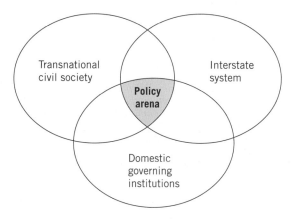

paved the way for the problems encountered by U.S. troops as they conducted their mission (see Mitchell and Massoud 2009).

The Impact of Civil Society

Like other democracies, the U.S. government provides many opportunities for citizens and groups to participate in public affairs. Early U.S. leaders looked to civil society as a hedge against future government repression, and modern-day societal groups continue to serve this function. In this process they enhance the openness, or transparency, of government and inform interested citizens about key issues and developments. Foreign policy makers may find this input difficult to manage, as in the case of antiwar protests during the Vietnam War and the more recent invasion of Iraq, but they cannot ignore the citizens who represent the ultimate power base in American politics.

Forces outside the government, and increasingly beyond the United States altogether, greatly complicate the American foreign policy process. These members of **transnational civil society,** including interest groups along with public opinion, the news media, and think tanks, collectively exert pressure continually on the United States to accommodate their policy preferences. Since U.S. elected officials must also heed domestic public opinion for electoral reasons, they must be sensitive to public opinion overseas, particularly in democratic countries whose support for American foreign policy is needed. In addition, the financial ownership of major news outlets has become increasingly transnational, and the impact of their news coverage is felt immediately in the White House.

Foreign Policy in a "Small State"

The United States is said to feature a "small state" that is overshadowed by a "large society" (Krasner 1978). This is a common characteristic of democracies, in contrast to authoritarian polities, in which the state dominates public life and represses or prohibits many forms of civic expression (see Figure 3.3). The U.S. government, which employs millions of people in a variety of civilian and military agencies, is by no means small on an absolute level. Still, the government's power to shape U.S. foreign policy is greatly constrained by the pressures imposed by influential groups outside the state. Such is to be expected in a government "by the people." In contrast, highly repressive governments tightly control their civil societies, a practice that makes their decision making more efficient at the cost of widespread neglect of individual freedoms and violations of human rights.

Although governments maintain sovereign powers to make foreign policy, "transnational actors crucially affect state interests, policies, and inter-state relations" (Risse-Kappen 1995, 15). Churches, organized ethnic groups, multinational corporations, and other groups have influenced foreign policy throughout U.S. history, but never before have they been so well organized,

Figure 3.3   Policy Influence and Control: Two Models of State-Society Relations

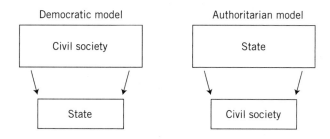

visible, and connected with their counterparts overseas. This "power shift," political analyst Jessica Mathews (1997, 50) has observed, affects all countries today:

> Increasingly, resources and threats that matter, including money, information, pollution, and popular culture, circulate and shape lives and economies with little regard for political boundaries. International standards of conduct are gradually beginning to override claims of national or regional singularity. Even the most powerful states find the marketplace and international public opinion compelling them more often to follow a particular course.

In this sense, transnational civil society serves as an extension of America's own civil society, which values public opinion and a free press while providing interest groups with access to the government through many channels—congressional committees, executive agencies, the White House, and political campaigns. As political theorist David Truman (1951, 502) observed more than half a century ago, "Such organized groups are as clearly a part of the government institution as are the political parties or the branches of government formally established by law or constitution." These forces exert enormous influence on political leaders, which is unseen in more insulated polities.

Each day, thousands of NGOs actively engage in foreign policy issues of concern to the United States. These organizations, with memberships increasingly drawn from multiple countries, pursue their policy preferences in many areas, including economic development, environmental protection, arms control, immigration, public health, and human rights (see Keck and Sikkink 1998). Although these organizations occasionally serve as agents of U.S. foreign policy, they frequently challenge U.S. positions and preferences. Indeed, the constraints on U.S. sovereignty posed by these organizations, particularly intergovernmental organizations associated with the UN, prompted the Bush administration's turn away from the international community when it came to power in 2001.

The U.S. political system lends itself to public scrutiny in several ways. First, in most cases the deliberations of Congress are open to the news media and are documented in publications such as the *Congressional Record*. Other government records, including the federal budget, are available on the Internet. Second, congressional committees often feature testimony from interest groups, some of which are also invited to high-level meetings of federal agencies that cannot gain sufficient information from public sources alone. Finally, by providing campaign donations to political candidates, publishing reports on pressing policy issues, organizing mass e-mail campaigns, and staging high-profile media events, these private citizens and groups have multiple ways to "shrink" the power of the state.

Iron Triangles and Issue Networks

The fragmentation of the U.S. political system and the nature of foreign policy allow government decision makers to maintain a high degree of autonomy from the public and even the president, who cannot possibly rein in the far-flung bureaucratic and societal forces that find niches in the political system. Powerful interest groups, for example, pursue their policy preferences by forming alliances with supportive government agencies and officials. Some aspects of the foreign policy process can thus be viewed as an **iron triangle** that links influential interest groups, congressional committees, and the corresponding executive branch agencies that carry out policies of mutual concern. At the same time, an iron triangle effectively excludes other members of Congress, the White House, and the general public from affecting key foreign policy decisions (see Figure 3.4).

A commonly cited example of an iron triangle is the U.S. defense industry, identified by President Eisenhower in his 1961 farewell address to the nation as a key element of the **"military-industrial complex."** Defense contractors such as General Dynamics and Lockheed Martin exert strong influence over members of Congress who control defense funding and the fate of individual weapons programs. These legislators, who are primarily on the Armed Services Committees of both the House and the Senate, have political and personal incentives to satisfy the contractors, because they represent many jobs (and possible votes) in their districts and provide large campaign contributions. The Pentagon's incessant need to maintain its high funding levels, coupled with the lobbying efforts of self-interested defense contractors, places ongoing pressure on congressional committees to increase military spending. Other iron triangles in the foreign policy process are in the areas of energy policy, foreign investment, veterans' affairs, and arms exports (see Hook and Rothstein 2005).

Decision making in other areas involves more actors and is more open to competing viewpoints. These **issue networks** bring together interested government and private actors with shared knowledge and expertise, if not similar policy preferences (Heclo 1978). At times, the groups that come together in *ad hoc* issue networks bitterly oppose one another, leading to a process of competition rather than collusion, which is the essence of iron triangles. The growth of issue networks in the 1970s followed structural reforms by Congress, which created more

Figure 3.4   The Iron Triangle

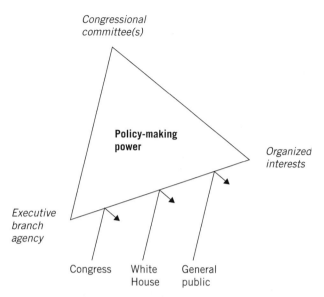

subcommittees and expanded the federal bureaucracy in response to public demands for more services and access to the decision-making process.

"Politics makes strange bedfellows," a popular axiom in the study of government, has been affirmed repeatedly in U.S. foreign policy. The antiglobalization protests during the 1999 WTO conference in Seattle, Washington, for example, involved anarchists, trade unions, environmentalists, feminists, and human rights activists. Proponents of the WTO's pro-globalization agenda included most governments and major corporations, as well as some liberal activists who viewed closer integration of the world economy as a step toward political cooperation and peace. Although these groups came from different backgrounds and pursued widely varying agendas, all were attempting to influence the same broad policy area. (The protesters succeeded in disrupting the conference and calling attention to their needs, but ultimately they failed to stop the WTO from furthering the cause of free trade.)

During this same period, a similar issue network formed around the issue of China's trading status with the U.S. government (see Figure 3.5). In this case, the Clinton administration strongly favored granting China most-favored-nation (MFN) status, a step that would lead directly to China's entry into the WTO. Clinton, who defended his initiative on behalf of "engaging" repressive governments, was supported by large corporations based in the United States that hoped

Figure 3.5   China MFN Issue Network

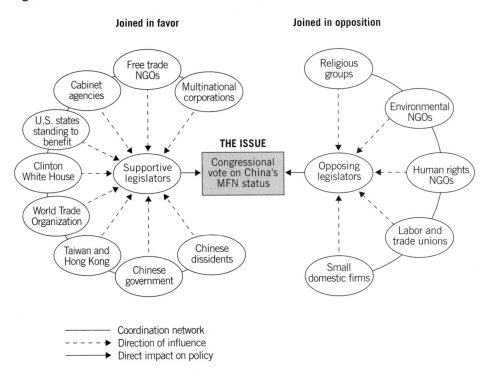

SOURCES: Steven W. Hook, "Sino-American Trade Relations: Privatizing Foreign Policy," in *Contemporary Cases in U.S. Foreign Policy: From Terrorism to Trade,* 3rd ed., ed. Ralph G. Carter (Washington, D.C.: CQ Press, 2008); Mary H. Cooper, "U.S.-China Trade," *CQ Researcher Online* (April 15, 1994), http://library.cqpress.com/cqresearcher; David Masci, "China after Deng," *CQ Researcher Online* (June 13, 1997), http://library.cqpress.com/cqresearcher; Washington Council on International Trade, "Issue Brief: China's MFN Status" (April 11,1997), www.wcit.org/resources/publications/issue_briefs/ib_china_mfn_status.htm.

to profit from heightened commercial relations between Washington and Beijing. The government of China, of course, favored the move, as did the WTO, recently created as the institutional locomotive of free trade. Opposing the president were conservative members of Congress and a variety of private groups that protested the move because it rewarded a Chinese Communist Party that had committed atrocities against its own people. A variety of labor and trade unions as well as many small manufacturers opposed the measure as well. Clinton ultimately won this policy debate, gaining Senate ratification of the trade measure and ensuring China's entry into the WTO (Hook and Lebo 2008).

Because interest groups have expanded their activism and the federal government has become more and more fragmented, decision making on domestic policies generally corresponds with the issue network model. Iron triangles do endure in many foreign policy areas, but issue networks are found more frequently in the process today as the boundaries between foreign and domestic policies erode and intermestic issues, which cross the line between international and domestic policies, demand a greater share of the government's attention. Thus, understanding issue networks is crucial to understanding how domestic politics and U.S. foreign policy converge.

Coping with Bureaucratic Politics

The decentralized structure of the U.S. government produces a high level of tension within the executive branch. The process of **bureaucratic politics** thus plays a crucial, though often dysfunctional, role in shaping U.S. foreign policy. This pattern, which afflicts all governments to varying degrees, is clear in the historical record. As societies modernized throughout nineteenth-century Europe, bureaucrats took on an ever-widening array of tasks and became powerful political actors as well. Their greater expertise, longevity in government, and direct access to the instruments of policy gave them significant advantages over elected leaders. These bureaucratic actors, however, were thrust into competition with one another over the control of major government functions, and their ensuing rivalries frequently undermined the coherence and effectiveness of state policies.

Contemporary scholars have applied these facets of bureaucratic politics in their analyses of the U.S. federal government, whose immense size, spending power, structural complexity, and global reach have no historical precedents and are unequaled by any other government today. For example, political scientist Terry Moe (1989, 267) pointed out that "American public bureaucracy is not designed to be effective." He found that "the bureaucracy arises out of politics, and its design reflects the interests, strategies, and compromises of those who exercise political power." Graham Allison was the first to apply bureaucratic politics systematically to U.S. foreign policy. According to Graham Allison (1971, 144), "The Governmental (or Bureaucratic) Politics Model sees no unitary actor but rather many actors as players—players who focus not on a single strategic issue but on many diverse intra-national problems as well; players who act in terms of no consistent set of strategic objectives but rather according to various conceptions of national, organizational, and personal goals; players who make government decisions not by a single, rational choice but by the pulling and hauling that is politics."

Patterns of Organizational Behavior

Critics of the bureaucratic politics model argue that it is *deterministic,* falsely identifying agencies with singular and predictable interests and policy positions (Welch 1992). The State Department, for example, was deeply divided over U.S. involvement in the Vietnam War; similar strains could be seen in more recent interventions in Somalia, Kosovo, and Iraq. While this critique is borne out by many studies of U.S. foreign policy, it affirms the overall image of bureaucratic politics that deprive the United States of a "united front" in its relations with other governments. In this respect, bureaucracies in the United States and other industrialized societies exhibit similar characteristics. Among the most important of these characteristics for understanding of U.S. foreign policy are resilience, autonomy, self-interest, conservatism, and inefficiency.

Resilience. "Once it is fully established," German sociologist Max Weber (1946, 228) once observed, "bureaucracy is among those social structures which are the hardest to destroy." The creation of U.S. federal agencies is a difficult, time-consuming task requiring public support, consensus within Congress, and presidential approval. Once formed, an agency becomes part of the institutional landscape, welcoming new missions and clients that have a stake in its future activities. Often an agency is "captured" by clients whose preferences for continuity, if not expansion, of its mission are embraced by the agency's managers. As described earlier, this pattern is clearly visible in the institutional momentum of American foreign policy agencies.

Autonomy. Bureaucracies enjoy a high level of freedom from outside interference. Agency managers have more expertise in their domains than elected leaders, giving the managers the upper hand in shaping and implementing policy. They also tend to last longer in their jobs, where they accumulate still greater expertise along with on-the-job training in mastering the political system. Finally, although agencies in the executive branch fall under the president's authority, they can elude presidential oversight even when monitoring measures exist. "Agencies can ignore presidential directives, delay implementation of presidential programs, and limit presidential options when it suits their needs to do so because presidents do not have the time or resources to watch them" (Zegart 1999, 47). The most troublesome aspects of bureaucratic autonomy led to the 1986 Iran-contra scandal, in which the National Security Council conducted "off-the-shelf" military operations in Central America with little or no oversight by President Reagan.

Self-interest. Thrust into a competitive relationship with other agencies, agency managers are often more concerned with their own preferences and needs than with what would best serve the national interest. Bureaucratic rivalries extend beyond competition for material resources to competition for intangible assets. Of particular importance among the latter are the greater *influence* over policy and the enhanced *prestige* within the policy community that come with such influence. During the Cuban missile crisis, for example, the advice of senior military leaders reflected their parochial concerns rather than an objective determination of the most effective means for defusing the conflict and preventing a nuclear war between the United States and the Soviet Union (see Allison and Zelikow 1999). More recently, in George W. Bush's first term, tensions between Secretary of State Colin Powell and Secretary of Defense Donald Rumsfeld over Iraq had as much to do with built-in bureaucratic rivalries as with substantive policy differences.

Conservatism. Agencies put in place **standard operating procedures (SOPs),** or consistent measures for addressing commonly encountered situations, as a matter of routine. These SOPs stress continuity over change, the execution of specialized roles, and a high level of internal order. Within bureaucracies, an organizational culture develops that further encourages business as usual and discourages innovation or changes of course (see Brehm and Gates 1997 and Drezner 2000). These problems plagued Donald Rumsfeld in 2003 as he sought to "transform" the U.S. military. Rumsfeld's frustration became so great that he fired Tom White, the army secretary. Rumsfeld did so in part because of White's refusal to support the cancellation of a pet project, the $11 billion Crusader artillery system, which Rumsfeld considered obsolete. Attempts to reform agencies, though occasionally successful, generally lead to frustration and failure (Abramson and Lawrence 2001).

Inefficiency. The fragmentation of bureaucracies leads to breakdowns in communication and coordination. This problem was illustrated during the 1983 U.S. invasion of the tiny Caribbean island of Grenada, launched by the Reagan administration to prevent a pro-Soviet regime from taking power. Despite their overwhelming force, the six thousand U.S. troops needed three days to subdue a small brigade of enemy fighters, many of them construction workers from Cuba. Eighteen Americans died in battle, partly as the result of a battle plan that guaranteed each of the armed services a role in the invasion. There were also severe problems with communications. One marine, unable to contact his superiors by radio, simply used a pay telephone to contact the Pentagon and provide the location of enemy forces.

These aspects of bureaucratic behavior suggest to many observers a U.S. government on automatic pilot, controlled by bureaucrats who are driven by institutional self-interests. It is important to note, however, that this bureaucratic politics model is hardly universal and is challenged by two other models of decision making. The **presidential control model** views presidents as "caretakers of the national interest" who can rise above domestic politics, particularly when U.S. security interests are at stake (Bendor and Hammond 1992; see also Krasner 1972 and Art 1973). The **congressional dominance model** holds that legislators make their preferences clear to agency managers, who then have a material incentive—in the form of future budget support—to ensure that those preferences are realized (see Shepsle 1979 and Weingast 1984). Once again, students can find evidence that supports both models in different areas of U.S. foreign policy, as revealed in the chapters that follow.

State and Local Governments

The pluralistic nature of U.S. foreign policy extends to the state and local levels as well. As described in Chapter 2, the original blueprint for American government—the Articles of Confederation—granted state governments control over most aspects of foreign policy. Placed in a system of domestic anarchy, the thirteen original states engaged in trade wars among themselves, pursued separate relations with foreign governments, and conducted their own military expeditions on the western frontier. As a result, the founders designed the Constitution in part to shift key foreign policy powers to the federal government, a system that remains in place today.

Under this system, however, state and local governments can still pass resolutions on foreign policy issues, pursue foreign investments, organize cultural exchanges, and manage the intermestic problems, such as pollution, that affect them. "As decisions are made and events transpire outside the boundaries of the nation-state that may have an immediate and profound effect on citizens at the grassroots level, these citizens demand that their interests be protected and enhanced not only by their national governments, but also by the subnational governments closest to where they live" (Fry 1998, 15). Likewise, Jessica Mathews (1997, 65–66), president of the Carnegie Endowment for International Peace, has observed, "Nation-states may simply no longer be the natural problem-solving unit."

Public activism in U.S. foreign policy frequently takes place at the state and local levels. It is there that Americans learn about problems overseas, discuss possible solutions to those problems, and take action to influence national policy makers. With more direct access to the political process at these levels, citizens frequently mobilize around the slogan "Think globally, act locally." State governments frequently respond to these pressures by speaking out or taking action on foreign policy issues. Among prominent examples:

- Nearly 1,000 localities called for a nuclear freeze by the time the Cold War ended in 1991, nearly 200 had demanded a halt to nuclear testing, and 120 had refused to comply with federal civil defense guidelines in the event of nuclear war (Shuman 1992).

- Twenty-eight state governments imposed trade and other commercial restrictions on U.S. and foreign businesses operating in South Africa by the time its government, in 1994, abolished its system of *apartheid* that denied political rights to the majority black population (Fry 1998).

- The governors of ten states met with the president of Mexico between 1995 and 2004 (McMillan 2008, 229). Governors also met during this period with the heads of state or government in Canada, China, the European Union, Israel, Spain, the United Kingdom, and twenty-two other foreign countries.

- Thirty governors visited Iraq in the first three years of the Iraq war (O'Connor 2006, B3). All fifty governors signed a letter in 2007 asking that President Bush provide additional federal funds to resupply their "depleted National Guards" (Scharnberg 2007, 1A).

To an extent previously unseen, the war on terrorism declared in 2001 brought local governments directly into the foreign policy process. These governments serve on the front lines of the homeland security effort in three ways. First, they must protect their citizens with enhanced police forces. Second, they must be prepared to respond immediately and effectively to terrorist attacks, a task managed with courage on September 11 by the New York City Fire Department and other first responders. Third, local governments and agencies must play an intelligence-gathering role in looking out for possible terrorist "cells" or suspicious activities in their jurisdictions. In all three areas, local governments must work closely with federal officials and, when necessary, secure additional resources from Washington.

In the economic realm, the annual output of many states exceeds that of most foreign countries. The overseas exports of U.S. manufacturing firms have grown tremendously in the past decades. As a result, most states now operate overseas offices in foreign countries, while promoting joint ventures, sponsoring trade conferences, and subsidizing export promotion at home. Governors compete intensely for foreign industries to locate within their borders, offering a variety of economic incentives, such as tax breaks, highway improvements, and regulatory relief, to make this happen. Members of Congress commonly support these efforts and provide federal resources where possible to attract industries. In addition, military bases provide a substantial boost to employment, tax revenue, and spin-off economic activity at the state and local levels.

State governments also may pursue environmental policies that have impacts far beyond their borders. In California, for example, a measure was placed on the November 2006 ballot to raise $4 billion in tax revenues from oil producers to fund research and development of alternative energy. The proposed Clean Alternative Energy Act, or Proposition 87 on the ballot, sought to reduce oil consumption by 25 percent in California, the nation's leading oil consumer. An array of politicians, including former President Bill Clinton, joined Hollywood celebrities and tycoons from Silicon Valley in supporting the measure, which was opposed largely by the oil companies that would have to pay the new taxes. The act would fill the gap left in federal energy policy, which by 2006 had yet to include stringent measures for energy conservation and reduced emissions of greenhouse gases (see Chapter 12). Though the measure was defeated, similar actions were proposed elsewhere as the threat of global warming increased.

Local governments are even more likely than states to voice their opinions on general foreign policy issues, attracting attention by approving resolutions on these matters. For example, more than 160 cities and counties approved resolutions opposing President Bush's preventive invasion of Iraq early in 2003. "Military action in Iraq will divert attention from economic issues and challenges confronting the American people and American cities," the city of Cleveland's resolution stated. Although this plea went unheeded by national policy makers—as such resolutions often do—the opposition of Cleveland, along with that of Chicago, Philadelphia, San Francisco, and other major cities, was made clear to a global audience.

Critics of local activism think foreign policy should be left to the experts in Washington and city councils should stick to their core responsibilities. "Local officials are elected because of their competency to manage local concerns, not because of their personal beliefs on national and international affairs," policy analyst Beth Waldron (2003) argued. "Hijacking local-government meetings for the debate of federal policy accomplishes painfully little and costs plenty. Municipalities should keep the 'local' in local government and leave national policy up to the appropriate duly elected federal officials." Despite these complaints, cities and towns remain outspoken advocates on global issues.

The Human Factor

Foreign policy is made by people, not by inanimate entities such as nation-states or bureaucracies. Despite efforts to understand world politics by focusing on such abstractions, the simple fact remains that individuals respond in different ways to similar problems. Individual actions are more likely to have significant consequences "when leaders have an inordinate amount of power" (Mintz and DeRouen 2010, 19), but such actions can have impacts even in complex democratic polities such as the United States. The human factor, therefore, can never be eliminated from the policy-making equation (see Hill 2003, chs. 4–5). The field of **political psychology** recognizes this central fact "by asserting the importance of individual psychological processes to political outcomes" (McDermott 2004, 3).

In this world of **bounded rationality,** foreign policy makers cope as best they can with the personal as well as the institutional limitations facing them (Simon 1957). In this decision-making environment, the characteristics of individual actors are vital. This link between psychology and political behavior, as demonstrated in recent studies of American presidents (see Table 3.4), shapes the U.S. foreign policy process in important ways. It is therefore critical that the political psychology of foreign policy be examined in four areas: the beliefs and perceptions of key decision makers, their personalities and styles of leadership, the dynamics of decision making in groups, and the dynamics of crisis decision making.

Table 3.4 The Political Psychologies of Presidents Bill Clinton and George W. Bush

Bill Clinton	George W. Bush
• Favorable view of policy-making environment	• Moralistic worldview
• Optimism regarding political goals	• Need to control or dominate others
• Cooperative approach to problem solving	• Sensitivity to criticism
• Reliance on rewards rather than punishments	• Tendency to take impulsive action
• Aversion to taking risks	• Willingness to take risks

SOURCES: Stephen G. Walker, Mark Schafer, and Michael Young, "William Jefferson Clinton: Operational Code Beliefs and Object Appraisal," in *The Psychological Assessment of Political Leaders,* ed. Jerrold M. Post (Ann Arbor: University of Michigan Press, 2003), 324–328; and Aubrey Immelman, "The Political Personality of U.S. President George W. Bush," in *Political Leadership for the New Century: Personality and Behavior Among American Leaders,* ed. Linda O. Valenty and Ofer Feldman (Westport, Conn.: Praeger, 2002), 81–103.

Beliefs and Cognitive "Shortcuts"

According to political psychologists, decision makers come to their positions of authority with distinctive **belief systems** that directly influence their foreign policy goals and strategies as well as their responses to specific problems (Holsti 1962). Belief systems, which are formed early in life and are stubbornly resistant to change, link the fragmented impressions people have of the outside world into a coherent whole (see Mowle 2003). These beliefs shape the manner in which leaders identify the nature of each problem that arises in foreign policy, a vital step in determining a nation's response (Sylvan and Thorson 1992, Knecht 2009).

Two types of beliefs guide the judgment of policy makers (see Goldstein and Keohane 1993, ch. 1). Every individual maintains **principled beliefs** regarding the virtues and limitations of human nature, the proper roles of governments, and the national and global problems that are of greatest concern. Each person also maintains **causal beliefs** about the best means available for solving these problems. President Obama, for example, maintained principled beliefs that the United States should provide moral leadership in conducting U.S. foreign policy. His causal beliefs led him to revive diplomatic cooperation, affirm U.S. support for international law, and call for nuclear disarmament. These beliefs combined to form an **operational code**—that is, "a political leader's beliefs about the nature of politics and political conflict, his views regarding the extent to which historical developments can be shaped, and his notions of correct strategy and tactics" (George 1989, 486; see also Schafer and Walker 2006).

In managing foreign policy, decision makers are guided unconsciously by both sets of judgments. Woodrow Wilson's moralistic approach to world politics, for instance, was shaped profoundly by his childhood as the son of a Presbyterian minister (George and George 1956). Early in the Cold War, Christian beliefs led Secretary of State John Foster Dulles to assume the worst about the "atheistic" regime of the Soviet Union (Holsti 1962). As for Secretary of State Henry Kissinger, his conception of world politics as an arena of great-power manipulation dictated his approach to the Vietnam War (Walker 1977), just as the "black-and-white" thinking of Ronald Reagan shaped that president's confrontational approach toward the Soviet Union (Glad 1983). Such links between operational codes and foreign policy behavior continued to shape the course of U.S. foreign policy during the Clinton years (Walker, Schafer, and Young 2003). The same link could be seen in George W. Bush's forceful response to the September 2001 terrorist attacks (Renshon and Larson 2003).

Perceptions, therefore, are critical to the ways in which decision makers define and respond to foreign policy problems. This assertion, borne out by historical research, leads to consideration of **cognitive psychology,** the process by which individuals obtain and process information about the world around them (see Jervis 1976 and Vertzberger 1990). Due to the sheer enormity of information available, individuals can absorb even less than a tiny fraction of it. They must, therefore, constantly make choices about what information they will expose themselves to and how they will act on what they have learned. These "shortcuts," described below, help foreign policy makers function in an environment that would otherwise be overwhelming.

Cognitive consistency. People feel most comfortable when events in the "outside world" correspond with their existing beliefs and operational codes. Developments that contradict these beliefs are often ignored or dismissed altogether. Along the same lines, foreign policy makers tend to exaggerate the extent to which their interests converge with those of their allies and the depth of hostility adversaries have to those same interests. In distorting the true nature of friends and foes, both tendencies hinder the process of reconciling differences among states.

Selective perception. Once their belief systems have formed during the socialization process, people tend to seek out information that reinforces their views while ignoring information that contradicts them. In making foreign policy, this selective use of information discourages presidents from weighing information evenly or considering contrary evidence. Senior officials in the Bush administration appear to have engaged in selective perception as they prepared for war against Iraq early in 2003, relying primarily on intelligence reports that claimed Saddam Hussein had weapons of mass destruction and posed an imminent danger to the United States (Rieff 2003a).

Use of analogies. Decision makers often search familiar precedents in history that allow them to "match new pieces of information against their stored memories" (Yetiv 2004b, 59). Cold War presidents frequently drew on the analogy of the U.S. "appeasement" of Adolf Hitler in justifying U.S. intervention in Korea and Vietnam (Khong 1992). The same analogy was revived prior to the Gulf War in 1991 by President George H. W. Bush, who repeatedly compared Saddam Hussein to Hitler. In still another case, Bill Clinton's memories of his failed 1993 military intervention in Somalia paralyzed his judgment during the onset of the genocides in Rwanda and Burundi the following year (Brunk 2008).

Cognitive closure. Policy makers find the process of decision making a stressful one, particularly when the information they receive is incomplete and contradictory. Their desire to make a decision quickly leads them to adopt a given solution to a problem before the available information has been fully examined and alternative strategies have been considered. For example, President Lyndon Johnson's strategy in the Vietnam War became increasingly rigid despite mounting problems on the battlefield and the intensification of domestic opposition to the war.

Bolstering. Once a decision is made, policy makers often use these decisions to "bolster" their claims regarding the problem at hand. As Deborah Larson (1985) discovered, Truman's anti-Soviet beliefs became more pronounced *after* he had settled on the containment policy and was compelled to sell the strategy to Congress and the public. A similar pattern was evident after the September 2001 terrorist attacks as President Bush demanded quick action. "Once on a course, he directed his energy at forging on, rarely looking back, scoffing—even ridiculing—doubt and anything less than 100-percent commitment. He seemed to harbor few, if any, regrets" (Woodward 2002, 256).

In summary, how government leaders see the world has an important impact on how they are likely to conduct foreign policy. Their perceptions of the external environment, which are ingrained at an early age and then reinforced through selective perception, bolstering, and other cognitive shortcuts, relate directly to how they will respond to individual problems facing the United States overseas (Hermann 1984). Because such perceptions are highly personal and vary widely, foreign policy choices cannot be predicted reliably on the basis of rational calculations. This is a central claim of **prospect theory,** which emphasizes individual limitations in gauging the likely risks and rewards of policy choices (see Levy 1997, McDermott 1998, and Below 2008).

The Power of Personality

A second general area of political psychology involves the outward, observable behavior of policy makers, which serves as an expression of their beliefs and perceptions of the outside world. Most analysts assume that the personality of a president, or that of an organizational leader in any setting, plays an important role in the decision-making process (Hermann 1984, Howell 2003). In short, it matters whether a leader is aggressive or passive, gregarious or withdrawn, competitive or cooperative, or emotionally stable or temperamental. These and other personality traits directly, if subtly, shape the social environment in which decisions are made. More specifically, the personality traits and leadership styles of top policy makers often determine the roles played by secondary members of the decision-making team in policy discussions and debates (see Warshaw 1996). A study of President George W. Bush, for example, found that his high need for power, sense of control over events, and lack of trust toward others contributed directly to his decision to invade Iraq in 2003 (Shannon and Keller 2007). The quality of Bush's decision making was also problematic because, compared with other political leaders, he exhibited a lack of confidence and curiosity about the details of important foreign policies (see Schafer and Crichlow 2010).

One prominent study divided U.S. presidents into four categories based on where they fit along two dimensions (Barber 1992). The first dimension addresses whether presidents take an "active" or "passive" approach to their jobs. Of particular interest is how much energy presidents invest in their work and how strongly they assert themselves in decision making. The second dimension addresses whether presidents maintain a "positive" or "negative" view of their working environment. Is their work "a burden to be endured or an opportunity for personal enjoyment"? The study found that the personalities of

IN THEIR OWN WORDS: JOHN F. KENNEDY

President John F. Kennedy clearly expressed the liberal view of U.S. foreign policy when he took office in January 1961. His inaugural speech, parts of which appear below, highlighted changes in world politics that he believed required a new, more cooperative approach by the United States. Kennedy challenged foreign leaders, including U.S. adversaries in the Cold War, to work together in creating a more just and peaceful world. He also challenged American citizens to become actively engaged in changing the course of U.S. foreign policy.

Let the word go forth from this time and place, to friend and foe alike, that the torch has been passed to a new generation of Americans—born in this century, tempered by war, disciplined by a hard and bitter peace, proud of our ancient heritage—and unwilling to witness or permit the slow undoing of those human rights to which this Nation has always been committed, and to which we are committed today at home and around the world.

Let every nation know, whether it wishes us well or ill, that we shall pay any price, bear any burden, meet any hardship, support any friend, oppose any foe, in order to assure the survival and the success of liberty. . . .

To those peoples in the huts and villages across the globe struggling to break the bonds of mass misery, we pledge our best efforts to help them help themselves, for whatever period is required—not because the Communists may be doing it, not because we seek their votes, but because it is right. If a free society cannot help the many who are poor, it cannot save the few who are rich. . . .

To that world assembly of sovereign states, the United Nations, our last best hope in an age where the instruments of war have far outpaced the instruments of peace, we renew our pledge of support—to prevent it from becoming merely a forum for invective—to strengthen its shield of the new and the weak—and to enlarge the area in which its writ may run.

Finally, to those nations who would make themselves our adversary, we offer not a pledge but a request: that both sides begin anew the quest for peace, before the dark powers of destruction unleashed by science engulf all humanity in planned or accidental self-destruction. . . .

And if a beachhead of cooperation may push back the jungle of suspicion, let both sides join in creating a new endeavor, not a new balance of power, but a new world of law, where the strong are just and the weak secure and the peace preserved. . . .

Now the trumpet summons us again—not as a call to bear arms, though arms we need; not as a call to battle, though embattled we are—but a call to bear the burden of a long twilight struggle, year in and year out, "rejoicing in hope, patient in tribulation"—a struggle against the common enemies of man: tyranny, poverty, disease, and war itself. . . .

And so, my fellow Americans: ask not what your country can do for you—ask what you can do for your country.

My fellow citizens of the world: ask not what America will do for you, but what together we can do for the freedom of man.

SOURCE: Inaugural address, January 20, 1961. John F. Kennedy Presidential Library and Museum, Speeches of John. F. Kennedy, www.jfklibrary.org.

"active-positive" presidents such as Franklin Roosevelt and John Kennedy were best suited to their tasks. By contrast, those presidents who fell into the "active-negative" category, including Woodrow Wilson, Lyndon Johnson, and Richard Nixon, often met with personal frustration and professional failure. The impact of personality on foreign policy is certainly not confined to the United States, however. Indeed, a measurable link can be found between the personality traits and foreign policy decisions of leaders in a wide range of countries (see Hermann 1984, 1993).

One might also ask what is the impact of presidential personality on U.S. foreign policy, especially in light of the president's broad powers in times of national crisis and war? Also of concern is whether the U.S. political system attracts "high-dominance individuals with a greater personal disposition to use force" (Etheridge 1978, 451). In his own study, foreign policy scholar John Stoessinger (1985, xiii) divided U.S. presidents into two general categories: crusaders and pragmatists. *Crusaders* demonstrate a "missionary zeal to make the world better" and "tend to make decisions based on a preconceived idea rather than on the basis of experience."

Among the twentieth-century presidents examined by Stoessinger, those fitting the crusader profile were Woodrow Wilson, Lyndon Johnson, Jimmy Carter, and Ronald Reagan. *Pragmatists,* by contrast, confront foreign policy problems more flexibly. They try to make decisions based on the available evidence, weigh the pros and cons of alternative policies, and are quick to reverse themselves if those policies prove unsuccessful. Franklin Roosevelt fit this category, and Richard Nixon's foreign policy was driven by the pragmatism of national security adviser Henry Kissinger. From this historical review, Stoessinger concluded that pragmatists are better equipped to manage foreign relations, which demand that presidents adapt quickly to rapidly changing circumstances.

The Dangers of "Groupthink"

The third dimension of political psychology is group behavior—an important object of scrutiny because much of the day-to-day formulation of U.S. foreign policy occurs in group settings. Often, the pressures imposed by collective decision making prevent individuals from simply demanding that their policy preferences be followed. Some sort of collaboration and compromise among several individuals, whose beliefs and personalities meld with those of other decision makers in the decision process, are usually involved. Although among these actors cohesion rather than discord is generally preferred, dangers arise when group pressures force individuals to reach and support a consensus before they are prepared to do so.

In the 1970s, psychologist Irving Janis introduced the concept of **groupthink** and the policy problems it presents. In his view, major U.S. foreign policy "fiascoes" such as the failure to anticipate Japan's attack on Pearl Harbor and the poor prosecution of the Vietnam War could be attributed to the dysfunctions of collective decision making. Specifically, Janis (1982, 174–175) identified three characteristics of groupthink:

- Overestimation of the group's power and morality, "inclining members to ignore the ethical or moral consequences of their decisions"
- Closed-mindedness, or a collective reluctance to question basic assumptions about the problems at hand
- Pressures toward uniformity, or "a shared illusion of unanimity," combined with "direct pressure on any member who expresses strong sentiment against any of the group's stereotypes, illusions, or commitments."

Later studies reinforced and refined the concept of groupthink. For example, one study found that "structural deficiencies" in group deliberations hindered the outcome of major U.S. foreign policy decisions from 1975 to 1993 (Schafer and Crichlow 2002). Another study discovered that newly formed groups appear most vulnerable to reaching premature consensus (Hart, Stern, and Sundelius 1997). And yet another pointed out that the dangers of groupthink are not limited to foreign policy crises; they apply to routine decision making as well (Hart 1994). Indeed, the problems associated with groupthink may be observed within government bodies at all levels and in private organizations.

Reports on the Bush administration's deliberations before the March 2003 invasion of Iraq offer additional evidence of the persistent problems associated with groupthink. In particular are reports claiming that, shortly after taking power, senior administration officials reached a consensus that Saddam Hussein should be overthrown and then searched for an appropriate pretext in which they could make this happen (Woodward 2004, 2006). As Greg Cashman and Leonard Robinson (2007, 355) observed, "The net effect of the bureaucratic struggle was something that looked like groupthink. The moderates in the State Department had been allowed to play in the game, but they were driven into self-censorship and into confining their criticism to tactical issues in order to stay on the playing field. Thus a small group of decision makers were able to control the agenda and the options and ensure that nothing stood in the way of the president's predisposition for a preventive war against Iraq."

Crisis Decision Making

A final dimension of political psychology is the behavior of presidents and other key decision makers in times of heightened stress or crisis. International crises are crucial because they occur at a midpoint "between peace and war" (Lebow 1981). The actions taken by political leaders in such crises often determine whether long-standing differences will be resolved peacefully or through violent conflict. Legal constraints and institutional structures play an important, but relatively indirect, role in such stressful circumstances. Of greater consequence are the psychological and behavioral orientations of the decision makers. To political psychologists

Members of the National Security Council consider U.S. options during the October 1962 Cuban missile crisis. In carefully weighing advice from multiple advisers, then adopting a forceful, but flexible posture in his negotiations with Soviet leaders over their nuclear missiles in Cuba, President John Kennedy (facing forward, third from left) avoided a catastrophic clash between the world's two superpowers.

Jonathan and Stanley Renshon (2008, 511), "no crisis or war is understandable without direct reference to the decision making of individual leaders."

Several factors converge in a crisis to shape the response of foreign policy makers (Hermann 1993). These include the following:

- The element of surprise
- A perceived threat to vital national values and interests
- A compressed time frame that demands quick action.

These circumstances hinder a "rational" policy response. Information on the nature and cause of the crisis is very limited, as are precise calculations about the costs and benefits of possible responses. Emotions run high in crisis situations, further impairing the process. Normal decision-making routines are often suspended, and presidents are likely to consult only members of their inner circle of advisers. Leaders must make the final decisions, however, and they often do so by relying on their existing beliefs about the foreign governments and leaders, by focusing on short- rather than long-term goals, and by adopting a rigid stance that discourages dissent or a protracted search for alternative actions. Another common response is to shift the burden of escalating the conflict to the foreign adversary (George 1980 and Holsti 1984).

All these conditions and policy responses were evident in the Bush administration's response to the September 11, 2001, terrorist attacks. Although government officials had long been aware that terrorism posed a danger to the nation, the attacks took the Bush administration by surprise and shattered the sense of national security felt by government leaders and the general public. The prospects of additional attacks, affirmed by an outbreak of anthrax poisonings in the weeks to come, compelled Bush to respond quickly by ordering an invasion of Afghanistan and the overthrow of its government. As Bush's advisers acknowledged, the ordeal strained the emotional capacities of all government officials, who had to respond immediately and forcefully with only limited information about the proposed invasion and the viability of other responses.

International crises pose the most acute challenge to rational foreign policy making. In some cases, presidents have managed crises in a way that produced a favorable outcome. Most notable among these cases were John F. Kennedy's patience and careful attention to conflicting advice during the 1962 Cuban missile crisis, and his selection of a "measured" U.S. response that offered the Soviet Union a peaceful way out of the crisis. Even the best efforts of leaders, however, cannot prevent the pressures of time, combined with the dynamics of individual and group psychology, from hindering the rational conduct of U.S. foreign policy.

Conclusion

As this chapter suggests, the conduct of U.S. foreign policy derives from pressures that arise not only from overseas, but also from within the country's borders. Events in key areas—the start of the Korean War in 1950, the Iranian hostage crisis under President Carter, or the terrorist attacks of September 2001—focus the attention of foreign policy makers. How they respond, however, depends on the outcome of a complex deliberation process that engages powerful figures in civil society, multiple federal agencies, and individual decision makers who draw upon their own belief systems and personal experiences. These dynamics of decision making occur within the "black box" of U.S. foreign policy, which is a primary concern of this chapter and those that follow.

In analyzing these dynamics of decision making, it is worth recalling that each foreign policy decision is made in a unique time and place, the contextual features of which define the problems facing the United States, establish alternative solutions, and determine final choices (Farnham 2004). The range of choices is restricted not only by their anticipated outcomes, but also by whether a given course of action will be acceptable politically to important domestic stakeholders within and outside the federal government (George 1980). These *political* factors have a logic of their own and may be related indirectly, if at all, to accepted *policy* goals. Although such political pressures vary widely and are difficult to discern in specific cases, they are keenly familiar to the players in the "two-level game" of U.S. foreign policy.

Consideration of the president's vital role, outlined in Chapter 4, demonstrates further the power of the human factor located in the White House. Yet the institutional constraints on this power, based in Congress and in the various federal agencies engaged in foreign policy, guarantee that other agendas will be represented in the policy process. These agendas may be either shared or resisted by external actors whose affiliations and agendas are increasingly transnational in their scope. One thing is certain, however. Making "rational" decisions, always a difficult task in view of the limitations of human nature and political psychology, proves especially difficult in the complex institutional environment in which U.S. foreign policy is made.

Key Terms

anarchy, p. 70

balance of power, p. 71

belief systems, p. 91

bolstering, p. 92

bounded rationality, p. 90

bureaucratic politics, p. 85

causal beliefs, p. 91

cognitive closure, p. 92

cognitive consistency, p. 92

cognitive psychology, p. 91

congressional dominance model, p. 87

constructivism, p. 73

crisis decision making, p. 96

game theory, p. 77

global governance, p. 72

groupthink, p. 95

identity, p. 75

interdependence, p. 71

iron triangle, p. 82

issue networks, p. 82

levels of analysis, p. 69

military-industrial complex, p. 82

national interest, p. 71

negative-sum game, p. 78

neoliberal institutionalism, p. 72

norms, p. 72

operational code, p. 91

political psychology, p. 90

positive-sum game, p. 78

presidential control model, p. 87

principled beliefs, p. 91

prospect theory, p. 93

rational actors, p. 77

rational choice, p. 77

regimes, p. 73

security community, p. 72

security dilemma, p. 70

selective perception, p. 92

sovereignty, p. 70

standard operating procedures (SOPs), p. 87

structural realism, p. 70

transnational civil society, p. 80

Treaty of Westphalia, p. 70

two-level game, p. 79

unitary actors, p. 77

zero-sum game, p. 77

Internet References

The **Center on Budget and Policy Priorities** (www.cbpp.org) focuses on federal and state budget priorities, including research on taxes and spending. Projects of interest include analysis of military spending, specific foreign policy spending, and tax burdens for national security.

Hosted by Dalhousie University, the **Centre for Foreign Policy Studies** (www.dal .ca/~centre) provides useful information on conferences, seminars, and publication series, as well as specific links to policy, government, and international institutions. The center's recent research seminars and publications analyze unilateralism and multilateralism decisions after the Cold War.

The **CRS Reports and Issue Briefs** (http://fpc.state.gov/c18185.htm) produced by the Congressional Research Service, the research arm of Congress, provide briefings on specific policy issues that include background information, chronologies, bibliographic references, and budget statistics. Two of the larger policy domains within the CRS are "Foreign Affairs" and "Defense and Trade." *CRS Reports* on particular topics are often updated each year. Current examples of such topics are terrorism, international and free trade, foreign aid, global finance, arms trade and control, missile defense, energy policy, and U.S.-Russia and U.S.-Israel relations.

The **International Action Center** (www.iacenter.org) critically considers international labor, poverty, militarization, and multinational corporations. This site lists dozens of links to books, journals, and Web resources on antiwar and antiglobalization activities and efforts to improve the standards of living in poverty-stricken countries.

The **International Studies Association** (www.isanet.org) provides conference papers, journal articles, and relevant links to timely and scholarly research on empirical testing and analysis of issues in foreign policy and international politics in general. Included are syllabi collections, which contain additional readings and links from various professors around the globe. The Foreign Policy Analysis Section of the ISA publishes *Foreign Policy Analysis*, a multidisciplinary, peer-reviewed journal on the process, outputs, and empirical testing of foreign policy (www.isanet.org/publications/2007/04/foreign_ policy_.html).

The **National Center for Policy Analysis** (www.ncpa.org) is a nonprofit, nonpartisan public policy research center that promotes market-based solutions to public problems. Areas of concern to U.S. foreign policy include immigration, energy, trade, and environmental issues.

The **National Center for Public Policy Research** (www.nationalcenter.org) is a conservative foundation that researches current international and national events with a free-market and individual liberty orientation. Topics of interest for foreign policy researchers are environmental and energy policy, national security, national sovereignty, and defense procurement.

The **Policy Section, American Political Science Association** (www.apsapolicysection .org), designed by a group of scholars in that field, provides useful links to journals,

(continued)

Internet References *(continued)*

think tanks, and centers for those interested in studying public policy. The site also provides links to recent conferences where papers and roundtables on public policy issues were presented; full-text downloading capabilities are available.

The **Woodrow Wilson International Center for Scholars** (www.wilsoncenter.org) provides a research hub for scholars and students to review current events and how they relate to relevant theories of policy. In addition to specific regional coverage and research, the center engages in ongoing projects on security and peace strategies along with research on conflict prevention and international trade and finance. The center publishes books in each area of research, together with the *Wilson Quarterly*.

4

Presidential Power

President Barack Obama fields questions on health care reform in the East Room of the White House on March 5, 2009. The president, who took office in the midst of a severe economic crisis, sought to change the course of U.S. foreign policy even while focusing on domestic priorities.

The president of the United States maintains a position of power that is unequaled in the United States and possibly the world. No other person has a greater capacity to mobilize the nation's vast political, economic, and military resources, or to affect the tenor of global politics. The extent of presidential power is greater in foreign policy than in domestic policy because presidents are regarded, at home and overseas, as living symbols of the United States. The increasing concentration of White House control over foreign policy in the two decades after World War II led one scholar to conclude that **two presidencies** operate simultaneously: a constrained president on domestic issues and a president who reigns supreme in foreign affairs (Wildavsky 1966).

Like the leaders of other countries, U.S. presidents know that foreign affairs can be a safe haven from their troubles at home. Status as head of state carries with it unmatched prestige and provides an opportunity to "rise above politics" in the pursuit of national interests. State visits abroad, as well as high-profile visits by foreign dignitaries, boost the president's approval ratings. For this reason, presidents "have a natural inclination to escape the frustrations and controversies of domestic policy making by seeking opportunities to strut their stuff in the realm of foreign and national security policy" (Rockman 1997, 26).

As we will find, presidents have a variety of formal and informal powers that reinforce their preeminence in the foreign policy process. This stature increased steadily during the past century as Congress, recognizing the emerging U.S. role as a major world power, ceded much of its authority in foreign policy to the executive branch. During this period, presidents have freely utilized a variety of unilateral tools at their disposal—executive orders, military orders, executive agreements, proclamations, and national security directives, among others—that strengthen their ability to control U.S. foreign policy (see Howell and Kriner 2008). Recent examples include the following:

- President Bill Clinton signed an executive order on June 25, 1994, that outlined measures for implementing the Chemical Weapons Convention.

- On October 25, 2001, President George W. Bush issued a national security directive that outlined plans for the U.S. invasion of Afghanistan in retaliation for the government's role in sponsoring the September 11 terrorist attacks. Bush later signed a military order creating military commissions for the prosecution of suspected terrorists, and he lifted an executive order signed by President Gerald R. Ford that banned CIA-backed political assassinations.

- President Barack Obama, in one of the first acts of his administration in January 2009, issued an executive order that banned military commissions and the "coercive interrogation" of war prisoners, both of which proved highly controversial in the Bush years.

Even with these broad powers, presidents face a variety of constraints in conducting foreign policy. Democratic control of Congress under the Republican administrations of Dwight Eisenhower, Richard Nixon, Ronald Reagan, and George H. W. Bush led to frequent clashes over foreign policy, and the Republican-led Congress of 1995–2001 waged a vigorous campaign to blunt the "neo-Wilsonian" aspects of Clinton's foreign policy. Further complicating matters, presidents must navigate their way through multiple power centers within the executive branch whose interests routinely conflict with one another (see Figure 4.1). The judicial branch can also constrain presidential power, although the courts are generally "content to function as an arm of the executive branch on matters concerning foreign affairs and national security" (Fisher 2007, 59). Finally, presidents are engaged daily with foreign governments along with nongovernmental agencies of "global governance" that have their own stakes and preferences in the U.S. foreign policy process.

Presidents have much to win or lose with each decision they make, but they retain considerable freedom to make such choices as they see fit. Successful presidents exploit their status and authority by effectively persuading subordinates in

Figure 4.1 Influences on the President in Foreign Policy

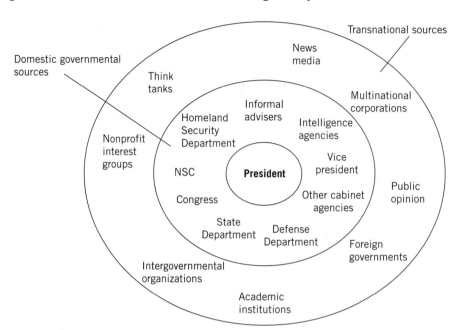

the executive branch, along with members of Congress, to support their policy preferences. According to Richard Neustadt (1960, 34), who became an adviser to President John Kennedy, "The essence of a president's persuasive task is to convince [others] that what the White House wants is what they ought to do for their own sake and on their own authority."

The Constitution's Mixed Blessing

Understanding the president's role in foreign policy begins with the U.S. Constitution, which calls for the sharing of powers between the executive and legislative branches of government and for legal questions to be resolved by the judicial branch.[1] This central principle of **codetermination** reflects the twin fears of tyranny at home and adventurism abroad that preoccupied the founders of the United States (see Chapter 2).

Much of the Constitution has less to do with the scope of federal authority than with its distribution among the branches of government. On this point, the

---

1. This notion of *sharing* powers is more accurate than the widespread concept of the *separation* of powers, because according to Article II, section 2, of the Constitution, the president, with the advice and consent of the Senate, is required to make joint decisions on key foreign policy matters.

founders were deeply divided. Alexander Hamilton believed a strong president was needed to guide the United States in the unpredictable and often perilous realm of world politics. Hamilton's nemesis in this debate was James Madison, the primary author of the Constitution, who believed a legislature must be empowered to prevent the emergence of a tyrannical head of state.[2] Madison, taking his lead from the French political philosopher Baron de Montesquieu, insisted that national powers be shared by the executive and legislative branches of government and that an independent judiciary be established to ensure that government action, as well as private behavior, complied with the rule of law.

Although the Constitution did not emphasize foreign policy, these checks and balances were intended in large part as restraints on the U.S. government in world politics. In particular, the empowerment of Congress directly curbed the president's power to plunge the country into foreign "entanglements" without popular consent. Not only would these restrictions prevent the rise of a European-style monarch, but they also would make the formulation of foreign policy so cumbersome that the United States would only rarely take aggressive action in foreign affairs. Such self-discipline seemed entirely appropriate for the new nation, whose primary concerns at the time involved the consolidation of domestic order, the creation of effective government agencies, and economic development.

Modern presidents have not questioned this constitutional design, but they have consistently resisted efforts by Congress to tie their hands. Among twentieth-century presidents, Theodore Roosevelt was the most outspoken advocate of strong presidential power in war and peace (see In Their Own Words box). Roosevelt's **stewardship theory** called for a dominant president in domestic and foreign policy. Although his successors adopted a more balanced view of presidential power, they have asserted, and generally have been granted, considerable discretion, or **prerogative powers,** in managing foreign affairs (Silverstein 1997). This freedom to make independent and binding judgments extends beyond national emergencies to include day-to-day decisions that do not require the blessing of Congress or the courts. Yet the Constitution still provides the essential framework for the formulation of foreign policy.

The Sharing of Foreign Policy Powers

The powers of Congress and the president are defined in Articles I and II of the Constitution, respectively (see Table 4.1). The language on foreign policy is very brief and sufficiently vague to provoke widely varying interpretations of the framers' intent. References to foreign policy powers do not appear in separate sections of either article, but are interspersed among references to powers in domestic policy. The president has formal powers in foreign policy in four key

---

2. This public debate over the Constitution, which took the form of essays written by the two men along with John Jay, another founder, was published anonymously in various newspapers during the ratification process. The essays, later published as the *Federalist Papers*, remain an eloquent statement of the complex logic underlying the U.S. political system (see Rossiter 1999).

IN THEIR OWN WORDS: THEODORE ROOSEVELT

Among twentieth-century U.S. leaders, Theodore Roosevelt was one of the strongest advocates of presidential power. He believed that the president, who alone serves the nation as a whole, should be a "steward" of the people. To act as one, the president must have broad authority to exercise power without interference from Congress or the courts. According to political scientist Michael Nelson, Roosevelt's stewardship theory rests on the assumption that "the president could do anything that the Constitution or laws did not expressly forbid," a view of presidential power in sharp contrast to that held by many nineteenth-century presidents. Roosevelt explained the theory himself in his autobiography.

The most important factor in getting the right spirit in my Administration . . . was my insistence upon the theory that the executive power was limited only by specific restrictions and prohibitions appearing in the Constitution or imposed by the Congress under its Constitutional powers. My view was that every executive officer, and above all every executive officer in high position, was a steward of the people bound actively and affirmatively to do all he could for the people, and not to content himself with the negative merit of keeping his talents undamaged in a napkin. I declined to adopt the view that what was imperatively necessary for the Nation could not be done by the President unless he could find some specific authorization to do it. My belief was that it was not only his right but his duty to do anything that the needs of the Nation demanded unless such action was forbidden by the Constitution or by the laws. Under this interpretation of executive power I did and caused to be done many things not previously done by the President and the heads of the departments. I did not usurp power, but I did greatly broaden the use of executive power. In other words, I acted for the public welfare, I acted for the common well-being of all our people, whenever and in whatever manner was necessary, unless prevented by direct constitutional or legislative prohibition.

SOURCES: Michael Nelson, ed., *Historic Documents on the Presidency: 1776–1989* (Washington, D.C.: Congressional Quarterly, 1989), 170; *Theodore Roosevelt, An Autobiography* (New York: Macmillan, 1913), also available online at www.bartleby.com/55 (Bartleby.com, 1998).

areas: (1) directing the conduct of warfare, (2) negotiating and signing treaties and international agreements, (3) appointing cabinet secretaries and ambassadors, and (4) conducting diplomacy.

Directing the conduct of warfare. The rationale for the Constitution's division of labor for war powers is clear: sending troops to war, widely considered the most crucial decision any government can make, must be a collective, not an individual, undertaking. A declaration of war, therefore, must follow reasoned discussion of alternatives. Furthermore, hostilities must proceed only after most legislators determine war to be the best available option. Once war has been

Table 4.1   The Sharing of U.S. Foreign Policy Powers

	Executive	Legislative
Actors	President, cabinet, NSC, bureaucracy, White House advisers	House of Representatives and Senate, committees and subcommittees
Advantages	Coherence, speed, secrecy, national constituency, control of information	Deliberation, compromise, openness
War powers	Commander in chief of the armed forces, authority to repel attacks	Power to declare war, authorize ongoing deployment per War Powers Resolution
Diplomatic powers	Recognize and conduct routine relations with foreign governments	Initiate "fact-finding" missions
Appointment powers	Nominate ambassadors and cabinet secretaries	Confirm nominees
Treaty powers	Negotiate and sign treaties	Ratify treaties
Administrative powers	Oversight through cabinet, bureaucracy, and staff	Appropriations, oversight of executive branch
Economic powers	Lead economic agencies; adopt fiscal, monetary, and trade policies	Regulate commerce, power of the purse
Special powers	Declare national emergencies, sign executive orders	Impeach president

declared, however, the president as commander in chief must be free to direct the conflict. As a result of the need for prompt, unified, and decisive leadership, military conflicts require centralized command rather than legislative deliberation. Thus, once the United States has become engaged in warfare, the government checks and balances deemed so essential by the framers no longer pertain to the actions of the commander in chief.

No area of U.S. foreign policy has been as controversial as the president's war powers. Three factors account for this unending controversy. First, formal declarations of war are no longer standard practice in diplomacy. The United States has declared war in only five conflicts: the War of 1812, the Mexican-American War, the Spanish-American War, World War I, and World War II. Since December 1941, the U.S. government, despite intervening in dozens of armed conflicts—including those in Korea, Vietnam, Panama, the Persian Gulf, the former Yugoslavia, Afghanistan, and Iraq—has not issued a formal declaration of war. This is possible because presidents can resort to military force with little concern for the preferences of Congress. Even when war declarations were customary, American presidents unilaterally deployed troops overseas when they felt national interests were at stake. Thomas Jefferson, for example, dispatched U.S. naval forces to the Mediterranean Sea without congressional authorization in a mission to repel attacks on shipping.

Point/Counterpoint
GOVERNMENT WAR POWERS VS. PRIVACY RIGHTS

During his second term, President George W. Bush provoked legal debates in waging the war on terrorism beyond the question of detaining and interrogating alleged terrorists. One of the most contentious issues was the National Security Agency's surveillance of communications among suspected al Qaeda operatives and supporters of the terrorist group in the United States. In defending this practice, the White House cited the president's constitutional power as commander in chief as well as the congressional resolution in September 2001 that authorized the president to "use all necessary and appropriate force" in the conflict.

Critics charged that the Bush administration's practice violated the Foreign Intelligence Surveillance Act (FISA) of 1978, which requires the government to first gain warrants from a special FISA court created for this purpose. More generally, critics charged that the practice violated the Constitution's Fourth Amendment, which protects "the right of the people to be secure in their persons, houses, papers, and effects, against unreasonable searches and seizures." In response, the White House asserted that the process of repeatedly justifying warrants would severely burden its ability to gain the upper hand against enemies of the United States.

The two sides in this debate presented their arguments in the February 24, 2006, edition of the *CQ Researcher*. Robert Turner, cofounder of the Center for National Security Law at the University of Virginia Law School, argued that the Fourth Amendment "binds in peace and war, but in neither is it absolute. It prohibits only 'unreasonable' searches and seizures—a standard obviously affected when Congress authorizes war—and the idea that warrantless surveillance of our enemies during wartime is 'unreasonable' finds no support in historic practice or judicial opinions."

This position was rejected by Kate Martin, director of the Center for National Security Studies: "The president now claims the power to act in violation of FISA as well as the Fourth Amendment's warrant requirement, citing his commander-in-chief authority. But the president's authorization for such wiretapping—done in secret and deliberately withheld from the public and the Congress—is unprecedented. Nothing in the Constitution authorizes the president to violate the law or to decide on his own to secretly wiretap Americans—even during wartime."

In August 2006, a federal judge supported Martin's view and ordered the surveillance program to be shut down. "It was never the intent of the Framers to give the president such unfettered control," wrote Judge Anna Diggs Taylor, who sided with the American Civil Liberties Union in its lawsuit against the government. The Justice Department then appealed Taylor's decision, and an appeals court in October allowed the practice to continue until the matter was settled. Meanwhile, the White House appealed to Congress to enact legislation that would permit "warrantless" domestic surveillance throughout the war on terrorism.

SOURCE: Kenneth Jost, "Is Bush Overstepping His Executive Authority?" *CQ Researcher* 16 (February 2006): 169–192.

Second, military interventions provide a *fait accompli* for presidents. Once troops are deployed, domestic opposition not only appears unpatriotic but also may weaken the mission and threaten the lives of American servicemen and women. For this reason, members of Congress are reluctant to question presidential uses of force even when they believe their own prerogatives have been blocked. President James Polk established this precedent in 1845 by sending U.S. troops into disputed territory along the U.S.-Mexico border. The deployment quickly provoked skirmishes between U.S. and Mexican forces that led to war between the two countries.

Third, presidents have broad discretion to conduct wars in whatever ways they deem appropriate. Although such discretion is clearly within the authority as commander in chief, critics have frequently assailed presidents whose military actions were seen as immoral or illegal. During the Civil War, for example, Abraham Lincoln suspended many constitutional freedoms for the sake of military necessity. Harry Truman did not seek congressional approval for the use of atomic bombs against Japan. Richard Nixon openly defied Congress during the Vietnam War, withholding vital information about U.S. incursions into Cambodia and Laos. In the war on terrorism, domestic critics charged the Bush administration with abusing Iraqi prisoners, violating the civil rights of Muslims in the United States, and unjustly restricting the civil liberties of all Americans (see Roth 2004).

President Harry Truman poses at his desk, which features a sign with the blunt message, "The buck stops here!" Although Truman came to power as a result of the death of President Franklin Roosevelt, he quickly emerged as a strong president. He took decisive action in ending World War II, including the atomic bombing of two Japanese cities in August 1945. Truman also laid the foundations for the U.S. campaign against the Soviet Union during the Cold War.

Negotiating and signing treaties and international agreements. Presidents and Congress share the power to conclude agreements with foreign governments. Whereas the executive branch negotiates treaties, the U.S. Senate must approve them with a "super majority" of two-thirds support (or sixty-seven votes). The Senate has complied with the president's wishes in virtually every historical case. The exceptions to this rule—the Senate's rejection of the Treaty of Versailles in 1919, for example, and of the Comprehensive Test Ban Treaty in 1999—illustrate how delicate the constitutional balance between branches can be.[3]

The framers expected senators to play a role throughout the treaty-making process, and for this reason the Senate's advice and consent were written into the Constitution. Such collaboration is helpful, and often essential, for a smooth and successful ratification process. A president's failure to consult with Congress can prove disastrous. After World War I, Woodrow Wilson insisted on negotiating the Treaty of Versailles personally and took no members of Congress with him to Paris for the peace conference. The ambitious treaty, which called for the creation of the League of Nations, was rejected by the Senate. More recently, President Clinton in 1996 signed a path-breaking global ban on nuclear weapons testing but paid little attention to the ratification process in the Senate. This proved to be a serious misjudgment: the Senate later rejected the Comprehensive Test Ban Treaty.

Formal treaties, however, represent only a small fraction of the agreements reached between the United States and foreign governments. Between 1939 and 2000, more than 90 percent of international agreements took the form of **executive agreements** that did not require Senate ratification (Congressional Research Service 2001). Although most executive agreements involve routine matters such as bilateral trade and scientific exchanges, many are related directly to defense and national security (see Caruson and Farrar-Myers 2007, 635). These include Franklin Roosevelt's lend-lease agreements with the country's European allies during World War II, the various commitments made by Roosevelt at the Yalta Conference and by Truman at the Potsdam Conference, the agreement between the United States and North Vietnam ending the Vietnam War, and many agreements during the Cold War granting U.S. military forces access to overseas bases.

Ronald Reagan signed more executive agreements—2,840—than any other U.S. president, while approving just 125 treaties during his eight years in office (1981–1989). George H. W. Bush signed 1,350 executive agreements, and Bill Clinton signed another 2,048. George W. Bush greatly slowed the pace of all U.S. pacts with foreign countries, with only 274 executive agreements concluded during his first term and just over one-quarter as many treaties (72) approved during the same period (Stanley and Niemi 2006, 339). To some observers, this use of executive agreements represents a "power grab" by presidents seeking to defy the

---

3. Many other governments share this foreign policy power and face clashes between heads of state and legislatures over the ratification of treaties (see Lantis 2009).

Constitution. To others, however, the sheer volume of agreements with foreign governments makes it impossible for Congress to act formally on every one. In this sense, Congress is a willing partner in an "institutional bargain grounded in requirements for efficiency that are demanded by modern realities" (Krutz and Peake 2009, 10).

Appointing cabinet secretaries and ambassadors. Under the Constitution, presidents must submit their choices for top positions in the foreign policy bureaucracy to Congress. Senate approval of presidential appointees, like treaties, is granted in virtually every case. Observers widely agree that presidents, upon being elected, deserve to select the people they believe best equipped to promote presidential agendas in foreign as well as domestic policy. In the rare instance a nomination is rejected, it and the surrounding circumstances capture the national attention. One of the bitterest of these setbacks came in 1989 when the Senate refused to confirm Sen. John Tower, R-Texas, as George H. W. Bush's secretary of defense. Many senators believed Tower's highly publicized personal problems made him unfit to lead the Pentagon.

Unpopular nominations are usually withdrawn before the formal votes are cast. In the Clinton administration, these nominations included those of Anthony Lake (director of central intelligence), Robert Pastor (ambassador to Panama), and Morton Halperin (assistant secretary of state for democracy and peacekeeping). Another Clinton nominee, former Massachusetts governor William Weld, was denied the post of ambassador to Mexico in 1997 by Sen. Jesse Helms, R-N.C., the chairman of the Senate Foreign Relations Committee. Helms refused to allow Weld's nomination even to come before the committee. An outspoken conservative critic of President Clinton's foreign and domestic policies, Helms rejected Weld's liberal positions on social issues such as gay rights and abortion. The personal—and highly public—dispute between the two men poisoned any chance for compromise.

Although Congress has usually deferred to the president in nominations, confirmation hearings in these uncontroversial cases still serve important functions. Nominees have a chance to outline their goals and strategies and to promote the president's agenda. For their part, committee members relish the opportunity to advance their own ideas about U.S. foreign policy and to enlist a nominee's support for their proposals. For example, in 2007 Robert Gates, President George W. Bush's choice to succeed Donald Rumsfeld as defense secretary, confronted a Senate Foreign Relations Committee dominated by Democrats who were deeply critical of the administration's actions in Iraq and other parts of the world.

Another Bush appointment illustrated the bitter ideological rivalry and partisan politics that afflicted U.S. foreign policy during the president's two terms. Bush's 2005 appointment of John Bolton as the U.S. permanent representative to the United Nations provoked widespread opposition in Congress because of Bolton's previous criticism of multilateral diplomacy in general and the UN in particular. Faced with an imminent defeat in Congress, Bush gained Bolton's ascension to the office through a **recess appointment,** a constitutional measure permitting the temporary installation of political appointees when Congress is not in session. Bolton, who remained in his post through the congressional session ending in January 2007, failed to gain the political support necessary for confirmation after the November 2006 midterm elections.

Conducting diplomacy. The Constitution is especially vague about the day-to-day conduct of U.S. foreign policy. There is little doubt, however, that the president, as head of state, is empowered to represent the United States in foreign relations and to manage the routine functions of diplomacy. Indeed, the strongest presidential powers may be found in the conduct of these routine interactions.

Those who believe the president should dominate this process refer to the wording in Article II, section 3, of the Constitution that the president "shall receive Ambassadors and other public Ministers." This wording is considered significant because, according to international law, "the reception of an ambassador constitutes a formal recognition of the sovereignty of the state or government represented" (Adler 1996b, 133). George Washington set the precedent for U.S. recognition of newly installed foreign governments in 1793, when he invited the French envoy Edmond Charles Genêt for a state visit to Philadelphia, then the U.S. capital. Washington's invitation represented "tacit recognition" of the new revolutionary regime in Paris (Jones 2002, 34). Early in the twentieth century, Theodore Roosevelt recognized the government of Panama without first consulting Congress—even before Panama had formally freed itself from Colombian rule.

More recent presidents have generally taken it upon themselves to recognize foreign governments or to deny recognition to regimes they consider illegitimate. Franklin Roosevelt's recognition of the three Baltic republics after they were annexed by the Soviet Union in 1940 became U.S. policy for the entire Cold War. Richard Nixon's "opening" to the People's Republic of China in 1972 reversed the long-standing U.S. policy that denied the legitimacy of China's communist government. In the early 1990s, Bill Clinton's recognition of the breakaway Yugoslav republics of Croatia, Slovenia, and Bosnia-Herzegovina paved the way for U.S. assistance to all three governments. Clinton refused, however, to recognize the Taliban regime in Afghanistan, a position also taken by his successor, George W. Bush, as the two countries went to war in 2001.

For any president, the power of diplomatic recognition is vital to future relations between the United States and the other government—and to the president's ability to have a strong influence on U.S. foreign policy. Presidential discretion in this area extends far beyond simple recognition or nonrecognition of foreign governments. Formal recognition by the United States brings with it a wide array of potential economic, military, cultural, and political arrangements that are part of routine bilateral relationships. In contrast, nonrecognition is often accompanied by economic sanctions and other punitive measures. Presidents have broad control over these arrangements, as well as the timing and tone of official U.S. contacts with foreign governments.

White House Advantages over Congress

Aside from the president's formal powers, the office enjoys a variety of informal advantages over those of Congress. The following six advantages of the presidency have helped the White House to strengthen its hold on the foreign policy process:

- *A national constituency.* The president is the only elected official who represents a national constituency and can claim to speak for "all the people." Senators and House members represent states and congressional districts, respectively, and thus are obliged to promote the relatively narrow self-interests of their constituents in these areas even if they conflict with perceived national interests. Presidents face no such dilemma in their foreign policy choices.

- *Use of the "bully pulpit."* As noted elsewhere, presidents have unparalleled access to the general public in making their case for their chosen foreign policies. The news media follow every word and deed of the president on a daily basis, which gives the White House an opportunity to communicate directly with citizens through interviews and press briefings (see Chapter 8). The **bully pulpit,** a term coined by President Theodore Roosevelt, can influence public opinion and, consequently, congressional support for the president's foreign policies.

- *Status as the party leader.* As party leader, presidents generally can rely on support from within their own political party, not only in Congress but also among state and local officials. Party members who openly oppose presidents from "within the ranks" run the risk of appearing disloyal. George W. Bush's strong support among congressional Republicans, for example, strengthened his resolve to press forward on his plans to invade Iraq in 2003.

- *The perpetual "session."* The presidency, unlike Congress, is always in session. Thus, the president can respond to foreign policy problems at any time and with little notice. Congress lacks this element of expediency. It is often in recess and, except for times of national emergency, operates by means of a legislative calendar that is comparatively slow and rigid.

- *The bureaucracy's CEO.* The president serves as the chief executive officer of the federal bureaucracy and its employees. Presidents can expect that the general principles and policy goals they adopt will be supported by federal employees. "The political machinery will simply not work without effective presidential control over it" (Rodman 2009, 275).

■ *Information dominance.* The president's control of information is extensive and closely protected. The intelligence agencies, diplomatic corps, and armed services, all located within the executive branch, collect the vital information on foreign affairs that the president uses in making decisions. In most routine areas of foreign policy, members of Congress are kept out of this loop. Even when Congress is consulted, the White House is able to provide selective intelligence findings that support its policy preferences (Richelson 2008).

Constraints on Presidential Power

Although the framers of the U.S. Constitution set up a complex system of checks and balances for the formulation of U.S. foreign policy, in the modern era this delicate sharing of powers has been overridden frequently. As a global superpower, the United States has found itself in a nearly perpetual state of crisis, faced with two "hot wars" of global proportions, a protracted Cold War, and, more recently, a string of regional conflicts and a two-front war (domestic and overseas) against terrorism. These circumstances have produced major changes in the institutions of U.S. foreign policy, which have, in turn, given the president unprecedented influence in the foreign policy process.

Despite these changes and all the other presidential advantages just noted, the president faces many constraints in managing U.S. foreign policy. In coming to grips with the possibilities for and limitations of presidential power, three closely related and constantly fluctuating factors must be considered:

■ *Developments overseas.* U.S. foreign policy is often a reactive process. International crises cannot be anticipated with confidence, nor can changes within foreign governments and their consequences for U.S. bilateral relations. In recent years, the al Qaeda terrorist attacks, Russia's invasion of Georgia, and nuclear tests in North Korea have altered the short- and long-term priorities of U.S. foreign policy.

■ *Domestic politics.* The ability of presidents to achieve their foreign policy goals depends largely on whether the president's party controls one or both houses of Congress (see Fleisher, Bond, and Wood 2008). Further, presidents seeking reelection are tempted to show greater "toughness" in foreign policy even if this approach contradicts their previous styles of leadership or foreign policy agendas (see Stoll 1984 and Nincic 1990).

■ *Personal limitations.* As described in Chapter 3, presidents cannot be expected to act "rationally" amid the wide array of foreign and domestic problems facing the United States at any given time. They must take cognitive "shortcuts" to simplify this bewildering environment. Presidents' foreign policy decisions are shaped by their underlying sense of national identity and the international system, as well as by their ideologies and beliefs about friends and foes.

This framework for analysis highlights the central reality that the president's role in foreign policy cannot be determined without reference to the details of specific policy problems and solutions. In short, one cannot generalize about presidential powers, nor can one predict how these powers will express themselves in given situations with a high degree of certainty. The *context* of foreign policy is crucial in this respect, framing the possibilities as well as the limitations of presidential power.

Presidential Prerogative in the "Zone of Twilight"

The president enjoys a great degree of discretion, or prerogative, in managing U.S. foreign policy. This is important given the high level of mutual distrust between the two branches of government that is woven into the nation's institutional fabric and reinforced by historical experience. Many foreign policy powers of the president and Congress—those not explicitly written into the Constitution—are not clearly apportioned. As Supreme Court Justice Robert Jackson observed in 1952 in his famous concurring opinion in *Youngstown Sheet and Tube Co. v. Sawyer* (343 U.S. 579), "[T]here is a **zone of twilight** in which [the president] and Congress may have concurrent authority, or in which its distribution is uncertain." Most routine actions by the U.S. government in foreign affairs fall within this twilight zone, and presidents have consistently filled the void by wielding "power without persuasion" (Howell 2003).

The vast scope of presidential prerogative is evident in three areas of foreign policy: setting the agenda of U.S. foreign policy, organizing the chain of command, and taking the initiative. Effective presidents exploit all these applications to determine the course of foreign policy.

Setting the Foreign Policy Agenda

The president is uniquely equipped to set the nation's foreign policy agenda. Only the president can approve and articulate the grand strategy of the United States in global affairs, and only the president can make the most critical decisions about the tactics of foreign policy derived from this chosen grand strategy. In setting the agenda, presidents may not gain immediate consensus on what actions should be taken about a particular foreign policy problem. They can, however, use their unrivaled stature to influence what problems will receive the greatest attention in Congress, the press, and public opinion (Blinder 2007, 326).

Presidents' public statements related to the ends and means of foreign policy are a core element of this informal power. It is widely accepted that these statements "give authoritative articulation to the nation's foreign policy" (Robinson 1996, 118). This presidential agenda-setting power—promoted actively through deeds as well as words—was evident throughout the Cold War. Harry Truman launched the containment strategy that guided U.S. foreign policy until the

Table 4.2 Post–World War II Presidential Doctrines

Year	Presidential doctrine	Description
1947	Truman Doctrine	Committed U.S. support to foreign governments facing internal or external subversion
1957	Eisenhower Doctrine	Declared the Middle East to be a vital region of the United States
1969	Nixon Doctrine	Shifted U.S. involvement in Asia to a more limited role by encouraging allies to fight communism on their own
1985	Reagan Doctrine	Pledged U.S. support for countries fighting communism through insurgents or "freedom fighters"
1994	Clinton Doctrine	Identified global engagement and "enlargement" of democratic rule as a central goal of U.S. foreign policy
2002	(George W.) Bush Doctrine	Defended preventive attacks on state terrorists; identified U.S. primacy as a key goal of grand strategy

collapse of the Soviet Union in 1991 (see other doctrines in Table 4.2). In the late 1960s, Richard Nixon adopted the "realpolitik" model of statecraft championed by national security adviser Henry Kissinger, and in the 1970s Jimmy Carter revived the moralism of Woodrow Wilson. Carter's successor, Ronald Reagan, placed the revival of Soviet containment at the top of his agenda and, with a supportive Congress and favorable public opinion, enjoyed practically free rein to manage the superpower conflict at its pivotal moment (see Scott 1996).

Conversely, the lack of presidential vision in foreign policy can be costly. George H. W. Bush acknowledged that his failure to identify a coherent post–Cold War grand strategy contributed to his unsuccessful reelection campaign in 1992. For his part, Bill Clinton remained preoccupied with domestic reforms long after taking office in 1993. He finally decided on the guiding principle of his foreign policy—the "enlargement" of global democracy—but the doctrine never caught on with Congress or the public (Brinkley 1997). By the time the Republican Party captured both houses of Congress in November 1994, Clinton had largely relinquished his ability to set the foreign policy agenda (Dumbrell 2002).

Although presidents have a great deal of discretion over their foreign policy agendas, unforeseen global events "can blow the president's foreign-policy ship into seas the president never planned to enter" (Brenner 1999, 187). The Japanese attack on Pearl Harbor in 1941, for example, shattered Franklin Roosevelt's efforts (and promises) to stay out of World War II. The same can be said for President Carter's foreign policy, which assumed a more aggressive stance after three developments abroad: the takeover of Nicaragua's government by Marxist rebels, the taking of U.S. hostages in Iran, and the Soviet Union's invasion of Afghanistan (Rosati 1987).

This pattern repeated itself with George W. Bush, for whom the terrorist attacks of September 11, 2001, provided the defining focus not only of his foreign policy but also of his presidency.[4] The Bush Doctrine that followed, detailed in the administration's National Security Strategy (White House 2002), contained four primary principles: (1) the promotion of democracy, (2) the need for preventive measures against grave threats to U.S. security, (3) unilateralism, and (4) the benefits of U.S. primacy not only for the United States but also for international security (Jervis 2003). In appealing to long-standing themes of American nationalism, Bush "was able to provide a context in which America could understand and accept a set of foreign-policy goals far broader and more ambitious than a simple response to the immediate attacks would have suggested" (McCartney 2004, 400; see also Blinder 2007 and Tunç 2009).

President Obama set his administration's foreign policy agenda by pledging to the United Nations in September 2009 "a new era of engagement based on mutual interest and mutual respect." The president, drawing on the liberal tradition of international relations summarized in Chapter 3, promised to "re-engage" the UN after years in which Washington and the world body maintained an adversarial relationship. Although Obama's immediate attention was forced inward by the near collapse of the U.S. economy just prior to his election, he sent a strong signal to the UN that the United States would pursue its national interests, including the struggle against Islamic extremism, within the "rule of law." Obama's emphasis on transnational problems, particularly the threat posed by climate change, departed from his predecessor's agenda, which focused more narrowly on U.S. national interests.

Organizing the Chain of Command

A second informal power of the president in foreign policy is the ability to organize the chain of command. Presidents have a great deal of flexibility in determining the roles played by various government institutions in formulating and conducting U.S. foreign policy. These institutions include the National Security Council, the Departments of State and Defense, the intelligence agencies, and the many agencies concerned with conducting foreign economic policy (see Chapter 6 for an elaboration).

With the concentration of foreign policy power in the executive branch after World War II, a new and more complex framework was established for the institutions of national security, which grew in number and in size during the late 1940s and early 1950s. Presidents have since assumed a crucial role in coordinating the activities of these institutions, in mediating their occasional conflicts, and, most important, in deciding which of them will have the greatest influence over specific policy choices.

---

4. In his February 2004 appearance on NBC's *Meet the Press,* Bush repeatedly said that ever since September 11, 2001, he had considered himself a "war president."

The creation of the National Security Council after World War II permanently shifted the locus of foreign policy decision making into the White House. The national security adviser, who was originally a coordinator and "gatekeeper" (controlling access to the Oval Office), soon displaced the secretary of state as the primary consultant to the president on foreign policy matters. This escalation of the adviser's role began in the Kennedy administration and peaked in the Nixon years, when Henry Kissinger overshadowed all the cabinet secretaries in shaping and personally conducting U.S. foreign policy. In George W. Bush's first term, national security adviser Condoleezza Rice enjoyed direct access to the Oval Office and was granted considerable freedom to orchestrate the president's advisory system. Obama's national security adviser, Gen. James Jones, assumed a more modest position as an "honest broker" in policy deliberations.

Finally, the president closely controls a large personal staff located within the Executive Office of the President (EOP). The office, created in 1939 under Franklin Roosevelt, resulted from the president's "frank recognition that the sprawling federal bureaucracy, which he had helped create, was beyond his control" (Lewis 2008, 238). Among the thirteen agencies located within this office, several involve foreign policy directly, including the National Security Council, National Economic Council, Office of the U.S. Trade Representative, White House Military Office, and the President's Intelligence Advisory Board and Intelligence Oversight Board. As in other areas of the chain of command, the president has wide discretion over these agencies, paying close attention to some while neglecting others. With more than 2,000 federal employees, however, the office provides direct assistance to the president and must be considered among the primary power centers in the foreign policy bureaucracy.

Taking the Initiative

Finally, presidents can dominate the foreign policy process by taking the initiative, or dictating the flow of events. Presidents wield this power simply by conducting U.S. foreign policy on a day-by-day basis. They are granted considerable discretion in doing so, and they choose from many options in deciding which issues should receive their attention, which foreign countries they should consider friends or foes, and which actions they should take to achieve their goals. Their decisions set the foreign policy process in motion, determining the roles to be played by other government officials and forcing leaders overseas into a reactive posture.

This informal power often involves military action. Presidents must constantly manage tensions with foreign adversaries, and depending on circumstances they may choose to ease those tensions through diplomacy or escalate them with a show of military force. In the latter case, **saber rattling** is a common technique used to intimidate adversaries through hostile rhetoric, arms buildups, or the deployment of forces into contested territories. Such actions, intended to coerce adversaries into making concessions favorable to the United States, also run the risk of sparking a military conflict, upsetting regional power balances, or creating fears at home that stymie economic growth (Wood 2009).

As noted earlier, the Constitution permits presidents, as commanders in chief, to deploy forces in response to imminent threats without the consent of Congress. Ronald Reagan took the initiative in 1983, when he invaded the Caribbean nation of Grenada, where domestic turmoil that year led to the rise of a neo-Marxist government. Reagan claimed the mission was essential to rescue U.S. medical students stranded on the island. The mission served a larger purpose, however, of demonstrating Reagan's resolve to prevent such regimes from taking power on his watch. In overthrowing the government of Panama in 1989, George H. W. Bush showed that he was serious about the "war on drugs." In 1992, Bush's relief mission to Somalia symbolized the benevolent use of U.S. military force after the Cold War. For his part, Bill Clinton believed he had to act decisively to end the ethnic cleansing of Bosnia (1995) and Kosovo (1999), because Congress and the public opposed both interventions in the former Yugoslavia.

President George W. Bush also seized the initiative to change the course of U.S. foreign policy (Gregg 2004). He accelerated the "unilateral turn" in U.S. foreign policy that began in 1994 when the Republican Party captured congressional control. Emboldened by his legislative majority, Bush implemented a "forward-leaning" security strategy that included the invasion of Iraq in March 2003. For his part, President Obama prohibited the use of torture and called for the closing of the Guantánamo Bay detention center in his first days in office. He later appointed a special envoy—former Democratic senator George Mitchell of Maine—to pursue a resolution of the Arab-Israeli conflict, and dispatched Richard Holbrooke, a longtime foreign policy adviser and former UN ambassador, to lead the U.S. effort to reach a political settlement of the conflicts in Afghanistan and neighboring Pakistan.

In taking the initiative, presidents regard the **unilateral powers** implicitly granted by the Constitution to be within the range of presidential prerogative. Such powers, including the issuance of executive orders and the approval of executive agreements, "create policies that assume the weight of law without the formal endorsement of a sitting Congress" (Howell 2005, 417). Presidents may interpret new laws as they wish and may adhere to them selectively by attaching "signing statements" to approved legislation. President George W. Bush adopted this tactic more than 750 times in his first five years in office, far more often than his predecessors. When congressional leaders, led by Republican senator John McCain of Arizona, sought to moderate the president's policies about the treatment of war prisoners, Bush signed the measure in question but attached a signing statement that declared, "The executive branch shall construe [the law] in a manner consistent with the constitutional authority of the President . . . as Commander in Chief."

The consequences of such assertiveness can be enormous. Taking action alters the strategic landscape and changes the calculus of future foreign policy decisions. Some options open and others close under these circumstances, determining outcomes. Lyndon Johnson's decision to force the Vietnam issue through the Tonkin Gulf resolution, for example, started the United States down the slippery slope to war in Southeast Asia. More positively, Ronald Reagan's plans for a "Star Wars" antimissile system pushed the Soviet Union beyond its limits in the arms race, hastening the end of the Cold War.

Structures of the "Presidential Branch"

The White House serves as the institutional nucleus of the foreign policy process (Hart 1987). This status was codified in the 1930s, when Franklin Roosevelt convinced Congress to expand the administrative capacity of the White House and to establish "a responsible and effective chief executive as the center of energy, direction, and administrative management" (Presidential Committee on Administrative Management 1937, 2). Members of Congress, persuaded that the president required a larger staff to accommodate the nation's arrival as a major global power, created the EOP in 1939. As noted earlier, this office has expanded steadily since then. Under President Obama, more than a dozen units comprise the EOP, ten of which are involved to some extent in foreign policy making (see Figure 4.2). Other units, including the offices of the chief of staff, first lady, White House counsel, and press secretary, comprise a separate White House office.

This expansion of White House power has led to the emergence of a "presidential branch separate from the executive branch" (Polsby 1990). Institutional momentum in the White House had its greatest impact on U.S. foreign policy with the creation in 1947 of the National Security Council (NSC). The NSC was designed in part to constrain presidents by ensuring that they collaborate with other senior government officials—particularly the vice president and the secretaries of state and defense—in making major foreign policy decisions (Hammond 1960). Presidents have consistently rejected this role for the NSC and have instead used the council and its staff as an independent policy-making center (Daalder and Destler 2000). The NSC system has proven highly malleable over the years and "is properly the President's creature. It must be left flexible to be molded by the President in the form most useful to him" (Tower Commission 1987, 4).

While facilitating decisions and reducing interagency disputes, the White House–centered model has several drawbacks. First, the political appointees in these offices, including the national security adviser, are not subject to Senate confirmation, which deprives Congress of a constitutional means of advice and consent. Second, decision making in the White House tends to be highly secretive, with staffers hidden from public view more than their counterparts elsewhere in the federal government. Finally, the creation and expansion of White House agencies has inevitably led to redundancy in the foreign policy process. It was no secret in Washington, for example, that the White House Council on Environmental Quality, whose leaders were handpicked by President George W. Bush in 2001, engaged in constant policy struggles with the Environmental Protection Agency as well as the State Department's specialists in this area (Jehl 2003).

Figure 4.2 Foreign Policy in the White House: Selected Units Engaged in Foreign Policy

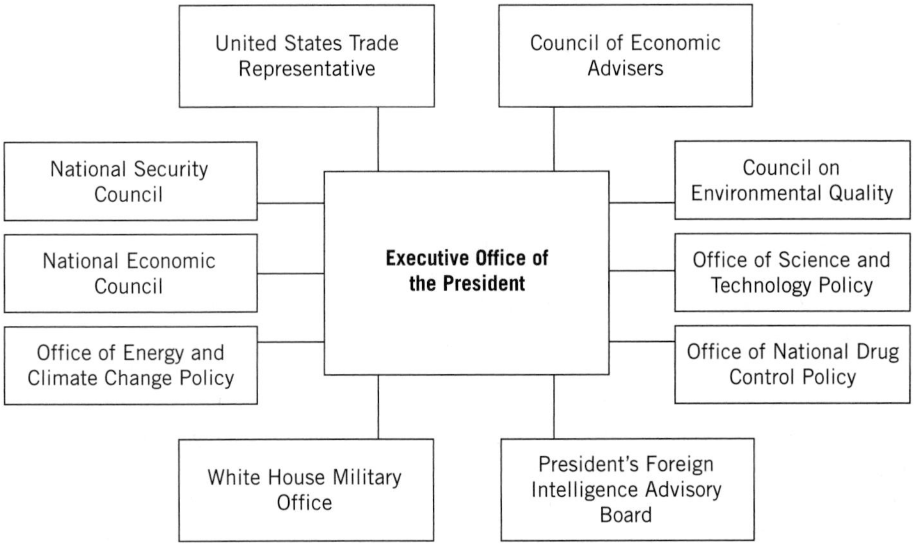

SOURCE: The White House, http://whitehouse.gov/administration/eop.

Advisory Systems in the Inner Circle

As described in Chapter 3, the president's organizational skills are vital to sound decision making. Each president constructs an **advisory system** of trusted aides and confidants who have the most direct impact on the president's final decisions (George 1980; Hermann and Preston 1999; Hess and Pfiffner 2002). The structure of these advisory systems may be rigid, with the president listening selectively to like-minded aides, or they may be more open, with conflicting views welcomed. In either case, presidential decisions can often be traced to such input from the president's "inner circle," which can take multiple forms and adopt widely varying tactics in influencing foreign policy (Garrison 1999).

The president's inner circle often includes advisers outside the cabinet. Woodrow Wilson listened most closely to adviser Edward House, who lacked a formal title but did have his own living quarters in the White House. Wilson was later blamed, during the debilitating League of Nations debate, for elevating the counsel of his personal adviser above that of Congress. Karl Rove, George W. Bush's senior policy adviser and deputy chief of staff, similarly enjoyed unequaled access to the Oval Office. His influence was so great that Rove seemed to act as "co-president" on critical policy decisions (Moore and Slater 2003). Rove, whose aggressive campaign strategies vaulted Bush to the governorship of Texas in the 1994 election, used the same formula in directing Bush's 2000 presidential campaign and his reelection campaign in 2004. His advice focused less on the intrinsic merits of alternative policy options than on their likely political impact on the president's standing among valued constituents and interest groups. In this respect, Rove's endorsement of forceful action against "Islamic extremists" was based in part on the enthusiasm for such an approach displayed by Christian conservatives, a crucial element of Bush's electoral base (see Chapter 9).

The **management style** of presidents shapes the role their advisory systems play—that is, the procedures, working relationships, and standards of behavior among their foreign policy advisers. The working environment within advisory networks plays a key role in shaping policy outcomes in war (Crabb and Mulcahy 1995; Haney 1997) and peace (Best 1992). Although the management styles of presidents vary widely, three general models have been identified (Johnson 1974). As depicted in Figure 4.3, the **formalistic model** is orderly and hierarchical, with advisers adhering to narrowly defined roles and channeling their advice through a "gatekeeper" in the White House. President Nixon used this model and relied on Henry Kissinger, his national security adviser, to represent the views of other advisers and present his own perspective. This model was well suited to George W. Bush, who positioned himself at the top of a rigid hierarchy rather than at the center of a "spoke-and-wheel" policy-making system (Walcott and Hult 2004).

Presidents adopting the **competitive model** of management encourage open debate and conflict among advisers. Franklin Roosevelt, an exemplar of this model, found that the best ideas emerged from this unfettered, occasionally chaotic competition among viewpoints. He felt comfortable presiding over such competition and choosing the policies and rationales he believed had been argued most persuasively in White House debates. Dwight Eisenhower also adopted this approach and once observed: "I know of only one way in which you can be sure you've done your best to make a wise decision. That is to get all of the people who have partial and definable responsibility in this particular field, whatever it may be. Get them with their different viewpoints in front of you, and listen to them debate" (quoted in Pfiffner 2005, 220).

Finally, the **collegial model** encourages the same openness while searching for areas of common ground. Unlike the competitive model, this model encourages consensus that reconciles the differences among advisers. Unlike the formalistic model, the collegial model encourages open debate regardless of hierarchical rank. Most recently, Bill Clinton adopted this management style, often encouraging open-ended policy debates that ran long into the night (Renshon 1996; Stephanopoulos 1999).

A president's management style can have direct consequences for U.S. foreign policy (Rodman 2009). Nixon's reliance on his national security adviser, for example, excluded many other top advisers from his inner circle and left them demoralized.[5] Jimmy Carter's attempt to balance the input provided by his

---

5. Kissinger maintained his White House presence under President George W. Bush, who frequently called on Nixon's protégé for foreign policy advice (Woodward 2006).

Figure 4.3   Management Styles in U.S. Foreign Policy

Formalistic model (Nixon)

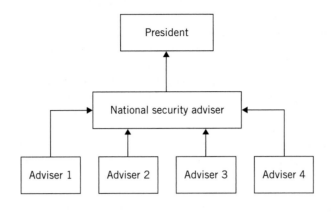

Competitive model (F. D. Roosevelt)

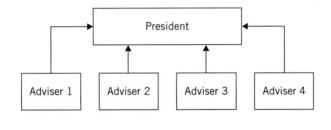

Collegial model (Clinton)

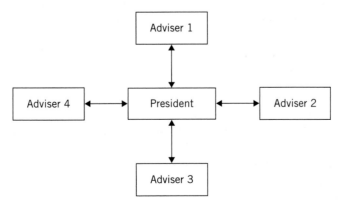

NOTE: Arrows denote the direction of policy input.

national security adviser (Zbigniew Brzezinski) and secretary of state (Cyrus Vance) created strong tensions between them (Rosati 1987). A study of Clinton's foreign policy making found that the president relied increasingly on his inner circle as his attention became focused not on foreign policy, but on his own defense in the Monica Lewinsky scandal (Redd 2005).

For his part, George W. Bush turned to a "small, tightly controlled group of loyalists" in making his decision to invade Iraq in 2003 (Haney 2005, 296), particularly Rice, Defense Secretary Rumsfeld, and Vice President Dick Cheney. Their dominance of Bush's advisory system "was enormously frustrating to [Secretary of State] Colin Powell, who found himself the odd man out" (Gordon and Trainor 2006, 39). The favored position of Rumsfeld and other civilian leaders of the Pentagon also came at the expense of the uniformed officers and the Joint Chiefs of Staff, whose efforts to build an invasion force for Iraq comparable to that deployed in Operation Desert Storm were rebuffed by the secretary. Even Gen. Tommy Franks, commander of U.S. Central Command in the Middle East, was reduced to a note taker in Bush's chain of command (Ricks 2006, 32–34).

The Vice President's Varying Roles

The Constitution says little about the powers of the vice president and nothing about the office's role in foreign policy, a fact that has given presidents enormous flexibility in utilizing the "second in command." Among other innovations of the George W. Bush White House, the vice president's office assumed unprecedented stature in the foreign policy process (see Lemann 2001; Kengor 2004; and Mayer 2004). Dick Cheney, who served as secretary of defense in George H. W. Bush's administration, assembled his own national security team with direct connections to the Pentagon. Cheney, a protégé of Donald Rumsfeld in the Ford administration, succeeded Rumsfeld as the president's chief of staff after Rumsfeld was appointed secretary of defense in 1975. Cheney later served in Congress as a representative from Wyoming before returning to the executive branch as defense secretary in 1989. He spent the Clinton years serving as chief executive officer of Halliburton Corporation, a Texas-based firm concerned primarily with supporting the oil and gas industry. A Halliburton subsidiary, Kellogg, Brown, and Root (now KBR), later became the primary commercial supplier of military services in Afghanistan and Iraq.

The role of previous vice presidents had been more modest, and often insignificant. Bush's father selected a vice president—Dan Quayle—who was little known nationally and is largely absent in historical accounts of U.S. foreign policy during the period. Although Vice President Al Gore implemented important Clinton initiatives during the 1990s—including the effort, in cooperation with Russian authorities, to enhance the security of post-Soviet nuclear stockpiles in Eurasia—he deferred to others in the inner circle on most foreign policy issues.

Cheney assumed a high profile early in the Bush administration by chairing the newly created National Energy Policy Development Group, whose mission was to chart the future course of U.S. energy policy. The work of the task force became controversial, however, when Cheney refused to identify its members or disclose the details of their deliberations. The General Accounting Office (GAO) filed a lawsuit against Cheney in February 2002 to gain this information, but the suit was rejected by the Supreme Court in June 2004. Nevertheless, the GAO (2003, 5) reported that Cheney's task force received most of its input from "petroleum, coal, nuclear, natural gas, and electricity representatives and lobbyists," while turning to nonprofit environmental groups "to a more limited degree." The task force's recommendations emphasized accelerated domestic oil and gas production and the construction of more than 1,300 power plants. Energy conservation, the favored course of most nonprofit groups, received relatively little attention in the report (see Chapter 12).

Cheney was among the administration's most forceful advocates of invading Iraq in 2003. He argued that the events of September 11 transformed the strategic environment of U.S. foreign policy and that Saddam Hussein's "cat-and-mouse game" with UN weapons inspectors could no longer be tolerated. Cheney's hold on the policy process remained firm even after his statements in 2002 and 2003 that Saddam maintained an active nuclear weapons program and that U.S. troops entering Iraq would be greeted as "liberators" proved erroneous. The vice president survived a scandal in his own office as his chief of staff, I. Lewis "Scooter" Libby, was indicted in October 2005 on charges related to the "outing" of a CIA agent (Valerie Plame) in apparent revenge for criticism of the Iraq invasion by her husband (Joseph Wilson), a former U.S. ambassador.[6] Elsewhere in the global war on terrorism, Cheney waged an intense campaign to stop domestic opponents from restricting President Bush's power as commander in chief (Priest and Wright 2005).

Cheney's successor, Joe Biden, came into office with a pledge of "restoring the Office of the Vice President to its historical role" (Allen 2008). Biden, a former senator and chairman of the Senate Foreign Relations Committee, said he would advise President Obama on domestic and foreign policy issues while limiting his actions within the legislative branch to breaking ties within the Senate. This low-key approach, contrasting sharply with Cheney's invasive operational role, reveals how malleable the White House is within the Constitution's system of shared government. As in other aspects of foreign policy, presidents have broad discretion to organize the executive branch as they see fit. This flexibility extends beyond the cabinet agencies to the White House itself.

---

6. Libby was convicted on several counts, including perjury and obstruction of justice, in March 2007. Although Cheney was brought before a grand jury on several occasions, he escaped prosecution in the scandal.

Judicial Interventions in Foreign Policy

Debates over how constitutional powers figure in U.S. foreign policy generally focus on the roles of the president and Congress. But what about the role of the judicial branch in tempering presidential power? The courts have assumed a relatively low profile in foreign affairs, leaving the executive and legislative branches alone so long as they do not directly violate the explicit terms of the Constitution or otherwise deny the rights of American citizens. As Louis Henkin (1996, 148), a leading scholar on the Constitution and foreign policy, has noted: "Overall, the contribution of the courts to foreign policy and their impact on foreign relations are significant but not large. The Supreme Court in particular intervenes only infrequently and its foreign affairs cases are few and haphazard. The Court does not build and refine steadily case by case, it develops no expertise or experts; the Justices have no matured or clear philosophies; the precedents are flimsy and often reflect the spirit of another day."

Although the Constitution does not make such a claim, courts have consistently dismissed issues relating to U.S. foreign policy as "political questions" and therefore beyond the scope of judicial review. In other words, struggles over the formulation and conduct of U.S. foreign policy are best waged in the political arena and should not be resolved by judges. In the Supreme Court case *Marbury v. Madison* (5 U.S. 137 [1803]), Chief Justice John Marshall defended the process of judicial review but argued that such review be limited. The Constitution, Marshall wrote, invested the president "with certain important political powers, in the exercise of which he is to use his own discretion, and is accountable only to his country . . . and to his own conscience."

Supreme Court Justice William Brennan restated this position in 1962: "Not only does resolution of such issues frequently turn on standards that defy judicial application, but many such questions uniquely demand a single-voiced statement of the Government's views" (quoted in Henkin 1996, 145). His view was generally shared by lower courts that felt ill-equipped to resolve matters of foreign policy. In this spirit, judges repeatedly refused to consider lawsuits that claimed U.S. presidents were waging an illegal war in Vietnam and later in the former Yugoslavia.

Judicial Rulings on Executive Power

Although the judicial branch has generally steered clear of disputes between the president and Congress, its occasional rulings have tended to support the executive branch (see Table 4.3). This tradition is traced to John Marshall, who as a member of Congress in 1800 claimed that "the President is the sole organ of the nation in its external relations. . . . Of consequence, the demand of a foreign nation can only be made on him" (quoted in Adler 1996a, 25–26). Importantly, Marshall was referring to the president's exclusive role as the contact between the United States and foreign governments. His view, however, was construed widely

Table 4.3 Major Supreme Court Rulings on Foreign Affairs, 1920–2008

Year	Court case(s)	Importance
1920	*Missouri v. Holland*	Established primacy of federal government over states in approving treaties
1936	*United States v. Curtiss-Wright Export Corporation*	Affirmed the president's foreign policy powers
1937 1942	*United States v. Belmont* *United States v. Pink*	Upheld executive agreements by the president
1952	*Youngstown Sheet and Tube Company v. Sawyer*	Restricted the power of the president to seize private assets in the name of national security
1971	*New York Times v. United States (Pentagon Papers)*	Ruled that First Amendment freedoms of the press outweighed presidential claims of national security
1979	*Goldwater et al. v. Carter*	Affirmed the president's power to terminate treaties
1983	*INS v. Chadha*	Ruled the legislative veto was unconstitutional
1983 1985 1987 1990	*Crockett v. Reagan* *Conyers v. Reagan* *Lowry v. Reagan* *Dellums v. Bush*	Affirmed presidential war powers
2004 2004 2006 2008	*Rasul v. Bush* *Hamdi v. Rumsfeld* *Hamdan v. Rumsfeld* *Boumediene v. Bush*	Upheld the right of prisoners in the war on terrorism to appeal their detentions in U.S. courts

as a rationale for broad presidential authority in foreign affairs. Marshall's language was applied much later in the landmark case of *United States v. Curtiss-Wright Export Corporation* (1936), in which the Supreme Court upheld Franklin Roosevelt's authority to enforce an arms embargo previously authorized by Congress.[7] In making this decision, Justice George Sutherland wrote that foreign policy should be considered "the very delicate, plenary, and exclusive power of the president as the sole organ of the federal government in the field of international relations."

Nevertheless, members of Congress have frequently turned to the courts to restrain presidents in foreign policy. In *Goldwater et al. v. Carter* (1979), for example, the Supreme Court supported President Jimmy Carter's right to terminate the U.S. Mutual Defense Treaty with Taiwan. In the Court's view, the case was "political" because no clear violations of the Constitution had occurred. Similarly, in *Crockett v. Reagan* (1984) and *Lowry v. Reagan* (1987), the Court again

---

7. In addition, in *Curtiss-Wright,* the Court affirmed the external sovereignty of the federal government. The delegation of power from Congress to the president was appropriate in this case, the Court ruled, because the issue at hand concerned foreign rather than domestic policy.

dismissed as "political" congressional claims that the president had overstepped his constitutional bounds by deploying troops into conflicts overseas.

On some occasions, the Supreme Court has acted to curb presidential powers. For example, in *Youngstown Sheet and Tube Co. v. Sawyer* (1952), the Court declared unconstitutional President Truman's seizure of American steel mills to avert a national strike during the Korean War. Such authority, the Court ruled, could be exercised only with the explicit consent of Congress. Then, in 1971, the Supreme Court ruled against the president in the *Pentagon Papers* case. The Court rejected Nixon's claim that damaging information possessed by the *New York Times* about U.S. involvement in Vietnam should be barred from publication on the grounds of national security.

The years immediately following the Cold War featured less intervention by the Supreme Court. The Court, however, passed judgments on a variety of cases that had direct consequences for the formulation and conduct of U.S. foreign policy. In 1993, for example, the Supreme Court endorsed President Clinton's policy of intercepting Haitian refugees in international waters and returning them to their homeland before they could seek asylum in the United States, a decision that angered human rights activists (see Rohter 1993). And in the case of *Crosby v. National Foreign Trade Council,* the Court ruled in 2000 that federal sanctions against the repressive government of Myanmar (formerly Burma) "preempted" or nullified similar sanctions that were later imposed by the Commonwealth of Massachusetts and were seen by the U.S. government as obstacles to enforcing the federal sanctions.

Controversies in the War on Terrorism

As noted earlier, presidents wield greater foreign policy authority in wartime, a historic pattern that continued with the onset of the war on terrorism. President Bush seized upon his constitutional role as commander in chief in casting the September 2001 attacks as a *casus belli* (cause of war) rather than a matter for law enforcement or diplomacy, and in declaring a national emergency three days after the attacks. These war powers were affirmed on September 18 by Congress, which granted Bush broad authority "to use all necessary and appropriate force . . . to prevent any future acts of international terrorism against the United States" (U.S. Congress 2001).

The war on terrorism differed from previous conflicts in many respects. In this war, the United States opposed an amorphous network of terrorists, not a sovereign nation-state such as Japan or Germany in World War II. This difference prompted Bush to issue an executive order in November that called for treating captured al Qaeda forces in Afghanistan not as prisoners of war, the designation used in conventional interstate conflicts, but as "unlawful enemy combatants." Bush's order also called for such "detainees" to be tried by military commissions, and it prevented them from seeking "any remedy . . . in any court of the United States, or any State thereof" (White House 2001a). As

John Yoo (2006, 151, 155), deputy director of Bush's Office of Legal Counsel, later observed in rejecting intervention by the courts, "The defense lawyer's first action would be to order his client to say nothing to the government. . . . [The U.S. legal system] should not allow detainees to use our own laws against us."

White House lawyers also declared that U.S. actions in the conflict fell outside the reach of the Geneva Conventions, the most recent of which, adopted in 1949, prohibited the "cruel treatment and torture" of war prisoners. Attorney General John Ashcroft believed the September 11 attacks constituted a "crime of war and a crime against humanity" that demanded extraordinary measures by Washington. These measures sparked protests and legal challenges after alleged terrorists were transferred from Afghanistan to a U.S. detention facility at the Guantánamo Bay Naval Station in Cuba. More than five hundred "high-value" detainees were regularly held after the facility opened early in 2002, although few were formally charged and none were tried during the first four years of the war. Reports of the mistreatment of these prisoners and of riots and hunger strikes at the facility, followed by revelations of abuses at Iraq's Abu Ghraib prison in 2004, fueled these legal challenges.[8]

Contrary to Bush's executive order, prisoners at the Guantánamo facility sought, and gained, support from U.S. courts to challenge the legality of their detention. In two separate cases—*Rasul et al. v. Bush* (542 U.S. 466 [2004]) and *Hamdi v. Rumsfeld* (542 U.S. 507 [2004])—the Supreme Court ruled that such appeals were permissible and should be heard in civilian courts. A central issue in both cases concerned the prisoners' rights of **habeas corpus,** a centuries-old legal principle that prisoners must be able to hear the charges against them in court and to challenge the legality of their detention (see Doyle 2006). In supporting the majority view on behalf of Yaser Hamdi, an American citizen, Justice Sandra Day O'Connor observed that the Supreme Court "made clear that a state of war is not a blank check for the president when it comes to the rights of the nation's citizens" (*Hamdi v. Rumsfeld,* 542 U.S. 507 [2004]).

The Supreme Court ruled against the White House again in June 2006. In *Hamdan v. Rumsfeld,* the Court asserted that government plans to place Guantánamo detainees on trial before military commissions were not authorized by federal law as it was currently written and violated international law. Writing for the majority, Justice John Paul Stevens argued that, in its prosecution of Salim Ahmed Hamdan, "the Executive is bound to comply with the Rule of Law that prevails in this jurisdiction." But Justice Clarence Thomas, who opposed the majority opinion, countered that the ruling "openly flouts our well-established

---

8. The International Committee of the Red Cross (2004) concluded that the prisoners at Guantánamo were placed "beyond the law . . . [with] no idea about their fate, and no means of recourse through any legal mechanism." A year later, the United Nations Economic and Social Council (2006, 12) complained that the extended detention of prisoners at the facility without charges or legal counsel marked a "radical departure from established principles of human rights," a practice that was made more troubling because of the widespread allegations of torture by former detainees.

U.S. military police keep a watchful eye on newly arrived Afghan prisoners at the Guantánamo Bay detention facility in January 2002. The Guantánamo Bay facility became controversial because its prisoners, known formally by the U.S. government as "enemy combatants," were not offered the same rights provided to prisoners of war in the conventional military conflicts of the past.

duty to respect the Executive's judgment in matters of military operations and foreign affairs" (*Hamdan v. Rumsfeld*, 548 U.S 557 [2006]).

The Bush administration responded to these rulings in two ways. First, it reversed its earlier position and announced that the detainees were entitled to protections under the Geneva Conventions. Second, the White House appealed to Congress for relief. Responding to the Supreme Court's concern that U.S. policies lacked formal authorization from the legislative branch, the Bush administration implored Congress to provide a legal basis for its use of military commissions and "coercive interrogations" of alleged terrorists. The White House strategy proved effective as legislators in both houses approved the Military Commissions Act of 2006. Although the act affirmed the Geneva Conventions as an appropriate international standard, it allowed the president to "interpret the meaning and application" of the conventions. The act also denied detainees habeas corpus rights and permitted coercive interrogations. Finally, the act immunized, or freed from prosecution, U.S. officials who were found to have committed acts of torture prior to 2006.

The legislation, signed by Bush on October 17, was viewed as a victory for the White House, but it hardly settled the issue. The American Civil Liberties Union, which had sued the government on behalf of detainee rights, condemned the new law as "one of the worst civil liberties measures ever enacted in American history." Once again, in June 2008, the Supreme Court addressed this issue in the case of *Boumediene v. Bush* (553 U.S. 723 [2008]). In a five-to-four vote, the Court ruled that the Guantánamo Bay detention center was not a legal vacuum in which detainees had no rights.[9] Instead, they must have the same rights, including habeas corpus, that defendants in American criminal courts deserve. Even legislation passed by Congress and signed by the president could not overcome this legal reality. When Bush left office in January 2009, the conflicts over presidential war powers and the "laws of war" in the fight against terrorism remained for future presidents—and courts—to resolve.

The Impact of International Law

As we have seen, the judicial branch has an occasional, but significant, impact on U.S. foreign policy. Rulings by the Supreme Court have directly affected the assertion of presidential war powers, the ability of state governments to negotiate with foreign leaders, and the freedom of the press to cover sensitive areas of foreign policy. While judicial intervention is most often limited to rulings on domestic disputes over foreign policy powers, its scope has widened considerably in recent years. International law, or the accumulated body of legal agreements and rulings across national boundaries, has exerted greater influence on U.S. foreign policy in the current era of globalization. "The Court, like the State Department and the Pentagon, now makes decisions on cases that directly change and shape our relationship with the world," Noah Feldman (2008) observed. "And as the justices decide these cases, they are doing as much as anyone to shape America's fortunes in an age of global terror and economic turmoil."

National governments have long adhered to international laws and customs that make cooperation possible among sovereign states. Foreign embassies and consulates, for example, are considered the property of the governments that operate them, a principle of **extraterritoriality** that has prevented "host" governments from raiding these offices on a regular basis. Governments have also adhered to long-standing customs, such as civilian immunity in wartime, that constrain the behavior of governments even in the absence of outside enforcement. The flourishing volume of world trade, meanwhile, would not be possible without universal adherence to the principle of "freedom of the seas" that was first adopted by trading states in the seventeenth century. Finally, as human rights

---

9. The Court's split vote on this issue was typical. Chief Justice John Roberts voted with other conservatives, including Samuel Alito Jr., Antonin Scalia, and Clarence Thomas, in opposition to the view held by liberal judges Stephen Breyer, Ruth Bader Ginsburg, David Souter, and John Paul Stevens. The ninth and most "centrist" member of the court, Anthony Kennedy, broke the tie by voting with the liberals on this case. Souter, who retired in June 2009, was later replaced by a like-minded judge, Sonia Sotomayor, ensuring that the delicate balance between conservatives and liberals would continue.

became a global concern after World War II, the UN's Universal Declaration of Human Rights set standards for personal freedom that are largely consistent with U.S. political values and provide a basis for citing violations by "rogue states."

The notion of **global jurisprudence** was first raised at the Hague conferences of 1899 and 1907. Since then, the U.S. government has actively pursued a variety of global agreements and conventions that are viewed as favorable to the nation's values and interests. American leaders have accepted rulings by the International Court of Justice along with the authority of intergovernmental organizations, including the World Trade Organization, to establish standards of state behavior and oblige governments to follow them. But the growing shadow of international law has drawn concern among many U.S. foreign policy makers in recent years. President George W. Bush's unilateral turn in foreign policy revealed the deeply embedded ambivalence in U.S. political culture regarding the relationship between the United States and the international system (see Chapter 1). This schism can be seen in the current debate between two groups of legal scholars, each of which seeks to uphold the spirit of the U.S. Constitution.

The first group, comprising **legal nationalists,** believes that the Constitution has one narrow but essential aim: to advance the well-being of the United States through carefully prescribed government institutions and powers. Protecting national sovereignty is critical to achieving this goal, as is the "prerogative of the United States to act as if it is responsible to no one but itself" (Feldman 2008). The same view rejects international laws intended to restrain state actions in warfare. To legal scholars Eric Posner and Adrian Vermeule (2007, 261, 271), "The United States should comply with the laws of war in its battle against al Qaeda only to the extent that these laws are beneficial to the United States. . . . The determination that it is in America's interest to comply or not should be made by the president, and not by the courts."

This position is rejected by **legal internationalists** who believe the Constitution represents principles of individual freedom and justice that are universal in scope. In this view, the founders sought not merely a just and orderly United States, but also a harmonious world order based on the same liberal principles— "life, liberty, and the pursuit of happiness"—that guided the American Revolution. The rule of law in other countries, meanwhile, would contribute to domestic stability and better relations with the United States. To legal internationalists, this is not just a pipedream but an accurate depiction of the "constitutional" world order (Ikenberry 2001) that already exists through the array of international laws and institutions that regulate state actions.

These conflicting views have very different implications for presidential power. Legal nationalists believe the executive branch must be preeminent, particularly in the state of war that has become nearly permanent in the United States. In contrast, internationalists believe the courts at all levels—state, national, and global—should hold the upper hand to ensure that legal rights are protected in an era of global governance. In this view, U.S. leaders can only "do their jobs properly at the national level by interacting—whether in cooperation and conflict—at the global level" (Slaughter 2004, 270). Presidents, therefore, must not be free to conduct wars as they see fit. Instead, they must operate within an evolving system of checks and balances that extends beyond the U.S. Constitution. As in many other areas of U.S. foreign policy, this debate has deep roots in the nation's political culture and will likely reinforce the paradox of America's world power long into the future.

Conclusion

President Obama came to office in January 2009 after eight years in which his predecessor, George W. Bush, revived fears of an "imperial presidency" that were first raised by Richard Nixon's actions in the Vietnam War. Obama set a new agenda for U.S. foreign policy that included greater engagement not only with foreign powers, but also with his political opponents at home, including those in Congress. The new president hoped to take advantage of this "honeymoon period" in which his popular and political support was very high (Beckmann and Godfrey 2007). The near collapse of the U.S. economy late in 2008, however, forced Obama's attention inward toward domestic recovery and reform. The strains of the wars in Iraq and Afghanistan also limited the president's options in foreign policy. Even with a Democratic majority in both houses of Congress, Obama struggled to gain support for many of his initiatives at home and abroad, leaving one journalist (Hill 2009) to declare him "Obama the Impotent."

Bush, who will long be known for his assertion of presidential power, also discovered that his unrivaled stature did not free him from the many constraints imposed by the U.S. political system. His decline in public approval, which began in 2002 and continued throughout his presidency, repeated a pattern that is common among presidents in their second terms (Dunn 2006b). The domestic backlash against Bush's foreign policies, which contributed directly to Obama's election in 2008, suggested a pendulum-like swing back to moderation and liberal internationalism.

Despite these ebbs and flows in presidential power, one prediction can be made with confidence: the "invitation to struggle" written into the U.S. Constitution will remain a permanent and defining aspect of foreign policy making. As when the United States was founded, a fundamental tension exists between two contradictory principles deeply ingrained in American political culture: the fear of an overzealous and authoritarian central government and the need for decisive leadership in the face of an often menacing international system. Politics, therefore, will never truly stop "at the water's edge" in the United States; conflicts of interest are embedded in its foreign policy institutions. As Louis Henkin (1996, 85–86) noted, "The Executive is sometimes carried away by ready opportunity and initiative, by expertise, by responsibility, and by the security of secrecy, to invade where Congress has its claims. Congress, frustrated by separation and secrecy from the means and channels of diplomacy, distrustful of executive assertions of expertise, and sensitive to domestic implications or responding to domestic 'pressures,' is sometimes tempted to tie the president's Constitutional hands."

Within the "zone of twilight" of political power, the informal and personal aspects of presidential decision making become central to the foreign policy process. The president's character, worldview, and management style play vital roles in determining the primary goals to be pursued by the United States and the means chosen to achieve them. The success or failure of the United States in world politics, therefore, is largely a by-product of the president's use of power at home.

Key Terms

advisory system, p. 121

bully pulpit, p. 113

codetermination, p. 104

collegial model, p. 122

competitive model, p. 122

executive agreements, p. 110

extraterritoriality, p. 131

formalistic model, p. 122

global jurisprudence, p. 132

habeas corpus, p. 129

legal internationalists, p. 132

legal nationalists, p. 132

management style, p. 122

prerogative powers, p. 105

recess appointment, p. 112

saber rattling, p. 118

stewardship theory, p. 105

two presidencies, p. 102

unilateral powers, p. 119

zone of twilight, p. 115

Internet References

The **American Presidency Project** Web site (www.presidency.ucsb.edu), maintained and researched by political scientists at the University of California, Santa Barbara, presents a wealth of data, links, statistics, and multimedia clips on the presidency. Included are presidential speeches, public papers, and statistics on specific policy areas. A variety of documents related to the 2008 election are also on the site.

The Web site for the **Center for Congressional and Presidential Studies** (www.ameri can.edu/spa/ccps) is hosted by American University and provides access to conferences, speeches, and articles on the presidency. Of particular interest to the center is the relationship between the executive and legislative branches, as well as presidential and congressional campaigning. The center publishes books and series on these issues as well as the peer-reviewed journal *Congress and the Presidency* (the journal's index is available at www.american.edu/spa/ccps/journal.cfm).

The **Center for the Study of the Presidency and Congress** (www.thepresidency.org) provides useful links to White House documents as well as research opportunities and tips on studying the presidency. In addition to sponsoring internship and fellowship

(continued)

Internet References *(continued)*

opportunities, the center publishes *Presidential Studies Quarterly,* which investigates all aspects of the institution of the presidency (the contents of each issue are available on the site).

The University of Virginia's **Miller Center of Public Affairs** (http://millercenter.virginia .edu) has compiled historical biographies and recordings of the presidents. The center directs much of its research toward study of the media and the presidency. It also produces the *Miller Center Papers,* which describe presidential public policy making.

POTUS, on the Internet Public Library (www.ipl.org/div/potus), is a site hosted by the University of Michigan. It provides full biographical data, timelines, and descriptions of the major actions of all the presidents.

The National Archives hosts a Web site on the **Presidential Libraries** (www.archives .gov/presidential_libraries/index.html) that includes links to a dozen presidential librar- ies. The Web sites of most libraries contain speeches, memoirs, and research links to the specific policies of the respective presidents.

Presidents of the United States (www.presidentsusa.net), a site hosted by CB Presiden- tial Research Services, serves as a comprehensive resource, with monthly updates, on presidential speeches, salaries, quotes, military history, and major policies. This site also includes specific vetoes, appointments, and election data on each president.

The Web site for the **White House** (www.whitehouse.gov) lists links to presidential speeches, executive agencies and committees, and issue information released by the president and White House advisers. Of particular interest to foreign policy researchers is the "foreign policy" link (www.whitehouse.gov/issues/foreign-policy) to progress updates on U.S. policy endeavors throughout the world.

The **White House Historical Association** (www.whitehousehistory.org) is committed to teaching citizens and providing links for scholars studying the presidency. It serves as a "hub" for information on presidential administrations and includes timelines related to the presidency, information about first ladies, and the biographies of each president.

5

Speaker of the House Nancy Pelosi, D-Calif., holds up her gavel upon the opening of the 110th Congress in January 2007. Pelosi became the first woman to hold this position as Democrats regained majority control of both houses of Congress for the first time since 1995. Foreign policy was a main reason for the Democrats' success; public frustration over the U.S. war in Iraq reached record levels during the fall 2006 congressional campaigns.

Congress beyond the "Water's Edge"

Alongside the president, Congress plays a vital role in the formulation and conduct of U.S. foreign policy. Despite the long-standing maxim that politics must "stop at the water's edge," the legislative branch confronts presidents on a wide variety of international issues, from military interventions to foreign aid and arms control. Even U.S. trade, long shielded from interbranch rivalry, frequently falls prey to domestic politics. Although claims of an "imperial Congress" (Jones and Marini 1988) are overstated, as demonstrated by George W. Bush's almost free rein in the war on terrorism, presidents know their global objectives cannot be realized without the blessing of Capitol Hill.

As noted in Chapter 4, early U.S. leaders looked to Congress as a crucial hedge against potential abuses of executive power. Article I of the Constitution assigns "the first branch of government" more explicit grants of authority than Article II does presidents. Among the authorities granted to Congress are the powers to declare war, raise military forces, regulate commerce, and provide "advice and consent" on treaties and key appointments. Congressional activism in foreign policy is therefore expected in a system of "separate institutions sharing power" (Neustadt 1960). Besides curbing presidential power, such activism provides opportunities for the public to be heard, encourages open deliberation, and rewards compromise on foreign policy issues.

Congress is the U.S. government's institutional home for partisan politics, or the competition between the two dominant political parties. Whether Republicans or

Democrats hold the most seats in Congress has proved especially crucial since the Vietnam War because **unified government,** with one political party controlling the executive and legislative branches, has been an exception to the general rule of **divided government** (see Table 5.1).[1] This pattern has profound implications for both foreign and domestic policy: "When the two branches are controlled by opposing parties, gridlock increases. When government is divided, presidents are forced to oppose a greater number of foreign policy bills initiated by Congress" (Peake 2002, 80). Unified government, by contrast, encourages legislative activism and tempts the dominant party to cement its advantages in new laws and policy actions. Partisan support in Congress also affects the gravest decision made by presidents: whether to send military forces into battle (Howell and Pevehouse 2005).

Legislative activism has a downside, however. Despite the concerns raised on Capitol Hill over President Bush's "abuse of power" in foreign policy, legislators have strong self-interests in focusing on domestic issues that relate more directly to the needs of their constituents. As congressional scholar Barbara Hinckley (1994, 13) has observed: "This is a legislative body where time and influence must be carefully expended, where conflict must be kept within tolerable levels, and where many other policies can fulfill the goals of members better than foreign policy programs do. Seen in this light, foreign policy making by Congress should be the exception and not the rule."

As we will find in this chapter, Congress's role has varied over time and across the many domains of foreign policy. Developments overseas—such as civil and interstate wars, regime changes, and economic crises—shape the policy options and opportunities available to congressional legislators in any given period (Henehan 2000). Domestic factors also come into play. As discussed previously, such pressures have led to foreign policy "mood swings" among legislators, who historically have alternated between global engagement and detachment in reaction to U.S. public sentiment (Klingberg 1952; Holmes 1985). Significant as well is the domestic balance of power between political parties and the related shifts in the population of states and congressional districts (Rohde 1994). For example, the mid-twentieth-century mass migration of Americans from the Rust Belt states of the Northeast to the Sun Belt states of the South and Southwest eventually transformed the partisan balance in Congress, as evidenced by the 1994 Republican takeover of both chambers (Trubowitz 1992).

In their attempt to meet Republican challenges in foreign policy, Democrats face a central problem: the widespread public perception that they are "soft on defense." This perception has many sources, including the fact that in the previous century Democrats were more inclined than Republicans to favor diplomacy

---

1. Republican presidents have had to deal with divided government far more often than have Democratic presidents in the past several decades (Ornstein, Mann, and Malbin 2002). This pattern recurred with the Democratic Party's takeover of both houses of Congress in November 2006.

Table 5.1   Balance of Power: White House and Congress, 1961–2010

Years	Congress session number	President and political party	House			Senate			Gover-nance
			Majority	Minority	Other	Majority	Minority	Other	
1961–1963	87	Kennedy (D)	D-263	R-174		D-65	R-35		UG
1963–1965	88	Kennedy/L. Johnson (D)	D-258	R-177		D-67	D-33		UG
1965–1967	89	L. Johnson (D)	D-295	R-140		D-68	R-32		UG
1967–1969	90	L. Johnson (D)	D-246	R-187		D-64	D-36		UG
1969–1971	91	Nixon (R)	D-245	R-189		D-57	R-43		DG
1971–1973	92	Nixon (R)	D-254	R-180		D-54	R-44	2	DG
1973–1975	93	Nixon (R)	D-239	R-192	1	D-56	R-42	2	DG
1975–1977	94	Ford (R)	D-291	R-144		D-60	R-37	2	DG
1977–1979	95	Carter (D)	D-292	R-143		D-61	R-38	1	UG
1979–1981	96	Carter (D)	D-276	R-157		D-58	R-41	1	UG
1981–1983	97	Reagan (R)	D-243	R-192		R-53	D-46		DG-H
1983–1985	98	Reagan (R)	D-269	R-165		R-54	D-46		DG-H
1985–1987	99	Reagan (R)	D-252	R-182		R-53	D-47		DG-H
1987–1989	100	Reagan (R)	D-258	R-177		D-55	R-45		DG
1989–1991	101	G. H. W. Bush (R)	D-259	R-174		D-55	R-45		DG
1991–1993	102	G. H. W. Bush (R)	D-267	R-167	1	D-56	R-44		DG
1993–1995	103	Clinton (D)	D-258	R-176	1	D-58	R-43		UG
1995–1997	104	Clinton (D)	R-230	D-204	1	R-54	D-48		DG
1997–1999	105	Clinton (D)	R-226	D-207	2	R-55	D-45		DG
1999–2001	106	Clinton (D)	R-222	D-212	1	R-55	D-45		DG
2001–2003	107	G. W. Bush (R)	R-221	D-211	2	D-50	R-49	1	DG-S
2003–2005	108	G. W. Bush (R)	R-229	D-205	1	R-51	D-48	1	UG
2005–2007	109	G. W. Bush (R)	R-232	D-202	1	R-55	D-44	1	UG
2007–2009	110	G. W. Bush (R)	D-233	R-202		D-49	R-49	2[a]	DG
2009–2010	111	Obama (D)	D-258	R-177		D-57[b]	R-41[b]	2	UG

SOURCES: For 87th to 110th Congresses, U.S. Census Bureau, *Statistical Abstract of the United States* (Washington, D.C.: Government Printing Office); for 111th Congress, TheCapitol.net, "Congress by the Numbers, 2nd Session," www.thecapitol.net/FAQ/images/Congress%20by%20the%20numbers.pdf.

NOTE: D = Democrat; R = Republican; DG = divided government; UG = unified government; DG-H = divided government (House only); and DG-S = divided government (Senate only). Data are for beginning of first session of each Congress (as of January 3), except as noted.

[a]In the 110th Congress, both independent senators, Joseph Lieberman of Connecticut and Bernard Sanders of Vermont, pledged to caucus with the Democratic Party and vote with Democrats on procedural matters.

[b]The Senate's partisan balance changed in January 2010 when Scott Brown, a Republican, replaced the late Sen. Ted Kennedy, D-Mass., in a special election.

over the use of military force, global problems over domestic interests, and multilateral cooperation over going it alone. The Republican Party has exploited the image of Democratic "softness" ever since congressional Republicans accused President Truman of "losing China" in 1949 and Sen. Joseph McCarthy, R-Wis., accused Democrats of being communist sympathizers in the early 1950s.

Foreign policy, in short, cannot be divorced from domestic politics. Although this feature of U.S. foreign policy is a timeless one, the current period has been unusually volatile. The partisan balance of power swerved from unified Republican rule in the first six years of Bush's presidency to divided government after the 2006 midterm elections. Barack Obama's victory in the 2008 national elections revived unified government—this time led by the Democratic Party. The return of unified government, however, only brought continued partisan attacks and public alienation. Three characteristics of recent legislative sessions will be significant as the corresponding changes in U.S. foreign policy unfold:

- *Longevity.* Members of Congress are more likely than ever to make careers out of legislative office. Frequently holding "safe seats" with little inter-party competition, legislators have been reelected in more than 80 percent of cases since the 1950s (Davidson and Oleszek 2006, 62, 32). Whereas most members of Congress served only one term in the nation's first century, fewer than 10 percent did so in the 109th Congress that ended in January 2007. Although many safe seats in 2006 proved less durable than expected, cutting legislative careers short, most incumbents stayed in office and, as in the past, the realignment did not alter the pattern of increased "careerism" in Congress.

- *Polarization and party unity.* In contrast to the public, whose political beliefs cluster near the center of the ideological spectrum, members of Congress are increasingly holding more rigid liberal or conservative views. This "unprecedented disappearance of the political center" has left Congress highly polarized (Binder 1996, 36). Rather than searching for middle ground, legislators have voted along party lines at record levels in recent years. Indeed, loyalty in the Republican Party ensured the swift passage of Bush's foreign policy agenda. Continued polarization under divided government would likely produce stalemate, an outcome that is not optimal for either party but that increases the prospects for checks and balances across the branches of government and within Congress itself.

- *Public discontent.* Highly polarized debates on Capitol Hill, combined with a wave of recent corruption scandals involving legislators and lobbyists, have left Americans deeply cynical about the legislative branch, whose public approval ratings fell to nearly 19 percent in 2009 (see Figure 5.1). Although much of this public discontent involved the legislative branch's management of domestic issues, the same foreign policy problems that steadily drove down Bush's approval ratings after the September 11 terrorist attacks clearly spilled over into dissatisfaction with Congress.

Each of these features of recent legislative sessions affects the capacity of Congress to "codetermine" U.S. foreign policy, as the U.S. Constitution requires. Despite calls for consensus from leaders on both sides of the aisle, party loyalty rather than accommodation is often a safer bet for legislators engaged in virtually

Figure 5.1 Plunging Public Approval of Congress, 2000–2009

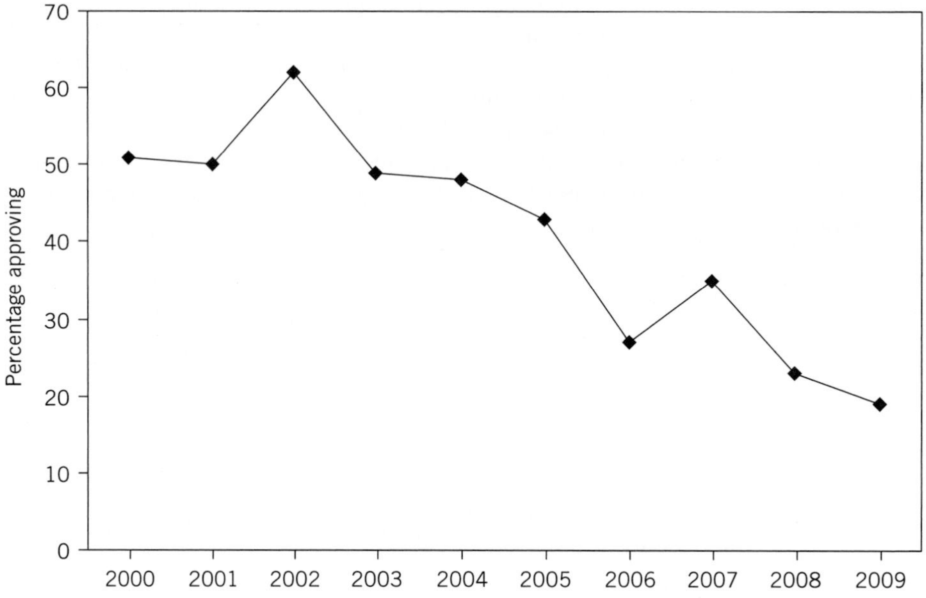

SOURCE: Gallup Polls, Congress and the Public, January ratings, www.gallup.com/poll/1600/congress-public.aspx.

constant reelection campaigns. Taking care of business in their states and districts, furthermore, is commonly more valued by legislators than dabbling in foreign policy. Careerists on Capitol Hill—those who survive the ebb and flow of majority rule—know that foreign policy is no exception to the general rule that "all politics is local."

Trends in Legislative-Executive Relations

This section reviews the ebb and flow of legislative-executive relations over foreign policy matters since World War II.[2] The early years of the Cold War featured broad cooperation between the White House and Capitol Hill that stemmed from a consensus between the branches on the ends and means of foreign policy. However, the nation's failure in the Vietnam War ruptured this consensus and, along with the Watergate scandal, led Congress to become more assertive in the foreign policy process. After the Cold War, with the United States facing no direct threats from other great powers, heightened interbranch conflict continued as a Republican majority captured both houses of Congress and subsequently challenged Bill Clinton's foreign policy agenda (McCormick and Wittkopf 1998). A brief interlude of cooperation between the branches occurred when George W. Bush took office in January 2001 with a Republican-controlled Congress—and ended again

---

2. Diplomatic histories of U.S. foreign policy rarely focus on Congress, but rather on the president or socioeconomic forces outside of government (Johnson 2001).

Figure 5.2 Spectrum of Congress's Attitude toward the White House

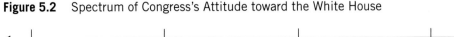

| Compliance | Resistance | Rejection | Independence |

SOURCE: James M. Scott and Ralph G. Carter, "Acting on the Hill: Congressional Assertiveness in U.S. Foreign Policy," *Congress and the Presidency* 29 (autumn 2002): 151–169.

when Vermont senator James Jeffords left the GOP to become an independent in May 2001 and the Democrats gained control of the Senate. The terrorist attacks of September 2001 engendered bipartisanship and renewed congressional support for the White House. Congress supported the U.S. invasion of Afghanistan, new measures for homeland security, increases in the defense budget, and the overthrow of Saddam Hussein in Iraq.

The historical record suggests that Congress's relationship with the White House runs along the entire spectrum from legislative compliance at one end, through resistance and rejection, to independence at the other (see Figure 5.2). What accounts for these fluctuations? Scholarly studies suggest that the situational context of policy making is critical. Two sets of factors must be taken into account when considering the situational context of foreign policy: the *nature* of issues and the *timing* of decisions.

As for the first factor, Congress tends to play a more active role in economic issues and other issues with a strong domestic component, such as immigration, whereas presidents hold more sway over issues pertaining to national security. When it comes to the timing of decisions, presidents generally enjoy freedom of action during the "honeymoon" period—the period shortly after taking office when they have strong public and political support. Taking advantage of this support, they announce their foreign policy agendas and expect Congress to provide the necessary resources to convert these agendas into programs. Presidents also exert more power over foreign policy during crises, such as the Japanese attack on Pearl Harbor in 1941 and the terrorist attacks on New York and Washington, D.C., in 2001. In these cases, members of Congress usually defer to the commander in chief.

Like the situational context, **congressional diplomacy** plays a critical role in legislative-executive relations in foreign policy matters. Congressional diplomacy concerns the degree of presidential leadership in and attention to the legislative process, a vital aspect of a president's foreign policy goals (LeLoup and Shull 2003). In short, presidents ignore members of Congress at their peril, as Bill Clinton learned. For example, by lobbying key legislators intensely, he successfully gained ratification of the North American Free Trade Agreement and of the treaty permitting NATO expansion. However, Clinton neglected Congress in the weeks before its vote on the Comprehensive Test Ban Treaty (Schmitt 1999). After discovering that he lacked the necessary votes to ratify the treaty, the president made a last-minute attempt to delay the vote, but was blocked by Republican leaders.

Collaboration and Discord in the Cold War

As described in Chapter 2, the post–World War II threat posed by the Soviet Union led congressional leaders to support President Harry Truman's efforts to put the containment doctrine into practice. Some of the important measures approved by Congress were the Bretton Woods accords, the Marshall Plan, the Truman Doctrine, and the creation of NATO. Of greatest institutional significance was the National Security Act of 1947, which created the Department of Defense, the National Security Council, and the Central Intelligence Agency. Exploiting this support on Capitol Hill, Truman deployed U.S. troops to South Korea in 1950 without a declaration of war from Congress. He justified this unilateral action on the grounds that the deployment was part of a UN peace-making mission. His decision to sidestep the legislative branch set a precedent for future U.S. military deployments in Vietnam, Central America, the Middle East, and other areas.

Like his predecessor, President Eisenhower encountered little resistance from Capitol Hill as he created new military alliances, expanded the U.S. nuclear arsenal, and allowed the CIA to organize and sponsor military coups in countries such as Iran and Guatemala. The foreign policy role of Congress during this period was reduced to "the legitimizing of presidential decisions" (Bax 1977, 887–888). Such support not only reflected broad agreement on the containment strategy, but also stemmed from the ample benefits flowing to congressional districts in the form of military contracts, the building of military bases, and the construction of a massive interstate highway system, which was justified on national security grounds.

The domestic consensus continued through the presidency of John Kennedy. Congress funded the launch of Kennedy's Alliance for Progress, a development program aimed at strengthening U.S. allies and promoting economic reforms in Latin America and the Peace Corps, an agency of paid volunteers trained to help developing countries. On the military front, Kennedy made the fateful decision to send U.S. military advisers to Vietnam to help southern forces resist unification under communist leadership. Congress later affirmed the intervention in the 1964 **Gulf of Tonkin Resolution,** which authorized Kennedy's successor, Lyndon Johnson, to "take all necessary measures" to protect U.S. forces supporting the government of South Vietnam.[3] The protracted fighting that followed and the eventual U.S. defeat ruptured legislative-executive consensus on foreign policy. President Richard Nixon's secret invasions of Cambodia and Laos and his attempts to spy on domestic opponents further fueled the challenge by Congress. Sen. J. William Fulbright, D-Ark., chairman of the Senate Foreign Relations Committee from 1959 to 1974, declared the United States to be under "presidential dictatorship" (Franck and Weisband 1979).

The 1970s and 1980s saw the passage of a wide range of legislation designed to enhance the legislative branch's **oversight** role—that is, its ability to monitor

---

3. The resolution, based on Johnson's claim that two U.S. ships were attacked in the Vietnamese waterway, passed 416–0 in the House and 88–2 in the Senate. However, evidence uncovered later raised doubts about the reported attacks (see Karnow 1983, 366–373).

the president's conduct of foreign policy. The following measures, among others, provided explicit guidelines for congressional oversight:

■ The **Case-Zablocki Act** (1972), which required presidents to report all international agreements to Congress within sixty days of their entering into force

■ The **War Powers Resolution** (1973), described shortly, which required presidents to inform Congress about U.S. military deployments and authorized Congress to order the troops home after sixty days if a majority of legislators opposed the deployments

■ The **Nelson-Bingham Amendment** to the 1974 Foreign Assistance Act, which authorized Congress to review foreign arms sales of more than $25 million and to reject such sales through a concurrent resolution of both chambers

■ The **Jackson-Vanik Amendment** to the Trade Act of 1974, which prevented presidents from granting most-favored-nation (MFN) trade status to foreign countries that restricted the emigration of their citizens[4]

■ The **Intelligence Oversight Act of 1980,** which empowered House and Senate committees to oversee U.S. intelligence activities and required presidents to notify Congress about covert (secret) operations in foreign countries.

Clinton versus the Republican Congress

The post-Vietnam animosity between Congress and the White House continued long after the Cold War. Despite the collapse of the nation's primary adversary and the emergence of the United States as the world's "lone superpower," distrust between the branches persisted. Partisan and interbranch debates revealed deep divisions over the nation's grand strategy and how it should balance foreign and domestic priorities. In place of overriding security issues, **intermestic policy** concerns—the merger of international and domestic policy concerns such as trade and the environment—surfaced after the sudden end of the Cold War in 1991 (Manning 1977). Such issues, which mobilized local- and state-level interest groups, proved of great electoral importance to Congress.

In the 1990s, various factors combined to intensify the polarization of Congress. The absence of superpower tensions after the Cold War "removed the ready guide for responding to events that had promoted bipartisanship" (McCormick, Wittkopf, and Danna 1997, 135). At the same time, a generational shift was rapidly diminishing the number of legislators with military experience in World War II or the Korean or Vietnam Wars (Greenberger 1995/1996). The new members of Congress also had no legislative experience with the politics and struggles of the Cold War. The defining military memory for many of them was the 1992

---

4. The Soviet Union was the amendment's primary, if unstated, target.

U.S. intervention in Somalia, a humanitarian rescue mission that degenerated the following year into bloody street fighting and attacks by Somali militias against U.S. and UN peacekeepers.

Most of the period's new congressional members came from the Republican Party, which became dominant in the South after more than a century in which Democrats, liberal and conservative, controlled the region's politics.[5] This partisan shift shattered the Democratic coalition of southern conservatives and northern liberals that had produced consensus on U.S. foreign policy during much of the Cold War. The Republican takeover of both houses of Congress in 1994 resulted in an entirely new slate of committee chairs, many of whom were "the ideological opposites of their Democratic predecessors" (Rosner 1995, 2). The Republican majority gained control of Congress at a time when national attention had turned from overseas concerns to domestic ones, a pattern typical in the United States in the aftermath of major wars. Republican Dick Armey of Texas, the second most powerful House member, captured the inward-looking sentiment on Capitol Hill when he declared, "I've been to Europe once. I don't have to go again" (quoted in Barone and Ujifusa 1999, 1583).

In the divisive years that followed, Clinton failed to gain congressional support for a string of U.S. military interventions. Congress, led by Sen. Jesse Helms, R-N.C., the conservative chair of the Senate Foreign Relations Committee, also forced cutbacks in foreign aid and demanded, unsuccessfully, that the U.S. Agency for International Development be shut down. Under congressional pressure, the United States refused to pay the United Nations more than $1.5 billion in overdue contributions during this period, a striking development in view of Clinton's general enthusiasm for the world body and multilateral foreign policy. Furthermore, Congress denied Clinton "fast-track" authority to negotiate trade agreements, a power first granted in the mid-1970s to President Gerald Ford, and it ensured that several of Clinton's appointments to foreign policy posts were rejected.[6]

Most devastating to Clinton was the Senate's rejection in 1999 of the Comprehensive Test Ban Treaty, "the international issue where partisan conflict surfaced in rawest form" (Destler 2001a, 326). The treaty, which sought to discourage nuclear proliferation by outlawing the testing of such weapons, had already been ratified by fifty foreign governments. The 48–51 vote, with all but four Republicans voting against the pact, marked the first time since the Treaty of Versailles that the Senate had defeated a major international security agreement.[7] Clinton

---

5. This shift resulted in part from racial issues, particularly the passage of the Civil Rights Act (1964) and Voting Rights Act (1965), which, especially in the South, prompted "white flight" from the Democratic Party. See Jacobson (2000) for an elaboration.

6. Prominent casualties of the confirmation process included Morton Halperin, a liberal critic of the Vietnam War, whose nomination for the new position of assistant secretary of state for democracy and peacekeeping was withdrawn by Clinton in 1994.

7. As noted in Chapter 4, the votes of at least two-thirds of the Senate, or sixty-seven members, are needed to ratify a treaty.

viewed the Senate rejection as evidence of a new isolationism in Congress—that is, the country was again turning away from global engagement.

Deference in the War on Terrorism

Republicans maintained control of both houses of Congress in the bitterly contested presidential election of November 2000 that brought George W. Bush to power. However, the narrow Republican advantage dissolved in May 2001, when Sen. James Jeffords of Vermont left the Republican Party and became the Senate's then-lone independent member. The move by Jeffords, who complained that the Bush White House did not represent his moderate views, gave the Democrats majority control of the Senate. Renewed partisan conflict appeared inevitable in the weeks after Jeffords's defection, and the president found his ability to implement his foreign policy agenda greatly constrained (Nelson 2004).

The terrorist attacks on the World Trade Center and the Pentagon in September 2001 quickly ended the period of discord between Congress and the White House. An overwhelming majority of legislators authorized President Bush to "use all necessary and appropriate force" in responding to the terrorist attacks against New York City and Washington, D.C. The resolution did not specify the targets of this military response, an omission "unprecedented in American history, with the scope of its reach yet to be determined" (Grimmett 2001, 46). In addition, Congress passed sweeping legislation, known as the **USA PATRIOT Act** (short for Uniting and Strengthening America by Providing Appropriate Tools Required to Intercept and Obstruct Terrorism), that increased the federal government's ability to investigate suspected terrorists in the United States.

Bush expected an equal level of deference from Congress in 2002 when he sought its support to wage war against Iraq. Fearful of being perceived as unpatriotic and hoping to neutralize Iraq as an election issue, most Democrats went along with the war resolution and gave Bush wide discretion in initiating hostilities. The House of Representatives approved the resolution by a vote of 296–133, the Senate by 77–23. Neutralizing the war issue did not help Democrats, however, because the Republican Party regained control of both chambers in the November midterm elections. After the United States launched its war against Iraq in March 2003, legislators approved $87 billion in additional military funding to pay for the war effort. In the opinion of Louis Fisher (2004, 120), a well-known constitutional expert, "Congress failed to discharge its constitutional duties when it passed the Iraq Resolution."

Congress's patience with the president's foreign policies wore thin by the end of Bush's first term. Sen. John Kerry, D-Mass., a decorated Vietnam War veteran and the Democratic Party's nominee for president in 2004, repeatedly criticized Bush's management of the war in Iraq. After Kerry's narrow loss to Bush in the November election, a continuing Republican majority allowed the president to pursue his foreign policy agenda. But dark clouds were gathering over the White

House. A wave of corruption scandals, which coincided with rising antiwar pressures, created a perfect storm for congressional realignment in 2006.

Electoral Backlash and Realignment

The outcome of the November 2006 congressional elections reflected the public's growing unease over Iraq. After twelve years in the minority, the Democratic Party regained its majority status in both houses of Congress: 51 seats in the Senate (which included two independents who declared they would caucus with the Democrats) and 233 seats in the House of Representatives. Exit polls in both races revealed deep differences over the war in Iraq, with supporters of the Democratic candidates favoring a reduction or complete withdrawal of U.S. troops from the country. Sen. Harry Reid, D-Nev., the new majority leader, and Rep. Nancy Pelosi, D-Calif., the new Speaker of the House, vowed to revive Congress's "coequal" role in foreign policy. More ominously, the new congressional leaders announced they would investigate actions by the Bush administration that they claimed were badly planned and poorly implemented and may have violated national or international laws.

The 110th Congress that came into power in January 2007 was determined to restore the legislative branch's oversight role, which had "virtually collapsed" during the first six years of the Bush presidency (Ornstein and Mann 2006, 67). Even before this period, the number of legislative oversight hearings had fallen steadily, particularly on matters related to U.S. foreign policy. Few hearings, for example, were held on the wars in Afghanistan and Iraq despite the ongoing problems U.S. troops encountered in achieving their goals on both fronts. The same lapse occurred on such controversial issues as the treatment of war prisoners, domestic surveillance of private U.S. citizens, and the creation of the Department of Homeland Security. To legal analysts Victor Hansen and Lawrence Friedman (2009, 5), "Such inquiries represent a critical structural check on executive power."

Barack Obama's victory in the 2008 presidential elections, combined with the strengthening of the Democratic Party's majority in both houses of Congress, ushered in a new period of united government in Washington. Democrats now held 57 of the 100 seats in the Senate and 257 of the 435 seats in the House of Representatives. Obama had good reason to expect Capitol Hill's support for his foreign policy agenda. Left unclear, however, was whether the 111th Congress would also uphold its constitutional duty to maintain a "watchful eye" over the executive branch.[8] Despite their minority status, congressional Republicans harshly criticized Obama's approach to the war on terrorism and other security issues.

---

8. Early signs suggested this would be the case. On July 9, 2009, for example, the House of Representatives voted 429–2 to rebuke Obama for his June 24 signing statement that declared he could disregard key aspects of a bill that expanded U.S. assistance to the World Bank and the International Monetary Fund. Like Bush, Obama argued that parts of the measure "would interfere with my constitutional authority to conduct foreign relations" (Savage 2009).

IN THEIR OWN WORDS: SEN. MITCH McCONNELL

Although the partisan battles that faced President Obama when he took office in January 2009 focused primarily on domestic issues, foreign policy also figured prominently in attacks by Republican leaders in the 111th Congress. Senate minority leader Mitch McConnell, R-Ky., took aim at Obama's approach to the war on terrorism in a February 3, 2010, speech to the Heritage Foundation, a conservative think tank. McConnell echoed his party's rejection of the president's shift in foreign policy toward greater emphasis on diplomacy, "soft power," multilateral cooperation, and international law. The senator's critiques of the president continued and were likely to become central topics in the 2012 presidential election.

More than eight years have passed since September 11th. Yet we are continually reminded of the need to remain as vigilant now as we were in the weeks and months after that terrible day. The past few months have offered ample proof of that. . . .

Again and again, the administration's approach has been to announce a new policy or to change an existing one based not on a careful study of the facts, but as a way of conspicuously distancing itself from the policies of the past, even the ones that worked. In short, it has too often put symbolism over security.

This is a very dangerous route. And it reflects a deeper problem; namely, the return of the old idea that terrorism should be treated as a law-enforcement matter. An administration that puts the attorney general in charge of interrogating, detaining, and trying foreign combatants has a pre-9/11 mindset. . . .

Some have described the administration's penchant for formulating new policies before thinking them through as a ready, fire, aim approach. Whatever you call it, it must not continue. The safety and security of our nation is at stake. And we will not hold the American people hostage to the good opinion of our critics in Europe or the pet theories of liberal academics. The Global War on Terror is not a theory to be discussed. It is a war to be won against Al Qaeda and other extremists. And that means our policies must be formulated, first and foremost, with an eye toward defeating these enemies. Nothing is more important. . . .

The good news is this: if the administration adjusts course, there is good reason to hope historians will look back on 2010 as a turning point not only in our fight with the Taliban, but also as the year in which America achieved a balance in the war against Al Qaeda, as the year in which the pendulum swung back into its proper place.

To that end, Republicans will continue to advocate for a strong, principled foreign policy that keeps America on the offense in this war and provides our intelligence professionals and servicemen and women with all the tools they need. Part of that effort is pointing out mistakes as we see them.

The war on Al Qaeda will continue for years to come. In order to prevail, we must continue to use all the reasonable tools that have served us well in the past and remain focused on the threat. Republicans will work with the Administration to strike the right balance in fighting terror both at home and abroad. This is not too much to hope for, and it's not too much to expect. Bipartisanship is not always easy to come by in Washington. But it is achievable. And in this war, my view is that it's absolutely necessary.

SOURCE: Sen. Mitch McConnell, address to Heritage Foundation, February 3, 2010, Washington, D.C., http://blog.heritage.org/2010/02/03/watch-live-sen-mitch-mcconnell-r-ky-addresses-the-war-on-terror.

Constraints on Congressional Action

As we have seen, the role played by Congress in U.S. foreign policy has varied widely since World War II, depending on circumstances in the global environment as well as the partisan balance of power at home. These variations, however, mask a general trend of congressional deference to the executive branch. Several factors deprive Congress of the vital role in foreign policy the founders designed it to play in the U.S. Constitution:

- **Passing the buck.** Legislators know the White House, not Congress, will receive credit for any breakthroughs in foreign policy. By distancing themselves from foreign policy, they protect themselves from blame if the president's actions fail. "Taking a position on a difficult issue leaves a member of Congress politically exposed and complicates his or her next election," noted Lee Hamilton (2009, 9), who served in the House of Representatives from 1965 to 1999. "The far easier route is to delegate the tough decisions to the president."

- **Structural weaknesses.** The sheer size of Congress hinders its efforts to compete with the president, who sits alone atop the executive branch. Unity within Congress has proved to be a rare exception to the rule of partisan division, because Democrats and Republicans disagree chronically over the primary goals of U.S. foreign policy and the means to achieve them. The laborious and time-consuming nature of the legislative process further constrains legislators' ability to influence foreign policy. Presidents have greater access than Congress to intelligence on foreign policy issues, and the command of the "bully pulpit" gives presidents an additional advantage in shaping public opinion.

- **Judicial noninterference.** As noted in Chapter 4, Congress has received little help from the judicial branch in foreign policy disputes. Court rulings have consistently acknowledged the president as the "sole organ" of foreign policy or dismissed as political the turf battles between the White House and Congress. The Supreme Court's refusal to rule on the constitutionality of the War Powers Resolution (see the next section), despite repeated appeals by Congress that it do so, has encouraged presidents to dismiss the legislation.

- **Constituent service.** Recognizing their limitations in the foreign policy arena, legislators have strong incentives to meet the material needs of the citizens in their states and districts rather than focus on "abstract" foreign policy concerns (Weissman 1995; Silverstein 1997). Legislators receive more immediate gains by delivering tangible benefits, such as highway projects and defense contracts, to their constituents. Meeting these needs is especially vital to House members, whose two-year terms in office force them into nearly perpetual reelection campaigns.

Point/Counterpoint
THE IRAQ WAR: HAWKS VS. DOVES IN CONGRESS

In the aftermath of the events of September 2001, members of Congress gave President George W. Bush broad powers to use force against Iraq and to topple its dictator, Saddam Hussein. Their patience wore thin, however, as U.S. forces failed to find weapons of mass destruction in the country (a chief argument for the war) and confronted an unexpectedly large insurgency.

On Capitol Hill, supporters of the war continued to defend the commander in chief's rationale for invading Iraq, if not his management of the conflict. Their views were summed up in August 2004 at the Republican National Convention by Sen. John McCain, R-Ariz., a Vietnam veteran and former prisoner of war: "Whether or not Saddam possessed the terrible weapons he once had and used, freed from international pressure and the threat of military action, he would have acquired them again. We couldn't afford the risk posed by an unconstrained Saddam in these dangerous times. By destroying his regime we gave hope to people long oppressed that if they have the courage to fight for it, they may live in peace and freedom. . . . I believe as strongly today as ever, the mission was necessary, achievable, and noble" (McCain 2004).

As the Iraqi insurgency evolved into civil war and as the U.S. death toll rose, legislative critics of the war became more outspoken. "The war in Iraq is not going as advertised," Rep. John Murtha, D-Penn., pointed out in November 2005. "It is a flawed policy wrapped in an illusion. The American people are way ahead of us. The United States and coalition troops have done all they can in Iraq, but it is time for a change in direction. . . . It is evident that continued military action in Iraq is not in the best interest of the United States of America, the Iraqi people, or the Persian Gulf region" (Murtha 2005).

Despite charges of favoring a "cut-and-run" war strategy, critics of the war gained the upper hand in the midterm elections of November 2006, when Democrats retook control of both houses of Congress. As consensus neared that the rationale and execution of the war were both deeply flawed, the debate shifted to the question of how best to extricate U.S. forces from Iraq without leaving the region vulnerable—not just to civil war but to an even deadlier conflagration across the Middle East.

Legislating Foreign Policy

Despite these limitations, Congress has an inescapable role to play in U.S. foreign policy. In any consideration of this role, it is helpful to recall the basic features of the legislative body. In the Senate, two senators, who serve six-year terms, represent each of the fifty states. In the House of Representatives, 435 members, who serve two-year terms, represent congressional districts within each state. The number of House members assigned to each state is based on the state's population. In structuring Congress, the framers chose the bicameral (two-chamber) design in order to create checks and balances *within* the legislative branch. More broadly, they purposefully made the passage of bills difficult in order to inhibit governmental activism.

In addition to the partisan balance of power and general tone of legislative-executive relations, other institutional factors determine the extent to which Congress engages in foreign policy. Legislation comes from many sources and takes many forms, some of which favor Capitol Hill at the expense of the executive branch. Members of Congress must balance a variety of factors in voting on legislation, the primary means by which they influence policy. Finally, the congressional committee system serves as the incubator of legislation and a revealing forum for congressional hearings and debates.

Dynamics of the Legislative Process

Congressional action on foreign policy originates from many sources. The executive branch, for example, often writes laws on such matters as defense appropriations, the terms of proposed treaties, and new human rights standards, and then submits the bills to Congress for consideration. Prominent interest groups and think tanks also take part in drafting legislation that, not surprisingly, advances their own foreign policy goals. In still other cases, **foreign policy entrepreneurs** within Congress "have chosen to lead the way on the foreign policy issues they care about without waiting for the administration to take action" (Carter and Scott 2009, 221). For example, as Senate majority leader in the late 1950s, Lyndon Johnson filled this role when he proposed creating the National Aeronautics and Space Administration (NASA) in response to the Soviet Union's launching of the Sputnik satellite. William Fulbright, chair of the Senate Foreign Relations Committee in the 1960s, led the way in organizing congressional opposition to the Vietnam War. After the Cold War, Sens. Sam Nunn, D-Ga., and Richard Lugar, R-Ind., designed the Cooperative Threat Reduction Program that provided funds to Moscow for controlling the former Soviet Union's nuclear arsenal.

The framers of the Constitution discouraged governmental activism by erecting high procedural hurdles to the passage of legislation. These hurdles, designed to protect individual freedoms, continue to constrain the legislative process today. A new piece of legislation must first be deemed worthy of consideration by both chambers; if it jumps that hurdle, the chambers assign the drafting of proposed language to the appropriate committees or subcommittees. If approved at this level, the two bills are introduced on the floors of the Senate and the House. Should both versions of the legislation pass, a joint conference committee between the two houses of Congress must resolve any differences in the bills' provisions. The final, joint version of the legislation then goes to the White House for the president's approval. The president may choose to veto, or reject, the bill, in which case at least two-thirds of the membership in each chamber must vote to override the veto for the measure to become law.

Congress's role in legislating U.S. foreign policy extends beyond consideration of specific problems facing the nation at a given time. **Substantive legislation,** such as the imposition of sanctions on South Africa during its period of apartheid rule, has proved difficult to pass because of the time-consuming nature and partisan realities of the legislative process. Faced with this restriction, Congress has often turned to **procedural innovations** that provide members with "a way to build their preferences into the policy-making process" (Lindsay 1994, 282). Three of these innovations are of primary interest: (1) creating new agencies; (2) imposing reporting requirements; and (3) enacting laws to ensure legislative participation.

First, Congress can create new federal agencies that strengthen its ability to shape U.S. policy in all areas, including foreign policy. For example, in 1921 legislators established the General Accounting Office (since 2004 known as the Government Accountability Office) to act as their investigative arm for examining the operation of federal agencies. The Congressional Research Service conducts studies for the House and the Senate on foreign and domestic policy. Its annual reports on arms sales, for example, include timely data on the global military trends of critical importance to legislators considering future sales and transfers of military assistance. Another agency, the Congressional Budget Office, analyzes trends in federal spending and tax revenues, thereby lessening the legislature's dependence on the executive branch's Office of Management and Budget.

Without congressional action, the creation of other federal agencies is impossible. The 2002 birth of the Department of Homeland Security, for example, stemmed from a joint effort by the Bush administration and Congress. Legislators can also modify the structures of—or even abolish—existing agencies. For example, in the 1990s Congress forced the State Department to absorb two formerly independent agencies, the U.S. Information Agency and the U.S. Arms Control and Disarmament Agency. During this same period, Sen. Jesse Helms tried to abolish the U.S. Agency for International Development. He finally agreed to allow the foreign aid agency to survive, but only under greater State Department scrutiny.

Also, Congress can impose reporting requirements on the executive branch. These reports may include special notifications to Congress on matters such as military deployments and covert operations. The executive branch also may be asked to provide one-time reports on specific issues, such as the likely impact of military base closings on neighboring communities or sectors of the U.S. economy. Periodic reports, too, are required by legislators. Since 1975, for example, the Defense Department has submitted annual reports on the impact of U.S. weapons programs on global arms control. Legislators have frequently imposed such reporting requirements to gain control over federal agencies.

Finally, Congress can enact laws that ensure legislative participation in U.S. foreign relations, as it did with the Trade Act of 1974. The act required that five members of the Senate Finance Committee and the House Ways and Means Committee serve as official advisers to the executive branch in international trade negotiations. Through such participation, Congress hoped to regain at least part of its constitutional power to regulate commerce, power it had surrendered to the White House decades earlier (see Chapter 11).

The Calculus of Voting Behavior

A central question of interest to students of Congress is related to the motivations of legislators. Why do they support some policies and programs and oppose others? What factors do they consider when determining their positions on specific issues and deciding how much time and attention to devote to these issues? Four sets of factors converge to shape voting behavior: situational, ideological, electoral, and strategic (see Figure 5.3). Each set affects decisions to varying degrees in different cases.

Situational factors. In lawmaking, legislators must assess the objective details of the problem at hand and the costs and benefits of the proposed legislative solution—that is, the **situational factors**. According to rational models of decision making, such costs and benefits can be estimated with some confidence and weighed against the status quo. In this respect, legislators approved President George W. Bush's request for $87 billion in additional military spending in November 2003 after calculating that the benefits of providing the funds outweighed the costs.

Ideological factors. Voting behavior is commonly assumed to reflect the **ideology** of legislators—that is, their general principles and beliefs about human nature, the relationships between states and society, and the nation's roles and responsibilities in world politics (see Chapter 3). From this perspective, the political activity of legislators serves as a natural extension of their deeply held worldviews.

Figure 5.3   Sources of Congressional Voting Behavior

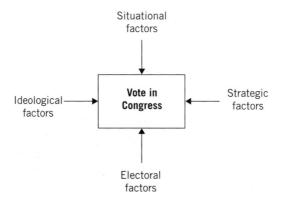

Academic studies consistently reveal a link between the ideology of legislators and their behavior on such foreign policy issues as U.S.-Israeli relations (Rosenson, Oldmixon, and Wald 2009), Taiwan (Kastner and Grob 2009), and human rights (McCormick and Mitchell 2007).

Such **ideological factors** may lead legislators to vote in different ways over time. For example, Senate conservatives discouraged foreign policy activism prior to the 1960s but later became the leading advocates of intervention in Vietnam and other frontline states during the Cold War (see Cronin and Fordham 1999). Liberals, who resisted military interventionism during these years, later led the charge for increased U.S. involvement in multilateral peacekeeping operations and relief for "failed" states. The tides turned again during the war in Iraq. Republicans remained largely loyal to President Bush's military campaign, whereas Democrats criticized the war and many called for U.S. withdrawal. Aside from partisan politics, these apparent contradictions reflect differing ideas in Congress about the appropriate use of U.S. military force. Republicans have been more likely to support interventions that pursue *nationalist* ends tied closely to U.S. self-interests, whereas Democrats have more often identified *internationalist* goals, such as the prevention of "ethnic cleansing" in the former Yugoslavia, as rationales for military intervention.

Electoral factors. The link between ideology and voting patterns hardly seems surprising. Citizens expect members of Congress to act on the principles and beliefs expressed in their campaigns once they are elected to the House or the Senate. However, viewing legislative action only in terms of ideology oversimplifies the equation. Scholars today pay closer attention to the electoral calculations of legislators. An early advocate of the importance of such **electoral factors,** David Mayhew (1974, 5, 16) defined legislators as "single-minded seekers of reelection" whose survival at the polls "must be achieved over and over if other ends are to be entertained." In this view, members of Congress are "strategic actors" whose choices are determined by rational calculations of political costs and benefits (see Kingdon 1981 and Fiorina 1989). These actors undertake extensive research on the likely political consequences of various actions. After consulting this research, legislators take the issue positions they believe will please a majority of their constituents, who will then presumably reward the legislators with votes in the next election.

Studies of congressional voting on foreign policy issues generally support this electoral connection. Eileen Burgin (1993), for example, interviewed dozens of House members about their foreign policy positions in the early 1980s. She found the influence of "supportive constituents"—those who voted for the legislators in past elections and would be inclined to do so in the future—to be the decisive factor in 90 percent of these votes. A similar study of the Reagan administration found that every one-point variation in public views on the defense buildup in the 1980s was associated with a $13 billion variation in legislators' preferences for military spending programs (Bartels 1991). Other studies have revealed that late in the Cold War electoral influences played a role in legislation on a freeze in the nuclear arms race (Overby 1991), defense spending increases (Carter 1989), and military base closings (Twight 1989).

Usually members of Congress can simultaneously satisfy their ideological preferences as well as the needs of their constituents. The reason for this is simple: the majority of voters tend to elect legislators who share their views about public policy, both foreign and domestic. Representatives of liberal congressional districts, for example, will likely hold liberal positions on issues such as arms control and foreign aid, and they will be rewarded at the polls for doing so. The same can be said for conservative members of Congress, whose preferences for military over welfare spending are shared by a majority of their constituents. Unsurprisingly, members holding such views are likely to be found in districts or states with large military bases or defense-related industries. Thus, in general, legislators are not forced to "sell their souls" to maintain the support of their constituents.

Strategic factors. In deciding foreign policy positions, congressional members also consider **strategic factors,** such as the probable consequences of individual votes for the outcome of legislation. Legislators examine the linkage between votes on different bills coming to the floor of the House and the Senate and routinely engage in **logrolling,** a practice in which they "support one measure for later support for another measure" (see Davidson and Oleszek 2004). But such behavior, combined with electorally driven voting, casts doubt on Congress's presumed capacity, as a "study and deliberative body," to play a responsible role in advancing U.S. national interests in foreign policy. Under these conditions, legislators are more inclined to advance parochial interests or those confined to the political advancement of individual legislators. When its members succumb to pressures for reelection, Congress becomes "inordinately responsive without being responsible" (Jacobson 1987, 73).

Voting on legislation, of course, is only one duty of members of Congress. To demonstrate their service to constituents, members engage in more symbolic acts, such as making speeches, cutting ribbons, and appearing on television talk shows. In addition, legislators please constituents by sponsoring bills that constituents favor, even if the bills never get out of committee. Constituents also expect their representatives and senators to speak out for them on issues of acute concern, such as trade protections and military base closings, even when the chances that this advocacy will have any impact seem slim (see Deering 1996). Symbolic activism is particularly common in foreign policy matters, where details and stakes are often far removed from constituents. "On foreign policy matters, legislators can engage in activities that appeal to constituents without expending much effort, political capital, or time. They can take stands without taking action, and they can make pronouncements, hold hearings, and run investigations without having to produce results" (Zegart 1999, 32).

Foreign Policy by Committee

Majority status within Congress brings with it great advantages, beyond the simple fact that the majority will win votes cast strictly along party lines. The majority party also receives the most seats in congressional committees and controls these committees by designating its members to chair them. The fact that Congress conducts its primary mission of drafting legislation in dozens of committees and subcommittees makes this control particularly important (see Deering and Smith 1997).

Reforms during the 1970s sought to strengthen the committee system, thereby weakening the seniority system that had previously concentrated congressional power in a few hands. The reforms opened doors to junior legislators and encouraged policy "entrepreneurs" to promote individual causes that, in turn, furthered their own political ambitions (Wawro 2000; Carter and Scott 2009). The reforms also granted greater powers and staff to subcommittees (see Figure 5.4). As a consequence of these changes, members of Congress became knowledgeable about a wider range of foreign and domestic policy issues. They also became better acquainted with individual constituents and interest groups in these specialized areas. Congressional influence and activism increased naturally as a result of these reforms, although the fragmented committee structure made it more difficult for legislators to identify and pursue common priorities.

Among the congressional committees with primary concern over foreign policy are the Senate Foreign Relations Committee and the House Committee on Foreign Affairs (see Figure 5.4). The Senate Foreign Relations Committee is especially important because its members consider treaties and presidential appointments before the full Senate votes on them. With their focus on global affairs, both committees offer members public visibility, as well as exposure to foreign leaders, intergovernmental organizations, and transnational interest groups. However, the issues the committees address rarely have material ties to constituent needs, a deficiency that has made membership less attractive to legislators in recent years. In short, approving a treaty is not likely to "bring home the bacon" and thereby enhance legislators' prospects of reelection in their home states or districts. "Foreign Relations has been kind of a wasteland," Sen. Chuck Hagel, R-Neb., said in 1998. "It is not a particularly strong committee to fundraise from" (quoted in Pomper 1998, 3203).

The Senate and House Armed Services Committees are concerned primarily with Department of Defense matters. Their jurisdictions include the development of weapons systems; structure of the army, navy, and air force; benefits for active and retired military personnel; and the selective service system. The Armed Services Committees, unlike the Senate Foreign Relations Committee and the House Committee on Foreign Affairs, attract legislators because of the large financial stakes involved in the operations of the Pentagon. Committee members frequently represent states or districts with sizable military bases or defense contracting

Figure 5.4 Key Congressional Foreign Policy Committees and Subcommittees: 111th Congress, 2009–2010

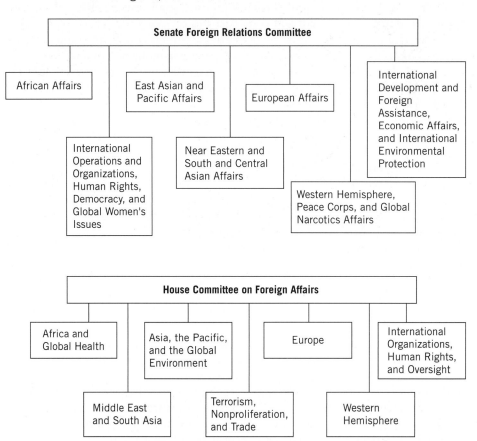

SOURCES: Senate Foreign Relations Committee, www.senate.gov/general/committee_membership/committee_memberships_SSFR.htm; House Committee on Foreign Affairs, www.internationalrelations.house.gov.

firms, both of which pressure legislators to maintain or increase the levels of support coming from Washington. On average, legislators on these committees tend to be more conservative than their congressional colleagues, favoring strong military forces as a primary national goal.

After the Vietnam War, both congressional chambers created "select" intelligence committees, providing the legislative branch with a structural role in an area previously managed almost exclusively by the president. In addition to receiving information about conditions and developments overseas from the executive branch, these committees monitor the activities of the CIA and other intelligence-gathering agencies. Of particular concern to committee members are

No member of Congress had more impact on U.S. foreign policy during the Cold War than J. William Fulbright, D.-Ark., who chaired the Senate Foreign Relations Committee from 1959 until 1974. During his long tenure on the committee, Fulbright led the legislative effort to ensure U.S. entry into the United Nations and supported most presidential measures to implement the containment policy against the Soviet Union. Fulbright later became a harsh critic of U.S. involvement in Vietnam and of the "militarized economy" in the United States.

covert operations by the U.S. government, which occurred frequently during the Cold War without congressional knowledge (see Smist 1990). After September 11, 2001, the Senate committee conducted an investigation into the events leading up to the terrorist attacks (U.S. Senate 2004). They concluded that the CIA and other agencies had failed to act on mounting evidence that Islamist terrorists were planning a major attack on the United States. Congressional investigators also concluded that intelligence agencies, with prodding from the White House, later exaggerated the threat posed by Saddam Hussein to solidify domestic support for the preventive invasion of Iraq in March 2003.

Appropriations Committees in each chamber designate the amount of money to be spent on individual federal programs. In foreign policy, these programs include the operations of the State and Defense Departments and foreign aid. Other congressional committees play roles in specific areas of U.S. foreign policy. Trade policy, for example, is handled primarily by the Senate Finance Committee and the House Ways and Means Committee.[9] Agriculture Committees approve the terms

---

9. At least a dozen other congressional committees and subcommittees are concerned with U.S. trade. As in other areas of U.S. foreign policy, the overlapping jurisdiction of committees in trade matters further complicates the policy-making process.

Table 5.2 Selected Congressional Oversight Hearings on U.S. Foreign Policy, Senate Foreign Relations Committee, 110th Congress (First Session, 2007)

Hearing date	Subject	Administration representative
January 10	The Administration's Plan for Iraq	Condoleezza Rice, Secretary of State
April 11	Darfur: A "Plan B" to Stop Genocide?	Andrew Natsios, Special Envoy to Sudan
June 21	Strategic Assessment of U.S.-Russian Relations	Daniel Fried, Assistant Secretary of State
July 25	Pakistan's Future: Building Democracy or Fueling Extremism?	Nicholas Burns, Under Secretary of State
August 1	Exploring the U.S. Africa Command and a New Strategic Relationship with Africa	Theresa Whelan, Deputy Assistant Secretary of Defense
November 8	Syria: Options and Implications for Lebanon and the Region	David Welch, Assistant Secretary of State
December 12	North Korea: Update on the Six-Party Talks	Christopher Hill, Assistant Secretary of State

SOURCE: Senate Foreign Relations Committee, http://foreign.senate.gov/hearings.

of commodity exports and overseas food aid, and Judiciary Committees consider matters relating to international crime and terrorism. Legislation in the areas of energy and environmental policy, agricultural programs, and military construction is also channeled through the vast network of congressional committees.

Presidents who resist congressional interference usually prevail in keeping legislators at bay. The practical difficulties of monitoring the executive branch in highly complex and secretive areas further hinder Congress's oversight role. Still, legislators are free to hold hearings on foreign policy issues of interest, and these sessions offer them a chance to criticize the executive branch and demand changes in policy. After Democrats regained majority control of Congress in 2006, for example, members of the Senate Foreign Relations Committee frequently called in Bush administration officials to explain their actions in a variety of areas (see Table 5.2). Even though the hearings rarely produced changes in policy or further congressional action, they offered legislators vital "voice opportunities" in the foreign policy process.

The most powerful legislative committees quickly became more assertive when Democrats gained a majority of seats in both houses in 2006. Sens. Joseph Biden, D-Del., and Carl Levin, D-Mich., outspoken critics of Bush's handling of the war in Iraq, regained their chairmanships of the Senate Foreign Relations and Armed Services Committees, respectively. In January 2009, Biden became Obama's vice president and John Kerry, the defeated Democratic

Sen. Carl Levin, D-Mich., steps out of an armored military vehicle during a March 2008 visit to the Diyala province of Iraq. As chairman of the Senate Armed Services Committee, Levin had direct influence over U.S. military operations throughout the world.

candidate in the 2004 presidential election, took over as chair of the Senate Foreign Relations Committee. Levin maintained his powerful role on the Armed Services Committee and played a crucial role in gaining Congress's support for Obama's military policies.

Ongoing Struggles over War Powers

The question of war powers is the most critical and controversial area of legislative-executive relations. As noted previously, although the Constitution explicitly bestows the power to declare war on Congress, since World War II presidents have frequently deployed troops without a congressional declaration. This apparent breach of the spirit and the letter of the Constitution led to the passage of the War Powers Resolution, over President Richard Nixon's veto, on November 7, 1973. Congressional leaders at the time were highly critical of Nixon's conduct of the Vietnam War, particularly his secret invasions of Cambodia and Laos, his massive bombing of civilian areas, and his approval of domestic surveillance of antiwar activists. Also important, in 1973 Congress was in the midst of investigating the Watergate scandal, which would lead to Nixon's resignation in August 1974.

The legislators' goal in passing the resolution, as stated in its introductory section, was to "fulfill the intent of the framers of the Constitution of the United States . . . that the collective judgment of both the Congress and the President will

Table 5.3 The War Powers Resolution in Practice, 1974–2009

President	Time period	Military interventions reported	Unreported interventions	Sixty-day clock activated
Ford	1974–1977	4	1	1
Carter	1977–1981	1	3	0
Reagan	1981–1989	14	8	0
G. H. W. Bush	1989–1993	7	5	0
Clinton	1993–2001	60	1	0
G. W. Bush	2001–2009	39	2	0

SOURCE: Richard F. Grimmett, "War Powers Resolution: Presidential Compliance," Congressional Research Service, Washington, D.C., September 23, 2009.

apply to the introduction of United States Armed Forces into hostilities." To fulfill this goal, congressional members crafted a resolution with two key requirements: the president must *consult* with Congress before deploying troops into possible armed conflict in other countries and must *report* to Congress "periodically on the status of such hostilities." Upon receiving an initial notification from the president of such a deployment (which may be sent up to forty-eight hours *after* the mission has been launched), Congress, through a majority vote of its members, can order that the troops be withdrawn after sixty days. The White House may extend this deadline by up to thirty days.

Presidents have dismissed the War Powers Resolution as unconstitutional, claiming that their powers as the commander in chief permit them to deploy troops overseas into armed conflicts without a formal declaration of war from Congress. Despite these assertions, between April 1975, the end of the Vietnam War, and October 2001, the beginning of the war on terrorism, presidents chose to comply with the resolution ninety-two times by submitting reports to Congress on U.S. troop deployments (Grimmett 2001, 53–68). President Clinton alone submitted sixty reports during his two terms, and George W. Bush filed thirty-nine such reports during his presidency (see Table 5.3). Bush repeatedly informed Congress, "consistent with the War Powers Resolution," about ongoing military operations in the former Yugoslavia and the Middle East. Other reports to Congress described U.S. military activities in Haiti and in such African nations as Djibouti, Eritrea, Ethiopia, and Kenya that were little known to the general public as well as most legislators (see Grimmett 2006, 11–12).

Only once during this period has the sixty-day "clock" actually been activated. In May 1975, President Ford cited the crucial section of the resolution, Section 4(a)(1), in ordering the rescue of the U.S. merchant ship SS *Mayaguez*, which had been seized by a Cambodian naval patrol. Under that section, presidents acknowledge the introduction of U.S. troops "into hostilities or into situations where imminent involvement in hostilities is clearly indicated by the circumstances." Since the *Mayaguez* rescue (which was completed by the time

Ford notified Congress), no president has cited Section 4(a)(1) to trigger the time limit. In avoiding this crucial step, presidents have prevented the legislative branch from using the War Powers Resolution for its primary purpose: forcing an end to military actions deemed contrary to U.S. national interests.

During the 1990s, congressional efforts to retain some measure of codetermination over military deployments failed consistently. In 1993, legislators threatened to cut off funding for the U.S. intervention in Somalia if its mission was not completed by March 31, 1994, but U.S. troops remained in Somalia a year beyond this deadline as part of a UN mission. In 1995, the House and the Senate approved "sense-of-the-Congress" resolutions stating that U.S. combat troops should not be deployed to Bosnia-Herzegovina without congressional approval. But Clinton ignored these resolutions and ordered the deployment of 32,000 troops to the former Yugoslav republic. When Clinton deployed troops to Kosovo in March 1999, several members of Congress filed suit against him to force a withdrawal. Three months later, the U.S. Court of Appeals dismissed the suit, ruling that the legislators lacked "legal standing" to sue the president. The U.S. Supreme Court upheld the ruling in October 2000. These and other legal cases affirmed the authority of presidents to send troops into combat in the absence of a declaration of war from Congress.[10]

As the Supreme Court has held consistently, these disputes over war powers are largely political in nature. Appeals to the judicial branch are muted when presidents enjoy a legislative majority, and they are silenced altogether when foreign threats or crises loom. At all times, legislators are rewarded less for their rhetorical flourishes on global diplomacy than for their delivery of tangible benefits to their states and districts. Acting on this electoral impulse, then, Congress "has virtually abdicated its constitutional war powers to the imperial presidency" (Irons 2005).

The Power of the Purse

One of Congress's most potent weapons in foreign policy relates to its taxing and spending power, or its "power of the purse." Article I, section 8, of the Constitution explicitly provides Congress with authority to "lay and collect taxes, duties, imposts and excises, to pay debts and provide for the common defense and general welfare of the United States." The framers of the Constitution, whose primary concern was restraining a potentially tyrannical head of state, viewed this control over government spending as a crucial hedge against excessive presidential ambition. As James Madison wrote in *Federalist* No. 58, power over government spending is "the most complete and effectual weapon with which any constitution can arm the representatives of the people."

---

10. Some members of Congress have acknowledged the failure of the War Powers Resolution to support a meaningful role for Congress in this process. Their views were reflected in a House bill, narrowly defeated in June 1995, to repeal the central features of the resolution.

The power of the purse is not important simply as a matter of checks and balances. Decisions about the amount of money received by the government, and how that money will be spent, dictate what is possible in public policy. In short, those who hold the keys to the treasury establish both the opportunities and the limitations of government action. Indeed, the failure of past world powers to keep their fiscal houses in order precipitated their decline. Economic crises may result from the overwhelming commitments associated with "imperial overstretch" (Kennedy 1987). Alternatively, in modern democratic governments the demands of domestic interest groups may drain public treasuries and deprive military forces and diplomatic services of the funds they need to maintain a strong posture in foreign affairs (Olson 1982).

Government spending has special significance in foreign policy. Foreign leaders closely watch the amount of money the United States directs toward military programs and other operations abroad, viewing it as a sign of the government's priorities and future intentions. "If budget levels are thought to affect the behavior of potential foreign threats, budget totals then become an instrument of foreign policy" (Wildavsky and Caiden 1997, 232). Similarly, the U.S. government's financial commitments to allies, whether in the form of military or development aid, often speak louder than the rhetorical statements of presidents and diplomats.

Conflicts between the legislative and executive branches over foreign policy frequently come down to matters of dollars and cents. In 1907, President Theodore Roosevelt dispatched the Great White Fleet on a symbolic cruise around the world, and then dared Congress not to appropriate the funds to bring the fleet home. In the 1970s, Congress forced President Nixon to end the Vietnam War by cutting off funds for further U.S. military action. During the 1990s, the Republican-led Congress repeatedly cut the foreign aid budget and refused to pay past U.S. dues to the United Nations. Likewise, after the return of divided government in 2007, congressional debate over the war in Iraq focused increasingly on military appropriations. Resolutions in both chambers linked supplemental appropriations for the war to "redeployments" of U.S. troops out of the country, although legislators could not agree on timetables for such withdrawals and President Bush promised to veto any bills that would tie his hands as commander in chief.

Congressional spending authority in foreign policy comes into play in two distinct areas. First, Congress approves the *defense* budget, by far the largest single spending category in the federal budget. Second, it approves the *international affairs* budget, which finances the State Department and related agencies. As part of this budget, the legislative branch also decides how much money the United States will spend on assistance to foreign governments and international financial institutions such as the World Bank and the International Monetary Fund.

Both branches of government engage in the budget process from beginning to end. At the start of a congressional session, the president submits a series of budget proposals to Congress, which then develops its own budget. Members base that budget in part on the president's proposals as well as on their own judgments about how much money the nation should spend and how that spending should be divided among the various government agencies. Finally, Congress submits its budget proposals to the president, who then has a choice of approving or vetoing the budget. Negotiations continue between the White House and Capitol Hill throughout the process, with both sides recognizing that failure to reach a final agreement may lead to a shutdown of the federal government. In most cases, this stark reality is sufficient to force the president and Congress to split their differences over federal spending.

Managing the Defense Budget

Though the share of the federal budget devoted to defense spending has dropped considerably since the mid-1950s, as has the share of U.S. economic output represented by defense spending, the government still devotes the largest share of its discretionary spending to national defense. Annual spending in this area averaged $282 billion during the first post–Cold War decade (1992–2001). After the September 2001 terrorist attacks, the defense budget increased by $100 billion in the next two years (from $305 to $405 billion) and continued rising steadily to nearly $700 billion by fiscal year 2009 (see Figure 5.5). Described by Aaron Wildavsky and Naomi Caiden (1997, 219) as the "largest organization in the free world," the Department of Defense employs more than 2 million people, or about three

Figure 5.5 National Defense Outlays, Fiscal Years 2000–2009

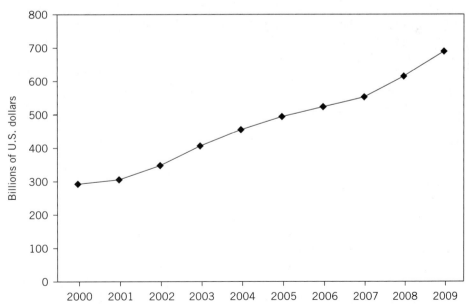

SOURCE: U.S. Office of Management and Budget, *Budget of the United States Government: Historical Tables Fiscal Year 2010*, "Outlays by Function and Subfunction, 1962–2014," www.gpoaccess.gov/USbudget/fy10/hist.html.

out of every four federal employees. Nearly 1.5 million have served in the armed forces in recent years; the rest are civilian employees working largely in administrative positions.

Defense spending is not only the largest component of the federal budget, but also one of its most controversial. Four factors in particular account for this controversy. First, proposed legislation for defense spending routinely provokes **guns-or-butter debates** within Congress and among the general public. In short, critics of higher defense spending argue that domestic needs are being sacrificed in the name of national defense. Generally speaking, Republicans in Congress are more likely than Democrats to support military spending over nonmilitary programs such as Medicare, education, and foreign aid.

Second, presidents and members of Congress nearly always disagree about the amount of money needed for national defense and engage in acrimonious public debates over the issue. In fiscal year 2001, for example, Republicans in Congress charged President Clinton with neglecting both the combat readiness of active U.S. troops and the living standards of veterans. The $291 billion approved for defense in that year included $5 billion in spending beyond the amount proposed by Clinton. Similarly, the U.S. armed services compete with each other over the distribution of military spending. Gen. David Jones found that this "intramural scramble for resources" distracts the armed services from their core mission of promoting national defense (quoted in Wildavsky and Caiden 1997, 224).

Third, government and private studies frequently expose cases of overpriced weapons systems and wasteful spending practices in the Pentagon (see Goodwin 1985; Gregory 1989; and Mayer 1992). As noted in Chapter 3, critics charge that three elements—Congress, the Defense Department, and military contractors—form an "iron triangle" that conspires to increase weapons spending beyond the levels needed to maintain U.S. security. This problem is compounded when former legislators and military officials pass through a "revolving door" and become lobbyists for defense contractors with direct access to Capitol Hill. This issue gained national attention in 2003, a year that otherwise witnessed national consensus over military spending. A subsidiary of Halliburton, a major military subcontractor, admitted to overcharging the federal government for its services in Iraq. Vice President Dick Cheney once ran the oil services firm, which garnered more than $15 billion in grants to support the U.S. occupation (Jehl 2003).

Finally, influential members of Congress are frequently able to gain spending approval for pet military projects in their states or districts. In 2000, for example, Senate majority leader Trent Lott, R-Miss., won approval for $460 million in spending on a helicopter carrier in Pascagoula, his hometown. Congress appropriated another $400 million that year to produce F-15 fighter jets in St. Louis, the hometown of House minority leader Richard Gephardt, D-Mo., and a politically vital source of support for Sen. Christopher Bond, R-Mo., a member of the Senate Appropriations Committee. Most observers view members of the Armed Services Committees as "uncritical supporters of the military establishment who receive, in exchange for that support, a continuous flow of defense spending in their districts" (Deering 1993, 175).

After their party captured both houses of Congress in 1994, Republican leaders sought to boost defense spending beyond the levels proposed by President Clinton. Rep. Floyd Spence, R-S.C., chair of the House National Security Committee, took the unusual step in 1996 of asking the four service chiefs how they each would spend up to $3 billion in additional funds that Congress might give them. Not surprisingly, the chiefs quickly provided detailed proposals for new spending projects, and Congress came through with a defense budget of $267 billion, $13 billion higher than the president's requested budget (see Weiner 1996).

The September 2001 terrorist attacks transformed the domestic debate over U.S. defense spending. Congress consistently supported President Bush's calls for sharp increases in the defense budget, including large supplemental appropriations for the wars in Afghanistan and Iraq. As noted earlier, this spike in military spending continued even after the Democrats gained control of the Pentagon's budget after the 2006 midterm elections. As in the past, Democratic legislators avoided being labeled "soft on defense" or unsupportive of U.S. troops by voting for the increases despite their stated misgivings about the progress being made in the war on terrorism and in the war in Iraq.

The U.S. defense budget approached $700 billion in fiscal year 2010 after Congress approved a 3.4 percent increase in pay for the armed forces. President Obama, who signed the appropriations bill in October 2009, viewed the new funding level as a decrease since the wars in Iraq and Afghanistan were no longer listed as supplemental appropriations. The president also gained congressional approval to reduce or eliminate funding for some weapons systems that the White House did not consider to be vital. Foremost among these was the F-22 fighter jet, the world's costliest aircraft, which was designed in the 1980s to repel the Soviet Union's air force. By cancelling future purchases of the F-22, the Senate in July 2009 supported the president's view that U.S. forces should be prepared for the unconventional wars of the future rather than the superpower showdowns that seemed imminent during the Cold War (see O'Hanlon 2009). Still, the U.S. defense budget remained, by far, the largest in the world.

The Price of Diplomacy

The second primary arena of congressional spending power in foreign policy is the budget for international affairs. This budget comprises the costs of running the State Department and other nondefense agencies, as well as U.S. spending on foreign aid and contributions to international organizations. Together, these expenses nearly tripled between fiscal years 2001 and 2009, from about $16 billion to nearly $48 billion (U.S. Office of Management and Budget 2009). Still, these figures represented just 7 percent of the Pentagon's budget and 2 percent of the federal budget in fiscal year 2009 (see Figure 5.6).

The State Department claims only a small part of the international affairs budget—about $9 billion annually in President Bush's second term. These funds cover the operating costs of the State Department headquarters and foreign

Figure 5.6 Distribution of Federal Spending as a Percentage of Total, Fiscal Year 2009

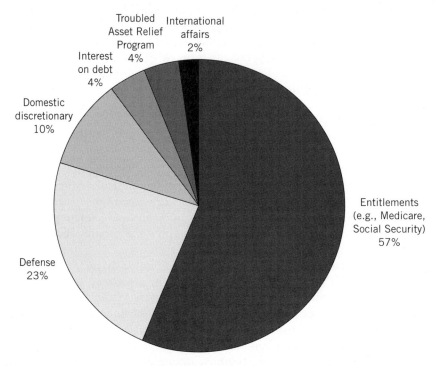

SOURCE: U.S. Office of Management and Budget, Summary Tables, pp. 149–150, www.whitehouse.gov/omb/budget/fy2011/assets/tables.pdf.

service, the support costs of public information campaigns and exchange and democratization programs, and U.S. contributions to international organizations and peacekeeping. (Foreign aid programs overseen by the State Department consume a far larger portion of this budget, as described in Chapter 11.) Despite the global scope of these activities, the diplomatic service has long faced a skeptical and sometimes hostile Congress during budget deliberations, particularly since the end of the Cold War. Congressional hostility toward the State Department stems from several sources. To legislators, the diplomatic service is poorly managed, does not make efficient use of federal resources, and resists a close working relationship with Congress. State's lack of a domestic constituency further reduces its position on the priority list of most legislators.

Congress's resistance to State Department funding has deep roots in U.S. history and political culture (see Hook 2003). Public disregard for diplomacy, in general, and the State Department, in particular, reflects a long-standing skepticism of traditional statecraft that extends beyond immediate circumstances or individual relations with foreign governments. As described in greater detail in Chapter 11, U.S. foreign aid programs, the objects of deep congressional cuts in the 1990s, rank among the least popular in the federal budget. Legislators have few electoral incentives to champion the causes and costs of diplomatic engagement, so far removed from the day-to-day lives of average U.S. citizens.

As a result, the State Department has been routinely neglected in each of its primary areas of responsibility: the development and articulation of foreign policy, the conduct of private and public diplomacy, and the transfer of foreign assistance. A study by the Overseas Presence Advisory Panel (1999) found U.S. embassies, consulates, and specialized missions to be "near a state of crisis." The panel reported "shockingly shabby and antiquated building conditions" in overseas missions, which were increasingly being staffed by personnel from other U.S. agencies. After the September 2001 terrorist attacks, Congress increased funding for counterterrorism efforts and assistance to law enforcement in foreign countries. Upon taking office in January 2009, President Obama supported greater funding for diplomacy, recognizing the importance of nonmilitary international programs in enhancing the "soft power" of the United States (Nye 2004).

Conclusion

Tensions between Congress and the White House are hardwired into the U.S. political system and foreign policy process. If today's national security architecture is a relic of the early Cold War, legislative-executive conflicts are creatures of the American Revolution and the ill-fated Articles of Confederation. Both experiences shaped the political culture of the United States in profound ways, placing individual freedoms above the orderly and efficient exercise of state power. The framers merely codified this arrangement in the U.S. Constitution, providing enough central governance to keep the new republic intact while allowing the dynamism and centrifugal forces of federalism and civil society to be expressed freely. The fragmentation and diffusion of government power, of which legislative-executive relations is but one element, ensure the erratic exercise of world power by the United States.

The climate of perpetual war that has prevailed for most of the past century enhances presidential power and rewards congressional deference. Unified government, the state of affairs for most of the George W. Bush years and at least the first two years of the Obama administration, provides the chief executive with additional leverage. Regardless of the balance of partisan power, however, presidents have repeatedly claimed the authority to put U.S. forces in harm's way without a congressional declaration of war, and have done so freely. Yet, whatever the rationale invoked by presidents and whatever the positions taken by legislators, the unilateral exercise of war powers by a U.S. president contradicts the spirit of the U.S. Constitution, which explicitly calls on Congress to make this most fateful decision. "If the goal is a long-term, stable set of legal structures for a conflict of indefinite duration against a novel adversary, neither the judiciary nor the executive can ultimately deliver," Benjamin Wittes (2008, 132–133) observed. "Only Congress can effectively constrain the executive in its exercise of the powers of presidential preemption and at the same time constrain the courts in their ambitions for a greater role in foreign and military affairs."

Even in the comfort zone of unified government, presidents cannot maintain the support of Capitol Hill indefinitely if their foreign policies fail. As legislative scholar James Lindsay (2003, 545) has observed, "The fact that members of Congress defer to the White House when [the president's] foreign policy takes off does not mean they will be deferential when it crashes." This insight was affirmed in 2006 as recurring setbacks in Iraq battered Bush's approval ratings and encouraged legislators in both parties to challenge the commander in chief. Although Obama began his presidency with a clean slate and enjoyed broad support in Congress, his ability to achieve his goals was constrained by a legislative branch no longer willing to write a blank check for executive action.

The lesson of history is clear: mutual accommodation between the White House and Congress is essential for the nation's global ambitions to be realized and, equally important, for the day-to-day functions of foreign policy to take place in an orderly fashion (see Hersman 2000). Presidents may test the limits of their executive power, particularly in times of war, but they inevitably confront resistance from Capitol Hill when legislators are left out of the loop. For its part, Congress may gain politically by avoiding foreign policy entanglements, but congressional deference to the White House leads inexorably to foreign policies that are poorly conceived, improperly planned, and carried out recklessly, often with disastrous results. Both branches of government, therefore, must accept the Constitution's "invitation to struggle" (Crabb and Holt 1992) in U.S. foreign policy.

Key Terms

Case-Zablocki Act, p. 143

congressional diplomacy, p. 141

constituent service, p. 148

divided government, p. 137

electoral factors, p. 153

foreign policy entrepreneurs, p. 150

Gulf of Tonkin Resolution, p. 142

guns-or-butter debates, p. 164

ideological factors, p. 153

ideology, p. 152

Intelligence Oversight Act of 1980, p. 143

intermestic policy, p. 143

Jackson-Vanik Amendment, p. 143

judicial noninterference, p. 148

logrolling, p. 154

Nelson-Bingham Amendment, p. 143

oversight, p. 142

passing the buck, p. 148

procedural innovations, p. 151

situational factors, p. 152

strategic factors, p. 154

structural weaknesses, p. 148

substantive legislation, p. 151

unified government, p. 137

USA PATRIOT Act, p. 145

War Powers Resolution, p. 143

Internet References

The **Almanac of Policy Issues** (www.policyalmanac.org) is an independent public resource that provides background information and Web links on a host of U.S. policy issues such as foreign affairs and national security, education, public health and social welfare, and the environment. The Web site also includes an archive of policy documents from a variety of sources such as the Congressional Research Service and the Congressional Budget Office.

TheCapitol.Net (www.thecapitol.net) is a nonpartisan firm that provides seminars, workshops, and publications to assist government and business personnel in understanding policy making in Washington, D.C. It focuses on, among other things, congressional operations, media and testifying training, and business etiquette. The site includes links to legislative reports, records, and schedules.

The **Center for Congressional and Presidential Studies** (www.american.edu/spa/ccps) is hosted by American University and provides access to conferences, speeches, and articles on Congress, the presidency, and their interaction. Elections, ethics, and lobbying are just some of the topics addressed in the publications, such as *Congress and the Presidency: A Journal of Capital Studies,* that are available through this site.

The **Center on Congress** (http://congress.indiana.edu) at Indiana University is a nonpartisan organization dedicated to increasing civic engagement by improving the understanding of the general citizenry about how Congress works. Articles, e-learning modules, and commentaries available through the Web site are not highly technical. Rather, they focus on matters such as the impact of Congress on the daily lives of Americans.

The Politics page on **CNN**'s Web site (www.cnn.com/politics) is a comprehensive news source for information on current events and political topics. The interplay between Congress and the presidency is often the subject of discussion.

Congress.org (www.congress.org) is a private, nonpartisan company that provides descriptions and analyses of the latest issues and votes on Capitol Hill to improve civic participation. Links enable visitors to search current bills and research congressional voting patterns.

The **Congressional Budget Office** (www.cbo.gov) provides recent and historical data, along with economic forecasts on U.S. government spending. Available are links to testimony, letters, budget reviews, and reports related to government expenditures on a wide range of policy areas, from the war on terrorism to Medicare.

CQPolitics.com, a product of Washington, D.C.–based publisher Congressional Quarterly, fulfills its mission ("Every District. Every State. Every Day") by complementing staff-written articles on congressional electoral politics with links to Congress and its members and to fund-raising data.

(continued)

Internet References *(continued)*

The **Library of Congress: THOMAS** (http://thomas.loc.gov) makes federal legislation freely available to the public by means of the site's links, which are helpful for exploring bills, resolutions, the *Congressional Record,* committee information, schedules, and legislative calendars. Links are also provided to both houses of Congress, as well as to every committee and subcommittee.

Organized and maintained by the Public Broadcasting Service (PBS), the **Weekly Political Wrap** (www.pbs.org/newshour/political_wrap/index.html) reports on salient political issues in Congress and in the media more generally. Audio and transcribed testimony are especially helpful for researchers.

6

The Foreign Policy Bureaucracy

America's emergence as a global superpower after World War II gave rise to a large foreign policy bureaucracy that sustained U.S. primacy during and after the Cold War (see Stuart 2008). New global roles and responsibilities prompted leaders to overcome the nation's traditional distaste for standing armies, worldwide diplomatic outposts, and trade bureaus. The institutions created during this period are even larger today, and far more complicated. As described in Chapters 4 and 5, the White House and Congress *formulate* U.S. foreign policy—that is, deciding on the nation's primary goals and providing the means to achieve them. Once adopted, however, executive branch agencies *implement* these policies, a task that places them on the front lines of U.S. foreign policy.

Although bureaucrats behave in similar ways across industrialized countries, the distinctive features of the U.S. political system must be taken into account. The government's authority is disbursed vertically among local, state, and federal agencies; horizontally across the three branches of government; and internally within the bureaucracies themselves. The agencies represent strong and often independent power centers that can determine the success or failure of foreign policy initiatives. As described in Chapter 3, negotiations among bureaucracies over foreign policy powers and missions can be as exhausting as negotiations with foreign governments. Three factors make bureaucratic managers especially powerful:

No federal department is nearly as large as the Department of Defense, whose headquarters—the Pentagon—creates its own small city across the Potomac River from Washington, D.C. The military leaders and other people who work in the Pentagon, mostly civilians, oversee the global deployment of U.S. troops and the ongoing U.S. military operations in Iraq, Afghanistan, and dozens of other countries.

- *Congressional deference.* While legislators play a central role in creating government agencies, they tend to leave them alone afterwards. "Legislators know that presidents take their foreign policy agencies seriously," Amy Zegart (1999, 34) has observed. "Any move to eliminate, reform, or significantly reduce the funding of these organizations without presidential approval is bound to incur executive wrath and invite inter-branch conflict—a fight that presidents almost always win."

- *White House constraints.* The president is hampered by the sheer mass of policy issues and institutions that must be overseen by the executive branch at any given time. This gives bureaucracies substantial autonomy, or freedom of action. In contrast to the regular turnover of presidents, federal agencies are semi-permanent structures with deeply entrenched self-interests, preferences, and standard operating procedures. According to a popular aphorism, "Presidents may come and go, but the bureaucracy lives forever."

- *Organizational expertise.* As specialists in their functional areas, often with many years of experience, bureaucrats "become more expert about their policy responsibilities than the elected representatives who created their bureau" (McCubbins, Noll, and Weingast 1987, 247). Elected officials, who stand to gain little by meddling in day-to-day bureaucratic functions, routinely trust agencies to implement foreign policies as they see fit. In most cases, politicians intervene only after policy breakdowns have occurred.

Because bureaucratic structures are easier to build than dismantle, the foreign policy architecture has not changed significantly since the signing of the National Security Act of 1947 (see Chapter 2), which created the National Security Council, the Department of Defense, and the CIA. Since then, the foreign policy bureaucracy has exhibited **path dependency,** a pattern by which past structural choices, informed by their architects' values and goals, push future policies in particular directions. For example, the massive size of the Defense Department relative to that of the State Department may lead foreign policy makers toward military rather than diplomatic solutions. Conversely, advocates for global environmental protection have difficulty gaining traction because of the lack of a formidable federal agency charged with that mission.

The foreign policy bureaucracy is loosely arranged within four complexes, or bureaucratic clusters, which manage diplomatic relations, national security, intelligence, and economic affairs, respectively (see Figure 6.1). Each complex features "a smorgasbord of institutional types," including cabinet-level departments, subordinate agencies, diplomatic posts, military services, and special units within the Executive Office of the President (Seidman 1986, 249). Although the work of these complexes overlaps, their specialized roles give them advantages in their areas of expertise—and a strong basis for maintaining the institutional rivalries that afflict U.S. foreign policy on a regular basis.

Figure 6.1   The U.S. Foreign Policy Bureaucracy

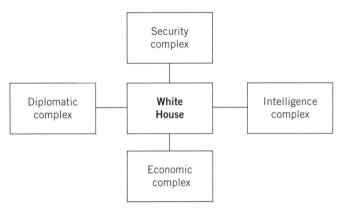

Agency Dysfunctions and the Paradox of World Power

Bureaucracies provide ballast, or stability, to government. They lend "continuity and constancy" to the federal government, which is otherwise prone to recurring changes that stem from shifting political alignments and external demands (Rockman 1997, 21). Yet, as students and practitioners of bureaucratic politics well know (see Chapter 3), such organizations often fall short of the standards of "rationality" they were designed to achieve. This is especially true for democratic states, with their vibrant civil societies, and for major powers, with their elaborate military forces, intelligence services, and diplomatic networks. Rather than working as partners toward a common vision of the national interest, bureaucrats frequently compete with each other for resources and influence while resisting changes that threaten their institutional turf. Clashing goals, dominant self-interests, and overlapping responsibilities contribute to the fragmentation of bureaucratic authority and reinforce the paradox of world power as exercised by the United States.

Two models of foreign policy, both of which have many historical precedents, shed light on this pattern. The first, bureaucratic politics, highlights the competition, or "pulling and hauling," among agencies in the foreign policy process (Allison and Zelikow 1999). These conflicts produce "winners" and "losers" that shape the future direction of policy. For example, in planning the Iraq war, a coalition of bureaucrats in Vice President Dick Cheney's office, the Defense Department, and the CIA managed to keep the State Department and National Security Council out of the loop (Woodward 2008). In other cases such struggles are literally built in. In Mexico City, the presence of the many state and federal agencies represented in the U.S. embassy produce bureaucratic rivalries "so complex, so multilayered, so conflicting, that it hamstrings, frustrates, and often paralyzes policy and makes it virtually impossible for the United States to carry out a successful foreign policy there" (Wiarda 2000, 175).

The second model, **organizational process,** refers to the standard operating procedures (SOPs) that bureaucratic managers follow. These SOPs may be rational in terms of meeting each agency's objectives, but the lack of interagency coordination prevents the government from seeing the big picture. The September 2001 terrorist attacks, for example, combined domestic and international elements, including suspicious visa requests and flight training in the United States (FBI concerns) and heightened "chatter" among al Qaeda operatives in Europe and Asia (a CIA concern). Compounding this overlap in jurisdiction was reluctance by CIA and FBI counterterrorism units to communicate with each other. "Everybody who does national security in this town knows the FBI and CIA don't talk," observed former senator Bob Kerrey (quoted in *New York Times* 2004, 25), a member of the 9-11 Commission, during his questioning of national security Adviser Condoleezza Rice.

Bureaucratic behavior in U.S. foreign policy reflects differences in **organizational culture,** or the shared values, goals, and functional priorities of the members of a government agency. According to James Q. Wilson (1989, 91), an expert on bureaucracy, "Culture is to an organization what personality is to an individual. Like human culture generally, it is passed from one generation to the next. It changes slowly, if at all." The presence of many foreign policy agencies in the U.S. government inevitably leads to clashes of organizational cultures. The tendency of diplomats to favor negotiated settlements over military coercion contributes to the State Department's reputation for excessive caution and timidity. Similarly, the inherent secrecy of intelligence gathering creates a highly insular organizational culture within the CIA and other intelligence agencies.

A foreign policy institution encompassing many agencies can feature multiple, and clashing, organizational cultures. Within the Department of Defense, each of the armed services considers its own mission to be the most vital to the national interest and its forces superior to those in other services. Such differences can energize the morale of each unit and serve as valuable recruiting tools across the foreign policy bureaucracy. But they also can create problems by sparking public disputes over funding allocations, deployments, and the assignment of operational missions in military conflicts. Such ruptures also extend beyond the government. The distinctive culture of military life, for example, produces strains in **civil-military relations.** The "persistent peacetime tensions between military imperatives and American liberal society" keep the armed services disconnected from many other facets of U.S. society, in stark contrast to other countries in which uniformed military officers are integrated into civilian life (Huntington 1957, 345).

Today's foreign policy bureaucracy displays many of the same operational flaws that have hindered the U.S. government's actions in the past. Seven chronic problems, detailed recently by the Congressional Research Service (Dale et al. 2008), are familiar to foreign policy makers: (1) domination of policy input by the Pentagon, (2) lack of resources for civilian agencies, (3) weak central leadership, (4) poor planning, (5) inadequate reporting across agencies, (6) lack of budget coordination, and (7) poorly structured congressional oversight. Solving all these

IN THEIR OWN WORDS: CONDOLEEZZA RICE

National security adviser Condoleezza Rice, along with other Bush administration officials, testified before the 9-11 Commission in April 2004. In her testimony, Rice emphasized the institutional barriers that had prevented the U.S. government from "connecting the dots"—the numerous clues that had indicated a large-scale terrorist attack was imminent.

The threat reporting that we received in the spring and summer of 2001 was not specific as to time, nor place nor manner of attack. Almost all of the reports focused on al Qaeda activities outside the United States, especially in the Middle East and in North Africa. In fact, the information that was specific enough to be actionable referred to terrorist operations overseas. Most often, though, the threat reporting was frustratingly vague.

Let me read you some of the actual chatter that was picked up in that spring and summer:

"Unbelievable news coming in weeks," said one.

"Big event . . . there will be a very, very, very, very big uproar."

"There will be attacks in the near future."

Troubling, yes. But they don't tell us when; they don't tell us where; they don't tell us who; and they don't tell us how. . . .

Throughout the period of heightened threat information, we worked hard on multiple fronts to detect, protect against and disrupt any terrorist plans or operations that might lead to an attack. For instance, the Department of Defense issued at least five urgent warnings to U.S. military forces that al Qaeda might be planning a near-term attack, and placed our military forces in certain regions on heightened alert. The State Department issued at least four urgent security advisories and public worldwide cautions on terrorist threats, enhanced security measures at certain embassies, and warned the Taliban that they would be held responsible for any al Qaeda attack on U.S. interests.

The FBI issued at least three nationwide warnings to federal, state and [sic] law enforcement agencies, and specifically stated that although the vast majority of the information indicated overseas targets, attacks against the homeland could not be ruled out. . . .

In looking back, I believe that the absence of light, so to speak, on what was going on inside the country, the inability to connect the dots, was really structural . . . the legal impediments and the bureaucratic impediments. But I want to emphasize the legal impediments. To keep the FBI and the CIA from functioning really as one, so that there was no seam between domestic and foreign intelligence, was probably the greatest [impediment]. . . . [W]hen it came right down to it, this country, for reasons of history and culture, and therefore, law, had an allergy to the notion of domestic intelligence, and we were organized on that basis. And it just made it very hard to have all of the pieces come together. . . .

SOURCE: Condoleezza Rice, "Hearing of the National Commission on Terrorist Attacks upon the United States" (April 8, 2004), www.9-11commission.gov/archive/hearing9/9-11Commission_Hearing_2004-04-08.pdf.

problems will be difficult, especially as those who must reform the policy process are entrenched in their bureaucratic bunkers, favoring institutional survival above all else.

The Diplomatic Complex

A central element of U.S. foreign policy is the conduct of **diplomacy**—the interactions among representatives of two or more sovereign states on official matters of mutual or collective concern. In particular, diplomats seek to maintain stable and functional relations with as many foreign governments as possible and to resolve interstate differences without resorting to force. The absence of tensions offers openings for constructive relations, particularly for commerce in which the citizens and governments of all parties involved may profit. Diplomats posted overseas also serve as the "eyes and ears" of their governments, providing leaders at home with timely firsthand information about developments in host countries.

Governments have maintained some sort of diplomatic ties since the dawn of international politics. As far back as 3,000 BC, ancient city-states in Mesopotamia, a region near the Persian Gulf that is now part of Iraq, "were in constant dispute over water rights, boundaries, and trade relations, which occasioned much mediation and arbitration" (Leguey-Feilleux 2009, 25). In the centuries that followed, governments commonly assigned representatives, or ambassadors, to resolve such differences and negotiate peace treaties, a practice that continues in much the same manner today. Modern diplomacy emerged in the seventeenth century as France's prime minister, the Cardinal Richelieu, was the first to create a large and permanent foreign service. This system became a model for other great powers, including the United States.

In the country's first decades, the post of chief U.S. diplomat, or secretary of state, served as a stepping-stone to the presidency. Thomas Jefferson, James Madison, James Monroe, and John Quincy Adams all became chief executives in this manner. Yet, despite this impressive showing of strong secretaries, early U.S. leaders, including the nation's third president, frowned on the routine practice of diplomacy. Jefferson, the first secretary of state, described eighteenth-century diplomacy as "the workshop in which nearly all the wars of Europe are manufactured" (quoted in Morris 1966, 43–44). Rep. Benjamin Stanton of Ohio declared in 1858 that he knew of "no area of public service that is more emphatically useless than the diplomatic service—none in the world" (U.S. Department of State 1981, 9–10). In the popular imagination, the nation's early foreign policy achievements, particularly the rapid pace of continental expansion, resulted from a *rejection,* rather than an embrace, of diplomatic relations.[1]

---

1. Foreign policy analysts from the constructivist perspective (see Chapter 3) reject many U.S. diplomatic practices as "myth." To Walter Hixson (2008, 307), widespread notions of U.S. exceptionalism contributed directly to "the nation's pathological militancy and hostility to multilateral diplomacy."

Largely for this reason, the U.S. government did not create a full-scale foreign service until after World War I. American leaders agreed, however reluctantly, that the nation's arrival as a global power required it to "dirty its hands" in diplomatic activity. Even then, State Department budgets and salaries were kept at minimal levels, and the travel and schedules of diplomats were scrutinized closely. Once the United States achieved the status of a great power, other government agencies became enmeshed in the foreign policy process. Since 1947 the U.S. government has maintained "two foreign ministries," in the State Department and the National Security Council, respectively (Rockman 1981). This blurring of foreign policy authority created problems over jurisdiction and access to the president that continue to plague the foreign service today.

Department of State

The State Department, created in 1781 as the Department of Foreign Affairs, is the U.S. government's oldest executive agency. Officials at Foggy Bottom (the State Department's Washington, D.C., headquarters, which got its informal name from the area of the city in which it is located) manage a diplomatic complex that includes foreign policy specialists based abroad as well as at home. As many as 60,000 federal employees from thirty agencies have been stationed in State Department offices in recent years. Duties of department employees include representing U.S. positions to foreign governments, international organizations, and private citizens, while also serving as contacts for representatives of foreign governments who wish to convey their views to the U.S. government. Beyond these diplomatic tasks, the State Department serves the following five functions:

- Advising presidents on the ends and means of U.S. foreign policy

- Gathering and sharing information about recent developments overseas

- Providing representation and services to U.S. citizens abroad

- Regulating and managing foreign travel to the United States

- Investigating solutions to transnational problems such as environmental decay, large-scale poverty, and weapons proliferation (see Chapters 11 and 12).

The secretary of state, who oversees the U.S. diplomatic complex, serves as the ranking member of the president's cabinet and stands fourth in line of presidential succession. This official serves as the government's chief diplomat while also advising the president and overseeing the State Department bureaucracy. Beyond these formal duties, secretaries of state have played widely varying roles in presidential administrations—roles determined by the officeholder's relationship with the president and other top leaders, communications skills, and management style. Further affecting the secretary of state's role is the blurring of foreign policy authority that began after World War II, as presidents chose to rely on a larger group of foreign policy advisers. This fragmentation of authority has made life difficult for the secretary of state, who "has to use a great deal of time and energy to get anything done" (Rubin 1985, 263).

The experience of Secretary of State Colin Powell illustrates this point. Just prior to the terrorist attacks of September 11, 2001, Powell had such a low profile in the George W. Bush administration that *Time* magazine asked on its cover, "Where have you gone, Colin Powell?" (Lemann 2002). Although formally part of the president's inner circle, Powell did not play a decisive role in Bush's strategic choices in the war on terrorism and was among the last to be informed of the decision to invade Iraq (Woodward 2004). Even though Powell offered to serve a second term, he was rebuffed by the president, and so he retired. His chief of staff, Lawrence Wilkerson (2005), later complained that a "little-known cabal" led by Vice President Cheney and Donald Rumsfeld, the defense secretary, commandeered U.S. foreign policy. The group's use of power was "efficient and swift—not unlike the decision-making one would associate more with a dictatorship than a democracy."

The secretary of state oversees an elaborate worldwide bureaucracy organized along regional and functional lines (see Figure 6.2). In 2009, the State Department employed nearly 19,000 people, including about 11,500 specially trained **foreign service officers** (FSOs) who conduct the day-to-day administrative and diplomatic tasks through a network of about 180 embassies (in foreign capitals), hundreds of consulates (in other major cities), and specialized missions located in nearly every foreign country.[2] Face-to-face interactions between FSOs and their counterparts overseas make up much of the business of U.S. foreign policy.[3] The ambassador serves as the president's official representative and the "leading protagonist, protector, and promoter" of U.S. interests within each foreign country (Kennan 1997, 207). Second in command at an embassy is the deputy chief of mission, who is responsible for the routine operation of overseas posts. This task is an imposing one, because embassies include many functional sections routinely staffed by officials from other federal agencies. Military officers serve in most posts, along with trade representatives, development specialists, and intelligence agents.

In addition to the FSOs, more than 7,000 civil service workers manage State Department activities in Washington. These include offices with a regional focus (for example, African and Near Eastern affairs) and others with functional tasks, including arms control, economic affairs, and democracy promotion. Still other specialists manage policy planning, counterterrorism efforts, intelligence gathering, and other functions from the State Department headquarters. Two offices operate autonomously but within the secretary of state's statutory authority: the

---

2. The United States has maintained diplomatic relations with about 90 percent of the roughly two hundred countries in the world in recent years. Among the few countries with no formal U.S. diplomatic representation are Cuba, Iran, and North Korea.

3. See Kopp and Gillespie (2008) and Dorman (2003) for detailed descriptions of the work of FSOs in the State Department.

Figure 6.2 U.S. Department of State

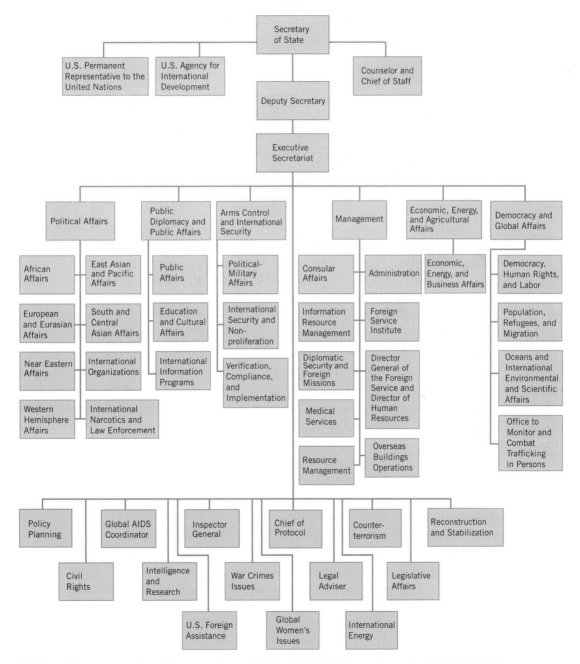

SOURCE: U.S. Department of State, "Department Organization Chart: May 2009," www.state.gov/r/pa/ei/rls/dos/99494.htm.

A relief worker unloads U.S. emergency supplies following the devastating earthquake in Haiti that killed more than 200,000 people in January 2010. The food shipments were provided by USAID, an arm of the State Department, which also coordinated relief efforts of other governments and hundreds of nongovernmental organizations.

U.S. Agency for International Development (USAID) and the U.S. Permanent Representative to the United Nations.

Whereas the State Department represents the institutional core of the diplomatic complex, other government agencies as well as a growing network of private actors play a role in this area. This trend has increased the types of diplomacy that are now a part of U.S. foreign policy (see Table 6.1). The national security adviser, secretary of defense, and U.S. trade representative, for example, routinely negotiate with their foreign counterparts. It is not uncommon, furthermore, for private citizens, including wealthy philanthropists such as Bill Gates, to undertake diplomatic missions on behalf of the U.S. government. As described further in Chapter 8, U.S. leaders often engage the news media to provide favorable coverage of its efforts in "public diplomacy" (see Cowan and Cull 2008). Hollywood actors and actresses, meanwhile, have furthered the rise of **celebrity diplomacy** (Cooper 2008) by speaking out against U.S. foreign policy positions. Richard Gere, for example, led numerous rallies against the Iraq war, and Angelina Jolie criticized the Bush administration's sluggish response to the campaign of genocide in the Sudanese region of Darfur. Rapid developments in communications, particularly the Internet, have eroded the monopoly on diplomatic activity formerly held by government officials, often pushing U.S. foreign policy in unexpected directions.

Table 6.1 The Many Faces of U.S. Diplomacy

Type	Description	Example
Celebrity	Highly publicized efforts by celebrities that draw attention to foreign policy issues	Visit to Sudan by actress Angelina Jolie to publicize ongoing genocide in Darfur and gain U.S. support for intervention (2004)
Conference	Organized events, often multilateral, that concern specific areas of U.S. foreign policy	United Nations Climate Change Conference in Copenhagen, Denmark (2009)
Digital	Use of modern telecommunications to facilitate U.S. foreign policy goals	State Department creation of Diplomatic Outreach Team to "explain U.S. foreign policy and to counter misinformation" in Muslim countries (2008)
Gunboat	Shows of force that compel foreign governments to support U.S. foreign policy positions	Deployment of U.S. naval forces to coast of Japan to compel opening of trade relations with United States (1853)
Public	Efforts by U.S. leaders to gain public support for foreign policy goals	"Listening tour" of Muslim countries by Karen Hughes, manager of public diplomacy in Bush administration (2005)
Shuttle	Direct mediation by U.S. leaders to foster agreements between warring parties	Mediation by Secretary of State Henry Kissinger to end Yom Kippur War between Israel and its Arab neighbors (1973)
Special mission	Assignment of U.S. negotiator, often not in government, to manage a specified foreign policy problem	Appointment of Richard Holbrooke to manage U.S. foreign policy efforts in Afghanistan and Pakistan (2009)
Summit	Role of U.S. presidents to sign treaties already approved by foreign governments	Signing of Intermediate-Range Nuclear Forces (INF) Treaty by President Reagan and Soviet President Mikhail Gorbachev (1987)
Two-track	Coordinated diplomacy conducted by government and private actors	U.S. relations with East Asian countries (ongoing)

Criticism and Reform at Foggy Bottom

For all its constitutional stature, the State Department is among the most embattled of federal agencies. Its budget, though rising to $16.3 billion in fiscal year 2010, is still less than 2 percent of the national defense budget and far less than that for intelligence and homeland security. Though its problems stem in large part from the widespread skepticism of "old world" diplomacy that is deeply embedded in U.S. political culture, the department faces criticism for a variety of other reasons, all further limiting its prestige, influence, and budgetary support. Three criticisms in particular continue to plague the State Department:

- *Elitism.* Political leaders and the general public often see diplomats as "objects of suspicion" because of "their arcane interests as well as their cosmopolitan behavior and manners" (Rubin 1985, 6). A recruitment pattern in which affluent white males from Ivy League universities have disproportionately filled the foreign service and top appointed positions has fueled this perception. In response to this criticism, Colin Powell increased the proportion of women and minorities at the State Department. Condoleezza Rice, who followed Powell and Madeleine Albright to the secretary of state's office, became the third consecutive secretary to break these gender and racial barriers.

- *Excessive caution.* Critics often complain that foreign service officers resist making changes or taking chances in diplomatic relations because of their determination to maintain stable relations with foreign governments. Furthermore, critics say, they avoid initiatives that may not be popular among members of Congress whose support may be needed in the future. State Department officials respond that U.S. national interests are served by maintaining congenial and reliable diplomatic relations, a point demonstrated, to the nation's detriment, in the Iraq war. Officials recognize their political weakness relative to the Pentagon and many domestic agencies, so they choose their battles with Congress carefully.

- *Clientitis.* Foreign service officers are prone to develop close relationships with governments and citizens overseas that may cloud their judgment about U.S. global priorities. "It's a disease not unique to the Foreign Service," former secretary of state James Baker (1995, 29) observed. "Some of the worst cases of clientitis I encountered involved politically appointed ambassadors who fell so thoroughly in love with their host country and its government that they sometimes lost sight of what was in the national interest." To help prevent such compromising ties from forming, FSOs rotate every four years among overseas posts and domestic offices.[4]

In view of these criticisms and cross pressures, it is not surprising that State Department morale—long a major problem—has slumped to new lows in recent years. This morale problem persisted in George W. Bush's administration despite Powell's success in increasing diversity, improving working conditions, and enhancing employee compensation. As a result, attracting and keeping skilled employees, particularly those with greatly needed language skills, has been difficult for the department. Filling vacant "hardship" posts, such as in Beirut, Lebanon, and Peshawar, Pakistan, is a constant problem. According to the U.S.

---

4. Such rotation has produced its own criticism—that FSOs lack the necessary knowledge about the countries and regions in which they work.

Point/Counterpoint
DEFENSE DEPARTMENT VS. STATE DEPARTMENT

Relations between the two agencies at the forefront of U.S. foreign policy, the Defense Department and the State Department, are fraught with institutional tensions. True to the nature of their institutions, Pentagon officials focus on military solutions to foreign policy problems, whereas their counterparts at Foggy Bottom emphasize diplomatic measures.

These built-in tensions were exposed shortly after the terrorist attacks of September 11, 2001. On September 13, Paul Wolfowitz, the deputy secretary of defense, outlined a large-scale military response. "It's not just simply a matter of capturing people and holding them accountable," Wolfowitz told reporters at a Pentagon press conference, "but [also of] removing the sanctions, removing the support systems, [and] ending states who sponsor terrorism."

At a press conference soon after Wolfowitz spoke, reporters asked Secretary of State Colin Powell what he thought of "ending," or overthrowing, state sponsors of terrorism. "We're after ending terrorism," Powell replied, "and if there are states and nations, regimes that support terrorism, we hope to persuade them that it is in their interest to stop doing that. I think ending terrorism is where I'd like to leave it, and let Mr. Wolfowitz speak for himself."

Powell's reference to persuasion, rather than force, typifies the State Department's mindset. As in most other interagency policy disputes during that period, however, the Defense Department gained the upper hand. President George W. Bush, who ultimately chose the course of action to be followed, made it clear that the United States would attack not only terrorists, but their state sponsors as well. The Bush Doctrine allowed little room for diplomacy, a fact affirmed by the U.S. invasion of Afghanistan in November 2002 and the overthrow of Saddam Hussein's regime in Iraq in March 2003, the latter without the support of the UN or key U.S. allies.

SOURCE: Public Broadcasting Service, "The War behind Closed Doors" (*Frontline* documentary, February 20, 2003), www.pbs.org/wgbh/ pages/frontline/shows/iraq.

Government Accountability Office (Ford 2009, 2), "[the Department of] State's diplomatic readiness remains at risk."

Despite these obstacles, President Obama's appointment of Sen. Hillary Clinton, D-N.Y., as his secretary of state signaled a heightening of the State Department's prominence in the foreign policy complex. Clinton shared the president's desire to promote diplomatic cooperation after many years in which military forces seemed to be the primary face of U.S. foreign policy. She also shared Obama's worldwide popularity, gained in her overseas travels as first lady in the 1990s. Her efforts garnered support from an unlikely source—the Defense

Department (see below)—as foreign aid programs to build schools, hospitals, and public utilities were seen as vital to winning the "hearts and minds" of ordinary citizens in countries paralyzed by civil wars and insurgencies (see Klein 2009). As a well-known expert on national security (Rothkopf 2009a) observed, "The secretary has quietly begun rethinking the very nature of diplomacy and translating that vision into a revitalized State Department, one that approaches U.S. allies and rivals in ways that challenge long-held traditions."

The Security Complex

In contrast to the agencies of the diplomatic complex, the agencies of the U.S. security complex cast an immense shadow over the entire federal government, consuming much of its discretionary funding and controlling its largest workforce. In the years following World War II, the security complex grew enormously. The framework for national defense had been established early on with passage of the National Security Act of 1947 (see Chapter 2). The legislation and subsequent amendments created the National Security Council (NSC) and the National Military Establishment, which later became the Department of Defense. These institutions, which played a crucial role in waging and ultimately winning the Cold War, remained intact after the collapse of the Soviet Union in 1991. The terrorist attacks on the United States a decade later prompted a new expansion of the security complex—creation of the vast Department of Homeland Security.

National Security Council

The greatly enlarged world role of the United States after World War II, combined with the onset of the Cold War, required a more centralized system of foreign policy making. This need led to the creation of the NSC, which since 1947 has served as the nerve center of the foreign policy process. The council comprises four statutory members, four statutory advisers, top presidential aides, and a variety of other senior government officials who attend meetings involving their areas of expertise (see Table 6.2). Based in the White House, the NSC serves three primary functions:

- *Agent of policy coordination.* The NSC attempts to establish an orderly working relationship among the many federal agencies involved in U.S. foreign policy, particularly the Defense and State Departments along with the intelligence agencies. The special assistant for national security affairs, more commonly known as the **national security adviser,** serves as a gatekeeper in the White House, controlling access to the president. Policy coordination is further promoted through an array of interagency "principals" (cabinet-level) and "deputies" committees that meet regularly on foreign policy matters.

Table 6.2 Members of the National Security Council (NSC)

Statutory members	Statutory advisers	Nonstatutory members, invited to all meetings	Nonstatutory members, attend as necessary
President (chair)	National security adviser	President's chief of staff	Attorney general
Vice president	Chair, Joint Chiefs of Staff	Council to the president	Director, Office of Management and Budget
Secretary of defense	Director of national intelligence	Assistant to the president for economic policy	Other government officials invited by president
Secretary of state	Secretary of the Treasury		

SOURCE: White House, www.whitehouse.gov/nsc.

- *Source of neutral policy guidance.* The national security adviser meets regularly with the president to review and interpret recent developments in U.S. foreign policy, a role formerly filled by the secretary of state. The president receives additional staff support from NSC policy experts in the White House. Of critical importance is the neutrality, or lack of institutional bias, underlying this guidance, which is an essential alternative to the parochial, self-interested advice of cabinet heads and agency directors.

- *Forum for crisis management.* Finally, the NSC provides an organizational setting for the management of national security crises. The breakout of the Cold War and the ensuing nuclear arms race created a nearly perpetual state of crisis that solidified the NSC's crisis management role. Although recent occupants of the White House have preferred ad hoc meetings of selected advisers to formal NSC meetings, the council remains a useful forum for presidents.

The NSC system has proved highly malleable over the years, assuming different shapes and roles in each presidential administration (see Inderfurth and Johnson 2004). The rationale is that the council "must be left flexible to be molded by the President in the form most useful to him" (Tower Commission 1987, 4). Presidents Harry Truman and Dwight Eisenhower, for example, viewed the NSC warily, relying instead on their secretaries of state for advice. John Kennedy was the first president to use his national security adviser, McGeorge Bundy, as an active policy *advocate*. The national security adviser's power peaked in the Nixon administration, when Henry Kissinger dominated the U.S. foreign policy process as no one did before or has since. He eventually served as both national security adviser and secretary of state—a dual role that proved unworkable. National security advisers have since assumed a lower profile while retaining their advantage of direct access to the president.

The NSC frequently has been an object of controversy and criticism. Three issues are of primary concern. The first is the council's emergence as an independent power center within the security complex and a rival, rather than a partner, of other federal agencies, most notably the State Department. Critics allege that NSC staff members have overstepped their bounds by taking formal policy positions, interacting with foreign governments, and appealing to the public through the news media (Daalder and Destler 2000, 7). A second, related concern is that Congress is left out of the workings of the NSC, negating the checks and balances written into the U.S. Constitution. Unlike cabinet secretaries and other high-level presidential appointees, the national security adviser and other high-level NSC staff members do not require Senate confirmation. The secretive nature of the NSC raises the third issue of concern—potential abuses from the concentration of power within the White House. This fear was realized in the 1980s when NSC staffers conducted secret, "off-the-shelf" military operations in the Middle East and Central America, which led to the Iran-contra affair.

Department of Defense

The Department of Defense is by far the largest and most expensive organization within the U.S. government. It is also the largest single employer in the United States. In 2009 about 1.5 million men and women served in the active forces, another 1.5 million served in the reserve forces, and nearly 700,000 civilians supported the military effort. Defense spending in the United States, averaging less than $300 billion in the 1990s, rose to more than $500 billion after the 2001 terrorist attacks and amounts to about $700 billion today. The "military-industrial complex," which includes the contractors that provide goods and services to the DoD, employs millions of other workers, further compounding its economic impact (see Chapter 3).

Because of its vast scale, the DoD has a predictably complex structure (see Figure 6.3). At the top of the hierarchy stands the secretary of defense, a civilian appointed by the president and confirmed by the Senate. The secretary and the secretary's deputy oversee the three armed services—the U.S. Army, the U.S. Navy, and the U.S. Air Force—which in 2009 operated out of 5,570 military installations in the United States and overseas (U.S. Department of Defense 2009).[5] The DoD maintains military installations and alliances around the globe that are organized through six regional commands (see Maps 7–9 in map section).

The Joint Chiefs of Staff (JCS), composed of the leaders of all the armed services, provides guidance to the secretary of defense on military strategy and operations. This role has heightened as the Pentagon has made several changes to encourage "jointness" in military missions. The Defense Reorganization Act of 1986 (more commonly known as the **Goldwater-Nichols Act** after its congressional sponsors) altered the balance of power within the Pentagon in two distinct ways. First, the act strengthened the power of the JCS chairman, who became the

---

5. A fourth armed service, the U.S. Marine Corps, is based within the Department of the Navy but operates its own network of commands and agencies. The U.S. Coast Guard, formerly controlled by the U.S. Navy, is overseen by the Department of Homeland Security.

Figure 6.3   U.S. Department of Defense

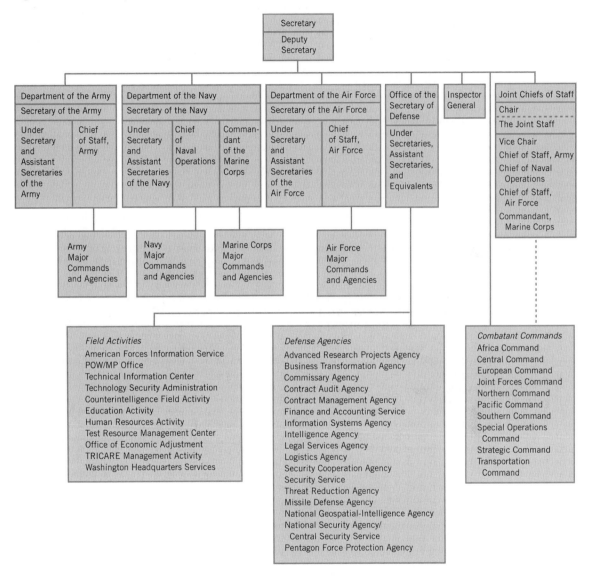

SOURCE: Director of Administration and Management, U.S. Department of Defense, "Organization and Functions Guide," http://odam
.defense.gov/omp/pubs/guidebook/pdf/dod.pdf.

primary military adviser to the president and secretary of defense and was thus
better able to prevent "end runs" by the individual service chiefs. Second, Goldwater-Nichols increased the power of the regional commanders in chief, who
manage forces across the armed services.

The first direct beneficiary of Goldwater-Nichols was Gen. Colin Powell, chairman of the JCS under Presidents George H. W. Bush and Bill Clinton. Powell used his clout to devise a blueprint for U.S. military forces after the Cold War that included large-scale cutbacks in military personnel and installations. By the mid-1990s the U.S. Army had reduced its divisions from eighteen to ten and the U.S. Navy had reduced its fleet from 551 to fewer than 400 ships. The Pentagon closed about 20 percent of U.S. military bases between 1998 and 2002, saving the government an estimated $30 billion initially and $6 billion a year afterward. In 2005 another twenty-two bases—twelve for the army and five each for the navy and air force—were scheduled for closure.

Upon taking office in 2001, Defense Secretary Donald Rumsfeld made it clear that the gradual downsizing of U.S. military facilities served his overriding goal of **military transformation,** a process designed to allow U.S. military forces to compete more effectively on the battlefields of the future (see MacGregor 2003). Like his predecessors, Rumsfeld believed the DoD should exploit the **revolution in military affairs** that had changed the nature of conventional warfare (Galdi 1995; O'Hanlon 2002). Rapid changes in military technology had fueled this revolution. Automated weapons systems and surveillance, satellite-guided munitions, lighter and faster transport vehicles, and advanced networks of command and control had allowed modern militaries to increase the potency of their armed forces without making them larger or more expensive.

The September 2001 terrorist attacks provided the boost Rumsfeld needed to revive his transformation campaign. His calls for higher defense spending after September 11 provided something for everybody—higher pay for troops, the extension of existing weapons programs, more military sales for weapons contractors, and all the support Rumsfeld needed to accelerate the research and development of new military technologies. He gained further momentum after U.S. troops proved effective in overwhelming Afghanistan in 2001 with a withering display of "shock and awe," a bombing campaign that also produced a prompt overthrow of Saddam Hussein's regime in Iraq in 2003. The Pentagon's subsequent problems in occupying and restoring order to both countries suggested, however, that even the most sophisticated armed forces could not overcome intelligence failures, tactical miscalculations, and "unconventional" warfare on the ground. Col. Ken Allard, former dean of the National War College, complained that the latest Quadrennial Defense Review Report (U.S. Department of Defense 2006) wrongly assumed "that we could continue to substitute high-tech 'systems' for those low-tech things called 'soldiers' " (quoted in Beehner 2006).

The DoD, with its global military commands, also plays a lead role in a variety of alliances that are extensions of the U.S. security complex. Growing concerns about the Cold War prompted the United States to join forces with its Western European allies in 1949 through the creation of the North Atlantic Treaty Organization (NATO). Lord Hastings Ismay, NATO's first secretary general, succinctly captured the alliance's threefold mission: "NATO was designed to keep the Americans in, the Russians out, and the Germans down" (quoted in Yost 1998, 52). More broadly, NATO advanced the process of **regional integration** in

Europe—that is, closer economic and political cooperation that offered a remedy for the chronic wars that had long ravaged the continent.

The persistence of NATO after the Cold War posed a central challenge to alliance theory, which held that alliances naturally dissolve when their stated adversaries are defeated (see Walt 1987, 26–27). NATO has not only endured since 1991, but it has steadily grown larger as well (see Asmus 2002). The first round of NATO "enlargement" added the Czech Republic, Hungary, and Poland in 1999 (see Map 8, NATO Expansion, in map section). Seven other Eastern European countries—Bulgaria, Estonia, Latvia, Lithuania, Romania, Slovakia, and Slovenia—joined the alliance in 2004, bringing the total membership to twenty-six. The "enlargement" process unfolded as NATO members identified new roles for the alliance long after the accomplishment of its original primary mission—containing Soviet expansion. In taking command of the International Security Assistance Force in Afghanistan in August 2003, thousands of NATO troops embarked on the alliance's first "out-of-area" mission in its history.

The DoD also continues to support other alliances. These include the Rio Treaty, formed in 1947 with Latin American states as part of the U.S. effort to contain Soviet communism. The same motives led the United States to create a three-way alliance with Australia and New Zealand in 1951. Finally, the United States maintains formal bilateral alliances with Japan and South Korea, two countries whose strategic importance and security ties to Washington also have endured beyond the Cold War. These alliances, combined with dozens of informal security agreements with allies, reflect past U.S. commitments while foreshadowing future military interventions.

The massive size and scope of the Pentagon make institutional reform a continuous, but exceedingly difficult, process. To one critic, a retired U.S. Marine officer (Sayen 2008, 2), recent U.S. military setbacks can be traced to "a climate of intellectual laziness and complacency that prefers the glories of the past over the unpleasant realities of the present and future." In a recent study entitled *America's Military Meltdown,* he and other analysts charged that internal turf battles continue to preoccupy U.S. military officials. Most often, these battles lead to a stalemate and a reliance on standard operating procedures that, in the Pentagon's case, result in continued spending on massive defense forces, worldwide bases, and elaborate missions. This practice pleases the many stakeholders in the security complex, but it neglects the most basic challenge facing the United States today: adapting to the **complex irregular warfare** that has plagued the nation since September 11 and that continues to confound military tacticians in Afghanistan and Iraq.

Department of Homeland Security

The September 11 terrorist attacks shattered the sense of invulnerability Americans had enjoyed throughout the nation's history. Suddenly the United States found itself joining dozens of other countries for which the trauma of global terrorism was a fact of life. Seven months before the attacks, the U.S. Commission

Figure 6.4 U.S. Department of Homeland Security

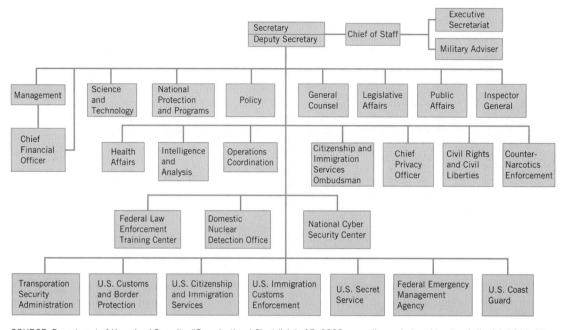

SOURCE: Department of Homeland Security, "Organizational Chart," July 17, 2008, www.dhs.gov/xabout/structure/editorial_0644.shtm.

on National Security/21st Century (2001) had found the U.S. government to be "very poorly organized to design and implement any comprehensive strategy to protect the homeland." The onset of the war on terrorism produced calls for new institutions to bolster the country against its enemies. In this case, the institutions were intended to guard against future catastrophic attacks at home while supporting rapid responses to such attacks should they occur.

One of President Bush's first actions after the events of September 11 was to create the Office of Homeland Security by executive order. Based in the White House, the office was to take a lead role in protecting the United States against future attacks on U.S. territory. Bush appointed Tom Ridge, the former governor of Pennsylvania, to the new position of homeland security adviser. The president's executive order also created the Homeland Security Council, which was to be responsible for "advising and assisting the President with respect to all aspects of homeland security." It soon became obvious, however, that the U.S. government needed more than a White House office to assume the formidable burdens of homeland security. This realization prompted the creation in March 2003 of the Department of Homeland Security (DHS), which brought more than 180,000 employees from twenty-two federal agencies together under one institutional roof (see Figure 6.4). These agencies included, among others, the U.S. Coast Guard, U.S. Customs and Border Protection, Secret Service, Citizenship and Immigration Services, Transportation Security Administration, and Federal Emergency

Management Agency (FEMA). The department's budget, much of which originally came from those of the existing agencies, grew steadily to $43 billion by fiscal year 2007.

The vast scope of this endeavor guaranteed that the DHS would face serious problems during its start-up years (see Glasser and Grunwald 2005). As noted throughout this chapter, efforts to merge federal agencies and functions often succumb to clashing organizational cultures, disputes over budgets and missions, and other forms of bureaucratic rivalry. These problems were compounded with the DHS, an unwieldy department that many agencies did not want to join. Officials and legislative allies of the FBI, for example, made it clear that proposals to add the bureau to the DHS roster would be dead on arrival, a fate that also would have awaited an attempted takeover of the National Guard by the DHS. Further complicating matters, the department found itself at the center of disputes over the protection of civil liberties in the war on terrorism (see Nakaya 2005, ch. 4).

External problems, too, plagued the DHS as a series of high-profile missteps diminished public support for the new department. A color-coded national alert system, for example, only seemed to confuse Americans, as did remarks by Ridge that they should stock up on plastic sheeting and duct tape to survive biochemical attacks on their neighborhoods. And long delays prevented the timely release of a terrorist "watch list." Local first responders, border patrols, and federal air marshals, who had expected more federal funds for stepped-up efforts, instead suffered budget *reductions* in 2004. "Far from being greater than the sum of its parts," journalist Michael Crowley (2004, 17) observed, "DHS is a bureaucratic Frankenstein, with clumsily stitched together limbs and an inadequate, misfiring brain. . . . [E]ven allowing for inevitable transition problems, DHS has been a disaster: underfunded, undermanned, disorganized, and unforgivably slow moving."

Progress reports from other sources have also been critical. The Gilmore Commission (2003) reported to Congress and the White House that because of "the lack of a clear articulated vision from the federal level," each of the fifty states and the five U.S. territories "has been moving to combat terrorism in its own way." The 9-11 Commission, in its follow-up report, gave the White House a "D" or a failing grade in areas such as "critical infrastructure assessment," cargo screening, airline passenger prescreening, and "international collaboration on borders and document security" (9/11 Public Discourse Project 2005a). The DHS was criticized further for allocating funds on the basis of pork-barrel politics rather than security concerns. "What money is appropriated receives little or no oversight," columnist Eric Alterman (2006) observed in *The Nation*. "Columbus, Ohio, is free to spend homeland security funds on bulletproof vests for fire department dogs; Newark, New Jersey, on air-conditioned garbage trucks; and the District of Columbia, on leather jackets and self-improvement seminars for sanitation workers."

The lethargic response by FEMA to Hurricane Katrina in August 2005 further illustrated the U.S. government's homeland security problem. The hurricane, the worst national disaster in American history, diverted DHS's attention from counterterrorism. A "second-stage review" by Ridge's successor, Michael Chertoff, promised prompt reforms, but it was overshadowed by reports of the department's cutbacks in antiterror funding for New York City and Washington, D.C. Morale sunk to ever lower levels in the department, whose first headquarters in a decrepit navy complex several miles from the White House symbolized its inferior status within the security complex.

The Intelligence Complex

Foreign policy makers have long relied on the gathering of timely information about conditions and developments in other countries that might affect their national interests. Intelligence gathering, the "first line of defense" in foreign policy, has been especially critical for the United States since its arrival as a global superpower after World War II. The attack on Pearl Harbor in 1941 revealed the tragic consequences of faulty intelligence. By contrast, sound intelligence gathering, as demonstrated during the Cuban missile crisis, has proved to be invaluable. The phrase "knowledge is power" is nowhere more applicable than in the field of intelligence.

Many government officials and outside experts believed the collapse of the Soviet Union in 1991 would lessen the need for foreign intelligence. The outbreak of regional crises in the early 1990s and the subsequent rise of Islamist terrorism, however, soon revealed that gathering such information must remain a critical element of U.S. security policy (Hilsman 2000). Terrorists pose very different challenges to U.S. intelligence than the adversaries of the Cold War—sovereign nation-states "bounded" by established diplomatic practices and transnational codes of conduct (Treverton 2009).

Today's intelligence does not come primarily from rival governments, but from a highly diffuse array of terrorist groups, drug cartels, criminal syndicates, clans, provincial warlords, religious organizations, and transnational banks. In confronting the Soviet Union, Washington's main obstacle was a lack of information. The current challenge is polar opposite: making sense of an unending tidal wave of intercepted phone conversations, financial records, news media reports, Internet postings, and other data, many of which must be translated or decoded.

Paradoxically, America's open society makes it an "open book" for its current adversaries, which closely guard information, operate in secret, and are extremely difficult to penetrate. In contrast, these groups and their state sponsors find it relatively easy to learn about developments in the United States. To identify internal divisions within the government or to learn about new foreign policy initiatives, these adversaries need look no further than the twenty-four-hour U.S. news networks or the televised congressional hearings and debates on C-SPAN (see Chapter 8). This **intelligence gap** contributed directly to al Qaeda's successful attacks in September 2001. To Eleanor Hill (quoted in Best 2009, 8), staff director of a congressional inquiry into the attacks, U.S. officials received numerous warnings of imminent danger. Sorely lacking, however, was "information prior to September 11 that identified precisely where, when and how the attacks were to be carried out."

Although their missions vary, intelligence agencies are involved primarily in the process of converting **raw intelligence**—information collected from various sources usually without their knowledge or permission—into **finished intelligence**—information made useful to policy makers. The information gathered in this process takes three forms: **human intelligence** (or **HUMINT**), which comes from informants and other personal sources; **signal intelligence** (or **SIGINT**), which is derived from intercepted communications; and **image intelligence** (or **IMINT**), which comes from the recorded surveillance of satellites, manned aircraft, and unmanned "drones." Each intelligence agency manages an **intelligence cycle** that includes five stages:

- *Planning and direction*—identifying what information policy makers require

- *Collection*—gathering information from various sources

- *Processing*—transcribing, translating, and decrypting information, and processing digital images and other visual data

- *Analysis*—clarifying and interpreting messages to guide policy makers

- *Dissemination*—sending intelligence to the proper authorities, a task undertaken with great care given the huge volume of potentially vital information that is collected.

In addition to these standard functions, intelligence agencies engage in two other activities. The first, **counterintelligence,** involves the "acquisition of information or activity designed to neutralize hostile intelligence services" (Richelson 1985, 3). Although much of this information can be found by intercepting the internal messages of foreign governments, U.S. agents must in many cases penetrate these governments, often by recruiting—and rewarding—informants in their own bureaucracies. The second activity, executing secret or **covert operations,** is designed to force changes in foreign governments that are favorable to the United States (Prados 1996). These operations, while not originally intended to be a key function of the intelligence complex, played a major role in the Cold War and are conducted regularly in U.S. foreign policy today.

Features of the Intelligence Community

The chronic tensions between centralized authority and bureaucratic fragmentation that characterize the federal government are particularly troubling to the intelligence complex, whose member agencies have long demanded strict independence in carrying out their missions. This pattern emerged during World War II and continued into the Cold War. President Harry Truman, more determined to unify the armed services than the intelligence agencies after World War II, made the latter a low priority (Zegart 1999). Consequently, the National Security Act of 1947 paved the way for the establishment of the CIA but left other intelligence units intact. These agencies maintained their independence in order to protect their sources and avoid interference from other agencies. While such parochialism was natural for intelligence agents who prided themselves on secrecy, it impeded the U.S. government's effort to anticipate and respond to overseas threats.

The attacks of September 11 offered foreign policy makers a golden opportunity to bring order to the government's far-flung intelligence community. Acting on the recommendations of the 9-11 Commission, Congress approved and President Bush signed the Intelligence Reform and Terrorism Prevention Act of 2004. The measure created the Office of the Director of National Intelligence (DNI) to oversee the activities of each agency and to serve as the primary source of intelligence to the president, military commanders, and Congress. In addition, the act created the National Counterterrorism Center, based in McLean, Virginia, to integrate intelligence findings and anticipate future attacks.

Despite these changes, the intelligence complex has retained its complicated Cold War structure, which today includes seventeen separate agencies with a combined budget of nearly $50 billion in fiscal year 2008 (see Figure 6.5). This complex is "by any measure the largest in the free world and certainly the most complicated, bureaucratic, convoluted, and expensive system anywhere. . . . No one could have invented such a system, but because it grew in bits and pieces, it has become the complicated structure we have today" (Hulnick 1999, 191–192). The CIA maintains its roles as the primary source of intelligence and a sponsor of foreign operations. Most other agencies are overseen by the Defense Department, which continues to protect its missions from outside control (Best and Bazan 2006). The Pentagon manages its own Defense Intelligence Agency, intelligence units in each of the four armed services, and three other agencies that support its intelligence mission:

- The National Security Agency, which employs "codemakers" and "codebreakers" to provide intercepted electronic communications to foreign policy makers

- The National Reconnaissance Office, which manages the nation's spy satellites that provide data from around the world

- The National Geospatial-Intelligence Agency, which supplies "map-based intelligence" used by U.S. leaders for tracking troop deployments, refugee flows, and other information.

Several nondefense agencies are also part of the intelligence complex. The Energy, State, and Treasury Departments manage their own intelligence units, as does the DHS and its subsidiary, the Coast Guard. Within the Justice Department, the FBI and the Drug Enforcement Agency have also expanded their intelligence functions in recent years. Although these agencies pursue distinctive missions and specialized roles, they often fall prey to the pattern of bureaucratic competition

Figure 6.5   Hub and Spokes: The Intelligence Complex

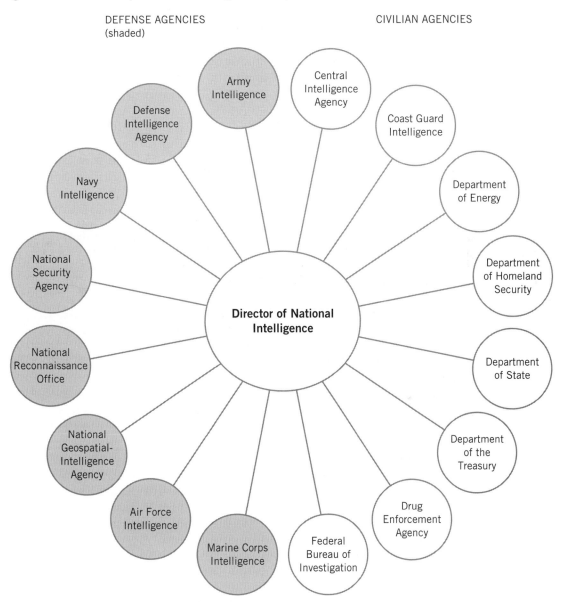

SOURCE: Office of the Director of National Intelligence, "Seventeen Agencies and Organizations United under One Goal," www.intelligence.gov/about-the-intelligence-community.

that became a defining feature of the intelligence complex at its inception. For this reason, the post–September 11 reforms described earlier have failed to transform this complex into an intelligence "community," a term that is used widely by the U.S. government but that remains on oxymoron.

Rather than streamlining the intelligence complex, the Director of National Intelligence has become just another rival for bureaucratic power with a staff that has grown to nearly fifteen hundred (Thomas 2006). The Pentagon, meanwhile, has challenged the CIA's exclusive control over intelligence operations—those involving spies in the field rather than analysts within the Beltway—as its Special Operations Command began "rapidly expanding its own global spying and terrorist-tracking operations, both long considered CIA roles" (Schmitt 2006, 1A). The most recent reforms have also failed to resolve the simmering tensions between the CIA and the FBI, which immediately adopted counterterrorism as its primary function. This shift did not come easily to the FBI, which had formerly focused on fighting crime that crossed U.S. state borders. Legal restrictions also limited the extent to which the FBI could meld its intelligence and criminal investigations. Finally, despite the heightened urgency of its counterterrorism mission, the FBI faced chronic shortfalls in its intelligence budgets and failed to recruit enough new agents to achieve its goals (see Zegart 2009).

Despite these problems, the FBI has claimed success in thwarting several plots to commit terrorist attacks in the United States. In May 2009, for example, FBI agents along with detectives from the New York City Police Department arrested four men who were allegedly planning a series of bombing attacks on synagogues in the city. Two months later, another team of FBI agents arrested seven "home-grown terrorists" in North Carolina who had allegedly amassed a large weapons arsenal in preparation for a series of attacks on behalf of Islamist causes. And in September, the FBI arrested a Jordanian citizen who, in the presence of undercover agents, attempted to detonate an inactive car bomb that was intended to destroy a Dallas skyscraper.

The heightened importance of domestic intelligence also requires greater cooperation among federal, state, and local agencies. In many areas, police and sheriff's departments are called upon to monitor suspected terrorist cells. In the event of a terrorist attack, these first responders may obtain crucial evidence that leads to the apprehension of those responsible. Once again, however, bureaucratic frictions often arise as local law enforcement agencies lack the resources and training necessary to conduct such missions. These agency managers also maintain a long-standing animosity toward the FBI, whose agents had previously consulted them only when convenient and ignored their requests for information about potential security threats in their jurisdictions.

Intelligence Failures and Scandals

The CIA and other intelligence agencies played vital roles in achieving the central goals for which they were created during the Cold War: "containing" communism and contributing to the demise of the Soviet Union. In some instances, including the 1962 Cuban missile crisis, intelligence breakthroughs saved the United States from imminent threats. In the 1980s, CIA-sponsored assistance to anti-Soviet militants in Afghanistan played a significant role in hastening Moscow's withdrawal from that country a decade after its 1979 invasion.

From 2001 to 2004, a primary target of criticism in the U.S. war on terrorism was George Tenet, the director of central intelligence. Tenet, who was appointed to the post by President Clinton, fought an uphill battle defending the CIA's record prior to the attacks of September 11 and gathering intelligence about the threat posed by Saddam Hussein's regime in Iraq. Congressional investigators concluded that faulty intelligence contributed to U.S. setbacks in the war on terrorism. Tenet resigned from his post in June 2004, citing "personal reasons."

Accompanying this success, however, has been a variety of problems that have damaged the intelligence complex's credibility. To defense analyst John Diamond (2008, 15), "The sixty-year history of the CIA is pockmarked with failures, whether botched or illegal covert operations, failures to warn of foreign invasions, or lying by Agency officers in testimony to Congress or to government investigators." Five problems in particular remain acute:

■ *Strategic surprises*. U.S. security interests have been damaged repeatedly by events overseas that intelligence agencies were expected to anticipate and, if possible, prevent (see Table 6.3). Japan's 1941 attack on U.S. naval forces at Pearl Harbor, Hawaii, and the al Qaeda attacks on the U.S. homeland in September 2001 remain the most notorious such surprises. Among other prominent examples, U.S. presidents were surprised by North Korea's attack on South Korea in 1950, by the overthrow of the shah of Iran and the Soviet invasion of Afghanistan in 1979, and by the entry of India and Pakistan into the nuclear club in 1998 (Auster and

Table 6.3   Caught by Surprise: Major U.S. Intelligence Failures, 1941–2009

Year	Event
1941	Japanese attack on Pearl Harbor
1950	Outbreak of Korean War
1956	Soviet military crackdown in Hungary Outbreak of Suez Canal crisis
1957	Soviet launch of Sputnik satellite
1962	Soviet nuclear weapons in Cuba
1968	Tet Offensive in Vietnam Soviet military crackdown in Czechoslovakia
1973	Outbreak of Six-Day War in Middle East
1979	Soviet invasion of Afghanistan Iranian revolution; takeover of U.S. embassy
1980	Iraqi invasion of Iran
1982	Terrorist attack on U.S. marines in Lebanon
1990	Iraqi invasion of Kuwait
1991	Collapse of Soviet Union
1994	Genocide in Rwanda and Burundi
1998	Nuclear tests in Pakistan and India
2001	Terrorist attacks on New York City and Washington, D.C.
2003	Absence of weapons of mass destruction in Iraq following U.S. invasion
2009	Attempted destruction of U.S. commercial jet by Nigerian terrorist

SOURCES: Amy B. Zegart, *Spying Blind: The CIA, the FBI, and the Origins of 9/11* (Princeton: Princeton University Press, 2009); Melvin A. Goodman, *Failure of Intelligence: The Decline and Fall of the CIA* (Lanham, Md.: Rowman and Littlefield, 2008); other sources.

Kaplan 1998). Other, more subtle, lapses have been significant. Estimates of the Soviet Union's military and economic power, for example, were exaggerated repeatedly throughout the Cold War, a pattern that swelled Pentagon budgets and provoked U.S. interventions in regional conflicts that may not have been necessary (see Goodman 2008, ch. 6).

■ *Operational failures.* Efforts by intelligence agents to influence political and military developments overseas frequently create additional problems for the United States. When a lightly armed brigade of Cuban "freedom fighters" was crushed by government forces in 1961, for example, it turned out that the CIA had trained and armed the rebels before their tragic assault at the Bay of Pigs. As a result, U.S. credibility was immensely damaged throughout the world as the failed overthrow of Fidel Castro's regime revealed not only that the U.S. government was secretly involved but did so in an incompetent fashion. Similarly, secret U.S. missions to arm antigovernment rebels in Nicaragua in the 1980s failed to unseat the communist regime while provoking widespread criticism of the United States for meddling in the internal affairs of a sovereign country.

■ *Internal security.* The nation's interests are also damaged when agents in the intelligence complex are found to be working on behalf of foreign governments. One of the most troubling cases was the arrest in 1994 of Aldrich Ames, a career CIA officer who sold military secrets to the Soviet Union and Russia for more than $2 million. Ames compromised dozens of CIA missions, and his leaks to Moscow led to the deaths of at least ten Soviet agents secretly working for the United States. The CIA was not alone in failing to maintain internal security. Robert Hanssen, an FBI agent, passed more than six thousand pages of highly classified documents to the Soviet and Russian governments over a twenty-one-year period in return for payments exceeding $1.4 million.

■ *Politicized intelligence.* The deliberate manipulation of findings about conditions overseas to promote an administration's foreign policy preferences creates additional problems for members of the intelligence community. A common complaint during the Cold War was that the exaggerated estimates of Soviet power were intended to generate domestic support for higher levels of U.S. military spending. The same charges were articulated during the Vietnam War, when investigators found that the Nixon administration had encouraged CIA reports that exaggerated the communist influence in Southeast Asia. More recently, congressional investigators concluded that the George W. Bush administration had distorted intelligence on the presence of weapons of mass destruction in Iraq, a charge strongly denied by the White House (U.S. Senate 2004).

■ *Domestic surveillance.* The National Security Agency recently drew criticism when it engaged in domestic surveillance of American citizens, primarily by tapping phone lines and Internet transmissions, without the requisite court orders. These actions violated the Foreign Intelligence Surveillance Act of 1978, which sought to ease the fears of many Americans that a "Big Brother" in Washington, D.C., would violate their privacy rights and individual freedoms. President Bush circumvented these restrictions, however, claiming that it would be perilous for the White House to seek court permission to spy on the large number of suspects who, in the government's view, posed an imminent danger to the United States.[6]

Defenders of the intelligence complex claim that the record of U.S. intelligence agencies during and after the Cold War is stronger than generally believed. According to former CIA director Robert Gates (1996, 562), who later served as

---

6. See Jackson (2009) for a useful summary of arguments regarding the need for, and obstacles to, domestic intelligence in the war on terrorism.

secretary of defense, the fact that there were "no significant strategic surprises" in the Cold War owed much to sound intelligence reporting. The lack of a second terrorist attack on the United States after September 11 is also seen as evidence that the intelligence complex is working effectively. Still, these advocates argue, expectations of foolproof intelligence provide a false sense of security. "Good intelligence diminishes surprise, but even the best cannot possibly prevent it altogether. Human behavior is not, and probably never will be, fully predictable" (Andrew 1995, 538).

Ongoing Controversies over Covert Operations

When the CIA was created in 1947, its mission statement identified the gathering of intelligence as its primary role. Little was said about the agency's operational role, which expanded steadily and in the early Cold War attracted a great deal of attention for its covert operations. Such operations included the CIA-backed overthrows of elected leaders in Iran (1953), Guatemala (1954), Indonesia (1965), and Chile (1973), among other countries.[7] President John F. Kennedy approved several CIA attempts to assassinate Cuba's leader, Fidel Castro, all of which failed. In 1963 Kennedy supported coups in South Vietnam and the Dominican Republic that led to the murders of their leaders—Ngo Ninh Diem and Rafael Trujillo, respectively. The CIA's covert operations extended internally as well, as the Johnson and Nixon administrations approved domestic spying and censorship of critics of the Vietnam War.

American policy makers justified these covert operations as vital to the nation's effort to "contain" communism. Even so, the tactics employed by CIA agents often contradicted the political values widely promoted by the United States, not to mention violating national and international laws. The uncovering of CIA involvement in these cases proved embarrassing to the agency and provoked anti-American backlash in the countries involved. In response to these spillover effects of covert operations, the Senate and the House of Representatives created select committees in 1976 to oversee the intelligence complex in general and the CIA in particular, which Sen. Frank Church, D-Idaho, charged had become a "rogue elephant."[8] The **Church Committee,** as the Senate body became known, found many CIA operations to be abuses of presidential power. President Gerald Ford later signed an executive order that prohibited political assassinations by the U.S. government.

After September 11, the Bush administration gained renewed congressional support for covert operations to penetrate and destroy terrorist cells around the world (see Cumming 2006). Controversy soon arose, however, after the CIA was

---

7. The CIA conducted more than nine hundred major covert operations and thousands of smaller ones between 1961 and 1974 (U.S. Senate 1976, 445).

8. The status of these intelligence committees as "select" rather than "standing" gives the party leadership in each chamber greater power to appoint members—a power deemed necessary because of the sensitive nature of national intelligence.

found to be holding suspects in secret overseas prisons, also known as "black sites" (Priest 2005). The CIA, in conjunction with the Pentagon, also engaged in a practice known as **extraordinary rendition** by which suspected terrorists were transported to foreign governments whose interrogation practices did not have to comply with U.S. laws. Of greatest concern, however, were the tactics CIA agents used in "coercive interrogations" such as extended sleep deprivation, intimidation by attack dogs, sexual humiliation, and "waterboarding," a method whereby prisoners are forced to ingest large volumes of water, which brings them to the verge of drowning (see Goodman 2008, ch. 10). These and other interrogation techniques violated the terms of the *U.S. Army Field Manual,* updated in 2006, which held that that no person in custody "shall be subject to torture or cruel, inhuman, or degrading treatment or punishment. . . . Any unlawful act or omission by the Detaining Power causing death or seriously endangering the health of a prisoner of war in its custody is prohibited" (U.S. Department of the Army 2006, viii, 5–19).[9]

The CIA's operational role also expanded in the war on terrorism. The agency managed its own fleet of unmanned "drones" in Pakistan that conducted remote-controlled bombing attacks on suspected leaders of al Qaeda and other terrorist groups (Mayer 2009). Although the attacks often reached, and killed, their targets, they claimed other victims, including family members and neighbors of the terrorists. The bombing attacks, which President Obama accelerated after he took office in 2009, were unknown to the public and most government officials in Congress and the foreign policy complex itself. The practice also defied President Ford's ban on political assassinations, noted earlier.

Neither Congress nor the courts have effectively challenged these practices, and press reports of recent covert operations have elicited little concern among the general public. Although the select committees on intelligence have enhanced Congress's oversight role, the executive branch's refusal to provide full disclosure has frustrated this role (see Lowenthal 2009, ch. 10). As in the past, fears of appearing unpatriotic in wartime discourage criticism of the White House and compel members of Congress to leave further reforms of the intelligence complex for a later day—which may be far in the future, given the seemingly perpetual nature of the war on terrorism.

The Economic Complex

This chapter now turns to the fourth component of the U.S. foreign policy bureaucracy, the economic complex. The end of the Cold War permitted American leaders to broaden their foreign policy agendas from concerns based primarily on

---

9. The U.S. actions, since acknowledged by government officials, also violated the UN Convention against Torture and Other Cruel, Inhuman or Degrading Treatment or Punishment. The convention, signed by President Reagan in 1988, declared that "no one shall be subjected to torture or to cruel, inhuman or degrading treatment or punishment."

military security, or geopolitics, to include concerns regarding the growing inter-action of national markets in the world economy, or **geoeconomics.** Among other consequences of the end of the Cold War was the widening support among gov-ernments for market-based economies rather than those dominated or strictly controlled by states. In short, the U.S. model of free enterprise and open markets became a role model of sorts for the postcommunist states of Eastern Europe, as well as for the industrialized states in East Asia, Latin America, and other areas. Economic globalization reinforced the rise of economic affairs on the U.S. foreign policy agenda, as did the nation's commanding lead in many sectors of the globalized economy.

Promoting national prosperity is, of course, an intermestic concern, with both international and domestic components. Well-organized groups represent the interests of private actors in the federal government, which provides many points of access within the executive and legislative branches. Congress plays a bigger role in economic affairs than in national security. The regulatory powers approved by Congress in areas such as labor practices, environmental standards, and product safety affect business activity in the United States and the commer-cial relations of U.S. firms with their foreign counterparts. Congress also must approve major trade agreements, although it has largely deferred to the executive branch in this area.

Finally, federalism is a major factor in foreign economic policy. American governors and mayors eagerly pursue foreign markets for the goods and services produced by their constituents. At the same time, states and cities compete with one another for the attention of foreign-owned firms planning to set up shop in the United States. The outcome of this internal competition has long-lasting implications for American political, as well as economic, relations abroad. At the federal level, various agencies such as the Treasury and Commerce Depart-ments have long engaged in different aspects of economic affairs. The most important institutional change in the economic complex occurred after World War II with the creation of the World Bank and the International Monetary Fund (IMF).

Taken together, these organizations form a highly fragmented economic com-plex with no discernible center of gravity (Destler 1994, 132). At the federal level, "different bureaucratic actors will assume leadership roles depending on the issue at hand and the strength of personal relationships between agency heads and the president's inner circle" (Cohen, Blecker, and Whitney 2003, 113). This structure, even more decentralized than the other foreign policy complexes described earlier, reflects a unique aspect of foreign economic policy, which is highly dependent on private firms and capital markets. Indeed, in the liberal global economy long pro-moted by U.S. leaders, the "invisible hand" of market forces should produce effi-ciency and prosperity without government intervention. While such a pure vision of free markets has proved to be an impossible dream in the real world, it remains embedded in the U.S. economic complex.

Key Players in Economic Policy

Among the array of agencies that play a role in advancing U.S. economic interests overseas (see Table 6.4), four merit special attention: the National Economic Council, the Office of the United States Trade Representative, and the Treasury and Commerce Departments. Taken together, these and other bureaucratic actors aim to improve U.S. competitiveness in world trade, capital, and labor markets, which have become so interconnected that one can now speak of a single world marketplace. The United States, which maintains the largest national economy, confronts serious problems in the form of massive budget and trade deficits and the decline of its manufacturing base. Meanwhile, the rapid growth of East Asian competitors and of those in India, Brazil, and the European Union have created a "multipolar" world economy—in stark contrast to the unipolar balance of military power that continues to favor the United States.

Table 6.4   Agencies of Foreign Economic Policy

Agency	Function
Council of Economic Advisers	Provides guidance to the White House on foreign economic policy
Department of Agriculture	Supports efforts by farmers and agricultural firms to sell products overseas
Department of Commerce	Promotes and manages interests of firms doing business overseas
Department of State	Manages day-to-day economic relations with foreign countries
Department of the Treasury	Manages U.S. financial issues such as private investment, monetary policy, and global debt
Federal Reserve Board	Makes decisions about the money supply and "prime rate" of interest offered to major borrowers
National Economic Council	Plays a coordinating role with the White House to align policies of all the agencies in the economic complex
National Security Council	Integrates economic issues into its consideration of national security policy
Office of Management and Budget	Manages fiscal policy for the federal government and develops the president's budget proposals for federal spending
Office of the U.S. Trade Representative	Gains access to foreign markets by negotiating bilateral and multilateral trade agreements

National Economic Council. Among Bill Clinton's first acts as president in 1993 was the creation, through executive order, of the National Economic Council (NEC). The eighteen members of the council include the president and vice president; the chair of the Council of Economic Advisers; the U.S. trade representative (see below); the director of the Office of Management and Budget; and the secretaries of agriculture, commerce, energy, labor, transportation, and the Treasury.[10] An assistant to the president for economic policy serves as director of the NEC and provides direct guidance to the president on all matters related to economic policy, foreign and domestic. President Clinton's executive order assigned four tasks to the NEC: (1) coordinate policy making on economic issues, (2) coordinate the flow of economic policy advice to the president, (3) ensure that economic policies are consistent with the president's goals, and (4) monitor implementation of economic policies. The NEC director has become more outspoken on policy issues in recent years. This more independent role "challenges the original notion of the NEC serving as an honest broker of the policy-making process" (Dolan and Rosati 2006).

U.S. Trade Representative. Concern about U.S. competitiveness in overseas trade markets has been a constant in the nation's history. This concern became more acute after World War II as the United States sought to preserve its status as the world's predominant economic power. In 1962, Congress created the Office of the United States Trade Representative (USTR), whose primary task is gaining access to foreign markets by negotiating bilateral and multilateral trade agreements. Contrary to the nation's free-market values, the USTR draws much of its political support from advocates of **protectionism**—that is, the manipulation of trade by governments in order to serve the interests of domestic stakeholders, including producers and consumers, at the expense of foreign competitors (Dryden 1995). The trade representative, who holds the rank of ambassador and sits on the president's cabinet, promotes the interests of producers who want to see the U.S. market closed to foreign countries that discriminate against their goods.

Treasury and Commerce Departments. Although many federal agencies support U.S. economic growth, two are most directly involved in foreign economic policy. First, the Treasury Department is considered the "steward" of the U.S. financial system. Its core duties, in addition to advising the White House on economic policy, include producing currency, collecting and disbursing federal funds, and borrowing money to cover the government's functions. In the foreign policy process, the Treasury Department imposes sanctions on foreign governments that are seen as threatening U.S. global interests (see Chapter 11). Second, the Commerce Department serves as an ally of U.S. firms, banks, and other private economic actors. Its officials support the USTR by promoting U.S. exports, by seeking new markets for U.S. goods and services, and by opposing tariffs and other barriers to overseas trade. The pro-business orientation of the Commerce Department is clear in the mission statement of its "Export.gov" program, which "brings together resources from across the U.S. government to assist American

---

10. Two deputy assistants serve on the NEC as specialists on domestic and foreign economic policy, respectively. In addition, a team of special assistants provides guidance on issues such as agriculture, energy, and global financial markets.

businesses in planning their international sales strategies and succeed in today's global marketplace."

International Financial Institutions

The conduct of U.S. foreign economic policy, like military alliances in the security complex, extends to financial institutions that are based in the United States but that have members, stakeholders, and ongoing programs worldwide. Two international financial institutions—the World Bank and the IMF—arose from the Bretton Woods conference of 1944 (see Chapter 2) and continue to hold a central position within the economic complex.

The World Bank offers low-interest loans, grants, and technical assistance to struggling economies for long-term development projects. Two agencies form the core of the World Bank Group, which has provided more than $510 billion in low-interest loans since World War II (World Bank 2007). The largest of these agencies is the International Bank for Reconstruction and Development, created in 1946 to manage the distribution of Marshall Plan loans to U.S. allies, primarily in Western Europe. The bank's focus then moved on to developing nations, many newly freed from colonial rule. The second agency, the International Development Association, helps the world's poorest countries to address immediate problems such as malnutrition and the HIV/AIDS epidemic. All World Bank presidents have been U.S. citizens appointed by the federal government, which located the bank's headquarters near the U.S. Treasury for more than symbolic reasons. The United States' contribution to the bank's budget (about 17 percent) is more than twice that of the second-largest contributor, Japan. Because the weight of member votes is based on their financial contributions, the United States effectively has veto power over loans, which must be supported by at least an 85 percent share of votes cast.

The IMF also plays an important role in the U.S. economic complex. A central lesson of the Great Depression was that governments must have confidence in the currencies and long-term stability of their trading partners. These governments quickly lose this confidence when they see those partners accumulating such large debts and suffering such high inflation rates that they cannot pay for routine government programs. The economic calamities that follow, including deep cuts in public services, defaults on foreign debts, political disarray, and social unrest, extend far beyond the individual debtors and creditors to include the world economy as a whole. In addition to helping the global system of "floating" exchange rates operate smoothly, the IMF serves three other functions: (1) monitoring the fiscal and monetary policies of member states; (2) lending money at "concessional" rates to IMF members in financial distress; and (3) providing technical assistance or advice on matters such as national accounting, tax policies, and the strengthening of individual economic sectors.

Both Bretton Woods institutions are widely perceived, first and foremost, as instruments of U.S. economic power (see Blustein 2001). To its critics, the World Bank has unfairly required foreign governments to adopt U.S. free-market policies in return for emergency loans, has repeatedly "subsidized" repressive governments, and has supported numerous development projects that harm the environment. The IMF, labeled by one analyst the "poster child for the evils of globalization" (Willett 2001, 594), is blamed for a variety of economic calamities, including the collapse of market reforms in Russia, the East Asian economic crisis in the late 1990s, and the more recent outbreak of social unrest in Argentina and other Latin American states. Defenders of both institutions counter that they enforce discipline that is often lacking in cash-strapped governments and that their refusal to aid governments such as those of Russia, Mexico, and South Korea would have produced greater distress to their people and the world economy (see Eichengreen 2002 and Rogoff 2003).

Another international financial institution—the World Trade Organization (WTO)—is not formally part of the U.S. government, unlike the World Bank and the IMF. Still, the WTO advances a cause long embraced by American leaders: unrestricted cross-border trade in goods and services. As described more fully in Chapter 11, after World War II the White House favored the creation of such a trade body, but protectionists in Congress rejected this plan. A series of multilateral trade agreements widened the scope of free trade for nearly fifty years, after which the WTO came into being as a permanent international financial institution based in Geneva, Switzerland. For the managers of the U.S. economic complex, the WTO supports U.S. geoeconomic goals by encouraging the "invisible hand" of market forces to determine trade practices rather than restrictions imposed by self-interested states. Although the United States has been sanctioned by the WTO for its own protectionist policies, the WTO's penalties against dozens of other governments have benefited U.S. exporters and the nation's larger foreign policy interests.

Conclusion

In implementing foreign policy, bureaucrats maintain their places on the front lines of the policy process and continue to determine, in large measure, the success or failure of policy initiatives adopted by the president and Congress. And yet, while actively pursuing more personnel and greater influence, agencies have resisted the sweeping changes in their organizational structures and missions long advocated by critics inside and outside the U.S. government. Despite the creation of an intelligence "czar," the intelligence agencies remain highly antagonistic toward one another. Meanwhile, the National Security Council rarely meets formally as originally planned because presidents freely consult with various members of their inner circles as needed.

Similarly, despite moves toward "jointness," the Pentagon continues to struggle with rivalries among the armed services and public disputes over funding, arms programs, and missions. Only the September 11 terrorist attacks and subsequent arms buildup prevented Defense Secretary Rumsfeld from succumbing to pressure from the armed services and giving up on military transformation. Even so, a truly unified military, as envisioned in the 1947 National Security Act, remains a distant and remote possibility. "The conspicuous silence of defense experts on this issue at the end of the Cold War can only be understood as proof of the institutionalized clout that the separate services had acquired over the previous five decades" (Stuart 2003, 305).

The U.S. foreign policy bureaucracy exhibits two entrenched but contradictory patterns: the *centralization* of authority within the White House and the *fragmentation* of control across a far-flung bureaucracy. From managing military crises to negotiating trade deals, presidents and their advisers have sought, and have generally been granted, greater authority to conduct foreign policy. As a result, this authority has shifted within the executive branch from the State Department and other federal agencies to the White House. At the same time, the size, scope, and intricacy of the foreign policy complexes described in this chapter have increased steadily since the current structure was devised after World War II.

In summary, national security concerns reinforce the *centripetal forces* (those centralizing power) of U.S. foreign policy, while bureaucratic politics and organizational processes propel *centrifugal forces* (those decentralizing power). These tensions between centralization and fragmentation reflect the paradox of world power wielded by the United States today. The sources of these tensions—unprecedented global clout, a dynamic civil society, and a political system designed to hinder foreign policy making—are likely to become even more pronounced in the years to come. To some observers, the sheer mass of the foreign policy bureaucracy makes the United States a "headless monster" that is incapable of acting in a coherent and consistent manner. To others, such a bureaucracy is inevitable—and generally effective—in the world's most powerful nation. How these tensions and contradictions are reconciled, therefore, will have long-lasting implications for the formulation and conduct of U.S. foreign policy.

Key Terms

celebrity diplomacy, p. 180

Church Committee, p. 200

civil-military relations, p. 174

clientitis, p. 182

complex irregular warfare, p. 189

counterintelligence, p. 193

covert operations, p. 193

diplomacy, p. 176

elitism, p. 182

extraordinary rendition, p. 201

finished intelligence, p. 193

foreign service officers, p. 178

geoeconomics, p. 202

Goldwater-Nichols Act, p. 186

human intelligence (HUMINT), p. 193

image intelligence (IMINT), p. 193

intelligence cycle, p. 193

intelligence gap, p. 192

military transformation, p. 188

national security adviser, p. 184

organizational culture, p. 174

organizational process, p. 174

path dependency, p. 172

protectionism, p. 204

raw intelligence, p. 193

regional integration, p. 188

revolution in military affairs, p. 188

signal intelligence (SIGINT), p. 193

Internet References

The **Center on Budget and Policy Priorities** (www.cbpp.org) focuses on federal and state budget priorities, including research on taxes and spending. Projects of interest deal with analysis of military spending, specific foreign policy spending, and tax burdens for national security.

The **Central Intelligence Agency** (www.cia.gov) operates a Web site that provides detailed information on the CIA's mission as well as about global developments. The *CIA World Factbook,* available online, contains comprehensive political, economic, military, and other data on all nation-states.

CRS Reports (http://fpc.state.gov/c18185.htm; www.fas.org/sgp/crs/index.html) from the Congressional Research Service, the research arm of Congress, provide briefings on specific policy issues and include background information, chronologies, bibliographic references, and budget statistics.

The Web site for the **Department of Defense** (www.defenselink.mil) presents reports on defense-related activities and specific programs, along with information on the military and its past operations. In addition, news releases, speeches, and transcripts from defense officials on topics such as casualties, funding, and officer assignments are available. Also included are links to agencies within the Defense Department as well as a list of online publications such as the defense budget, *Defense Almanac,* and reports on capabilities and security measures.

The newest cabinet agency, the **Department of Homeland Security** (www.dhs.gov), offers consistent updates on the war on terrorism as well as missions to contain and combat domestic terrorism. The site also has information on immigration, border control, and policies related to emergency actions. Speeches, documents, and research links are provided as well.

The **Department of State** (www.state.gov) is vested with many aspects of diplomacy, including foreign aid, peace building, democratization, and disease and poverty reduction, as well as other aspects of the U.S. foreign policy process. The State Department's Web site includes speeches, policy descriptions, and issue explanations for those studying U.S. foreign policy.

The **Government Accountability Office** (www.gao.gov) evaluates and reports on congressional and presidential decision making, budgets, and policies. Included on its Web site are audits, evaluations, and policy analysis reports on intergovernmental relations and policy decisions.

The **International Monetary Fund** (www.imf.org) promotes a more stable global economy by enhancing monetary cooperation and aiding countries in distress. The IMF's Web site provides details on its financial programs, along with country-by-country economic data and reports on current issues such as globalization, rural poverty, financial regulation, and debt relief.

(continued)

Internet References *(continued)*

The Web site of the **Office of the United States Trade Representative** (www.ustr.gov) provides links and access to bilateral and multilateral trade data and events. Researchers will find the information on NAFTA, the WTO, and free trade negotiations particularly helpful. Speeches, testimony, trade legislation, and daily updates on international trade are also posted on this site.

The Web site for the **U.S. Intelligence Community** (www.intelligence.gov) offers information on the organization of all U.S. intelligence agencies and their relationships toward each other and the government as a whole. Meetings and special report findings on national and international intelligence are summarized on this site, which is broader in scope than the CIA Web site.

The **World Bank** (www.worldbank.org) is an intergovernmental organization that focuses on economic development and growth. Its Web site includes speeches, project summaries, regional analyses, and data resources on global trends for all countries.

CHAPTER 7

Public Opinion at Home and Abroad

A Filipino surplus vendor watches President Barack Obama's January 2010 State of the Union address from his shop in Manila. Obama sought not only the support of Congress and American citizens in his speech; he also reached out to global public opinion for approval as he began his second year in the White House.

The previous section of this book focused on the government actors engaged in the formulation and conduct of U.S. foreign policy. This section shifts to the "outside-in" forces—public opinion, the news media, and interest groups—that seek to influence the foreign policy process from many vantage points, domestic and foreign. Trends in world politics increase the importance of this external dimension, which blurs common distinctions between domestic and foreign policy and between private and public life.

This chapter explores the impact of public opinion on U.S. foreign policy. This is a critical concern given the central place of private citizens in the governance of a democratic polity. For a nation "of the people, by the people, for the people"—Abraham Lincoln's famous construction in his Gettysburg Address—public opinion provides an essential guide for government action. As we will find, however, this role is controversial and has varied significantly over time. Moreover, since the American "public" is highly fragmented among diverse groups with differing interests, it rarely sends a unified signal to policy makers. Deepening U.S. trade with China, for example, has pleased corporate and banking interests while angering religious groups and human rights activists (see Chapter 3). Finding consensus in such a fragmented environment is a difficult, often futile task. Political leaders do not passively await the public's verdict on their actions. Instead, they actively *gauge* citizens' attitudes in advance and base their decisions, at least in part, on the likely response. In this respect, public opinion plays the productive role envisioned by democratic theorists—that of increasing the likelihood that government policies will reflect public preferences. Yet leaders also *manipulate* public opinion in several ways: by focusing on particular issues in speeches and interviews, by strategically timing their actions to gain political advantage, and by creatively interpreting (or "spinning") developments overseas. Policy makers, well aware of the general population's lack of knowledge about most foreign policy problems, can expect their depictions of friends and foes to be accepted readily (Ginsberg 1986).

The manipulation of public opinion is hardly unique to the current period. As Seymour Martin Lipset (1966, 20) noted more than four decades ago, the president "makes opinion, he does not follow it. The polls tell him how good a politician he is." Such efforts have become more refined in recent years with the emergence of more sophisticated polling techniques, the use of carefully targeted focus groups, and new outlets of mass communication, particularly the Internet. A **public relations presidency** exists today as presidents "act in deliberate ways to achieve heightened popularity in the polls and in elections" (Brace and Hinckley 1993, 383). The ability of presidents to "make" public opinion is especially strong in foreign policy because of their high profile and expansive powers in this area and because of Americans' general preoccupation with domestic affairs. Foreign policy provides further leverage for presidents since most issues have little material impact on citizens and groups, unlike domestic issues such as health care, unemployment, education, and tax policy, in which citizens are direct stakeholders.

Still, foreign policy makers cannot ignore public opinion if they wish to maintain domestic support for their actions overseas. Those who voted for the president expect that his campaign promises on foreign policy will be honored. This is especially true of societal groups—based on common ethnicities, economic needs, devotion to human rights, and other shared interests—that follow closely the foreign policies that affect them directly. The foreign policy behavior of U.S. leaders is constrained not simply by explicit societal demands, but also by **latent public opinion**—that is, the unstated but deeply held views of private citizens that apply to ongoing policy problems (Stimson 1991). Such views create a range of publicly acceptable policy actions; those "likely to generate widespread public opposition are dismissed from active consideration" (Powlick and Katz 1998, 44).

Public opinion matters increasingly outside the United States as well, as foreign policy makers appeal to citizens and governments overseas for support. This has been especially true since the end of the Cold War, which, paradoxically, not only left the United States unmatched in power but also highly vulnerable to external scrutiny and criticism by foreign observers. The growing impact of world public opinion stems from several sources: the advance of information technologies, the growth of civil societies in response to democratic reforms, and the wider array of issues and problems that cross national borders, to name a few. In addition to making global public opinion more important, these trends have created and solidified transnational norms regarding appropriate foreign policy behavior and raised expectations that political leaders will follow them.

President Bill Clinton's adoption of "assertive multilateralism" during the 1990s was designed, in part, to strengthen the U.S. government's appeal overseas. The United States, however, dismayed other governments and mass publics in the new millennium by turning away from the international community. The surge in anti-American sentiment extended to the typically friendly states of Europe, whose citizens differed with U.S. policy makers on global threats, the merits of higher levels of military spending, and—most troubling for Washington—the long-term costs and benefits of U.S. world power (Kennedy and Bouton 2002). George W. Bush's decision to invade Iraq in 2003 without the endorsement of the UN Security Council incited anti-American movements overseas far beyond Europe (Pew Research Center 2005).

These trends have important consequences for U.S. foreign policy. Widespread antagonism toward Washington erodes the legitimacy of U.S. world power. Actions by American leaders that ignore the views and interests of allies discourage cooperation on counterterrorism and other issues that demand joint effort for effective problem solving. Anti-Americanism, meanwhile, provides an opening for adversaries that wish to weaken U.S. alliance ties. These dangers have become apparent to American citizens and a cause for strong concern. In a statistical review by the Council on Foreign Relations (2009, 1, 4), dozens of recent surveys produced consistent findings that

> Americans support an international order based on international law. A majority believes that international laws create normative obligations like domestic law and rejects the view that nations should not feel obliged to abide by international law when doing so is at odds with their national interest. . . . Americans favor a world order either based on a balance of regional powers or led by the United Nations, rather than a system based on hegemony or bipolarity. Large majorities reject a hegemonic role for the United States, but do want the United States to participate in multilateral issues.

President Obama, upon accepting the Nobel Peace Prize in December 2009, acknowledged the need for restored U.S. credibility in domestic and global public opinion. "America—in fact, no nation—can insist that others follow the rules of the road if we refuse to follow them ourselves," he said. "For when we don't, our actions appear arbitrary and undercut the legitimacy of future interventions, no matter how justified." The president's return to a multilateral foreign policy, and one favoring diplomatic cooperation over military competition, reflected not just his political principles and priorities as laid out in his long 2008 presidential

Table 7.1 Global Public Opinion of U.S. Foreign Policy, 2009

Question: "In our government's relations with the United States, do you think the U.S. more often treats us fairly or abuses its greater power to make us do what the U.S. wants?"

Country	Treats us fairly	Abuses its great power
China	14%	76%
France	26	68
Great Britain	27	68
Indonesia	21	63
Mexico	10	87
Pakistan	6	90
Poland	20	65
Russia	12	75
South Korea	17	81
Turkey	9	86

SOURCE: World Public Opinion, "America's Global Image in the Obama Era," July 7, 2009, p. 3, www.worldpublicopinion.org.

campaign. His shift in U.S. foreign policy also was eagerly sought by the general public, which elected Obama to office with this priority in mind.

Although this return to the international community had great appeal, Obama faced an uphill battle in overcoming the distrust and resentment that lingered in most countries. From Great Britain to China and Russia, large majorities of citizens still felt unfairly treated and abused by the United States (see Table 7.1). Foreign leaders closely followed the president's response to these pressures. While allies looked hopefully for leadership from Washington, adversaries sought to exploit gaps between Obama's words and deeds. These leaders also considered the president's statements as signals for their own foreign policy decisions, well aware that "bandwagoning" with Washington can produce added security and economic benefits but may also spark bitter dissent and challenges to their own political power.[1] In all cases, the United States retained its unique ability to gauge the mood and temperament of global public opinion.

Democracy and the Paradox of World Power

Since its beginnings, the U.S. government has expected individuals and groups to insert themselves into the policy process, expressing their wishes to policy makers. In the democratic model, elected leaders are servants, rather than masters, of the private citizens who voted those leaders into office. For this reason, recognizing

---

1. The most prominent recent victim of close relations with the United States was Tony Blair, Great Britain's former prime minister, whose support for the U.S. war in Iraq led to his political demise.

public preferences and providing "constituent service" are viewed as essential responsibilities of elected officials.

Fundamental tensions often exist, however, between democratic governance and foreign policy. Short-term electoral pressures divert the judgment of policy makers and legislators from long-term concerns, including transnational problems that affect the "global commons" (see Chapter 12). Openness, an essential quality of democratic governance, can also be a liability when intelligence secrets are leaked to the press for partisan advantage or when domestic debates reveal a lack of national unity. These inescapable by-products of modern democracy are confronted by all countries with internally fragmented governments and robust civil societies. The costs are magnified in the United States, whose foreign policies profoundly affect other countries and the overall climate of world politics.

Americans' influence on government action is also highly uneven, which further impairs the democratic process. As one analyst (Schattschneider 1960) observed half a century ago, most American citizens are "semi-sovereign" given the dominance of powerful interest groups, particularly corporations, in shaping domestic and foreign policies (see Chapter 9). Few observers dispute that the U.S. government maintains **procedural democracy** in the form of regular elections, but many doubt whether a **substantive democracy** exists that truly empowers the majority of citizens on a day-to-day basis (Key 1961). This problem is reflected in studies of public opinion, which find that U.S. citizens, in their impact on foreign policy, can be divided into three categories:

- The **foreign policy elite,** who comprise no more than 1 percent of the general public but hold powerful positions in government, business, and interest groups. These elites, also known as opinion leaders, are often engaged directly in issues relating to U.S. foreign policy and are able to guide or manipulate public opinion as they see fit.

- The **attentive public,** about 15 percent of the population, includes policy analysts, government bureaucrats, scholars, journalists, and political activists with substantial knowledge of global issues. This group is "inclined to participate, but still lacks the access or opportunity to do so" (Rosenau 1961, 33).

- The **mass public,** the vast majority of American citizens, are neither well informed about nor interested in most foreign policy issues. Because these issues generally have little salience, or direct impact on citizens, they open the door for elites and special interests to determine policies.

On key issues such as war and peace, the mass public takes a strong interest but generally defers to the views of elites as covered in the news media (Zaller 1992). Otherwise, foreign policy elites direct most of their efforts at the attentive public, whose concurrence on policy matters may be reflected in favorable news coverage, supportive research findings, and financial contributions to political campaigns. In this respect, the attentive public serves as a courier of elite "signals"

Figure 7.1   Interest and Influence in U.S. Foreign Policy: A "Semi-Sovereign" Public?

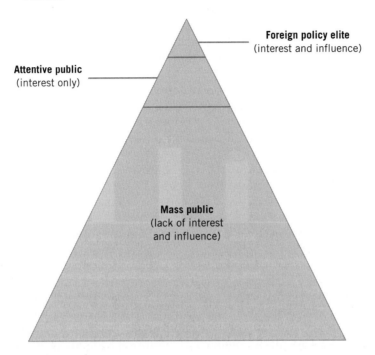

Foreign policy elite
(interest and influence)

Attentive public
(interest only)

Mass public
(lack of interest
and influence)

to the mass public, a crucial role that renders this group a pivotal source of public opinion (see Figure 7.1). For most Americans, these signals are sufficient to inform their own views on specific issues; further scrutiny of most matters of foreign policy is best left to the experts.

Rival Views of Political Leadership

Political theorists have long disagreed about the public's ideal role in shaping policy. Two general models of political representation capture this schism in democratic governance. The **delegate model** holds that elected officials should reflect the general public's preferences on a given issue, making decisions based on the majority view. In short, officials should act as they believe their "constituents should want" (Pitkin 1967, 147) and not allow their personal preferences to enter into the equation. Abraham Lincoln expressed this view to the House of Representatives in July 1848, when he declared as the "primary, the cardinal, the one great living principle of all democratic representative government—the principle that the representative is bound to carry out the known will of his constituents."

By contrast, the **trustee model** prefers that elected officials be granted greater flexibility and autonomy than is envisioned in the more restrictive delegate model.

This more conservative view is most often associated with Edmund Burke, the eighteenth-century British statesman and political theorist who did not consider the mass public qualified to make informed judgments about public policy. Burke, living in an era of widespread illiteracy and ignorance, argued that representatives should follow their own, more "enlightened" beliefs about what is best for the body politic. He believed that "your representative owes you not his industry only, but his judgment; and he betrays, instead of serving you, if he sacrifices it to your opinion" (quoted in Hofman and Levack 1949, 115). Vice president Dick Cheney applied this view to the current era when, in response to a press question regarding whether he follows public opinion, he replied, "No. . . . I think you cannot be blown off course by the fluctuations in the public opinion polls" (World Public Opinion 2008).

This historic debate about the role of political leadership in democratic governance is related directly to the two primary bodies of international relations theory, realism and liberalism (see Chapter 3). Recall that realists have a pessimistic view of world politics and the prospects for peaceful cooperation. They base this pessimism, in part, on a bleak assessment of human nature, which they believe to be plagued by momentary passions, ignorance, and hostility toward others. For this reason, realists cast a skeptical eye on public opinion as a reliable guide to foreign policy. "The government is the leader of public opinion, not its slave," observed Hans Morgenthau (1967, 547–548), a prominent realist and proponent of the trustee model. "Especially when foreign policy is conducted under conditions of democratic control and is inspired by the crusading zeal of a political religion, statesmen are always tempted to sacrifice the requirements of good foreign policy to the applause of the masses."

Realists believe citizens may be competent to participate in matters of local governance that touch their day-to-day lives, such as education, but that most are not competent to do so in foreign policy matters, which are more removed from daily life, as well as generally more complex, than local issues. Furthermore, foreign policy makers rely on classified information that, by necessity, gives them a more informed view about the problems faced and alternative solutions. The need for quick, decisive action also works against a strong public role in the foreign policy process.

Liberal theories of world politics provide a more positive view of the public's role in foreign policy. During the Enlightenment era, liberal European theorists such as Jeremy Bentham, Immanuel Kant, and Jean-Jacques Rousseau had great confidence in the reason and judgment of the mass public, whose views of foreign as well as domestic affairs, they believed, should be followed closely by elected leaders. In modern times, Woodrow Wilson is the president most closely associated with the liberal view and its application to U.S. foreign policy. In a September 1918 speech entitled "America's Purpose," Wilson argued that private citizens rather than political leaders had the stronger grasp of the war's true meaning:

> It is the peculiarity of this great war that, while statesmen have seemed to cast about
> for definitions of their purpose and have sometimes seemed to shift their ground and

their point of view, the thought of the mass of men, whom statesmen are supposed to instruct and lead, has grown more and more unclouded, more and more certain of what it is they are fighting for. National purposes have fallen more and more into the background; and the common purpose of enlightened mankind has taken their place. . . . That is why I have said that this is a people's war, not a statesman's.

This debate over the public's role in the governance of democracies continues today. In going to war against Iraq in 2003, President Bush acted contrary to polls that showed the public opposed military action in the absence of widespread support from U.S. allies and the UN Security Council. Bush's rationale—that decisive leadership was needed, even if it was unpopular—placed him squarely in the trustee camp. For those favoring the delegate model, the problems that subsequently plagued the U.S. occupation of Iraq reinforced their position that the "general will" of American citizens must be heard and heeded.

Mood Swings or Pragmatism?

The penchant for U.S. citizens to look inward is nothing new. When French sociologist Alexis de Tocqueville toured the United States in the early 1830s, he found Americans to be far less interested in public affairs than their European counterparts. "Intent only on getting rich, they do not notice the close connection between private fortunes and the general prosperity. They find it a tiresome inconvenience to exercise political rights which distract them from industry" (Tocqueville [1835] 1988, 540).

Scholars in the early twentieth century echoed Tocqueville's concerns about the public's role in U.S. public affairs. Walter Lippmann (1922), a prominent journalist and social commentator, faulted Americans for ignoring German expansionism in Europe until it threatened their own country and forced the U.S. entry into World War I. The same criticism came after World War II, when popular commentators and prominent scholars cited the U.S. public's apathy during the interwar period as a contributing factor in the rise of fascist regimes in Europe and Asia (see Bailey 1948; Kriesberg 1949; and Almond 1950).

Gabriel Almond's 1950 book, *The American People and Foreign Policy,* provided a bleak view of the connection between public attitudes and U.S. foreign policy. Drawing on survey data provided by the newly founded Gallup Organization, Almond (1950, 71) complained that Americans generally felt so secure at home that "foreign policy, save in moments of grave crisis, has to labor under a handicap; it has to shout loudly to be heard even a little." Making matters worse, he argued, were the "mood swings" in public opinion that led to constantly shifting demands for global activism and withdrawal.[2]

The similarities between this view and Lippmann's produced what became known as the **Almond-Lippmann consensus,** which is based on three assumptions (Holsti 1992). First, public opinion is *volatile,* shifting erratically in response to

---

2. See Holmes (1985) and Klingberg (1983) for later analyses of "mood swings" in U.S. public opinion.

Point/Counterpoint
MASTERS VS. PAWNS OF U.S. FOREIGN POLICY

A primary and enduring debate in the realm of public opinion and U.S. foreign policy is whether the general public is fit to guide political leaders in managing relations with other countries. Skeptics such as political scientist Gabriel Almond find that Americans tend to be well informed only about immediate concerns. "But on questions of a remote nature, such as foreign policy, they tend to react in more undifferentiated ways, with formless and plastic moods which undergo frequent alteration in response to changes in events," Almond wrote in 1950. "The characteristic response to questions of foreign policy is one of indifference. A foreign policy crisis . . . may transform indifference to vague apprehension, to fatalism, to anger; but the reaction is still a mood, a superficial and fluctuating response."

According to political scientist Bruce Jentleson, more recent studies have contradicted "the traditional view of the public as boorish, overreactive, and generally the bane of those who would pursue an effective foreign policy." Citizens are not easily manipulated by presidents, these studies suggest, and citizens are able to distinguish between vital U.S. interests worth defending and nonvital interests that should not be pursued at the cost of American lives. "It is difficult to explain much of the foreign policy behavior of the United States during the mid- to late-1970s," political scientist Eugene R. Wittkopf has observed, "without some sense of the constraining forces of the Vietnam Syndrome that the Ford and Carter administrations must surely have perceived."

Nevertheless, the debate over public opinion continues today. Surveys conducted in 2003–2004 revealed widespread public misperceptions about the U.S. invasion of Iraq, including the view that Saddam Hussein had been an accomplice in the September 11 terrorist attacks. These erroneous views proved remarkably persistent despite a steady stream of evidence to the contrary. As Almond predicted, U.S. leaders continue to exploit gaps in public attentiveness to foreign affairs and pursue their own course in foreign policy, knowing that citizens will follow their lead.

SOURCES: Gabriel Almond, *The American People and Foreign Policy* (New York: Harcourt, Brace, 1950), 53; Bruce W. Jentleson, "The Pretty Prudent Public: Post Post-Vietnam American Opinion on the Use of Military Force," *International Studies Quarterly* 36 (March 1992): 71; Eugene R. Wittkopf, *Faces of Internationalism: Public Opinion and U.S. Foreign Policy* (Durham: Duke University Press, 1990), 219.

---

the most recent developments. Mass beliefs early in the twentieth century were "too pacifist in peace and too bellicose in war, too neutralist or appeasing in negotiations or too intransigent" (Lippmann 1955, 20). Second, public opinion is *incoherent*, lacking an organized or a consistent structure to such an extent that the views of U.S. citizens could best be described as "nonattitudes" (Converse

Table 7.2 Support for Active U.S. Participation in World Affairs, 1974–2000 (percentage of support by each group)

Year	Public	Elites/leaders
1974	74%	99%
1978	67	99
1982	61	99
1986	70	99
1990	69	98
1994	69	99
1998	68	97
2000	70	98

SOURCE: Chicago Council on Foreign Relations, "Worldviews 2002: American Public Opinion and Foreign Policy" (2002), www.worldviews.org/detailreports/usreport/index.htm.

1964). Finally, public opinion is *irrelevant* to the policy-making process. Political leaders ignore public opinion because most Americans can neither "understand nor influence the very events upon which their lives and happiness are known to depend" (Kris and Leites 1947, 393).

In contrast, more recent research challenges this gloomy assessment, detecting greater consistency and coherence in mass attitudes and greater concern among decision makers with public opinion than the early pessimists allowed. Surveys conducted since 1974 by the Chicago Council on Foreign Relations register ongoing support among the public, as well as foreign policy elites, for active U.S. participation in foreign affairs (see Table 7.2). Although the mass public tends to be more nationalistic on economic issues than elites, especially the protection of U.S. jobs against foreign competition (Page and Barabas 2000), both groups favor U.S. engagement in the United Nations and other forms of multilateral cooperation. Small segments of the public do consider themselves to be "isolationist," but most favor an internationalist foreign policy. The only question among these citizens is whether the United States should pursue a policy of **militant internationalism** or **cooperative internationalism** (Wittkopf 1990). Whereas realists, embracing a competitive and zero-sum worldview, prefer the former approach, liberals favor active government collaboration and pooling of resources.

At its core, public opinion is reducible to the belief systems of individual citizens, whose normative values and presumptions about human nature, the state, and society shape their judgments about foreign policy (see Chapter 3). In this respect, the dichotomy between militant and cooperative internationalism reflects a more subtle difference in the level of **international trust** felt by individuals. An extension of political trust (Hetherington 1998), which is a generalized faith in government, international trust hinges on the perception that "most foreign countries behave in accordance with normative expectations regarding the conduct of nations" (Brewer et al. 2004, 96, 105). Although many Americans—the cooperative internationalists—see the world as generally benign, the majority "believe the United States is surrounded by untrustworthy nations seeking their own advantage." Such perceptions dictate policy opinions on a broad spectrum of global issues such as UN peacekeeping, foreign aid, and nuclear proliferation.

Other surveys contradict the notion of incoherent public opinion. Even though test scores and survey research find the public to be generally ill informed, citizens seem to approach foreign policy problems with deeply held principles, values, and standards of evaluation (Graber 2006). Public opposition to the Korean and Vietnam Wars, for example, corresponded logically with growing U.S. casualties in each conflict (Mueller 1970; 1973). At other times, citizens responded pragmatically to perceived excesses in presidential behavior. For example, whereas Jimmy Carter's "dovish" foreign policies in the late 1970s prompted public calls for a tougher response to Soviet aggression, Ronald Reagan's "hawkish" approach alarmed many Americans and led to public appeals for moderation (Nincic 1988). Both presidents altered their approaches to foreign policy in part because of public dissatisfaction.

From this perspective, Americans do not suffer from "mood swings," but instead react in a reasoned and predictable manner to problems facing the United States (Mayer 1992). Unless they are experts in world politics, private citizens evaluate a problem on the basis of their underlying beliefs and values (Page and Shapiro 1992). During the Cold War, Americans evaluated possible military interventions on a case-by-case basis rather than supporting or opposing the use of force across the board (Jentleson 1992; see also Peffley and Hurwitz 1992).

The same can be said of public opinion since the Cold War. One of the public's core beliefs—that U.S. power should be applied only to repel clear threats to vital national interests—produced support for military intervention in some situations (such as the Persian Gulf War and Afghanistan) and calls for restraint in others (such as Rwanda, the former Yugoslavia, and Iraq). Once an intervention is under way, support for its continuation has hinged largely on public assessments of whether the mission would ultimately succeed or fail (Kull and Ramsay 2001). Fluctuations in public opinion thus have more to do with the *context* of foreign policy problems than with the general population's lack of understanding (see Larson 1996).

The Almond-Lippmann assumption that public opinion is irrelevant in the policy process is contradicted by elected officials' vigorous efforts to gauge and manipulate that opinion in recent years. All presidents since John F. Kennedy have created elaborate polling operations within the White House to guide their decisions in foreign and domestic policy (see Jacobs and Shapiro 1995). In the 1990s, Bill Clinton was so concerned about public opinion that he shaped the nation's military strategy in Bosnia and Kosovo around the need to maintain support for both interventions (Stephanopoulos 1999). The growing reliance of presidents on public diplomacy, described in Chapter 8, further demonstrates the relevance of public opinion—even to "trustees" prone to override majority preferences.

America's Knowledge Gap

Paradoxically, despite their ready access to the policy process, U.S. citizens tend to be poorly informed about the world around them. Although most Americans believe the nation should play an active role in world politics, they commonly focus their energies on local and state problems unless the United States is directly threatened with or involved in an international crisis or major military conflict (Sobel 2001). For example, as is typical when the country is enjoying peace and prosperity, U.S. public interest in foreign affairs declined in the 1990s, after the Cold War ended. The September 2001 terrorist attacks disrupted this period of complacency, although domestic issues and scandals soon captured most headlines—and public attention. "Today, the apparent political ignorance of the ordinary citizen is one of the most thoroughly documented and lamented facts about U.S. politics" (Lee 2002, 297; see also Neuman 1986).

Cultural detachment from the "outside world" has a long tradition in the United States, reflecting the nation's geographic distance from other major powers as well as an "exceptional" national identity deeply rooted in U.S. political culture (see Chapter 1). This lack of knowledge about global events has held constant throughout the nation's geographic expansion and subsequent emergence as the world's predominant power—and despite the nation's pervasive overseas presence (see Table 7.3). The U.S. educational system has reinforced rather than remedied this problem. In nationwide tests conducted in 2001, more than three-quarters of high school students failed to demonstrate proficiency in history and geography, two areas consistently neglected in public schools (U.S. Department of Education 2002).[3]

The latest National Geographic (2006) survey, discussed in Chapter 1, revealed deeper problems than a nationwide inability to locate Afghanistan and Iraq on a world map. Nearly 30 percent of the sample of young adults aged eighteen to twenty-four estimated the U.S. population to be, not at the actual level of about 300 million, but at 1–2 *billion*. Nearly half believed India, whose massive population is predominantly Hindu, has the world's largest *Islamic* population. Nearly two-thirds could not recall, less than three months after the event, that the catastrophic earthquake that claimed seventy thousand lives in October 2005 occurred in Pakistan. And nearly three-quarters wrongly identified English as the most widely spoken primary language in the world (it is Mandarin Chinese).

The lack of public knowledge about foreign affairs has tangible consequences for public opinion. Almost 60 percent of Americans in another survey reported having little or no knowledge about Islam (Council on American-Islamic Relations 2006). The same pool of respondents reported widespread antagonism toward Muslims, with an average of 25 percent agreeing with the following state-

---

3. Raising concerns about future trends, a 2010 survey by the Annie E. Casey Foundation, entitled "Early Warning," found that 67 percent of American fourth graders were "below proficient" in reading.

Table 7.3 U.S. Public Knowledge about World Affairs: Nationwide Survey Results, 1942–2008

Question topic (survey year)	Percentage able to answer
India a British colony (1942)	51%
Role of foreign aid (1958)	48
U.S. secretary of state (2008)	42
Soviet Union not in NATO (1964)	41
Purpose of NATO (1988)	40
President of Russia (2007)	36
President of France (1986)	34
Two signatories of SALT (1979)	30
Prime minister of Great Britain (2008)	28
Serb genocide in Bosnia (1994)	27
Location of Persian Gulf (1988)	25
U.S. secretary of defense (2007)	21
U.S. national security adviser (1977)	17
Location of Common Market (1961)	13
Secretary general of UN (1953)	10
President of Mexico (1991)	3

SOURCES: Michael X. Delli Carpini and Scott Keeter, *What Americans Know about Politics and Why It Matters* (New Haven: Yale University Press, 1996), ch. 2; Pew Research Center for the People and the Press, *What Americans Know: 1989–2007* (April 15, 2007), http://people-press.org/reports/pdf/319.pdf; and Pew Research Center for the People and the Press, *Key New Audiences Now Blend Online and Traditional Sources* (August 17, 2008), http://people-press.org/reports/pdf/444.pdf.

ments: "Muslims value life less than others"; "Muslims teach children to hate"; and "Islam teaches violence."

Is this knowledge gap limited to the mass public? Apparently not. In 2006, when journalist Jeff Stein interviewed U.S. counterterrorism officials, his final question was, "Do you know the difference between a Sunni and a Shiite?" He expected that his sources would have considerable knowledge of the two Islamic sects that were primary antagonists in Iraq's burgeoning civil war. "But, so far, most American officials I've interviewed don't have a clue," Stein observed in the *New York Times*. "That includes not just intelligence and law enforcement officials, but also members of Congress who have important roles overseeing our spy agencies. How can they do their jobs without knowing the basics?" (Stein 2006).

When ordinary citizens lack knowledge about a particular U.S. foreign policy, they rely on "cues" from opinion leaders that are often misleading or simply false (Zaller and Chiu 1996). For example, surveys conducted in 2003–2004 revealed widespread public misperceptions about the U.S. invasion of Iraq, including the view that Iraqi leader Saddam Hussein had been an accomplice in the September 11 terrorist attacks. These erroneous views persisted despite a steady stream of evidence to the contrary. In this respect, the "marketplace of ideas," assumed to reveal the truth in democratic societies through rigorous public scrutiny and debate, broke down in the months preceding the 2003 invasion. The American public, still reeling from the September 2001 terrorist attacks, proved highly susceptible to White House claims that Iraq posed a clear and present danger. The societal forces expected to impose such scrutiny, including the press and the opposition political party, failed to serve this societal check-and-balance function (Kaufmann 2004). "All of this has contributed to a political and policymaking environment in which political leaders are (compared to previous historical periods) relatively free to ignore or misperceive public opinion on foreign affairs" (Shapiro and Jacobs 2002, 200).

Misperceptions plague U.S. public opinion and foreign policy in other ways as well. Research has shown, for example, that members of Congress, when considering future votes on foreign policy issues, wrongly perceive that the public favors unilateral policies (Kull and Destler 1999; Todorov and Mandisodza 2004). To the contrary, repeated surveys find that the public and elites share preferences for U.S. participation in the United Nations, the World Trade Organization, and the International Criminal Court, as well as U.S. support for the Kyoto Protocol on Climate Change and the Comprehensive Test Ban Treaty. On such issues, "leaders generally underestimate the consistency between their views and the general public" (Chicago Council on Foreign Relations, Program on International Policy Attitudes 2004, 11). Virulent congressional attacks on the United Nations and the more general U.S. isolation from the international community are fueled in part by these misperceptions.

Public Opinion since World War II

Because public opinion plays a crucial role in democratic nations, whose citizens decide at the polls who will lead them in times of war and peace, politicians clearly recognize that their survival relies on securing and maintaining the public's confidence. Such support provides a variety of secondary benefits as well. Aside from their improved prospects for reelection, popular presidents have generally enjoyed a more favorable partisan balance of power in Congress (Marra and Ostrom 1989). They have also been more successful in achieving the goals of their major policy initiatives (Rivers and Rose 1985).

American foreign policy goals are no exception. Indeed, the success or failure of presidents, who alone represent "all the people," often hinges on how the public reacts to events overseas and how the White House manages those critical situations. For example, the failure of President Woodrow Wilson to enlist public support for his activist agenda after World War I led to his political downfall. Since 1945, the ebbs and flows of public support for U.S. foreign policy have determined not only the political fates of presidents, but also the goals, tactics, and outcomes of their policies. Harry Truman and Lyndon Johnson watched their presidencies collapse under the weight of foreign entanglements in Korea and Vietnam, respectively, a lesson apparent to George W. Bush as the war in Iraq spiraled out of control during his second term.

Consensus and Discord during the Cold War

After World War II, President Truman faced a major policy problem: sustaining public support for an assertive foreign policy that matched the nation's military, economic, and political predominance. With peace, Americans had demanded, and received from Congress, sharp cutbacks in military spending, which dropped from $83 billion in 1945 to less than $10 billion in 1948 (U.S. Office of Management and Budget 2002, 44).[4] Yet, Truman felt the United States should be actively engaged overseas in restoring political stability and economic growth. The onset of the Cold War in the late 1940s gave Truman further impetus to shake the public out of its customary shift toward postwar disengagement. The start of the Korean War solidified the containment consensus that would propel U.S. foreign policy over the next two decades (Yergin 1977).

Public support encouraged Presidents Dwight Eisenhower and John Kennedy to continue Truman's military buildup and focus on anticommunism. Along with most members of Congress, the public supported Lyndon Johnson's early deployments of U.S. troops to Vietnam (Bardes 1997, 157). And that support continued until the 1968 Tet offensive revealed that the United States would not, as Johnson had promised, soon win the war. Opposition mounted as Richard Nixon instituted a lottery for drafting Americans into the armed services. By May 1970, the month in which National Guard troops killed four students at Kent State University during an antiwar demonstration, a majority of the public considered their nation's involvement in Vietnam a mistake. Controversy over U.S. covert operations, revelations of CIA abuses against domestic opponents, and a prolonged economic downturn contributed further to the Vietnam syndrome, a generalized aversion to U.S. military activism coupled with a sense of defeatism (Holsti and Rosenau 1979).

In this respect, President Jimmy Carter followed, rather than created, the national sentiment that identified human rights as a central pillar of U.S. foreign policy in the late 1970s. By the end of Carter's term, however, a combination of public pressure and overseas developments had forced the president to increase military spending and adopt a more confrontational foreign policy. The revival of Cold War tensions led to the 1980 election of Ronald Reagan, who hailed the Vietnam War as a "noble effort" and promised to rid the public and the government of the Vietnam syndrome. But the spiraling arms race of the early 1980s spawned a new generation of public protests and a "nuclear freeze" movement in the United States and Europe. Failing to generate public or congressional support for U.S. intervention in Central America, the Reagan administration turned to covert operations that ultimately produced the Iran-contra scandal (see Chapter 3).

President George H. W. Bush, who succeeded Reagan in 1989, inherited both a favorable international climate that accompanied the approaching end of the Cold War and the broad public approval that went with it. Bush declared the

---

4. Defense spending between 1945 and 1948 fell from 90 percent of overall federal spending to 31 percent.

Vietnamese children flee in terror from a napalm attack by the United States in June 1972. The nude girl in the center, nine-year-old Kim Phuc, had stripped off her burning clothes after the attack. Her brother, Phan Thanh Tam (left), lost an eye as a result of the napalm, a chemical defoliant used widely by the U.S. Air Force in an attempt to locate military targets. Behind the children are soldiers from the South Vietnamese army. This and other photographs fueled public opposition to the war and eventual U.S. withdrawal from Vietnam.

Vietnam syndrome a thing of the past at the time of the Persian Gulf War, which featured the largest deployment of U.S. troops since Vietnam. Ironically, though, Bush's preoccupation with foreign affairs proved his undoing after the war, when a recession at home prompted challenges in 1992 from former Arkansas governor Bill Clinton and Ross Perot, an independent candidate for president. Perot, who drew most of his votes from disillusioned Republicans, effectively handed the White House to Clinton, who received only 38 percent of the votes cast.

Ambivalence and Drift in the Clinton Years

The end of the Cold War brought about new patterns in public opinion—ones that reflected the demise of superpower tensions and the birth of U.S. predominance among the great powers. Considerable ambivalence among the public and government leaders about U.S. foreign policy provided the backdrop for these new dynamics. This uncertainty continued throughout the decade because no single foreign policy issue dominated the public's attention or played a decisive role in national elections (see Posen and Ross 1996/1997). Surveys in the early 1990s demonstrated that most Americans wanted their government to pay more

Table 7.4   Shifting Public Concerns, 1998 and 2002

Survey question	1998	2002
"What is the biggest foreign policy problem facing the country today?"	Don't know: 21%	Terrorism: 33%
	Terrorism: 12%	Middle East situation: 21%
	Middle East situation: 8%	Don't know: 11%
	Foreign aid: 7%	Foreign aid: 8%
	Getting involved in affairs of other countries: 7%	Getting involved in affairs of other countries: 7%
	Immigration: 3%	Immigration: 7%

SOURCE: Chicago Council on Foreign Relations, "Worldviews 2002: American Public Opinion and Foreign Policy" (2002), www.worldviews.org/detailreports/usreport/index.htm.

attention to domestic problems. By 1998, in the midst of an economic boom at home and no major perceived threats abroad, Americans generally felt little concern about foreign policy. When asked in a prominent survey what was "the biggest foreign policy problem facing the country today," the most common response was "Don't know" (see Table 7.4).

Although public opinion surveys revealed a low regard for his foreign policy performance, Clinton still received the highest approval ratings among the ten postwar presidents, in part because of his high sensitivity to the ebbs and flows of public opinion. Initially committed to completing the U.S. military intervention in Somalia, he quickly pulled the plug on the mission after U.S. troops were killed in October 1993. Similarly, he withdrew U.S. forces from Haiti after they confronted a hostile band of rebels in the nation's capital. From Clinton's perspective, such foreign policy problems could not be allowed to interfere with his primary goal as president—reviving the nation's economic output and competitiveness in markets abroad. Even though Clinton identified "enlargement" of global democracy as a top foreign policy goal, he did not vigorously pursue this goal because of limited public and congressional interest.

Recognizing the lack of public support for military intervention in the former Yugoslavia, Clinton avoided large-scale intervention in Bosnia-Herzegovina despite his stated concerns about "ethnic cleansing" in the region. Public and congressional opposition to U.S. involvement in Kosovo led the president in 1999 to adopt a "zero tolerance" policy for American casualties, which limited NATO's military role to high-altitude bombings of military targets and the Yugoslav capital of Belgrade. Clinton's refusal to consider deploying ground troops, further motivated by a lack of consensus among the western European allies, angered U.S. military commanders, who sought to keep all options open in order to secure a prompt and overwhelming victory (see Daalder and O'Hanlon 2000 and Clark 2001).

Although Americans generally resisted military intervention in the first post–Cold War decade, they still favored active involvement and multilateral cooperation in other areas of foreign policy. This consensus, however, was not reflected in U.S. foreign policies during the 1990s, which took a "unilateral turn" that continued into the new millennium (Kull and Destler 1999). Regarding foreign aid, a majority of the public favored cutbacks in aid levels, but this preference was based on a misreading of current spending levels. Whereas the majority of survey respondents believed the U.S. government was spending 15–20 percent of the federal budget on foreign aid—and believed this level should be reduced to 5–10 percent—the actual level of U.S. aid spending was just 1 percent of the federal budget. These and other findings revealed a foreign policy "disconnect" between mass opinion and U.S. foreign policies (Page and Bouton 2006).

Rallying around the Flag after September 11

Domestic issues dominated the 2000 presidential race between George W. Bush and Vice President Al Gore. A September 2000 survey conducted by ABC News and the *Washington Post* found that, of the seventeen election issues of potential concern to voters, "national defense" and "foreign affairs" ranked eleventh and thirteenth on the list, respectively. The four issues of greatest concern to the registered voters surveyed—education, the economy, Social Security, and health care—received the most attention in campaign advertisements and speeches. By contrast, foreign policy issues came up rarely during the presidential debates. Despite the significant differences between the two candidates in this area—Gore favored a broad global agenda, whereas Bush preferred a narrow focus on U.S. national interests—most voters believed the nation was sufficiently secure to make foreign policy a secondary concern.

Fears of terrorism predictably rose to the top of the public's list of concerns after the September 11 attacks (see Table 7.4), and the ensuing war on terrorism transformed Bush's presidency. Following a consistent pattern in U.S. public opinion, presidential approval rose sharply as the nation faced a major military conflict overseas. This **rally around the flag effect** is generally attributed to a patriotic sense among citizens that national unity must be maintained in times of crisis (Mueller 1970; 1973). For similar reasons, members of Congress usually avoid criticizing presidents when U.S. troops are in harm's way. The benefits from this rally effect are difficult to gauge, however, and the boost in public approval may be short lived if the missions falter (see Baker and Oneal 2001). But there is little doubt that presidents gain politically at the onset of international crises. Some scholars have gone so far as to put forth a **diversionary theory of war,** suggesting that presidents may *provoke* conflicts to boost their approval ratings (see Levy 1989). For example, Republicans accused President Clinton of resorting to this tactic in 1999, when his order to intervene in Kosovo temporarily shifted public attention from his impending impeachment over the Monica Lewinsky scandal.[5]

---

5. This episode was eerily reminiscent of the 1997 film *Wag the Dog,* a satire in which the U.S. president fabricated a foreign crisis—in this case on a Hollywood movie set—to distract the public's attention from a White House sex scandal.

Figure 7.2 George W. Bush Public Opinion and Rally Effects, February 2, 2001–April 18, 2004

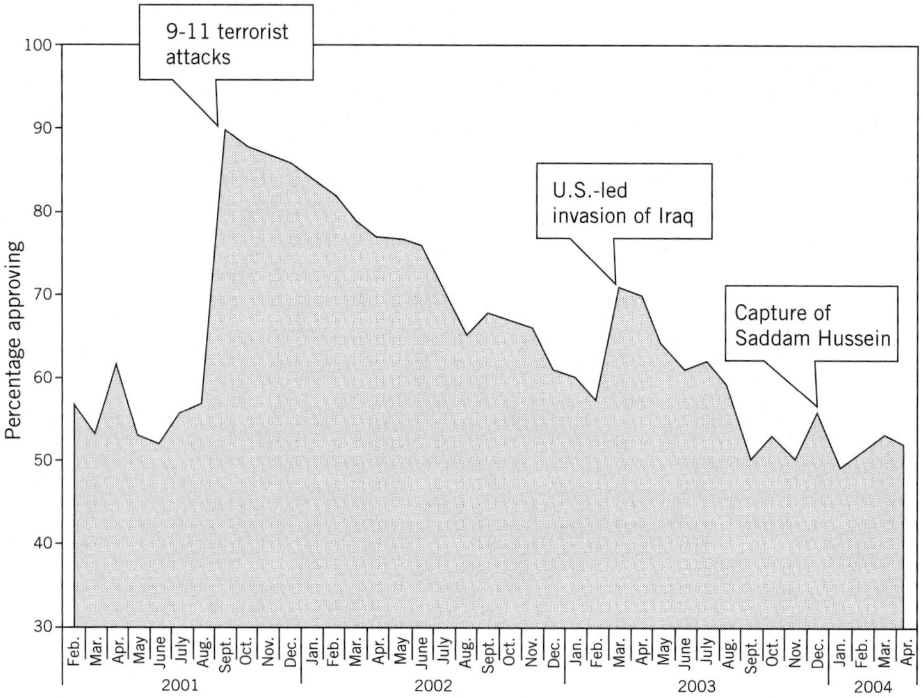

SOURCE: Gallup Organization surveys via the Roper Center for Public Opinion Research, "Presidential Approval Ratings" (2004), www.ropercenter.uconn.edu.

Bush clearly benefited from the rally around the flag effect. His public approval ratings before September 11 were lukewarm, averaging 53 percent in eight major surveys.[6] After the terrorist attacks, these ratings soared to an average of 82 percent and peaked at 90 percent, the highest enjoyed by any president. Bush retained his strong reservoir of public support in the months that followed, although his popularity sagged along with the U.S. economy and the military's failure to apprehend al Qaeda leader Osama bin Laden in 2002. Bush experienced a second rally effect in March 2003, when he ordered the invasion of Iraq. A third, but more modest and short-lived rally effect followed the capture of Iraqi leader Saddam Hussein in December 2003 (see Figure 7.2).

By any measure, the rally effect for Bush was enormous—three times the level experienced by President Franklin Roosevelt after the Japanese attack on Pearl Harbor in 1941. In investigating why Bush received such an unprecedented spike in public approval after September 11, scholars pointed to the president's

---

6. See www.pollingreport.com/BushJob.htm for details of these polls.

IN THEIR OWN WORDS: THE NATIONAL SECURITY COUNCIL

Facing an uphill battle in regaining public support for the Iraq war, the Bush administration turned to public opinion experts for assistance. These experts, led by Peter D. Feaver of Duke University, helped draft a November 2005 report by the National Security Council entitled "National Strategy for Victory in Iraq." The purpose of the report was to convince Americans that the White House's war plan was clear and was succeeding, despite highly publicized set-backs. According to the outside experts, both impressions would revive the public's confidence in the Bush administration and allow U.S. leaders and military forces more time to gain the upper hand in the conflict. Excerpts of the report's key points are listed below.

- Victory in Iraq Is a Vital U.S. Interest. Iraq is the central front in the war on terror. Failure in Iraq will embolden terrorists and expand their reach; success will deal them a decisive and crippling blow. The fate of the greater Middle East—which will have a profound and lasting impact on American security—hangs in the balance.
- Failure Is Not an Option. Iraq would become a safe haven from which terrorists could plan attacks against America, American interests abroad, and our allies. Middle East reformers would never again fully trust American assurances of support for democracy and human rights in the region—a historic opportunity lost.
- Our Strategy for Victory Is Clear. We will help Iraqis build a new Iraq with a constitutional, representative government that respects civil rights and has security forces sufficient to maintain domestic order and keep Iraq from becoming a safe haven for terrorists.
- Victory Will Take Time. **Our strategy is working.** Much has been accomplished in Iraq, including the removal of Saddam Hussein's tyranny . . . restoration of full sovereignty, holding of free elections . . . gradual restoration of neglected infrastructure, the ongoing training and equipping of Iraqi security forces, and the increasing capability of those forces to take on the terrorists and secure their nation.

SOURCE: National Security Council, "National Strategy for Victory in Iraq," November 2005, www.whitehouse.gov/infocus/iraq/iraq_strategy_nov2005.html.

relatively low public approval prior to the terrorist attacks, when he ranked third to last among postwar presidents at the same stage in their terms. Bush had several problems during his first nine months in office, including a stagnant economy and the defection of a Republican senator that effectively handed majority rule in the Senate over to the Democratic Party. Roosevelt, by comparison, was very popular before Pearl Harbor; his public approval rating of 72 percent gave him little room for a rally effect (see Baum 2002).

Strong public support bolstered Bush as he ordered the invasion of Iraq in March 2003. As noted earlier, the persistence of this support as the occupation wore on reflected widespread public misperceptions about Iraq and its leader, Saddam Hussein (Kull, Ramsay, and Lewis 2003/2004). Specifically, most Americans believed that (1) clear evidence had earlier linked Saddam to al Qaeda;

(2) weapons of mass destruction had been found recently in Iraq; or (3) global public opinion favored U.S. military action. The strength of these misperceptions, which endured despite daily revelations to the contrary, provided Bush with the domestic support he needed to sustain the war effort.

The Anti-American Backlash

This period of complacency did not last long. Escalating political violence in Iraq, combined with a deluge of critical reports on the lack of U.S. postwar planning, sent public support for the president's foreign policies into a tailspin. His overall decline in approval, no longer buoyed by rally effects, closely paralleled public dissatisfaction with the war in Iraq and the broader war on terrorism (see Figure 7.3). Opinion leaders in the news media and at think tanks, universities, and religious institutions all turned deeply pessimistic about the future (Pew Research Center 2005). The titles of many books, including *Fiasco* by Tom Ricks (2006) and *State of Denial* by Bob Woodward (2006), summarized their coverage of the bureaucratic infighting and strategic miscalculations that occurred before and during the Iraq invasion. By March 2006, Americans had concluded by a two-to-one margin that the war in Iraq was one of *choice*, not necessity, and that the U.S. position in the conflict was worsening (World Public Opinion 2006). Even a

Figure 7.3   Bush's Public Decline: The Foreign Policy Connection

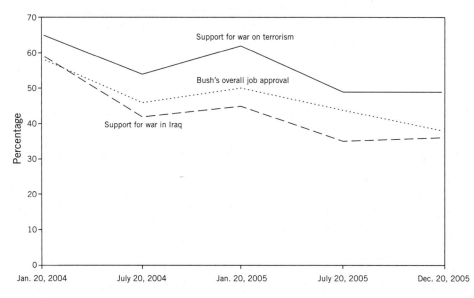

SOURCE: Pew Research Center for the People and the Press, "Iran a Growing Danger, Bush Gaining on Spy Issue" (February 7, 2006), http://people-press.org/reports/pdf/269.pdf.

majority of Republicans (53 percent) believed the United States should not have gone to war in Iraq without irrefutable evidence of an imminent threat.

Much of this public discontent was directed at the president, whose approval ratings fell from their peak of 90 percent late in 2001 to the mid-30s in 2006 (Pew Research Center 2006a). A September poll by *Time* magazine found that nearly 60 percent of respondents believed that Bush lacked a "clear policy for dealing with terrorism" (Schulman and Regan 2006). Although mounting U.S. casualties were linked to this decline in Bush's public approval, the numbers of troops killed in Iraq and Afghanistan were low compared with the numbers killed in the major wars of the twentieth century. Rising body counts in Korea and Vietnam, shown to be correlated with rising public opposition to U.S. involvement, prompted some analysts to conclude that Americans suffered from a "casualty phobia" (see Mueller 1973). This became even more acute after the Cold War, as U.S. presidents engaged in repeated military conflicts that could not be traced to threats by a rival world power.

In 2005, Bush's National Security Council sought to revive public support for the war in Iraq by shifting attention from past military setbacks to future prospects for victory (see Gelpi, Feaver, and Reifler 2005/2006). This "victory

Members of the UN Security Council approve a measure in June 2004 calling for the transfer of sovereignty back to Iraq after more than a year of occupation by U.S.-led forces. The Security Council had earlier opposed the U.S. government's call to use force against Saddam Hussein after UN inspectors failed to uncover weapons of mass destruction in the country late in 2002. The lack of support by the Security Council did not stop George W. Bush from ordering Saddam's overthrow in March 2003.

strategy" failed, however, to halt the drop in public support for the war. Instead, the White House message was drowned out by daily reports of sectarian strife, attacks on U.S. troops, and the rising costs of the war. By February 2007, fully two-thirds of Americans felt the U.S. mission in Iraq was not going well, a sharp rise from 51 percent a year earlier (Pew Research Center 2007). This situation demonstrated that, as in the past, outcomes as well as expectations drive public opinion on U.S. military interventions. Whereas failure is an "orphan," leaving policy architects alone to fend off critics, victory "has many friends" among policy makers and the general public (see Eichenberg 2005). Above all, private citizens base their judgments on results, not rhetorical flourishes and predictions of success—a pattern that should please skeptics of U.S. public opinion.

Anti-American sentiments registered deep concerns over many perceived shortcomings of U.S. foreign policy: its penchant for favoring military over diplomatic solutions, its failure to consider or consult with other countries, and its perceived control by multinational corporations.[7] By the end of 2006, citizens in thirty-three of thirty-five countries surveyed believed the U.S. war in Iraq had increased the likelihood of terrorist attacks around the world (World Public Opinion 2006). Predictably, Bush became a lightning rod for discontent overseas. Ninety-eight percent of European Commission members and 68 percent of members in the European Parliament disapproved of his foreign policies (Centre for the Study of Political Change 2006, 6). In these and other studies, actions by the United States prompted Europeans to favor strengthening their own defense forces and becoming more independent of Washington in foreign affairs.

The rise of anti-Americanism, also evident in public demonstrations and media coverage, was not lost on U.S. citizens. A survey by Public Agenda (2005) found three-quarters of Americans worrying that "there may be growing hatred of the U.S. in Muslim countries" and that the United States "may be losing the trust and friendship of people in other countries." More than 60 percent of Americans believed the accusation that the United States had been "too quick to resort to war" against Iraq was at least partly justified. And nearly 90 percent believed that "showing more respect for the views and needs of other countries would enhance security."

Revived Legitimacy in the Obama Era

Overseas surveys revealed some exceptions to the general rule of heightened anti-Americanism (see Applebaum 2005). In the Philippines, for example, nearly 90 percent of the population held positive views of the United States even after the Iraq invasion. Meanwhile, Japanese citizens were not greatly bothered by the

---

7. Public views of foreign government actions are often linked to personal, cross-cultural impressions. Although foreign citizens associate Americans with several positive traits—"hardworking," "inventive," and "honest"—Americans are also widely perceived as "greedy" and "violent." The negative impressions have been highest in Muslim countries; in those countries that are allied with the United States, including Canada and European nations, "rudeness" is identified as a common negative cultural trait. See Pew Global Attitudes Project (2005).

preventive attack and other manifestations of the Bush Doctrine. Government leaders and citizens in Eastern Europe also remained friendly toward Washington. Although Western Europeans were generally critical of Bush and his foreign policies, senior citizens continued to support U.S. foreign policy, a pattern that likely reflected enduring appreciation for the U.S. role in liberating the region from Nazi Germany in World War II. Most striking of all, global surveys found that U.S. "soft power" still resonated through movies, television shows, music, fashions, and Web sites. This pattern revealed that, in much of the world, anti-American sentiment was directed primarily toward the nation's leaders and their policies, not its people.

At home, a growing number of Americans had grown wary of the Bush Doctrine and the damage it was doing to U.S. credibility, moral leadership, and overall world power. A July 2008 survey found "improving America's standing in the world" to be the general public's top U.S. foreign policy priority (Chicago Council on Global Affairs 2009). The next two priorities—protecting American jobs and securing energy supplies—reflected the unease felt by Americans amid the economic crisis that lasted throughout Bush's last year in office. These concerns, along with those regarding nuclear proliferation, overshadowed the public's worries about international terrorism that previously dominated their attention.

The majority view of U.S. foreign policy aligned with the positions espoused by Barack Obama during his presidential campaign, providing him a clear public mandate to adopt a more liberal approach to foreign affairs. This alignment between public preferences and Obama's foreign policy was visible in four primary areas:

- *Diplomacy.* The United States should negotiate on foreign policy matters with all foreign governments, including those such as Cuba, Iran, and North Korea that are openly hostile to Washington.

- *Multilateral cooperation.* The United States should join the International Criminal Court and sign global agreements to combat climate change and prohibit the testing of nuclear weapons.

- *International law.* The U.S. government should conduct its foreign policy in accordance with international law, which establishes normative standards of behavior for all governments and a legal basis for sanctions in response to violations.

- *International institutions.* American leaders should support the creation of new global institutions that monitor energy supplies, enforce climate-change agreements, and regulate capital markets.

Group Identities and Foreign Policy Views

Citizens' political viewpoints come from a combination of sources, including their past experience, moral and social values, and exposure to current events. Public opinion is highly personal in this respect, an outcome of factors that are unique to each individual. Still, citizens share many common attributes with others that further define their ideas and interests in U.S. foreign policy. Surveys consistently affirm the strength of **group identity,** or a sense of common cause with other citizens with shared personal traits. According to Donald Kinder and Lynn Sanders (1996, 89), "The interests that enter into the formation of public opinion are collective rather than personal, group-centered rather than self-centered."

Public opinion regarding U.S. foreign policy tends to cluster in ways that reflect group identities in three primary areas: physical traits, social associations, and political belief systems (see Chapter 3). These group identities, detailed below, are reliable predictors of foreign policy views on a variety of issues. Support for U.S. internationalism is strongest, for example, among affluent Americans with higher levels of education and professional stature. Those with military experience, furthermore, have "systematically different opinions on whether and how to use force" (Feaver and Gelpi 2004, 184). Even the regions in which Americans live provide clues regarding public opinion, as residents of the South and western mountain states tend to favor unilateral and military-based foreign policies more than their northeastern, midwestern, and West Coast counterparts (Trubowitz 1992). Understanding the **demographics** of public opinion reminds us that this concept, like that of "national interest," is rarely monolithic and is instead a mosaic of ties that cut across American society.

Physical Identities: Gender, Race, and Generation

Shared physical traits provide a strong foundation for group identities. Men and women, studies show, consistently diverge in their opinions regarding foreign policy. This **gender gap** is clear on the most critical issues of war and peace, as surveys have found men to be more supportive than women of U.S. military involvement in the Korean, Vietnam, and Persian Gulf Wars (Mueller 1994, 1973; see also Caprioli 2000). These differences appeared in both key issues regarding U.S. military intervention: *whether* to intervene in a particular conflict and *how* such an intervention should proceed (Nincic and Nincic 2002, 550). "In practically all realms of foreign and domestic policy," Benjamin Page and Robert Shapiro (1992, 295) concluded bluntly, "women are less belligerent than men."

Many explanations have been offered for this gender gap. Those from the constructivist perspective emphasize the traditional roles that societies have long imposed on men and women, with the former assigned the role of "warriors" and the latter assigned the role of "caregivers" (Keohane 1989). Other explanations relate to biological differences, including the higher levels of male testosterone that are linked to aggressive behavior (Goldstein 2001). Finally, higher levels of support for military conflict among men may be explained by the fact that the majority of those displaced by war are women and children (Lindsey 2000). All these viewpoints explain not only why women are more likely than men to oppose wars, but also why women more frequently favor diplomatic and other nonviolent forms of conflict resolution (Tickner 1992).

Racial differences, though less often studied by scholars, are also significant in shaping foreign policy views. Compared with whites, African Americans are consistently more inclined to favor U.S. detachment in foreign policy (Holsti 1996) and more skeptical of U.S. military interventions (Mueller 1994). African Americans are also more likely than whites to oppose higher levels of defense spending, a pattern that may be explained by the economic gaps between the two races and the greater desire among African Americans for domestic spending on social programs. To one analyst (Bowser 2003, 19–20), these differences reflect deeper problems in American society that threaten its foreign policy ambitions: "A continued failure to face racial inequality and do something about it means continued isolation and hostility overseas tomorrow." This perspective suggests that African Americans, like women, suffer from **political alienation,** feeling less empowered in public affairs than white men and particularly lacking influence in U.S. foreign policy (see Figure 7.4).

Finally, generational differences among Americans have been found to "endow the individual with a common location in the social and historical process"

Figure 7.4 Societal Gaps in Public Knowledge: Percentage of Amercians Who Could Identify . . .

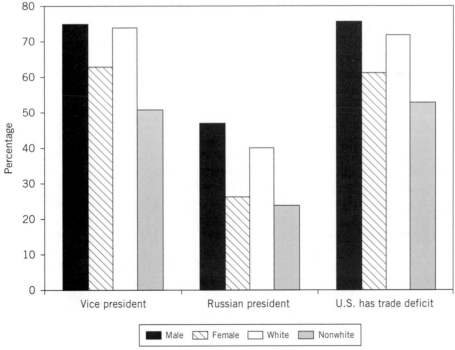

SOURCE: Pew Research Center for the People and the Press, "What Americans Know: 1989–2007," pp. 17, 19 (April 15, 2007), http://people-press.org/reports/pdf/319.pdf.

(Mannheim 1952, 291). It is widely assumed, for example, that those who experienced World War II learned distinct "lessons of history" that were not apparent to Americans born and raised after the war. The same can be said for the "Vietnam generation," which expressed greater reluctance about U.S. military interventionism than did those who grew up in the 1950s and 1960s (Roskin 1974). Public opinion polls provide modest support for this generational link, although other demographic attributes tend to have greater impact on foreign policy opinions (Holsti 1996).

Social Identities: Education, Wealth, and Religion

Unlike physical identities, social and political identities involve shared attributes that derive from personal experience. Two sources of social identity—education and wealth—have a clear impact on Americans' foreign policy views. These two attributes are so closely related in statistical studies, however, that they are commonly considered together. Religious affiliation, the other attribute considered in this section, has a different, but equally strong influence on public opinion and U.S. foreign policy.

Relatively high levels of wealth and education are defining features of the foreign policy elite and, to a lesser extent, the attentive public. In short, affluent Americans typically favor "cooperative internationalism" in U.S. foreign policy, a pattern that contrasts with the mass public's greater tendency to support isolationism or "militant internationalism" (Wittkopf 1990, 38). These differences extend to the economic realm, as those with more education and wealth are more likely than other citizens to favor open trade with other countries (Page and Barabas 2000). Taken together, these findings suggest that affluent Americans identify more closely with global issues than does the mass public, which views foreign affairs more skeptically and is more concerned with U.S. national interests. Affluent Americans, furthermore, may have more direct personal stakes in the global economy that compel them to favor open trade.

Religious beliefs, another source of social identity, also shape public views regarding U.S. foreign policy. This "faith factor" (Wald and Wilcox 2006) contributes to foreign policy views that stand apart from those of citizens who rarely, if ever, attend religious services. Public opinion surveys affirm this **divine divide** in public opinion. During the Bush years, regular churchgoers believed far more than their counterparts that the United States was "doing the right thing" in foreign policy (see Table 7.5). In Christian churches, active members commonly respond to surveys with views that "echo the traditional theme of American exceptionalism: Americans are a people chosen for a special mission in the world and especially blessed by God" (Yankelovich 2005). Not surprisingly, Jewish and Muslim Americans tend to favor Israel and Arab states in the Middle East, respectively, in their positions regarding U.S. foreign policy (Page and Bouton 2006, 91–96).

Evangelical Protestants formed a cohesive voting bloc that proved critical to Bush's reelection in 2004, demonstrating the importance of social movements in

Table 7.5 The "Divine Divide" in U.S. Foreign Policy (percentage who agree, based on attendance at religious services)

Statement	Frequency of church attendance			
	Never	Occasionally	Regularly	Frequently
Believe the U.S. is "generally doing the right thing with plenty to be proud of" in its relations with the rest of the world	28%	33%	49%	52%
"Worry a lot" that the war in Iraq is leading to too many casualties	63	60	50	45
Agree that the U.S. can help other countries become democracies	31	35	43	48
Give a high grade to the U.S. on giving the war on terrorism all the attention it deserves	48	56	64	64

SOURCE: Daniel Yankelovich, "Poll Positions: What Americans Really Think About U.S. Foreign Policy," *Foreign Affairs* 84 (September–October 2005): 2–16.

shaping U.S. foreign policy (see Chapter 9). By 2008, thousands of evangelical "mega-churches" served more than 5 million worshippers, a majority of whom were under thirty-five years old, middle class, and not formerly involved in church life (Thumma and Bird 2009). These citizens, primarily white-collar workers living in the suburbs, were also likely to have conservative political beliefs and a preference for Republican candidates in national elections. On national security matters, evangelical Protestants provided the strongest support among religious subgroups for Bush's aggressive response to the September 11 attacks and his decision to invade Iraq in 2003 (Pew Research Center 2006b). A more recent survey found that "rising death tolls, spiraling financial costs, and negative media reports about the Iraq war [had] the least effect on Evangelicals because of their firm religious beliefs that conflict in the Middle East is part of a divine plan" (Baumgartner, Francia, and Morris 2008).

Political Identities: Ideology and Political Party

A final source of group identity involves the general views citizens hold of politics, or ideology, and the political parties that they regularly support. The "basic attitudes" (Page and Bouton 2006, 238) of citizens, once formed early in life, tend to be highly stable over time and guide their judgments on a variety of specific issues. On foreign policy matters, for example, those who identify themselves as liberals express more concern over human rights, global poverty, and environmental decay than conservatives, whose primary concerns tend to focus on strengthening U.S. military power, restricting immigration, and promoting U.S. businesses overseas. The results of one prominent study (Wittkopf 1990, 34) "strongly confirm the view that ideology colors perceptions of the appropriate role of the United States in world affairs." Specifically, liberals were most closely identified with *accommodationist* foreign policy positions, whereas conservatives best fit the category of *hard-liners*. Gallup surveys during the 1991 Gulf War found a majority of conservatives favoring U.S. military action and most liberals favoring extended economic sanctions and negotiations (Holsti 1996, 152).

Citizens' ideological views have a direct impact on their party affiliations, with conservatives overwhelmingly aligning with the Republican Party and liberals supporting candidates from the Democratic Party. Like basic attitudes, these partisan identities are firmly embedded and show little fluctuation over time. Statistical studies demonstrate strong parallels between ideology and party identification. In 2002, for example, Democratic voters were far more likely than Republicans to favor strengthening the United Nations and to support the Kyoto Protocol on global warming (Page and Bouton 2006, 70). These positions "hardened" in the 1990s, with those aligned with each party growing less likely to adopt alternative positions on specific foreign policy issues.

Trends in public opinion reflect the "disappearance of the political center" (Binder 1996) in U.S. politics described in Chapter 5. The increased polarization of both mass and elite views has, in turn, produced unprecedented partisan conflict over U.S. foreign policy. As noted elsewhere, the Republican-led Congress in the late 1990s effectively overrode President Clinton's national security strategy of global "engagement" and democratic "enlargement." Congress also approved deep cuts in several areas of U.S. foreign policy including multilateral peacekeeping, financial support of the United Nations, and foreign aid. Although a majority of Americans supported these programs, most Republicans did not, a well-researched statistical finding that fueled legislative opposition to Clinton's foreign policies. With a Republican majority in both houses of Congress, George W. Bush claimed that he was fulfilling a national mandate to adopt a "muscular" response to the September 2001 attacks. Still, most Democrats in the general public were critical of the Bush Doctrine, particularly the invasion of Iraq. This lack of consensus, which continued into the Obama administration, casts further doubt on the once-popular proposition that "politics stops at the water's edge."

Conclusion

Political and technological trends have converged in the past fifty years to magnify the public's impact on U.S. foreign policy. American citizens expect the government to take their views and policy preferences into account (World Public Opinion 2008). For their part, political and military leaders routinely gauge public sentiments and likely responses to their foreign policy choices. Overseas, technological developments and the spread of democratic rule empower private groups and expand press freedoms, adding a potent transnational dimension to the pressures already imposed by domestic civil society.

As this chapter has described, public support for U.S. foreign policy has shifted from general acceptance during the early Cold War to greater skepticism since the Vietnam War. The views of citizens have also shifted from consensus to widespread contention over the ends and means of U.S. foreign policy. This polarization, which mirrors the political climate in Congress, virtually ensures that any foreign policy will face substantial and outspoken dissent among the public and on Capitol Hill. Beyond political realignments at home, the fallout from the most recent spike in anti-American sentiment will be felt for many years. Despite Barack Obama's popularity overseas since taking office in January 2009, global public opinion remains wary of the United States and the ways in which it exercises its world power.

The impact of U.S. public opinion will continue to be muted, however, by a political culture that remains stubbornly ignorant of world history, geography, and current events. Such aloofness breeds misperceptions of world politics and makes citizens susceptible to manipulation by political leaders. The lack of public scrutiny also gives elites considerable leeway to provide favors to special interests, particularly corporate leaders (see Jacobs and Page 2005). The insular character of U.S. public opinion, a throwback to the nation's "splendid isolation" at its founding, runs counter to its primacy and pervasive global presence today.

A central part of this paradox stems from the disconnect between public opinion and government behavior. As political scientist I. M. Destler (2001b, 75) describes that disconnect, "We seem to have a rational public and an ideological ruling class. Average Americans are basically centrist, prone to balance, compromise, fair shares, and reasonable resolutions. Their Congress is polarized, hyperpartisan, responsive to 'cause' activists of left and right." This argument is strengthened by several recent U.S. foreign policy decisions that ran counter to the prevailing public preferences. Among others, these actions included the government's refusal to pay past UN dues, rejection of the Comprehensive Test Ban Treaty, and invasion of Iraq in the absence of UN authorization. The mass public's general inattention to foreign affairs—reflected in test scores and public opinion surveys—surely made the government's decisions to defy the popular will easier and safer politically.

The domestic and foreign backlash against U.S. foreign policies associated with the Bush Doctrine may return the United States to the international community from which it has strayed. Whether or not this shift provides tangible benefits for the nation's global interests, it would reflect the public's foreign policy preferences better than the go-it-alone strategy pursued by U.S. leaders in recent years. Americans remain divided on many foreign policy issues but are generally united "on using talks and multilateral institutions to tackle problems, even while keeping the military strong" (Chicago Council on Global Affairs 2009). Most Americans also express a desire for greater government attention to domestic issues—primarily unemployment and other economic problems—that may revive the "guns-or-butter debates" that ignite repeatedly during hard times. Whatever the policy outcomes, public opinion at home and overseas is a force that must be reckoned with in the globalized U.S. foreign policy process.

Key Terms

Almond-Lippmann consensus, p. 217

attentive public, p. 214

cooperative internationalism, p. 219

delegate model, p. 215

demographics, p. 234

diversionary theory of war, p. 227

divine divide, p. 236

foreign policy elite, p. 214

gender gap, p. 234

group identity, p. 234

international trust, p. 219

latent public opinion, p. 211

mass public, p. 214

militant internationalism, p. 219

political alienation, p. 235

procedural democracy, p. 214

public relations presidency, p. 211

rally around the flag effect, p. 227

substantive democracy, p. 214

trustee model, p. 215

Internet References

The **Chicago Council on Global Affairs** (www.thechicagocouncil.org) is one of the world's largest groups organized for studying and informing the public about world affairs. The council publishes regular studies of public opinion and U.S. foreign policy that are closely followed by scholars and policy makers.

The **Gallup Organization** (www.gallup.com) has studied public opinion and behavior for more than half a century and continues to conduct nationwide and international surveys on political and social issues. Surveys focus on presidential approval, current events, and conflicts.

The **Inter-University Consortium for Political and Social Research** (www.icpsr.umich.edu) provides the world's largest archive of digital and social science data that are compatible with a variety of statistical software programs.

The **National Opinion Research Center** (www.norc.uchicago.edu) specializes in public opinion data and analysis. Recent research projects and special reports have focused on public responses to the terrorist attacks of September 11, 2001.

The **Pew Research Center for the People and the Press** (http://people-press.org) is an independent research center that studies public opinion, news media coverage, and political issues. The Pew Center conducts a wide range of surveys in the United States and overseas, focusing in recent years on global public attitudes toward U.S. foreign policy.

Polling Report (www.pollingreport.com) is an independent, nonpartisan group that offers public opinion data from a variety of sources. Of particular interest to foreign policy researchers are topics such as national security, presidential elections, and the role of the United Nations.

(continued)

Internet References *(continued)*

The **Program on International Policy Attitudes** (www.pipa.org), part of the School of Public Affairs at the University of Maryland, focuses on public opinion and media coverage related to U.S. foreign policy and international issues.

The **Roper Center for Public Opinion Research** (www.ropercenter.uconn.edu) offers access to public opinion and polling data through an archive of historical and current data. Reports include the General Social Survey, National Election Survey, and a variety of other polls.

The *Washington Post* (www.washingtonpost.com/wp-srv/politics/polls/polls.htm) features past articles related to public opinion. Included in the articles are survey data and direct links to past *Washington Post* surveys.

8

The Impact of Mass Communications

Jon Stewart (right), host of *The Daily Show* on cable television's Comedy Central, interviews Pakistani president Pervez Musharraf (left) in September 2006. The interview, alternating between light-hearted moments and serious discussion, is typical of the "soft news" featured increasingly in the media today. Such programs appeal to an audience that is often larger than that for conventional news broadcasts.

On the morning of November 27, 2006, host Matt Lauer of NBC's *Today* show made a dramatic announcement: "As you know, for months now the White House has rejected claims that the situation in Iraq has deteriorated into civil war. And for the most part, news organizations, like NBC, have hesitated to characterize it as such. But, after careful consideration, NBC News has decided the change in terminology is warranted—that the situation in Iraq, with armed militarized factions fighting for their own political agendas, can now be characterized as civil war" (quoted in Froomkin 2006).

The *Today* show's linguistic turn had less significance for Iraq, where political violence between Sunni and Shiite militias had already spun out of control, than for U.S. domestic politics and public opinion. Along with other news organizations, NBC effectively declared independence from the Pentagon, which clung to the view of Iraq as embroiled in a stubborn, but ultimately manageable, insurgency. In legitimizing the gloomier conception of Iraq, the news media fundamentally altered the public discourse on

U.S. foreign policy and, in so doing, stymied the White House's effort to revive public support for the war.

More generally, this episode illustrates the vital role played by the news media in U.S. foreign policy. No other country in the world possesses such a vast array of news outlets with direct access to national and, increasingly, global audiences. The range of news sources in the United States has grown wider with successive technological innovations—the mass production and distribution of newspapers, the invention of radio and television, and the creation of a World Wide Web of Internet sites. All these messengers of news coverage confront the foreign policy process on a daily basis and report what they find—the good, the bad, and, very often, the ugly—to a global audience.

The United States serves not only as a primary source of world news, but also as the most common subject of foreign-based news coverage. Nearly one in five news stories examined in a thirty-eight-country study covered the United States, or more than twice the frequency found for other countries (Wu 2000, 126).[1] This finding is not surprising in view of the United States' vast power and influence. It also reveals how media attention reflects the balance of power in world politics.

As with other countries that recognize press freedoms, in the United States the news media naturally foster a dynamic civil society by keeping citizens aware of current affairs, political struggles at all levels of government, and important social issues that spur mass movements and interest groups (see Chapter 9). At the same time, the capacity of other governments and societies to challenge U.S. foreign policies will increase as their news media reach and give voice to more citizens, a trend of likely significance given the high levels of anti-American sentiment overseas in recent years. The vast reach of the U.S. news media, and the financial windfall it produces, also incites daily charges of cultural imperialism. With the global spotlight cast on Washington, its political scandals, fissures in public opinion, and missteps in foreign policy become apparent to those in other countries. In this respect, the global expansion of press freedoms, while fulfilling a long-standing ambition of U.S. foreign policy, may also heighten U.S. vulnerabilities and reinforce the paradox of America's world power.

For most Americans, news reports are their primary if not only source of information about the "outside world." As discussed in Chapter 7, Americans have limited knowledge of world history and geography and are generally uninterested in foreign affairs unless the United States is facing a clear and present danger to its security (see Table 8.1). Local and national news consistently draw interest from Americans. By contrast, most respondents to a recent survey indicated that they follow world news only "when something important is happening" (Pew Research Center 2008, 111). In terms of ratings, the biggest U.S. news

---

1. The other countries most commonly covered were, in order, France, the United Kingdom, and Russia.

Table 8.1 Public (In)Attention to World News

Americans who follow...	Local news	National news	World news
Most of the time	57%	55%	39%
Only when important	40	41	56
Don't know	3	4	4

SOURCE: Pew Research Center for the People and the Press, "Key News Audiences Now Blend Online and Traditional Sources," p. 38 (August 17, 2008), http://people-press.org/reports/pdf/444.pdf.

story in the early 1990s was not the collapse of communism or the genocide in Rwanda, but rather the murder trial of former football player O. J. Simpson. The defining story of the late 1990s did not involve U.S. global primacy or its military interventions in the former Yugoslavia, but rather the sex scandal surrounding President Bill Clinton.[2]

The managers of U.S. news coverage respond to public interests by focusing primarily on domestic issues. This strategy, based on a desire for greater appeal to a mass audience, was clearly on display in September 2009 when nearly four times as many newspaper articles covered ongoing debates over Barack Obama's health care reforms than covered troubling developments in Afghanistan that later forced the president to escalate U.S. war efforts there (see Figure 8.1). In view of this weak appetite for world news, even the most cursory press reports give many citizens all the information they seek. Their lack of direct international exposure, through travel or personal contacts abroad, leaves Americans further dependent on the media for information and ideas about U.S. foreign policy.

Commercial and technological changes in the news industry compound the public's superficial understanding of global developments. The near collapse of the newspaper industry in recent years deprives Americans of detailed coverage of foreign affairs that is rarely offered by television networks and most Internet sources (Jones 2009). The Project for Excellence in Journalism (2006) identified a "paradox of journalism," by which the greater number of media outlets, including thousands of Internet sites, has actually *narrowed* the range of in-depth news coverage available to the public. "We tend to see more accounts of the same handful of stories each day. And when the big stories break, they are often covered in a similar fashion by general assignment reporters working with a limited list of sources and a tight time frame. . . . For the most part, the public—and the government—were learning from journalists who were discovering things for themselves."

---

2. James Fallows (1997, 247), a prominent journalist and author, found that superficial and scandal-driven news coverage simply adds to the public's cynical view of U.S. politics and foreign policy: "The press, which in the long run cannot survive if people lose interest in politics, is acting as if its purpose is to guarantee that people are repelled by public life."

Figure 8.1   Home Sweet Home: News Coverage of the Afghanistan War and Health Care Reform, August–September 2009

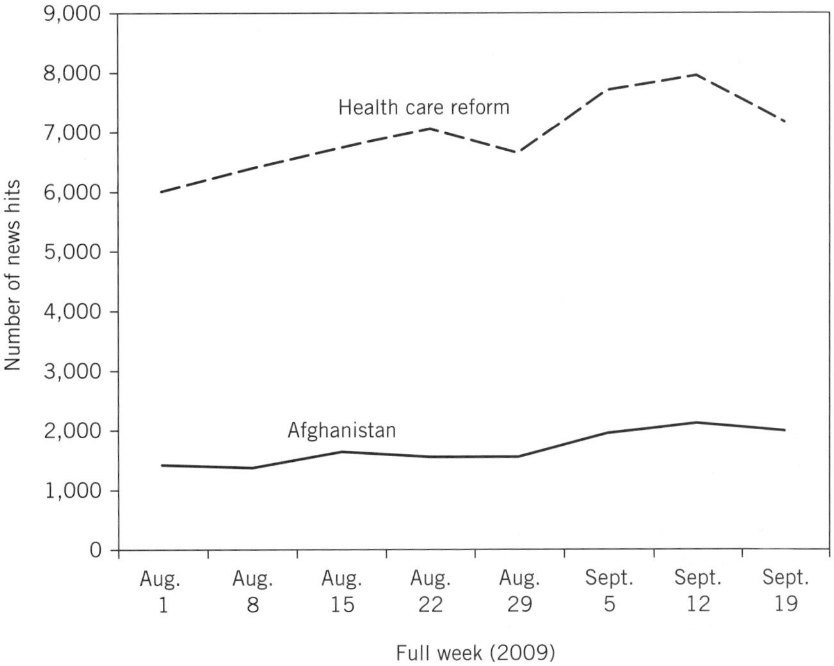

SOURCE: Compiled by the author, based on LexisNexis news database, www.lexisnexis.com.

Functions of the News Media

A free press stands as a pillar of democratic governance, providing civil society with a crucial check on government authority. The U.S. Constitution reflects this belief in its First Amendment, which explicitly protects freedom of the press. As Thomas Jefferson once mused, "Were it left to me to decide whether we should have government without newspapers or newspapers without government, I should not hesitate for a moment to prefer the latter." The news media play an even more vital role in modern, mass-based democracies. Because of the large scale of these political systems, most people do not participate directly in the political process. Instead, they learn what their government is doing primarily by following news reports in the electronic and print media. The public places even greater dependence on the news media when it comes to foreign policy issues, which commonly involve faraway and seldom-seen people and places.

Print and broadcast news outlets, as well as a rapidly widening array of Internet sources, fill three primary roles in the U.S. foreign policy process:

- *Source of information and opinions.* The most vital role played by the news media is to keep the public informed about developments at home and abroad. Throughout U.S. history, foreign correspondents have provided firsthand accounts of events overseas, including the many wars fought by the United States. Print and broadcast outlets also supplement news reports with commentaries on such foreign policy issues as the war on terrorism, U.S. relations with China, and global trade. Newspapers have long filled their editorial pages with such commentaries, whether written by staff editors or guest columnists. In recent years, debates over foreign policy have also become the staple of cable television news channels such as CNN, Fox News, and MSNBC. Millions of Americans also tune in daily to radio commentators such as Rush Limbaugh, whose conservative arguments and attacks on liberals appeal to millions of Americans every day.

- *Agenda setter.* Studies of the news media have consistently established a link between news coverage and the perceived importance by the public and governments of the issues covered.[3] In short, media coverage of a political problem, whether in domestic or foreign policy, increases the importance attached to that problem by citizens and foreign policy makers (see Page 1996 and Ghanem 1997). The same relationship holds for public perceptions of foreign countries. Extensive media coverage of Russia and Japan in the late 1990s, for example, was closely related to heightened public concern with those countries, whereas relatively few stories about Brazil, Mexico, India, Iran, and other significant world powers left them off the "public agenda" (Wanta, Golan, and Lee 2004). Similarly, extensive press coverage of foreign policy issues such as foreign aid tends to stimulate the U.S. government to pay greater attention to those issues (Van Belle and Hook 2000; Van Belle 2003).

- *Government watchdog.* A third and crucial role of a free press is to scrutinize government actions and to reveal wrongdoings when they occur. The CBS newsmagazine *60 Minutes II* served this function on April 29, 2004, when it featured horrifying photographs of Iraqi detainees at Abu Ghraib prison, which was once the site of brutal acts of torture under Saddam Hussein. Subsequent investigative reports disclosed that U.S. military officials had known for months about the abuses in Iraq as well as others in Afghanistan, some of which led to the deaths of detainees (see Hersh 2004). News stories on other problems related to the war on terrorism, including domestic surveillance by the National Security Agency and scandals involving defense contractors, also provided vital public information that was withheld by government sources.

---

3. For pioneering work on media agenda setting, see McCombs and Shaw (1972). For recent applications to U.S. politics, see Tedesco (2001) and Golan and Wanta (2001).

The functional role of the news media in the U.S. foreign policy process is a dynamic one in which influence runs in both directions between the news media and their partners in the information chain—the public and the government (see Figure 8.2). For government officials, the news media serve as means for explaining government policies, disseminating propaganda, and "leaking" confidential information officials want the public to know about. As Theodore White observed, "No major act of the U.S. Congress, no foreign adventure, no act of diplomacy, no great social reform can succeed in the United States unless the press prepares the public mind" (quoted in Graber 2006, 14). For the public, as noted earlier, news organizations serve as vital sources of information, opinions, and venues for governmental oversight. Citizens are also granted voice opportunities, or ways to express their viewpoints, through letters to the editor, op-ed articles, and other means of expression. They also convey feedback to the commercial news media by purchasing the goods and services they advertise.

The relationship between journalists and the government agencies they cover is inherently fraught with tension. By their very nature, reporters want to learn all they can about what the government is doing, and they stand to benefit greatly when they uncover evidence that government officials have acted improperly, illegally, or incompetently. Government officials are therefore understandably hesitant to open their doors to the news media. In the foreign policy arena, because of the secrecy that routinely surrounds diplomatic negotiations, military maneuvers, and other aspects of foreign policy, government officials are especially eager to keep journalists at arm's length.

Figure 8.2   The News Media's Bidirectional Impact

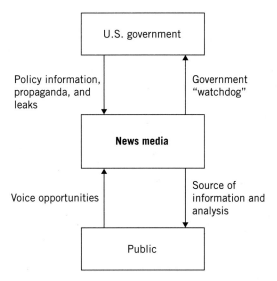

Yet despite this basic tension, the functional relationship between the media and the government can best be described as *symbiotic*—that is, one based on mutual need. Reporters rely on government sources to provide them with timely and accurate information. And for all their hostility toward the press, government officials depend on the news coverage to publicize their activities and generate support among citizens. Their ability to manipulate the media to turn public opinion in their favor "becomes moot if the media do not report what [they] are saying in the first place" (Powlick and Katz 1998, 38).

Patterns of Foreign News Coverage

The field of journalism, always in flux, has undergone unprecedented change in recent years. Within the past generation, a few open-air television networks have given way to hundreds of cable channels, satellite radio has shattered the dominance of local AM and FM stations, the Internet has assumed a central role in everyday life, and the local newspaper has become an endangered species. Many journalists, both practicing and aspiring, have gone "private" by creating their own blogs and engaging millions of citizens in unending dialogues. The nation's news outlets no longer compete just against each other, but also against those in Great Britain, India, Brazil, and most other countries.

This explosion of **new media**—the common term used to describe this new world of mass communications—greatly expands the news options available to citizens, who rely on familiar patterns of behavior in finding their media comfort zones. As in the past, they seek out and habitually follow "media outlets that match their beliefs and dispositions" (Stroud 2008, 342; see also Mutz 2006).[4] This pattern of **selective exposure** is important given the changing roles of the news media. Whereas journalists of the past viewed themselves as *messengers,* providing a general audience with objective updates of current events, most in the new media adopt the role of *advocates* of ideological, partisan, and policy positions.[5] Although news consumers pay close attention to the messages of like-minded media figures, they tend to adopt more rigid political beliefs that make national consensus unlikely. In this way, today's more diverse media contribute to the recent polarization of public opinion—and to the ideologically charged politics that have become a fact of life in Congress, the executive branch, and the courts.

As noted earlier, the U.S. media rarely cover international news unless the United States is facing a major crisis (Graber 2006). In the 1990s, the major broadcast and print outlets curtailed their foreign coverage in response to viewer preferences for domestic news and increased competition from cable networks.

---

4. This cognitive trait is linked closely to that of *selective perception* (see Chapter 3), by which citizens generally seek out information and "cues" that reinforce their existing belief systems.

5. By 2008, more television viewers watched news broadcasts on CNN, Fox News, and MSNBC than the daily news programs offered by ABC, NBC, and CBS (Pew Research Center 2008, 14).

According to one survey, foreign news coverage by the major networks dropped from more than 40 percent in the 1970s to less than 15 percent by 1995 (Dizard 2001, 173). Whereas a century ago dozens of U.S. newspapers maintained foreign news bureaus, today only major newspapers such as the *New York Times* and *Washington Post* employ foreign-based reporters. The others rely on wire services such as the Associated Press and Reuters.[6] Among the top twenty-five magazines sold in the United States in 2009, only two—*Time* (ranked thirteenth) and *Newsweek* (ranked twenty-first)—provided detailed coverage of international news (BurrellesLuce 2009). According to Neilsen Media Research (2009), the top twenty-five cable networks included just three that provided international news programs: Fox News Channel (ranked third), CNN (ranked twenty-third), and MSNBC (ranked twenty-fourth).

These trends reflect the intensifying market pressures imposed on U.S. news outlets, which must respond to audience preferences in order to maximize market share and advertising revenue. For a decade before the war on terrorism, news consumers sent the media the clear message that they had limited interest in foreign news. Newspaper readers consistently ranked their interest in news coverage as (1) state and local news, (2) national news, (3) foreign news involving the United States, and (4) foreign news not involving the United States (Rielly 2003). News organizations pay a price if they defy the public's general preference for domestic coverage.

The majority of Americans find only the most urgent news about events abroad worthy of their attention. Indeed, surveys find that the huge audiences that tuned into the evening news broadcasts in the pre-cable era were not actually interested in current events and public affairs. Instead, most viewers were habitually drawn to the *medium* of television itself, which in the 1950s was a novel source of relaxation after the workday, and the evening news on ABC, CBS, and NBC was all the local stations carried at this time of day. Once given opportunities to watch reruns of *Seinfeld, The Simpsons,* and other entertainment shows during this time period, most viewers abandoned the evening news on the open-air networks, all of which today serve a small fraction of their former audiences. "In a high-choice environment, lack of motivation, not lack of skills or resources, poses the main obstacle to a widely informed electorate" (Prior 2005, 577).

Opinion leaders and the attentive public, while relying on cable news to a limited degree, are more prone than the mass public to seek thorough news broadcasts from the Public Broadcasting Service (PBS) and National Public Radio (NPR), which are not owned by corporations fixated on making profits. These networks, which air programs such as, respectively, the *Frontline* documentary series and *All Things Considered,* win prestigious news awards every year but have far smaller audiences. Highly educated and affluent Americans are also

---

6. Although full-time foreign correspondents are less common today, news outlets find other ways to transmit firsthand information from overseas, including temporarily hiring foreign nationals or "parachute" journalists to report on current events on an ad hoc basis. See Hamilton and Jenner (2004) for an elaboration.

drawn disproportionately to foreign news networks and Internet sites. Although the explosion of new media has reduced the "knowledge gap" within this small share of the national population, it has widened the overall gap between rich and well-educated Americans and those at the other end of the socioeconomic spectrum.

Evolving Technologies and Media Coverage

Technological innovations historically have paved the way for mass communication in all forms, allowing more people to follow, understand, and become involved in public affairs. For example, Johann Gutenberg's invention of the printing press in 1450 allowed written messages of all kinds to be made available to readers, beyond the rulers who had previously monopolized the production and consumption of information within their provinces. Martin Luther, a leader of the Protestant Reformation, seized on this new technology in gaining popular support for his challenge to the Catholic Church in the early sixteenth century (Knutsen 1992, 46–50).

The linkages among technological advances, news coverage, and public opinion appear throughout U.S. history. The invention of the telegraph in the nineteenth century permitted newspapers to provide immediate coverage of the Civil War. In the months preceding the Spanish-American War, newspaper publishers learned to rally public opinion and thereby greatly expand their sales. Radio became an essential source of public information during World War II. Meanwhile, the newsreels shown at movie theaters and the photographs featured in popular magazines provided visual images of the fighting in Europe and Asia.

The Vietnam War became the first **living-room war,** bringing footage of U.S. military actions into American homes on a daily basis (Mandelbaum 1983). Graphic scenes of carnage in Vietnamese villages incited citizens already skeptical of the war. Such coverage also provided daily reminders that a U.S. victory in Vietnam was not "at hand," as had been stated repeatedly by the Johnson and Nixon administrations. Antiwar sentiment was fueled further when the *New York Times* (1971) published the **Pentagon Papers,** which detailed the administration's efforts to conceal its military activities throughout Southeast Asia.

The Vietnam War also represented a turning point in the news media's coverage of U.S. foreign policy. Before the war, reporters and editors generally had supported the government's stated goals in fighting the Cold War and had not subjected the tactics employed to close scrutiny. They limited their roles to conveying the government's viewpoints and describing its actions. However, the Vietnam War and the concurrent Watergate scandal produced a generation of skeptical journalists who openly questioned the motives and judgments of national leaders. Later in the decade, President Jimmy Carter could not escape saturation coverage of the Iranian hostage crisis, which began in November 1979 and continued through the rest of his presidency. The advent of cable television in the early 1980s expanded the range of news providers. The Atlanta-based Cable News Network (CNN) was the first to provide around-the-clock coverage of breaking news in the United States and abroad. Its coverage of the 1984 famine in Ethiopia generated widespread sympathy for the victims and prompted a series of benefit rock concerts, *Live Aid,* that were televised worldwide and raised tens of millions of dollars for emergency relief. Five years later, CNN transmitted live footage of the pro-democracy uprising in China that culminated in the government slaughter of protesters in Tiananmen Square, which outraged global public opinion and led to condemnations and sanctions by most industrialized states.

Globalized telecommunications from the United States and other industrialized countries also played a key role in the collapse of communist governments in Eastern Europe in 1989 and the subsequent demise of the Soviet Union. The leaders of these countries could not maintain their firm grip on information, which was increasingly being transmitted across their borders via satellite. As a result, citizens in the Soviet bloc became all too aware that their counterparts in the "first world" were enjoying political rights and living standards greater than their own. In this respect, the collapse of communism in these countries owed as much to the penetration of global telecommunications as to the foreign policies of the United States and its allies. Although the Chinese government, more distant and culturally detached from the West, suppressed the democracy movement in its country, communist leaders in the Soviet bloc succumbed to the pressures imposed by their newly enlightened and energized, if not empowered, citizens.

The end of the Cold War created a "new global optic" that included the absence of U.S.-Soviet ideological competition, the rise of regional conflicts, and accelerated economic globalization (Grunwald 1993, 14). The 1991 Persian Gulf War gave television networks their first opportunity to broadcast a major military conflict in "real time" (Bennett and Paletz 1994). The instigator of the war, Iraq's Saddam Hussein, reportedly tuned into CNN throughout the conflict, while U.S. officials relied on the same broadcasts for battlefield information. **Rooftop journalism** became a staple of televised war coverage, with flak-jacketed CNN reporters gaining celebrity status by narrating U.S. attacks on downtown Baghdad. CNN's audience increased tenfold during the war, and on some days it exceeded the sizes of the broadcast networks' audiences. Meanwhile, twenty of the twenty-five largest U.S. newspapers experienced sharp gains in circulation during the war (Hallin and Gitlin 1994).

The rapidity with which globalized news coverage prompts government action is often referred to as the **CNN effect.** Among the most vivid examples are Somalia's 1992 civil war and the resulting famine, which were covered extensively by CNN and other networks. President George H. W. Bush said the images of starving Somalis so disturbed him that he felt compelled to order a humanitarian intervention by U.S. military forces. Many analysts (for example, Strobel 1997 and Robinson 2001) found a reciprocal relationship between press coverage and U.S. foreign policy: responses by the U.S. government to problems overseas, provoked in part by media reports, greatly increased the volume of subsequent news coverage and public interest in the areas in question.

In the 1990s, the media repeatedly cut back coverage of international affairs despite the fact that the United States had emerged from the Cold War as

Table 8.2   Cable Networks and the Iraq War, Spring 2003

Network	Average viewership	Change of viewership since war started
Fox News	3.3 million	+ 236%
CNN	2.7 million	+ 313
MSNBC	1.4 million	+ 360

SOURCE: Nielsen Media Research, www.nielsenmedia.com.

the undisputed world leader in terms of military power, economic wealth, and political influence. Print and broadcast news organizations closed foreign bureaus and paid more attention to developments at home. Foreign news predictably regained its hold on media attention after the terrorist attacks of September 2001. In early 2003, news outlets provided saturation coverage of the invasion of Iraq, aided by the nearly three thousand journalists armed with videophones and laptop computers who received press credentials. While the "big three" broadcast networks—ABC, CBS, and NBC—recorded high ratings, the cable networks such as CNN and Fox News reported the largest increases in viewership (see Table 8.2).

Fox News emerged from the war as the most popular cable news network— and the most supportive of the Bush administration's war effort. Launched in 1996, Fox News overtook ratings leader CNN in 2002 by appealing to the same conservative sector of U.S. society that made talk radio, and commentator Rush Limbaugh in particular, a powerful cultural force in the 1990s. Among news consumers, Fox News viewers were the most enthusiastic about Operation Iraqi Freedom as well as the most likely to exaggerate the threat posed by Saddam Hussein's regime. A prominent survey conducted by Steven Kull, Clay Ramsay, and Evan Lewis (2003/2004, 585–586) found that among Fox viewers "greater attention to news modestly *increased* the likelihood of misperception" (emphasis in original). More recent survey data suggest that most Fox News viewers are conservative, whereas those of CNN and the broadcast news networks are politically moderate (Pew Research Center 2006c, 38).

Advances in media technology spurred an unprecedented global response to the January 2010 earthquake in Haiti, which killed more than 200,000 people and nearly leveled the capital city of Port-au-Prince. Within weeks of the disaster, nonprofit groups received more than $500 million in donations, most of which were transmitted electronically via the Internet. More than 80 million viewers tuned into the "Hope for Haiti Now" telethon, which raised more than $70 million in donations after being broadcast or streamed on dozens of television networks, Internet sites such as YouTube and Yahoo!, and social media outlets such as Facebook and Twitter. The download-only album of music performed on the telethon quickly reached the top of the Billboard chart, marking a milestone in the recording industry. Meanwhile, the American Red Cross raised more than $30 million by soliciting $10 donations for earthquake relief via cell phone text messages. This outpouring of relief complemented the efforts of the Obama White House, which assumed a lead role in raising funds from other governments and delivering aid supplies to Haiti.

Characteristics of World News

Technological developments thus play a critical role in shaping the form and content of news coverage, but a closely related factor is the growing concentration of media outlets (see Compaine and Gomery 2000). This trend has been hastened in recent years by media deregulation in the United States. In the name of free enterprise, government officials abolished a variety of rules designed to foster competition and diversity.[7] By 2007, eight conglomerates were dominating the U.S. news and entertainment industry.[8] Their holdings extended far beyond news providers to include movie studios, radio stations, music studios, local television stations, book and magazine publishers, and makers of consumer electronics.[9] Of concern as well are the close links between media conglomerates and business interests in other sectors of the economy. In the early 1990s, most major stockholders of ABC, CBS, and NBC were banks such as Chase Manhattan (Parenti 1993, 29). At the same time, CBS's board of directors included top executives from some large corporations (and major advertisers) such as IBM, Philip Morris, AT&T, Citibank, and Metropolitan Life. Such links threaten the editorial independence of each news outlet, whose reporting is presumed to be free from economic pressure. Political overlaps, too, are troubling, as many media outlets are owned by corporations that provide unrelated goods and services to the government. General Electric (GE), for example, not only owns NBC, its affiliated cable news networks, and more than two hundred local stations, but also serves as a primary defense contractor to the Pentagon. The potential conflicts of interest in these cases are obvious.

Beyond these points, news coverage of U.S. foreign policy features six common trends and characteristics:

From print to video. The emergence of CNN in the 1980s coincided with a long-term contraction in the newspaper industry, whose advertising revenues fell from nearly half of the national total to just 22 percent in 1998 (Compaine and Gomery

---

7. The George W. Bush administration encouraged this deregulation trend. Michael Powell, the son of Secretary of State Colin Powell, led the drive toward greater media concentration as head of the Federal Communications Commission.

8. These major conglomerates were AOL-Time Warner, AT&T, Bertelsmann, CBS, General Electric, Viacom, Vivendi Universal, and Walt Disney (Stop Big Media 2007; see also Miller 2002). Amid subsequent shifts in the balance of power among these firms, the concentration of media ownership has continued on a global scale.

9. A near monopoly over satellite radio would result from the proposed merger of the two industry giants, Sirius and XM, in February 2007. Consumer groups, along with the National Association of Broadcasters, expressed concern about this proposal, which also sparked opposition in Congress and required approval by the Federal Communications Commission.

Figure 8.3 Reliance on Sources of News, 2008 (percentage relying on each news source)

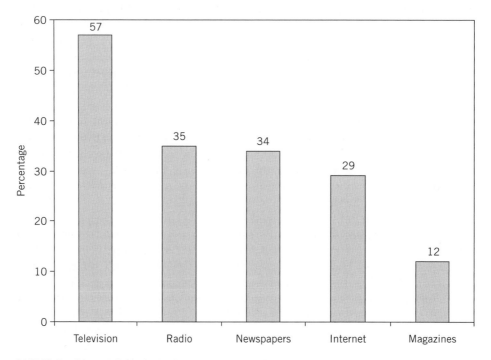

SOURCE: Pew Research Center for the People and the Press, "Key News Audiences Now Blend Online and Traditional Sources," pp. 7, 19 (April 17, 2008), http://people-press.org/reports/pdf/444.pdf.

2000, 3). By 2009, fewer than thirty U.S. newspapers managed bureaus in Washington, D.C., in contrast to the more than seventy bureaus in the 1980s (Project for Excellence in Journalism 2009).[10] Most Americans now rely on television as their primary source of news, with nearly 60 percent of survey respondents citing their reliance on television in June 2008 (see Figure 8.3). Televised news coverage, which provides dramatic, real-time visual images of events abroad, obviously has a strong advantage over the print media. Such coverage, however, naturally favors events with strong visual appeal. News executives downplay less telegenic, but equally important, events such as international summit conferences.

The rise of niche media. Not long ago, most Americans relied on their local newspapers, mass-circulation magazines such as *Time* and *Newsweek,* and three television networks—ABC, CBS, and NBC—for their daily news. These media outlets tailored their coverage for their millions of news consumers, providing them with

10. Leading newspapers such as the *Chicago Tribune, Baltimore Sun,* and *Los Angeles Times* had closed their Washington bureaus by the end of 2008.

news of general interest and avoiding controversies and debates. All this has changed in recent years. Whereas the number and circulation of local newspapers have plummeted since the 1980s, the number of specialty publications and news-letters (most delivered electronically) has increased by more than 50 percent (Project for Excellence in Journalism 2009). As detailed later in this chapter, news consumers are also more likely than ever to seek information from foreign news sources that may offer a different perspective from that offered by domestic news outlets and the U.S. government.

U.S.-centrism. News organizations have learned that foreign news, to interest most Americans, must have a "peg" to the United States, such as involving a possible deployment of U.S. forces or an impact on trade or immigration. Because general news about political developments overseas usually does not concern Americans, news managers avoid stories that do not relate directly to this audience. A recent study found foreign news on U.S. television networks significantly related to such factors as shared religious views, proximity to the United States, and trade and investment ties with the foreign countries covered on news programs (Golan 2010). This bias in news budgets produces coverage that may exaggerate a nation's importance in global affairs, while prompting readers and viewers to disregard important problems that affect much of the world's population, but not U.S. citizens. By contrast, major foreign outlets such as the BBC provide more coverage of foreign news, including a substantial volume of news about U.S. foreign policy.

Conflict orientation. Coverage of all news, foreign and domestic, tends to empha-size conflict rather than cooperation, chaos rather than order. "If it bleeds, it leads" is a popular standard used widely by local and national news editors in deciding what is worth covering. In foreign policy, such a standard leads to an emphasis on civil wars and international conflicts, whose dramatic images have the strongest impact on viewers and readers. Of secondary importance are nonvio-lent political conflicts, such as closely contested elections and struggles for power. This bias in news management distorts public understanding by subjecting citizens to the misperception that the "outside world" is plagued by unrest and disorder.

Superficiality. The preoccupation with visual images, conflict, and late-breaking news prevents reporters from providing in-depth coverage of their stories or paying attention to long-range problems such as global warming, economic inequalities, population growth, and weapons proliferation. News consumers thus have little context in which to understand day-to-day crises elsewhere and U.S. options in responding to them. Coverage of the Persian Gulf War, for example, rarely moved beyond breaking news to explore the underlying cultural and economic problems in the region that had fueled the conflict (Iyengar and Simon 1994, 79). Such cov-erage has given rise to **parachute journalism,** a pattern in which reporters descend on a trouble spot and then move on, never gaining a deep understanding of the problems in the areas that would have given their reporting greater substance.

Arbitrariness. Foreign news coverage in the United States tends to be guided by immediate developments rather than long-term priorities and principles. The news media's attention to a foreign country generally lasts only as long as the crisis of interest, after which journalists flock *en masse* to other trouble spots. This was clearly the case during and after the 1989 U.S. invasion of Panama, a tiny Central American country that suddenly became a focus of media attention and then, just as abruptly, disappeared from the radar screens of U.S.-based editors (see Figure 8.4). The arbitrary nature of U.S. news coverage can have direct consequences for U.S. foreign policy. The nation's responses to natural disasters overseas, for example, are significantly related to the amount of news coverage they receive. When other stories dominate the headlines—shootings at a U.S. high school, for example, or the Olympics—Washington provides less disaster assistance (Eisensee and Strömberg 2007).

As noted earlier, the U.S. military intervention in Somalia was prompted in large part by media coverage of the war-induced famine in the African nation. A similar crisis in nearby Sudan received little press or government attention. Even in areas that attract the media spotlight, however, the effects on government policy are skewed. "If you look at how humanitarian aid is delivered in Bosnia

Figure 8.4 News Articles about Panama before and after December 1989 U.S. Invasion

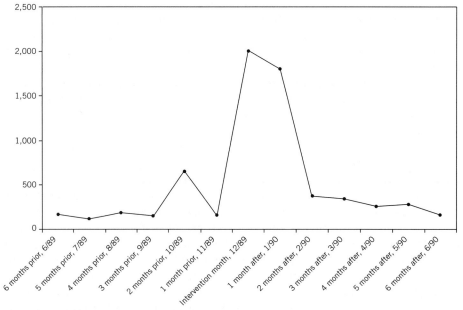

SOURCE: Compiled by the author, based on LexisNexis news database, www.lexisnexis.com.

you see that those areas where the TV cameras are most present are the ones that are best fed, the ones that receive the most medicine," observed Mohamed Sacirbey, Bosnia's ambassador to the United Nations. "While on the other hand, many of our people have starved or died of disease and shelling where there are no TV cameras" (quoted in Seib 1997, 90).

The ability of global news coverage to shape the agenda of U.S. foreign policy raises troubling questions, ones that Thomas Jefferson and other early advocates of a free press could not have anticipated. First, public and government attention is drawn only to trouble spots abroad that are readily accessible to camera crews. In other war-torn areas, such as Sudan and the former Zaire in the 1990s, the lack of news coverage precludes public pressure for action and discourages a U.S. response. Second, excessive reliance on news coverage leads foreign policy makers to ignore long-term problems and to focus instead on impending disasters (Van Belle and Hook 2000). For example, by the time ethnic conflict in Rwanda reached genocidal proportions in 1994, the time had passed for the United States and other governments to prevent massive death and destruction. Similarly, the lack of dramatic visual imagery on global warming hampers the news media in alerting the public about this growing problem (see Chapter 12). The U.S. government, which often takes its cue from the news media, thus has less incentive to confront the problem.

Most important, media-driven foreign policy erodes the capacity of diplomats and other public officials to pursue a clear, consistent, and coherent national strategy. As George Kennan (1996, 297) observed, "If American policy from here on out, particularly policy involving the uses of our armed forces abroad, is to be controlled by popular impulses . . . provoked by the commercial television industry, then there is no place—not only for myself, but for the responsible deliberative organs of government." Thus although the globalized news media have the capacity to bring citizens closer to world problems than ever before, such coverage may hinder as well as facilitate the U.S. government's effective use of world power.

Government Efforts to Control the Message

When it comes to the news media's coverage of its actions, the U.S. government is not a simple bystander. On the contrary, government officials work actively to shape that coverage in ways that show them in the best possible light. **Spin control,** or the elaborate efforts by government leaders to improve their public approval by influencing media reports, has become an art form in recent years (see Kurtz 1998).

By manipulating information, the government seeks to advance its agenda and control public opinion. The media historically have been a primary instrument of **propaganda**—that is, false and misleading public information designed to enhance the stature of the government or its policies. Jody Powell (1984, 223), Jimmy Carter's press secretary, believed the government "has not only the right but a positive obligation to lie" when national interests are at stake. Early in the war on terrorism, White House press secretary Ari Fleischer carried out an elaborate "system of disinformation—blunter, more aggressive, and in its own way, more impressive than spin" (Chait 2002, 20). Meanwhile, Defense Secretary Donald Rumsfeld proposed the creation of a new agency, the Office of Strategic Influence, that would spread information—some of it false—to audiences in the Islamic world. Although Rumsfeld quickly dropped his proposal in response to public protests, he retained the right of the CIA and other intelligence agencies to use false information as a strategic weapon.

The first and most common means by which the U.S. government controls information is *keeping secrets*. Secrets are especially common in foreign policy, which relies to a large extent on classified information and on necessarily private lines of communication between Washington and foreign governments. Most news outlets accept the need for secrecy, and they may even withhold from the public information they receive "off the record" from government officials.

The remains of U.S. casualties from the recent military conflicts in Afghanistan and Iraq are delivered to Delaware's Dover Air Force Base for subsequent release to families and burial. The Pentagon had earlier resisted the release of this and other photographs to the news media, fearing that such images would weaken public support for the ongoing conflicts linked to the global war on terrorism.

Journalists and government officials view this practice as essential, both to maintain national security and to preserve their mutually beneficial ties.

Government officials frequently reveal secrets in the form of **press leaks** to journalists. Some leaks, such as those used by Bill Clinton on a new trade pact with China, may serve as "trial balloons" to gauge public support for a possible policy change. Other leaks are used to punish dissenters by secretly providing embarrassing information about them to reporters. The Bush administration resorted to this tactic in 2003 by revealing to columnist Robert Novak that Joseph Wilson, a former ambassador and career foreign service officer, was married to a clandestine CIA agent. The leak, intended to discredit Wilson (2004) after he wrote a *New York Times* op-ed disputing Bush's claims about Iraq's pursuit of nuclear materials in Africa, ended Valerie Plame's intelligence career and placed her life in jeopardy (see Chapter 4).

Unofficial leaks, by contrast, are supplied by anonymous critics who hope to reform government behavior by revealing potentially harmful or illegal practices. Government "whistleblowers," for example, frequently alert reporters to cost overruns in the defense industry and failed weapons systems tests that would otherwise be unknown to the public. Government employees who find press leaks a useful way to affect policy from behind the scenes may apply the same tactics. According to journalist Hedrick Smith (1988, 81), "On Wall Street, passing insider information is standard operating procedure. In Washington, it is the regular stuff of the power game. Everyone does it, from presidents on down, when they want to change the balance of power on some issue."

"Framing" U.S. Foreign Policy

News organizations generally support government attempts at **framing** foreign policy problems—that is, structuring and simplifying these problems so that they are understood by U.S. citizens in ways that favor the government's position. As noted in Chapter 3, government officials routinely "construct" a particular image of allies and adversaries in order to garner support for their foreign policies, knowing that the vast majority of Americans with little knowledge of or interest in foreign affairs "can be routinely manipulated by alternative framings of a problem" (Chong and Druckman 2007, 103). Ronald Reagan's depiction of contra rebels in Nicaragua as "freedom fighters" in the 1980s served this purpose, as did George H. W. Bush's more recent portrayal of Saddam Hussein as "Hitler" before the United States ousted Iraq from Kuwait in 1991 (Norris, Kern, and Just 2003).

The process by which government frames penetrate the news media and public opinion is complex. As conceived by the White House, news frames "cascade" through the federal government and are adopted by the lower-level officials who maintain regular contact with the press. Only when internal divisions among U.S. officials are exposed—a relatively rare occurrence in foreign policy—do the news media depart from the government's frame and create their own images of the foreign policy problem (Lewis and Rose 2002; Entman 2004). Otherwise, news organizations freely grant government leaders access to audiences and adopt the government's ideology and viewpoints (see Hunt 1987).

This pattern applies not just to the United States. All governments have a keen interest in the content of news coverage because of its critical role in the formulation of public opinion. A government and its media outlets tend to frame foreign policy coverage in ways that adhere to their distinctive cultural traditions and political systems. For example, in 2001 a U.S. spy plane and a Chinese jet fighter collided off the coast of China, killing the fighter pilot and forcing the damaged U.S. plane to land on Chinese territory and the crew to suffer a prolonged period of detention and interrogation. Whereas U.S. media focused mainly on the diplomatic standoff over the stranded crew, the government-controlled Chinese press emphasized the crew's covert mission and framed news coverage in the context of U.S. hegemony and imperialism (Hook and Pu 2006).

The White House demonstrated its skill in "manufacturing consent" (Herman and Chomsky 1988) during the U.S. invasion of Iraq. Despite their expressed reservations about the invasion, the editorial boards of major U.S. newspapers "conditioned themselves to treat Bush's national security argument with deference" (Mooney 2004, 29). As the invasion began, the government "embedded" reporters within military units to provide firsthand accounts of the overthrow of Saddam Hussein's government. The White House correctly anticipated that the "**embeds**" would identify with the troops and thus produce favorable reports of the missions (see Katovsky and Carlson 2003).

Government officials also turned for support to powerful allies in media corporations that spent billions of dollars on print and broadcast advertising. Radio giant Clear Channel displayed this muscle in 2003 when it refused to play music by the Dixie Chicks after band members spoke out against the invasion of Iraq. A year later, the Sinclair Broadcast Group prevented its eight ABC affiliates from airing an episode of *Nightline* that was devoted exclusively to reciting the names of U.S. casualties in Iraq. These and other instances of politicized media content demonstrate further the close link between the U.S. government and like-minded corporations.

Public Diplomacy and Strategic Communications

Although foreign policy makers customarily conduct their statecraft through conventional diplomatic channels, they also resort to **public diplomacy** to achieve their objectives. In effect, public diplomacy goes "over the heads" of foreign leaders by appealing directly to the citizenry. The messengers of public diplomacy, whose ranks have included private citizens such as scholars, artists, and journalists, are uniquely positioned to project the nation's cultural values and demonstrate the vitality of its civil society. In doing so, they may strengthen international support for the United States in ways beyond the reach of the conventional diplomats and political leaders.

The U.S. government has sponsored programs of public diplomacy for many years. The Fulbright Program, for example, provides for the international exchange of scholars, teachers, and students in many fields of study. Another program is the Voice of America, a worldwide international radio service, which has been joined in recent years by regional broadcasters Radio *Martí* and TV *Martí* (to Cuba), Radio Free Europe/Radio Liberty, Radio Free Asia, and Radio *Sawa* (to Arab countries). As part of its public diplomacy mission, the State Department also operates press centers in the United States and funds democracy programs in foreign countries. Overseeing these efforts is the department's Office of International Information Programs, an agency created in 1999 to replace the U.S. Information Agency.

Government officials pursue public diplomacy as a peculiar form of public relations. Shortly after the September 2001 terrorist attacks, the Bush administration appointed Charlotte Beers, a Madison Avenue advertising executive, to serve as under secretary of state for public diplomacy. Beers spent millions of dollars on a campaign of radio and television documentaries, booklets, and wall posters that portrayed the U.S. government and society as open to multiple cultures and welcoming the participation of Muslims in public life. The point of these messages: the Islamic world has nothing to fear from the United States. "She got me to buy Uncle Ben's rice. There is nothing wrong with getting somebody who knows how to sell something," Secretary of State Colin Powell said of the Beers appointment. "We are selling a product. We need someone who can rebrand American foreign policy, rebrand diplomacy" (quoted in the *Economist* 2002).

This effort failed to rally global public opinion at a time when the U.S. government was found to be abusing war prisoners, ignoring treaties, and violating international laws—all difficult practices to "sell" to foreign governments and mass publics. Engaging civil societies was also hampered by the elaborate steps taken to protect U.S. embassies and consulates from terrorist attacks after September 11. These diplomatic compounds were transformed into modern-day fortresses, surrounded by electronic fences and dozens of machine gun–wielding guards. Although President Obama attained instant popularity upon taking office in January 2009, lingering anti-Americanism and ongoing security threats to the United States frustrated his effort to revive public diplomacy.

The State Department is not alone in trying to create a stronger image for the United States overseas. The same goal is pursued regularly by the Pentagon in the form of **strategic communications,** defined by the Defense Science Board (2004) as "the ability of the United States to communicate with and thereby influence worldwide audiences." Civilian and military officials around the world conduct **influence operations** directed toward "opinion leaders whose credibility and trustworthiness is judged to be high" (Larson et al. 2009, 6). These contacts include private briefings with foreign governments and media owners, conventional press

IN THEIR OWN WORDS: KAREN HUGHES, UNDER SECRETARY OF STATE FOR PUBLIC DIPLOMACY

The Bush administration's difficulties in gaining public support for its foreign policies prompted the president to pay greater attention to public diplomacy during his second term. In assuming leadership of this effort and conducting an extended "listening tour" of foreign countries, longtime Bush adviser Karen Hughes aggressively sought to reverse this trend. Among her priorities was ensuring that foreign service officers and other members of the State Department stationed overseas remained "on message" when communicating with government officials and citizens. A memorandum that she wrote, leaked to the Washington Post *in November 2006, included the following guidelines that became known as "Karen's Rules." Excerpts of her memo follow.*

Rule #1: Think Advocacy. I want all of you to think of yourselves as advocates for America's story each day. . . . I know that it is important to get out in front of an issue or at best have a strong response to a negative story. . . . We want you out there on television, in the news, and on the radio a couple of times a week and certainly on major news stations in your country and region.

Rule #2: Use What's Out There. You are always on sure ground if you use what the President, Secretary Rice . . . or senior USG spokesmen have already said on a particular subject. I always read recent statements by key officials on important subjects before I do press events.

Rule #3: Think Local. Because your key audience is your local—or regional—audience you do not need clearance to speak to any local media, print or television. . . . The rule of thumb to keep in mind is "don't make policy or pre-empt the Secretary or senior Washington policymakers."

Rule #4: Use Common Sense to Respond to Natural Disasters or Tragedies. You do not need to get Department clearance to express condolences in the event of a loss, or express sympathy and support in response to a national disaster.

Rule #5: Don't Make Policy. This is a sensitive issue about which you need to be careful. Do not get out in front of USG policymakers on an issue, even if you are speaking to local press.

Rule #6: No Surprises. You should always give [your supervisor] a heads-up in the event that you speak to U.S.-based media. This ensures that those who should know are in the loop on what is happening.

I encourage you to take advantage of opportunities to speak out, and look forward to our aggressive promotion of U.S. policy.

SOURCE: Elizabeth Williamson, "Karen's Rules on Diplomacy: Talk to the Media—If You Dare," *Washington Post*, November 8, 2006, A25.

releases, and other tools of public relations in order to "create, strengthen, or preserve conditions favorable to the advancement of U.S. government interests, policies, and objectives" (U.S. Department of Defense 2006, xii). These activities, which have become more elaborate in recent years, are seen by U.S. officials as vital in countering similar efforts in "influence warfare" (Forest 2009) undertaken by terrorist groups and other adversaries of the United States.

Television news coverage in recent years has increasingly consisted of bitter debates between hosts of rival cable networks. Arguments between conservative Bill O'Reilly (left) on Fox News and liberal Keith Olbermann (right) on MSNBC have drawn millions of viewers nightly. Their exchanges, however, have merely reinforced the opinions of their respective fans rather than encouraging consensus on key issues dividing the public.

The Seduction of "Soft News"

The dominance of television as a news source, combined with the proliferation of TV channels on cable and satellite systems, allows producers to offer many forms of news suited to different audiences. For "hard news" (breaking news stories), viewers turn to the major U.S. networks—ABC, CBS, and NBC—and the cable networks such as CNN, Fox News, or MSNBC. Viewers seeking entertainment turn to **soft news.** News magazines such as *60 Minutes,* video tabloids such as *Entertainment Tonight,* talk shows such as *The Oprah Winfrey Show,* and variety shows such as *The Tonight Show with Jay Leno* have attracted comparable, if not larger, audiences than the purveyors of hard news.

Soft news producers rely on celebrity stories—the O. J. Simpson trial in 1995, the 2000 marriage of Jennifer Aniston and Brad Pitt, and the death of Michael Jackson in 2009—for the huge audiences (and advertising revenues) they attract, but they also frequently address the most pressing issues of the day, including the September 11 terrorist attacks and the subsequent war on terrorism. In contrast to traditional news programs, which provide basic facts and details about the crises, soft news outlets emphasize human interest stories that highlight the role of the people caught up in the events. Soft news productions also frame foreign policy conflicts in moralistic terms to make the stories understandable and compelling to an audience that ordinarily avoids political news.

Packaged in this way, such **"infotainment"** highlights specific foreign policy issues without burdening its audience with their complex origins and political conflicts.

Like its hard news counterpart, soft news has a measurable impact on public opinion. The moralistic frames adopted by soft news producers, depicting the United States as a benevolent but besieged world power, reinforce viewers' suspicions about the "outside world." This image resonates especially with viewers of soft news, who tend to have less education and lower incomes than the national average. Surveys consistently find that this demographic group is more likely to hold isolationist views on U.S. foreign policy and to oppose U.S. interventions in foreign trouble spots. To media analyst Matthew Baum (2003, 291), the seductive presentation of soft news prompts "politically inattentive individuals to further recoil from foreign entanglements. Taken to an extreme, this could potentially lead to a substantial increase in public support for an isolationist American foreign policy."

The sources of soft news also include popular magazines, books, and Internet sites that examine U.S. military conflicts, the political travails of other countries, and other foreign policy issues. Recent films such as *The Hurt Locker, Lord of War,* and *The Messenger* may serve as a "gateway" to more detailed knowledge of world events, which in turn elicits more active participation in public affairs. Indeed, those less familiar with policy issues have proved especially receptive to new information and political causes (see Zaller 1992 and Iyengar 1991). Thus, the media can fill the nation's knowledge gap in many ways, even when the viewers, readers, and Internet surfers are less interested in reading than in being entertained.

Among young adults (aged eighteen to twenty-four years), a popular source of soft news in recent years is *The Daily Show,* a self-proclaimed purveyor of "fake news" airing on the Comedy Channel. As Bill Moyers, a former CBS News correspondent and respected media analyst, has observed, "You simply can't understand American politics in the new millennium without *The Daily Show*" (PBS 2003). The program's success, with each episode attracting an estimated 2 million viewers, lies not so much in the "fakeness" of its news; the major headlines are first presented accurately. Instead, viewers are drawn to the satirical insights of its host, Jon Stewart, and his team of "journalists," who pretend to report from remote locations. Presidential candidates routinely appear on *The Daily Show* knowing that young viewers, who generally are less politically active and unattached to traditional news sources, can be enlisted as voters or campaign volunteers.[11] Even foreign leaders yearn for an appearance on the program. When Pakistan's leader, Pervez Musharraf, appeared on *The Daily Show* in 2006 under heavy security, Stewart opened the interview by

---

11. A survey by the Pew Research Center (2004) revealed that young adults spend an average of thirty-five minutes a day following the news, or about two-thirds of the national average of fifty-one minutes. One-quarter of the young adults surveyed said they paid no attention to hard news.

offering tea and a Twinkie to his guest and then asking, with mock seriousness, "Where's Osama bin Laden?"[12]

In blurring news and entertainment, *The Daily Show* "represents an important experiment in journalism, one that contains much significance for the ongoing redefinition of news" (Baym 2005). Yet, the long-term effect of this media hybrid on political attitudes and behavior is unclear. One recent study, comparing viewers' exposure to *The Daily Show* with that to the *CBS Evening News,* found that those treated to "fake news" had more negative views of U.S. politics and less "faith in the system" after watching selected excerpts. The same study, however, found that exposure to *The Daily Show* "increased internal efficacy by raising viewers' perception that the complex world of politics was understandable" (Baumgartner and Morris 2006, 362). These two findings highlight the mixed blessings of soft news—superficial coverage that indulges Americans' impatience with public policy, foreign and domestic, while serving as a pathway to a more knowledgeable and attentive public.

The Internet's Window on the World

As described earlier, technological advances historically propel changes in relations between citizens and states, in the role and impact of the press, and in the day-to-day conduct of foreign policy. This pattern certainly applies to the Internet, a vital fact of life in the "brave new wired world" of the twenty-first century (Burton 1997). This technology, barely known a generation ago, provides new outlets for government and private expression, along with a nearly limitless range of information for students, observers, and practitioners of world politics. Web-based news providers, such as the Microsoft Network, Yahoo!, and AOL, are now primary sources of world news for most Americans (see Table 8.3).

As the centerpiece of the new media, the Internet has altered the landscape of U.S. foreign policy in all areas. The U.S. military's swift overthrows of the governments of Afghanistan (2001) and Iraq (2003) owed much to improvements in Web-based communications—a central element of the "revolution in military affairs" (see Chapter 6).[13] Meanwhile, managers of U.S. foreign economic policy are using the nation's technological superiority to capture a greater market share of overseas investments and exports. The Internet also has accelerated the pace of diplomatic communications within the foreign service and between the United States and foreign governments. This shift toward **digital diplomacy** marks "the most important innovation affecting diplomatic practices since the fifteenth century" (Dizard 2001, 1).

---

12. Tellingly, one of Musharraf's primary goals in appearing on the broadcast was to sell copies of his memoir, *In the Line of Fire* (Musharraf 2006).

13. The Defense Department was the primary sponsor of the development of the Internet during the 1960s and 1970s (Margolis and Resnick 2000, 25–51).

Table 8.3   Top Ten Online News Sites, 2008

News site	Percentage indicating use
Yahoo!	28%
MSN	19
CNN	17
Google	11
NBC/MSNBC	10
AOL	8
Fox	7
New York Times	4
Local news source	4
BBC	2

SOURCE: Pew Research Center for the People and the Press, "Key News Audiences Now Blend Online and Traditional Sources," p. 22 (August 17, 2008), http://people-press.org/reports/pdf/444.pdf.

The Internet combines the immediacy and visual impact of television with the substantive depth of the print media, offering its users a vast range of information at little or no cost. According to Netcraft (2009), a British Internet service company, the number of Web sites increased to 232 million in 2009, or more than double the number recorded in its 2006 survey. Only 1 million sites were identified in April 1997—a number that grew to 10 million by February 2000. E-mail and blogs, the second major component of the Internet, make the new technology interactive. Users gain ample opportunities to voice their opinions, ask questions, and share information with other users who have similar interests. This "two-way electronic street" is congested further by Internet-friendly cell phones and text-messaging systems. Military troops can now communicate instantaneously with their families at home, exchanging messages that used to take days or weeks to deliver.

The growth of Internet use since 2000 suggests that it has established a distinct niche—not as a primary source of news but as one that supplements traditional sources. Fewer than 10 percent of Internet users devote thirty minutes or more to reading news online, compared with the nearly half of television viewers who devote thirty minutes or more to viewing newscasts (Pew Research Center 2006c, 2). Internet users commonly turn to multipurpose Web sites for a quick scan of headlines rather than read the in-depth stories found in the electronic versions of national newspapers. As a result, the Internet is less an independent source of news than a carrier of news generated elsewhere. Overall, the rise of the Internet has not increased the overall level of news consumption in the United States, which rose slightly from sixty-six minutes daily in 1996 to sixty-seven minutes a decade later.

For the United States, the Internet represents, in addition to a source of news and communications, a powerful source of cultural influence, or "soft power"

Table 8.4   Global Online Populations, 2006

Country	Number of Internet users (millions)	Percentage of world users
United States	204	19%
China	111	10
Japan	86	8
India	51	5
Germany	49	5
United Kingdom	38	4
Rep. of Korea	34	3
Italy	29	3
France	26	2
Brazil	26	2
Russia	24	2
Canada	21	2
Indonesia	18	2
Spain	17	2
Rep. of China (Taiwan)	14	1

SOURCE: ClickZ Network, "Population Explosion!" (April 12, 2006), www.clickz.com/showPage.html?page=151151.

(Nye 2004): English is the dominant language of the Web, more than 80 percent of Web "visits" are to sites in the United States, and nearly 20 percent of all Internet communications involve participants in the United States (see Table 8.4). Although this domination of the Internet will undoubtedly decline in the coming years, the United States is expected to maintain its edge as this technology continues to advance and new applications are discovered.

Inevitably, this pattern will reinforce the U.S.-centric worldview that has characterized the Internet since its inception. According to Don Heath, president of the Internet Society, "If the United States government had tried to come up with a scheme to spread its brand of capitalism and its emphasis on political liberalism around the world, it couldn't have invented a better model than the Internet" (quoted in Lohr 2000, WK-1). The decentralized, loosely governed structure of the Internet encourages the kind of informal, uninhibited dialogue familiar to Americans. As Daniel Burton (1997, 33), former president of the Council on Competitiveness, observed, "The Internet is a tangible expression of the world coming together. If regionalism was the intermediate step toward a true global community, the World Wide Web is its consummation."

And what are the more direct, practical implications of the Internet for U.S. foreign relations? The new age of digital diplomacy affects U.S. foreign policy in four distinct ways:

- Internal communications among the hundreds of U.S. diplomatic posts improve greatly, thereby facilitating greater *coordination* in implementing the policies adopted in Washington, D.C.

- The *integration* of computer networks among the State Department and other federal departments produces greater consistency in the day-to-day conduct of foreign policy. With the Internet, distant embassies now have easy access to the latest press reports.

- The establishment of electronic ties between the United States and foreign governments encourages greater *responsiveness* to political problems and crises abroad, thereby accelerating the pace of diplomacy, which historically has been hampered by slow communications.

- Digital diplomacy fosters greater *mobilization* of nongovernmental organizations. Thousands of such groups—firms, religious institutions, research foundations, and public interest groups—use the Web as their primary source of communications. Internet campaigns, for instance, were instrumental in hastening East Timor's secession from Indonesia in 1999, in securing the arrest of Serbian leader Slobodan Milosevic in 2000, and in rallying global public opinion against the U.S. mistreatment of Iraqi prisoners in 2004.

A main concern about the Internet is maintaining **information security,** or unfettered flows of online communications. Computer "hackers" frequently disrupt such communications and introduce viruses that can cripple even the most advanced computer systems in the public and private sectors. In this respect, the growing reliance of U.S. government agencies on the Internet makes **cyberterrorism** a source of vulnerability and a threat to foreign policy (Stanton 2002). Of concern as well are the ways in which knowledge gained from Internet sources may be used. The Clinton administration placed massive volumes of government documents, including the *Congressional Record* and important government studies, on Web sites. This effort succeeded in making the U.S. government more "transparent" and accessible to citizens, thus serving a central function of democratic rule. Such transparency, however, may be equally useful to U.S. adversaries, including states and terrorist groups, which can draw on the same sites to better "know thy enemy."

Even before the terrorist attacks of September 2001, the Bush administration had begun reversing the Clinton administration's policy of placing most government documents and records online. This effort intensified after the attacks, because officials worried that terrorist groups were exploiting their easy access to government information that could be useful in planning and executing future attacks. In accordance with the USA PATRIOT Act, passed by Congress just weeks after the attacks of September 11, the Bush administration gained greater access to e-mail messages sent by U.S. citizens as well as resident aliens living in the United States. These policies, extended in the renewal of the act in March 2006, further revealed the tension between democracy—including the privacy of personal communications and citizens' right to know about government—and the maintenance of national security in a competitive and dangerous world. The control of information will become an even more controversial issue in the years to come as computer systems, operated by commercial firms as well as government agencies, amass greater volumes of personal data on citizens from innumerable sources.

The Foreign Policy Blogosphere

The Internet is often considered a more "democratic" news source than established media outlets because it allows individuals and groups an opportunity to engage actively in policy discussions and debates. Indeed, Internet content can be viewed more as a dialogue than a one-way stream of information from media or government elites to the general population. In this respect, the proliferation of Internet blogs represents a breakthrough in mass communications. This trend, which in the United States began in the mid-1990s with the online *Drudge Report,* has since spread to specialized areas of interest, including U.S. foreign policy. Andrew Sullivan (2008), a well-known author, magazine writer, and editor, launched his own blog, *The Daily Dish,* which received nearly 40 million visits in 2007. His description of blogging captures the unique nature of this new media form:

> This form of instant and global self-publishing, made possible by technology widely available only for the past decade or so, allows for no retroactive editing (apart from fixing minor typos or small glitches) and removes from the act of writing any considered or lengthy review. It is the spontaneous expression of instant thought—impermanent beyond even the ephemera of daily journalism. It is accountable in immediate and unavoidable ways to readers and other bloggers, and linked via hypertext to continuously multiplying references and sources. Unlike any single piece of print journalism, its borders are extremely porous and its truth inherently transitory. The consequences of this for the act of writing are still sinking in. . . . Every writer since the printing press has longed for a means to publish himself and reach—instantly—any reader on Earth. Every professional writer has paid some dues waiting for an editor's nod, or enduring a publisher's incompetence, or being ground to literary dust by a legion of fact-checkers and copy editors. If you added up the time a writer once had to spend finding an outlet, impressing editors, sucking up to proprietors, and proofreading edits, you'd find another lifetime buried in the interstices. But with one click of the Publish Now button, all these troubles evaporated.

Not surprisingly, *blogs,* a term derived from "Web log," have entered the realm of U.S. foreign policy. These sites generally extend beyond the host's personal views and provide links to a variety of supporting materials: newspaper and magazine articles, government reports, videos, and other foreign policy blogs. Those interested in current actions by the White House and underlying tensions in the foreign policy process—many of which are not covered by mainstream media outlets—can gain vital insights from a variety of these blogs, including:

- *Democracy Arsenal* (www.democracyarsenal.org), sponsored by the National Security Network, provides ongoing commentary on U.S. foreign policy issues written by a team of experts plus a useful link to other blogs.

- The *Foreign Policy Association* (www.fpa.org/blogs) offers timely and in-depth analyses of such issues as U.S.-China relations, global crime, and the Persian Gulf as part of the association's Great Decisions Global Affairs Education Program.

- *Foreign Policy Watch* (www.fpwatch.blogspot.com) features commentaries on U.S. foreign policy and global issues and invites readers to participate in online discussions of the issues raised. The site also provides hyperlinks to more than one hundred other foreign policy blogs.

- *Passport* (http://blog.foreignpolicy.com), a widely read blog sponsored by the magazine *Foreign Policy,* offers news updates, commentaries by leading experts, and a link to "The Cable," which provides "reporting inside the foreign policy machine."

- *Real Clear World* (www.realclearworld.com) provides daily links to newspaper and magazine articles from around the world on all aspects of world politics.

- The *Washington Note* (www.thewashingtonnote.com), sponsored by the New America Foundation, features commentary and reader responses on various issues regarding U.S. foreign policy.

As in the case of print and broadcast outlets, regular visitors to the **blogosphere** are highly selective. They tend to be dissatisfied with mainstream news sources run by corporations or governments, and they seek viewpoints that generally conform to their existing beliefs. "Few would deny that blogs are inherently subjective, in line with their authors' perspectives or predispositions; indeed, for many bloggers, a non-biased blog would be pointless, even if it was possible to achieve" (Allan 2006, 85). In this respect, blogs reinforce rather than challenge existing opinions, a pattern that reduces further the prospects for national consensus on key foreign policy issues. Still, by actively engaging in Internet "chat rooms" and other interactive venues, many people seize the opportunity to express

Point/Counterpoint
THE IRAQ WAR: HAWKS VS. DOVES
IN THE BLOGOSPHERE

Many foreign policy debates today are waged on the Internet, in blogs hosted by well-known experts that invite comments from readers. Thomas Ricks, a senior fellow at the Center for a New American Century, spurred such a debate on February 24, 2010, when he argued on his blog, "The Best Defense," that the United States should not withdraw all its forces from Iraq—a central goal of President Obama. His blog posting, "OK, Time to Think about Staying in Iraq," excerpted below, elicited dozens of rebuttals within hours, including those also featured below. Note the rapid pace of this debate, which continued for many days:

> (3:20 pm) *Thomas Ricks:* I have a piece in the *New York Times* today that contends that we need to think about keeping at least 30,000 troops in Iraq for many years to come, instead of getting them all out at the end of next year. . . . Do you know anyone who thinks that Iraqi forces will be able to stand on their own at the end of next year? Uh-huh, me neither.
>
> As I note in the article, it doesn't make me happy to say it, because I think that invading Iraq was a huge mistake, perhaps the biggest error in the history of American foreign policy. I mean, invading a country pre-emptively on the basis of false information? That would get you thrown out of night court. But I think that staying beats the hell out of the alternatives. We've had too much rushing to failure in the Iraq war.

Rebuttals

(4:25 pm) From *Rubber Duckey*: In all, it's one hell of a price to pay to protect our lost investment in the imperialism of the last Administration. If it feels bad, quit doing it. Put the money to work at home or send it back to the taxpayers. Fix the United States of America, not Bush's Iraq brainfart.

(5:38 pm) From *Tyrtiaos*: Keeping such a conventional force in place has its pluses, but also has its minuses. One negative consequence of such an American force, besides seen [sic] as an occupier, is being directed to pick sides and thus alienating other competing factions. At that point all neutrality is given-up and the force becomes an enemy to some.

(5:40 pm) From *Kieselguhr Kid*: I read the article this morning and was really irritated by one thing: you just barely tipped your hat to the fact that the troop drawdown is, well, something binding that was negotiated with the Iraqis.

(6:19 pm) From *Hunter*: Some of us who have done a tour in Iraq or two don't want to go back there again after it dissolves into civil war (again) or is annexed by Iran. Some of us know good people in Iraq who we don't want to see lost in the quagmire (like when we abandoned many nominal allies in Vietnam). We're there now, let's do it right.

(6:34 pm) From *NNELGL*: Tom: Your advocacy of maintaining a sizable American troop presence in Iraq for years to come is

(continued)

Point/Counterpoint
THE IRAQ WAR: HAWKS VS. DOVES
IN THE BLOGOSPHERE (CONT.)

cut from the same cloth as the original arguments for the Iraq war: Play up fears about not following your policy prescription, trump up the benefits of following your advice and talk little—if at all—about the costs.

(8:30 pm) From *Zathras*: Ricks ignores the question of opportunity cost. The resources we devote to Iraq can't be used to do other things. I can imagine that some of those other things might be more important to the United States than the evolving politics of one, mid-sized Arab country. Ricks cannot. Ricks ignores the possibility of an Iraqi civil war engulfing the much-reduced, less capable American force he proposes to leave as a deterrent to civil war.

SOURCE: Thomas Ricks, "OK, Time to Think about Staying in Iraq," *The Best Defense,* February 24, 2010, http://ricks.foreign-policy.com/posts/2010/ 02/24/ok_time_to_think_about_staying_in_iraq. Reproduced with permission from Foreign Policy.

their own ideas and concerns about foreign policy and make contacts, however "virtual," with like-minded citizens around the country and world.

Online News and Views from Overseas

For the relatively small segment of the American public that follows news of U.S. foreign policy on a regular basis, the Internet provides ready access to news coverage generated by journalists overseas. Approximately one-quarter of regular Internet users turn to these sources, which include online newspapers, magazines, blogs, and broadcast outlets.[14] This trend accelerated as the United States responded to the September 2001 terrorist attacks by invading Afghanistan in 2001 and Iraq in 2003, and then became mired in a series of military setbacks, scandals, and internal controversies over the use (and misuse) of intelligence. The Internet, and the innumerable foreign-based Web sites it hosts, provided a primary vehicle for the expression of anti-American sentiment that became commonplace during this period.

Foreign news, once beyond the reach of American news consumers, provides a valuable alternative to the dominant news frames generated by the White House and adopted by most domestic media sources. Whereas most Americans accept the media's generally uncritical coverage of U.S. foreign policy (Zaller and Chiu 1996), those with doubts about Washington's motivations or tactics are more likely to pursue these doubts on foreign news sites. "Never before has it been possible to gauge so many views—not only in the United States but from Europe and the Middle East" (Best, Chmielewski, and Krueger 2005, 52, 65). "Given that

14. The number of accredited foreign correspondents working in Washington, D.C., has increased from 160 in 1968 to nearly 2,000 today (Project for Excellence in Journalism 2009).

foreign news sources tend to represent a much wider range of perspectives than those offered by the U.S. media, those seeking to move outside of the U.S. ideological spectrum, whether it currently skews to left or right within this range, can use foreign news sources to investigate alternative perspectives."

Some foreign news outlets, including the BBC, rarely challenge Washington's foreign policies and media frames. More commonly, foreign media adopt a more skeptical view of the United States (Lehman 2005). These include al Jazeera ("the island" in Arabic), a news network based in Qatar whose video streams and online articles rejected the Bush administration's claims regarding Saddam Hussein's threat to the United States prior to the 2003 U.S. invasion of Iraq. The network provided extensive coverage of U.S. mistreatment of Iraqi prisoners and deadly terrorist attacks on U.S. forces while providing Arab and Islamic leaders daily opportunities to criticize and denounce the United States. Their verbal attacks centered on President Bush and his top aides, such as Condoleezza Rice and Donald Rumsfeld. More generally, the criticism extended to American and Western culture and societal values. American viewers had never before had such immediate exposure to the nation's adversaries and their views.

Conclusion

Like public opinion, mass communication plays a vital role in U.S. foreign policy, in keeping with the underlying virtues of democratic governance. News organizations, whether print, broadcast, or digital media, link events overseas and citizens at home. Their coverage shapes the agenda of foreign policy makers and, occasionally, brings attention to scandals and policy miscalculations that are otherwise unknown to the public. Although journalists may at times reveal internal dissension among foreign policy elites or gaping holes in the nation's intelligence or defense capabilities, such revelations are viewed widely as a reasonable price to pay for a free press.

The news media's role, however, is fraught with problems and complications. Even in the midst of the latest technology-driven "information revolution," public attention remains focused on immediate and local concerns, which means long-term problems in other parts of the world are neglected or ignored entirely. Only when these problems reach crisis proportions do they become apparent to the public, whose impulsive demands for action commonly fuel hasty and ineffective responses.

The news media reinforce this pattern by alternately ignoring foreign news and providing saturation coverage of crises overseas. Even though "soft news" is widely appealing to American news consumers, its content tends to ignore the complexity of ongoing foreign policy problems in favor of human interest stories, moralistic themes, and satirical forms of comic relief that entertain rather than inform.

The preoccupation of media conglomerates with profitability, combined with the growing concentration of media ownership, discourages news outlets from funding major news investigations that may offend audiences. The conglomerates' top officers also fear alienating the U.S. government officials, whether in the White House or Congress, on whom they rely for regulatory concessions or tax relief. Thus, the news media routinely fail to advance the *public interest,* a term cited widely in the past as the primary mission of a free press. As the Project for Excellence in Journalism (2006) observed recently, "At many old-media companies, though not all, the decades-long battle at the top between idealists and accountants is now over. The idealists have lost. . . . Meanwhile, at many new-media companies, it is not clear if advocates for the public interest are present at all."

Taken together, these problems add another societal dimension to the paradox of America's world power. Like public opinion, the news media often frustrate rather than enhance the coherent conduct of U.S. foreign policy. In the absence of greater mass participation, public involvement will continue to take place within narrow interest groups, whose members have high stakes in the outcomes of U.S. foreign policy choices and present their demands daily to the federal government. This third "outside-in" influence on the foreign policy process, mass movements and interest groups, is the subject of Chapter 9.

Key Terms

blogosphere, p. 270

CNN effect, p. 251

cyberterrorism, p. 268

digital diplomacy, p. 265

embeds, p. 260

framing, p. 259

influence operations, p. 261

information security, p. 268

infotainment, p. 264

living-room war, p. 250

new media, p. 248

parachute journalism, p. 255

Pentagon Papers, p. 250

press leaks, p. 259

propaganda, p. 257

public diplomacy, p. 260

rooftop journalism, p. 251

selective exposure, p. 248

soft news, p. 263

spin control, p. 257

strategic communications, p. 261

Internet References

Aljazeera (http://english.aljazeera.net) provides in-depth coverage of issues and events relevant to the Islamic world. Included on this Web site, which is an offshoot of the group's television network, are news reports about world events, survey results, and other information related to Islamic countries.

Based in England, the **BBC** (http://news.bbc.co.uk) is a media hub for worldwide news coverage. The BBC's Web site features detailed reports on all regions of the world and links to its television and radio broadcasts.

(continued)

Internet References *(continued)*

The **Center for Media and Democracy** (www.prwatch.org) examines the role of public relations advocacy and "spin control" in the dissemination of news coverage. Its Web site includes links to features, such as "PRWatch" and "Sourcewatch," that chronicle the impact of propaganda in news reports.

CNN (www.cnn.com) provides an Internet-based supplement to the global cable television news network. Its Web site includes print versions of broadcast reports as well as links to the network's broadcast outlets.

FreedomForum.org (www.freedomforum.org) is a nonpartisan research center that promotes the cause of press freedoms in the United States and overseas. Based in Arlington, Virginia, the group's Web site features reports and essays on issues related to the First Amendment, the creation of independent media outlets overseas, and newsroom diversity.

The **Media Research Center** (www.mediaresearch.org), a self-proclaimed "media watchdog," promotes the dissemination of conservative opinions and policy analyses that seek to counter the "liberal bias" in U.S. news coverage. The group's Web site features reports on media coverage and links to articles and broadcasts of programs that support its policy agenda.

MediaStudies.com (http://mediastudies.com), based in Vancouver, Canada, promotes research and education in media studies throughout the world. Its Web site provides links to global news outlets and organizations that examine the news media's role in foreign policies.

Netcraft (http://news.netcraft.com), a British Internet services company, offers detailed reports on the Internet, including survey results that document the rapid proliferation of Web sites. The firm also assists its clients, located throughout the world, in protecting their sites against piracy and fraudulent use.

Russia's largest news and media source, **Pravda** (http://english.pravda.ru), provides articles and news coverage of world affairs and Russia's relations with the United States and other countries. Its Web site features current and archived articles and feature stories, most of which are concerned with Russian domestic and foreign policies.

The **Project for Excellence in Journalism** (www.journalism.org) is a rapidly growing "fact tank" that focuses on trends in the American news media. Now part of the Pew Research Center, the project was previously affiliated with Columbia University and maintains the same focus on media coverage and industry trends.

9

CHAPTER

Social Movements and Interest Groups

Environmental activists rally at the White House in November 2009 to protest the involvement of multinational corporations at the upcoming Copenhagen Climate Conference. This protest pitted these activists against the more powerful economic interest groups in the United States that opposed new environmental treaties on the grounds that they would damage the U.S. economy, already in a deep recession.

Chapters 7 and 8 described how public opinion and the news media impose external pressure on the U.S. foreign policy process. As expressions of the nation's civil society, both shed light on public preferences and are watched closely by reelection-minded political leaders. At the same time, national surveys consistently reveal a mass public that is largely disengaged on foreign policy issues. Only a small elite and the attentive public have significant knowledge of world history, geography, and current events. Similarly, most Americans pay little attention to foreign news coverage on a regular basis, preferring instead entertainment programs, video games, and interactions on social media. Public interest and media coverage spike upward only during times of crisis and then quickly return to their tepid levels.

This seeming indifference of the American public, paradoxical for the dominant and most pervasive global power, leaves the field open to a relatively small segment of the population—social movements and interest groups—to influence U.S. foreign policy. These groups, which promote a vast array of causes, are highly diverse but share a common objective: to steer government action in directions favorable to their members, participants, and other perceived stakeholders. U.S. leaders may choose to ignore survey results or critical news coverage, but they cannot ignore the constant pressure exerted by vocal and well-endowed groups.

In many areas of public policy, group action fills a vacuum created by the neglect or inadequate resources of governments. At home, private charities provide food and shelter to those in need while grassroots environmental groups demand restrictions on commercial developments that would otherwise be promoted solely by business interests. The need for public action is even greater at the global level due to the absence of a centralized, authoritative body to ensure the provision and protection of global public goods (see Chapters 3 and 12). This **sovereignty gap** leaves critical transnational problems such as environmental decay and weapons proliferation without governmental stewards. In these and other areas, private groups contribute to global governance, or the management of transnational problems by a loose-knit network of public and private bodies, along with intergovernmental organizations such as the United Nations and the World Trade Organization (WTO), which also engage in global governance on a daily basis.

The issue of landmines was one such transnational problem. It barely registered on government radar screens until a coalition of groups, the International Campaign to Ban Landmines, called for a global ban on antipersonnel landmines in the mid-1990s. The coalition launched a well-orchestrated international campaign to raise public consciousness about these weapons, most placed in poor countries, where they maim civilians long after the end of the military conflict. By December 1997, 123 countries had signed a comprehensive ban on land mines.[1] When it took effect in March 1999, the ban became the most rapidly adopted and implemented international agreement of its kind in history. The campaign and its coordinator, Jody Williams, received the 1997 Nobel Peace Prize "in part for helping create a fresh form of diplomacy" (Rutherford 2000, 75). The United States found itself in a small minority of countries that opposed the ban, a distinction that fueled anti-American sentiment in the global community.

Social movements often assume an adversarial approach to government policies by demanding changes in existing practices. This is less often the case with interest groups, which are smaller in scale but tend to have greater organizational cohesion and clout. While conflicts between these groups and the U.S. government often capture media attention, lurking in the shadows are the "quiet and generally harmonious networks of relationships among interest groups and policy makers who share goals that few others care about.... In such policy subsystems, the goals of interest groups and policy makers are generally closely aligned and it is often

---

1. The full name of the agreement is the Ottawa Convention on the Prohibition of the Use, Stockpiling, Production and Transfer of Anti-Personnel Mines and on Their Destruction. By February 2010, 156 countries had ratified the accord (see www.icbl.org/treaty). The United States remained a nonsignatory.

not clear who is serving whom" (Lieberman 2009, 251). Interest groups have an easier time when they are "pushing on an open door," as in the case of Cuban and Iraqi exiles who recently teamed up with like-minded U.S. leaders in promoting foreign policies that affected their countries of origin (Vanderbush 2009).

This chapter presents an overview of the social movements and interest groups that have sought, and often gained, influence over the U.S. foreign policy process. The chapter begins by exploring how societal actors serve both as vital agents of America's democratic system and, on occasion, as obstacles to consistent or coherent policy. The next sections highlight the social movements that have mobilized large numbers of Americans in pursuit of changes in government policies and actions. Attention then turns to the interest groups, widely referred to as nongovernmental organizations (NGOs) in global politics, which often serve as the institutional offspring of these movements. Finally, the chapter examines economic interest groups, particularly those representing multinational corporations (MNCs), which enjoy a privileged status among other nonstate actors in U.S. foreign policy. The collective involvement of these private groups, their degree of interconnectedness, and their capacity to shape government agendas represent the "power shift" in global politics discussed in Chapter 1.

Group Action and the Paradox

Private organizations have always served as the backbone of the U.S. democratic system. Like public opinion and the news media, these groups represent alternative centers of power that can counteract government abuses while offering outlets for the expression of societal needs. As it is in economic markets, the *demand* for favorable government policies determines the *supply* of groups promoting them. "The public is not only represented in the formal political sense by a variety of elected officials," political scientist Gabriel Almond (1950, 231) noted long ago, "but there are few groups of any size in the United States today which do not have their interests represented."

Several features of U.S. society and its political system favor the development and persistence of private groups (see Risse-Kappen 1995):

- Fragmented *governmental structures* offer many points of access to the legislative and executive branches through which private groups can affect foreign policy.

- Robust *societal structures,* a result of the constitutional restraints on state power and the broad political and social freedoms granted to individuals and groups, provide a fertile environment for NGOs to recruit new members and affect policy.

- Numerous *policy networks* allow NGOs to join with issue-related government agencies that share a basic consensus on the merits of U.S. government and society.

As noted earlier, the membership of NGOs has increasingly crossed national boundaries, mobilizing like-minded citizens from several countries. The activism of transnational groups, though associated most often with liberal theories of world politics (see Chapter 3), is better understood as "an arena of struggle" among political actors than as a stepping-stone to world government (Keck and Sikkink 1998, 33). In this respect, the empowerment of NGOs is compatible with realist theories, whose emphasis on chronic conflicts of interest may be extended beyond the anarchic system of nation-states.

The United States is more often a target than an ally of these groups. For example, in 1999 President Bill Clinton faced the full wrath of certain NGOs when antiglobalization protesters disrupted the annual meetings of the WTO in Seattle, Washington. The relationship between Washington, D.C., and public interest NGOs became even more adversarial with the coming to power in 2001 of George W. Bush, who distanced his administration from these groups as well as from the many intergovernmental organizations that opposed key elements of his foreign policy. Yet at the same time, Bush reached out to a different set of NGOs: evangelical Christian churches whose members had funded his 2000 campaign and shared his policy priorities. The ideological complexion of active nonprofit NGOs shifted during this period as conservative groups, from the American Enterprise Institute to the Family Research Council, joined the NGO community once dominated by more liberal groups (Peterson 2004).

As the world's predominant power with unrivaled influence over the global economy, related ecological issues, weapons proliferation, and the protection of human rights, the United States naturally attracts the most NGO attention. Although constraints on state power were precisely what the Constitution's framers had in mind when they fostered a vigorous civil society at home, they could not have anticipated the challenges to U.S. autonomy, or freedom of choice, that transnational groups would pose two centuries later. Their challenges to state sovereignty, an important element of the paradox of world power, affect all democratic countries that open themselves to group pressures, especially the primary target of such pressure, the United States.

Dynamics of Social Movements

When citizens determined to change government policies join together in pressure groups and coalitions, their collective actions often take the form of social movements. Frequently, the issue of concern—whether it be war, human rights, globalization, or the environment, among other things—involves foreign policy. The goals of these movements vary widely, but they can be divided into two broad categories: those that seek to change *bad* policies already in place (such as an unpopular military intervention) and those that seek to create *good* new policies (such as sanctions to halt human rights abuses or measures to protect the environment). Unlike the self-interested campaigns of economically oriented groups, the motivations of social movements are not solely reducible to the material welfare

Figure 9.1 The Cycle of Public Pressure and Political Change

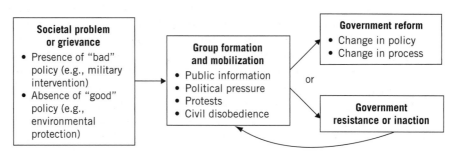

of their members, whose focus commonly extends to the welfare of peoples far beyond their shores.

The term **social movement** is notoriously vague and stubbornly resistant to a simple definition. Here, social movements are viewed as broad-based collective actions undertaken by citizens and groups to solve perceived societal problems through the reform of domestic or foreign public policy. This definition suggests a causal chain that begins with the perceived problem, which then stimulates the mobilization of like-minded advocates who hope for concrete policy reforms. These reforms may appear either in the policy itself or in the decision-making process used to make and enforce the policy (see Figure 9.1).

Social movements' prospects for success depend in large part on the type of political systems in which they operate. As noted in Chapter 7, democratic polities with dynamic civil societies are, by their nature, more receptive to social movements than authoritarian states that discourage or even outlaw group activism and dissent. Even among democracies, the prospects for success of social movements reflect the governing arrangements and political party structures that are unique to each polity. This framework clearly applies to the United States, whose two-party system and winner-take-all election rules stand apart from those of other democracies that feature proportional representation of multiple parties. In Germany, for example, the relatively small Green Party fueled by the environmental movement has gained considerable political clout by winning seats in the national legislature and forming coalitions with dominant parties. In the United States, to wield political influence a third party would have to win majorities in legislative or presidential elections, a highly unlikely outcome. For this reason, a U.S. social movement cannot gain an institutional foothold in the partisan system and must align with the Democratic or Republican Party to achieve its goals.

Aside from their concrete policy goals, social movements are driven by norms that represent their underlying values and visions of how the state and society *should* function. Norms on human rights and other transnational issues gain enduring value when they are codified in international law (Tornquist-Chesnier 2004). As such, transnational norms provide social movements with significant moral authority that often compensates for their lack of financial resources.

Advocates of human rights, for example, gained momentum during the Cold War by joining forces with like-minded groups in other countries. The resulting **transnational advocacy network** was crucial in elevating the role of human rights in the Jimmy Carter and Ronald Reagan administrations (Keck and Sikkink 1998).[2]

Social movements, then, play a vital role in converting widely held public aspirations into concrete government policies. Their impact varies widely, however, depending on circumstances at home and overseas and the problems they seek to resolve. The descriptions of two such movements in the United States—antiwar activists and religious organizations—in the sections that follow will reveal both the strengths and the limitations of this external influence on U.S. foreign policy.

Antiwar Protests from Vietnam to Iraq

One of the most familiar expressions of social movements is the antiwar demonstration in which protesters seek *en masse* to force governments to avoid military confrontations. As noted in Chapter 2, antiwar protests erupted frequently on college campuses during the Vietnam War, sometimes with tragic results. A weekend of protests in May 1970 at Kent State University in Ohio prompted government officials to impose martial law and deploy the National Guard to Kent. When protesters gathered again on the following Monday, confronting the armed forces in a bitter standoff, the National Guard opened fire on the protesters, killing four students and wounding nine others. The tragedy at Kent State literally "brought home" the war in Vietnam and hardened public opposition to the U.S. intervention. President Richard Nixon never regained public support for the Vietnam War after the Kent State shootings and spent the remainder of his presidency trying to extricate U.S. forces "with honor" from Southeast Asia.

No comparable antiwar movement has emerged in the United States since the Vietnam War, despite nearly constant U.S. military interventions. The small scale of these conflicts restricted mass opposition, and for many—such as those in Grenada, Panama, and Somalia—the abrupt timing and short duration of the interventions did not allow opponents time to mobilize. By contrast, the 1991 Persian Gulf War was much larger in scope and was preceded by months of sanctions, diplomatic negotiations, and legislative debates. Still, the creation of a thirty-six-country coalition, combined with a UN Security Council resolution to eject Iraqi forces from Kuwait, gave a legitimacy to the impending conflict that tempered antiwar sentiments.

The opposite conditions surrounded the U.S.-led invasion of Iraq in early 2003. The lack of regional and UN support for preventive war left the United States largely isolated in pressing for a military solution. These circumstances, combined with the profound implications and uncertain consequences of major

---

2. When transnational norms such as group rights clash with local customs, NGOs face ethical dilemmas that require them to "tolerate, without respecting" social inequities as they carry out vital development projects and other tasks (Bell and Carens 2004).

Table 9.1 The Iraq War Protest Coalition

Group type	Number of groups	Example
Antiwar	11	Peace Action
Religious	11	United Church of Christ
Identity (e.g., racial, ethnic)	8	NAACP
Social justice	8	MoveOn
International politics	5	Global Exchange
Environmental	2	Greenpeace

SOURCE: David S. Meyer and Catherine Corrigall-Brown, "Coalition and Political Context: U.S. Movements against Wars in Iraq," *Mobilization* 10 (October 2005): 327–344.

war in the Middle East, sparked a surge of peace activism in the United States and overseas. More than 1 million protesters took to the streets of London, Madrid, Rome, and other European cities on February 15. An estimated 500,000 demonstrated against the impending war in Washington, D.C., and dozens of city councils formally registered their opposition to the war. These actions, organized and carried out by a coalition of more than forty NGOs, constituted a discernible antiwar movement as the diplomatic struggle wore on (see Table 9.1).

All this pressure, however, failed to discourage the White House from carrying out its threat to overthrow Saddam Hussein's regime. The congressional authorization of force against Iraq the previous October muted the subsequent debate, which, in turn, discouraged critical media coverage of the planned attack. The U.S. invasion in March thus effectively silenced the peace movement, which remained dormant even as the rationale for war proved unfounded and even as U.S. forces struggled to prevent Iraq from descending into civil war.

What accounted for the different outcomes of the antiwar movements against the wars in Vietnam and Iraq? A prominent factor was the much higher death toll in Vietnam, which exceeded 50,000 by the early 1970s, in contrast to the approximately 3,200 Americans killed during the first four years of the Iraq war. Other factors were the larger troop deployments to Vietnam—nearly 500,000 at the height of the conflict—and the military draft that forced many Americans to fight in the unpopular war. Above all, the inability of transnational peace activists to prevent the U.S. invasion of Iraq demoralized the coalition and prompted many groups to disband or shift their energies to other issues (Meyer and Corrigall-Brown 2005). Their sense of futility was reinforced by the unified U.S. government in place early in the Iraq war, with Republicans controlling both the executive and legislative branches.

Still, small-scale efforts to oppose the war continued. After U.S. Army Specialist Casey Sheehan was killed in Iraq in March 2004, his mother, Cindy Sheehan, emerged as an outspoken war critic. Her protracted vigil outside President

Although no large-scale, organized antiwar movement emerged in the early years of the war on terrorism, several high-profile figures rallied opponents of the conflict to maintain pressure on the U.S. government. Two such figures, Cindy Sheehan (left), the mother of a slain U.S. soldier, and documentary filmmaker Michael Moore (right) led this opposition through public appearances that drew large audiences and extensive coverage in the news media.

Bush's Texas ranch in the summer of 2005 drew worldwide attention. Similarly, filmmaker Michael Moore produced a documentary, *Fahrenheit 9/11*, that depicted the Bush administration's war on terrorism as a misguided campaign driven by economic and military elites. After its release in June 2004, the documentary earned a record $200 million, nearly half of which came from foreign audiences. Meanwhile, more than twelve hundred local and national peace groups organized efforts to stop the war in Iraq and resist the calls for war against neighboring Iran.

The Christian Conversion on Foreign Aid

Long before the Iraq war, a very different social movement helped to change the course of U.S. foreign policy. The 1990s witnessed a surge in foreign policy activism among American religious, or faith-based, groups, whose interest in public policy had previously centered only on domestic social issues such as abortion, gay rights, and capital punishment (see Martin 1999). Debates over such issues reflected deeply held religious beliefs and moral values, which offered "ultimate perspectives, broad criteria, motives, inspirations, sensitivities, warnings, and moral limits" (Bennett 1966, 36). The same beliefs and values animated foreign policy discourse on a variety of post–Cold War foreign policy issues, particularly the persecution of Christians by foreign governments. The passage of the International Religious Freedom Act of 1998, which identified freedom of religion and conscience as a "core objective" of U.S. foreign policy, was driven by church groups.

Energized by their earlier success, the same groups compelled Congress to pass the Sudan Peace Act of 2002 and the North Korea Human Rights Act of 2004.[3]

The idea that religious institutions play a vital role in the civil society of democratic states can be traced to the writings of French political observer Alexis de Tocqueville ([1835] 1988) in the early nineteenth century. More recently, political scientist Robert Putnam found that U.S.-based churches serve as "agents of civic engagement" that represent an exception to the general rule of public detachment from public affairs. As he explains, "Religious conservatives have created the largest, best-organized grassroots social movement of the last quarter century" (Putnam 2000, 162). In shifting their focus to foreign policy, Christian groups were inspired further by deeply held concerns about the declining state of "family values" and lobbied aggressively to exclude abortion services from U.S.-funded family planning programs overseas. Elsewhere, their heightened concern for human rights and the end of religious persecution prompted such groups to embrace the promotion of democratic rule worldwide, a central foreign policy goal of the Clinton and Bush administrations.

Evangelical Christians figured prominently in the U.S. government's shift toward higher levels of humanitarian aid (Hook 2008). Once staunchly opposed to aid programs, this politically powerful constituency detached itself from other conservatives who considered aid spending a form of global welfare.[4] Two initiatives demonstrated the impact of this social movement on U.S. development policy. A worldwide campaign for debt relief, Jubilee 2000, prompted industrialized states to forgive more than $20 billion in loans to countries in extreme poverty. Earlier, the U.S. government had resisted calls for large-scale debt relief, but its views changed when faith groups united around the idea that crippling debt obligations amounted to a moral crisis that could no longer be ignored. The mass mobilization of these groups, combined with personal pleas to government officials by televangelists and celebrities such as Bono, the leader of the rock band U2, convinced U.S. leaders to commit $435 million in debt relief in fiscal year 2001. Even larger volumes of U.S. debt relief followed later in the decade, along with billions of dollars in relief from other governments.

The second aid initiative was aimed at economic support for victims of HIV/AIDS in the developing world. Christian conservatives again mobilized and aligned with African American groups that had unsuccessfully sought greater support from the Republican-controlled Congress (see Burkhalter 2004). In February

---

3. The impact of faith-based interest groups is attributable in part to the relatively high level of religiosity in American society. In a survey of forty-three societies conducted in the 1990s, Americans ranked first among all citizens in believing in a "personal God" (Inglehart, Basañez, and Moreno 1998). Americans also ranked first among citizens of industrialized countries in believing that there are "absolute guidelines about what is good and evil" and that religion plays a "very important" role in their lives.

4. Of the 150 members of InterAction, the largest association of development NGOs, about one-quarter were faith based in 2000. Faith-based groups can be differentiated from secular NGOs in that they make an "overt statement of religious faith" in their mission statements, are formally associated with a "religious hierarchy or theological tradition," and hire their staff members in part "on a creed or faith statement" (Natsios 2001, 190–191).

2002, the Christian relief organization Samaritan's Purse hosted a global AIDS conference in Washington that drew leaders from more than eight hundred Catholic and Protestant churches along with a variety of government leaders. Bush, a born-again Christian with close ties to evangelical groups on a variety of issues (see Fineman 2003), responded in January 2003 with an Emergency Plan for AIDS Relief that pledged $15 billion in funding over five years.

Although the September 2001 terrorist attacks and subsequent war on terrorism produced large increases in U.S. foreign aid, the scale of this shift in foreign policy cannot be understood fully without reference to the mobilization of religious groups. Evangelical Christians in particular demonstrated enormous political skill in organizing at the grassroots level and applying pressure on Washington to adopt the role of "good Samaritan" in poverty and AIDS relief. The strongly held religious convictions of these activists, shared by many born-again government officials, resonated with long-standing cultural values in the United States. In this sense, evangelicalism is "the classic entrepreneurial faith, thriving in the American open marketplace because it is constantly renewed by revivals and religious visionaries"

Two unlikely political allies, rock star Bono (left) and former senator Jesse Helms, enjoy a moment together before a December 2005 U2 concert in Charlotte, North Carolina. Years earlier, Bono had convinced Senator Helms to support massive increases in U.S. debt relief to the impoverished countries of sub-Saharan Africa. Helms, the former chair of the Senate Foreign Relations Committee who retired in 2003, also played a key role in gaining congressional support for greater funding to fight HIV/AIDS in the developing world. In his appeal to Helms, Bono emphasized the Christian values shared by both men, a strategy that also proved effective in gaining support among evangelical Christians who formed one of President George W. Bush's most influential and supportive interest groups.

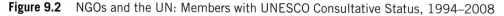

(Hertzke 2004, 33). Ironically, the enthusiasm displayed by evangelical Christians for the U.S. government's war on terrorism also contributed to the failure of peace groups to mobilize a successful campaign to prevent the U.S. invasion of Iraq.

Types of Foreign Policy NGOs

Social movements in the United States, like those just described, represent coalitions of individual groups that share concerns about foreign and domestic policy. The number of politically active NGOs, who are often loosely connected, cannot be stated with precision. Particularly at the transnational level, at which much of their foreign policy activism takes place, no formal mechanism exists for licensing or registering the vast majority of these groups. Further complicating matters, NGOs are continuously created and dismantled in response to shifting needs, unforeseen developments, and evolving stages of the policy process. However, the number of NGOs that have gained "consultative status" with the UN Economic and Social Council is known and offers a perspective on the growth of NGOs over the past decade. In 1948, just forty NGOs held this status; by 2008 the number had grown to 3,187 (see Figure 9.2).

Figure 9.2   NGOs and the UN: Members with UNESCO Consultative Status, 1994–2008

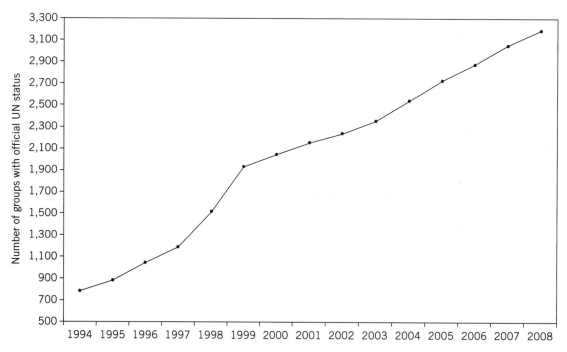

SOURCE: UN Department of Economic and Social Affairs, http://esa.un.org/coordination/ngo/new/index.asp?page=intro.

Nonprofit NGOs concerned with U.S. foreign policy assume a variety of institutional forms. Some are small, focus narrowly on single issues, and disappear when their policy preferences are satisfied. Others have large staffs and budgets, promote policies along a broad spectrum of issues, and maintain a permanent presence in Washington, D.C., and foreign capitals. The Worldwide Fund for Nature, for example, boasts a membership of 5 million and maintains a staff of more than 3,000. The development group CARE has an annual budget of more than $100 million (Bond 2000).

Most NGOs are considered to be **particularistic groups,** which serve a limited number of individuals who each have a stake in an NGO's mission. The rest are **cosmopolitan groups,** which address transnational problems that affect the general public, such as environmental decay and weapons proliferation. Both types of groups have a proven capacity to shape U.S. foreign policy, but they also suffer from four primary weaknesses:

- Limited resources, which forces groups to spend much of their time soliciting private donations to survive

- Lack of formal contacts with governments, which makes gaining access to key decision makers a constant challenge, particularly for smaller groups lacking political or economic muscle

- Inevitable divisions between NGOs with contrary or competing claims on governments (see Rogers 1993), which neutralizes the groups' overall impact

- A **democratic deficit** created by a lack of elected representation and openness in decision making, which are hallmarks of democratic states (see Christensen 2004).

The primary strength of these NGOs stems from their direct links to citizens at all levels of government—local, state, national, and transnational. These links often prove stronger than those between states and private citizens because U.S. citizens are more likely to participate politically through NGOs than through government programs or political parties. Furthermore, nonprofit NGOs benefit greatly from a sense of shared values among their members, who are determined to see these values reflected in tangible goals and political action. The high levels of commitment and solidarity within a group are the glue that holds its members together over an extended period of time. Finally, the members of NGOs have expertise in relevant policy areas that lends credibility and leverage when they attempt to influence government officials. Their expertise is also an asset when governments need help implementing or monitoring programs.

Religious and Ethnic Groups

Religious and ethnic groups play vital roles in the U.S. foreign policy process. Most Americans identify themselves as part of a faith community that is represented, in some form, by organizations that advance the group's interests. These religious NGOs provide massive campaign contributions to political candidates every year, along with a steady stream of policy briefs they expect their beneficiaries to follow. As a nation of immigrants, the United States is also sensitive to the needs of ethnic groups, whose members look to Washington for economic, political, and moral support. This relationship is fragile given that these groups "may find themselves conflicted on issues that could divide the motherland from the adopted country, the United States" (Newhouse 2009, 74). More often, "hyphenated Americans" find common cause with U.S. foreign policy and serve to cement friendly diplomatic relations with such countries as Ireland, Poland, India, and Armenia.

Most religious and ethnic groups form large, cohesive, and politically active organizations to advance the interests of their members. In addition, they appeal to all U.S. citizens within their groups to vote as a bloc for the most sympathetic political candidates. Because support from the general public can be crucial in advancing their interests, the groups also must espouse causes that apply to a population broader than their membership. Finally, such groups focus their lobbying efforts on Congress, not the White House, because of their greater access to Capitol Hill and legislators' greater responsiveness to parochial, rather than national, concerns (Haney and Vanderbush 1999, 344–345).

As described earlier, evangelical Christian groups were of particular importance to President George W. Bush, who in 2000 received about 40 percent of his votes from this segment of the population (Bumiller 2003). Bush repaid these core supporters by vigorously pursuing their policy preferences. His frequent references to biblical scripture in his speeches affirmed his link to the 43,000 congregations composing the National Association of Evangelicals, whose continued support he needed for reelection in 2004. The president and his senior political adviser, Karl Rove, kept a close watch on this vital constituency in charting the administration's course in foreign policy.

Jewish Americans have also organized politically to exert strong pressure on U.S. foreign policy. With 65,000 members residing in all fifty states, the American Israel Public Affairs Committee (AIPAC) has achieved a level of NGO influence exceeded only by the National Rifle Association (Cohen and Bell 2005). The group's Web site (http://AIPAC.org) claims credit for the passage of more than a hundred pro-Israel legislative measures every year, including the annual transfer of massive amounts of foreign aid and export credits to Israel. Also on the Web site is a link to the "Hill staff" that describes the current issues of concern to the Israeli government. These intimate ties prompted two prominent political scientists, John Mearsheimer and Stephen Walt (2006, 1), to charge that

> the centerpiece of U.S. Middle East policy has been its relationship with Israel. The combination of unwavering U.S. support for Israel and the related effort to spread democracy throughout the region has inflamed Arab and Islamic opinion and jeopardized U.S. security.... The overall thrust of U.S. policy in the region is due almost entirely to the activities of the "Israel Lobby." Other special interest groups have managed to skew U.S. foreign policy in directions they favored, but no lobby has managed

to divert U.S. foreign policy as far from what the American national interest would otherwise suggest, while simultaneously convincing Americans that U.S. and Israeli interests are essentially identical.[5]

Islamic and Arab American groups have had far more difficulty gaining influence over U.S. foreign policy, despite their large numbers in big cities and electorally important "swing" states such as Michigan. According to political scientist Eric Uslaner (2002, 362–364), these groups are less cohesive, affluent, and politically active than the members of AIPAC. In addition, whereas AIPAC members overwhelmingly support the Democratic Party, Arab Americans are more equally divided between Republicans and Democrats. Furthermore, the societal stature of these groups has suffered, not surprisingly, since the onset of the war on terrorism, and Arab Americans frequently have been "profiled" and singled out for government scrutiny.

Hispanic and Latino citizens, who now comprise the largest minority group in the United States, also have suffered from a lack of internal cohesion, economic power, and assimilation into mainstream U.S. society (Huntington 2004). Certain subgroups, however, have fared better. The Cuban-American National Foundation (CANF) offers an outstanding example. CANF, based in Miami, uses sophisticated promotional techniques to gain government support for Cuban exiles living in the United States. It also calls on the U.S. government to maintain harsh sanctions against Cuba's communist regime, which has remained in power since the Cuban people overthrew a U.S.-backed government in 1959. Meanwhile, the organization has pushed successfully for the creation of two government-run media outlets, Radio Martí (1985) and TV Martí (1990), which provide news and entertainment programs directly to the Cuban population. Political leaders in Florida, and even presidential candidates, routinely include CANF meetings in their campaign stops, fully aware that the group's endorsement can be vital to their chances of gaining or maintaining elected offices.

Since the end of the Cold War, ethnic groups linked to the former communist countries in Eastern Europe have become actively involved in U.S. foreign policy toward the region. For example, in 1998 Polish American groups mobilized in large numbers to support the eastward expansion of NATO.[6] During the Kosovo conflict of 1999, legislators were careful to address the concerns of Greek Americans about the possible spillover of the conflict into northern Greece. Although it would be an exaggeration to assert that these groups dictated the terms of U.S. foreign policy in these cases, their concerns undoubtedly carried enormous weight among elected officials. And such transplanted ethnic groups from all regions that

---

5. Not surprisingly, the study provoked strong reaction and debate in political circles, academia, and the news media. Critics (e.g., Dershowitz 2006) questioned Mearsheimer and Walt's research and claimed that their findings exaggerated the influence—and negative consequences—of the "Israel Lobby."

6. The U.S. government paid close attention to public opinion in the former Soviet bloc in considering two rounds of NATO expansion after the Cold War. See Kostadinova (2000) for an elaboration.

look to their adopted governments for support "as the independence, survival, or general welfare of [their] ethnic kin or homeland is threatened" will continue to seek influence (Ambrosio 2002, 8–9).

Public Interest Groups

As noted earlier, cosmopolitan NGOs confront a wide range of transnational problems ineffectively managed by national governments and intergovernmental organizations. Violations of human rights, threats to the environment, widespread economic disparities, and other problems routinely cross political boundaries and affect entire populations, not parochial interests. Lacking the traditional governing mechanisms to confront these problems, public interest groups appeal to the general public, either in one country or worldwide, to increase pressure on governments. Shared values play an especially strong role in the mobilization of public interest groups, whose actions cannot be simply reduced to material self-interests.

Human rights. The protection of human rights is one of the most pervasive concerns of public interest NGOs (see Welch 2001). This cause resonates strongly in the United States, where support for global human rights has historically been based on the constitutional foundations of its own government. Attention to human rights intensified during the Cold War. American leaders believed the denial of political and economic freedoms in communist countries amounted to a wholesale violation of human rights. American support for repressive governments around the world, however, prompted charges that the United States did not live up to its own standards of human rights.

In the 1970s and 1980s, the lapses of the U.S. government, combined with the widespread abuses of human rights by communist regimes and many developing countries, inspired millions of private citizens worldwide to join NGOs focusing on the issue (see Weissbrodt 1984 and Korey 1999). Private groups in the industrialized countries formed links with their counterparts in the developing regions. Private funding for these groups, from individuals as well as other public interest NGOs, grew rapidly during these decades. Economic support from foundations, for example, jumped from less than $1 million in the mid-1970s to more than $20 million in the early 1990s (Keck and Sikkink 1998, 99).

This growth occurred during a period—from the Vietnam War to the end of the Cold War—when many human rights groups viewed the United States with suspicion. The Reagan administration, in particular, maintained an adversarial relationship with these NGOs. By 1990, however, Congress was not only listening to them, but also, in some instances, using their reports as the basis for public hearings and possible sanctions. After Americas Watch, a prominent Latin American NGO, released findings in the late 1980s of widespread torture and political killings in Mexico, Congress held public hearings on the problem. The publicity generated by these hearings, combined with pressure from the U.S. government, prompted Mexican leaders to create the National Commission on Human Rights and, later, to reform their country's electoral system.

Advocates of human rights became even more assertive after the Cold War, as the world's earlier preoccupation with East-West conflict gave way to a range of transnational problems that were neglected previously, including widespread social inequities and government repression. Group rights, described by political scientist Karen Mingst (2004) as "second-generation" human rights (after the earlier acknowledgment of universal rights), became the rallying cry of ethnic and religious minorities. A global conference on women's rights, held in Beijing in September 1995, included 2,600 NGOs on the official program and another 35,000 NGOs at an alternative forum.

As noted elsewhere in this volume, beginning in 2003 human rights groups mobilized against the U.S.-led invasions and subsequent occupations of Afghanistan and Iraq. The most prominent of these groups, Amnesty International and Human Rights Watch, published dozens of critical reports on civilian casualties and the mistreatment of prisoners in both countries as well as in the U.S. detention center at its Guantánamo Bay Naval Base in Cuba. A confidential report by the International Committee of the Red Cross, which visited detention centers across Iraq in 2003, described widespread abuses by U.S. and British guards and interrogators. The report, leaked to the public, heightened criticism of the United States after its own reports of mistreatment at the Abu Ghraib prison, along with graphic photographs of the abuses, were made public.[7]

Environmental protection. Another primary concern of public interest NGOs is the global environment. Public activism in the environmental arena also increased in the late twentieth century, especially after the Cold War, when security concerns gave way to transnational problems previously neglected by the world powers. Prior to this time, environmental decay in the United States had been considered primarily a domestic problem to be solved by domestic measures such as the Clean Air Act and the Clean Water Act. However, mounting evidence that the effects of pollution could not be contained within political boundaries, along with scientific findings of a "greenhouse effect" and global warming, made it clear that the world needed cooperative solutions (see Chapter 12).

The memberships of environmental NGOs more than doubled during this period, as did the financial contributions from members and private foundations. The largest of these groups, including Greenpeace, the Environmental Defense Fund, the Nature Conservancy, and the Natural Resources Defense Council, formed chapters in dozens of countries. The 1992 UN Conference on Environment and Development, more commonly known as the Earth Summit, served as a catalyst for NGO activism. More than 1,400 NGOs and government leaders from more than 170 countries officially took part in the conference, held in Brazil. Thousands of other private groups staged an alternative forum at the Earth Summit, a practice that has since been repeated during annual meetings of the International Monetary Fund, the World Bank, and the WTO. Ten years later,

---

7. For the full report, see www.globalsecurity.org/military/library/report/2004/icrc_report_iraq_feb2004.htm.

the World Summit on Sustainable Development, held in Johannesburg, South Africa, also sparked NGO activism and urgent appeals for government action on global warming and other critical issues.

The U.S. government is chronically at odds with environmental groups. As the world's leading source of fossil fuel emissions and solid waste and its leading consumer of finite energy resources, the United States is the foremost object of criticism among the groups. The close ties that President George W. Bush and many of his senior advisers had to the oil industry, whose lobbyists called for greater oil extraction rather than conservation, added to the criticism. Private groups as well as many governments view with skepticism, if not disdain, the common assertion of U.S. officials that restrictions on private enterprise impair economic growth while violating economic liberties. Ironically, the environmental NGOs owe much of their rapid rise and growing influence to the damaging impact of the United States on the global ecosystem and its refusal to abide by the norms of conservation espoused by these groups.

International development. Hundreds of U.S.- and foreign-based NGOs engage daily in the transfer and delivery of humanitarian assistance to people in need. The most prominent of these groups, such as CARE, World Vision International, Oxfam Federation, and Doctors Without Borders, have each controlled more than $500 million of the estimated $8 billion in development aid disbursed annually to poor countries in recent years (Simmons 1998, 92). More than one-half of World Bank loans today involve NGOs in the development process.[8]

Groups based in industrialized countries routinely form partnerships with NGOs from developing countries to deliver food aid, conduct health programs, and plan long-term development projects. Government agencies in many developing countries are not equipped to manage the needs of their rapidly growing populations. In these cases, development NGOs fill a void in the public sector, drawing on resources from private sources as well as from wealthy governments that greatly exceed those available to the governments of poor states.

The United States has increasingly turned to NGOs to manage the aid programs it sponsors. The International Red Cross, for example, receives annual grants from the U.S. Agency for International Development to immunize the citizens of developing countries against infectious diseases such as polio, measles, and malaria. Through its offices in more than 175 countries, the Red Cross also provides emergency relief in the aftermath of hurricanes, earthquakes, and other natural disasters. From the U.S. government's standpoint, NGOs provide a more "neutral" vehicle for such programs than agencies affiliated with the United Nations, which many American policy makers see as politically biased and hostile to their country.

A major concern among many development NGOs in recent years has been the foreign debts of developing countries. As noted earlier, a global coalition of

---

8. The World Bank, like governments, benefits by outsourcing development projects to private groups rather than managing these projects itself with permanent staff. As the largest source of World Bank funding, the U.S. government has the most to gain from these arrangements.

private development agencies, church groups, human rights activists, and other groups mobilized around the issue of debt relief by forming a movement called Jubilee 2000. This movement led the World Bank and the International Monetary Fund to organize the Heavily Indebted Poor Countries Initiative, which coordinated the pledges of debt relief from wealthy countries. By February 2010, their governments provided $51 billion in debt relief to thirty-five countries, all but six of which were located in Africa (International Monetary Fund 2010a).

Think Tanks and Private Foundations

Public debate on U.S. foreign policy often originates within the dozens of "think tanks" located in Washington and elsewhere across the country. Although the news media provide the forum for debate, these private institutions supply the debaters in the form of academic specialists, former government and military officials, and outspoken figures from the private sector. The primary goal of these **idea brokers** is to influence public opinion and government policy through the dissemination of research findings and the airing of opinions on a variety of national issues (Smith 1991). Indeed, observers sometimes refer to major think tanks as "governments in waiting" that give those out of power an opportunity to remain active in the policy community while the rival political party controls the White House or Congress (see Figure 9.3).

The "politics of expertise" is particularly important in U.S. foreign policy, which is both highly complex and of limited concern to the general population

Figure 9.3   Select Foreign Policy Think Tanks: The Ideological Spectrum

Liberal	Centrist	Conservative
Center for Defense Information	Brookings Institution	American Enterprise Institute
Center for Nonproliferation Studies	Carnegie Endowment for International Peace	Cato Institute
Federation of American Scientists	Center for Strategic and International Studies	Ethics and Public Policy Center
Global Policy Forum	Council on Foreign Relations	Family Research Council
Institute for Policy Studies	Economic Policy Institute	Heritage Foundation
Interhemispheric Resource Center	Freedom House	Hoover Institution
Project on Defense Alternatives	Institute for International Economics	Hudson Institute
Union of Concerned Scientists	New America Foundation	Project for the New American Century
World Policy Institute	U.S. Institute of Peace	RAND Corporation

(Rich 2004). Among U.S.-based think tanks, the Council on Foreign Relations (CFR), formed in 1921, is the most influential in informing policy discussions and debates. The council limits its membership, valued as a sign of prestige in the policy community, to four thousand. Attendance at CFR-sponsored policy forums, which often involve current foreign policy makers and foreign leaders, also serves as an important status symbol. The journal *Foreign Affairs,* edited and published by the council, is a widely read source of elite opinion on U.S. foreign policy. The CFR and other moderate think tanks play a major part in the "revolving door" of policy elites. Richard Haass, for example, left the Brookings Institution in 2001 to become director of policy planning in the State Department, and then left the Bush administration two years later to become president of the CFR.

Other think tanks, some with institutional links to universities and government agencies, participate more directly in the U.S. foreign policy process.[9] The California-based RAND (an acronym for research and development) Corporation has received billions of dollars in grants since 1948 to conduct research on military technology for the Department of Defense. In recent years, however, its scope has broadened to include health care, education, and criminal justice, among other areas of public policy.

Finally, hundreds of private foundations in the United States provide grants for international research and programs in areas such as public health, education, environmental protection, development, and conflict resolution. The Ford Foundation, for example, has approved more than $10 billion in grants since 1950, primarily in economic development, political reform, and international cooperation. The Bill and Melinda Gates Foundation, with a $27 billion endowment from the founder and chairman of Microsoft Corp., has donated about $800 million annually in recent years for health care and literacy programs in the developing world. Recipients urgently needed the funds because of the growing income gaps between developed and less-developed countries and the cutbacks in aid programs from many countries, including the United States.

The Microsoft/Gates donations signal a new era in global development, with corporations stepping in to fund programs that governments are either unwilling or unable to support. Wealthy individuals also have filled the void in government funding. CNN founder Ted Turner, for example, announced in 1997 that he would donate $1 billion to the United Nations over ten years, in part to pay for development programs that faced cutbacks because of the lower contributions from the U.S. government. Another wealthy philanthropist, Warren Buffett, announced in June 2006 that he would provide $1.5 billion annually to the Gates endowment, effectively doubling its size.

---

9. The U.S. Institute of Peace, though technically considered an "independent" research organization, is funded by Congress. Its board of directors is appointed by the president and confirmed by the Senate.

Point/Counterpoint
GLOBAL COMPETITION VS. COOPERATION

Much of the public debate on U.S. foreign policy is held among think tanks, the private research NGOs that have become more sophisticated in shaping public opinion and influencing government policies. Many prominent think tanks focus on foreign policy, often drawing on the expertise of former (and possibly future) government officials who want outlets for their viewpoints. This has particularly been true in recent years as policy analysts have disagreed over the course of U.S. foreign policy, especially on the question of whether the United States should adopt a competitive or a cooperative posture in world politics.

The Project for the New American Century (PNAC) is one of the most outspoken advocates of a more "muscular" foreign policy. According to the PNAC statement of principles adopted at the group's founding in 1997, "We seem to have forgotten the essential elements of the Reagan Administration's success: a military that is strong and ready to meet both present and future challenges; a foreign policy that boldly and purposefully promotes American principles abroad; and national leadership that accepts the United States' global responsibilities." From this perspective, the United States should exploit its global primacy to make the world more hospitable to U.S. values and interests.

More moderate and liberal think tanks call for a "nonoffensive" approach to U.S.

foreign policy. The Project on Defense Alternatives (PDA), for example, promotes a "transitional security policy" that would curb military spending, encourage arms control, and foster "an increasing reliance on collective and global peacekeeping agencies and nonmilitary means of conflict prevention, containment, and resolution." Such cooperative measures are in keeping with Bill Clinton's grand strategy of global engagement and democratic reforms, with Jimmy Carter's emphasis on human rights, and with Woodrow Wilson's much earlier call for collective security.

PNAC gained the upper hand in this debate in 2001 when many of its founding members, including Dick Cheney, were appointed to high-level positions in the Bush administration. Other PNAC officers, including Donald Rumsfeld and Paul Wolfowitz, took command of the Pentagon and adopted the "neoconservative" principles espoused by the group. For its part, the PDA became a vocal critic of the Bush administration's preventive war strategy and its 2003 invasion of Iraq. The subsequent developments in that country only hardened the positions of the two think tanks, whose Internet studies continued to advocate very different strategies for U.S. foreign policy.

SOURCES: Project for the New American Century, www .newamericancentury.org; Project on Defense Alternatives, www.comw.org.

Group Strategies and Tactics

As described in this section, the tactics used by NGOs to influence U.S. foreign policy vary widely, depending on the type of NGOs involved, the resources at their disposal, and the foreign policy issues they seek to influence. Generally speaking, NGOs have become far more sophisticated as they have moved from the fringes to the mainstream of the policy process. They are now participating *within* the process—drafting legislation, serving on international commissions, and implementing government programs in areas previously monopolized by states.[10]

Consciousness Raising

Many NGOs simply want to call attention to their causes. They recognize that before a government will do something about problems such as global warming or the plight of political prisoners, large numbers of private citizens have to make government officials aware of these problems and forcefully call for government action.

By **shaming** governments through public information campaigns, NGOs raise normative doubts about the governments in question in the hope that the general public will follow their lead. Accomplishing this goal is particularly difficult in the United States, where thousands of NGOs compete daily for attention and support in a crowded, often bewildering, media environment. The continued existence of many NGOs depends on their success in taking hold of the media spotlight, if only for a brief time.

Well-organized private groups have been instrumental in shaping the agendas of states and intergovernmental organizations. The creation of the United Nations in 1945 and the UN's early emphasis on human rights and decolonization owed much to the work of churches, peace groups, and ethnic minorities. In the 1960s and 1970s, environmental groups mobilized effectively to force changes in automobile emission standards and enhance the protection of natural habitats. Peace groups in the 1980s rallied in favor of a nuclear freeze and in opposition to a new round of U.S. missile deployments. In the 1990s, private groups managed to place a treaty restricting the trafficking of small arms on the international agenda. Meanwhile, as discussed earlier, religious groups assumed a key role in promoting the causes of debt relief and AIDS treatment in the developing world.

The most effective of these groups exploit advances in communications technology, particularly the Internet, to get their messages across. Their Web sites serve as crucial sources of information about their organizations, their causes, and the strategies they use to achieve their objectives. These sites commonly provide

---

10. Permanent members of the UN Security Council, including the United States, regularly brief NGOs and seek their input on regional problems that may call for UN action. See the Security Council section of www.globalpolicy.org for a detailed listing of these collaborations.

links to related groups and information sources, encouraging the collaboration of NGOs and collective political action. Mass e-mailings also are a low-cost means used by groups to communicate with their members as well as with influential policy makers. Well-orchestrated media events, such as press conferences or demonstrations, have proved useful in attracting attention as well.

Like government officials, NGOs frame their adopted causes in dramatic and clearly understandable ways to gain media attention and public support. In the NGO campaign to ban landmines, for example, visual images of maimed victims proved more effective than hard numbers on the death toll produced by these weapons (Rutherford 2000). Similarly, members of Amnesty International found that the plight of political prisoners resonated more strongly among the public when individual cases were presented in graphic detail.

Because the problems of concern to NGOs tend to be ongoing, a primary function they fulfill is to *monitor* the extent of these problems and the U.S. government's response to them, and to *report* their findings on a regular basis to their members, policy makers, and the general public. Freedom House, a U.S.-based human rights group, accomplishes this task by publishing an annual volume called *Freedom in the World,* which rates the conduct of all governments in respecting human rights (see Map 11, Freedom in the World, in map section). Policy makers and activists from other groups watch the ratings closely because Freedom House, unlike a government agency, is an independent organization that stakes its reputation on its objective assessment of government practices. In a similar fashion, periodic reports by the Council on Economic Priorities review the practices of major corporations and provide needed guidance to political and business leaders.

Political Pressure and Lobbying

In addition to influencing government agendas, private groups directly intervene in the U.S. foreign policy process. Their tactics include direct-mail campaigns to congressional offices and the White House that ask for support on matters of immediate concern. Representatives of NGOs also appeal in person to legislators and key executive branch officials. In the process of **lobbying,** they present these officials with "carrots," or potential rewards, for support of their preferences, as well as "sticks," or potential punishments, for nonsupport.

Carrots and sticks generally come in two forms—electoral and financial support. The first relates to the central reality that elected officials need votes to gain and stay in office and that organized groups can deliver more votes than individuals. Politicians listen carefully to these groups, particularly large religious and ethnic NGOs, labor unions, and business groups that can mobilize multitudes of voters. In the 2000 presidential election, George W. Bush actively sought the support of Cuban Americans in southern Florida and promised to continue the economic embargo against Fidel Castro's communist regime that these voters widely supported. Florida governor Jeb Bush, who had close ties to the Cuban

Americans, helped his brother win the state (however narrowly, and after intervention by the U.S. Supreme Court) largely on the basis of an overwhelming majority of votes from this close-knit ethnic group.

Another way NGOs influence the policy process is by providing, or withholding, contributions to political campaigns through their affiliated **political action committees (PACs)**—the electoral arm of organized groups responsible for fund-raising and distributing money to promote the election of desired candidates. Despite recent reforms in campaign finance, money still speaks volumes in national politics (see Figure 9.4). The high price of campaigning—primarily the costs of producing and airing television commercials—forces candidates to rely heavily on financial contributions. Private groups needing help from the government—as almost all groups do—gain favor among political leaders by contributing money to their campaigns. In return for these funds, candidates assure the groups that their concerns will be taken into account.

Lobbying, a term used to describe the lobbies outside congressional offices and meeting rooms where personal contacts can be made, provides access to the foreign policy process that may not be possible through conventional diplomatic channels. Most foreign embassies lack the staff and resources necessary to get the attention of top policy makers, let alone members of congressional committees. Lobbying firms, clustered around K Street just a few blocks from the White House and Capitol Hill, also arrange business deals that benefit their foreign

Figure 9.4 Financial Contributions to Presidential Candidates, 1976–2008

SOURCE: www.opensecrets.org/pres08/index.php.

clients as well as the politicians who approve the deals. Recent examples of this "privatized" diplomacy abound (see Newhouse 2009):

- The BGR Group, led by former ambassador Robert Blackwill, earned $300,000 for providing "strategic counsel" to Ayad Allawi, Iraq's former prime minister who sought a return to power in 2010.

- Patton Boggs, another prominent lobbying firm, helped the U.S.-India Business Council promote the 2005 agreement between the two countries that called for U.S. shipments of nuclear fuel to India, a deal that alarmed the country's neighbors and nonproliferation advocates.[11]

- The Livingston Group, exploiting its personal links to George W. Bush's foreign policy advisers such as Douglas Feith and Richard Perle, worked successfully on behalf of its client, the Turkish government, which discouraged Congress from condemning Turkey's 1915 genocide of Armenians.

- Hogan & Hartson, still another powerful lobbying group, helped the Chinese government gain trade concessions and favorable changes in U.S. financial practices—deals that could not have been made alone by Chinese government officials.

Policy and Program Implementation

A rapidly growing arena of NGO activity is implementation of policies and programs approved by national governments. In these instances, which require shared preferences between the government and groups, NGOs serve as functional extensions of the governments they serve and as instruments of their policy ambitions. Development NGOs, for example, manage the shipment and delivery of U.S. foreign aid to governments in need. Human rights NGOs conduct voter registration drives sponsored by the State Department and monitor elections in countries undergoing transitions to democratic rule.

Government contracting, the "public financing of private provision," is attractive to all parties concerned (Berrios 2000, 23). Through NGOs that have acquired material resources as well as legitimacy in advancing their agendas, the federal government, by far the largest customer of such contracted services in the United States, can pursue its foreign policy goals, such as economic development and political reform, without adding to its permanent workforce. More broadly, the practice of contracting services is consistent with the nation's ideological bias in favor of limited government and free enterprise. **Public choice theory**, which argues that competitive private firms can supply goods and

---

11. As part of its effort to secure passage of the Hyde Act, which was approved by both houses of Congress in November 2006, the "India lobby" held fundraisers for key legislators such as Joe Biden, D-Del., chair of the Senate Foreign Relations Committee, and Hillary Clinton, D-N.Y., co-chair of the Senate India Caucus.

services more efficiently than government agencies, reinforces this bias (see Buchanan 1977).

Recent evidence demonstrates that the U.S. government takes these NGOs seriously in its conduct of foreign policy. After the Kosovo conflict in 1999, the State Department disbursed more than $10 million in grants to NGOs so that they could help refugees return to their homes and rebuild their communities. Shortly before leaving office in January 2001, Secretary of State Madeleine Albright announced nearly $4 million in grants to NGOs so that they could monitor working conditions in overseas "sweatshops." Private contractors manage U.S. foreign aid projects so commonly that an "aid lobby" has emerged among competing NGOs in such specialized areas as education, health care, environmental protection, and disaster relief (Lancaster 2007, 102–103).

As noted earlier, the outsourcing of U.S. foreign policy functions is also routine in the military sector. Of particular interest are **corporate warriors,** private companies that "trade in professional services linked to warfare" (Singer 2003, 8). Dozens of private military firms provide a wide range of military functions once reserved for the government, from food services to maintaining the grounds on U.S. military bases. In Iraq, private contractors built schools and hospitals, installed telephone and satellite systems, and advised Iraqi officials on effective ways in which to pursue political and economic reforms. Other countries also have turned to these companies for assistance, including for combat forces that are in some instances better trained and equipped than their own troops (Isenberg 1997).

The benefits of outsourcing defense, however, come at considerable costs. By their nature, private firms are more secretive and less accountable than public agencies, which must adhere to provisions for legislative oversight and public scrutiny. Controlling corporate warriors can also be difficult, as the U.S. government realized in the 2004 prison abuse scandals in Iraq. Only after the media reported the story did Congress and U.S. citizens learn that private contractors serving as prison interrogators had resorted to brutal tactics that violated the Geneva Conventions. Private contractors in Iraq, better paid than their military counterparts, provoked widespread resentment among U.S. troops during the conflict. Finally, contractors from the United States and other coalition forces became frequent targets of kidnappings in Iraq. Indeed, some of the most publicized U.S. casualties during the Iraq occupation, including the beheading of businessman Nicholas Berg, involved private contractors.

Civil Disobedience

When private groups feel their voices are not being heard through conventional channels of political discourse, they frequently resort to civil disobedience to get attention. According to Howard Zinn (1968, 119), civil disobedience involves "the deliberate, discriminate violation of law for a vital social purpose. It becomes not only justifiable but necessary when a fundamental human right is at stake, and when legal channels are inadequate for securing that right." The tactics of civil disobedience are considered most significant for their symbolic value.

Although a protester's arrest may have little immediate consequence for the policy process, protesters expect such arrests to attract public attention and to provoke sympathies, thereby building pressure for reform.

Civil disobedience has long been an important tactic of transnational NGOs. Greenpeace, for example, gained the world's attention by sending boats into restricted areas of the South Pacific where the French government was planning to conduct nuclear tests.[12] As noted earlier, violent protests by environmentalists, human rights advocates, anarchists, and labor unionists during the 1999 meetings of the WTO in Seattle stole the spotlight from the WTO delegates and altered the agenda and outcome of the meetings. Several months later, protesters in Davos, Switzerland, disrupted the annual meetings of the World Economic Forum. In response, the forum invited fifteen NGOs to the 2000 annual meeting. By 2002 more than one hundred private groups had joined the discussions, although they remained excluded from many events.

In the United States, during the late 1960s and early 1970s critics of the Vietnam War frequently resorted to civil disobedience to express their displeasure with the government's war effort. For example, the Students for a Democratic Society (SDS), an organization established by campus activists in several major universities, conducted "sit-ins," or the peaceful occupation of public spaces, to express their opposition to the war. Some SDS members burned their draft cards; others staged hunger strikes to raise public consciousness. Demonstrations against the war, while generally peaceful, sometimes led to violent clashes with police and mass arrests. In the 1980s, organized groups protested the escalation of the arms race and called for a nuclear freeze, much to the dismay of the Reagan administration.

Buying Power: The Corporate Connection

The largest and most powerful NGOs can be found in the business world. It is not unusual for a company to have its headquarters in one country and its other operations (such as research and development, production, marketing, and sales) in others. Profit-seeking firms with operations, subsidiaries, and markets in more than one country are known as **multinational corporations (MNCs)**. In responding to technological advances, primarily in the areas of research and development, telecommunications, and transportation, MNCs are both the by-products and the catalysts of globalization.[13] Indeed, these kinds of firms have grown rapidly in number, size, and global reach in the past century, to the point that the annual revenues of today's largest MNCs far exceed the economic output of most countries. Wal-Mart, for example, brought in more money in 2001 than the economy

---

12. Membership in Greenpeace soared in 1985 after the French Secret Services sunk the Greenpeace vessel *Rainbow Warrior* off the coast of New Zealand.

13. The increasingly blurred distinction between "home" and "overseas" ownership and management of MNCs had led some observers to adopt the term "globally integrated enterprise" in discussing these firms (see Palmisano 2006). See May (2006) for a recent anthology, *Global Corporate Power*.

of Austria. In that same year, General Motors and Ford had higher revenues than the economies of Indonesia, Poland, Venezuela, and dozens of other countries (Kegley and Wittkopf 2004, 175).

The U.S. government, whose founding principles include a belief in the virtues of free markets and global commerce, has long been an advocate of MNCs. In 2009, seven of the world's twenty largest MNCs in terms of total revenues were based in the United States (see Table 9.2). Other leading MNCs have most of their production and support facilities in the United States. Still others, such as the electronics firms based in Japan, derive most of their revenues from American consumers. These corporate interests flood the policy process, and political campaigns, with massive financial resources; financial firms alone contributed nearly $500 million to candidates in the 2008 national elections (Drum 2010). More generally, these corporations can serve as agents of U.S. foreign policy by embracing many

Table 9.2   The World's Twenty Largest Corporations, 2009

Rank	Company	Nationality	Revenues (billions of U.S. dollars)
1.	Royal Dutch Shell	Netherlands	$458
2.	Exxon Mobil	USA	443
3.	Wal-Mart Stores	USA	406
4.	BP	United Kingdom	367
5.	Chevron	USA	263
6.	Total	France	235
7.	ConocoPhillips	USA	231
8.	ING Group	Netherlands	227
9.	Sinopec-China Petroleum	China	208
10.	Toyota Motor	Japan	204
11.	Japan Post Holdings	Japan	199
12.	General Electric	USA	183
13.	China National Petroleum	China	181
14.	Volkswagen	Germany	167
15.	State Grid	China	164
16.	Dexia Group	Belgium	161
17.	ENI	Italy	159
18.	General Motors	USA	149
19.	Ford Motor	USA	146
20.	Allianz	Germany	142

of the interests, values, and beliefs about political economy held by government leaders. Three areas of convergence can be identified:

■ *Shared values.* Corporations and U.S. political leaders share the belief that a free market economy will foster political freedoms. In this view, firms will avoid doing business in countries that cannot guarantee the security of their assets, that tolerate corruption, and that repress political rights to such an extent that mass revolts pose constant dangers.

■ *Shared interests.* Corporate leaders and the U.S. government promote a world economy based on private property and open markets. The government's bias toward free trade favors U.S.-based MNCs that are wealthier and more technologically advanced than their competitors overseas.

■ *Economic peace.* Corporate and government officials agree that countries respecting economic and political freedoms most likely will engage in peaceful relations toward one another. This variant of democratic-peace theory (see Chapter 3) is driven by economic necessity, as private investors and firms require a stable, predictable environment, which is impossible in areas prone to violent conflicts and coups.

In addition to having economic clout, MNCs are powerful *political* actors. Business groups have always been influential at all levels of U.S. politics. Their prospects for higher profits depend on favorable government policy in several areas, including corporate taxation, health and safety regulations, defense spending, and labor rights. Trade policy is of particular importance to MNCs, which want access to foreign markets along with protection from foreign competition. Corporations also stand to gain from food aid and development projects overseas, many of which require the provision of U.S.-based goods and services.

The pervasive role of MNCs in U.S. foreign policy makes them frequent targets of criticism by nonprofit NGOs with more altruistic goals. Animosity is not limited to individuals and groups within the United States; foreign-based groups complain that MNCs are agents of cultural imperialism, force-feeding people consumer products such as Coca-Cola and McDonald's hamburgers through aggressive marketing and advertising campaigns. Groups also "name and shame" corporations for damaging ecosystems, mistreating workers, and intimidating the political leaders of foreign countries and communities. Exposés of oppressive labor practices in overseas sweatshops by companies such as Nike, Wal-Mart, Walt Disney, and the Gap prompted these corporations to establish codes of conduct for their suppliers (Gereffi, Garcia-Johnson, and Sasser 2001).[14] Pressure from environmental NGOs such as the Rainforest Network and the Natural Resources Defense Council forced major retail stores in the United States, including Home Depot and Lowe's Home Improvement Warehouse, to certify that the lumber they

---

14. See Roberts and Engardio (2006) for a discussion of recent attempts by Chinese manufacturers to defy these pressures for reform.

were selling was not furnished by suppliers who were inflicting irreversible damage on the natural world.

The Military-Industrial Complex

Among U.S.-based corporations, those involved in the defense industry have the closest ties to the foreign policy process (see Carroll 2006). The U.S. defense industry, by far the largest of its kind in the world, has grown rapidly in recent years, after a decade of post–Cold War cutbacks. Weapons production, a large segment of the U.S. economy, is a leading source of new technologies, many of which find their way into civilian industries.[15] The defense industry currently employs more than 2 million people. As the largest discretionary category of U.S. government spending, the defense budget has a strong impact on whether the overall federal budget ends each fiscal year with a surplus or deficit. As Sen. Everett Dirksen, R-Ill., once observed wryly, "A billion here, a billion there, sooner or later it adds up to real money."

Defense spending is also a major arena of competition for federal dollars. American military contractors such as Lockheed Martin, Boeing, and Northrop Grumman dominate the global defense industry (see Table 9.3). Although these industry giants produce the largest and most modern weapons systems for the United States and foreign governments, hundreds of smaller MNCs support the defense sector as well, providing ammunition, spare parts, uniforms, food, medical supplies, and other goods to the armed services. For some corporations, such as General Electric, defense products amount to a small fraction (about 2 percent) of

Table 9.3 Top Ten Military Contractors, 2008

Rank	Company	Country	Defense revenue, 2008 (billions of U.S. dollars)	Proportion of revenue from defense
1.	Lockheed Martin	USA	$40	93%
2.	BAE Systems	UK	33	95
3.	Boeing	USA	31	51
4.	Northrop Grumman	USA	27	78
5.	General Dynamics	USA	23	78
6.	Raytheon	USA	22	93
7.	EADS	Netherlands	16	26
8.	L-3 Communications	USA	12	82
9.	Finmeccanica	Italy	10	46
10.	United Technologies	USA	10	17

SOURCE: Defense News, "Defense News Top 100 for 2008," www.defensenews.com/static/features/top100/charts/rank_2008.php?c=FEA&s=T1C.

---

15. For example, the U.S. Department of Defense sponsored much of the research and development of the Internet during the Cold War.

revenue that nevertheless amounts to billions of dollars in government expenditures. Deciding which military contractors receive the massive volumes of money is part of an intense and often bitter political process within Congress, whose members affect large sectors of the U.S. economy with each defense appropriation.

The latest military buildup, focusing on high-technology weapons systems, accelerated after the terrorist attacks of September 2001. The steady increase in U.S. defense spending, detailed in Chapter 5, has benefited hundreds of U.S.-based corporations. The large size and political clout of these MNCs have been a central feature of U.S. society since World War II. During the Cold War, President Dwight Eisenhower worried that the U.S. "military-industrial complex" posed a danger to the economy by diverting a significant share of output from civilian production (see In Their Own Words box). In his view, the reliance of huge and politically influential corporations on arms manufacturing created a perverse incentive on the government's part to expand the nation's military arsenal. In such an environment, Eisenhower believed, both the arms merchants and their patrons in Congress were tempted to inflate the magnitude of foreign threats. Evidence that government officials exaggerated a "missile gap" favoring Soviet forces affirmed these concerns in the 1960s. In the 1980s, intelligence estimates of Soviet military capabilities proved inaccurate as well, raising doubts about the necessity of the huge U.S. military buildup.

Eisenhower's warning also highlighted the potential dangers iron triangles pose in the policy process (see Chapter 3). For many former military officers, who retire from active service in their forties and fifties, a logical next step in their careers is the defense industry, with its familiar products and functions. This crossing of career paths creates a strong bond between the Pentagon and defense contractors. Together, they are able to get the attention and support of powerful members of Congress, who receive campaign contributions and other forms of political support from the defense industry and its PACs. The groups in the military-industrial complex, as well as those in countless other areas, have proved to be highly influential in the U.S. foreign policy process.

With such huge volumes of money involved, conflicts of interest and potential corruption inevitably emerge, as documented abuses have shown. Some defense contractors have bribed members of Congress in return for lucrative contracts. Meanwhile, former Pentagon officials who have moved into lobbying jobs with military contractors have gained privileged access to legislators. Even though measures have been taken to reduce the impact of this "revolving door" on the procurement process—for example, legislators and senior officials in the executive branch must refrain from lobbying their former colleagues for at least one year after leaving government—the incentives of all concerned to maintain these ties persist within the military-industrial complex.

The case of Vice President Dick Cheney and Halliburton, the company he once headed, illustrates the dangers associated with the revolving door.[16] Cheney,

---

16. Halliburton employees gave $385,094 in campaign contributions between 1999 and April 2007, of which nearly $280,000 was paid to Republican candidates (www.campaignmoney.com/Halliburton.asp).

IN THEIR OWN WORDS: DWIGHT D. EISENHOWER

Although Dwight D. Eisenhower's farewell address in 1961 was the first such event to be tele-vised, observers registered surprise not so much at the medium of delivery as at the message sent. The man who had made his name as supreme Allied commander during World War II and then as supreme commander of NATO warned against the defense industry's unchecked influ-ence in the halls of government. Coining the term "military-industrial complex," Eisenhower offered a cautionary tale about some of the nation's largest and most powerful foreign policy interest groups. Although many political and business leaders agreed with Eisenhower, the military-industrial complex is even stronger today.

A vital element in keeping the peace is our military establishment. Our arms must be mighty, ready for instant action, so that no potential aggressor may be tempted to risk his own destruction.

Our military organization today bears little relation to that known by any of my pre-decessors in peacetime, or indeed by the fighting men of World War II or Korea.

Until the latest of our world conflicts, the United States had no armaments industry. American makers of plowshares could, with time and as required, make swords as well. But now we can no longer risk emergency improvision of national defense; we have been compelled to create a permanent armaments industry of vast proportions. Added to this, three and a half mil-lion men and women are directly engaged in the defense establishment. We annually spend on military security more than the net income of all United States corporations.

This conjunction of an immense military establishment and a large arms industry is new in the American experience. The total influence—economic, political, even spiritual—is felt in every city, every State house, every office of the federal govern-ment. We recognize the imperative need for this development. Yet we must not fail to comprehend its grave implications. Our toil, resources, and livelihood are all involved; so is the very structure of our society.

In the councils of government, we must guard against the acquisition of unwarranted influence, whether sought or unsought, by the military-industrial complex. The poten-tial for the disastrous rise of misplaced power exists and will persist.

We must never let the weight of this combination endanger our liberties or demo-cratic processes. . . .

SOURCE: Michael Nelson, ed., "Dwight D. Eisenhower's Farewell Address (1961)," *Historic Documents on the Presidency: 1776–1989* (Washington, D.C.: Congressio-nal Quarterly, 1989), 350–354.

who earned $44 million from the military contractor during his five years as CEO, received about $150,000 annually in deferred pay between 2001 and 2005 and held another $18 million in stock options (Mayer 2004). As secretary of defense in 1992, Cheney hired the company to study ways it could support U.S. military needs after the Cold War. A dozen years later, just prior to the 2003 Iraq inva-sion, which Cheney supported, Halliburton and its subsidiary—KBR—were the primary recipients of Department of Defense contracts to feed the troops, maintain their bases, construct new government buildings, and rebuild Iraqi oil wells (see Baum 2003). Halliburton received nearly $4 billion in government contracts in fiscal year 2003 alone for services in Iraq and Afghanistan (U.S. Department of Defense 2004). The administration did not advertise most of these contracts or receive competing bids on them, in part because few other firms were prepared to manage such a complex undertaking on short notice.

Not long after its Iraqi contracts received approval, Halliburton ran into trouble. In January 2004, the company announced that it would repay the U.S. government $6.3 million to cover "improper payments" two of its employees had received for their hiring of a subcontractor in Kuwait. In February, auditors found that a Halliburton subsidiary may have charged the government $16 million for meals it never served. Worse still, that same month the Pentagon launched a criminal investigation into allegations that Halliburton had overcharged U.S. taxpayers by $61 million for oil from Kuwait (Spinner 2004). Yet despite these problems, Halliburton continued to receive new government contracts after Iraq regained formal sovereignty in June 2004 and as the rebuilding and military support costs continued to mount.

Trade Associations and Labor Unions

Private groups that represent entire sectors of the U.S. economy or the business community in general promote business interests in the United States as well. Many of these groups are active in shaping not only U.S. foreign policy, but also the policies of governments abroad. Prominent among these groups is the U.S. Chamber of Commerce, which seeks business access to foreign markets by pressuring policy makers in the United States and their counterparts in other countries. In 2002, the Chamber, which represents more than three million firms and nearly one thousand business associations, had a presence in eighty-two foreign nations. Using many of the same tactics, foreign-based MNCs and trade associations maintain full-time staffs in Washington, D.C., to pursue favorable treatment in U.S. trade policy and other legislation.

Labor unions such as the United Auto Workers, the Teamsters Union, and the Communications Workers of America participate in this process as well, often as adversaries of the MNCs that employ their members. These groups are seeking to keep their workers' jobs in the United States. The clout of this sizable voting bloc, though weakening in recent years as the number and proportion of unionized workers have declined, remains beyond question. Proponents of the steel industry, for example, persuaded President Bush in 2002 to increase tariffs on foreign-made steel to keep domestic producers in business, a decision popular in U.S. steel-producing regions of the United States that play a critical role in national elections. However, Bush's decision angered foreign political and business leaders as well as the WTO, which criticized Bush for violating his own standards on free trade and WTO regulations. In the face of this criticism and the threat of imminent WTO and European Union sanctions, Bush lowered the steel tariffs.

The protection of U.S. jobs is a classic *intermestic* issue, as are other aspects of economic activity, such as environmental regulation and immigration. Policy makers in these cases play a two-level game (Putnam 1988) in which they negotiate simultaneously with representatives of foreign governments and those of U.S. interest groups with a stake in the outcome. Interests at the two levels frequently come into conflict. For example, after the U.S. government secures access to another country's domestic market, American firms are tempted to move their factories to that country to reduce labor costs, thereby laying off workers in the United States. Decision makers in these cases must walk a political tightrope, trying to find areas of agreement among the interested parties at home and abroad.

Conclusion

This chapter has described the many strategies and tactics pursued by social movements, NGOs, and profit-seeking firms in their attempts to influence U.S. foreign policy. Such activity can be highly effective given the lack of general public interest and engagement in the policy process, a pattern highlighted in Chapters 7 and 8. Whereas broadly based social movements seek policy changes that presumably benefit all citizens, most interest groups seek to advance the interests of a narrower range of stakeholders. The influence of these groups varies widely, and competition among them for resources and access is often fierce. Although their relationship with U.S. foreign policy makers is often contentious, interest groups frequently align with Washington on key issues, producing mutual benefits and a stronger U.S. position in diplomatic bargaining.

Organized group action is entirely consistent with American political values, but there is little doubt that the political and financial pressures imposed by such groups may steer U.S. foreign policy in directions that conflict with and sometimes contradict proclaimed national interests. Privatized diplomacy, which has become commonplace in U.S. foreign policy, reinforces "a uniquely American habit of sustaining the democratic process with money; [foreign governments] see a broad and deepening pattern of corrupt and corruptible members of Congress making self-serving deals with lobbyists working for foreign entities" (Newhouse 2009, 92). The same can be said for the pressure applied by MNCs, military contractors, and other groups with a material stake in security policies, whose proven influence over key decisions fuels the paradox of U.S. world power.

Whereas particularistic groups pose challenges to the democratic conduct of U.S. foreign policy, cosmopolitan groups that promote collective interests must overcome their own "democratic deficits," as described earlier, by permitting outsiders to observe their deliberations or have a voice in selecting their leaders (see McGann and Johnstone 2005). At the same time, the common deficiencies of nonprofit NGOs—their limited political clout compared with that of MNCs, their need for constant fund-raising, and their frequent conflicts with one another—will also persist. These strains will likely continue, however, as the spread of democracy to much of the world ensures that members of transnational civil society will become even more potent political actors (Slaughter 2004).

Broader social movements, including those demanding an end to military interventions or greater U.S. respect for human rights overseas, fail to achieve their goals at least as often as they succeed. Nevertheless, government officials ignore such forces at their peril and must constantly weigh the electoral and material costs and benefits of engagement with large-scale and well-organized advocates for change. The government must contend with the full range of societal actors, at home and abroad, whose proven capacity to disrupt the status quo and cut political careers short makes them inescapable players in the foreign policy process.

Key Terms

corporate warriors, p. 300

cosmopolitan groups, p. 287

democratic deficit, p. 287

idea brokers, p. 293

lobbying, p. 297

multinational corporations (MNCs), p. 301

particularistic groups, p. 287

political action committees (PACs), p. 298

public choice theory, p. 299

shaming, p. 296

social movement, p. 280

sovereignty gap, p. 277

transnational advocacy network, p. 281

Internet References

The **American Enterprise Institute** (www.aei.org), based in Washington, D.C., promotes a variety of causes related to "American freedom and democratic capitalism." Nearly two hundred researchers and prominent policy experts publish reports and organize conferences that advocate U.S. foreign policy based on the promotion of national interests rather than global concerns.

The **American Israel Public Affairs Committee** (www.aipac.org), one of the most influential lobbying organizations in the United States, promotes U.S. foreign policy in the Middle East that supports Israel. The group's Web site includes briefings on issues related to regional security and updates on AIPAC efforts to gain U.S. political, economic, and military support for Israel.

The **Brookings Institution** (www.brookings.edu) is a think tank that provides scholarly reports and in-depth research on domestic and international sources affecting U.S. foreign policy. Particular attention is paid to defense, the world economy, environmental issues, and global governance.

The **Center for Defense Information** (www.cdi.org) publishes reports and statistics on defense and security policy. In particular, the center focuses on U.S. arms sales and trade, missile defense, defense projects and budgets, and nuclear issues.

(continued)

Foreign Policy in Focus (www.fpif.org) is a "think tank without walls" that seeks to educate the public through Internet reports and public conferences on a variety of U.S. foreign policy issues. Sponsored by the Institute for Policy Studies, the group advocates the advancement of human rights and justice as a centerpiece of U.S. foreign policy.

MoveOn (www.moveon.org), a coalition of liberal grassroots organizations, gained national stature as a rallying point for critics of the Bush administration's domestic and foreign policies. Through its Web site, the group sponsors voter registration drives, neighborhood canvassing, and other activities on behalf of liberal candidates.

The **National Council of Churches** (www.ncccusa.org) represents an array of U.S.-based Christian denominations in advancing human rights, poverty relief, and other social causes. Recent resolutions have condemned U.S. mistreatment of prisoners and increased domestic surveillance in the war on terrorism.

The **NGO Global Network** (www.ngo.org) promotes collaboration among NGOs that maintain consultative status within the United Nations. Its Web site includes updates on pressing issues before the United Nations involving conflict resolution, international law, and sustainable development.

One.org, an Internet-based advocate for humanitarian relief, derives its influence from the more than 2 million signatories of its declaration to end extreme poverty. The group's petitions reveal mass-based support for debt forgiveness, increased treatment of HIV/AIDS, and the protection of human rights in the developing world.

Political Advocacy Groups: A Directory of United States Lobbyists (www.vancouver .wsu.edu/fac/kfountain/about.html), maintained by Washington State University, has links to a variety of issue advocacy groups. Of particular interest to U.S. foreign policy are the links for peace and war, the environment, international affairs, and political parties.

Political Science Resources: Think Tanks (www.lib.umich.edu/govdocs/psthink.html), a University of Michigan Web site, offers links to think tanks and working papers journals inside the United States and around the globe. The links are organized both alphabetically and by political ideology.

10 CHAPTER

National Security and Defense Policy

Secretary of Defense Robert Gates (center) testifies to members of the Senate Appropriations Committee to discuss the Pentagon's 2008 request for supplemental funding for the wars in Afghanistan and Iraq. Gates, accompanied by Deputy Secretary of State John Negroponte (left) and Joint Chiefs of Staff Chairman Peter Pace (right), maintained his position in the Obama administration in 2009.

The final three chapters of this book examine the primary domains of U.S. foreign policy—that is, the substantive issue areas that affect the nation's relations with governments and citizens overseas. The three domains—national security, global economic relations, and transnational issues—capture the diversity of foreign policy problems facing the United States today. They do not, however, exhaust the full range of issues that confront policy makers, who must respond to unanticipated events while managing routine functions and pursuing their long-term objectives on a daily basis.

This chapter considers the foreign policy problems related to **national security,** the freedom a nation-state enjoys from threats to its sovereignty, territory, and political autonomy. This term is inherently controversial because of the tendency of political leaders to justify their actions on security grounds. Dwight Eisenhower, for example, created the interstate highway system on the basis of national security, and Richard Nixon used the same rationale to defend his secret bombings of Cambodia during the Vietnam War. Yet, despite the ambiguity and manipulations surrounding the term, *national security* "has come into such broad usage since World War II that, like a boomerang, we cannot throw it away" (Jordan, Taylor, and Mazarr 1999, 3).

The security that states and their citizens experience derives from a variety of sources. Canadian scholar Barry Buzan (1991, 19–20) found that five elements combine to create a sense of national security:

- *Military security*—the strength and effectiveness of the armed forces

- *Economic security*—the productive use of natural and human resources, financial assets, technological advancements, and foreign markets

- *Political security*—the stability and legitimacy of government institutions

- *Societal security*—the vitality of civil society, including interest groups, mass culture, and the news media

- *Environmental security*—the degree to which natural resources are protected and human activity takes place on an ecologically sustainable basis.

This chapter focuses on the first of these elements, military security, and its contribution to U.S. national security through **defense policy,** or the organization and strategic deployment of armed forces to protect a state against foreign threats. Maintaining national defense is an essential responsibility of all governments. In the United States, determining which strategies to pursue is complicated by the highly fragmented security complex in which defense policy is managed. This security complex, as described in Chapter 6, includes the White House–based National Security Council, the Department of Homeland Security, and the four armed services overseen by the Department of Defense.

The Pentagon, with its massive budget and worldwide troop presence, has assumed greater responsibility for all aspects of U.S. national security in recent years. The war on terrorism, which has no discernible end, fuels this militarization of U.S. foreign policy. Top presidential advisers, including President Barack Obama's national security adviser, the head of the National Intelligence Council, and the ambassador to Afghanistan, are retired military officers. Even the provision of development aid is increasingly a Pentagon function. Indeed, U.S. foreign policy today is unique to the extent that it "is being crafted and implemented by the military," observed Michael A. Cohen (2009, 69), a research fellow at the New America Foundation. "Whether it's waging the war on terror or the war on drugs; nation-building in post-conflict environments, development, democracy promotion, or diplomacy; fighting cyber-criminals or training foreign armies, the global face of the United States is generally that of a soldier."

The balance of military power among the world's nations offers a useful starting point in any analysis of U.S. defense policy (see Table 10.1). In most measures of military strength, the United States maintains a wide lead over other great powers. As noted in Chapter 1, U.S. defense spending of more than $600 billion

Table 10.1 Global Military Balance of Power

Country	Military spending, 2008 (billions of U.S. dollars)	Armed forces, 2008 (thousands of active personnel)	Military aircraft, 2009	Total navy ships, 2009	Total land-based weapons, 2009	Nuclear warheads, 2010
United States	$616.0	1,385	13,641	1,559	29,920	9,400
China	121.9	2,255	4,695	760	31,300	240
Russia	70.0	1,245	5,053	526	79,985	12,000
United Kingdom	55.4	195	1,388	139	5,121	185
France	54.0	225	1,720	134	8,536	300
Japan	41.1	239	1,933	147	2,040	0
Germany	37.8	250	1,069	130	5,699	0
Italy	30.6	240	1,326	107	3,355	0
Saudi Arabia	29.5	124	622	31	5,695	0
South Korea	24.6	687	1,437	85	8,325	0
India	22.4	1,325	1,625	143	10,340	60–80
Brazil	16.2	287	1,036	89	1,676	0

SOURCES: U.S. Office of Management and Budget, *Budget of the United States Government: Historical Tables,* www.gpoaccess.gov/USbudget/fy10/hist.html; Christopher Hellman and Travis Sharp, "U.S. Military Spending vs. the World," Center for Arms Control and Non-Proliferation (February 22, 2008), www.armscontrolcenter.org/policy/securityspending/articles/fy09_dod_request_global; Global Firepower.com, www.global firepower.com; Global Firepower.com, Navy Ships, www.globalfirepower.com/navy-ships.asp; *AviationWeek.com,* www.aviationweek.com/aw/sourcebook/channelSB_profiles_military.jsp?channelName=pro; Hans M. Kristensen, "Status of World Nuclear Forces, 2010," Federation of American Scientists, www.fas.org/programs/ssp/nukes/nuclearweapons/nukestatus.html.

in 2008 nearly exceeded that of all other countries combined. Although other nations lead in some categories of military power, such as China in sheer numbers of military personnel and Russia in tanks and other land-based weapons, only the United States maintains a worldwide military presence that carves the globe into separate regional commands with military installations in nearly forty countries (see Map 7, Department of Defense Regional Commands, and Map 9, Nuclear Threats and U.S. Defense Installations, in map section). Through this pervasive reach, the United States dominates the "commons" of air, sea, and space (Posen 2003). Advances in U.S. military technology, clearly on display in Afghanistan, Iraq, Kuwait, and Kosovo during the past decade, significantly widen this gap in military power.

These indicators highlight the importance of military strength in the global balance of power. To Hans Morgenthau (1967, 26), who equated *world* politics with *power* politics, "Armed strength as a threat or a potentiality is the most important material factor making for the political power of a nation." In this regard, power represents more than a tangible resource, the identifiable and measurable sum of a country's military assets. It also represents an intangible capability to "effect the outcomes you want, and if necessary, to change the behavior of others to make this happen" (Nye 2002, 4).

Throughout its history, the United States has frequently employed its military forces to achieve a variety of foreign policy goals. A 2004 study by the Congressional Research Service identified 320 instances of overt military force between 1798 and March 2004, an average of more than 1.5 military actions per year (Grimmett 2010). Of this total, 168 occurred through 1945, an average of 1.14 per year. This rate slowed modestly during the Cold War, when the United States used military force "for other than normal peacetime purposes" fifty-three times between 1945 and 1991. After the Cold War, the pace of U.S. military involvement accelerated. Between 1992 and the end of 2003, ninety-five such instances were recorded, an average of nearly eight per year. This rapid pace has continued in recent years as the United States has maintained ongoing military operations in Iraq, Afghanistan, Pakistan, across the horn of Africa, and in other conflict zones associated with the war on terrorism.

The terrorist attacks of September 2001 forced military planners to reshape U.S. strategy around the concept of "asymmetric warfare"—that is, wars fought between adversaries of highly uneven material strength (see Chapter 1). The *National Defense Strategy* (U.S. Department of Defense 2008, 2) found the global security environment to be "defined by a global struggle against a violent extremist ideology that seeks to overturn the international state system." The weaker powers in such low-intensity conflicts "work around, offset, and negate" their targets' superiority as measured by standard calculations of military power (Gray 2002, 6). The advantages of even the most muscle-bound states, including the United States, may be undercut by weaker but highly determined terrorist groups that prey on civilian targets and mass psychology, staging attacks at times and places of their choosing. Asymmetric warfare also is unique in the way it blends high technology with primitive battlefield tactics, governments with private groups, and military with civilian targets. In such conflicts, "Microsoft coexists with machetes and stealth technology is met by suicide bombers" (Evans 2004). Such warfare is alien to U.S. military strategists, whose global military presence and nuclear stockpiles are of little relevance to U.S. troops fighting in the deserts of Iraq or the mountains of Afghanistan. To Defense Secretary Robert Gates (2009, 29), the United States "cannot kill or capture its way to victory" in the war on terrorism but must instead turn to instruments of soft power "aimed at promoting better governance, economic programs that spur development, and efforts to address the grievances among the discontented, from whom the terrorists recruit."

Real and potential military challenges confront U.S. leaders along a **spectrum of armed conflict** in which the chance of each type of conflict occurring is inversely proportionate to its destructiveness (see Figure 10.1). Nuclear war is the most lethal, yet least likely, form of warfare. Conversely, "military operations other than war" are less destructive but more common, as in the case of U.S. humanitarian relief efforts or peacekeeping missions. Conventional wars, such as that fought in Korea, fall in the middle of this spectrum. Military

Figure 10.1 Spectrum of Armed Conflict

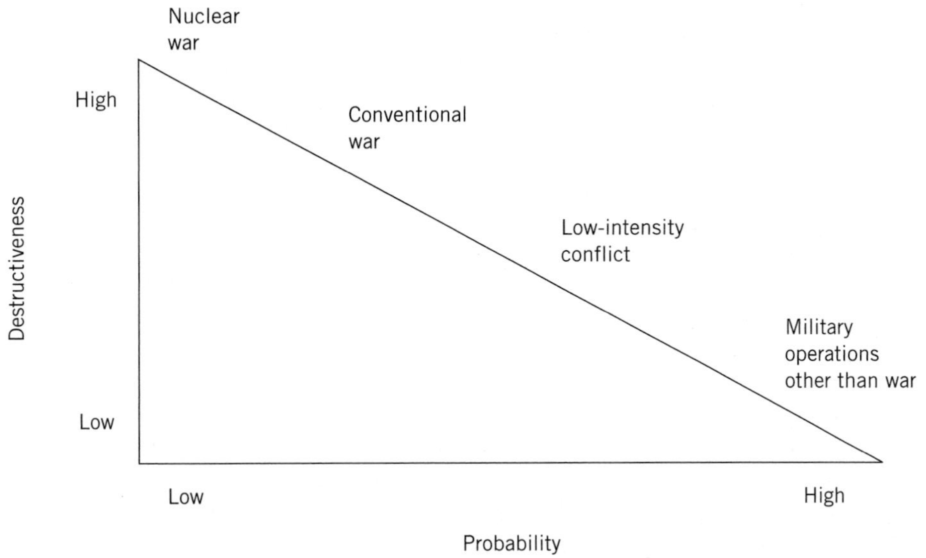

SOURCE: Peter L. Hays, Brenda J. Vallance, and Alan R. Van Tassel, eds., *American Defense Policy,* 7th ed. (Baltimore: Johns Hopkins University Press), 8 (figure 1). © 2005 The Johns Hopkins University Press. Reprinted by permission.

planners and their political masters must carefully gauge these ratios in considering the use of force.

The paradox of America's world power, which is firmly built into its democratic system and civil society, is clearly visible in its efforts to maintain military security. The very openness of the United States is a traditional strength that can also be a source of vulnerability in armed conflicts (see Barnett 2003). Nearly all government records are available to the public, including potential adversaries, and political debates over military strategies and deployments are broadcast to a worldwide audience. For example, the partisan disputes in 2007 over funding for the Iraq war and the possible timetables for U.S. withdrawal were followed closely by insurgents in Iraq and Afghanistan. The same could be said for President George W. Bush's declining public approval ratings in the United States and abroad, which were reported widely in the news media and on the Internet. President Obama's diminished public approval, combined with his preoccupation with domestic issues such as health care, was also portrayed in vivid detail overseas, revealing a power vacuum at the global level and in regional relations that adversaries of the United States were eager to fill.

The fragmented U.S. government, with its notorious turf battles, further hinders strategic coherence, a sense of common purpose, and the successful execution of military operations. Growing Pentagon budgets not only enhance U.S. military power; they also allow the already congested military bureaucracies to expand at a record pace. Such organizational growth enhances the military's stature in the U.S. foreign policy process, but it also heightens the likelihood of disabling bureaucratic rivalries and increases the costs of communication breakdowns and operational failures. "For every heroic and resourceful innovation by troops and commanders on the battlefield," Defense Secretary Gates (2009, 37) observed, "there was some institutional shortcoming at the Pentagon they had to overcome." These problems hampered military operations and prevented defense planners from adapting U.S. military strategy to the new challenges facing the United States (see Betts 2007).

More broadly, the challenges posed by asymmetric warfare require fundamental changes in the way U.S. security managers see the world and learn the lessons of recent experience. Unlike earlier periods in U.S. history, when a clear distinction could be made between wartime and peacetime, the current era finds the United States in a semi-permanent state of war. Adapting to this dramatic shift has proved difficult for the nation's political and military leaders. Prior to the September 11 attacks, "both civilian and military officials were misreading what really constituted threats to American national security interests, oriented as they were to idealized and outdated versions of warfare" (Hoffman 2006, 395). The problems that have since frustrated and at times paralyzed the Pentagon's war on terrorism can be traced ultimately to the oppressive weight of institutional and strategic momentum.

The Foundation of Strategy

Conflicts of interest, real and potential, are central realities of world politics and must be confronted and overcome on a regular basis. In facing such conflicts, political leaders devise a **grand strategy**—that is, a statement of the nation's essential objectives in world politics and the means of achieving those objectives. A clear statement of grand strategy "sets priorities and focuses available resources—money, time, political capital, and military power—on the main effort" (Posen 2001/2002, 42). An effective grand strategy is derived from the articulation of global objectives, as seen through the lens of the state's perceived threats and an assessment of its available resources (see Figure 10.2). Once applied strictly to military affairs, the scope of the grand strategy has broadened over time to include "*all* the resources at the disposal of the nation [and] attempts to array them effectively to achieve security in both peace and war" (Rosecrance and Stein 1993, 4, emphasis in original).

In the absence of a grand strategy, states approach international conflicts without a sense of purpose, and their military tactics bear little relation to the political stakes at hand in the conflict (Liddell Hart 1967). Carl von Clausewitz, who nearly two centuries after his death remains the most influential military strategist in history, believed that nations sever the link between politics and war at their peril. "Under all circumstances War is to be regarded not as an independent thing, but as a political instrument," wrote von Clausewitz ([1832] 1982, 121), a Prussian

Figure 10.2 The Strategic Matrix

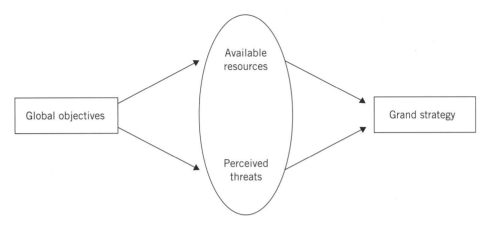

general and veteran of the Napoleonic Wars. "This view shows us how Wars must differ in character according to the nature of the motives and circumstances from which they proceed."

Elements of Strategic Thought

A state derives the elements of its grand strategy from a variety of external and internal sources. Among external sources, the **strategic environment** provides the context in which strategy must be applied. This term incorporates trends in global and regional balances of power and the degree to which a state considers other powerful nations and politically mobilized private groups to be friends or foes. Important developments in world politics, particularly those that challenge the state's vital security assets—its sovereignty, territorial integrity, and political autonomy—are also elements of the strategic environment and, as such, require immediate as well as long-term accommodation. The terrorist attacks of September 2001, for example, altered the strategic environment for the United States and called for a recasting of its foreign policy priorities and diplomatic relations. Of novel significance was the elevation of nonstate actors, in the form of Islamic terrorist groups, as proven threats to U.S. security, and the tactical challenges posed by terrorism as a form of warfare.

Still, U.S. global primacy remains the defining feature of the strategic environment. Even under the strains of the global war on terrorism, the unipolar balance of world power dominated by the United States has endured. Rather than expand their military forces (**internal balancing**) or form rival alliances (**external balancing**), other major powers have generally remained on the U.S. bandwagon—even as their leaders have, on many occasions, openly disputed and opposed U.S. foreign policies (Lieber and Alexander 2005). Even the most brazen actions by the White House have not been seen as threatening to most foreign governments, many of which enjoy considerable material benefits and security protections from their bilateral relations with Washington.

In addition to these external sources of a grand strategy, several internal factors must be taken into account for a fuller understanding of strategic thought. These domestic factors include geopolitical assets, strategic culture, state-society relations, and structural arrangements.

Geopolitical assets. **Geopolitical assets** pertain to a nation's available physical and human resources and their utility in foreign policy. The most basic of these assets—the size, location, and natural resources of the state—establish its possibilities, limitations, and strategic options. The United States' early grand strategy of strategic detachment was possible only because the young nation lay a considerable distance from the great powers of Europe and Asia. Other, more changeable factors include the size, structure, and growth of the country's economy; the perceived legitimacy of the government; the health and morale of the population; and some elements of "soft power" such as national education and cultural influence (see Nye 2004). Technological advances, particularly those in the information and military sectors, are increasingly vital to U.S. security (Paarlberg 2004). **Military alliances,** combined with the worldwide deployment of U.S. troops in regional commands (see Table 10.2), are an additional geopolitical asset of the United States.

Global power balances and statistical measures of capabilities do not fully explain the grand strategies adopted by states or the outcomes of international conflicts. If they did, perhaps the U.S. government would have anticipated and deterred the Japanese attack on Pearl Harbor in 1941 and North Korea's attack on South Korea in 1950. The United States also might not have lost the Vietnam War in the 1970s or been forced out of Somalia by a mob of irregular forces in 1993. A variety of domestic factors involving a nation's capacity to extract and

Table 10.2 Geographical Distribution of Active-Duty U.S. Military Personnel, as of September 30, 2009

Country where based	Number of troops
United States and territories	1,155,749
Iraq	164,100
Afghanistan	66,400
Germany	52,658
Japan	35,965
Italy	9,707
United Kingdom	9,199
Other foreign countries	155,264

SOURCE: U.S. Department of Defense, "Worldwide Manpower Distribution by Geographical Area," Defense Manpower Data Center (September 30, 2009), http://siadapp.dmdc.osd.mil/personnel/MILITARY/history/hst0909.pdf.

mobilize public resources for the attainment of proclaimed goals also enter into the equation. These factors are the strategic culture, state-society relations, and structural arrangements.

Strategic culture. **Strategic culture** refers to widely shared normative beliefs, attitudes, and policy preferences as they pertain to a country's foreign relations (see Snow 2004, ch. 3). As noted in Chapter 1, the United States has exhibited several distinct cultural traits throughout its history. These include a sense of *exceptionalism*, or standing apart from "ordinary" nation-states; a related sense of *moralism*, or a conception of world politics as a struggle between good and evil; and an *ambivalence* toward the nature and extent of U.S. global engagement (see Hook and Spanier 2010). These cultural traits help to explain the nation's erratic approach to foreign affairs—at times ignorant of and indifferent toward events abroad; at other times committed passionately to reforming foreign governments and international order, whatever the costs.[1] States do not passively absorb cultural values and act as neutral channels for their expression. On the contrary, leaders play a powerful independent role in promoting values widely shared within the government and with favored segments of the public (see Wendt 1999). In this respect, militarized states adopt a "culture of national security" that guides their calculations of a grand strategy (see Katzenstein 1996).

State-society relations. A grand strategy stems, too, from **state-society relations,** or the interaction of government and private actors in matters of foreign policy. As described earlier, the United States maintains a vibrant civil society, including private interest groups and a pervasive mass media that exert great influence over the foreign policy process. A prominent example in the 1990s was the Clinton administration's zero-tolerance policy toward combat fatalities after the Somalia mission in 1993, a mission cut short by mounting attacks on U.S. troops. Lukewarm public support for the NATO intervention in Kosovo greatly limited Clinton's military options, strengthening the hand of Serb leader Slobodan Milosevic and provoking a massive exodus of refugees. "Especially in a democracy," Arthur Stein (1993, 122) has noted, "politics can create a disjuncture between commitments and capabilities." [2]

Structural arrangements. A country's **structural arrangements,** or the governing bodies and legal system within which policy making takes place, shape a grand strategy as well. Constitutional provisions constrain the actions of political leaders

---

1. Meanwhile, American foreign policy makers must come to grips with the strategic cultures of their adversaries, which often reflect very different values, priorities, and long-term objectives (see Donnelly 2006).

2. A useful comparison can be made between the United States and most Western European governments, whose citizens expect more generous state services than their U.S. counterparts. This reliance on domestic social welfare spending limits the defense spending of European governments, a fact that causes ongoing tension with the U.S. government and within NATO.

in the United States. Powers shared by the executive and legislative branches extend beyond legal authority to include the appropriation of resources by Congress that may be required by a president's adopted grand strategy. Of consequence, too, are the roles and resources granted to the state's diplomatic corps, defense forces, and intelligence services, all of which must be aligned with the government's foreign policy objectives. The U.S. government's huge financial commitment to military forces relative to diplomacy and foreign assistance act as a structural constraint on the strategic choice of incoming presidents, whose ability to change course is also limited by standard operating procedures, ongoing commitments, and other forms of institutional inertia.

The Evolution of a U.S. Grand Strategy

Debates over U.S. grand strategy occur along two dimensions. The first dimension relates to the *degree* of U.S. involvement in foreign affairs. Should the United States impose its will on other states through an activist foreign policy? Or is the nation sufficiently secure to permit a more restrained posture, allowing most troubles abroad to work themselves out? The second dimension relates to the *nature* of U.S. involvement. Should the United States be concerned primarily with attaining its own national interests? Or does it have a greater responsibility to pursue transnational interests, some with little or no direct effect on the security or prosperity of American citizens?

As noted in Chapter 2, the geopolitical good fortune of the newly founded United States was the basis for its initial grand strategy of **strategic detachment.** Facing no large-scale military threat at home and protected at sea through a tacit naval alliance with Great Britain, the U.S. government did not have to build a large, permanent military force or even establish and deploy a large diplomatic corps. American strategic thought in the late nineteenth century was influenced profoundly by the "closing" of the continental frontier and the end of direct U.S. territorial expansion in the Western Hemisphere. Westward expansion did continue, however, by sea, into the Eastern Hemisphere. The principal figure behind this maritime strategy was Capt. Alfred Mahan (1897), who called for a rapid increase of U.S. naval forces and the creation of a network of U.S. bases in the Pacific Ocean.

Foreign events drove the nation's grand strategy during the world wars. When the European powers descended into mass violence, the United States altered its grand strategy, basing the new approach on the geopolitical premise that Americans would be secure only if no single power dominated Europe. But Germany's launch of its continental conquests in 1914 made the possibility of such domination all too real. The United States entered the war in 1917 and helped to end the threat. Between the world wars, the United States relapsed into strategic detachment, which lasted until Germany overran Europe once again and U.S. forces became the targets of submarine attacks in the Atlantic. The direct impetus for U.S. entry into World War II—the Japanese attack on Pearl Harbor—extended this strategic logic to East Asia, which, like Europe, the United States considered hospitable to its foreign policy only so long as a balance of power existed among the region's major countries.

The arrival of the United States as the world's strongest power after World War II and the onset of the Cold War demanded a new U.S. grand strategy. Though not explicitly, the government adopted a strategy of **sustained primacy,** which called for preserving the nation's military and economic predominance in the interstate system. American officials devised two tactics—global engagement and communist containment—to serve this strategy. First, the U.S. government would solidify its primacy by maintaining military activism, pursuing market-led economic expansion, and fostering the creation of multilateral organizations in which the United States would play a lead role. By doing so, the nation would preserve its advantages in relative power, while reassuring its allies through promises of economic aid, military protection, and the pursuit of shared social and political goals. Second, the United States would use George Kennan's containment doctrine as the tactical blueprint for waging the Cold War. This doctrine would help the nation avoid the pitfalls of renewed strategic detachment, on the one hand, and a potentially cataclysmic "hot war," on the other. The United States effectively used both tactics during the next forty-five years, sustaining its primacy through the support of allies and the eventual dismemberment of the Soviet bloc.

After the collapse of the communist threat brought an end to the Cold War, the U.S. government was determined to maintain the unipolar world that defined the new era. For the Pentagon's Joint Chiefs of Staff (2002, 4), the major challenge facing the United States was "instability and being unprepared to handle a crisis or war that no one predicted or expected." As noted earlier, under President George H. W. Bush the United States adopted a defense strategy whose primary goal was "convincing potential competitors that they need not aspire to a greater role" (*New York Times* 1992, A14). President Bill Clinton upheld this strategy in a modified form, focusing on U.S. "engagement" in multilateral organizations to further cement the nation's pivotal world role.[3]

This same global primacy, however, made the reappraisal of U.S. defense policy difficult. In view of its far superior military power, what should the United States consider an actionable threat? Did the ethnic conflicts, struggles over natural resources, and humanitarian crises in the "failed states" in Eastern Europe and Africa as the millennium approached represent serious threats to the nation? If so, the dangers were less clear-cut than those once posed by the Soviet Union's nuclear missiles and huge armies (see Blacker 1994). The conflicts of the immediate post–Cold War era were mostly fought *within* countries and thus did not directly threaten U.S. sovereignty, territory, or political autonomy. Many officials therefore believed the United States should allow such conflicts to run their course.

---

3. Alternative approaches, from neoisolationism to liberal internationalism and "selective engagement," focused more on the means of preserving U.S. primacy rather than on its merits (Art 2003). See Layne (2006) for a historical perspective of these debates.

The terrorist attacks of September 2001 again altered the strategic environment while leaving intact the U.S. grand strategy of sustained primacy. According to the National Security Council, "Our forces will be strong enough to dissuade potential adversaries from pursuing a military build-up in hopes of surpassing, or equaling, the power of the United States" (White House 2002, 21). The huge budget increases awarded to the Pentagon accelerated the modernization of military technology and the trend toward smaller but more lethal and more mobile force structures. In confronting terrorists and their state sponsors, Secretary of Defense Donald Rumsfeld argued, U.S. forces must be "forward leaning" and not allow their enemies to take the offensive. Rumsfeld's hawkish view was shared by most of the other presidential advisers, including national security adviser Condoleezza Rice and Vice President Dick Cheney. This consensus led directly to Bush's decision to overthrow Saddam Hussein in Iraq even as the United States conducted its war in Afghanistan (see Woodward 2004).

While remaining within the strategic boundaries of sustained primacy, Bush's shift in U.S. military doctrine after September 11 represented the boldest of its kind since the early days of the Cold War (see Gaddis 2005). His "National Security Strategy" assumed that the United States was embattled, not secure, and called on U.S. military forces to take the offensive in the global arena (White House 2002). These and other elements of the Bush Doctrine, discussed in previous chapters, remained in place even as the wars in Afghanistan and Iraq imposed mounting burdens on the nation. A year into Obama's presidency, the Pentagon upheld many aspects of Bush's security strategy while emphasizing broader changes in world politics that posed additional challenges to the United States. Its proposed responses to these challenges can be divided into three categories:

- *Adaptation*—responding to important and rapid changes in the strategic environment (see In Their Own Words box)

- *Integration*—furthering the trend toward joint operations among U.S. military services, while pursuing greater coordination among all foreign policy agencies and with like-minded foreign governments

- *Transformation*—developing a more technologically sophisticated military force that can respond promptly to attacks on the United States or shocks in the international system.

Beyond these general responses to changes in the global security environment, the Department of Defense (2010) emphasized a variety of specific tactics to advance U.S. military interests. These included measures such as enhancing homeland security, improving counter-insurgency operations, modernizing weapons systems, preventing the proliferation of weapons of mass destruction, and operating effectively in "cyberspace." Increased defense budgets, supported by Obama and approved by Congress, were designed to ensure a close connection between strategy and tactics, a subject addressed in the following section.

IN THEIR OWN WORDS: THE 2010 "QUADRENNIAL DEFENSE REVIEW"

Changes in the strategic environment play an important role in the formulation of any country's grand strategy. In 2010, the U.S. Department of Defense outlined a series of changes in the global strategic environment that required creative responses by the U.S. armed services. These changes, summarized below, called for continued U.S. predominance in all areas of potential military conflict while also acknowledging the growing need for the United States to cooperate with other governments in order to maintain the nation's security.

The United States faces a complex and uncertain security landscape in which the pace of change continues to accelerate. The distribution of global political, economic, and military power is becoming more diffuse. The rise of China, the world's most populous country, and India, the world's largest democracy, will continue to shape an international system that is no longer easily defined—one in which the United States will remain the most powerful actor but must increasingly work with key allies and partners if it is to sustain stability and peace.

Globalization has transformed the process of technological innovation while lowering entry barriers for a wider range of actors to acquire advanced technologies. As technological innovation and global information flows accelerate, non-state actors will continue to gain influence and capabilities that, during the past century, remained largely the purview of states.

The proliferation of weapons of mass destruction (WMD) continues to undermine global security, further complicating efforts to sustain peace and prevent harmful arms races. The instability or collapse of a WMD-armed state is among our most troubling concerns. Such an occurrence could lead to rapid proliferation of WMD material, weapons, and technology, and could quickly become a global crisis posing a direct physical threat to the United States and all other nations.

Other powerful trends are likely to add complexity to the security environment. Rising demand for resources, rapid urbanization of littoral regions, the effects of climate change, the emergence of new strains of disease, and profound cultural and demographic tensions in several regions are just some of the trends whose complex interplay may spark or exacerbate future conflicts.

SOURCE: U.S. Department of Defense, "Quadrennial Defense Review Report," February 10, 2010, pp. iii–iv, www.defense.gov/qdr/.

From Strategy to Tactics

The fate of nations is often decided on the battlefield. A grand strategy, therefore, is effective only if it provides direction to a military strategy. The organization of the armed services, in terms of size as well as tactical capabilities, must be compatible with the nation's strategic goals. This force structure, in turn, must deter external challenges to these goals or, if deterrence fails, overcome those challenges with superior military force. "To neglect strategy in defense planning or the conduct of war would be like trying to play chess without kings on the board; there would be no point" (Gray 1999, 44). Similarly, a military strategy must lead deductively to effective **tactics,** or the translation of political ends into military means. In short, strategists *plan* and tacticians *do*. A functional relationship therefore exists among all these elements of security policy. Only when the grand strategy, military strategy, force structure, and tactics are aligned can the United States or any other country pursue a sound defense policy.

How do these functional relationships apply to the ways in which the United States wages war? Modern warfare is fought on the ground, at sea, or in the air. The relative significance of each method varies over time, largely in response to technological developments. The U.S. military strategy during its first century was based on amassing adequate ground forces to defend the nation's territory and consolidate new acquisitions. Naval power, traditionally associated with the projection of power, became vital to the United States late in the nineteenth century. Air power emerged as a critical instrument of power projection during the world wars. Continued advances in aerial technology, particularly related to the accuracy and potency of strategic bombing, reinforce the predominance of air power, which is also favored politically when it reduces the need for large-scale ground troops. This preference for strategic bombing is especially obvious when the public does not regard the conflict as vital to U.S. national security.

Recent U.S. wartime experiences illustrate both the strengths and the weaknesses of air power in military strategy. More broadly, these experiences reveal the problems that arise when military strategy and political objectives clash. For example, the 1991 Persian Gulf War against Iraq featured an overwhelming demonstration of U.S. air power. Five weeks of intense bombing first decimated Iraq's military and industrial assets, and then pummeled the elite Republic Guard divisions in Kuwait. The subsequent ground offensive by the UN-sponsored coalition met little resistance as it gained control of Kuwait City four days after the offensive was launched. However, this overwhelming military victory did not establish a stable political order in the Persian Gulf; because a forced removal from power exceeded the UN mandate, Saddam Hussein remained as Iraq's leader. Later, his defiance of the United Nations produced a political breakdown within the UN coalition that overshadowed the military success of Operation Desert Storm.

The Balkan wars in Bosnia-Herzegovina (1995) and Kosovo (1999) further revealed the limitations of air power. In the first instance, the NATO air strikes designed to stop the Serbian government's "ethnic cleansing" of Muslims proved effective only after they were accompanied by a ground offensive by the rebels. In Kosovo, NATO responded to the breakdown of negotiations in March 1999 "with a bombing campaign that would last eleven weeks, involve 38,000 aircraft sorties (including almost 10,500 strike missions), and expend approximately 12,000 tons of munitions" (Lake 2009, 89). The high-altitude NATO bombing raids often missed their targets. Hundreds of Kosovar civilians died from errant bombs; other civilians, including Chinese, died when the United States mistakenly targeted the Chinese embassy in Belgrade. Only the prospect of NATO ground deployments, combined with diplomatic pressure from his patrons in Russia, persuaded Slobodan Milosevic to surrender. Although both missions in the former Yugoslavia ultimately ended the bloodshed, the victors were hardly in a mood to celebrate.

This pattern repeated itself in the war on terrorism. The swift U.S. overthrow of Afghanistan's Taliban regime was made possible by a new generation of munitions, including laser-guided "smart bombs" and "bunker busters." Such lethal firepower, however, failed to bring down al Qaeda leader Osama bin Laden, who eluded the U.S.-backed forces in the treacherous terrain along the 1,500-mile Afghan-Pakistani border (see Moore 2003). The military victory also proved of limited political value as the United States and its NATO allies still struggled to establish a new Afghan government and maintain control of the provinces long after their initial victory (see Katzman 2003). Similarly, the "shock and awe" blitzkrieg of Operation Iraqi Freedom in 2003 achieved its immediate objective, the overthrow of Saddam's government, but the low-tech mission of occupying a hostile population in the heart of Islam quickly overshadowed the initial success.

The September 2001 terrorist attacks also produced a major shift in the use of "unmanned aerial vehicles," or drones, whose missions escalated from surveillance to bombing missions in Afghanistan and Iraq. Sleek and slow-moving Predator and Reaper drones, equipped with remote-controlled video cameras, take off from hidden airfields and are then guided by civilian "pilots" in the United States to their high-value targets, usually top al Qaeda agents and insurgents. Since 2006, these attacks have killed an estimated 600 people, including their intended targets as well as civilians nearby. This new age of "push-button" warfare represents a "radically new and geographically unbounded use of state-sanctioned lethal force" (Mayer 2009).

The U.S. government operates two drone programs. The first, run by the Defense Department and publicly acknowledged, involves aerial strikes in Afghanistan and Iraq. The second, and covert, program is managed by the CIA and carries out attacks in other countries. The full range of these operations is unknown, but the repeated drone attacks on al Qaeda and Taliban leaders in Pakistan have yielded many successful "hits" along with high anxiety among civilians who have become accustomed to the drones hovering over their neighborhoods. "The drone war against Al Qaeda's leaders—and, increasingly, their Pakistani-based Taliban allies—has been waged with little public discussion or congressional investigation of its legality or efficacy, even though the offensive is essentially a program of assassination that kills not only militant leaders, but also civilians in a country that is a close ally of the United States" (Bergen and Tiedemann 2009).

The use of drones, described by CIA director Leon Panetta as "the only game in town," raises several broader questions regarding U.S. foreign policy. First, many legal experts believe the attacks, embraced by President Obama when he took office in 2009, violate President Gerald Ford's 1976 executive order that banned political assassinations. Second, the covert drone campaign is part of a security agreement with the government of Pakistan whose terms were not fully revealed to the American people. Third, the operations also involve a wide range

Unmanned aerial drones (inset) have become commonly used by the U.S. government in bombing suspected al Qaeda targets in Pakistan, including this location in North Waziristan, where two "high-value" terrorists were reportedly killed by a Hellfire missile attack in March 2009.

of private military contractors, including Blackwater Worldwide (now known as Xe Services LLC), which has been linked to clandestine attacks and "snatch and grab" operations in Iraq "on an almost nightly basis" from 2004 to 2006 (Risen and Mazzetti 2009, A1). The high ratio of civilian deaths to the intended targets of drone bombings raises additional questions about the practice, which has sparked protests by many Pakistanis and turned them against Washington. More broadly, the "virtual killing" inflicted by drones reveals the extent to which the United States is "wired for war" (Singer 2009) and disconnected from the human consequences of robotic destruction. To date, however, little concern has been raised in Congress or by the American public, due in part to the success of these operations in eliminating well-known enemies and in part to the general secrecy in which these attacks take place.

Justifying the Use of Force

The most crucial decision facing the leader of any country is whether to send military forces into combat (see Art and Waltz 2004). The outcome of armed conflicts is never certain, and unintended consequences—sneak attacks by the enemy, economic sabotage, third-party interventions, domestic uprisings, the introduction of weapons of mass destruction—overtake rational military strategy and tactics, shrouding them in the "fog of war" (see Betts 2002). In contrast to this ambiguity, leaders on the brink of war face the near certainty of casualties, widespread physical destruction, and economic liabilities. The choices they make at critical junctures "between peace and war" determine the fate of their nations for decades to come (Lebow 1981). The acceptable rationales for using force have changed dramatically over time, making these decisions even more difficult (see Weisburd 1997; Finnemore 2003; and Gray 2004).

The nature of U.S. military interventions varies widely. At times, such as in World War II, the United States fights **wars of necessity,** or conflicts arising from direct and unambiguous challenges to the nation's security. More commonly, such as in Panama in 1989 and Kosovo in 1999, U.S. forces fight **wars of choice,** or conflicts over nonvital interests.[4] Most frequently, U.S. power and influence are employed through **peaceful coercion**—that is, without the use of widespread violence—to compel foreign leaders to reverse acts of aggression, respect the human rights of their citizens, or protect U.S. citizens and assets from harm. Yet the nation's superior military strength never lies far from the surface in negotiations with its adversaries, even on nonmilitary issues.

Questions about the use of military force have become especially important today because of the overwhelming military predominance of the United States. Despite its clout, however, the nation remains ambivalent and divided about the use of force. These divisions, as well as the physical, political, and moral limitations of U.S. military policy, were exposed during the Vietnam War. The divisions deepened after the Cold War as national politics, particularly in Congress, became more polarized, and as the United States waded ever more deeply into the war on terrorism. The controversies surrounding the U.S.-led invasion of Iraq in 2003 raised troubling new questions about the use of military force when other options have not been exhausted, evidence of a clear and present danger is mixed, and an international consensus supporting war is lacking.

Considerations of War over Peace

The greatly expanded institutions of U.S. power after World War II—including the newly created Department of Defense, National Security Council, and CIA—ensured the presence of U.S. global military might for decades to come. Less clear, however, was under what circumstances that power should be used to

---

4. In many instances, including the 2003 Iraq war, supporters and opponents of U.S. interventions have disagreed about whether a conflict was a matter of need or of choice.

protect the nation's worldwide interests. The containment doctrine set forth a singular rationale for U.S. intervention—attempted expansion of the communist sphere of influence—that most Americans found acceptable, although some considered it too passive (see Lippmann 1947). In the 1950s, domestic debates about the use of force were shaped by Eisenhower's doctrine of **massive retaliation,** whose threat of nuclear annihilation understandably encouraged caution among would-be adversaries as well as among U.S. foreign policy makers.

The Soviet Union's achievement of nuclear parity in the 1960s, combined with the frustrations associated with the Vietnam War, ruptured any prospects for national consensus in the late 1960s and 1970s. Successive U.S. presidents tried, but failed, to outline a coherent rationale for the U.S. intervention in Vietnam, and the military strategies they devised ultimately made for a slow and debilitating defeat. Public protests, many of which turned violent, further ensured a lengthy period of introspection on the future course of U.S. defense policy.

Recognizing the persistent uncertainty about the use of force, Caspar Weinberger, Ronald Reagan's secretary of defense, outlined the conditions for military intervention. The **Weinberger Doctrine** called for the avoidance of "hot" wars while the United States was preoccupied with the Soviet Union and the Cold War, and it demanded that interventions be planned thoroughly, with all contingencies covered, before any offensive action is initiated. The doctrine enjoyed widespread support in the executive branch.

The end of the Cold War profoundly altered the calculations of defense policy makers about the use of force. Whereas the collapse of the Soviet Union clearly enhanced U.S. security, the shifting sands of global, regional, and subregional power balances created new fears and uncertainties not easily shunted aside. As chairman of the Joint Chiefs of Staff in the George H. W. Bush and Clinton administrations, Colin Powell (1992/1993) expressed doubts that a "fixed set of rules" could provide a definitive guide to military intervention. Nevertheless, Powell identified six questions for U.S. leaders to consider in making their decisions: "Is the political objective we seek to achieve important, clearly defined and understood? Have all other nonviolent policy means failed? Will military force achieve the objective? At what cost? Have the gains and risks been analyzed? How might the situation that we seek to alter, once it is altered by force, develop further and what might be the consequences?"

Powell (1992) insisted that once the United States committed to using force in a military conflict it must prevail *decisively*. As an architect of the 1991 Persian Gulf War, he argued that sufficient U.S. forces be deployed to the region to ensure the quick defeat of the Iraqi military. He further insisted that an **exit strategy,** a plan to conclude fighting and remove the U.S. presence, be adopted prior to the intervention so that U.S. troops would not be mired in a long-term, open-ended foreign occupation. These stipulations of the **Powell Doctrine,** like those identified by Weinberger, reflected the lessons of Vietnam, a war in which U.S. troops were deployed incrementally over many years, during which they found themselves supporting a vague political objective, lacking popular support, and unable to score a quick victory and complete their mission. Powell and Weinberger also shared an aversion to **mission creep,** the tendency of limited deployments to take on new tasks and open-ended commitments.

President George W. Bush came to power in 2001 favoring these more restrictive conditions for using military force. His only modification to the doctrine—that military interventions first and foremost serve U.S. national interests—signaled a turn away from the humanitarian and UN-sponsored peacekeeping missions of the Clinton years. After the September 2001 attacks, Bush committed U.S. troops to the open-ended war on terrorism. His invasion of Iraq, however, violated key elements of the Weinberger and Powell Doctrines. The ground forces, less than half the size of those used to eject Saddam from Kuwait, proved unable to prevent the rise of an insurgency and the onset of civil war. As the prospects of a stable political settlement eroded, no appealing exit strategy could be found. Most important, the absence of weapons of mass destruction in Iraq and of confirmed links between Saddam and the September 11 terrorists revealed that the use of force was not the last resort it was portrayed to be by the White House.

Threats and Coercive Diplomacy

Short of resorting to military force, U.S. officials often pursue their foreign policy goals through **coercive diplomacy**—the threat to use force to reverse an adversary's offensive action. "The attractiveness of coercive diplomacy as a tool of foreign policy is quite clear," political scientist Alexander George (2000, 80) observed. "It offers the possibility of achieving one's objective economically, with little bloodshed, fewer political and psychological costs, and often with much less risk of escalation than does resort to military action to reverse an adversary's encroachment." The Cuban missile crisis, which ended peacefully in 1962 largely on U.S. terms, is viewed widely as a textbook example of effective coercive diplomacy. The Kennedy administration skillfully combined five elements of this tactic to prevent the crisis from leading to a nuclear holocaust (George 2000, 84–85):

- *Clear demands.* The U.S. government issued clear demands with specific deadlines and penalties if the Soviet Union refused to remove its newly installed nuclear missiles from Cuba.

- *Severe penalty.* The penalty identified by President Kennedy—that the missiles would be removed forcefully and the Cuban government overthrown by U.S. forces—would obviously have "hurt" the Soviet Union and its leader, Nikita Khrushchev.

- *Credible demands.* The U.S. demands were credible. The presence of the nuclear warheads in Cuba clearly threatened U.S. security, and Kennedy had the political support and military capability to make good on his threat.

- ■ *Coherent plan.* The United States had a well-laid plan of action to remove the missiles if Kennedy's threats were ignored, a fact made known to the Soviet leader.

- ■ *Flexible application.* Kennedy offered Khrushchev a "carrot" as well as the "stick" of military retaliation. By offering to remove U.S. nuclear missiles from Turkey, an action already decided privately by the U.S. government, Kennedy provided the Soviet leader with a face-saving exit from the crisis.

Not all adversaries respond so well to coercive diplomacy. In fact, the United States has failed to resolve conflicts through coercive diplomacy more often than it has succeeded. Foreign leaders, even those of very weak states, commonly resist such threats, vowing instead to withstand U.S. pressure and hoping to "call the bluff" of their American counterparts. In doing so, adversaries present a threat of their own—a blow to the credibility of the United States should its threats be defied successfully. "There is a generation of political leaders throughout the world whose basic perception of U.S. military power and political will is one of weakness, who enter any situation with a fundamental belief that the United States can be defeated or driven away" (Blechman and Wittes 1999, 5).

Since the Vietnam War, foreign leaders have consistently defied the tactics of coercive diplomacy, forcing the United States to take costly military action against them. In 1989, for example, Manuel Noriega of Panama ignored U.S. demands to step down as president; ousting him required a large-scale invasion of the country (see Buckley 1991). Four years later, U.S. threats against Somalian warlords merely sparked more violent attacks on U.S. forces. The deaths of eighteen U.S. soldiers in Mogadishu, which sharpened U.S. domestic opposition to the mission, prompted President Clinton to withdraw from Somalia, thereby suffering a humiliating defeat.[5]

This pattern of U.S. threats, foreign resistance, and subsequent U.S. military interventions continued in Haiti (1994) and in the former Yugoslavia (1993–1995, 1999). In Haiti, rebels exploited the "Somalia syndrome," calculating—wrongly—that Clinton would not risk a second military humiliation. In the Yugoslav conflicts, Milosevic gambled that domestic opposition in the United States and Europe would undermine Clinton's effort to stop the "ethnic cleansing" of Muslims. In the end, Milosevic was defeated, but only after his country suffered large-scale bloodletting, physical devastation, and the displacement of millions of civilians.

Coercive diplomacy also failed to prevent the two U.S.-led wars against Saddam Hussein's Iraq in 1991 and 2003. In both conflicts, Saddam refused to meet the full range of U.S. demands and then suffered overwhelming military defeats, and ultimately his overthrow from power. Although speculation persists

---

5. "We have studied Vietnam and Lebanon and know how to get rid of Americans, by killing them so that public opinion will put an end to things," remarked Somali warlord Mohamed Farah Aideed, the primary target of Operation Restore Hope (quoted in Blechman and Wittes 1999, 6).

about his rationales for inviting such calamities, Saddam's fateful strategic choices demonstrated the limitations of coercive diplomacy and the inevitability of military conflict when threats are not sufficient to resolve fundamental differences.

Preventive War: The Iraq Precedent

Countries engage in interstate wars for many reasons. In offensive wars, they disrupt the status quo to gain resources, tangible or intangible, unavailable through peaceful or legal means. In defensive wars, states act in the face of external aggression. In outright attacks, they face the grim choice of responding with armed resistance to the attack or submitting to the demands of the attackers.

Not all defensive wars, however, are responses to outright, clear-cut attacks (see Walzer 1977, 74–85). Foreign intelligence may signal that an external attack is imminent, perhaps only days away, tempting leaders to strike first against the would-be invader. This recourse to **preemptive war,** rare in modern history, formed a key element of the Bush administration's "National Security Strategy" released in September 2002.[6] More commonly, an emerging challenger may be perceived by a more powerful rival as presenting a long-term threat to the security of that nation or the security of its allies, tempting the stronger state to launch a **preventive war** to eliminate the threat before it materializes (see Levy 1987). Although not using the term explicitly, the Bush administration launched a preventive war against Iraq, hoping to stem the nation's development of weapons of mass destruction, particularly nuclear weapons. In doing so, the White House opened a new and tumultuous era in U.S. foreign policy (see Glad and Dolan 2004).

Prior to the Iraqi invasion, the United States, like most other governments, had long renounced preventive war as a strategic option. "We do not believe in aggressive or preventive war," President Harry Truman proclaimed. "Such war is the weapon of dictators, not of free democratic societies" (quoted in Jordan, Taylor, and Mazarr 1999, 57). This restraint did not last long in the war on terrorism. In justifying the invasion of Iraq, President Bush characterized Saddam Hussein's regime as both an immediate and a long-term threat to Iraq's neighbors and the United States. Saddam's secret arsenal of biochemical weapons, Bush claimed, could be unleashed at any time. The invasion thus could be justified either as preemptive or preventive (Gaddis 2005). In both cases, national security adviser Condoleezza Rice argued, the United States could not afford to wait until a "mushroom cloud" awakened the United States to Saddam's menace.

Critics countered that U.S. officials produced no irrefutable evidence of Iraqi weapons of mass destruction, nor did they demonstrate strong links between Iraq and al Qaeda terrorists. Further, Iraq was exhausted by a decade of sanctions and exhibited neither a capability nor an intention to threaten the United States, a

---

6. According to political scientist Dan Reiter (1995), only three armed conflicts of the modern era qualify as preemptive wars: the start of World War I, China's 1950 intervention in the Korean War, and Israel's attack on Egypt in 1967.

point made earlier by Colin Powell. Finally, these opponents argued, U.S. officials did not exhaust all other options before deciding to overthrow Saddam. This debate between defenders and critics of the U.S. invasion will continue indefinitely and, like that about the Vietnam War, will probably never be settled conclusively. It is clear, however, that the United States established a dangerous precedent by initiating war against a sovereign state in the absence of compelling evidence of a clear and present danger.[7]

The Nuclear Shadow

A central task of U.S. security policy is to manage the nation's nuclear arsenal, by far the largest in the world. Nuclear weapons, which are *strategic* forces, play a vital role in military strategy that fundamentally departs from the role played by nonnuclear, or *conventional,* forces. Since their first and only wartime use—by the United States against Japan in August 1945—nuclear weapons have remained unused but "absolute weapons," capable of obliterating foreign enemies—and possibly the entire global population—in one swift blow (Brodie 1946). The Soviet Union's successful test of a nuclear bomb in 1949 transformed the Cold War balance of power into a "delicate balance of terror" (Wohlstetter 1959).

Despite the peaceful ending of the U.S.-Soviet arms race, the perils posed by nuclear weapons are more acute than ever. As of 2010, nine governments had the materials and means to deliver nuclear weapons (see Table 10.3 and Map 9, Nuclear Threats and U.S. Defense Installations, in map section). These countries include India and Pakistan, bitter rivals in South Asia, and North Korea, an impoverished dictatorship with an affinity for ballistic missile exports and nuclear blackmail. Israel also maintains a nuclear arsenal, although its government refuses to confirm this worst-kept secret in world politics.[8] Meanwhile, Iran's government has proclaimed its "nuclear rights," and private terrorist groups covet fissionable materials and ballistic missiles on transnational black markets (see Stern 1999). As two security experts (Daalder and Lodal 2008, 81) have concluded, the world has entered "an age of more nuclear weapons states, more nuclear materials, and more nuclear facilities that are poorly secured—making the job of the terrorists seeking the bomb easier and the odds that a nuclear weapon will be used greater."

The enduring menace posed by nuclear weapons, a standard feature of twenty-first-century world politics, was not inevitable. Just after World War II, the United States proposed placing all the world's nuclear materials, including its own, under the control of a UN-sponsored international authority. The Soviet

---

7. The U.S. government's subsequent problems in Iraq, however, may also discourage future preventive attacks (Dunn 2006a).

8. The deteriorating condition and questionable security of Russia's nuclear arsenal prompted a major U.S. assistance program in the 1990s, the Cooperative Threat-Reduction Program (see Krepon 2003).

Table 10.3 Nuclear Balance of Power, 2010 Estimates

Country	Total nuclear warheads
Russia	12,000
United States	9,400
France	300
China	240
United Kingdom	185
Israel	80
Pakistan	70–90
India	60–80
North Korea	<10
Total	23,300

SOURCE: Hans M. Kristensen, "Status of World Nuclear Forces, 2010," Federation of American Scientists, www
.fas.org/programs/ssp/nukes/nuclearweapons/nukestatus.html. Used courtesy of the Federation of American Scientists.

Union opposed this **Baruch Plan,** named after U.S. financier and presidential adviser Bernard Baruch, because it allowed the U.S. government to maintain its monopoly of nuclear weapons technology. Soviet leaders, who were three years away from testing their own nuclear weapon, also distrusted the United Nations and U.S. allies in the Security Council. By the 1970s, Soviet nuclear as well as conventional forces had reached parity with those maintained by the United States. The U.S. nuclear arsenal, though, was more accurate and better protected within its "triad" of delivery systems—underground silos, strategic bombers, and nuclear submarines.

Efforts to restrain this arms race quickly became a foreign policy priority. Beginning in the early 1970s, the SALT and START treaties placed limits on U.S. and Soviet stockpiles and delivery systems, and then provided for deep cuts after the Cold War. The Treaty of Moscow signed by the United States and Russia in 2002 called for ten-year reductions in active nuclear stockpiles to between 1,700 and 2,200 warheads on each side.[9] As for multilateral accords, the United States signed the Treaty on the Non-proliferation of Nuclear Weapons that came into force in 1970 and that by 2010 had gained the signatures of 189 governments. Earlier, the U.S. government had signed the 1963 Limited Test Ban Treaty, which prohibited nuclear tests in the atmosphere, under water, and in outer space. However, Congress's rejection in 1998 of the Comprehensive Test Ban Treaty, which called for a ban on *all* nuclear testing, signaled a U.S. turn away from multilateral cooperation in nuclear arms control.

---

9. The treaty allowed both sides to store thousands of inactive warheads, which could be reactivated quickly in a crisis.

This policy deepened under George W. Bush, who also widened the possible uses of nuclear weapons by abolishing the long-held "firewall" between these and conventional weapons. Under the revised plan, "low-yield" nuclear warheads would be used to destroy underground military facilities in such countries as Iran, which was busily constructing such sites during the Bush years. Meanwhile, calls for nuclear abolition grew louder and came from unlikely sources. Henry Kissinger, an architect of U.S. nuclear strategy long before his appointment as Richard Nixon's national security adviser in 1969, joined other former leaders in advocating disarmament.[10]

Upon taking office in 2009, President Obama vowed to reverse this trend and called for the destruction of all nuclear stockpiles—including that of the United States. Obama reached an agreement with Russia in March 2010 to reduce the number of deployed nuclear warheads on both sides to 1,550. Although this represented a step forward in the president's plan for arms control, the revised START treaty required confirmation by the Senate, an uncertain outcome in the midst of bitter partisan conflicts over health care and other domestic issues (see Chapter 12). Obama's "Nuclear Posture Review," released in April, maintained the central role of these weapons in protecting U.S. national security.

Deterrence in Theory and Practice

Since the 1945 bombings of Hiroshima and Nagasaki, nuclear weapons have had a unique functional distinction among military weapons—they are not meant to be used. Such use would not only invite nuclear retaliation from the target government or its nuclear-equipped allies, but also threaten the habitat of the entire world population (see Sagan 1983/1984). The primary goal of nuclear strategy, therefore, is to gain concessions from an adversary through the threatened use of nuclear weapons. Maintaining **nuclear deterrence,** the prevention of hostilities through the threat of using nuclear weapons, is vital to securing a nuclear power's interests while preventing an apocalypse (see Snyder 1961). Both Cold War superpowers refined the concept of nuclear deterrence by building massive nuclear arsenals and ensuring that the victim of a first strike would survive to hit back—that is, had "second-strike capabilities." The United States and Soviet Union also engaged in **extended deterrence** by vowing nuclear retaliation against attacks not only on their territory but also on the territory of their allies. "The threat of retaliation does not have to be 100 percent certain," nuclear strategist Bernard Brodie (1946, 74) wrote at the dawn of the nuclear age. "It is sufficient if there is a good chance of it, or if there is belief that there is a good chance of it. The prediction is more important than the fact."

American leaders believed a promise of massive retaliation was sufficient to deter challenges to the United States as long as it maintained nuclear superiority.

---

10. See George P. Shultz, William J. Perry, Henry A. Kissinger, and Sam Nunn, "Toward a Nuclear-Free World," *Wall Street Journal,* January 15, 2008, A15. Their embrace of the "zero option" was later endorsed by most former secretaries of defense, secretaries of state, and national security advisers.

When the Soviet nuclear arsenal "caught up" with the United States, however, a new era of **mutual assured destruction (MAD)** opened: both superpowers had to be effectively "self-deterred." In the MAD world, foreign policy makers, in the face of the compelling prospect of nuclear Armageddon, became even more cautious and strove to reduce the danger of a head-on collision between the two countries. Some U.S. officials complained, however, that their military options had become unduly constrained by this all-or-nothing strategic stalemate. President Kennedy approved a strategy of **flexible response,** intended to resolve this problem by condoning U.S. involvement in "limited wars," such as that in Vietnam, which could be fought below the nuclear threshold.[11]

The strategy of flexible response survived into the post–Cold War era as U.S. military forces intervened repeatedly in regional conflicts without threatening to use nuclear weapons or risking nuclear attack by the nation's adversaries (Daalder 1991). Meanwhile, relations within the "nuclear club" warmed to such an extent after the Cold War that nuclear war and deterrence seemed irrelevant. Still, the long-term intentions of China and Russia were unclear, as were the prospects for the Indo-Pakistani nuclear standoff, Israel's unclaimed nuclear arsenal, and proliferation threats from Iran. In East Asia, North Korea's underground tests in October 2006 heralded the arrival of the nuclear club's eighth official member. The same actions tempted Japanese leaders to follow suit and come out from under the U.S. nuclear umbrella.

These developments will severely test the stabilizing effects of nuclear deterrence in the twenty-first century. Unfortunately, the longevity of the "nuclear peace" will be threatened further by changes in the strategic environment. The war on terrorism raises the open question about the extent to which some adversaries, particularly religious extremists without allegiances to any country, can be deterred. For suicide bombers in the "age of sacred terror," self-destruction through mass political violence is an act of divine will, a principle that seems readily applicable to the use of nuclear and other unconventional weapons (Benjamin and Simon 2002).

The Missile Defense Controversy

U.S. advances in strategic missile defense make the balance of terror more uncertain. Among other paradoxes of nuclear strategy, for deterrence to succeed states must be defenseless against nuclear attacks. "Shielded" nations would be free to inflict overwhelming harm on their enemies without fear of retaliation. Recognizing this paradox, the United States and Soviet Union signed the **Anti-Ballistic Missile (ABM) Treaty** in 1972, which kept both superpowers vulnerable to nuclear attack beyond the end of the Cold War. In the United States, critics of the ABM Treaty longed for the day they would no longer be held hostage to

---

11. For prominent studies of nuclear strategy during this critical period, see Henry Kissinger (1957), Robert Osgood (1957), Thomas Schelling (1960), and Morton Halperin (1963). Lawrence Freedman (2003) provides a useful review of Cold War nuclear strategies.

threats of nuclear annihilation. Among these critics was President Ronald Reagan, whose 1983 **Strategic Defense Initiative (SDI),** better known as "Star Wars," called for space-based interceptors that would destroy long-range nuclear missiles in midflight. Congress approved $26 billion for the development of SDI, which Reagan promised to share with other nuclear powers once the system became operational.

Reagan's Star Wars program marked the beginning of the end of the ABM Treaty. Research on missile defense continued under President Clinton, then accelerated under George W. Bush. The United States officially withdrew from the ABM Treaty in 2002, the first U.S. renunciation of an arms control treaty in the nuclear era. With the consent of Congress and appropriations that reached $10 billion in fiscal year 2005, the White House created the Missile Defense Agency within the Department of Defense to develop and deploy a ballistic missile defense system that would be "layered" to intercept missiles in all phases of their flight, from liftoff through reentry into the lower atmosphere (Hildreth 2005).

President Bush based his decision to suspend the ABM Treaty on three key assumptions. First, even in the absence of nuclear tensions with Russia and China, the risk of an accidental launch of those nations' intercontinental ballistic missiles (ICBMs) could not be ignored. Second, as mentioned earlier, "rogue states" and their allied terrorist groups could not be reliably deterred from launching surprise attacks on the United States. Religious extremists viewed suicide, even mass suicide, as a form of spiritual or national salvation and thus lacked the capacity for the rational decision making that nuclear deterrence presumes. Finally, U.S. missile defense research had advanced sufficiently to warrant reliance on such a system.

Opponents of missile defense, including many legislators, strategic analysts in think tanks and universities, and peace groups, challenged the president's arguments for missile defense with three arguments of their own. The first argument challenges the presumed reliability of missile defense, a presumption that leaves no margin for error. Experimental tests, critics point out, have thus far produced, at best, mixed results. The General Accounting Office, for example, reported evidence of "immature technology" and faulty testing of missile defense systems. A rush to deploy these systems, the GAO warned in 2003, "places the Missile Defense Agency in danger of getting off track early and impairing the effort over the long term" (GAO 2003). Subsequent tests of missile interceptors failed to destroy their targets; in two such tests, the interceptors never got off the ground (Coyle 2006).

Second, critics warn that even a perfect ABM system would leave the United States vulnerable to nuclear attacks not delivered by missile. "Suitcase bombs" made in the United States or smuggled into its territory could prove just as deadly. Finally, it is not clear how other governments will react if the United States comes close to having both a massive nuclear arsenal and the certainty of nuclear defense. Such a combination in the hands of any other government would surely be viewed in Washington as an invitation to nuclear blackmail. Would other leaders feel the

Point/Counterpoint
NUCLEAR DETERRENCE VS. JUST WAR

One of the central dilemmas facing U.S. military strategists is the use of nuclear weapons in defending vital national interests. Because of their immense lethality, nuclear weapons are not designed to be *used*; rather, they are intended to *deter* attacks on their owners by assuring the destruction of enemies.

Yet the mere prospect of employing nuclear weapons raises serious moral questions that continue to confront military strategists today. Such use would violate two key elements of the just-war doctrine. The first element, *proportionality,* calls for the harm inflicted by a military retaliation to be proportionate, or roughly equal, to the damage inflicted by the initial attack. The first use of nuclear weapons would, by its very nature, be disproportionate to any attack using conventional weapons.

The second key element of the just-war doctrine, *discrimination,* calls for military attacks to spare the lives of noncombatants to the fullest extent possible. Nuclear weapons, however, inevitably target civilians and military personnel alike, particularly because the ecological damage caused by such weapons would remain for decades, if not centuries, to come.

During the Cold War, these considerations did not discourage U.S. strategists from giving nuclear weapons a central place in the nation's military arsenal. Henry Kissinger, whose 1957 book *Nuclear Weapons and Foreign Policy* caught the attention of then–vice president Richard Nixon, believed nuclear weapons gave the states that possessed them great advantages. The more likely it appeared to the enemies of nuclear states that these weapons would be used, Kissinger argued, the less likely it was that these states would resort to aggressive behavior. The moral "end" of nuclear deterrence, in this view, justified the immoral "means" of threatening mass annihilation.

Such views prompted a challenge as nuclear tensions heightened in the early 1980s. The National Conference of Catholic Bishops published a pastoral letter in 1983 that rejected notions of a protracted nuclear stalemate. The following year, Jonathan Schell declared in *The Abolition* that nuclear weapons were an "evil obsession" that must be eliminated if any hopes of world peace could be sustained.

Although the prospect of large-scale nuclear war appears remote today, the United States and other nuclear powers continue to rely on the logic of nuclear deterrence in protecting themselves and their allies. A new concern—that nuclear terrorists will not follow the same "rational" logic of deterrence—adds to the uncertainty about these ultimate weapons of mass destruction.

SOURCES: Henry Kissinger, *Nuclear Weapons and Foreign Policy* (New York: Harper and Row, 1957); National Conference of Catholic Bishops, *Challenge and Peace: God's Promise and Our Response* (Washington, D.C.: United States Catholic Conference, 1983); Jonathan Schell, *The Abolition* (New York: Knopf, 1984).

same way about the United States, despite its professed good intentions, especially within the anti-American climate in the wake of the 2003 Iraqi invasion?

Waging War on Terrorism

Since September 2001, U.S. foreign policy makers have elevated terrorism to the top of the U.S. security agenda. President Bush declared such attacks to be acts of war, not incidents to be turned over to criminal investigators and courts. Rather than taking on a conventional, sovereign nation-state, the global war on terrorism features elusive, loosely connected private groups whose members share an intense hatred of the United States and its allies and a determination to resist their political, economic, and cultural influence by any means, including mass violence against civilians. Terrorism, it should be recalled, is a tactic of political violence; terrorists are not a tangible enemy who can be readily identified, located, and defeated. A prompt resolution of this conflict is thus highly unlikely.

Until 2001, foreign terrorists had spared the U.S. homeland from large-scale attacks. When they did strike, the terrorists generally chose targets overseas such as the 1995 and 1996 attacks on U.S. troops in Saudi Arabia, the 1998 bombings of U.S. embassies in Kenya and Tanzania, and the 2000 attack on the USS *Cole* off the coast of Yemen. The most prominent exception to this rule, a failed initial attempt by Islamic militants to topple the World Trade Center with an underground detonation in February 1993, left six people dead and more than a thousand injured. Although all these attacks alarmed U.S. government officials and dominated news coverage for a few days, other concerns soon recaptured the attention of the White House, the Pentagon, and Congress. This complacency was encouraged in part by a general decline in the number of international terrorist attacks since the mid-1980s, even though the casualties from such attacks spiked every few years. In 2001, the year in which the September 11 attacks ended U.S. complacency, terrorist attacks worldwide claimed 5,799 victims.

The scale of terrorist attacks grew considerably in the years following the September 11 attacks. Worldwide, the number of reported attacks increased from 208 in 2003 to more than 11,000 in 2005. The death toll from these attacks also soared, from 625 in 2003 to nearly 15,000 two years later (Perl 2006, 7). Total casualties in 2005, including deaths and injuries, approached 40,000. Nearly half of the terrorist incidents and related deaths occurred in Iraq and Afghanistan, demonstrating both the blurred lines between terrorism and warfare and the centrality of these two countries to the U.S.-led global war on terrorism.[12] Several patterns remained consistent through 2008, including the predominance of the Near East and South Asia regions as frequent targets of terrorist attacks (see Figure 10.3).

---

12. Beyond these two frontline states, the number of large-scale terrorist attacks remained relatively stable in the years following the attacks of September 11. Prominent exceptions included grisly attacks on commuters in Madrid (March 2004) and London (July 2005), and a series of coordinated attacks in Mumbai, India's largest city, that left nearly 500 people killed or wounded in November 2008.

Figure 10.3 Geographical Distribution of Terrorist Attacks, 2008

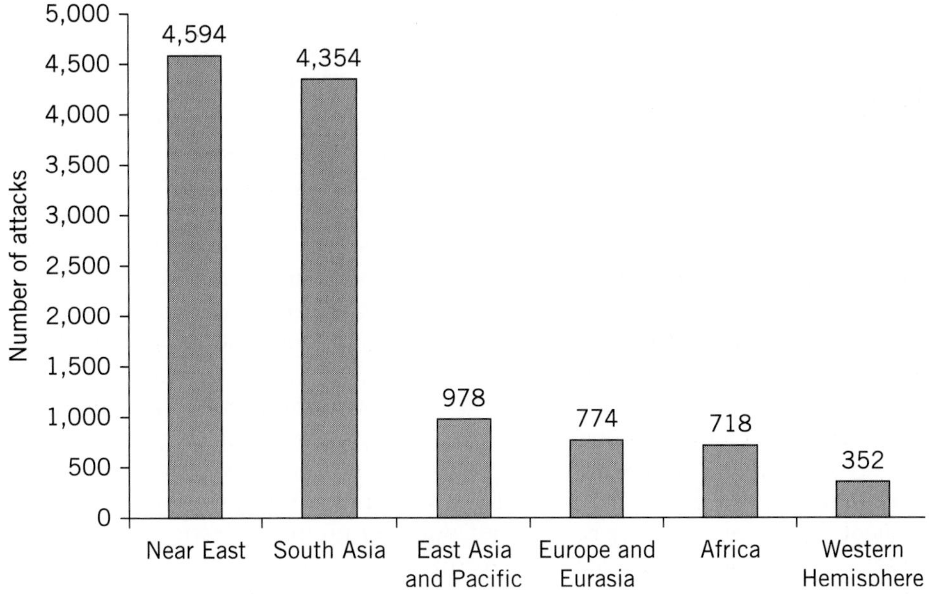

SOURCE: National Counterterrorism Center, *2008 Report on Terrorism,* p. 20 (April 30, 2009), www.nctc.gov.

The Western Hemisphere, by contrast, experienced far fewer terrorist incidents. Indeed, the lack of attacks on the United States in the five years after September 11, 2001, contradicted the dire predictions made by government officials and many media pundits. Despite stepped-up domestic surveillance, federal officials made few arrests of suspected members of al Qaeda "sleeper cells." Nor did they uncover evidence of al Qaeda spinoffs—other terrorist organizations with the capacity to inflict harm to the homeland. The record from this half-decade led political scientist John Mueller (2006) to charge that the threat posed by terrorists had been "grossly exaggerated" by government officials, much as their predecessors in the Cold War and earlier tended to depict ominous foreign threats that failed to materialize.

The Nature of Terrorism

The lack of large-scale domestic terrorism in the half-decade after September 11 was not fully reassuring to most Americans, for whom the brazen airliner assaults on the World Trade Center and Pentagon were irreversibly etched in their memories. For this and other reasons, terrorism continues to pose acute challenges to U.S. foreign policy as well as to broader conceptions of international security (Shultz and Dew 2006) and law (Duffy 2005). Simply defining the term has proved difficult, because one person's "terrorist" may be another's "freedom fighter" (see Combs 2003). In its definition of *terrorism,* the U.S. government identifies the essential elements: terrorism involves "premeditated, politically motivated violence perpetrated against noncombatant targets by subnational groups or clandestine agents, usually intended to influence an audience." [13]

The psychological effect of terrorism is crucial to this type of warfare. The perpetrators of seemingly random acts of violence find that raising public anxieties and doubts about the government's ability to protect its citizens represents a victory in and of itself (Wardlaw 1989). Another distinctive aspect of terrorism is its use of a single violent act to send a symbolic message. In Greece and Peru, for example, antiglobalization groups have bombed McDonald's, Pizza Hut, and other restaurant chains as the embodiment of U.S. economic and cultural imperialism. Osama bin Laden acknowledged the symbolic function of terrorism when he said that the September 11 attacks "were not targeted at women and children. The real targets were America's icons of military and economic power" (quoted in Esposito 2002, 22).

Although terrorism is usually associated with nonstate actors, **state terrorism,** too, has been practiced throughout history. Roman and Greek emperors publicly tortured their rivals to scare off further opposition. And during the "reign of terror" that followed the French Revolution, Robespierre found the guillotine a convenient device for pacifying his enemies. Another useful distinction can be made between domestic and international terrorism. Whereas the terrorist attacks of September 11, 2001, the deadliest in U.S. history, came from overseas, the second deadliest came from within. The American Christian Patriots revealed the dangers posed by **domestic terrorism** in 1995, when they destroyed the Murrah Federal Building in Oklahoma City, killing 168 people and injuring hundreds more.

The Oklahoma City attacks also revealed the growing role of religion in motivating terrorist activity. This perverse relationship dates back to the first and second centuries, when Jewish zealots and Islamic assassins used terror tactics to advance their spiritual ideals. Terrorism in the nineteenth and early twentieth centuries focused more on secular causes, as anarchists and Marxist revolutionaries attempted to overthrow governments through assassinations and other acts of violence. The revival of "sacred terror" came late in the twentieth century, as ideological conflicts associated with the Cold War gave way to heightened tensions between the proponents of different world religions (Benjamin and Simon 2002; see also Laqueur 1999). According to Bruce Hoffman (1998, 87), a leading expert on terrorism, "The religious imperative for terrorism is the most important defining characteristic of terrorist activity today." Militant Islamic groups such as al Qaeda openly embrace armed struggle as a matter of self-defense against encroachments by Western "infidels." As bin Laden (quoted in Esposito 2002, 24) has said:

> We are carrying out the mission of the prophet, Mohammad (peace be upon him). The mission is to spread the word of God, not to indulge in massacring people. We ourselves are the target of killings, destruction, and atrocities. We are only defending

13. See *U.S. Code* 22 (2000), § 2656f (d).

ourselves.... [Western powers] rob us of our wealth and resources and of our oil. Our religion is under attack. They kill and murder our brothers. They compromise our honor and our dignity and dare we utter a single word of protest against the injustice, we are called terrorists.

Bin Laden's religious justification for unleashing attacks on the United States and its allies renders **suicide terrorism**—the detonation of deadly explosions that take the lives of their perpetrators as well as targets—an act of ultimate sacrifice. These attacks, often committed by young people recruited by terrorist organizations with the blessing of their parents and local clerics, commonly seek the liberation of territories that are seen as unjustly occupied by foreign powers (Pape 2005). Suicide terrorists, who attach the explosives to their bodies before igniting them in population centers such as markets and cafes or who detonate vehicles laden with explosives in crowded areas while driving them, may also be driven by ideological passion, a desire for vengeance, and a belief that their sacrifice will be rewarded by a utopian afterlife (Moghadam 2008/2009). While such a practice is viewed as abhorrent in the United States and most other countries, terrorist groups relish the attention they gain from suicide attacks and the fears they incite among citizens who may consider siding with the opponents of Islamist *jihad*.

Osama bin Laden, machine gun at hand, conducts an interview with a Pakistani journalist in November 2001. Bin Laden, leader of the al Qaeda terrorist group at the time of the September 2001 attacks, eluded U.S. efforts to capture him in Afghanistan and elsewhere after the attacks. The shadowy nature of al Qaeda, with official and unofficial cells in many countries, typifies the new era of "irregular" warfare that confronts, and often confounds, U.S. military planners.

The uncertain moral status of the war on terrorism is reflected in **just-war doctrine,** a moral code of conduct in war that originated in the Middle Ages and is widely accepted by states and international law in theory, though often violated in practice (see Johnson 1981). A central condition of "just" wars is that they must be declared by *proper authorities,* a term that applies exclusively to sovereign states. Terrorist attacks conducted by private groups such as al Qaeda clearly violate this condition. They also violate another element of just-war doctrine, which prohibits the targeting of civilians. Terrorists believe, however, that attacks on civilian targets are essential to demonstrate the gravity of their concerns.

Figure 10.4 Primary Methods Used in Terrorist Attacks, 2008

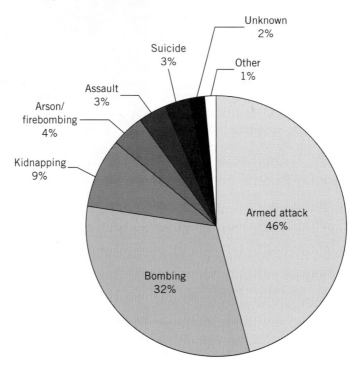

SOURCE: National Counterterrorism Center, *2008 Report on Terrorism*, p. 28 (April 30, 2009), www.nctc.gov.

Although such acts of terrorism take many forms, the vast majority of them involve armed attacks and bombings (see Figure 10.4). This latter category includes explosives ignited by suicide bombers and by "improvised explosive devices" that are generally hidden underground and triggered by a passing motor vehicle. In 2008, more than one thousand people died from terrorist attacks in Iraq, Afghanistan, India, Pakistan, Somalia, and India; hundreds more died in the Democratic Republic of Congo, Sudan, Thailand, Sri Lanka, and other countries (National Counterterrorism Center 2009, 24). Of the thirty-three American citizens killed by terrorists in 2008, the vast majority died in Iraq.

Aside from these general characteristics of terrorism, the U.S. Department of State (2006a, 12) recently identified three trends in terrorism of particular importance for the United States: a growing number of "micro-actors," or small terrorist organizations, that have sought to fill the void left by the capture and killing of many al Qaeda leaders by the United States and its allies; greater sophistication among terrorist groups in exploiting telecommunications, particularly the Internet, and global financial networks; and greater overlap between politically motivated terrorist activities and the work of national and global criminal syndicates. Each of these trends creates additional problems for U.S. counterterrorist efforts, which are described in the next section.

Elements of U.S. Counterterrorism

Because of the increasing destructiveness and sophistication, as well as the religious character, of international terrorism, it is difficult to contain and virtually impossible to eliminate (see Lesser et al. 1999). In cutting across political jurisdictions and state-societal boundaries, terrorists hinder their enemies' efforts to identify, pursue, apprehend, and prosecute suspects. In this respect, the United States faces great difficulties and chronic uncertainties in the war on terrorism. Two things have become clear. First, the war will be a long one, with success coming from "attrition, not a blitzkrieg" (Posen 2001/2002, 42). Second, the U.S. response will be multifaceted, involving many elements of counterterrorism: military combat, law enforcement, diplomacy, intelligence, finance, foreign aid and arms sales, and homeland security.

Military combat. In declaring "war" on terrorism after September 11, the White House granted the nation's military forces a lead role in the counteroffensive. The invasions of Afghanistan and Iraq required large-scale deployments of U.S. and allied troops, complex tactical alliances with supportive indigenous forces, and long-term military occupations in hostile environments. The initial military offensives effectively routed the state sponsors of terrorism (Afghanistan) and the state terrorists themselves (the ruling Baath Party in Iraq). By engaging in asymmetric warfare, however, the terrorists and their supporters prevented occupying forces from gaining full control of both countries. Their hit-and-run attacks in Iraq heightened public anxieties in the United States and pressure for withdrawal. Nevertheless, the Bush administration insisted that U.S. military forces would remain in Iraq indefinitely, even after the country regained its sovereignty in June 2004.

Law enforcement. The United States employed its domestic law enforcement agencies at all levels—federal, state, and local—to support the counterterrorism effort. Most prominent, the FBI assumed substantial authority to investigate terrorist attacks in the United States and abroad. The government encouraged cooperation between the FBI and local law enforcement agencies, which previously was limited, to create a more united front against domestic terrorist cells. On another front, Attorney General John Ashcroft expanded domestic surveillance, the "profiling" of potential terrorists, and other measures authorized by the USA PATRIOT Act, which was approved by Congress shortly after the September 11 terrorist attacks (see Chapters 5 and 12). The act expanded the power of some government agencies beyond terrorism. The Justice Department used its new powers "to investigate suspected drug traffickers, white-collar criminals, blackmailers, child pornographers, money launderers, spies, and even corrupt foreign leaders" (Lichtblau 2003).

Diplomacy. Conventional diplomacy has little value in resolving differences directly with terrorist groups, which, as noted earlier, typically operate outside the standard channels of statecraft. National governments may benefit, however, by cooperating with each other in counterterrorist efforts and engaging in public diplomacy (see Chapter 6) that isolates the terrorists politically. The experience of the United States clearly demonstrates the need for effective diplomacy. As noted, widespread global support for the U.S. government after September 2001 crumbled when Bush chose Iraq as the next major front in the war on terrorism. The diplomatic rupture, which was most pronounced in the United Nations, left the United States virtually isolated at a time it needed help from other governments, as well as the world body, in bringing its enemies to justice and rebuilding war-torn Iraq.

Intelligence. A central goal of counterterrorism, like conventional wars, is to "know thy enemy." But it is especially difficult to "know" terrorists, because they rely on stealth and deception to protect themselves. High-tech electronic intelligence may prevent al Qaeda operatives from communicating by phone or computer, but only human intelligence can penetrate terrorist cells and expose them to retaliation by the U.S. government. This reality prompted U.S. intelligence agencies to step up recruiting of foreign agents and to offer large rewards for information leading to the capture of key suspects, a tactic that produced mixed results. As described in Chapter 6, the tangle of U.S. intelligence agencies, and their traditional reluctance to compare notes with one another, greatly hinders the potential role of intelligence in fighting terrorism. The selective use of intelligence for political purposes creates another problem, as members of Congress learned in their multiple investigations of prewar intelligence on Iraq.

Finance. The U.S. and other governments further attempt to weaken terrorist groups by seizing control of their financial assets. This form of **financial statecraft,** or the manipulation of capital flows to achieve foreign policy goals, commonly involves seizing any assets of terrorists that are "laundered" in bank accounts, often in the United States (Steil and Litan 2006, ch. 3). Federal agents have long relied on this tactic in battling organized crime and drug traffickers, whose leaders similarly funnel huge volumes of cash through U.S. financial institutions. Another common target of U.S. agents is the network of charitable organizations that frequently serve as fronts for terrorist groups, including Hamas and Hezbollah in the Middle East.

Foreign aid and arms sales. It is widely assumed that distressed living conditions create hotbeds of discontent, rebellion, and international terrorism. Although the evidence for this assumption is mixed—many terrorists such as Osama bin Laden come from affluent backgrounds—there is no doubt that al Qaeda and other groups exploit the turmoil in "failed states" to expand their operations. Thus, the U.S. and other governments have increased their economic aid to many developing countries, citing the prospect of terrorism as a motivating force. The United States has also expanded its military aid programs and arms sales to "frontline" states, such as Pakistan and Tajikistan, for the same reasons. Bolstering these governments, officials believe, will allow them to support U.S. efforts while better preparing them for terrorist attacks on their own soil.

Homeland security. The September 2001 attacks proved especially traumatic for Americans because they demonstrated, once and for all, that the geographical separation of the United States from other world power centers no longer guaranteed the nation's security. The heightened sense of vulnerability required "new vigilance in the most fragile corners of the transportation, energy, power, and communications systems and closer attention to the security of government buildings" (Posen 2001/2002, 45). In addition to patrolling borders and protecting "high-value" targets in the United States, homeland security involves pursuing domestic terrorist cells and preparing "first responders" for future attacks (see O'Hanlon et al. 2002). The U.S. government's push for homeland security resulted in a reorganization in which dozens of federal agencies formed a new cabinet department (see Chapter 6), and federal efforts were coordinated with those of thousands of state and local government agencies. Despite these efforts, the U.S. government continues to warn agencies and citizens that new attacks are possible at any given time or place.

More broadly, the war on terrorism requires that the United States come to grips with the complex social tensions that fuel political violence in this form. **Counter-insurgency,** the suppression of military challenges to established governments, applies directly to terrorist groups that target citizens as well as political figures in their quest to disrupt the status quo. This is a complex and difficult task, however, as gaining public support and confidence is vital to victory. After years of frustration in Iraq, U.S. military planners led by Lt. Gen. David Petraeus shifted U.S. counter-insurgency strategy from a reliance on overwhelming force to one focused on training government security forces and on meeting the needs of civilian populations. By turning Iraqi resentment away from the United States and toward the al Qaeda terrorists who kept their country in a constant state of chaos, the "Sunni Awakening" of 2007 turned the tide in the war. The success of the new counter-insurgency strategy demonstrated that U.S. leaders are capable of learning from past experience—a welcome lesson given the short memories that have plagued many U.S. military operations in the past.

President Obama's adoption of a similar strategy for Afghanistan in 2009 and 2010 sought the same outcome but faced greater resistance from the dominant Pashtun tribes, which, along with their Taliban allies, controlled most of the country by the time Obama took office (see West 2009). Insurgent attacks increased steadily after the U.S. invasion late in 2001, from 65 in 2002 to more than 400 in 2007 (Jones 2008, 7). The new Afghan government, which was shattered and without resources during the U.S. occupation, was powerless to stop an uprising that sprang from a variety of sources, from terrorist groups to ordinary citizens who demanded the restoration of government services. Winning the "hearts and minds" of this population would prove especially difficult for Obama, as would keeping his promise to train self-sufficient Afghan forces and then begin withdrawing U.S. troops by 2011.

Obstacles to U.S. Victory

By nature, terrorist groups are extremely skilled at avoiding capture. Their members are highly motivated and unswervingly loyal to one another and their cause. They conceal themselves in remote, inaccessible areas or within the political and social chaos of failed states. They also limit their internal communications to prevent detection. Terrorist groups form clandestine alliances with governments that share their political agendas and provide safe havens and logistical support. The groups also form ad hoc alliances with like-minded terrorists and political movements. With their widely disbursed memberships and "flat" organizational structures, terrorist groups are especially elusive (see Arquilla, Ronfeldt, and Zanini 1999).

All governments share the challenges posed by terrorist groups, and the United States, in particular, faces several special obstacles in combating terrorism. A central obstacle is the very global primacy that served as a cornerstone of the National Security Council's 2002 "National Security Strategy." Such claims to dominance naturally fuel resentment within foreign countries, particularly among frustrated societal groups in the developing world that link their impoverished living standards to U.S. wealth and power. Such groups may mobilize against all forms of U.S. primacy—military, economic, and cultural—and resort to terrorism whenever they feel other avenues of protest are closed to them. A second and related obstacle facing the United States stems from the nation's high profile overseas, which creates its own vulnerabilities to terrorism. As Paul Pillar (2001, 59) noted before the war on terrorism, the thousands of Americans stationed in overseas military bases and diplomatic posts, along with thousands more conducting business overseas, are attractive targets for anti-American terrorists.

Finally, with its open, liberal government and civil society, the United States finds it difficult to gain the upper hand against terrorists. The fragmented U.S. political system—its checks and balances, federalism, and loosely connected bureaucracies—hampers effective planning and coordination. Private groups, including those bent on harming the government and its citizens, have considerable freedom to organize, express their views, and recruit new members. Even after new restrictions were imposed, these groups retained ample access to government facilities. Further obstacles are posed by the general public, which has viewed even modest preventive measures such as restrictions on curbside baggage check-in at airports to be burdensome impositions.

These domestic obstacles hinder a coherent, aggressive U.S. response to the terrorist challenge. Overreaction poses a greater danger to the counterterrorism effort, however. A common tactic of asymmetric warfare is to transform the victim of attack into the aggressor and to bait the victim into violent backlashes that damage its credibility and presumed moral authority. "The temptation to do something, for the sake of being seen to be doing something—even something strategically stupid—can be politically irresistible" (Gray 2002, 12). Prudence is essential in responding to terrorism, which is something that does not come easy for a global superpower that often relies on overwhelming military force to achieve its foreign policy goals.

Conclusion

Like other countries, the U.S. government considers the protection of national security to be its essential function, one that makes other policy goals at home and abroad attainable. This chapter has focused on the ends and means of security and defense policy and its relationship to the nation's evolving grand strategy. As the chapter has described, for more than half a century this strategy has focused on sustaining U.S. primacy in the interstate system. A combination of hard-power assets, including vast natural resources, a productive population, and cutting-edge military power, made this primacy possible after World War II. These resources and the nation's soft-power assets—the legitimacy of governmental institutions, economic freedoms, and a dynamic civil society—extended the unipolar balance of power past the Cold War and into the new millennium.

Many warning signs, however, suggest that sustained U.S. primacy is not a given. The readiness of U.S. military forces eroded during the Iraqi and Afghan conflicts to such an extent that by February 2007 "virtually all of the U.S.-based army combat brigades [were] rated as unready to deploy" (Tyson 2007, A13). Active forces were strained by accelerated rotations and multiple combat tours without the standard intervals of rest and training, and military recruiters found it impossible to fill many highly skilled positions (see GAO 2007). The wear and tear on military equipment was costing U.S. taxpayers about $2 billion a month by the end of 2006, or about one-quarter of the overall cost of the wars in Iraq and Afghanistan (Kelley 2006).

Similar problems weakened and ultimately paralyzed earlier hegemonic powers (see Kennedy 2003, 1987). Although claims of impending U.S. decline have been commonplace since the arrival of *pax Americana* after World War II, the hazards in the current strategic environment are unprecedented in their scope and complexity. Maintaining U.S. military security will be especially difficult in view of the variety of armed conflicts, conventional and irregular, likely to engage U.S. forces in the future. The "revolution in military affairs" emphasized by Pentagon officials, featuring high-tech intelligence gathering and weaponry, cannot convince Afghans to resist Taliban rulers or Osama bin Laden's call for *jihad*. Nor can the military revolution help the U.S. reconcile the simmering tensions among Islamic Sunnis and Shiites and ethnic Kurds that make long-term stability in Iraq an elusive if not impossible dream.

As noted previously, President Obama came into office in 2009 with a broad public mandate to change the direction of U.S. foreign policy—and military policy, in particular—in a more cooperative direction. Economic problems at home, however, dominated the president's time and energy during his first year, a common fate among many of his predecessors. Continuity rather than change marked U.S. defense policy during this period, a pattern that was personified by Defense Secretary Gates, a holdover from the Bush administration. With Obama's attention riveted on problems at home, a former national security adviser warned, "his grand redefinition of U.S. foreign policy is vulnerable to dilution or delay by upper-level officials who have the bureaucratic predisposition to favor caution over action and the familiar over the innovative" (Brzezinski 2010, 18).

All this suggests that preserving U.S. national security will depend on learning the lessons of the past that provided foreign policy makers with both the blessings and burdens of world power. Of these lessons, perhaps the most important is that "capabilities do not easily translate into influence" (Pressman 2009, 151). American primacy is not reducible to tanks and nuclear warheads. These instruments of destruction may subdue enemies, but they do not create the conditions that will ultimately make the United States secure. Force must be balanced with reason, dialogue, and a search for common understanding. Stated another way, the United States cannot be a "leader without followers" (Buzan, 2008). These and other lessons—the importance of U.S. moral leadership, for example, and the dangers of searching "for monsters to destroy"—may yet right the course of a nation that has consistently overcome past perils and upheavals.

Key Terms

Anti-Ballistic Missile (ABM) Treaty, p. 335

Baruch Plan, p. 333

coercive diplomacy, p. 329

counter-insurgency, p. 345

defense policy, p. 312

domestic terrorism, p. 340

exit strategy, p. 328

extended deterrence, p. 334

external balancing, p. 317

financial statecraft, p. 344

flexible response, p. 335

geopolitical assets, p. 318

grand strategy, p. 316

internal balancing, p. 317

just-war doctrine, p. 341

massive retaliation, p. 328

military alliances, p. 318

mission creep, p. 329

mutual assured destruction (MAD), p. 335

national security, p. 311

nuclear deterrence, p. 334

peaceful coercion, p. 327

Powell Doctrine, p. 328

preemptive war, p. 331

preventive war, p. 331

spectrum of armed conflict, p. 314

state-society relations, p. 319

state terrorism, p. 340

strategic culture, p. 319

Strategic Defense Initiative (SDI), p. 336

strategic detachment, p. 320

strategic environment, p. 317

structural arrangements, p. 319

suicide terrorism, p. 341

sustained primacy, p. 321

tactics, p. 324

wars of choice, p. 327

wars of necessity, p. 327

Weinberger Doctrine, p. 328

Internet References

The **Center for Defense Information** (www.cdi.org) publishes reports and statistics on defense and security policies, including information on interest groups and private companies involved in U.S. foreign policy. Among other topics featured on its Web site,

(continued)

the center examines U.S. arms sales and trade, missile defense, defense projects and budgets, and nuclear issues.

The **Center for Strategic and International Studies** (www.csis.org) is a bipartisan, non-profit organization whose Web site includes numerous reports on defense and security issues and related policy problems regarding demographics and population, energy security, and the international financial and economic system. The center publishes the *Washington Quarterly* (www.twq.com), which analyzes global changes and foreign policies with an emphasis on the U.S. role in the world, defense procurement, terrorism, nuclear proliferation, and regional issues.

The **Federation of American Scientists** (www.fas.org) is a nonprofit organization committed to researching the causes and tactics of war. Areas of research featured on the group's Web site include nuclear arms, terrorism, intelligence gathering and reporting, government secrecy, small arms trade, and the connection between technology and weaponry. In addition to providing facts and figures on these areas, FAS also publishes a newsletter, *Arms Sales Monitor* (www.fas.org/asmp), and a journal, *Public Interest Report* (www.fas.org/faspir/index.html), along with short books on each research topic.

The **International Institute for Strategic Studies** (www.iiss.org), a London-based company and registered charity, conducts research on political and military conflict. The IISS focuses its research on grand strategy, armed forces, technological and military equipment, and regional relations. The group's Web site, featuring updates on the global balance of power and recent reports on other security issues, is available only to members, however.

The **North Atlantic Treaty Organization** is the world's largest international defense organization. Its Web site (www.nato.int) hosts an online electronic library (www.nato.int/docu/home.htm) with links to numerous reports detailing NATO activities around the globe. Also available for additional research are platforms and data on, among other things, NATO's history, missions, partnerships, organizational capabilities, command structure, and defense expenditures.

The **RAND Corporation** (www.rand.org) is a private, nonprofit think tank established by the U.S. Air Force in the 1940s. It specializes in international affairs, terrorism, and U.S. national security issues. The group's Web site also maintains a database on international terrorism that is a vital resource for researchers. RAND, an acronym for research and development, also publishes the *RAND Review* (www.rand.org/publications/randreview), a magazine that covers current security and defense issues.

The **World Policy Institute** (www.worldpolicy.org/wpi/index.html) is a research organization that focuses on the connection between the domestic and international factors that drive foreign policy. WPI's research topics, which are also covered in its *World Policy Journal* (www.worldpolicy.org/journal/index.html), include counterterrorism, arms trade, U.S. grand strategy, cultural relations, and relationships between military superpowers. The group's Web site highlights its most recent activities and includes links to other sources of information on international security.

11

Economic Statecraft

Floor traders at the New York Stock Exchange scramble to manage the crash in stock prices in November 2008. The Dow Jones Industrial Average, which peaked at 14,165 in October 2007, lost more than half its value by March 2009. Foreign stock markets also plummeted during this period, revealing the global impact of developments in the U.S. economy.

American leaders, like their counterparts overseas, consider national prosperity essential to achieving broader strategic goals. The military preponderance currently enjoyed by the United States would not be possible in the absence of a productive population, vast natural resources, advanced technology, and commercial links to other markets. Indeed, U.S. troop deployments in foreign countries, including peace-keeping missions, have been linked to greater trade with their governments (Biglaiser and DeRouen 2009). Economic strength is also a source of the nation's "soft power," much of which is wielded by consumers and expressed, in part, by their material well-being (Nye 2004).

Beyond the functional benefits of a vibrant U.S. economy, the day-to-day conduct of foreign economic policy is regarded as a worthy end in itself. Productive economic ties tend to moderate the behavior of U.S. trading partners, which are more stable and reliable if they rule justly and "play by the rules" of interstate relations. At home, commercial activity harnesses the energies of private citizens, whose dogged pursuit of material self-interest contributes to the realization of national goals. In this respect, the domain of foreign economic policy is more *democratic* than security policy, which often takes place beyond the view or reach of civil society.

The notion that "the business of America is business" is deeply engrained in the nation's cultural identity. Americans have long been regarded abroad as highly materialistic, or driven by the acquisition of wealth. Alexis de Tocqueville, who toured the United States in 1831 and 1832, captured this materialistic spirit in his classic cultural study *Democracy in America*:

> The desire to acquire the good things of this world is the dominant passion among Americans.... It is odd to watch with what feverish ardor the Americans pursue prosperity and how they are ever tormented by the shadowy suspicion that they may not have chosen the shortest route to get it. Americans cleave to the things of this world as if assured that they will never die, and yet are in such a rush to snatch any that come within their reach, as if expecting to stop living before they have relished them. They clutch everything but hold nothing fast, and so lose grip as they hurry after some new delight (Tocqueville [1835] 1988, 534, 536).

As we will find, regulating commerce is a highly political enterprise because of the routine interaction of public and private actors in the U.S. economic complex (see Chapter 6). The makeup of Congress is determined in large part by the economic interests of constituents (Fordham and McKeown 2003), and presidential candidates know that "pocketbook" issues typically concern voters more than any others. Political intervention in private markets is inevitable because the economic affairs of Americans, diffused across business sectors, routinely come into conflict and cannot be fully reconciled. Amid the cross-pressures imposed by competing, self-interested investors, firms, and workers, the U.S. government must act as the final arbiter of these conflicts of interest (see Ikenberry, Lake, and Mastanduno 1988).

Paradoxically, the U.S. government has far less control over the market-driven world economy, which it played a lead role in creating. Economic globalization, which melds national and regional markets into a single world market, expands the field of competition and provides advantages to emerging economies that import technologies invented elsewhere and produce goods with lower costs and fewer regulations found in industrialized states.[1] The flow of private capital across national borders, a crucial part of globalization, also hinders the U.S. government's economic ability to control its fortunes in the global marketplace. Furthermore, as U.S.-based multinational corporations expand into new markets and join forces with foreign firms, they are less likely to align themselves automatically with U.S. foreign policy goals. All these trends suggest that, as in other areas of foreign policy, the United States may be the victim of its own success.

The fusion of the U.S. and foreign economies was apparent in the financial crisis of 2008. Triggered by reckless lending practices of American banks and

---

1. See Steger (2010) for a recently published volume of classic essays on economic globalization.

mortgage brokers, the crisis spread quickly to the major economies of Europe and East Asia, many of which had adopted the same financial structures and policies as Washington. As a result, national output plunged and unemployment surged worldwide in the most severe recession since the 1930s. Millions of U.S. citizens suffered severe personal losses, and the stature of the United States as the "locomotive" of global prosperity was tarnished badly. Barack Obama, who spent the first months of his presidency containing this damage, was forced to delay other national and foreign policy priorities.

This chapter begins by identifying the key models of political economy and then reviews the current status of the United States in the world economy. It then considers the two dimensions—global and domestic—of U.S. trade policy. Finally, the chapter examines two other aspects of U.S. foreign economic policy, foreign aid and economic sanctions, which also advance the nation's global interests. As we will find, all these elements of **economic statecraft** (Baldwin 1985) are crucial to the overall success or failure of U.S. foreign policy.

Models of Political Economy

Understanding U.S. foreign economic policy requires a firm grasp of **political economy,** an arena of public life located at the crossroads of states and markets. As noted earlier, regulating commerce is inherently a political process because of the state's role in deciding which economic system will be in place at any particular time, what the rules of the system will be, and how its costs and benefits will be distributed across society. These questions become matters of foreign economic policy when they involve the government's commercial, financial, and regulatory ties with other countries. The **international political economy** is the arena in which governments engage with an array of private actors—firms, workers, investors, and public-interest groups—as well as foreign governments and intergovernmental organizations such as the World Bank and the World Trade Organization (WTO). This engagement is partly competitive, as each nation seeks benefits for itself at the expense of others, but cooperation is also needed if the global economy is to function in the orderly manner required by financial managers.

An essential function of all governments is to organize economic activity within their societies and establish the relationships among economic actors in the public and private sectors. In doing so, political leaders adopt different models of political economy that feature distinctive trade-offs between labor and capital, political liberty and economic equality, and the power of states versus civil society. The model of political economy chosen by each nation determines the role it will play in the global economy and the broader relations it will maintain with other governments. Three models of political economy have been adopted in modern times: economic liberalism, socialism, and economic nationalism.[2] In managing economic affairs, governments commonly draw on the elements of more than one model.

---

2. See Gilpin (1987) for a similar breakdown of political economic models.

The United States is widely considered the primary proponent of **economic liberalism,** a system of free enterprise that protects private property and commercial activity from government intervention (see Lal 2006). Adam Smith ([1776] 2000), a leading proponent of this model during the Enlightenment era, believed that free markets offer an ideal environment in which entrepreneurs can take risks, introduce technological innovations, and expand production, thereby improving societal living standards beyond what governments can provide. In this view, a natural "harmony of interests" exists between states and markets, and among the producers and consumers of goods and services. This model became known as *capitalism,* a term reflecting the importance of private wealth (capital) in driving economic activity.

The second model of political economy, **socialism,** rejects the liberal notion of a harmony of interests and argues instead that free markets inevitably produce disparities in wealth and the exploitation of workers by business owners and managers. This critique, identified with Karl Marx and often known today as neo-Marxism, considers the political leaders of liberal states to be co-conspirators with business firms in the exploitation of workers. A socialist system seeks to ensure economic equality through social welfare programs and government ownership of vital enterprises, while also allowing citizens to own private property and operate firms. The Soviet Union adopted a stronger version of this model, **communism,** by assuming ownership of all economic activity and dominating political control. Although this model failed to improve living standards, the neo-Marxist critique of liberal economics persists and modified versions of socialism exist in many parts of the world.[3]

Finally, **economic nationalism** considers commercial activity fruitful only if it serves the interests of the state, whose power depends on the accumulation of wealth. Political actors adopting this model, also known as **mercantilism,** view the world economy as a "zero-sum game" in which the losses suffered by one country offset the gains enjoyed by another. During the Renaissance era, the maritime empires of Europe adopted this model by accumulating vast amounts of specie, or mineral wealth, which they used to enhance their military defenses and domestic political power. The revival of economic nationalism in the 1920s led to the closing of world trade markets, a severe global depression, and the onset of World War II. More recently, Japan and other East Asian countries have been accused of "neo-mercantilism," flooding global export markets with their goods while protecting their domestic producers from foreign competition. At home, critics charge that U.S. economic sanctions rarely work because security concerns routinely prevail, forcing American leaders to make concessions to strategically vital governments that ignore U.S. policy preferences (Pape 1997).

---

3. Several countries in Europe manage economies that resemble the socialist model, although they have moved toward liberalism under pressure from the European Union's central bank. Still, governments such as Austria, Hungary, and Italy spent more than 40 percent of national output on public programs in 2002; the United States spent less than 20 percent (World Bank 2004b, 222–224).

The United States first adopted a mercantile approach to foreign economic policy while simultaneously preaching the gospel of open markets. This behavior changed as the nation emerged from World War I as the world's economic powerhouse. Woodrow Wilson, who included free trade as one of his "fourteen points" for restoring global stability, pledged to dismantle U.S. trade barriers and encouraged others to follow his lead. The trade wars of the interwar period, however, delayed this transition to market liberalism. The calamity of the Great Depression and World War II prompted Franklin Roosevelt's secretary of state, Cordell Hull, to observe later, "Unhampered trade dovetailed with peace; high tariffs, trade barriers, and unfair competition with war. If we could get a freer flow of trade—freer in the sense of few discriminations and obstructions ... we might have a reasonable chance of lasting peace" (quoted in Gardner 1980, 9).

This spirit of free trade animated the U.S. government's foreign economic policy after World War II and continues to do so today. Yet, traces of economic nationalism remain, such as when President George W. Bush raised steel tariffs in 2002. The country's highly subsidized agricultural sector also exhibits the characteristics of socialism. Contradicting the liberal rhetoric of government leaders, such practices expose the United States to charges of hypocrisy. Critics of globalization also point out that the U.S. government's exaltation of free markets can be construed as a tactic of economic nationalism. After all, U.S. economic primacy would grow even stronger if U.S. firms, with their superior technology, huge marketing and advertising budgets, and economies of scale, were to swamp their challengers with agricultural and manufactured goods on open trade markets, a prospect that prompts aggressive countermeasures by trading states overseas.

As it is for security policy, institutional arrangements play a central role in shaping the foreign economic policies of all countries. In the United States, corporations enjoy a privileged place in the policy process, while workers in Great Britain and Germany have greater political influence over trade and foreign investment than their American counterparts. Meanwhile, the central governments of Japan and France are better equipped to overcome pressure from either of these societal groups (Hart 1992), although nongovernmental organizations have more recently gained in both popularity and power in Japan's foreign aid policies (Hirata 2002). These comparisons reveal the extent to which foreign economic relations reflect the bargains struck daily among contending actors in domestic society.

The Balance of Economic Power

Strengths of the U.S. Economy

The United States has managed the world's largest economy for nearly a century. Its output eclipsed those of Great Britain and other economic rivals early in the twentieth century, and the lead widened with the decimation of U.S. competitors in the two world wars. By 1945 and the start of the Cold War, U.S. firms were producing roughly as much economic output as the rest of the world combined.

Although this percentage fell predictably as other economies recovered, the U.S. share of world output, which leveled off at between one-quarter and one-third, remains unsurpassed today.

In the 1990s, record levels of foreign investment contributed to the rapid pace of U.S. economic growth, which averaged nearly 4 percent annually. The economic boom, aided further by the creation of new capitalist states in the former Soviet bloc, put to rest (temporarily at least) widespread expectations of a U.S. decline. The economies of the nation's most serious challengers—the newly industrialized countries of East Asia—peaked in the mid-1990s and then suffered a dramatic fall at the turn of the century (see Clifford and Engardio 2000). This reversal of fortunes coincided with a boom in the high-tech sectors of the U.S. economy and unprecedented growth in stock prices. A recession that began early in 2001, followed by the economic shocks of the September 11 terrorist attacks, disrupted this period of national prosperity, which resumed on a more modest scale in 2004.

As noted in Chapter 1, the **gross domestic product (GDP)** of the United States in 2009 was $14.3 trillion, or about one-fifth of the global total of $70 trillion. This proportion is especially striking because at the time the U.S. population of about 305 million represented less than 5 percent of the global population of 6.8 billion. Japan, which managed the world's second-largest national economy in 2009, produced about one-third of U.S. GDP. The volume of U.S. output exceeded the combined totals of more than 140 lower-income countries. As for Russia, the geopolitical rival of the United States in the Cold War, nearly two decades of economic and political upheavals had cut its GDP to about 10 percent of U.S. levels (International Monetary Fund 2010b).

Other statistics illustrate the magnitude of U.S. economic abundance. The per capita income of the United States, the nation's economic output divided by its population, amounted to $46,716 in 2008 (World Bank 2009). Only eleven other countries exceeded this level of affluence. The average life expectancy of Americans reached seventy-eight years in 2008, significantly higher than the world average of sixty-seven years. Americans today can expect to live nearly twice as long on average as the citizens of several African countries, including Botswana, Mozambique, and Zambia.

The United States maintains its status as the leading world trader. Overall U.S. trade in 2008 amounted to about $4.3 trillion, a level that exceeded that of the second-largest trading power, Germany, by more than a trillion dollars (WTO 2009). The nation's preponderance in trade, however, was driven primarily by its imports of manufactured goods ($2.2 trillion), which greatly exceeded the volume of U.S. manufacturing exports ($1.3 trillion). Germany retained its distinction as the world's largest exporter of these goods in 2008, a vital sign of economic strength (see Table 11.1). The United States, however, led the world in both the import and the export of commercial services, a relatively small but growing category of trade.

The United States maintains a close but contradictory relationship with other major economic powers. China, for example, is both a chief *competitor* of the

Table 11.1 Top Ten World Merchandise Traders, 2008

Exporter	Value of exports (billions of U.S. dollars)	Importer	Value of imports (billions of U.S. dollars)
Germany	$1,462	United States	$2,170
China	1,428	Germany	1,204
United States	1,287	China	1,133
Japan	782	Japan	763
Netherlands	633	France	706
France	605	United Kingdom	632
Italy	538	Netherlands	573
Belgium	476	Italy	555
Russia	472	Belgium	470
United Kingdom	459	South Korea	435

SOURCE: World Trade Organization, *World Trade Developments* (2009), www.wto.org/english/res_e/statis_e/its2009_e/its09_world_trade_dev_e.pdf.

United States and a *partner* in maintaining a stable global economy that, according to the guiding liberal model, benefits all parties. The Chinese economy, which grew by an astonishing 10 percent annually between 1979 and 2008 (Morrison 2009), has benefited greatly from manufacturing exports, particularly to the United States. Meanwhile, Chinese leaders have bolstered the U.S. economy by investing in U.S. treasury bonds, the volume of which approached $800 billion in 2009. During the same period, China has emerged as the world's leading destination of foreign direct investment. These trends make China an economic peer of the United States, one that simultaneously seeks the upper hand in the relationship while depending on a healthy U.S. economy to advance its own national prosperity. Continuing economic growth is vital for China's huge population, but it has come at a price—including political repression, high levels of pollution, and growing economic disparities—that will likely keep Beijing's attention focused on domestic issues rather than overseas rivalries.

Like China, other major industrialized countries maintain a highly interdependent relationship with the U.S. economy. Japan, for example, ranked second in 2008 in its imports to and exports from the United States, in its volume of incoming U.S. foreign investment, and in its holdings of U.S. treasury bonds. The Japanese economy, however, has suffered sluggish growth for more than a decade and, in 2009, sunk into its worst recession since World War II (Chanlett-Avery 2009). These problems generated political upheaval at home as voters in August unseated the dominant Liberal Democratic Party in favor of the newly created Democratic Party of Japan, whose leaders promised to maintain close economic relations with Washington while assuming a more independent role on diplomatic and security issues. Germany meanwhile maintains its status as Europe's largest economy and foremost trading partner of the United States. Although this trade relationship is imbalanced—Germany routinely exports twice as much to the United States as it imports—both governments share a common view regarding the need for stable economic relations and a liberal world economy. Close security relations between the United States and other members of the European Union—primarily France and Great Britain—further propel economic cooperation rather than competition across the Atlantic.

American Decline: The Financial Crisis of 2008

Despite its predominant role in the world economy, the United States confronts profound changes in the world economy that pose direct challenges to its sustained primacy. Cracks in the post-war U.S. economy first appeared in the early 1970s, when a spike in oil prices created double-digit inflation, high unemployment, and stagnant levels of output. The United States previously maintained a favorable **balance of trade,** or an equilibrium between imports and exports. But in the 1980s the nation began buying more goods from foreign countries than it was selling to them (see Figure 11.1). The U.S. trade deficit grew steadily during the boom years of the 1990s and then soared in the new millennium. By 2005, the trade deficit stood at $717 billion, an increase of $222 billion from its level two years earlier (U.S. Department of Commerce 2006, 1). The U.S. trade deficit fell to $696 billion by 2008, but the gap between the nation's imports and exports remained a fixture of its global economic relations (U.S. Census Bureau 2010). Consumer spending fueled the surge in imports as Americans rushed to buy the lowest-cost goods they could find, regardless of national origin. Their spending spree continued alongside a declining national savings rate that, remarkably, fell below 0 percent during this period.

These worrisome trends paled in comparison to the disruption of the U.S. and world economies that followed the financial crisis of 2008. The deep recession began a year earlier, when a "bubble" burst in the real estate market, which had experienced such rapid growth in property values that banks and mortgage brokers offered home loans at "sub-prime" interest rates with little regard for the credit worthiness of borrowers (see Schwartz 2009). When millions of these homeowners, faced with unexpected job losses or other economic problems, suddenly defaulted on their mortgages, the foreclosures triggered a cascade of bank failures and the collapse of major investment firms. The bankruptcy of Lehman Brothers in September 2008, valued at $639 billion, marked the largest such bankruptcy in U.S. history. President Bush, whose economic philosophy had always discouraged government intervention, pleaded with Congress to approve a federal bailout to prevent the collapse of the U.S. financial system. "What surprised most observers was how severe the reaction was—how deep into the economy the shock waves penetrated: beyond housing, beyond finance, deep to the core" (Veseth 2010, 67).

The crisis quickly assumed global proportions, as global stock markets tumbled alongside steep declines in national output (see Figure 11.2). The International

Figure 11.1 U.S. Balance of Trade, 1964–2005

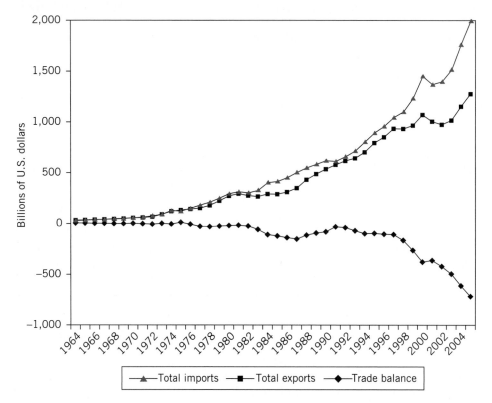

SOURCE: U.S. Census Bureau, "U.S. International Trade in Goods and Services," U.S. Department of Commerce, Washington, D.C., June 9, 2006, http://bea.gov/bea/newsrelarchive/2006/trad1306.pdf.

Monetary Fund (IMF), which along with the World Bank had long served as agents of globalization (Woods 2006), provided emergency loans to prevent the governments of Hungary, Iceland, and Ukraine from running out of money. Major economic powers such as Australia, India, and Russia also endured months of financial chaos. "Everything happening now in the economic and financial sphere began in the United States," Russian prime minister Vladimir Putin (quoted in Jagger 2008) declared on October 2. "This is not the irresponsibility of specific individuals but the irresponsibility of the system that claims leadership." While his view was shared by other world leaders at a November 15 global economic summit, they had no choice but to approve similar bailouts for their own faltering financial institutions. For the first time, Chinese leaders expressed concerns about their huge investments in U.S. treasury bonds, the withdrawal of which would effectively bankrupt the U.S. government.

President Obama avoided a greater calamity with the help of a second "stimulus" package from Congress, this one directed toward construction and other projects

Figure 11.2 Falling Fortunes: Index of Four Global Stock Markets, September 30–October 27, 2008

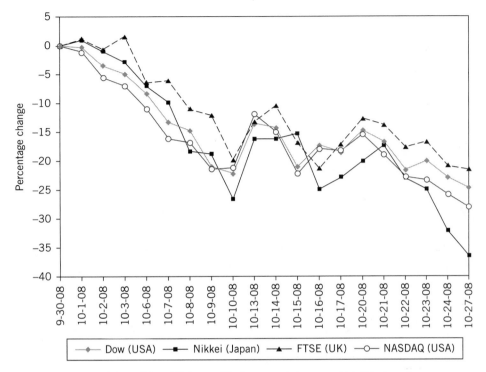

SOURCE: Data from MSN.com "Money" Web page, http://moneycentral.msn.com/detail/stock_quote.

that would stem rising unemployment across the United States. Still, industrialized and developing countries spent a combined total of nearly $12 trillion in recovery costs—a price tag that amounted to about $2,000 for every woman, man, and child on the planet (Jess 2009). The U.S. budget deficit grew rapidly under President Bush due to sweeping tax cuts in 2001 and the unexpected costs of fighting the war on terrorism after September 11. The financial crisis in Bush's last year sent this deficit soaring further—from $459 billion in 2008 to nearly $1.6 trillion in 2009. This total represented 11.2 percent of national output, the highest such level since World War II (Congressional Budget Office 2009). The national debt, meanwhile, skyrocketed to more than $12 trillion in 2009, nearly the value of U.S. goods and services produced in that year (Austin and Levit 2010, 4). Trade levels between the United States and other countries plummeted from $4.3 trillion in 2008 to $3.5 trillion in 2009, a clear sign that the financial crisis had quickly "gone global."

Above and beyond these staggering costs, the financial crisis raised profound doubts about the liberal model of political economy and its most boisterous

IN THEIR OWN WORDS: GROUP OF 20

The global financial crisis of 2008 had caught world leaders by surprise when they convened in Washington, D.C., in November for a summit meeting of the Group of 20 (G-20) economic powers. By this point in the crisis, the leaders—including French president Nicolas Sarkozy, German chancellor Angela Merkel, Chinese president Hu Jintao, and Indian prime minister Manmohan Singh—were forced to adopt wide-ranging and costly measures to prevent an even greater catastrophe. Still, the G-20 delegates agreed on a closing declaration that, however technical its language, openly summed up the underlying causes of the crisis.

We, the Leaders of the Group of Twenty, held an initial meeting in Washington on November 15, 2008, amid serious challenges to the world economy and financial markets. We are determined to enhance our cooperation and work together to restore global growth and achieve needed reforms in the world's financial systems.

Over the past months our countries have taken urgent and exceptional measures to support the global economy and stabilize financial markets. These efforts must continue. At the same time, we must lay the foundation for reform to help to ensure that a global crisis, such as this one, does not happen again. Our work will be guided by a shared belief that market principles, open trade and investment regimes, and effectively regulated financial markets foster the dynamism, innovation, and entrepreneurship that are essential for economic growth, employment, and poverty reduction....

During a period of strong global growth, growing capital flows, and prolonged stability earlier this decade, market participants sought higher yields without an adequate appreciation of the risks and failed to exercise proper due diligence. At the same time, weak underwriting standards, unsound risk management practices, increasingly complex and opaque financial products, and consequent excessive leverage combined to create vulnerabilities in the system. Policy-makers, regulators and supervisors, in some advanced countries, did not adequately appreciate and address the risks building up in financial markets, keep pace with financial innovation, or take into account the systemic ramifications of domestic regulatory actions.

Major underlying factors to the current situation were, among others, inconsistent and insufficiently coordinated macroeconomic policies, inadequate structural reforms, which led to unsustainable global macroeconomic outcomes. These developments, together, contributed to excesses and ultimately resulted in severe market disruption.

SOURCE: Group of 20, "Declaration: Summit on Financial Markets and the World Economy," November 15, 2008, www.g20.org/Documents/g20_summit_declaration.pdf.

advocate, the United States. The government's financial deregulation, which accelerated in the Clinton administration and continued under George W. Bush, may have "unleashed" private enterprise. The same policy, however, also enabled the most profit-hungry bankers, brokers, and bond traders to lead the U.S. economy, once known as the locomotive of global prosperity, into a train wreck that could be repaired only by massive government intervention. To Paul Krugman

(2009, 43), a Nobel Prize–winning economist, money managers must "face up to the inconvenient reality that financial markets fall far short of perfection, that they are subject to extraordinary delusions and the madness of crowds."

Trade Policy as a "Two-Level Game"

By far the most important aspect of U.S. foreign economic policy is trade with other countries. As noted earlier, Americans have robust appetites for foreign goods, even those that come at the cost of shuttered factories in U.S. cities. Although the United States is no longer the world's dominant exporter, the nation enjoys a commanding lead in many sectors of foreign trade, particularly services, military equipment, and the high-technology goods associated with the computer industry. Whereas trade accounted for about 10 percent of U.S. economic output in 1960, about one-fourth of the goods and services produced today are destined for foreign customers.

An examination of U.S. bilateral trade flows reveals the far reaches of the nation's trade deficit (see Table 11.2 and Map 10, U.S. Foreign Economic Relations, in map section). Of the top ten U.S. trading partners in 2009, all but Brazil and the Netherlands maintained a trade surplus with the United States. The trade gap was most severe in the case of China, whose imports to the United States amounted to four times the value of U.S. exports to the People's Republic. Canada and Mexico, wedded to the U.S. markets by proximity and the North American Free Trade Agreement (NAFTA), remained the leading destinations of U.S.

Table 11.2 Top Ten U.S. Trading Partners, 2009

Country	Total trade (billions of U.S. dollars)	Import volume (billions of U.S. dollars)	Export volume (billions of U.S. dollars)	Bilateral trade balance (billions of U.S. dollars)
Canada	$430	$225	$205	−$20
China	413	325	88	−237
Mexico	306	177	129	−48
Japan	147	96	51	−45
Germany	114	71	43	−28
United Kingdom	94	48	46	−2
South Korea	68	39	29	−10
France	61	34	26	−8
Netherlands	48	16	32	16
Brazil	46	20	26	6

SOURCE: U.S. Census Bureau, *Foreign Trade Statistics: Top Trading Partners*, Year-to-Date, December 2009, www.census.gov/foreign-trade/statistics/highlights/top/top0912yr.html.

exports while adding a combined $68 billion to the U.S. trade deficit. The United States, meanwhile, continued to manage close trade relations—and a chronic trade deficit—with Japan, despite long-standing efforts by Washington to reach "fair trade" with Tokyo. Other major trading partners, including India, Italy, and Venezuela, also enjoyed trade surpluses with the United States in 2009.

The conduct of trade policy is a prime example of a "two-level game" (Putnam 1988). In this game, officials in the executive branch negotiate simultaneously with foreign leaders and domestic stakeholders, including business firms, labor unions, and members of Congress. Because the terms of prospective trade agreements must be acceptable to parties at both levels if those agreements are to be approved and ratified, negotiators must be sure to resolve everyone's concerns to the greatest extent possible. At the same time, the foreign governments and domestic actors involved recognize the benefits of expanded trade and know compromises and trade-offs have to be made (see Chapter 3).

Global Trade Politics

As economic globalization has broken down the walls between domestic, regional, and world markets, the global politics of trade has become increasingly vital to the security of the United States. Cooperative trade relations foster goodwill between the United States and other nations, while creating incentives for stable political ties and the coordination of security policies. The interdependence resulting from economic ties, though creating occasional tensions, enhances the prospects for broader bilateral cooperation. Conversely, economic interdependence allows disruptions in one region to spread more easily to other regions, which happened during the 1997 East Asian economic crisis that continues to suppress global demand today. Increases in foreign tariffs evoke strong reactions in other countries, making trade wars a constant possibility (Krueger 1996). The United States and the European Union, representing the two largest centers of world trade, engage in a contentious trade rivalry, even while cooperating on most matters of international security.

The management of foreign economic relations, always a vital aspect of U.S. foreign policy, assumed even greater importance after the United States established itself as a formidable agricultural and industrial power early in the twentieth century. The nation's population had recently surpassed 100 million, in large part because of a wave of European immigration at the turn of the century, which brought a much-needed influx of workers to support the country's rapid industrial expansion. By the early 1920s, the United States was producing more steel, oil, and automobiles than the rest of the world combined.

The decimation of other major economies during World War II allowed the United States to assume a decisive role in creating today's market-driven world economy. American banks financed much of Europe's reconstruction in the post-war period, and the emerging threat of Soviet-style communism only reinforced Washington's drive to promote capitalism and open trade markets. In 1947 the industrialized states met in Havana, Cuba, and created the International Trade

Organization (ITO) to encourage and regulate world trade. But the U.S. Senate found this organization, like the League of Nations in 1919, too threatening to U.S. sovereignty and refused to ratify its founding treaty. As a fallback position, the United States supported the General Agreement on Tariffs and Trade (GATT), which later served as the primary vehicle of market reforms and the forerunner of the WTO. The GATT negotiations, or "rounds," were based on the principle of **most-favored-nation trading status**—that is, the provision of equal market access and terms of trade to all states participating in the GATT system.

As described elsewhere, the United States assumed primary responsibility for managing global monetary policies through the IMF and development policies through the World Bank. After World War II, the United States supported foreign currencies by basing their values on the U.S. dollar, which the nation backed up with its gold reserves. Then in 1971, rising inflation, along with the high costs of the Vietnam War, prompted President Richard Nixon to abandon this **gold standard.** In its absence, a system of **floating exchange rates** came into being that determined the value of one country's currency on the basis of the value of other currencies on foreign exchange markets. Meanwhile, the U.S. government still provided the largest share of IMF and World Bank funds and maintained the greatest influence over their policies.

In 1973, the Nixon administration confronted an economic challenge posed by the Organization of the Petroleum Exporting Countries (OPEC), the cartel whose embargo on oil exports sparked high inflation and a protracted economic recession across the industrialized world for the next decade. As the largest oil importer, the United States was especially hard-hit by the OPEC embargo, which was directed toward all supporters of Israel in its latest military conflict against neighboring Arab countries. The dependence of the United States on Middle East oil led President Jimmy Carter, in the late 1970s, to accelerate the development of new sources of supply, reward energy conservation, and promote the development of renewable energy such as solar power. To Carter, the energy crisis was "the moral equivalent of war" (see Rothgeb 2001, ch. 7).

Subsequent strains on the U.S. economy in the 1980s chipped away at the nation's commitment to free trade. The United States became a victim of its own success during this period as newly industrialized countries took advantage of open U.S. markets to hasten their own economic growth. Japan and other East Asian states kept their markets largely closed to foreign competition while flooding export markets with low-cost, highly subsidized goods. The result was a rapidly growing trade deficit in the United States, whose industries stagnated in several key sectors such as steel, textiles, and consumer electronics. Although the U.S. automobile industry retained its sales edge with the help of federal assistance, Japan enjoyed a steadily growing market share by selling smaller and more fuel-efficient vehicles than those sold by the "big three" U.S. automakers, Chrysler, Ford, and General Motors (see Nelson 1996).

The end of the Cold War in 1991 prompted President Clinton to base U.S. foreign policy on "geoeconomics." Bolstered by his success in 1993 in launching the NAFTA trade bloc, Clinton succeeded again in 1995 by securing congressional support for the creation of the WTO (see Lanoszka 2009). His push for free trade, however, produced its own counterreaction in the form of the antiglobalization movement. By taking to the streets during the 1999 WTO meetings in Seattle, antiglobalization protesters drew considerable public support from workers, environmentalists, human rights advocates, and other transnational interest groups. These protesters, supported by mass publics in many developing countries, argued that the WTO-sponsored trade agreements neglected environmental concerns and the rights of workers. Furthermore, these critics charged, open markets were fine for the United States, with its huge corporations, technological superiority, and economies of scale, but perilous for their own countries. *Globalization,* in this view, was a code word for *Americanization* (see Hayden and el-Ojeili 2005).

The resulting tensions boiled over in September 2003, when the representatives of dozens of developing countries walked out of global trade talks in Cancun, Mexico. These delegates, angry over barriers to the U.S. and European agricultural markets, refused to negotiate further on a sweeping accord with the WTO. The more than $12 billion in annual U.S. farm subsidies, they claimed, negated the comparable levels of U.S. foreign aid to these impoverished regions. But the WTO, with 150 member states, proved unable to convince the United States and the European Union to live up to their liberal principles and expose their farmers to the "invisible hand" of global competition.[4] The formal suspension of trade talks in 2006 halted a half-century of progress toward open trade markets, a primary catalyst of economic globalization.

Still, the United States is inextricably bound by the rulings of the WTO, which wields enormous *supranational,* or legal, authority over its member states. Just as Congress effectively waived its constitutional power to regulate trade, the White House routinely defers to WTO demands for changes in U.S. trade policies, even when they have harmed important domestic groups. In its first decade, the WTO ruled against the United States in sixty-eight of seventy-one cases brought before the trade body. The fact that the U.S. government made the required changes in fifty-nine of those cases, opening its markets more fully to foreign competition, represents a "triumph of globalism" over domestic politics in U.S. trade policy (Kirshner 2005, 498). As the next section reveals, however, the WTO cannot supplant domestic politics and interests entirely, because they represent essential elements of democratic governance and civil society.

Domestic Trade Politics

Trade policy is also contested domestically within all levels of U.S. government and across civil society. President Bush illustrated this point in March 2002 when he raised tariffs on foreign-made steel to satisfy the demands of domestic producers who had complained about low-cost steel from overseas. Although Bush

---

4. During a time when nearly half the world's population survived on less than $2 a day, *Time* magazine reported that a European cow received an estimated $2.50 a day in farm subsidies from the European Union (Robinson 2005).

gained political support in Pennsylvania, a "battleground state" he needed for reelection, he alienated automakers in Michigan, another battleground state, because the higher tariffs forced them to pay more for steel. When the president reversed his decision and lowered the tariffs in 2003, he experienced equal, but opposite gains and losses politically. Domestic politics are also at play when individual states compete with each other to lure foreign firms and the jobs their ventures would create.

Early in the history of the United States, two opposing views of trade policy vied for government support. Economic nationalists believed the nation should protect its domestic market from foreign competition and seek to become economically self-sufficient. Alexander Hamilton, the first U.S. Treasury secretary and a strong proponent of this view, felt the United States required a strong industrial base that could be used for military purposes in case of a challenge from abroad. By contrast, economic liberals favored a free trade policy more in keeping with the nation's distrust of an activist federal government, especially in economic affairs. Thomas Jefferson, for example, believed that living standards everywhere would be enhanced by the creation of a global division of labor in which each country's producers would

A striking U.S. autoworker pickets outside the Ford Motor Company's Dearborn, Michigan, world headquarters in January 2005. The worker, Danny Hearod, joined a thousand other members of the United Auto Workers in protesting Ford's plan to relocate production of Lincoln sedans from Wixom, Michigan, to Mexico. Labor prices are relatively low in developing countries, and workers are rarely supported by unions, which makes these areas attractive destinations for jobs "exported" by U.S. firms.

contribute in areas drawing on their unique strengths. David Ricardo and other early advocates of economic globalization later refined this notion of **comparative advantage** (see Heilbroner 1999).

Although early U.S. leaders embraced Jefferson's view in principle, Hamilton prevailed in practice. The government subsidized and protected "infant industries" from foreign competition, while encouraging large-scale agricultural production that would make Americans self-sufficient in this crucial economic sector. These policies remained in place as the United States expanded its territory throughout the nineteenth century and completed the transition to an industrialized society. By the early twentieth century, the United States had become a formidable economic power that was capable of tipping the balance of two world wars in its favor.

Since the United States has become an economic giant, Congress, despite its constitutional power to "regulate commerce," has largely deferred to the executive branch. This deference has stemmed from a painful chapter in U.S. economic history in the 1920s, when trade wars broke out among the major industrial powers. Members of Congress jumped into the fray in 1930 by passing the **Smoot-Hawley Tariff Act,** which dramatically increased tariffs on goods coming into the country.[5] The act, designed to strengthen domestic firms and bolster the nation's economic strength, instead reduced the volume of U.S. trade by nearly 70 percent and helped to plunge the U.S. and world economies into the Great Depression.

Two lessons emerged from the Smoot-Hawley debacle. First, members of Congress learned that the United States bore the primary responsibility for promoting and sustaining global economic growth. As the locomotive of the world economy, the United States could not engage in the trade wars so common among the smaller economic powers. Second, legislators recognized that constituent pressure for trade protections prevented them from living up to this global responsibility. Although protecting domestic firms from overseas competition made political sense, such actions stunted global commerce and economic growth.

This second lesson led Congress to pass the Reciprocal Trade Agreement of 1934, which shifted responsibility for trade agreements to the executive branch. The legislation presumed that presidents, in representing the "national interest," could better withstand the parochial pressures than legislators, with their closer contact to constituents. In the decades that followed, the occupants of the White House became the chief advocates of a liberal trade regime in which all countries were encouraged to open their markets to foreign goods and services.

Support for this position among Republicans and Democrats changed drastically in the last half-century. During the late nineteenth century, Republicans generally favored government intervention in the economy, while Democrats believed the "invisible hand" of market forces should dictate foreign economic relations. The parties then reversed roles as the United States emerged as an industrialized society early in the twentieth century. These alignments solidified late in the twentieth century with the expansion of the Republican power base across the southern and interior western states. Republicans also established voting blocs in the sprawling suburban areas surrounding major cities. The political power of Democrats was concentrated in the Northeast and Pacific Coast states and in the inner cities. Unfortunately for the Democratic Party, the clout of labor unions began to fade as factories closed in large numbers, either moving to non-unionized southern states, exporting their jobs to low-cost labor markets abroad, or shutting down entirely.

---

5. This measure raised the average tax on imports from 39 percent to 53 percent of their value. Other countries retaliated with higher tariffs of their own, prompting the volume of global exports to plummet from $5.2 billion in 1929 to $1.6 billion in 1932. Unemployment in the United States soared, peaking at 32 percent in 1932 and idling nearly one in every three workers (Rothgeb 2001, 38–39).

Point/Counterpoint
FREE TRADE VS. FAIR TRADE

A major fault line in U.S. foreign economic policy is that between free trade and fair trade. The two approaches have been in conflict since the United States emerged as a major trading power. But historical experience has hardly resolved this conflict, which remains stronger than ever in the globalized economy of the twenty-first century.

Advocates of free trade contend that the United States should promote a world economy in which goods and services move freely across national boundaries. "Wherever globalization has taken hold, there has been a measurable improvement in incomes and working conditions," claims the Center for Trade Policy Studies, an offshoot of the Cato Institute. "The historical record is very clear that free trade bestows many benefits to the average person.... While there are inevitable short-term transition costs in some sectors of the economy, the long-term benefits of free trade for all far outweigh such costs."

Opponents of free trade argue that open markets are not "fair" because they benefit the United States and other major industrialized nations at the expense of less-developed countries. The U.S. Green Party believes that trade rules "must always comply with higher laws of human rights, as well as economic and labor rights established by the Universal Declaration of Human Rights.... In a Fair Trade regime ... the United States would acknowledge the protection of human rights, ecological systems, and local cultures, as an essential first principle."

The Cato Institute, a conservative think tank, believes that while fair trade "sounds good in theory, in practice, the term is really a code word for protectionism. Fair trade, as the term is now used, usually means government intervention to direct, control, or restrict trade." The Green Party and other fair trade proponents agree that trade must be "restricted" in many cases—against countries that abuse human rights and exploit workers, for example. They also agree that U.S. trade should be "protectionist" if it means protecting the economic rights and living conditions of workers in the United States and abroad.

The U.S. government generally upholds the principle of free trade, reflecting the nation's political culture, which favors private property over government regulation. This position creates tensions on the international level, however, as the U.S. system draws in citizens of other countries through closer economic ties. As a result, trade policy in the United States has consequences throughout the world.

SOURCES: Center for Trade Policy Studies, "Free Trade FAQs," www.freetrade.org/faqs/faqs.html; Green Party of the United States, "International Resolution of the Green Party of the United States, Calling for Fair Trade and Opposing 'FTAA'—Free Trade of the Americas" (November 2003), www.gp.org/committees/intl/ftaa_declaration.htm.

Free marketers remained dominant in the executive branch until economic growth stagnated in the 1970s. Japan's rapid rise as the second-largest world economy during this period was fueled by neomercantilist government policies, including high tariffs and **nontariff barriers** such as industry subsidies, import quotas, and favorable regulations that effectively shut out foreign products. Japanese car manufacturers such as Toyota and Honda captured much of the U.S. market share by producing fuel-efficient, reliable, and relatively inexpensive vehicles, which were in high demand as gasoline prices soared. Despite this challenge, automakers in the United States continued to produce larger, gas-guzzling vehicles.

Heightened trade competition in the 1970s prompted Congress to provide presidents with "fast-track authority," later renamed **trade promotion authority,** for use in negotiating trade agreements with foreign governments. Congress first granted President Gerald Ford this authority with the Trade Reform Act of 1974, and legislators renewed this authority five times over the next three decades (O'Halloran 1993; Destler 1995). Under these provisions, the relevant committees were given no more than forty-five days to review trade agreements once the president submitted them. The House and the Senate then had fifteen days to approve or reject the deals without amendments. The act also elevated the role of the U.S. trade representative, who gained cabinet rank (Dryden 1995).

As plants closed across the United States, eliminating the jobs of millions of U.S. workers, the free trade consensus quickly gave way to "a recurring suspicion that free trade is not necessarily desirable at all costs" (Gibson 2000, 114). Appeals for relief were directed largely at Congress, which responded in the 1980s and 1990s by passing several bills designed to stabilize the U.S. trade balance. The Omnibus Trade and Competitiveness Act of 1988 required presidents to identify the most serious violators of free trade and propose steps to retaliate against violations that went beyond formal tariffs to include a variety of nontariff barriers. The bitter domestic politics of the Clinton years extended to the trade realm, as Republicans joined with labor-backed Democrats in denying Clinton the trade promotion authority granted to his predecessors.[6]

After George W. Bush came to power in 2001, the Republican-led Congress promptly granted him trade promotion authority. While pledging allegiance to free trade, Bush maintained the agricultural subsidies and tariffs that angered developing countries and led to the collapse of WTO talks. Bush also faced domestic resistance after the 2006 midterm elections that brought Democrats control of Congress. Their calls for "fair trade" signified their opposition to future deals that would cost U.S. workers their jobs or allow foreign producers to expand their markets by keeping out foreign competition, exploiting workers, or harming the environment. President Obama supported this position when he took office in January 2009, although his energies were focused initially on

---

6. The two groups did so for very different reasons. Democrats were concerned that the president would not protect U.S. jobs in his pursuit of economic globalization. As for the Republicans, some feared that Clinton would surrender too much power over U.S. trade to the WTO; others simply wanted to embarrass the president by tying his hands on the foreign policy issue most important to him.

stabilizing U.S. financial institutions and providing stimulus funds to private firms and government agencies at the federal, state, and local levels. Amid the chaos that accompanied the financial crisis, the U.S. government assumed primary ownership of the ailing automakers General Motors and Chrysler, whose imminent bankruptcies would have greatly increased unemployment while sharply accelerating the erosion of America's manufacturing sector.

National Interests and Foreign Aid

Another major component of U.S. foreign economic policy is **foreign aid,** or the economic resources that affluent governments give to developing countries on terms unavailable to the recipients in commercial markets. Virtually every nation-state, rich or poor, is an aid donor or recipient. This pattern continues amid sweeping changes in world politics during the past two decades, including the end of the Cold War, the onset of the war on terrorism, and the more recent financial crisis.

The high levels of poverty that continue to plague much of the world necessitated this global aid network. As noted previously, nearly half of the world's population lives on less than $2 a day. More than 80 percent live in low- or middle-income countries, where they produce less than a quarter of global output. Although many parts of the world experienced unprecedented prosperity during the globalization boom of the 1990s, and although many developing countries joined the ranks of "emerging markets," the gap between the richest and poorest peoples has continued to widen. Wealthy governments have responded to these inescapable facts, due to growing pressure from transnational interest groups, the United Nations, and regional organizations. The higher aid volumes of recent years are directed toward five general objectives:

- Stimulating market-based economic growth along the lines of liberal theory described earlier

- Combating the spread of HIV/AIDS and other infectious diseases, particularly in sub-Saharan Africa

- Easing the burden of international debt facing nations in extreme poverty

- Supporting emergency response and reconstruction after natural disasters, including the January 2010 earthquake in Haiti that left more than 200,000 dead, another 300,000 injured, and about 1 million homeless

- Countering the threat of international terrorism.

The United States, which provided the largest volume of foreign assistance during the Cold War, continues to maintain that status today. Its $26.8 billion contribution of development aid in 2008 was more than double the $13.1 billion in aid provided by Japan, the second-largest aid donor (OECD 2010). Still, the

Figure 11.3 Levels of Sacrifice among Top Fifteen Major Aid Donors, 2008

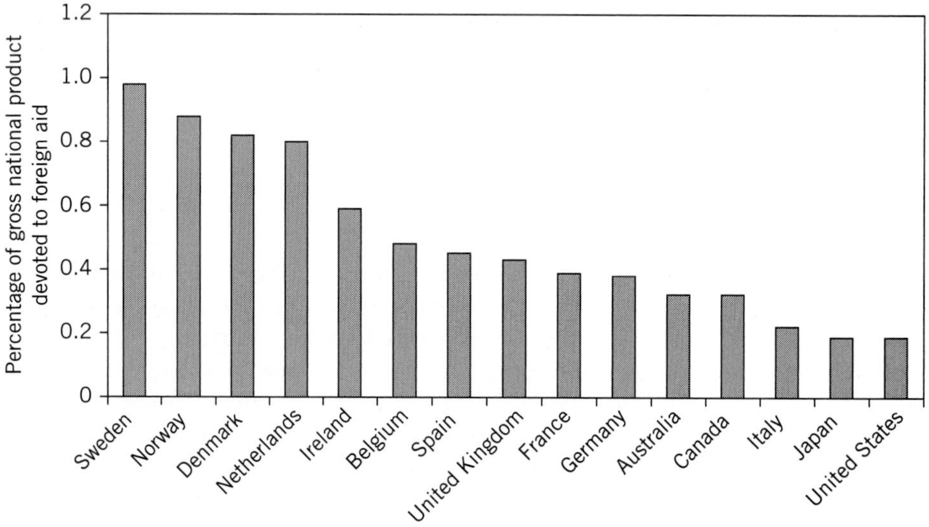

SOURCE: Organisation for Economic Co-operation and Development, *Statistical Annex of the 2010 Development Co-operation Report* (Paris: OECD, 2010).

United States ranks near the bottom of industrialized countries in terms of the proportion of national output devoted to foreign aid (see Figure 11.3). As a result, the world's most prolific aid donor is also widely considered its biggest miser.[7]

Although foreign aid represents less than 1 percent of the U.S. federal budget, this highly controversial program generates strong opposition from many political leaders and private citizens. As John Montgomery (1962, 197) observed nearly half a century ago, "In few areas of American public life is there so little national consensus on purposes as in foreign aid." Today's critics of foreign aid make three central arguments: (1) domestic needs should be taken care of first; (2) aid funds only reward incompetence and corruption abroad; and (3) past programs have not prevented the developing world from slipping further into poverty and social distress (Easterly 2006). A fourth, related argument is that the private agencies delivering the most aid-funded programs place their institutional interests above the interests of the starving and war-torn societies they serve (Maren 1997).

Supporters of foreign aid acknowledge the failure of past aid programs to stem the poverty of developing countries. They believe, however, that commercial

7. Spending by the U.S. government on foreign aid falls into five functional categories (listed in order of volume in 2005): development assistance, designed to hasten recipients' long-term economic growth; economic support funds, given to countries of strong political and security interest; military assistance, including military supplies and training; humanitarian relief, provided to nations recovering from natural disasters, epidemics, or other forms of acute stress; and multilateral aid, or the funds given to UN agencies, the World Bank, and other intergovernmental organizations.

markets contain insufficient capital to cover the basic human needs of billions of citizens worldwide, and that effective and well-coordinated programs can create the conditions for long-term growth. A world without foreign aid, they argue further, would constitute a moral breakdown among the world's affluent governments and societies.

Motivations for U.S. Aid

Tensions have always existed between the humanitarian and self-serving functions of U.S. foreign aid. At one level, generosity by the United States toward impoverished peoples is consistent with its historic self-image as a messianic "city on the hill." At another level, U.S. aid contradicts the self-help principles of many Americans as reflected in their historic distrust of government and their skepticism toward social welfare programs. To garner support for foreign aid from a skeptical public, the U.S. government has consistently identified national interests as a primary rationale for aid programs. After the Cold War, the U.S. Agency for International Development (USAID) issued a report entitled *Why Foreign Aid?* The agency answered this question bluntly: "Because it is in the United States' own interest" (USAID 1992, 1).

As a reluctant but leading contributor of foreign aid on an absolute level, the United States closely ties its aid contributions to the pursuit of its own prosperity and military security. This linkage between self-interest and the needs of aid recipients is not unique to the United States. Japan, for example, has routinely used foreign aid as an instrument to expand its trade ties across East Asia, while France and Great Britain have used aid to retain influence within their former African colonies (Hook 1995). That said, all aid donors expect a certain degree of political allegiance from their recipients. These patterns were evident more than four decades ago to political economist David Baldwin (1966, 3), who observed that "foreign aid is first and foremost a technique of statecraft. It is, in other words, a means by which one nation tries to get other nations to act in desired ways.... Thus, foreign aid policy is foreign policy, and as such it is a subject of controversy in both the international and the domestic political arenas."

Prior to the Cold War, U.S. foreign aid generally "consisted of admonition and was consequently neither expensive nor effective" (O'Leary 1967, 5). Examples of early U.S. initiatives included security assistance to Greece in the 1820s and disaster aid for victims of Ireland's famine in the 1840s. In the early stages of World War II, U.S. military hardware to Great Britain bolstered the Allied defense against Nazi Germany. Not until after the war did the U.S. aid program assume global proportions. Through the Marshall Plan, the United States helped to rebuild decimated states in Western Europe and Asia.[8] And through the military

---

8. The Marshall Plan is widely regarded as one of the most successful efforts in the history of U.S. foreign policy. The reason, Samuel P. Huntington (1970/1971) believed, was that the Marshall Plan was "(a) directed to specific and well-defined goals; (b) limited to a geographic area of vital concern to the U.S.; and (c) designed for a limited period of time."

Coffee growers in Yalí, Nicaragua, learn a new milling technique during an exhibition sponsored by the U.S. Agency for International Development. The agency, which has helped these growers gain access to the expanding market in specialty coffees, conducts similar economic development programs in many other poor countries. When funds for these programs are combined with multilateral and military assistance, the United States is by far the largest source of foreign aid in the world.

aid programs derived from the Truman Doctrine, the United States utilized a second form of foreign assistance in the pursuit of its foreign policy goals.

Two motivations propelled U.S. foreign aid during this period. First, aid flows were designed to strengthen anticommunist regimes throughout the world and ultimately to tip the balance of world power in favor of the capitalist states. Second, the United States sought to help emerging nation-states it hoped would become allies. The Cold War coincided with the decolonization of Africa and the creation of new nation-states in other developing regions, such as India in South Asia and the Philippines and Indonesia in the Pacific region. These new states faced many obstacles on the path to political and economic development— obstacles they could not overcome without external assistance.

In this respect, the East-West struggle of the Cold War intersected with emerging North-South tensions, or those between wealthy, industrialized countries (located largely in the Northern Hemisphere) and the poor nations of the developing world (located largely in the Southern Hemisphere). The United States had strong interests along *both* dimensions: in defeating the communist powers, in the first, and in creating allies and potential trading partners among the developing countries, in the second. Through foreign aid, the United States supported almost every country outside of the Soviet Union's sphere of influence. By 1990, the U.S. government had transferred $374 billion in loans and grants to more than a hundred developing countries, of which $233 billion was in the form of economic assistance (USAID 1992).

The U.S. aid efforts in the post–World War II period that focused on the reconstruction of industrialized states and the establishment of a global alliance of anticommunist states shifted, beginning in the 1960s, to emphasize the social and economic aspects of decolonization and "state-building" as well (see Packenham 1973). President John Kennedy redirected U.S. aid toward broader developmental goals. In doing so, he supported the Foreign Assistance Act of 1961, the Alliance for Progress, the Peace Corps, and other initiatives aimed at promoting political and socioeconomic development in developing countries, particularly in Latin America. However, the United States largely discarded these goals as it became mired in the Vietnam War, which claimed nearly half of all U.S. aid flows until the mid-1970s.

President Jimmy Carter hoped to revive the humanitarian elements of U.S. foreign aid, but other strategic concerns overtook his aid plans. The Camp David Accords between Israel and Egypt, although a major foreign policy achievement, came at a huge price tag: about $5 billion annually in foreign aid to the two countries. These commitments overwhelmed the U.S. aid budget, reducing funds available for other regions and development priorities. Strategic concerns prevailed during the 1980s as well. The Reagan administration used foreign aid, along with steep increases in defense spending, to support anticommunist regimes and thus increase pressure on the Soviet Union in the revived Cold War.

The Cold War's demise in 1991 deprived many bilateral aid programs—and U.S. foreign policy in general—of their previously stated rationales. The absence of the containment of communism as the guiding principle behind U.S. policy raised new doubts about many established programs, and the needs of the former Soviet Union and its Eastern European clients imposed new demands on limited aid funds. Bill Clinton's efforts to direct funds toward "sustainable development" and democracy in the developing world fell victim to deep cuts imposed by Congress. Not until after the September 2001 terrorist attacks did the government revive its aid program, as President Bush sought to reward allies in the war on terrorism with economic and military assistance and to reward the developing countries that followed the U.S. model of economic and political development.

Like his predecessors, President Bush came into office with his own agenda for U.S. foreign aid. Skeptical of past programs, Bush demanded that future recipients be held accountable for the money received from Washington. Aid recipients, in his view, should establish democratic governments and market economies freed from government intervention at home and barriers to foreign trade. After

Table 11.3 Top Recipients of U.S. Development Aid, 1984–2005

1984–1985	1994–1995	2004–2005
Israel	Israel	Iraq
Egypt	Egypt	Afghanistan
El Salvador	Haiti	Egypt
Sudan	Jordan	Sudan
Bangladesh	Somalia	Ethiopia
Costa Rica	Palau	Jordan
Pakistan	Rwanda	Colombia
Northern Marianas	Philippines	Palestinian Admin. Areas
India	India	Uganda
Peru	Bolivia	Pakistan

SOURCE: Organisation for Economic Co-operation and Development, *Statistical Annex of the 2006 Development Co-operation Report* (Paris: OECD, 2007), www.oecd.org/document/9/0,2340,en_2649_33721_1893129_1_1_1_1,00.html.

the terrorist attacks, Bush identified international development as one of the three "pillars" of his national security strategy, along with diplomacy and defense. A policy paper released by USAID (2004, 14) called for "far-reaching reforms ... that [would] enable a country to sustain further economic and social progress without depending on foreign aid."

The 2001 terrorist attacks and subsequent global war on terrorism forced radical changes in U.S. foreign aid. Iraq and Afghanistan emerged quickly as the primary destinations of U.S. assistance, replacing the two previous leading recipients, Israel and Egypt (see Table 11.3). Iraq alone consumed more than $28 billion in aid funds in 2004 and 2005, in addition to the military costs of resisting the insurgency and growing civil war in that country. Despite the differences in aid distributions over these years, one pattern has remained consistent since the Vietnam era: significant U.S. aid to the Middle East and southern Asia (see Sharp 2006). This pattern reveals the enduring importance of these regions to U.S. foreign policy interests, in stark contrast to the more impoverished, but less strategically vital, states of sub-Saharan Africa.

Other donors, whose aid programs are coordinated by the Organisation for Economic Co-operation and Development (OECD) from its Paris base, closely monitor the U.S. government's aid policies. During the 1970s, the OECD set a standard for aid contributions, suggesting that all donors should devote at least 0.7 percent of national output to official development assistance. Only five countries—Denmark, Luxembourg, the Netherlands, Norway, and Sweden—have surpassed this level on a regular basis. The failure of the United States to meet the OECD standard—its level has averaged less than 0.2 percent in recent years—has proved to be a chronic source of tension between the United States and other aid donors.

The Millennium Challenge

The liberal critique of U.S. foreign aid is that market forces, not government programs, are the primary engines of economic growth in the developing world, and that foreign aid programs merely reward government corruption and economic mismanagement. These beliefs compel U.S. officials to require foreign aid recipients to adopt market-based economic reforms, including cutbacks in state spending, privatization and deregulation of industries, and the opening of domestic markets to foreign trade and investment. Such practices, associated collectively with the "Washington consensus," are also used as conditions for aid from international financial institutions. As a prominent World Bank (1998, 2) study concluded, "Improvements in economic institutions and policies in the developing world are the key to a quantum leap in poverty reduction."

In 2002, President Bush seized on this consensus to propose the most dramatic change in U.S. foreign aid since the passage of the Foreign Assistance Act of 1961. He proposed the creation of a new government corporation, the Millennium Challenge Corporation (MCC), to provide development assistance only to countries with a proven track record of economic reform. Unlike USAID, with its large staff of development experts and its global network of private consultants, the MCC would resemble a philanthropic foundation whose "lean" staff would be limited to considering and approving grant applications, known as development "compacts." Also unlike USAID, the MCC would be free of the political concerns or foreign policy interests closely associated with other aid programs. The MCC's scope would be strictly economic, and its standards and performance requirements would be stated explicitly and applied universally. For their part, recipients of its aid would be left alone in proposing and carrying out approved projects such as modernizing farms, improving transportation networks, or expanding media coverage.

Like the Pentagon, which the White House sought to "transform" through a revolution in military technology, Bush proclaimed that the MCC would transform global development. His proposed annual budget of $5 billion by fiscal year 2006 would make the MCC the primary source of U.S. foreign aid, with USAID relegated to the roles of disaster relief, rescuing "failed states," and funding foreign governments of special geopolitical concern to the United States. The MCC's contributions, Bush predicted, would greatly exceed the volume of funds provided by other governments. Furthermore, its promotion of a "business model" of development would quickly take hold globally. The Republican-led Congress approved the creation of the MCC in January 2004. Like those of other profit-making corporations, the MCC's headquarters were located in a commercial district of Washington, D.C., not in a government complex.

The MCC got off to a slow start, however. Members of Congress, despite their general enthusiasm for the new corporation, approved funding at a far lower level than that proposed by the White House (Tarnoff 2007, 28). Fewer than one hundred staff members were hired in the MCC's first year, and only eight aid compacts were approved by the end of 2005. Several reasons account for this slow start. Many of the poor countries that applied for help proved ill-equipped either to plan or to carry out elaborate development projects at the fast pace projected by U.S. officials. Meanwhile, the MCC's "lean" staff quickly fell behind schedule in approving MCC-sponsored projects, and it was forced to compete "with a multitude of other funders and programs" (Herrling and Radelet 2005, 2–3). Still, "the incentive structure created by the MCC has captured the attention of candidate countries and has begun to stimulate positive political reform" (Collins 2009, 374).[9]

In 2006, Secretary of State Condoleezza Rice created a Bureau of Foreign Assistance that was designed to centralize the U.S. government's far-flung aid programs. This effort, however, proved discouraging, as rivalries among USAID, the MCC, and other agencies continued. Recent struggles between USAID and the Defense Department over the delivery of aid programs have further hindered a united front on foreign aid. Proposals to rewrite the Foreign Assistance Act of 1961 (Radelet 2008) and to create a cabinet-level Department of Global Development (Brainard 2007) failed to spur reform. To three former USAID directors (Atwood, McPherson, and Natsios 2008, 123), rhetorical calls by U.S. leaders to make global development a central priority of U.S. foreign policy have "not been realized because of organizational and programmatic chaos." The persistent lack of focus in U.S. aid policy, a by-product of conflicting national priorities and multiple centers of power, prevents the United States from achieving its goal of "transforming" global development.

Economic Sanctions as a Policy Tool

Economic sanctions are material penalties imposed on target countries in the areas of trade, aid, investments, or other aspects of foreign economic relations. Presidents may impose sanctions by executive order, or sanctions may originate in congressional legislation. The United States, whose vast wealth and domestic markets make its sanctions especially costly, uses its economic leverage in these cases to modify the behavior of foreign countries in ways consistent with U.S. foreign policy objectives (Cox and Drury 2006).

Economic sanctions are an attractive foreign policy tool because they provide the United States with a means to exert pressure on foreign governments without resorting to war.[10] In this sense, sanctions send a signal to their targets that the U.S. government is serious about the dispute in question (Lektzian and Sprecher 2007). Sanctions play a strategic role when they are backed up by

---

9. By the end of 2009, the MCC had completed economic support programs for eight countries: Albania, Burkina Faso, Jordan, Malawi, Paraguay, the Philippines, Tanzania, and Zambia. Another thirteen countries remained engaged in such projects, whose overall cost approached $500 million.

10. Democratic governments resort to economic sanctions more often than nondemocracies, and their sanctions target repressive states much more often than democracies. This pattern suggests a separate "economic peace" among democracies that is similar to their historic lack of military conflict (see Lektzian and Souva 2003 and Cox and Drury 2006).

promises of military action in the event the sanctions do not produce the desired changes in behavior. More generally, sanctions serve a symbolic function by identifying the target state and establishing the moral supremacy of the "sanctioning community" (Addis 2003).

In addition to the mixed motives underlying specific sanctions, their costs and benefits cannot be calculated simply in terms of trade and investment volumes (the "costs") or the required reforms demanded of target states (the "benefits"). A complete assessment must take into account indirect costs and benefits, including the symbolic value of placing the offending states on notice. Also difficult to measure, but critical nevertheless, are the relative costs and expected benefits of the alternative foreign policy tactics that may be used in the absence of sanctions (Baldwin 1999/2000).

Forms and Functions of Sanctions

Economic sanctions, which may assume several forms, are often used by governments in various combinations (see Table 11.4). The most common types of sanctions are trade embargoes and boycotts, increases in export quotas, revocation of most-favored-nation status, and other measures that restrict bilateral trade. These measures are *negative* in nature, involving the "stick" of economic penalties. The United States also may employ the "carrot" of *positive* sanctions, such as increases in foreign aid or trade, to modify the behavior of other governments (Baldwin 1985, 40–44).

Economic sanctions vary in other ways as well. In some instances, the United States joins with other countries, intergovernmental organizations, or both to

Table 11.4 Types and Examples of U.S. Economic Sanctions

Type	Description	Historical example
Boycott	Restriction on the import of another country's goods or services	Ban on diamond imports from Sierra Leone, used to finance domestic insurrection (2001)
Divestment	Withdrawal of assets from a foreign country; ban on future investments	Ban on investments from South Africa to penalize its apartheid policy of minority rule (1986)
Embargo	Refusal to provide one's own goods and services to a potential customer abroad	Grain embargo against the Soviet Union following its invasion of Afghanistan (1979)
Freezing assets	Impoundment of domestically held financial assets owned by the government or citizens of target country	Freezing of Iraqi assets in the United States following Iraq's invasion of Kuwait (1990)
Suspending foreign aid	Refusal to honor previous commitments to provide economic or military assistance	Aid to Pakistan suspended because of concerns about its nuclear ambitions (1977)

impose *multilateral* sanctions. In the 1990s, for example, sanctions imposed by the United Nations globally isolated the economies of the former Yugoslavia and Iraq. Otherwise, the United States acts alone in imposing *unilateral* sanctions. Although other countries may act independently to impose their own sanctions against the offending state, there is no concerted effort to do so in these cases. Finally, sanctions may be imposed with very specific demands—that a country withdraw from a country it invaded recently, for example. Or the sanctions may be accompanied by broader demands, such as when the imposing state insists on a change in the policies, or even the regime type, of the offending state.

During the Cold War, economic sanctions served as one of the most potent weapons used by the United States against the Soviet Union. American officials imposed stringent restrictions on commercial relations with Moscow, and they expected their allies to do the same. As the Cold War thawed, these allies resumed trade across the iron curtain, though at a lower level than before the conflict began. Earlier, the United States had temporarily eased sanctions against Moscow as part of the Nixon administration's **linkage strategy,** which tied a promise of future economic concessions to improved Soviet behavior on human rights and key foreign policy issues.

Prominent Cases of U.S. Sanctions

The Soviet Union hardly stood alone as a target of U.S. economic sanctions during the Cold War, as the examples noted in Table 11.4 demonstrate. After the Cold War, the use of sanctions continued, often preceding U.S. military actions against a nation, such as Iraq and the former Yugoslavia. In many other instances, such as in Pakistan, threats of sanctions became a routine part of bilateral diplomacy both during and after the Cold War.

Cuba. Fidel Castro's rise to power in 1959 and his creation of a communist government in Cuba, formerly a close U.S. economic and military ally, prompted sweeping economic sanctions by the United States. The Trading with the Enemy Act of 1963 prohibited nearly all trade with the Castro regime. The penalties for breaking these laws were substantial: up to ten years in prison, $1 million in corporate fines, and $250,000 in individual fines. The **Helms-Burton Act,** passed by Congress in the 1990s, imposed even stronger penalties. The act targeted foreign countries benefiting economically from confiscated U.S. property in Cuba. These measures, politically popular in Congress and the White House, still sparked criticism that they had done little to weaken Castro's hold on power after nearly half a century. In addition, countries accused the United States of maintaining a double standard, isolating Cuba while economically "engaging" China, another communist state.

Pakistan. The case of Pakistan reveals that, in some instances, the U.S. government must be careful not to alienate less affluent, but strategically vital countries (see Kux 1998). In 1977, fears of nuclear proliferation in South Asia prompted the Carter administration to suspend aid deliveries to Pakistan. The Soviet invasion of Afghanistan later that year, however, changed the strategic calculus and prompted Ronald Reagan to renew aid to Pakistan in 1981. This aid stopped once again when the Soviets withdrew from Afghanistan in 1989. Pakistan's detonation of a nuclear device in 1998 prompted the United States and other UN members to impose sanctions against both Pakistan and India, whose nuclear weapons test provoked the Pakistani response. The terrorist attacks of September 11, 2001, elevated Pakistan once again to the status of a U.S. "strategic partner." The Bush administration lifted the sanctions shortly after the attacks, while providing millions of dollars in military equipment and training to the regime of President Pervez Musharraf.

Iraq. The UN-sponsored sanctions against Iraq, which were imposed upon Saddam Hussein's invasion of Kuwait in 1990 and lasted until the U.S.-led invasion of Iraq in 2003, remain controversial. President George H. W. Bush first acted by declaring a national emergency and issuing an executive order forbidding future trade with Iraq. Later, however, critics labeled these sanctions against Iraq as "one of the decade's great crimes" (Rieff 2003b, 41). The denial of aid eventually led to the deaths of hundreds of thousands of Iraqi civilians from malnutrition and disease. Critics of the sanctions found the scope of these casualties especially troubling because Saddam and his advisers continued to enjoy lavish lifestyles, clearly undisturbed by the sanctions. The worldwide sanctions, among the most comprehensive in history, were viewed as successful by observers who credited them with preventing Saddam from developing weapons of mass destruction (Lopez and Cortright 2004).

Libya. Although lifting economic sanctions attracts less attention than imposing them, both steps are equally significant to U.S. foreign policy. In April 2004, for example, the Bush administration lifted many of the sanctions against Libya that had been in effect for nearly a decade. The White House praised Muammar Qaddafi, Libya's leader, for dismantling his nation's manufacturing facilities for weapons of mass destruction and for renouncing terrorism. The move represented a major reversal for the United States. It had previously linked Qaddafi to a variety of terrorist attacks, including the December 1988 bombing of Pan Am flight 103 over Lockerbie, Scotland, that killed 259 people. President Bush cited the transformation of Qaddafi from state terrorist to trading partner as evidence that the U.S. war on terrorism was bearing fruit. In making its concessions to U.S. demands, including financial restitution to the families of the Lockerbie victims, Libya was also freed from UN sanctions.

Taken together, these and other instances of economic sanctions provide three important lessons about the utility of these measures as instruments of U.S. foreign policy. First, economic sanctions rarely have the immediate impact that their advocates desire—the collapse of Cuba's communist government, for example, or Saddam Hussein's withdrawal from Kuwait. Just 4 percent of economic sanctions examined by Robert Pape (1997) produced "significant political concessions" from their targets. A more recent study (Lektzian and Sprecher 2007) found that sanctions, rather than preventing military conflicts, make them more likely. Sanctions may, however, politically weaken the leaders in target countries (Marinov 2005), and the mere threat of sanctions often compels potential targets to change their behavior (Drezner 2003; Lacy and Niou 2004). A key factor in this regard is whether the sanctioning country has the willpower to enforce sanctions that affect its own citizens negatively (Blanchard and Ripsman 2008).

A second and morally troubling lesson is that the leaders of targeted states rarely suffer directly from sanctions, which instead tend to victimize citizens with little political power (Major and McGann 2005). American sanctions against Myanmar, passed in 2003 by Congress in the Burmese Freedom of Democracy Act, produced sharply higher poverty rates while prompting the military junta to align with China (Rarick 2006). Even **smart sanctions,** designed to punish elites rather than their most vulnerable citizens, have limited effect (Heine-Ellison 2001; Cortright and Lopez 2002; Tostensen and Bull 2002). From the perspective of utilitarian ethics, such sanctions are unethical because "the losers exceed the winners" (McGee 2003, 43). Sanctions may also be considered immoral because "using people as a means represents an inhuman form of public policy" (Rarick and Duchatelet 2008, 50).

A third and final lesson is that multilateral sanctions have a greater probability of succeeding than unilateral measures. When the United States acts alone, its targets can readily turn to other trading partners to fill the gap (see Haass 1998). As an alliance leader and a dominant presence in international financial institutions, the United States can compound its impact when like-minded states join in the imposition of sanctions. This lesson was apparent to the Bush administration as it sought over several years to compel Iran's government to suspend its development of nuclear power. The wide-ranging sanctions imposed by the United States would have little effect without similar sanctions from Russia and European countries that maintained economic relations with Iran. Still, multilateral sanctions imposed by the UN Security Council in 2006 and 2007 failed to persuade Iran's government to promptly suspend its uranium enrichment and reprocessing activities.

Conclusion

As this chapter has shown, the U.S. government pursues commerce abroad with the same vigor it promotes economic development within its borders. American leaders have always looked forward to a world in which people and governments will be intimately connected to one another by the bonds of trade and foreign investments. They have envisioned the United States as a catalyst of global commerce by producing an abundance of goods for export while craving goods from abroad and stimulating foreign economies. This vision appeared to be realized with the victory of the United States in the Cold War and the triumph of capitalism over communism as the superior form of political economy.

Recent developments, described earlier, place this economic superiority in doubt. The United States itself has suffered the downside of globalization as millions of manufacturing jobs have moved to foreign countries with lower wage rates. The chronic trade deficits still being experienced today provide further evidence that globalization is a mixed blessing for the United States. Another cause for concern is the nation's budget deficit—a result, in part, of the security costs borne by the United States to keep the peace globally and to keep oil flowing to other industrialized countries. These problems were compounded by the financial crisis of 2008, which left U.S. and other market economies close to collapse.

For now, the United States retains its status as the engine of global economic activity. This status, however, relies on the seemingly limitless appetite of American consumers for goods and services produced in other countries. Their desire for products at the lowest possible price, exemplified by the emergence of Wal-Mart as the world's largest company in terms of revenue, is entirely consistent with the borderless logic of capitalism (see Brunn 2006). Nevertheless, the reality persists that jobs must be found for American workers to replace those exported every year. As laid-off factory workers well know, service industry jobs at Home Depot and Starbucks do not pay nearly as well as those on the assembly line. Unfortunately, such jobs in heavy industry are not likely to return in large numbers, and cutbacks in state and federal budgets have reduced government support for retraining and college educations.

Meanwhile, growing challenges from overseas, however consistent with the transnational logic of capitalism, may ignite pressures at home to resurrect trade barriers in order to prevent the further hemorrhaging of American jobs. Political leaders know their careers depend on economic growth that benefits a broad cross-section of the U.S. population, not simply corporate leaders and stockholders. Despite the decline in union membership in the United States, from its high of 20 percent of the U.S. workforce in 1983 to less than 13 percent in 2003, "big labor" still provides a strong voice for economic nationalism (U.S. Department of Labor 2004). Avoiding a return to protectionism and trade wars requires effective restructuring of the U.S. economy and the revival of worldwide demand in vital areas such as East Asia, Russia, and Latin America.

As globalization inevitably spreads, the U.S. government loses the considerable leverage it enjoyed during its peak years of economic hegemony just after World War II. The nation must now contend with other states, as well as foreign-based corporations, on a more equal footing. In short, the United States must come to grips with a globalized world economy of its own making. As in the past, the outcome of the ongoing struggle over U.S. foreign economic policy will be decided in the political arena, at home and abroad.

Key Terms

balance of trade, p. 357

communism, p. 353

comparative advantage,
p. 365

economic liberalism,
p. 353

economic nationalism,
p. 353

economic sanctions, p. 376

economic statecraft,
p. 352

floating exchange rates,
p. 363

foreign aid, p. 369

gold standard, p. 363

gross domestic product
(GDP), p. 355

Helms-Burton Act, p. 378

international political
economy, p. 352

linkage strategy, p. 378

mercantilism, p. 353

most-favored-nation
trading status, p. 363

nontariff barriers,
p. 368

political economy, p. 352

smart sanctions, p. 380

Smoot-Hawley Tariff
Act, p. 366

socialism, p. 353

trade promotion
authority, p. 368

Internet References

The **Economic Policy Institute** (www.epinet.org) conducts research on global trade, globalization, NAFTA, and U.S.-China relations, as well as on other economic and budgetary policies. EPI's Web site presents statistics and policy reports on various research topics including free trade, U.S. agricultural/commercial relations, fast-track powers, and other trade and globalization issues.

The **Institute for International Economics** (www.iie.com) is a nonprofit, nonpartisan research center that focuses on international economic policy. In addition to offering statistics and information on globalization, U.S. economic policy, debt, international trade, and international investment, IIE's Web site includes policy briefs, speeches, working papers, and links to relevant topics.

The **International Monetary Fund** (www.imf.org) is a 186-member international organization that seeks to ensure international monetary cooperation, financial stability, and temporary financial assistance to needy countries. IMF's Web site provides fact sheets on lending, country statistics, glossaries of financial terms, and links to other banks and international organizations.

The **International Trade Administration** (www.ita.doc.gov) is a government agency committed to providing U.S. export and import data. ITA's Web site includes data on export growth and market expansion as well as information on national and state trade levels, balances, sectors, and regions.

The home page of the **Office of the United States Trade Representative** (www.ustr.gov) offers links and access to bilateral and multilateral trade data and events. The information on the site on NAFTA, the WTO, and free trade negotiations, in addition to speeches, testimony, trade legislation, and daily updates on international trade, is particularly helpful for further research.

(continued)

Internet References *(continued)*

The **Organisation for Economic Co-operation and Development** (www.oecd.org) is an international organization of thirty-one member countries that share a commitment to democracy and free economic markets. Included on this Web site are data links on national wealth, foreign aid and investment, and development regimes.

The **U.S. Agency for International Development** (www.usaid.gov) provides information and statistics on U.S. foreign and military aid to other countries. USAID's Web site includes detailed information on humanitarian efforts and specific mission programs to other countries. Additional research topics covered are agriculture, democratization, global health, and humanitarian mission projects. A full database of U.S. foreign aid is available for all years of aid allocation.

The mission of the **World Bank** (www.worldbank.org) is to reduce poverty and economic disparities by providing loans and financial assistance to countries around the globe. The World Bank's Web site describes the bank's specific projects and missions and provides statistics on trade, aid, poverty, and other demographic issues.

The **World Health Organization** (www.who.int), based in Geneva, Switzerland, is a significant UN agency that seeks the "attainment by all peoples of the highest possible level of health." WHO's Web site offers links describing health issues in each member country as well as detailed summaries of health care topics and problems concerning all countries.

The **World Trade Organization** (www.wto.org) is an international organization that promotes open trade relations among countries. The WTO's Web site includes information on trade regulations, industry and business sector descriptions, currency and trade statistics, and annual growth reports.

12

Transnational Policy Problems

Residents of Kunming, China, walk city streets amid dense air pollution that threatens public health across the country and contributes to global warming. Government officials in China, which has overtaken the United States as the world's leading producer of carbon dioxide emissions, argue that such pollution is a necessary cost of economic development—an argument earlier made by U.S. leaders during their own industrial revolution.

The United States manages a variety of foreign policy problems that extend beyond national defense and the pursuit of gains in the global economy. Transnational policy problems, which do not respect political boundaries and cannot be solved in isolation from other states, also confront U.S. leaders. This chapter examines the U.S. government's response to four sets of transnational problems: (1) threats to the global commons, (2) illegal immigration, (3) weapons proliferation, and (4) restrictions on human rights and democratic freedoms. Although a matter of domestic governance, the fourth problem is also transnational because of the presumed link between the treatment of citizens at home and the promotion of national values abroad. The spread of democracy has always been a stated goal of U.S. leaders, who pursue political reforms overseas by a variety of means, including military force.

The United States has a mixed record in managing transnational problems. Although government officials rhetorically support cooperative problem solving in the four areas listed, domestic self-interests often stand in the way, especially when the solutions require sacrifices by influential domestic groups or reelection-minded politicians. Throughout his presidency, George W. Bush viewed transnational civil society, including intergovernmental organizations such as the United Nations and public interest groups such as Amnesty International, as a threat to U.S. sovereignty—an ironic twist given that the United States played a catalytic role in the rise of these actors. This estrangement, which President Barack

Obama sought to overcome when he took office in 2009, prevented the nation from using its vast resources and immense clout in pursuing solutions to global problems, while giving smaller powers a ready excuse to neglect such problems themselves. These tensions are explored in greater detail in this chapter, which concludes with a general assessment of the paradox of world power as the United States wields it today and will likely do so far into the future.

Managing the Global Commons

The **global commons** is the fragile ecosystem that sustains the earth's plant and animal life. But today that system is being threatened by the world's soaring population, the depletion of finite natural resources, rampant deforestation, and the fouling of the air and water—all of which have forced countries to confront environmental decay as a major foreign policy issue. These problems are inherently transnational in scope in that pollution, as well as the loss of habitat and nonrenewable resources, ultimately affect the entire human population, not just a single nation. The rapid destruction of the Amazon rain forest, for example, is removing a vast area of vegetation needed to absorb the toxic gases in the atmosphere.

The bleak future of the Amazon rain forest is a stark lesson in the **tragedy of the commons,** a situation in which a population stands to lose a common resource from overuse unless some limiting measures are taken. In this South American region, the pace of deforestation has accelerated; between 1995 and 2000 nearly 5 million acres of land were destroyed each year (Laurance, Albernaz, and Da Costa 2001). Even worse, under a new government program, Advance Brazil, a nationwide network of highways and rail lines would open the surviving 40 percent of the rain forest to logging, housing and industrial development, and hydroelectric projects. The demise of the rain forest has grave implications for the global climate. Yet, Brazil's decision to put its own urgent and immediate needs for economic growth before long-term global concerns can be seen as rational politically. Its behavior is also consistent with the actions of the world's affluent countries, including the United States, during and after their own periods of industrialization.

In the United States, the environmental protection movement was launched at the grassroots level in the 1960s and 1970s. Citizens demanded that the government give priority to regulating and enforcing environmental quality. Rapid industrial growth earlier in the century had left urban areas shrouded in smog and many waterways so contaminated that they could not sustain marine life. Congress responded by passing landmark legislation in the early 1970s, including the Clean Air Act and the Clean Water Act, that improved the quality of both public goods. The Environmental Protection Agency (EPA) also came into being during this period, as did similar state and local agencies.

The United States, however, has been less assertive in seeking global remedies. Political leaders resist global environmental agreements because they feel such pacts threaten the nation's sovereignty as well as its economic well-being. At the 1992 **Earth Summit** in Brazil, the largest gathering of heads of state in history, President George H. W. Bush was a reluctant participant—he knew that the United States, as the world's richest country and chief source of pollution, would be a lightning rod. His hesitation proved well founded. Delegates singled out the United States as a primary obstacle to environmental protection. More recent U.S. actions have lent credence to their accusation. For example, the United States has opposed the Convention on Biological Diversity, which by 2010 had been approved by all other national governments.[1]

Barack Obama promised to reverse the U.S. government's antagonistic approach to environmental policy when he took office in January 2009. His first months in office witnessed several achievements, including greater fuel efficiency requirements for cars and trucks, an explicit EPA recognition of the harmful effects of greenhouse gas emissions, and a prohibition of oil drilling on almost all public lands.[2] The House of Representatives, meanwhile, approved a "cap-and-trade" program for emission control similar to that established by the European Union.[3] This momentum halted promptly, however, as Obama struggled with the financial crisis and launched a major effort to reform the U.S. health care system—an effort that finally succeeded despite opposition from Republicans in Congress. To stimulate the sluggish economy, the White House approved massive increases in federal spending that sparked public protests and congressional opposition. With the U.S. government paralyzed by partisan strife—Senate Republicans refused to cast a single vote in favor of the health care plan—the White House's plan to champion the cause of global environmental protection sputtered and stalled. The gigantic oil spill in the Gulf of Mexico in 2010, which brutally demonstrated the ecology-energy link, was widely attributed to previous neglect and corporate "capture" of federal agencies.

Population Growth and Family Planning

One of the most critical problems facing the global commons today is the world's burgeoning population, which during the past century more than tripled, to 6 billion. The global population is expected to increase to 9 billion by 2050, before leveling off at between 11 and 13 billion by the century's end (United Nations 2005). The population explosion raises questions about the world's **carrying capacity**—that is, the limits to which existing natural resources can meet

---

1. Leading the successful opposition to this treaty were property rights activists and the American Sheep Industry Association. For more information on the provisions and membership of the Convention on Biological Diversity, see the convention's Web site at www.biodiv.org.

2. The U.S. Environmental Protection Agency (2009) found that "the current and projected concentrations of the six key well-mixed greenhouse gases ... in the atmosphere threaten the public health and welfare of current and future generations."

3. Under this program, nations establish a "cap" on carbon emissions, assign credits to major industrial sources of these emissions, and then allow heavy polluters to "trade" these credits with cleaner firms in order to stay within the national limits.

Figure 12.1 Trends in Global Population Growth

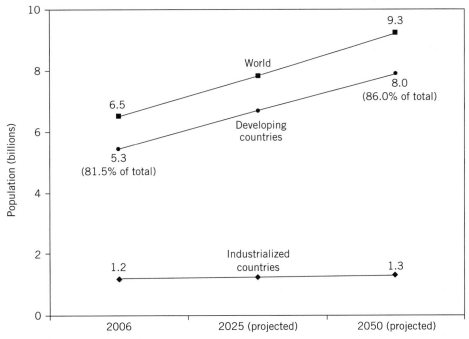

SOURCE: Population Reference Bureau, "2006 World Population Data Sheet," www.prb.org.

the demands and withstand the strains imposed on them by human development (see S. B. Cohen 2003).

The most rapid rates of population growth are concentrated in the world's poorest regions (see Figure 12.1). Growth rates in developing countries averaged 2.1 percent a year between 1980 and 2002, compared with 1.3 percent in middle-income countries and 0.7 percent in high-income countries (World Bank 2004b, 40, 98). The rate of growth in the United States during this period was 1.1 percent, with the most rapid growth in economically depressed areas. Fertility rates, or the average number of births per woman, were twice as high in poor countries (3.5) as in affluent countries (1.7). These trends illustrate the effects of the **demographic transition** that societies experience as their birthrates fall and life expectancies rise during the process of industrialization.

The United Nations and other international organizations also recognize the link between population growth and economic development. The first UN-sponsored global conference on family planning was held in 1974, and subsequent meetings in 1984 and 1994 placed the issue squarely in the context of development. Hundreds of nonprofit nongovernmental organizations (NGOs) offer family planning services in the developing world, focusing their efforts on the distribution of contraceptives and the education of women about their reproductive rights and choices. Among aid donors, the U.S. government has provided the largest share of family planning assistance in the past few years.

Americans generally agree about the merits of family planning, but the funding of programs that include abortion counseling and services continues to be highly controversial. Opposition to abortion in many segments of U.S. society has not subsided since the Supreme Court's *Roe v. Wade* decision in 1973, which ruled that in most cases abortion was constitutional. Since *Roe,* the opposition to abortion has been well represented in Congress and the White House, and it has emerged as a foreign policy issue as well.

The Reagan administration first took the offensive against abortion funding overseas at the 1984 UN International Conference on Population, held in Mexico City. The administration announced that the United States would no longer provide aid to agencies that endorsed or performed abortions "as a method of family planning." The policy also suspended grants to private hospitals and clinics, women's groups, and health research centers that engaged in political lobbying to decriminalize or legalize abortion. Although family planning agencies protested the decision, most decided to accept the restrictions.

Reagan's decision, known as the **Mexico City policy,** was significant because of the lead role played by the United States in providing family planning funds worldwide and the centrality of abortion in the population policies of many developing countries (see Cincotta and Crane 2001). The policy, which remained in place throughout the Reagan and George H. W. Bush administrations, became a fixture of interest-group politics in the United States, with Republicans siding with religious and pro-life groups and Democrats drawing support from women's groups and civil libertarians. Among President Clinton's first acts upon taking office in January 1993 was the restoration of funding for family-planning programs. George W. Bush was just as prompt in reinstating the restrictions, as was Barack Obama in quashing the Mexico City policy in January 2009.

Obama also restored U.S. funding to the UN Population Fund and gained legislative approval for steep increases in bilateral U.S. aid for family-planning and reproductive health programs. To Secretary of State Hillary Clinton (2009), U.S. foreign policy changes that strengthen the rights of women are not just morally vital but important to U.S. security in the war on terrorism: "A society that denies and demeans women's roles and rights is a society that is more likely to engage in behavior that is negative, anti-democratic, and which often leads to violence and extremism."

Heightened Concerns over Global Warming

A second threat facing the global commons is the effects of air pollution on the world's climate. Scientific evidence suggests that fossil fuel emissions, in addition to creating health problems and habitat loss in industrialized areas, contribute to **global warming,** or the gradual increase in surface temperatures due to, according to the scientific evidence, human actions. The UN's Intergovernmental Panel on Climate Change (IPCC) has reported that eleven of the twelve years between 1995 and 2006 were the warmest on record (IPCC 2007, 4). If the current trends continue, global surface temperatures will increase by four to eight degrees over the next century and continue rising thereafter in the absence of reductions in heat-trapping greenhouse gas emissions. The IPCC's report, based on the findings of hundreds of independent scientific studies, contains the most conclusive evidence of global warming to date. Among many other findings, the IPCC (2007, 12) observes the following:

- Mountain glaciers and snow cover are "retreating" across the northern and southern hemispheres.

- Sea levels are likely to increase by between seven and twenty-three inches by 2100, threatening crowded urban areas along shorelines, including American cities such as Miami, New Orleans, and San Diego.

- Many parts of the world have experienced "more intense and longer droughts" in recent years, while others have suffered flood-producing rains and "intense cyclone activity." The report notes that "it is very likely that hot extremes, heat waves, and heavy precipitation events will continue to become more frequent."

Earlier evidence of global warming prompted delegates at the 1992 Earth Summit to ratify the UN Framework Convention on Climate Change. The agreement, supported by the U.S. government, called on industrialized countries to voluntarily reduce their emissions of greenhouse gases.[4] These governments met again in Kyoto, Japan, in 1997 to strengthen the earlier agreement with legally binding standards and timetables for emission cutbacks. The **Kyoto Protocol,** signed by eighty-four governments in 1998 and 1999, required industrialized nations to reduce these emissions to 5 percent below their 1990 levels by 2012.

The United States signed the Kyoto Protocol in December 1998. The nation's support for the measure was crucial because the United States is a leading source of greenhouse gases, second only to China in 2006 (see Figure 12.2). The hopes of all countries for coming to grips with global warming thus hinged on U.S. actions. The treaty, however, faced strong opposition in Congress. Earlier, the Senate had passed, 95–0, a nonbinding resolution rejecting the Kyoto Protocol if it would harm the U.S. economy. Lawmakers also refused to ratify the agreement if it exempted major developing countries, including China and India, from the

4. These greenhouse gases include carbon dioxide, methane, nitrous oxide, hydrofluorocarbons, perfluorocarbons, and sulfur hexafluoride. The primary sources of these gases are gasoline-powered vehicles, coal-burning electric utilities, and large factories. The gases raise the earth's surface temperature by trapping the sun's heat and preventing it from returning to space, similar to the process that occurs in a greenhouse.

Figure 12.2 Top Seven Sources of Carbon Dioxide Emissions, 2006

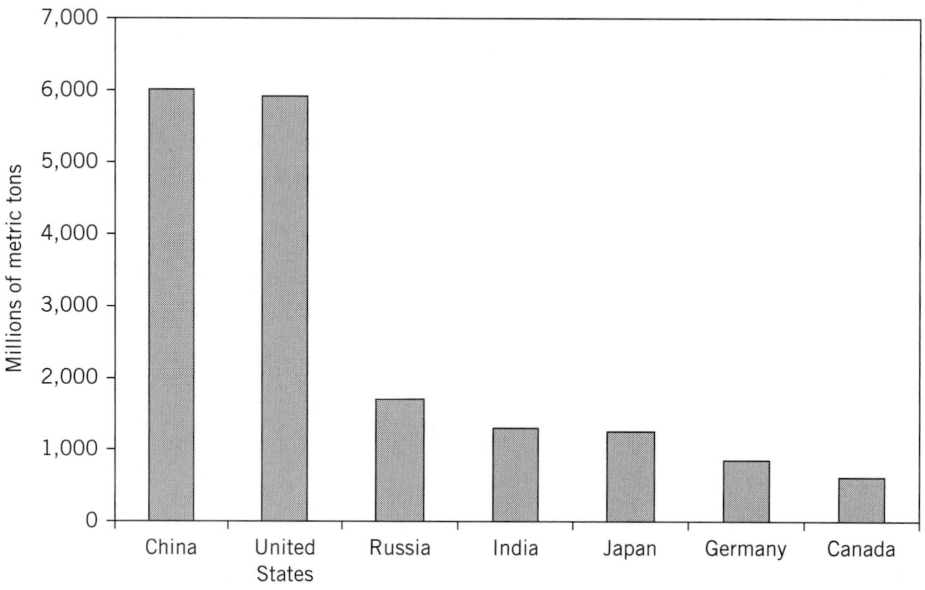

SOURCE: Energy Information Administration, *International Energy Annual 2006* (Washington, D.C., 2008).

required cutbacks.[5] With these exemptions written into the protocol, Clinton knew the treaty would be "dead on arrival" and did not submit it to the Senate.

As a presidential candidate, George W. Bush expressed concern about global warming and pledged to seek reductions in carbon dioxide (CO_2) emissions, which most scientific studies linked to global warming. However, Bush reversed his position in March 2001, when he announced that the U.S. government would not seek to reduce CO_2 emissions. The White House later declared the Kyoto Protocol to be so "fatally flawed" that the United States would no longer participate in climate change negotiations. The president restated the objections widely held in Congress, questioning the scientific evidence that included CO_2 among greenhouse gases and disputing the dire forecasts of climatologists. Bush's position was supported by an industry NGO, the Global Climate Coalition, which claimed that adherence to the treaty would reduce U.S. economic output by 1–2 percent and cause widespread layoffs of industrial workers.

Bush proposed instead a series of alternative measures to manage fossil fuel emissions. First, he called for voluntary efforts that would reduce U.S. emissions

---

5. These nations were allowed to waive the Kyoto restrictions for a limited time on the grounds that other economic powers, including the United States, had not faced such barriers during their periods of "dirty" industrialization.

as a percentage of U.S. economic output rather than in absolute terms. Under Bush's plan, the volume of U.S. greenhouse gas emissions in 2010 would be about 28 percent *higher* than their levels in 1990, though lower as a percentage of the nation's output. The president also proposed a "Clear Skies Initiative" that would limit emissions from electric power plants, the largest industrial source of air pollution, and would allow them to trade "pollution credits" so that the overall level of air pollution in the United States would decline. Finally, Bush called for the development of hydrogen-powered "Freedom Cars" that would rid U.S. motorists of their dependence on foreign oil by 2020, the target date for the widespread sales of these cars.

Despite the U.S. government's withdrawal, the Kyoto Protocol gained new signatories and came into force in February 2005. By March 2010, 189 countries had formally approved the protocol (United Nations Framework Convention on Climate Change 2010). Hopes that the United States, nearly alone in rejecting the agreement, would reverse this stance under Obama were dashed by the time world leaders met at the Copenhagen climate summit in December 2009. Instead, the leaders pledged to honor their existing commitments to the Kyoto Protocol and to further reduce their emissions of greenhouse gases voluntarily. For his part, Obama vowed that the United States would curb its own emissions by 17 percent by 2020 compared to 2005 levels. Achieving this distant goal, however, required a vital first step: domestic and congressional support for the measure, neither of which could be found while economic problems and political gridlock at home stymied the federal government.

Stalemate over Energy Policy

The debate over global warming is linked closely to U.S. energy policy. Historically, the United States has enjoyed a steady and relatively inexpensive energy supply, attributable in large part to its low taxes on gasoline and friendly relations with major oil exporters in the Middle East (see Yergin 1991). But when "oil shocks" occur, they keenly demonstrate U.S. vulnerability to fluctuations in the global energy market. American motorists are especially affected because the nation's per capita ownership of motor vehicles is the highest in the world.

This statistic reveals the towering presence of oil consumption in U.S. energy policy. Americans consumed nearly 20 million barrels of oil a day in 2008, almost one-quarter of the global total (British Petroleum 2009). The nation's seemingly insatiable appetite for oil not only exacerbates global warming, but also renders the United States dependent on oil imports, which represented 57 percent of its oil consumption in 2008 (U.S. Energy Information Administration 2009). Although nearly half of these imports come from the Western Hemisphere, it is well understood that the oil fields of the Middle East contain 60 percent of the global volume (see Figure 12.3).

For more than a century, U.S. oil companies, in cooperation with government officials, have aggressively pursued access to these fields (Randall 2005).

Figure 12.3 Global Oil Reserves by Region, 2008 (percentage of total known global reserves)

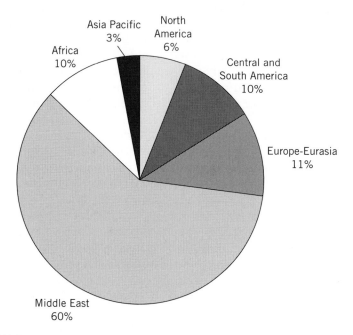

SOURCE: British Petroleum, *Statistical Review of World Energy 2008* (London: British Petroleum Company, 2009).

The hazards of such dependence were first revealed in 1973, when the members of the Organization of the Petroleum Exporting Countries (OPEC) embargoed oil exports to the United States and other allies of Israel, and then greatly increased the wholesale price of crude oil. The OPEC embargo, combined with fiscal problems in the United States linked to the war in Vietnam, plunged the U.S. and European economies into a prolonged economic recession. A second oil shock occurred in 1979–1980, when the revolution in Iran led to another disruption in OPEC supplies.

Although these oil shocks spurred efforts to improve energy conservation, the U.S. government and consumers later relaxed their conservation measures when oil prices began to fall. A decline in fuel prices during the 1980s prompted the Reagan administration to cut federal funding for conservation by 70 percent; federal support for the research on and development of new energy sources was cut by nearly two-thirds (Prestowitz 2003). The low energy prices and stable supplies of the 1990s literally fueled the U.S. economic boom that took place under President Clinton. The fuel efficiency of U.S. automobiles peaked at 26.2 miles per gallon (mpg) in 1987 but then fell to 24 mpg by 2002 (Joskow 2002). Congress prohibited any changes to fuel efficiency as sport-utility vehicles (SUVs) became the passenger vehicles of choice by the turn of the century.[6] President Obama's executive order in May 2009 to raise the average mileage of cars and light trucks to 35.5 mpg by 2016 made a reversal of this trend mandatory. The measure, which took effect in 2010, did not please domestic automakers, who struggled to remain solvent and remained dependent on the sales of their largest, and least fuel-efficient, vehicles.

Shortly after taking office in January 2001, President Bush sought to ease concerns over U.S. "energy security" by creating a National Energy Policy Development Group to devise a strategy for making the United States less vulnerable to oil shocks and other threats to energy supplies. Vice President Dick Cheney chaired the task force, whose report in May declared that "a fundamental imbalance between supply and demand defines our nation's energy crisis" (White House 2001c, 5). The work of this task force proved controversial for two reasons. First, Cheney did not reveal who had helped to draft the task force's report, which called for accelerated domestic oil and gas production and the construction of more than thirteen hundred power plants. The second criticism of the task force was its emphasis on increasing production rather than conservation as a means of expanding the nation's energy independence. By emphasizing oil production, critics charged, U.S. leaders dismissed the possibility that Americans could be encouraged to conserve energy by modifying their lifestyles or turning to renewable sources of energy such as solar or wind power.

With no end in sight for U.S. oil dependence, the United States must continue to rely on oil from the Middle East while it seeks new sources of oil elsewhere (Yetiv 2004a). In the other oil-producing areas, however, producers face internal problems that hinder their capacity to serve U.S. energy needs (see Klare 2004 and 2002). The oil-rich Caspian Sea region of central Asia, for example, is fraught with ethnic conflicts and concerns about the installation of pipelines across disputed territories. Meanwhile, Nigeria and its neighbors in western Africa are plagued by widespread poverty, human rights abuses, and government corruption, all of which have caused disruptions in oil exports (Forest and Sousa 2006). In Latin America, U.S. leaders must contend with Venezuela's Hugo Chávez, who in 2007 announced plans to nationalize his country's oil industry.

At home, partisan disputes have made it impossible for the U.S. government to overcome its energy insecurity. The Energy Policy Act of 2003, reflecting the views of the Cheney task force, did not pass muster in Congress. Revised legislation was passed in July 2005 but was dismissed widely as a "piñata of perks for energy industries" (Grunwald and Eilperin 2005). The Democratic-controlled Congress that came into power in January 2007 vowed to redirect U.S. energy policy toward conservation and alternative energy sources, but this policy shift failed to gain traction in the Bush White House. Obama's revival of this effort in 2009 also faced strong domestic opposition due to the deep and protracted economic recession that, even for leaders of the president's own party, made true "energy security" an unaffordable luxury for the United States.

---

6. These SUVs were exempt from the efficiency standards for passenger cars because they were regarded as "trucks" by the federal government, a regulatory loophole that pleased automakers.

The Immigration Debate

Americans have long relished the nation's rich history as a "melting pot" for those from elsewhere who are seeking economic opportunities and greater political freedom. The rapid industrial expansion of the United States a century ago would have been impossible without millions of European immigrants. After World War II, Latin Americans became the largest group of immigrants, taking advantage of a seemingly unlimited U.S. demand for agricultural and industrial labor. By 2003, they made up more than half of the 35 million foreign-born inhabitants of the United States (U.S. Census Bureau 2004).[7] More than 2 million other foreign citizens were granted citizenship later in the decade, either as new arrivals to the United States or, more commonly, as documented aliens previously living in the United States on a conditional basis (U.S. Department of Homeland Security 2006).

In recent years, the rapid pace of immigration has come under close scrutiny, because it has become obvious that the U.S. government is simply not able to control much of the influx of workers. An estimated 12 million people, or about one-third the total number of foreign-born citizens living in the United States in 2006, entered the country illegally, and today most continue to live and work in the nation without the government's permission (Passel 2006). Most of these undocumented aliens are migrant workers who toil for low wages on American farms, or in factory and service jobs, and then send, or "repatriate," their earnings home to their families. The size of their paychecks is paltry by American standards, because most undocumented workers receive less than the minimum wage and do not receive health or other benefits. Still, the sums sent to their families greatly exceed what those workers would have earned in their own communities.

Immigration, legal or otherwise, is a classic *intermestic* issue that fuses international and domestic elements. Immigrants engage in a broader process of **migration** that has profound consequences for economic development and political arrangements. Both commercial firms and governments are stakeholders in the ongoing resettlement of populations, although the costs and benefits of these changes are difficult to measure and future population shifts are difficult to predict. In some cases—for example, the massive refugee flows in the former Yugoslavia during its breakup during the 1990s—such migration occurs unexpectedly, overwhelming "host" communities across national borders. More often, human migration proceeds at a much slower and less perceptible pace.

Public opinion in the United States, like that in other countries, has long been divided on the question of immigration. Those in favor of open labor borders, the "pluralists," would like to see as many foreign workers in the United States as there are jobs available to them. Coming from the liberal economic tradition, pluralists believe that market forces, including the movements of labor toward the most dynamic areas of production, provide the "greatest good for the greatest

---

7. Asia accounted for another 25 percent of the total of foreign-born U.S. residents, and Europe for 14 percent. The rest came from other regions, primarily Africa.

number." By contrast, the labor "nationalists" accuse immigrants of "stealing jobs" from domestic workers. Backed by large labor unions such as the AFL-CIO, these nationalists claim further that, by working within a black market, undocumented workers drive down wage rates for law-abiding employees. Finally, nationalists are more likely than pluralists to resist the cultural changes that accompany large-scale immigration, such as the use of Spanish as a second language in California and other border states.

The focal point of the U.S. immigration controversy is Mexico, the birthplace of the largest number of foreign-born citizens in recent years (see Table 12.1). According to the Pew Hispanic Center, more than 6 million Mexicans worked illegally in the United States in 2005, nearly half the total of undocumented aliens (Passel 2006, 4). These illegal Mexican workers outnumbered those with "green cards," or work permits, by a ratio of four to one. Further aggravating U.S.-Mexico ties, it is widely understood that border cities such as Tijuana serve as major transit points for smuggling narcotics into the United States from Latin America. From the Mexican perspective, access

A Mexican girl is apprehended by U.S. border patrol agents near Laredo, Texas, in June 2006. Congress has authorized the federal government to build a massive network of fences spanning most of the nation's border with Mexico, a measure justified by proponents on the basis of homeland security as well as economic grounds. The flows of migrant workers, as well as refugees and other displaced populations, create a global problem that demands the attention of world leaders.

to the U.S. labor market is an economic necessity. Each year, migrant and seasonal workers send billions of dollars in remittances to their families in Mexico, an infusion of foreign capital second only in size to that produced by the nation's oil industry.

In Congress, the labor nationalists effectively gained control of U.S. immigration policy in the 1990s. With their newfound electoral base in the Southwest and a Republican majority in Congress beginning in January 1995, the advocates of more restrictive legal immigration and a crackdown against illegal aliens took the offensive. The 1996 Illegal Immigration Reform and Immigrant Responsibility Act gave the attorney general greater authority to fortify the U.S. border with Mexico, particularly in the heavily congested region between San Diego and Tijuana. With the September 2001 terrorist attacks adding further urgency to the need for greater border control, Congress passed in 2005 the REAL ID Act, which

Table 12.1 Top Ten Populations Granted U.S. Permanent Resident Status, 2008

Country of origin	Number of immigrants (to nearest thousand)
Mexico	190
China	80
India	63
Philippines	54
Cuba	50
Dominican Republic	32
Vietnam	31
Colombia	30
South Korea	27
Haiti	26
Global total	1,107

SOURCE: U.S. Department of Homeland Security, *2008 Yearbook of Immigration Statistics* (Washington, D.C.: DHS, 2009), 12–15.

authorized the attorney general to waive all legal impediments to securing the U.S. border from terrorists. President Bush deployed thousands of U.S. National Guard troops to support this effort, and thousands of armed private citizens, known as "Minutemen," organized their own border patrols.[8]

Popular sentiments related to the war on terrorism fueled even more draconian measures in 2006. Under the Secure Fence Act, approved by Congress and signed by Bush, the U.S. government would erect seven hundred miles of fencing along Mexico's border with California, Arizona, New Mexico, and Texas. The project, to cost an estimated $1.2 billion, would include the installation of remote cameras across the border and the deployment of unmanned aerial drones to observe the region and alert border patrols to illegal crossings. Bush, who favored a less restrictive guest worker program that would give Mexican immigrants an opportunity to gain U.S. citizenship, was compelled to support the measure in the face of partisan pressure in the November 2006 congressional elections. Among the critics of the Secure Fence Act were the past and present leaders of Mexico. President Vicente Fox, an ally of Bush on the proposed guest worker program, called the fence "shameful" before he left office on December 1, 2006. His successor, Felipe Calderón, expressed the same view: "Humanity made a huge mistake by building the Berlin Wall, and I believe the United States is committing a grave error in building the wall on our border" (quoted in Stout 2006).

8. The Minutemen also organized to patrol the Canadian border, which was not facing the problems associated with illegal aliens but was experiencing large volumes of illegal drug trafficking and financial flows involving crime syndicates (see Turnbull and Tu 2005).

By January 2010, the Army Corps of Engineers had completed 643 miles of fencing along the U.S.-Mexican border (Global Security 2010). While the success of this project would take years to assess, ongoing economic distress in Mexico and the continuing demand for low-cost workers in the United States ensured that tensions along the border would continue. Further complicating matters, Calderón launched a virtual civil war in his country by deploying more than 45,000 troops to fight drug cartels (Thompson and Booth 2009). The U.S. government supported these actions, citing a rise in drug-related violence in border states. Human rights advocates, meanwhile, charged that Mexican forces committed widespread human rights violations—including homicides, torture, rape, and illegal detentions—in the name of national security.[9] This conflict created a further impetus for many Mexicans to seek refuge in the United States.

As for Obama, reforming U.S. immigration policy also meant resolving a wide range of complaints regarding the treatment of resident aliens accused of immigration violations. An estimated 400,000 people are detained annually in these cases, an average of 32,000 per day (*New York Times* 2009). Given the lack of a centralized detention system in the United States, these aliens are held in a makeshift network of state and county jails that are designed to punish convicted criminals. Obama used his executive powers to investigate the deaths of more than 100 aliens in U.S. detention centers since 2003 (Bernstein 2010). He could not, however, stop states, such as Arizona, from passing harsh laws aimed at suspected illegal aliens.

The Dangers of Weapons Proliferation

Another transnational problem facing all governments today is the proliferation of weapons, from small arms to weapons of mass destruction. The spread of these weapons, whose accuracy and destructive power increase each year, aggravates internal and regional power balances, while diverting scarce economic resources from productive uses. A more militarized world poses clear risks to the United States, a primary target of resentment among many foreign governments and terrorist groups. And yet the United States has sent mixed messages on this front, serving as both a vocal opponent and an enabler of global weapons proliferation.

The prospect of nuclear proliferation is a paramount global concern, and preventing rogue states and terrorist groups from gaining access to such weapons is a central goal of U.S. foreign policy. As described in Chapter 10, for most of the late twentieth century the number of acknowledged nuclear powers stood at five: the United States, Great Britain, France, China, and the Soviet Union/Russia. Israel's nuclear arsenal, which the world has known about since the late 1960s, but whose

---

9. As in the United States, human rights NGOs have become more powerful foreign policy actors in Mexico in recent years. Among these groups, Center Prodh (www.centroprodh.org.mx/english) has assumed a lead role in defending the rights of women, ethnic minorities, and the poor.

existence the Israeli government officially denies, raised the membership of the nuclear club to six.[10] The group reached eight in 1998 when India and Pakistan conducted underground tests, and North Korea joined the club with similar tests in 2006 (see Sutcliffe 2006).[11]

The United States supports multilateral efforts to prevent the spread of these weapons through the Nuclear Non-proliferation Treaty (NPT), which by 2010 had been signed by 189 countries. Since the NPT was first signed in 1968, many would-be nuclear powers have shunned these weapons. These states include the major regional powers in South America and Africa, which feel more secure in nuclear-free zones. Yet the possibility that Russia may sell nuclear material to the highest bidder on the black market, or that China may export ballistic missile technology to nuclear terrorists, worries U.S. leaders. Especially troubling is the growing possibility of an Iranian nuclear bomb—the proclaimed "right" of its government—because of the effects of such a development on Egypt, Saudi Arabia, and other states in the region.

As with environmental issues, arms control featured prominently in Obama's presidential campaign and early public statements from the White House. "The existence of nuclear weapons is the most dangerous legacy of the Cold War," he told a public audience in Prague in April 2009. "I state clearly and with conviction America's commitment to seek the peace and security of a world without nuclear weapons." The president's *Nuclear Posture Review,* released in April 2010, proclaimed that "the United States will not use or threaten to use nuclear weapons against non-nuclear weapons states that are party to the Nuclear Non-Proliferation Treaty (NPT) and in compliance with their nuclear non-proliferation obligations" (U.S. Department of Defense 2010, 15). The "fundamental role" of nuclear weapons would be "to deter nuclear attack on the United States, our allies, and partners," a statement that seemed to rule out the use of nuclear weapons for tactical use, in small-scale conflicts, or against countries that used chemical or biological weapons but did not pose a direct threat to the United States.

While he expressed doubts that global nuclear disarmament would be achieved in his lifetime, Obama and his Russian counterparts agreed in March 2010 to further cuts in their strategic warheads. More frustrating for the president was his effort to gain the Senate's support of the Comprehensive Test Ban Treaty, whose defeat on Capitol Hill in 1999 crippled Bill Clinton's nonproliferation efforts. A decade later, with Republicans voting in lockstep against most of Obama's policies, getting the sixty-seven votes needed to ratify the treaty appeared an impossible dream for the White House. Many defense "hawks," however,

---

10. Although U.S. officials have declared nuclear proliferation in North Korea and Iran to be unacceptable, they have tolerated Israel's nuclear arsenal. This double standard in U.S. nuclear policy angers Arab nations, which would be the likely targets of an Israeli nuclear attack.

11. The duration of North Korea's status as a nuclear power came into question in February 2007, when its leader, Kim Jong-il, agreed to dismantle the program in return for foreign economic aid and political concessions. The agreement, which included China and Russia, was similar to that reached among North Korea, the United States, and Japan in the early 1990s. That deal languished, however, amid mutual charges of treaty violations.

Point/Counterpoint
ARMS SALES VS. ARMS CONTROL

The issue of U.S. arms sales raises questions about the nation's foreign policy: Should the United States be concerned primarily with its own interests or with global concerns? To what extent should economic factors influence decisions on national security? Are U.S. arms sales a help or a hindrance to the cause of international stability?

As regulator of the world's leading arms sales industry, the U.S. government argues that such sales promote national, as well as global, interests. Government officials, therefore, have been highly sympathetic to complaints from arms contractors that their exports are hindered by bureaucratic obstacles at home and growing competition from abroad. "From an industry perspective, the current U.S. defense trade regulations are complex and restrictive, seriously inhibiting cooperation with this nation's closest allies," observed *National Defense,* an industry magazine. "Current defense trade laws and policies must be revised to balance rational national security concerns and strategies with the need to enhance both the international competitiveness of the U.S. defense industry and the military effectiveness of U.S.-led international coalitions."

Critics of U.S. arms sales, however, dispute this claim, asserting instead that exports suffer from too *few* regulations and controls. According to Rachael Stohl of the Center for Defense Information, "The lack of controls on the global arms trade is fueling conflict, poverty and human rights violations worldwide. Every government around the world is responsible in stopping these horrors and abuses. In some cases, arms are being transferred to illegal groups that are terrorizing governments and civilians. The United States, as the world's largest exporter, has a special duty to lead the world in pushing for stronger arms controls."

SOURCES: Dennis Kennelly and Ben Stone, "Bush Team Reviewing Defense Trade Policy," *National Defense* (May 2003), www.nationaldefensemagazine.org/article.cfm?Id=1086; Rachael Stohl, "Control Arms Campaign," Center for Defense Information, www.cdi.org/friendlyversion/printversion.cfm?documentID=1765.

---

supported Obama's plans to continue the modernization of U.S. nuclear weapons and to maintain missile-defense systems in North America, an effort viewed in Moscow as an attempt to paralyze its own nuclear arsenal.

The U.S. government has also turned to global agreements to discourage the proliferation of chemical and biological weapons. The Chemical Weapons Convention, ratified by the Senate in 1997, prohibits the "development, production, acquisition, stockpiling, transfer, and use" of such weapons. By May 2009, 188 countries had made this pledge. The United States, along with more than 170 other governments, is also a signatory of the Biological Weapons Convention, which was ratified by Congress in 1975. The U.S. government's support for both measures has been controversial, however. Its own use of chemical and biological agents in Vietnam is often cited by critics, as are U.S. shipments in the 1980s of such agents to Saddam Hussein, who later used them against Iranian troops and his own Kurdish population (see Arms Control Association 2006). American leaders also resisted stringent measures to enforce these treaties, fearing the intrusion of international weapons inspectors in U.S. domestic firms.

The credibility of the United States has also been questioned in three other areas of weapons proliferation:

- *Trafficking in small arms.* These are the weapons of choice in military conflicts, with more than 600 million such weapons currently in circulation (Small Arms Survey 2007). Thus restricting the flow of small arms across national borders is a priority of most governments and arms control NGOs. The United States, however, has resisted the strong measures endorsed by most other states. Supported by a powerful gun lobby, the National Rifle Association, both Republican and Democratic presidents have argued that global measures to restrict the commercial sale of small arms would violate U.S. law, because the right to bear arms is protected by the Second Amendment of the U.S. Constitution.

- *Weapons in space.* In August 2006, President Bush approved a revised U.S. National Space Policy that declared, "Freedom of action in space is as important to the United States as air power and sea power.... The United States will oppose the development of new legal regimes or other restrictions that seek to prohibit or limit U.S. access to or use of space" (U.S. Office of Science and Technology Policy 2006, 1–2). Most other governments fear the consequences of a U.S. monopoly on such weapons and worry that they will spark a military "space race" with other world powers. Upon taking office, President Obama called for a ban on such weapons but refused to cancel the U.S. program in the absence of a global agreement.

- *Arms sales.* As in other areas of military power, the United States maintains a dominant position in the global arms industry (see Hook and Rothstein 2005). Between 2001 and 2008, the United States claimed more than one-third of the global arms market (see Figure 12.4).[12] Its deliveries to developing nations, which amounted to more than $12 billion, represented nearly 40 percent of the worldwide total. Presidents Clinton and George W. Bush defended exports not only as a means of strengthening U.S. allies overseas, but also as an opportunity to close the U.S. trade deficit in other sectors. Obama, faced with economic stagnation and entrenched support for these exports, continued the policies of his predecessors. His approval of a $6 billion arms sale to Taiwan in 2010 provoked angry protests by the Chinese government, but the action was justified in Washington as business as usual.

---

12. These forms of security assistance include foreign military sales, financing, and training (U.S. Defense Security Cooperation Agency 2007).

Figure 12.4 Top Seven Global Arms Merchants, 2001–2008 (according to the value of arms deliveries)

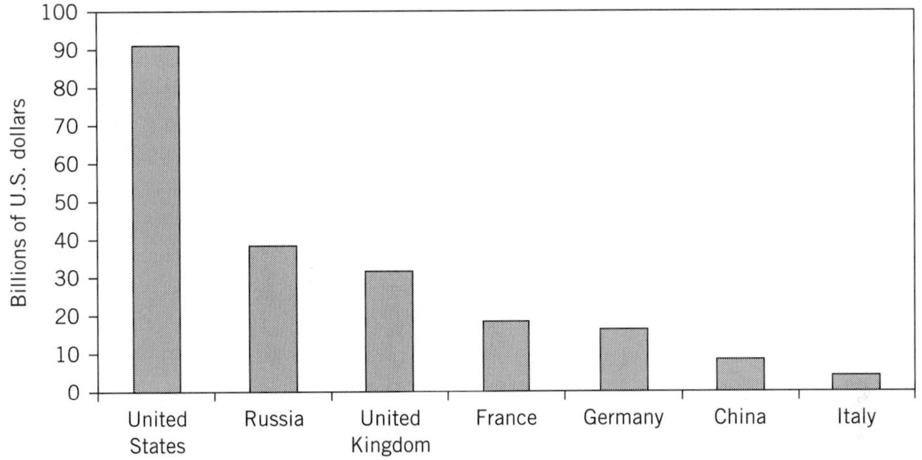

SOURCE: Richard F. Grimmett, "Conventional Arms Transfers to Developing Nations, 2001–2008," Congressional Research Service, Washington, D.C., September 4, 2009, 75.

Promoting Human Rights and Democracy

Military ties to repressive governments overseas reveal many tensions between U.S. national security interests and the promotion of democracy abroad. As noted elsewhere, American leaders have historically believed that the nation cannot be secure as a democratic "island" in a sea of despotic regimes. The twin victories of the United States during the twentieth century, first against the fascist powers of World War II and then against Soviet communism in the Cold War, reinforced the consensus among U.S. foreign policy makers that repression at home leads to adventurism abroad. Since then, the "most consistent tradition in American foreign policy ... has been the belief that the nation's security is best protected by the expansion of democracy worldwide" (Smith 1994, 9).

This formula for **democratization** received new validation with the terrorist attacks of September 2001—but with a significant twist. The attackers on that day were not government agents, but rather Islamic terrorists who harbored intense hostility toward the U.S. government and Western society in general. Most of the al Qaeda terrorists were from Saudi Arabia, whose ruling monarchy had long excluded rival groups from power, while maintaining cordial relations with the United States, the primary destination of its petroleum exports and the primary source of the royal family's extravagant wealth (Yergin 1991). Thus the attacks on the United States were linked, however indirectly, to a dictatorial regime overseas.

Until recently, the number of democracies had grown steadily in number and global influence. This progress, however, halted abruptly in 2005. According to Freedom House (2010), whose index of political freedoms is watched closely by governments and NGOs, the erosion of political freedoms from 2006 to 2009 represented the longest period of decline since the index was first published in 1972. Forty countries imposed new restrictions on political rights in 2009, and four countries—Honduras, Madagascar, Mozambique, and Niger—lost their status as electoral democracies. Virtually all the countries in the former Soviet Union denied their citizens democratic freedoms, China's one-party state harshly punished political dissidents, elections in Iran and Afghanistan were marred by corruption, and leaders in the Philippines clung to power only after regional authorities massacred dozens of journalists in November and imposed martial law. The Middle East remained the most repressive region in the world, a fact that Freedom House attributed to the numerous military regimes in the region and the continued hold on power by monarchs with little interest in sharing their immense power and wealth.

In response to the uncertainties surrounding these autocratic regimes as well as "failed states" in the developing world, U.S. foreign policy makers regularly give priority to the promotion of democracy. But this is an act of enlightened self-interest, not of altruism. According to democratic peace theory, a more democratic world would be a more peaceful one (see Doyle 1986b and Rasler and Thompson 2005). Governments that uphold political freedoms will escape the ravages of war with like-minded states and are likely to establish productive and profitable trade relations. President Bush relied on this theory in launching his "freedom agenda" in the Middle East, an effort that included militarized regime change in Iraq.

A Distinctive View of Human Rights

These linkages among regime type, economic productivity, and foreign policy behavior reinforce a historic tendency of American leaders to promote the respect for human rights beyond the country's shores. Yet the United States maintains a conception of human rights that differs from that adopted by most other countries. Human rights are applied primarily to *political* and *civil* rights, requiring tight constraints on government power in order for individuals to enjoy the "inalienable" rights to "life, liberty, and the pursuit of happiness." The more widely accepted view of human rights is broader, encompassing *social* and *economic* rights as well as political freedoms. From this perspective, citizens cannot be truly free if many of them suffer from deep economic inequalities and the societal disadvantages produced by gaps in material welfare.

Stated another way, the U.S. conception of human rights focuses on *liberty,* whereas the conception favored by most other governments emphasizes both *equality* and liberty. This more inclusive perspective was written into the Universal Declaration of Human Rights, adopted by UN members in 1948. Its thirty articles include the political rights familiar to Americans, such as freedom of thought and assembly and the ownership of private property. The declaration also includes social and economic rights, such as the right to equal pay for equal work, an "adequate" standard of living, assistance for child care, and sufficient opportunities for "rest and leisure."

Distancing itself from the language of the UN declaration during the Cold War, the United States seized upon communism, in its Soviet and Chinese forms, as a primary threat to human rights. Meanwhile, most European governments and developing countries adopted the broader conception of human rights, leaving the United States virtually alone in the UN General Assembly in its views of what constituted such rights. Further complicating matters, the U.S. government anxiously sought allies in the bipolar balance of power, few of whom had strong democratic credentials. American leaders resolved this dilemma by choosing the lesser of evils—"authoritarian" states that oppressed their people while providing some political and economic openings, as opposed to "totalitarian" communist regimes that dominated all aspects of public life. Military dictators across Latin America, Africa, and Asia maintained cordial relations with the United States, which provided enough military aid to protect these rulers against their domestic enemies.

In the late 1970s, Congress began to raise the profile of human rights as a foreign policy priority. Among other things, it suspended foreign aid to countries that engaged in "gross violations" of human rights, and it created the Office of Humanitarian Affairs, also requiring the secretary of state to submit annual reports on the human rights behavior of all foreign governments. President Jimmy Carter embraced this emphasis on human rights. "Because we are free we can never be indifferent to the fate of nations elsewhere," Carter declared in his 1977 inaugural address. "Our commitment to human rights must be absolute" (quoted in Schlesinger 1978, 514). But even Carter could not avoid double standards. His support for the despotic shah of Iran not only contradicted the president's moral standards, but also led to the shah's overthrow and replacement by an Islamic theocracy hostile to the United States.

Although the collapse of Soviet communism represented a geopolitical victory for the United States, today the nation remains vastly outnumbered by foreign countries that oppose its narrow conception of human rights. If anything, those nations' focus on socioeconomic equality has strengthened as globalization pressures have sparked new tensions between the world's rich and poor. President George W. Bush, remaining true to the traditional stance of the United States, replaced the term *human rights* in his speeches with *human dignity,* a term that emphasizes the individual's freedom *from* state interference rather than an obligation *by* the state to provide for the material welfare of its citizens (Mertus 2003).

Much of this book has examined the tensions, and frequent contradictions, between the stated principles and the actions of U.S. foreign policy makers. Such gaps between values and practices, or words and deeds, are hardly unique to the United States. In the American case, however, these gaps are more visible because of the nation's early role in fostering democratic development and its more recent ascension to global primacy. The gaps are also more troubling because they send important signals to other governments and affect the lives of much of the world's population (see Liang-Fenton 2004).

Political theorist Andrew Moravcsik (2005) believes these gaps between U.S. principles and practices represent a "paradox of American exceptionalism" in which the U.S. government serves as the world's most outspoken champion of human rights while actively resisting legal restraints on its own power to uphold them. Stated more simply, the United States is "simultaneously a leader and an outlier" in the area of human rights (Ignatieff 2005, 2). This paradox has four primary sources. First, U.S. primacy encourages its leaders to take or leave global commitments to human rights and other issues—a luxury not available to weaker states that benefit more from multilateral ties. A second source of the paradox is the messianic nature of U.S. political culture, which traditionally views the United States as a universal model of political and economic freedom that can be readily exported. Third, because the executive and legislative branches in the United States share powers, the ratification of global treaties is difficult and rare. Finally, the U.S. system of federalism concentrates legal authority at the local and state levels. Thus the federal government is wary of signing global accords that may infringe on domestic jurisdictional boundaries.

These forces have paradoxical outcomes, including the U.S. failure to ratify the 1919 treaty creating the League of Nations, despite Woodrow Wilson's leading role in establishing the body. The more recent U.S. refusal, along with that of only the failed state of Somalia, to sign a global treaty protecting children's rights reflected not the government's moral opposition to such rights, but its legal and political concerns that state and district courts would have to surrender control over the regulation of households to global tribunals. In two other prominent cases—the Kyoto Protocol and the International Criminal Court—U.S. leaders emerged as early and forceful advocates, only to oppose the multilateral treaties that resulted. Overall, then, the U.S. government's numerous double standards on human rights—such as demanding reform in Iraq while tolerating despotism in Saudi Arabia—"diminishes U.S. power to persuade through principle" (Koh 2005, 118).

The result is that the United States today remains caught between "two worlds" that cannot be reconciled (Forsythe 1995). The first world relates to the liberal tradition of U.S. moral exceptionalism and to the nation's self-image as an inspiring "city upon a hill." Beyond serving as the exemplar of human rights, the United States should, in this view, commit its vast resources to the cause of global reform. The United States also should embrace the trend toward global governance—that is, the emerging system of shared sovereignty among states and supranational organizations in which broad powers to influence and implement public policies are granted to NGOs (see Slaughter 2004 and Barnett and Finnemore 2004).

The second world corresponds to the bleak vision of realism that foresees endless conflicts among states and the primacy of national defense above other foreign policy goals, including the promotion of human rights (see Chapter 3). The United States must make moral compromises in this darker world, allying itself with dictators and foreign monarchs whose interests align with those of U.S. defense and security policy. American forces abroad must play by the ruthless rules of this world, even if those rules compel close trade relations with the chronic human rights violators in China and Saudi Arabia, as well as the "coercive interrogation" of suspected terrorists, according to realists.

The United States inhabits both of these worlds. Moral appeals to human rights, which have contributed to democratic reforms in many countries, are as central to the nation's political culture as its resort to the law of the geopolitical jungle. As noted in Chapter 3, although the stated *principles* of U.S. foreign policy are consistent with liberalism, its *practice* is more often compatible with realism. This dilemma cannot be overcome easily. The United States appears destined to be plagued by the mismatch between its words and deeds, all of which contributes to the paradox of U.S. world power, itself a by-product of the competing demands of global ambitions and national self-interests.

Prospects for "Exporting" Democracy

American leaders often feel compelled to impose "democracy by force" (von Hippel 2000). The 2003 U.S.-led invasion of Iraq was only the latest in a long project of **state building,** or the creation of the political institutions that facilitate the orderly and democratic conduct of governance (see Fukuyama 2004). Whereas **nation building** refers to the development of a harmonious civil society, state building involves the brick and mortar of public administration. In both cases, the major world powers have consistently endeavored to reform the governments of small countries that do not have the resources needed to manage the task themselves.

The U.S. government does not merely proclaim the benefits of human rights, American-style; it actively supports political reforms in other countries. The longevity of the nation's own democratic system, however strained it is by internal contradictions and double standards, provides a powerful basis and temptation for the "export" of its system (Muravchik 1991). This proactive effort, which has been a central element of U.S. foreign policy for three decades, stands in contrast to the more passive approach favored earlier in the country's history, when the United States sought to inspire democratic revolutions by example alone. As Secretary of State John Quincy Adams declared about the United States in 1821, "Where the standard of freedom and independence has been unfurled, there will her heart, her benedictions and her prayers be. But she goes not abroad, in search of monsters to destroy. She is the well-wisher to the freedom and independence of all. She is the champion and vindicator only of her own" (quoted in Merrill and Paterson 2000, 167).

More than a century later, President Franklin Roosevelt framed the growing U.S. involvement in World War II in the context of a global conflict between tyranny and democracy. He identified "four freedoms"—freedom of expression, freedom of religion, freedom from want, and freedom from fear—that would be essential to a lasting peace after the conflict (see In Their Own Words box). Rather than

IN THEIR OWN WORDS: FRANKLIN D. ROOSEVELT

American presidents have historically cast U.S. military interventions in the context of the nation's moral ideals. Franklin Roosevelt, while avoiding the sweeping rhetoric of Woodrow Wilson, told Congress in January 1941 that the United States would strive to ensure that "four freedoms" were protected by all governments after World War II. Although the United States had not yet entered the conflict directly, Roosevelt needed legislative and public support for aid packages to its European and Asian allies. In seeking this support, the president made it clear that the United States would pursue outcomes in the war that extended beyond national self-interests. Indeed, Roosevelt's desired world order pertained equally to the outcome of the Cold War.

In the future days which we seek to make secure, we look forward to a world founded upon four essential human freedoms.

The first is freedom of speech and expression everywhere in the world.

The second is freedom of every person to worship God in his own way—everywhere in the world.

The third is freedom from want, which, translated into world terms, means economic understanding which will secure to every nation a healthy peacetime life for its inhabitants—everywhere in the world.

The fourth is freedom from fear, which, translated into world terms means a world-wide reduction of armaments to such a point and in such a thorough fashion that no nation will be in a position to commit an act of physical aggression against any neighbor—anywhere in the world.

That is no vision of a distant millennium. It is a definite basis for a kind of world attainable in our own time and generation. That kind of world is the very antithesis of the so-called "new order" of tyranny which the dictators seek to create with the crash of a bomb.

To that new order we oppose the greater conception—the moral order. A good society is able to face schemes of world domination and foreign revolutions alike without fear.

Since the beginning of our American history we have been engaged in change, in a perpetual, peaceful revolution, a revolution which goes on steadily, quietly, adjusting itself to changing conditions without the concentration camp or the quicklime in the ditch. The world order which we seek is the cooperation of free countries, working together in a friendly, civilized society.

SOURCE: Michael Nelson, ed., *Historic Documents on the Presidency, 1776–1989* (Washington, D.C.: Congressional Quarterly, 1989), 283–284.

relying solely on the power of the nation's democratic example, Roosevelt proposed that the United States offer its like-minded allies material support. The postwar Marshall Plan and other aid programs heralded the arrival of a new era in which the U.S. government shaped the domestic political institutions of foreign governments.

The U.S. occupations of the western portion of Germany and of Japan after World War II are still regarded as the most successful state-building enterprises to date. The United States built new governments virtually from scratch in these countries, writing constitutions that separated powers, produced independent judiciaries, and protected the freedoms of speech, press, and religion. Foreign aid funds were then used to construct government buildings and to train civil servants, military and police officers, journalists, and trade unionists. The German and Japanese efforts became role models for subsequent state-building missions, although none would compare in scope or in the significance of their outcomes.

The postwar hegemony of the United States later encouraged its leaders to pursue dozens of state-building missions. This effort took on a new urgency in the early 1960s with the decolonization of Africa and growing concerns about poverty in Latin America. President John Kennedy's Peace Corps, Alliance for Progress, and foreign aid programs supported political reform as well as economic development in these areas. The focus of U.S. foreign policy soon shifted to Cold War concerns in Vietnam, which consumed most of the foreign aid budget. In the late 1970s, Jimmy Carter revived the State Department's democracy programs; and in 1983 the Reagan administration created the National Endowment for Democracy, a nonprofit NGO designed to fund political reforms abroad, primarily in the developing world.

After the Cold War, Bill Clinton sought to "enlarge the circle of nations that live under … free institutions" as a central element of his grand strategy (Clinton quoted in Brinkley 1997, 119). The U.S. Agency for International Development's budget for democracy assistance jumped from $165 million in fiscal year 1991 to $637 million eight years later, with the largest share of funds allocated to the former communist states of Eastern Europe (Carothers 1999, 50–51). Most of this funding supported independent news media, interest groups, labor unions, and other elements of civil society. But the 1992 U.S. intervention in Somalia, while successful in providing emergency relief to the thousands of starving victims of a war-induced famine, fell apart after U.S. and UN peacekeeping forces failed to create a viable government that would prevent a recurrence of humanitarian crises once the peacekeepers left. Subsequent frustrations in the former Yugoslavia, which splintered into several independent states amid widespread violence and U.S. military intervention, sapped the nation's appetite for new state-building missions.

After the September 2001 terrorist attacks, President Bush launched his "freedom agenda" to further the spread of democratic rule that began during the Cold War. The U.S. invasion of Iraq, first justified on security grounds, was later described as an effort to remake Iraq as a democratic state that would spur reforms throughout the Middle East. However noble this latter rationale appeared, global public opinion and most world leaders condemned the invasion, which lacked the endorsement of the UN Security Council. Subsequent problems restoring order, let alone creating democracy from scratch, further discredited the Bush administration's "muscular" approach to democracy promotion.

President Obama hoped to restore the U.S. government's credibility in several ways, primarily by seeking to make the United States a role model for other countries. By acknowledging the U.S. government's past misdeeds, by proclaiming the return of the United States to the international community, and by relying on U.S. "soft power" rather than military force to advance its foreign policy goals, Obama believed the United States would once again lead the world toward freedom. As in the past, however, the new administration made vital exceptions to its calls for political reform. The United States, for example, continued to embrace the government of Saudi Arabia, whose vast oil resources and strategic support for the United States in the Persian Gulf overshadowed its monarchy's repressive rule. As for China, Secretary of State Clinton (quoted in Kessler and Shear, 2009) insisted that pressing Beijing on human rights "can't interfere with the global economic crisis, the global climate crisis, and the security crisis." Her views on China extended to Turkey, Egypt, and other "vital" allies with dubious human rights records. The United States, therefore, once again pursued a foreign policy informed by liberal principles but guided as well by the dictates of realism: national interests must prevail, military force cannot be forsaken, moral principles are not absolute in world politics, and successful outcomes in foreign policy most often justify their means.

Several other lessons emerge from these attempts by the U.S. government to export democracy. First, state-building efforts are unlikely to succeed without public support. President Clinton's efforts to "enlarge" global democracy occurred at a time when the public had little interest in foreign policy activism. Thus it was predictable that when Clinton intervened in Haiti in 1994 to restore an elected regime, the initiative received little public support and later failed to restore democratic order.

Second, free and fair elections do not ensure that democratic leaders will come to power or government policy will respect domestic freedoms or international norms. Elections may instead produce an **illiberal democracy** in which elected leaders such as Russia's Vladimir Putin suppress the political rights of their citizens (Zakaria 1997). This point was demonstrated further in 2006, when Palestinian voters in Gaza elected candidates from Hamas, a militant organization linked to terrorist attacks on Israel, to lead their legislature.

Third, security concerns almost always override concerns about democratic governance in the allocation of U.S. foreign aid. The government of Egypt, whose recognition of Israel is a linchpin of the Arab-Israeli peace process, remains a primary aid recipient despite its repressive government (see Hook 1998). As noted earlier, Saudi Arabia remains a close ally of the United States despite its brutal repression of women, ethnic minorities, and political opponents.

Finally, external support is most helpful to governments that have already initiated their democratic transitions. In countries in which attempted transitions "are stagnating or slipping backward, democracy aid has few chances of reversing this trend" (Carothers 1999, 306). The prospects for jumpstarting reforms in countries with no experience with democratic rule are even more remote.

This final lesson offers a crucial reminder that democracy must ultimately originate *within* countries, not from outside persuasion or coercion. Domestic political leaders and citizens must have the will to undertake these difficult transitions. Although external support can increase the chances that democratic reforms will succeed, no amount of foreign aid can transform a repressive state into a viable democracy without the support and engagement of that state's own people.

The International Criminal Court

The trend toward global democratization is featuring new efforts to punish governments for the most egregious crimes they commit against their citizens and those of other countries. Legal precedents for the International Criminal Court (ICC), which came into being in 2002, date back to the Nuremberg and Tokyo tribunals after World War II (see D. Jones 2002). In the mid-1990s, international support for such a court was revived when ad hoc tribunals were established for the former Yugoslavia and Rwanda, scenes of large-scale ethnic warfare that left more than 1 million people dead, almost all civilians. A 1998 agreement produced by a conference in Italy and therefore known as the **Rome Statute** identified four categories of crimes that would be handled by the proposed ICC:

- *Genocide,* which includes mass attacks "with intent to destroy, in whole or part, a national ethnic, racial, or religious group"

- *Crimes against humanity,* a category that covers systematic violence against citizens, including murder, enslavement, torture, rape, and other inhumane acts

- *War crimes,* or the use of indiscriminate violence against civilians in pursuit of military goals

- *Unlawful acts of foreign aggression* (see Schmitt and Richards 2000).

As of October 2009, 110 countries had ratified the Rome Statute and become active members of the ICC. Under the statute, the court considers only those cases that governments are unable or unwilling to handle on their own, thereby upholding the vital principle of national jurisdiction. A panel of ICC judges determines which cases will be referred to the court, and in some instances the UN Security Council has influence over the selection of cases. A central presumption in creating the court is that its mere presence encourages governments to strengthen their own legal protections and court systems so that outside intervention is not necessary (Mayerfield 2003).

As in the cases of the Kyoto Protocol and the Convention on Biological Diversity described earlier, the United States is conspicuously absent from the ICC. American leaders, who once championed such a court, claimed it would violate U.S. sovereignty. Their opposition was rooted in fears that the nation's global primacy inevitably creates resentments elsewhere. Specifically, the deployment of U.S. troops in numerous regional conflicts, some under the UN flag, gives adversaries many opportunities to target the United States with charges of war crimes and foreign aggression. It is this fear of being singled out by the many countries hostile toward Washington that has kept the United States out of the ICC. Still, President Clinton signed the Rome Statute on his last day in office so that the United States could participate in negotiations on the structure of the court and the scope of its authority. Although the delegates made many concessions demanded by the United States, the concessions did not go far enough to prevent President Bush from "unsigning" Clinton's commitment and pulling out of future ICC negotiations.

President Obama adopted a more cooperative stance toward the court and looked for ways to support its investigations and prosecutions of major human rights violations. In his view, joining the ICC was not only politically impossible at home—the Senate showed no interest in ratifying the treaty—U.S. membership also threatened to disrupt the court's political balance and agenda. As Samantha Power (quoted in Greco 2008), an adviser to Obama during his campaign, observed, "Until we've closed Guantánamo, gotten out of Iraq, renounced torture and rendition, and shown a different face for America, American membership in the ICC is going to make countries around the world think the ICC is a tool of American hegemony." Even as the ICC charged Sudanese president Omar Hassan al-Bashir with genocide in Darfur—the first case of a sitting president facing an arrest order—the world's foremost superpower found itself in the paradoxical role of being more effective out of the ICC than part of it.

Threats to Democracy at Home

The September 2001 terrorist attacks caused a seismic shift in how Americans perceived threats to the nation. Among these changes was a greater willingness to grant the federal government more powers in combating terrorism within the nation's borders. This support gained strength after investigations revealed that the hijackers had spent months in the United States preparing for the attacks. Many Americans thus felt that government officials at all levels should be granted heightened powers to prevent a recurrence of terrorist attacks, even if the new measures encroached upon individual freedoms and civil rights. In construing the terrorist attacks as acts of war, the Bush administration pursued and eagerly accepted this strengthening of federal powers. The primary missions of the Department of Justice and the FBI turned abruptly to fighting terrorism. Attorney General John Ashcroft (2001) testified before Congress that the "wartime reorganization" of the Justice Department was necessary for federal agents to conduct "the largest, most comprehensive criminal investigation in history."

Reflecting this shift in the national mood, Congress quickly and overwhelmingly passed the USA PATRIOT Act in October 2001. The measure, an acronym for "Uniting and Strengthening America by Providing Appropriate Tools Required to Intercept and Obstruct Terrorism," expanded federal powers of surveillance, detention, and search and seizure. Considering its vast scope, the rapid passage of the PATRIOT Act was unprecedented. The act was introduced in the House of Representatives on October 23, 2001, and passed the next day by a vote of 357–66. On October 26, the Senate approved the bill without amendment by a vote of 98–1. President Bush signed the bill later that day. In March 2006, President Bush approved legislation that made most measures in the act permanent.

Among the PATRIOT Act's most contested provisions was Section 215, which expanded the kinds of records the federal government can search in investigating suspected terrorists. Before the act, the FBI had to demonstrate "probable cause" when requesting search warrants against such suspects, and the domains of FBI searches were largely limited to hotels, airlines, storage lockers, and car rentals. The PATRIOT Act, however, expanded the list of searchable items to include "any tangible thing," such as financial statements, library records, travel receipts, telephone logs, medical information, and memberships in religious institutions. Under the act, rather than having to make the case for probable cause, FBI agents had to merely assert that the requested search would protect the United States against terrorism. Despite being passed by huge margins in Congress, the act drew fire from civil libertarians (see Brown 2003; Leone and Anrig 2003; Dadge 2004). The American Civil Liberties Union sued the federal government, charging that many stipulations of the PATRIOT Act violated constitutional guarantees to privacy and equal protection under the law. Meanwhile, the American Library Association protested federal inspections of library records.

Other U.S. responses to the September 11 attacks raised concerns about the government's adherence to the very democratic values that distinguished the United States from despotic regimes and terrorist groups. As noted earlier, in 2002 President Bush authorized the National Security Agency (NSA) to eavesdrop on international telephone calls and e-mail transmissions without the court-approved warrants that were legally required for such domestic surveillance. Although the White House justified this practice in part on its limited scope—only suspected terrorists were being monitored—it later became known that the NSA had amassed the phone records of tens of millions of ordinary Americans. Several telecommunications firms, including AT&T, Verizon, and BellSouth, reportedly provided this information to the federal government without first getting permission from their customers (Cauley 2006). Although Bush agreed in January 2007 to suspend the government's program of domestic surveillance, he did not rule out a return to the practice if the nation's security were sufficiently threatened.

This is not the first time in U.S. history that domestic political rights have been curbed in response to perceived threats from abroad (see Parenti 2003). The Alien and Sedition Acts of 1798, passed by Congress in anticipation of a war with France, made it illegal to "print, utter, or publish" criticism of government policies. During World War II, the U.S. government placed Japanese Americans in detention camps solely on the grounds of their heritage. Some two decades later, Richard Nixon's efforts to suppress criticism during the Vietnam War provoked Supreme Court intervention on behalf of press freedoms in the *Pentagon Papers* case (see Chapter 4).

U.S. Attorney General Alberto Gonzales testifies before the Senate Judiciary Committee in July 2007. Gonzales became a central figure in defending President George W. Bush's authority, as commander in chief, to conduct the war on terrorism—and the "coercive interrogation" of war prisoners—on his terms rather than on the basis of international laws and conventions.

The U.S. government's "coercive interrogation" of suspected terrorists, also described earlier, extends these concerns to the global level. An internal report by the Central Intelligence Agency (2004), made public in 2009 under court order, revealed that between September 2001 and October 2003 CIA interrogators beat a prisoner to death with a metal torch, threatened another with a power drill, staged a fake execution of another prisoner, threatened to rape and kill the families of prisoners, and routinely conducted "waterboarding" exercises in which bound suspects were nearly drowned while being ordered to divulge secret information. Khalid Sheikh Mohammed, the alleged mastermind of the September 2001 terrorist attacks, received this treatment 183 times; another al Qaeda operative, Abu Zubaydah, was subject to waterboarding on 83 occasions (Shane 2009). Critics, supported by a large body of international law, alleged that these practices amounted to torture, a practice commonly employed by the most repressive foreign governments and frequently condemned by previous U.S. leaders.

More modest forms of coercive interrogation gained legislative approval with the passage of the Military Commissions Act of 2006. The measure, which overcame the Supreme Court's reservations, provided the president broad powers to designate "enemy combatants" and to establish his own standards for what constitutes torture. The act also sanctioned the suspension of *habeas corpus,* the centuries-old principle that prisoners deserved, at a minimum, the right to face their accusers. Lacking this right, hundreds of prisoners were held for years at Guantánamo Bay and other detention centers without being formally charged with any crimes or having access to legal counsel. Further troubling, the U.S. government was found to be "hiding and interrogating" suspected terrorists in secret prisons located in eight European and Asian countries (Priest 2005, A1). The harsh tactics used in these prisons would have been illegal in U.S. detention centers.

Upon taking office in 2009, President Obama issued executive orders to close the Guantánamo Bay detention center by 2010, end the use of torture, and abolish the use of secret prisons overseas. Human rights advocates celebrated these measures, but internal arguments over where the Guantánamo prisoners would be relocated and how they would be prosecuted kept the Cuban facility open into 2010. And although the torture of prisoners ended, Obama permitted the continuing "rendition" of prisoners to third countries for interrogation so long as host governments pledged to treat them humanely. Obama's decision to extend key provisions of the PATRIOT Act in February 2010 also disappointed his supporters, as did his reversal of an earlier decision to hold the trials of Khalid Sheikh Mohammed and four other top al Qaeda operatives in civilian courts in Manhattan, just blocks away from "ground zero."

Political realities led to these policy changes. As noted earlier, the financial crisis consumed Obama's energies during his first year in office, and the president's proposed health care reform cost him much of his political capital. Approving any international treaties, which requires a "super-majority" of sixty-seven votes in the U.S. Senate, was out of the question in this environment. Further, Obama had become vulnerable to the same charges of being "soft on defense" that proved to be the undoing of past efforts by Democratic leaders to change the course of U.S. foreign policy. These home-grown challenges to Obama's authority, which sent his public approval ratings in a downward spiral, left the president less optimistic about solving transnational problems such as global warming, extreme poverty, weapons proliferation, and human rights abuses in faraway places.

Conclusion

The United States has long been a catalyst for the two most vital forces in modern world politics: democratization and economic globalization. The first of these forces empowers citizens and civil societies, inviting them to serve as counterweights to the power of the state. The second of these forces provides the technological means for these private actors to connect with each other, both within their polities and increasingly across national borders. While enabling mass movements to gather momentum, globalization also encourages the pooling of financial resources and the dissemination of weaponry and techniques of political violence. Paradoxically, the pivot of world power shifts from the nation that most effectively *stimulated* these forces to transnational actors who consider that country to be the primary *obstacle* to their political aspirations. Thus the greatest threat to continued U.S. primacy comes from the very political and economic forces the United States inspired and actively supports.

Amid these changes in the structure and scope of transnational institutions, the United States maintains a system of governing institutions largely unchanged from the days of its founding. Here as well the objective is to fragment and fracture state power in order to prevent tyranny. The diffusion of policy-making authority across a widening array of federal agencies, however, inhibits the government from advancing a coherent set of principles and priorities. This pattern is especially visible in the formulation and conduct of U.S. foreign policy, a domain that features cross-cutting powers spanning the three branches of government and multiple centers of decision making within the diplomatic, security, intelligence, and economic bureaucracies.

The decentralized U.S. political system, with many access channels open to citizens and groups, also ensures that societal pressures will penetrate the policy process and shape the course of government action within the United States and elsewhere. Because interest groups are not created equal, however, their influence is skewed. Under the George W. Bush administration, for example, corporate influence over U.S. foreign policy, always considerable, was particularly visible in the administration's resistance to energy conservation, in its push for arms exports, and in its calculations behind the invasion and rebuilding of Iraq. Although Obama rhetorically distanced himself from corporate pressures, he filled his economic team with executives from major banks, many of which turned to Washington for relief during the financial crisis of 2008.

Meanwhile, little guidance can be expected from public opinion because many Americans not only pay little attention to world politics, but also are the products of an educational system that has long neglected world history and geography. As described in Chapter 8, the most recent revolution in mass communications—including the tidal wave of Internet and social media outlets—has been accompanied by reduced coverage of, and interest in, world news. These trends reinforce the nation's long-standing political culture, which still exhibits a chronic ambivalence about the global roles and responsibilities of the United States. As in the nation's early years, the U.S. government alternately seeks to detach itself from the outside world and to transform that world in its own image. A middle ground between the two, cooperating with other states on the basis of sovereign equality, seems to be ruled out by an ingrained sense of American exceptionalism.

These troublesome aspects of U.S. foreign policy proved manageable during the Cold War, whose bipolar balance of power had a "double disciplining" effect on the policy process. "The external threat disciplined American society, leading interest groups and the public generally to defer to central decision makers on the definition of national interest and how best to achieve it," G. John Ikenberry,

Michael Mastanduno, and William Wohlforth (2009, 17) observed. "The Cold War constrained American decision makers as well, forcing them to exercise caution in the international arena and to assure that public opinion or interest groups did not capture or derail foreign policy for parochial reasons." The luxury of a unipolar world has also "loosened the political discipline engendered by the Cold War threat, leaving U.S. foreign policy more vulnerable to growing partisanship at home. 'Red' and 'Blue' America disagree about the nature of U.S. engagement in the world; growing disparities in wealth have reawakened class tensions; and political pragmatism has been losing ground to ideological extremism" (Kupchan and Trubowitz 2007, 9).

Such constraints have not applied since the Soviet Union's collapse in 1991, when the United States assumed an unprecedented degree of global primacy. Two decades after the Cold War, no single foreign government appears capable of upending the current unipolar balance of power. China, Russia, and Japan remain preoccupied with domestic concerns, and the member states of the European Union continue to focus primarily on easing the strains that come with "dual sovereignty." Internal problems also preoccupy third-tier powers such as India and Brazil. In the absence of any other major power or alliance that can match the U.S. government's economic, military, and political assets, it is likely that the United States will retain its predominant status in the generation to come. Although this likelihood may be reassuring to those who value U.S. primacy, the extension of unipolarity also ensures that the domestic strains on coherent policy making will stymie American leadership.

The United States must come to grips with a world that has grown wary of U.S. foreign policy ambitions. Although pretensions of manifest destiny may have rationalized the expansion of U.S. hegemony from the nineteenth century through the Cold War, such claims ring hollow today. Given recent setbacks and lingering memories of the Bush Doctrine, Americans cannot assume that allies will "bandwagon" with the United States. Doubts about U.S. world power are especially strong now that the nation faces unprecedented national debts, chronic trade deficits, and the tactical limitations of its military power in the face of unconventional threats and low-intensity wars. The open-ended nature of the war on terrorism makes it difficult, if not impossible, for the United States to declare "victory" over its adversaries.

Whether the United States overcomes the paradox of its own world power will determine its fate in the twenty-first century. The nation's success will depend on its management of a world order largely of its making—a turbulent order that is at once more closely interconnected and more disjointed than ever before. Such contradictions, integral elements of the United States' own political system and society during the nation's rise to global primacy, should now be familiar to foreign policy makers. The ability of past leaders to embrace these contradictory forces at home offers a fitting lesson for the future navigation of U.S. foreign policy.

Key Terms

carrying capacity, p. 386

democratization, p. 401

demographic transition,
p. 387

Earth Summit, p. 386

global commons, p. 385

global warming, p. 388

illiberal democracy, p. 408

Kyoto Protocol, p. 389

Mexico City policy, p. 388

migration, p. 394

nation building, p. 405

Rome Statute, p. 409

state building, p. 405

tragedy of the
commons, p. 385

Internet References

The **Carnegie Council: The Voice for Ethics in International Affairs** (www.cceia.org/index.html) is an independent, nonpartisan organization that focuses on ethics, war and peace, global social justice, and religion in politics. The Carnegie Council produces, among its other publications, the journal *Ethics and International Affairs,* with many articles available online through the link to "publications" on its home page.

The **Carnegie Endowment for International Peace** (www.carnegieendowment.org) is a private, nonprofit, and nonpartisan organization with offices in Moscow, Beijing, Beirut, Brussels, and Washington, D.C. The endowment promotes international cooperation between nations and greater U.S. involvement in international affairs. The organization also addresses global change by examining international organizations, bilateral relations, and the various political-economic forces affecting change. Its publication *Foreign Policy* (www.foreignpolicy.com) is one of the leading periodicals on world politics and foreign policy.

Europa (http://europa.eu.int), the portal to the main Web site for the European Union, offers information on the integration of European countries. It provides links to maps, to an online library of EU documents, and to institutions such as the European Parliament and the EU's central bank.

The **Foreign and International Law Library** (www.washlaw.edu/forint), maintained by Washburn University School of Law Library, provides access to international and foreign law topics and journals as well as links to sites to facilitate further research.

Foreign Policy in Focus (www.fpif.org) is a think tank allied with "progressive" interests that emphasizes citizen-based foreign policy issues. FPIF researchers compose short policy briefs on U.S. foreign policy issues and global involvement such as trade, energy, environment, security, human rights, and labor. Much of their work is directed toward understanding the connection between private actors and the government.

Freedom House (www.freedomhouse.org) is an independent, nongovernmental research organization committed to promoting and understanding civil and political freedoms around the world. The organization conducts research at the national,

(continued)

regional, and global levels of analysis. Many of its publications, including *Freedom in the World,* which uses an ordinal scale to measure civil and political freedoms, are available on the Freedom House Web site.

The **Global Policy Forum** (www.globalpolicy.org) integrates information and research on globalization, security issues, and the United Nations. Resources on the Web site focus on UN and state accountability, issues of sovereignty, questions of empire, and the crisis in Iraq.

The **Globalization Website** (www.emory.edu/SOC/globalization), maintained by Emory University, provides links to international organizations, NGOs, and other resources related to globalization such as data links, newsletters, quick reference guides, glossaries, and debates on international governance and globalization.

The **Institute for Global Communications** (www.igc.org) is a network for NGOs wishing to discuss, promote, and influence transnational policies. Subject areas on the Web site include human rights, peace promotion, environmental protection, women's rights, and workers' rights, which are found through the portals of four central networks: PeaceNet, AntiRacismNet, WomensNet, and EcoNet.

The list of **International Affairs Resources** (www.etown.edu/vl/research.html) from the World Wide Web Virtual Library provides links to think tanks, international organizations, and NGOs to facilitate research into matters pertaining to international law, global governance, human rights, peacekeeping operations, and international economic affairs. The site is organized by data, journal, and electronic resources, with full descriptions of each link.

The **NGO Global Network** (www.ngo.org) seeks to enhance the collaboration of nongovernmental organizations throughout the world, thereby improving cooperation between NGOs and the United Nations. The organization's Web site has links to NGOs around the globe, organized by their missions and categories of operation.

The Web site of **Sovereignty International** (http://sovereignty.net/p/gov/ggmenu.htm), titled "Global Governance," offers links and articles on global governance and country cooperation. Included are commission reports, speeches, and treaty descriptions of policy areas such as the International Criminal Court, UN bureaus, and environmental regimes.

The **United Nations** (www.un.org) is the largest intergovernmental organization in the world. The UN's Web site provides links to further information on its councils, bureaus, and governing resources. Data resources on member countries and missions are also included.

U.S. Public Interest Research Group (www.uspirg.org), the federation of state Public Interest Research Groups, seeks to represent the interests of the American public on large-scale policy issues. U.S. PIRG focuses on the environment, energy, democratic governance, and health care, among other things. Research reviews and policy reports, as well as congressional and presidential "scorecards" on multiple issues, are available on the Web site.

U.S. Administrations since World War II

President	Secretary of State	Secretary of Defense	National Security Adviser
Harry Truman 1945–1953	Edward Stettinius James Byrnes George Marshall Dean Acheson	James Forrestal Louis Johnson George Marshall Robert Lovett	
Dwight Eisenhower 1953–1961	John Dulles Christian Herter	Charles Wilson Neil McElroy Thomas Gates	Robert Cutler Dillon Anderson Robert Cutler Gordon Gray
John F. Kennedy 1961–1963	Dean Rusk	Robert McNamara	McGeorge Bundy
Lyndon Johnson 1963–1969	Dean Rusk	Robert McNamara Clark Clifford	McGeorge Bundy Walt Rostow
Richard Nixon 1969–1974	William Rogers Henry Kissinger	Melvin Laird Elliot Richardson James Schlesinger	Henry Kissinger
Gerald Ford 1974–1977	Henry Kissinger	James Schlesinger Donald Rumsfeld	Henry Kissinger Brent Scowcroft
Jimmy Carter 1977–1981	Cyrus Vance Edmund Muskie	Harold Brown	Zbigniew Brzezinski
Ronald Reagan 1981–1989	Alexander Haig George Shultz	Caspar Weinberger Frank Carlucci	Richard Allen William Clark Robert McFarlane John Poindexter Frank Carlucci Colin Powell
George H. W. Bush 1989–1993	James Baker Lawrence Eagleburger	Dick Cheney	Brent Scowcroft
Bill Clinton 1993–2001	Warren Christopher Madeleine Albright	Les Aspin William Perry William Cohen	Anthony Lake Samuel Berger
George W. Bush 2001–2009	Colin Powell Condoleezza Rice	Donald Rumsfeld Robert Gates	Condoleezza Rice Stephen Hadley
Barack Obama 2009–	Hillary Clinton	Robert Gates	James Jones

The War Powers Resolution of 1973

JOINT RESOLUTION CONCERNING THE WAR POWERS OF CONGRESS AND THE PRESIDENT

Resolved by the Senate and House of Representatives of the United States of America in Congress assembled,

Short Title

SECTION 1. This joint resolution may be cited as the "War Powers Resolution."

Purpose and Policy

SEC. 2. (a) It is the purpose of this joint resolution to fulfill the intent of the framers of the Constitution of the United States and insure that the collective judgment of both the Congress and the President will apply to the introduction of the United States Armed Forces into hostilities, or into situations where imminent involvement in hostilities is clearly indicated by the circumstances, and to the continued use of such forces in hostilities or in such situations.

(b) Under article I, section 8, of the Constitution, it is specifically provided that the Congress shall have the power to make all laws necessary and proper for carrying into execution, not only its own powers but also all other powers vested by the Constitution in the Government of the United States, or in any department or officer thereof.

(c) The constitutional powers of the President as Commander-in-Chief to introduce United States Armed Forces into hostilities, or into situations where imminent involvement in hostilities is clearly indicated by the circumstances, are exercised only pursuant to (1) a declaration of war, (2) specific statutory authorization, or (3) a national emergency created by attack upon the United States, its territories or possessions, or its armed forces.

Consultation

SEC. 3. The President in every possible instance shall consult with Congress before introducing United States Armed Forces into hostilities or into situations where imminent involvement in hostilities is clearly indicated by the circumstances, and after every such introduction shall consult regularly with the Congress until United States Armed Forces are no longer engaged in hostilities or have been removed from such situations.

Reporting

SEC. 4. (a) In the absence of a declaration of war, in any case in which United States Armed Forces are introduced—

(1) into hostilities or into situations where imminent involvement in hostilities is clearly indicated by circumstances;

(2) into the territory, airspace or waters of a foreign nation, while equipped for combat, except for deployment which relate solely to supply, replacement, repair, or training of such forces; or

(3) in numbers which substantially enlarge United States Armed Forces equipped for combat already located in a foreign nation; the President shall submit within 48 hours to the Speaker of the House of Representatives and to the President pro tempore of the Senate a report, in writing, setting forth—

(A) the circumstances necessitating the introduction of United States Armed Forces;

(B) the constitutional and legislative authority under which such introduction took place; and

(C) the estimated scope and duration of the hostilities or involvement.

(b) The President shall provide such other information as the Congress may request in the fulfillment of its constitutional responsibilities with respect to committing the Nation to war and to the use of United States Armed Forces abroad.

(c) Whenever United States Armed Forces are introduced into hostilities or into any situation described in subsection (a) of this section, the President shall, so long as such armed forces continue to be engaged in such hostilities or situation, report to the Congress periodically on the status of such hostilities or situation as well as on the scope and duration of such hostilities or situation, but in no event shall he report to the Congress less often than once every six months.

Congressional Action

SEC. 5. (a) Each report submitted pursuant to section 4 (a) (1) shall be transmitted to the Speaker of the House of Representatives and to the President pro tempore of the Senate on the same calendar day. Each report so transmitted shall be referred to the Committee on Foreign Affairs of the House of Representatives and to the Committee on Foreign Relations of the Senate for appropriate action. If, when the report is transmitted, the Congress has adjourned sine die or has adjourned for any period in excess of three calendar days, the Speaker of the House of Representatives and the President pro tempore of the Senate, if they deem it advisable (or if petitioned by at least 30 percent of the membership of their respective Houses) shall jointly request the President to convene Congress in order that it may consider the report and take appropriate action pursuant to this section.

(b) Within sixty calendar days after a report is submitted or is required to be submitted pursuant to section 4 (a) (1), whichever is earlier, the President shall terminate any use of United States Armed Forces with respect to which such report was submitted (or required to be submitted), unless the Congress (1) has declared war or has enacted a specific authorization for such use of United States Armed Forces, (2) has extended by law such sixty-day period, or (3) is physically unable to meet as a result of an armed attack upon the United States. Such sixty-day period shall be extended for not more than an additional thirty days if the President determines and certifies to the Congress in writing that unavoidable military necessity respecting the safety of United States Armed Forces requires the continued use of such armed forces in the course of bringing about a prompt removal of such forces.

(c) Notwithstanding subsection (b), at any time that United States Armed Forces are engaged in hostilities outside the territory of the United States, its possessions and territories without a declaration of war or specific statutory authorization, such forces shall be removed by the president if the Congress so directs by concurrent resolution.

Congressional Priority Procedures for Joint Resolution or Bill

SEC. 6. (a) Any joint resolution or bill introduced pursuant to section 5(b) at least thirty calendar days before the expiration of the sixty-day period specified in such section shall be referred to the Committee on Foreign Affairs of the House of Representatives or the Committee on Foreign Relations of the Senate, as the case may be, and such committee shall report one such joint resolution or bill, together with its recommendations, not later than twenty-four calendar days before the expiration of the sixty-day period specified in such section, unless such House shall otherwise determine by the yeas and nays.

(b) Any joint resolution or bill so reported shall become the pending business of the House in question (in the case of the Senate the time for debate shall be equally divided between the proponents and the opponents), and shall be voted on within three calendar days thereafter, unless such House shall otherwise determine by yeas and nays.

(c) Such a joint resolution or bill passed by one House shall be referred to the committee of the other House named in subsection (a) and shall be reported out not later than fourteen calendar days before the expiration of the sixty-day period specified in section 5 (b). The joint resolution or bill so reported shall become the pending business of the House in question and shall be voted on within three calendar days after it has been reported, unless such House shall otherwise determine by yeas and nays.

(d) In the case of any disagreement between the two Houses of Congress with respect to a joint resolution or bill passed by both Houses, conferees shall be promptly appointed and the committee of conference shall make and file a report with respect to such resolution or bill not later than four calendar days before the expiration of the sixty-day period specified in section 5 (b). In the event the conferees are unable to agree within 48 hours, they shall report back to their respective Houses in disagreement. Notwithstanding any rule in either House concerning the printing of conference reports in the Record or concerning any delay in the consideration of such reports, such report shall be acted on by both Houses not later than the expiration of such sixty-day period.

Congressional Priority Procedures for Concurrent Resolution

SEC. 7 (a) Any concurrent resolution introduced pursuant to section 5 (c) shall be referred to the Committee on Foreign Affairs of the House of Representatives or the Committee on Foreign Relations of the Senate, as the case may be, and one such concurrent resolution shall be reported out by such committee together with its recommendations within fifteen calendar days, unless such House shall otherwise determine by the yeas and nays.

(b) Any concurrent resolution so reported shall become the pending business of the House in question (in the case of the Senate the time for debate shall be equally divided between the proponents and the opponents) and shall be voted on within three calendar days thereafter, unless such House shall otherwise determine by yeas and nays.

(c) Such a concurrent resolution passed by one House shall be referred to the committee of the other House named in subsection (a) and shall be reported out by such committee together with its recommendations within fifteen calendar days and shall thereupon become the pending business of such House and shall be voted upon within three calendar days, unless such House shall otherwise determine by yeas and nays.

(d) In the case of any disagreement between the two Houses of Congress with respect to a concurrent resolution passed by both Houses, conferees shall be promptly appointed and the committee of conference shall make and file a report with respect to such concurrent resolution within six calendar days after the legislation is referred to the committee of conference. Notwithstanding any rule in either House concerning the printing of conference reports in the Record or concerning any delay in the consideration of such reports, such report shall be acted on by both Houses not later than six calendar days after the conference report is filed. In the event the conferees are unable to agree within 48 hours, they shall report back to their respective Houses in disagreement.

Interpretation of Joint Resolution

SEC. 8. (a) Authority to introduce United States Armed Forces into hostilities or into situations of wherein involvement in hostilities is clearly indicated by the circumstances shall not be inferred—

(1) from any provision of law (whether or not in effect before the date of the enactment of this joint resolution), including any provision contained in any appropriation Act, unless such provision specifically authorizes the introduction of United States Armed Forces into hostilities or into such situations and states that it is intended to constitute specific statutory authorization within the meaning of this joint resolution; or

(2) from any treaty heretofore or hereafter ratified unless such treaty is implemented by legislation specifically authorizing the introduction of United States Armed Forces into hostilities or into such situations and stating that it is intended to constitute specific statutory authorization within the meaning of this joint resolution.

(b) Nothing in this joint resolution shall be construed to require any further specific statutory authorization to permit members of United States Armed Forces to participate jointly with members of the armed forces of one or more foreign countries in the headquarters operations of high-level military commands which were established prior to the date of enactment of this joint resolution and pursuant to the United Nations Charter or any treaty ratified by the United States prior to such date.

(c) For purposes of this joint resolution, the term introduction of United States Armed Forces includes the assignment of members of such armed forces to command, coordinate, participate in the movement of, or accompany the regular or irregular military forces of any foreign country or government when such military forces are engaged, or there exists an imminent threat that such forces will become engaged, in hostilities.

(d) Nothing in this joint resolution—

(1) is intended to alter the constitutional authority of the Congress or the President, or the provisions of existing treaties; or

(2) shall be construed as granting any authority to the President with respect to the introduction of United States Armed Forces into hostilities or into situations wherein involvement in hostilities is clearly indicated by the circumstances which authority he would not have had in the absence of this joint resolution.

Separability Clause

SEC. 9. If any provision of this joint resolution or the application thereof to any person or circumstance is held invalid, the remainder of the joint resolution and the application of such provision to any other person or circumstance shall not be affected thereby.

Effective Date

SEC. 10. This joint resolution shall take effect on the date of its enactment.

SOURCE: *Statutes at Large,* 93rd Cong., 1st session, Nov. 7, 1973, 555–560.

Glossary

advisory system A closely knit network of trusted aides and confidants who have the most immediate impact on the president's foreign policy decisions.

Almond-Lippmann consensus A widespread negative view jointly articulated by Gabriel Almond and Walter Lippmann that U.S. public opinion is volatile, incoherent, and irrelevant to the policy-making process.

analogies A cognitive "shortcut" by which leaders make sense of current foreign policy problems by seeing them as replications of similar problems in the past.

anarchy The lack of a world government to regulate and restrain the behavior of countries, a condition emphasized by structural realists as the defining feature of world politics.

Anti-Ballistic Missile (ABM) Treaty A 1972 agreement between the United States and the Soviet Union restricting each side's deployment of antimissile systems. Designed to enhance deterrence by keeping both superpowers vulnerable to nuclear attack, the agreement was nullified by the United States in 2002.

asymmetric warfare A type of armed conflict between two sides of unequal strength characterized by the weaker side's exploiting the vulnerabilities of the stronger.

attentive public The small segment of the U.S. general public that pays close attention to foreign policy issues but has little influence on the government's policy making.

balance of power The distribution of resources and capabilities among nation-states. Also, in realist theory, a belief that global stability can be maintained when the strongest nation-states have roughly equal levels of power.

balance of trade The relationship between the value of a state's imports and exports. A surplus indicates a higher level of exports, whereas a deficit indicates a higher level of imports.

bandwagon A strategy by which less powerful states align diplomatically with a global or regional hegemon in exchange for security and economic benefits provided by the hegemon.

Baruch Plan Proposal by the United States in 1946 to outlaw nuclear weapons and create common stocks of fissile material for the development of peaceful nuclear programs. The terms of the plan were later rejected by the Soviet Union.

belief systems Individual worldviews, formed early in life, that directly influence decision makers' foreign policy goals and strategies as well as their responses to specific problems.

bipolar balance of power A global power structure in which two countries maintain a predominant share of resources and form rival blocs to offset each other's advantages.

blogosphere The vibrant and rapidly growing network of electronic discourse involving Internet-based blogs and individuals who engage in discussions and debates on a variety of issues, including U.S. foreign policy.

blowback Hostile actions against a powerful state that are motivated largely by perceived wrongdoings and mistreatment by the targeted state.

bolstering A theory in cognitive psychology holding that, once a decision is made, policy makers later use that decision to "bolster" or lend additional support to their original argument regarding the problem at hand.

bounded rationality A decision-making environment characterized by an influx of more information than can be managed effectively, leading to policy decisions that do not fully conform to standards of rationality.

Bretton Woods agreements A series of agreements approved by the United States and other market economies in 1944 that led to the creation of the World Bank and the International Monetary Fund.

bully pulpit A term coined by Theodore Roosevelt to describe a president's unique ability to shape public opinion by speaking out forcefully on important issues.

bureaucratic politics A model of policy making that emphasizes inherent conflicts of interest among government agencies. The state is perceived as an arena of bureaucratic struggle rather than a "unitary actor."

Bush Doctrine A set of foreign policy principles and strategies, including the possible launching of preventive wars, devised by President George W. Bush in the aftermath of the September 2001 terrorist attacks.

carrying capacity The physical limit of the earth's ecosystem to sustain human life threatened by population growth, resource depletion, and environmental degradation.

Case-Zablocki Act Congressional bill passed in 1972 requiring presidents to report all international agreements to Congress within sixty days of their entering into force.

causal beliefs The perceptions that an individual decision maker holds regarding the most likely functional links among policy problems, their sources, and alternative solutions to solve them.

celebrity diplomacy The involvement of famous actors, pop musicians, and other celebrities in foreign policy issues such as HIV/AIDS and the genocide in Darfur that raises public awareness of the issues and often spurs government action.

Church Committee A select committee of the U.S. Senate created by Sen. Frank Church, D-Idaho, in 1975 to investigate a wide range of recent operations conducted by the CIA and other intelligence agencies, many of which were determined by the committee to be abuses of power. A series of intelligence reforms were enacted in response to these findings.

civil-military relations The vital but often awkward relationship between American civil society and the armed services that reflects underlying differences in backgrounds, values, and policy priorities.

civil society A loose-knit conglomeration of citizens and groups that interacts outside formal government boundaries and frequently applies pressure on state policies.

clientitis State Department employees' overly close relationships with foreign governments and citizens that may cloud their judgment about U.S. global priorities.

CNN effect A pattern in which globalized news coverage of a crisis abroad prompts government action in U.S. foreign policy.

codetermination A principle expressed in the U.S. Constitution calling for the sharing of foreign policy powers between the executive and legislative branches of government.

coercive diplomacy The threat to use force to reverse an adversary's offensive action. Often used by stronger powers to achieve foreign policy goals without violence.

cognitive closure The adopted conception of a problem before all the available information has been fully examined and alternative strategies have been considered.

cognitive consistency The common, subconscious tendency of individuals to perceive new information as consistent with their preexisting belief systems.

cognitive psychology The study of means by which individuals obtain and process information about the world around them.

Cold War The protracted conflict between the United States, the Soviet Union, and their respective allies from World War II until 1991 that was labeled "Cold" because it never led to direct military combat between the nuclear superpowers.

collective security A system of preventing interstate conflict in which world leaders renounce war as an instrument of statecraft and then pledge to defend each other in the case of aggression. A hallmark of the League of Nations.

collegial model A management style that encourages open dialogue among presidential advisers in order to gain consensus.

communism An economic system in which the state owns the primary means of production in order to ensure the equitable division of wealth among a nation's population, as in the case of the former Soviet Union.

comparative advantage A global division of labor in which each country's producers contribute to the world economy in areas that draw on their unique strengths. According to Ricardian economics, such a division would lead to a prosperous global market economy.

competitive model A management style that encourages open debate among advisers, often without regard to rank, allowing the president to select the policy that is defended most persuasively.

complex irregular warfare An emerging form of militarized conflict that fuses conventional warfare with state and nonstate terrorism, attacks on information and financial assets, alliances with criminal syndicates, and other tactics.

congressional diplomacy Efforts by the president to consult members of Congress at various stages of the foreign policy process. Seen as crucial to achieving White House goals in foreign policy.

congressional dominance model A model of policy making that views legislators in Congress as masters of the federal bureaucracy, capable of ensuring that their policy preferences are carried out in the policy process.

constituent service Legislators' primary attention to the needs of citizens in their states and districts as opposed to more general national concerns.

constructivism A critical body of social and political thought that argues that public problems, including those related to foreign policy, do not have fixed or "objective" properties but rather are socially constructed, primarily through public discourse.

containment The U.S. strategy devised by U.S. diplomat George Kennan at the start of the Cold War to prevent Soviet expansion. A midrange alternative to the extremes of U.S. withdrawal from global activism and direct military conflict with the Soviet Union.

cooperative internationalism A form of active engagement in foreign policy that emphasizes diplomacy and multilateral collaboration rather than military confrontation.

corporate warriors Private contractors engaged in the provision of military services, from cooking meals to interrogating prisoners, in theaters of armed conflict. Used increasingly by the United States and some smaller governments.

cosmopolitan groups Nongovernmental organizations that seek to influence transnational problems in world politics, such as environmental decay and weapons proliferation, which affect people in all areas.

counter-insurgency The ongoing effort by the United States and other governments to anticipate, resist, and destroy insurgent groups, as in the ongoing U.S. military efforts in Afghanistan and Pakistan.

counterintelligence Efforts by intelligence agents to obstruct attempts by foreign agents to infiltrate a country's political process or compromise its national interests.

covert operations Secret efforts by U.S. intelligence agencies to effect changes that are favorable to the United States within foreign governments.

crisis decision making The distinctive aspects of decision making exhibited by presidents and other foreign policy makers during times of heightened international stress.

Cuban missile crisis A dangerous standoff between the United States and the Soviet Union in October 1962 sparked by Soviet shipments of nuclear missiles to Cuba. The crisis, which brought the superpowers as close as ever to nuclear war, was settled peacefully after two weeks of tense negotiations.

cyberterrorism Form of nonmilitary political conflict by which an adversarial state or private group gains access to and disrupts a government's computer systems.

defense policy The organization and strategic deployment of armed forces to protect a state against foreign military threats.

delegate model One of two models of political representation (the other is the trustee model). Holds that elected officials should act on the general public's preferences on a given policy issue.

democratic deficit The lack of legal requirements for openness and elected representation in many nongovernmental organizations.

democratic peace A theory of international relations arguing that a world of democracies would be more cooperative and less prone to interstate violence.

democratization The process by which states adopt and implement democratic reforms. Also, a foreign government's promotion of democratic reforms in other states, often through the use of foreign aid or moral suasion.

demographic transition The process by which societies experience falling rates of population growth and rising life expectancies as they undergo the transition from agricultural to industrial economies.

demographics The characteristics (for example, ethnicity, religion, age, and wealth) of a given population that are known to affect opinions on U.S. foreign policy and other matters.

détente A policy devised by Henry Kissinger, national security adviser and secretary of state under Presidents Richard Nixon and Gerald Ford, to ease tensions between the United States and the Soviet Union.

digital diplomacy Increased contact among governments made possible by advances in telecommunications technology.

diplomacy The negotiations among representatives of two or more sovereign states involving official matters of mutual or collective concern.

diversionary theory of war A possible cause of war in which political leaders provoke armed conflicts to divert public attention from domestic problems or to boost their public approval ratings.

divided government A political deadlock that often results when Congress and the White House are controlled by different political parties.

divine divide The consistently reported differences in public opinion between religiously devout Americans and others, a gap reflected in the war in Iraq whose greatest source of public support came from evangelical Christians.

domestic terrorism Acts of terrorism in which the perpetrators and their targets are located within the same nation-state.

domino theory Widespread view within the U.S. government early in the Cold War that a communist victory in one country would lead to a succession of additional victories in neighboring states.

Earth Summit A major UN-sponsored environmental conference held in 1992 in Brazil that identified "sustainable development" as a central objective in the post–Cold War era.

economic liberalism A political-economic system that protects private property and commercial activity from government intervention. Identified with Adam Smith, an Enlightenment theorist.

economic nationalism A political-economic system that considers commercial activity fruitful to the extent that it serves the interests of the state, whose power depends on the accumulation of wealth and its use for military armament.

economic sanctions Material penalties imposed by states or intergovernmental organizations on foreign countries involving trade, aid, foreign investments, or other aspects of economic relations. Imposed to force adherence to political demands.

economic statecraft The use by national governments of a variety of economic tools, including trade, foreign aid, and sanctions, to advance their foreign policy goals.

electoral factors Calculations regarding the likely effects of a vote in Congress on a legislator's future prospects for constituent approval and reelection.

elitism A challenge to pluralist theory that argues that political power even in democratic systems is highly concentrated among a few government leaders and the wealthiest citizens.

embeds Reporters "embedded" with U.S. military troops during the 2003 invasion of Iraq to provide firsthand accounts. A practice accurately anticipated by government leaders to produce more favorable media coverage.

empire A form of domination by a world power that includes direct control over the domestic and foreign policies of other political entities.

engagement and enlargement President Bill Clinton's national security policy emphasizing U.S. global activism and the promotion of political reforms abroad that would "enlarge" the sphere of democratic rule.

exceptionalism A widely held sense of national distinctiveness or superiority, exemplified by Americans' traditional view of their nation as a "city upon a hill."

executive agreements Formal agreements negotiated by the executive branch with foreign governments that do not require Senate ratification. Often serve as an alternative to treaties.

exemplarists Advocates of a school of thought that believes the United States should lead primarily by example rather than by intervening directly in foreign affairs.

exit strategy A coherent plan to conclude military hostilities and remove a country's presence from a theater of conflict in a way that preserves the country's political and military interests in the conflict.

extended deterrence Avowed nuclear retaliation against attacks not only on a country's territory, but also on the territory of its allies.

external balancing The formation of military alliances and other tactics that allow relatively weak states to counter the ambitions and influence of a dominant power.

extraordinary rendition A tactic used by the United States and other governments to transfer suspected terrorists or other enemies of the state to third countries for detention and interrogation on terms selected by the third-party governments.

extraterritoriality A central principle of international law that designates foreign embassies and other properties as the sovereign territory of the country occupying the properties, thus protecting them from encroachments by host governments.

failed states National governments that are incapable of maintaining order or providing even minimal services to their citizens.

financial statecraft A form of foreign policy coercion that includes the seizure, freezing, or manipulation of the assets and capital flows of adversaries.

finished intelligence The end result of collecting and processing raw information, commonly presented to intelligence directors and White House officials for consideration of foreign policy action.

flexible response A security strategy adopted by the U.S. government during the Cold War that allowed for a range of military actions—nuclear and conventional—in response to offensive threats posed to the United States and its allies.

floating exchange rates A system in which the value of a country's currency is determined by market forces rather than government intervention, based largely on the relative value of other currencies.

foreign aid Economic resources provided by affluent governments to developing countries on terms unavailable to the recipients through commercial markets. May take the form of development or security assistance.

foreign policy elite The small segment (less than 5 percent) of the U.S. population that has both the interest and the means to influence U.S. foreign policy.

foreign policy entrepreneurs Members of Congress who adopt U.S. foreign policy as a major concern and take individual actions to advance their policy agendas.

foreign service officers Permanent State Department officials who work in overseas embassies and consulates on routine matters such as handling visas, hosting delegations, and advancing U.S. foreign policy priorities in their "host" countries.

formalistic model A presidential management style characterized as orderly and hierarchical, featuring the structured discussion of issues following well-defined procedures, roles, and communication channels.

framing Government attempts to simplify and represent foreign policy problems so that they are understood by citizens in ways that favor the government's position. Generally supported and perpetuated by news organizations.

game theory An approach to problem solving, drawing on economics and mathematics, that applies assumptions of rational choice and cost-benefit analysis to negotiations and bargaining on foreign policy issues.

gender gap The consistently reported differences between men and women in public opinion regarding U.S. foreign policy, with women found to be more supportive of diplomacy and other nonmilitary approaches to conflict resolution.

geoeconomics The interaction of national economies in the world economy. Also the global production and distribution of economic output as a national priority.

geopolitical assets A nation's available physical and human resources, such as its size, location, and natural resources, and their utility in foreign policy.

geopolitics The impact of geographical factors on the distribution of global power and the foreign policies of states.

glasnost Political reforms adopted by Soviet president Mikhail Gorbachev in the late 1980s that called for greater openness in the political system and a loosening of control by the Communist Party.

global commons The earth's fragile ecosystem that sustains animal and plant life. Generally includes physical resources shared by all inhabitants.

global governance Combines traditional state-to-state diplomacy with policy collaboration among private groups and intergovernmental organizations.

global jurisprudence Legal standards and restrictions applied above the nation-state level.

global warming The rising average temperatures on the earth's surface produced by population growth, industrialization, and the resulting fossil fuel emissions.

globalization The melding of national and regional markets into a single world market with limited political barriers to commerce.

gold standard A system of "fixed" exchange rates in which the values of national currencies are based on the value of gold. An alternative to "floating" exchange rates that currently set currency values.

Goldwater-Nichols Act Legislative measure approved in 1986 that altered the balance of power within the Pentagon by strengthening the power of the chairman of the Joint Chiefs of Staff and increasing the power of regional commanders in chief who manage forces across the armed services.

grand strategy A statement of a nation's essential objectives in world politics and the means to achieve those objectives.

gross domestic product A key measure of a nation's wealth, the sum total of goods and services produced in that nation during a given year.

group identity The tendency of individual citizens to adopt opinions regarding U.S. foreign policy and other issues that reflect their affiliation with larger groups such as churches, professional associations, and public interest groups.

groupthink Dysfunctional collective decision making characterized by a strong sense of a group's moral righteousness, closed-mindedness, and pressures toward conformity.

Gulf of Tonkin Resolution Resolution approved by Congress in 1964 authorizing President Lyndon Johnson to "take all necessary measures" to protect U.S. forces supporting the government of South Vietnam.

gunboat diplomacy The use of deployed military forces as a means of political intimidation in order to achieve a nation's foreign policy preferences without resorting to violence.

guns-or-butter debates Ongoing policy disputes about federal spending for defense versus social programs and domestic needs.

habeas corpus A centuries-old legal principle that prisoners must be able to challenge the lawfulness of their arrests before an independent court.

hegemon One nation-state that exerts a controlling influence over other countries and societies that falls short of formal political authority.

Helms-Burton Act Congressional legislation passed in 1996 imposing penalties on foreign countries that benefit economically from confiscated U.S. property in Cuba.

human intelligence (HUMINT) Information gained by intelligence agencies from foreign informants working undercover.

idea brokers Nongovernmental actors in policy debates who attempt to influence public opinion and government action through the dissemination of research findings and the airing of opinions on a variety of issues.

identity The definition and widely held conception of an individual or group as considered apart from others. A central element of constructivist theory.

ideological factors Aspects of policy makers' world views that influence their foreign policy decisions.

ideology A person's general principles and normative beliefs about human nature, the relationships between state and society, and the nation's roles and responsibilities in world politics.

illiberal democracy A form of government in which an elected governmental regime adopts policies that repress political freedoms and human rights.

image intelligence (IMINT) Information gathered by the CIA and other U.S. intelligence agencies that provides imagery of buildings, troop deployments, potential military targets, and other items that are of interest to the United States.

imperial presidency A critique of the U.S. political system advanced in the 1970s by historian Arthur M. Schlesinger Jr., who described the president as governing virtually "by decree."

influence operations Efforts by U.S. military, diplomatic, and intelligence agencies to shape public opinion in foreign countries in a way that enhances their governments' and citizens' support for the United States.

information security Unfettered communication flows protected from disruption by computer hackers, particularly within governmental agencies.

infotainment The common result of "soft news" that blends information regarding public affairs, including U.S. foreign policy, and media content designed to entertain an audience, as in *The Daily Show with Jon Stewart*.

intelligence cycle The five-stage intelligence process, moving from planning and direction to collection, processing, analysis, and, finally, dissemination to policy makers.

intelligence gap The stark contrast between the openness of democracies such as the United States and repressive societies such as North Korea, a gap that makes democracies more vulnerable to penetration by foreign intelligence services.

Intelligence Oversight Act of 1980 Legislative measure empowering House and Senate committees to oversee U.S. intelligence activities and requiring presidents to notify Congress about covert operations in foreign countries.

interdependence In contrast to anarchy, a model of world politics devised by liberal theorists based on mutual reliance among states and their need to cooperate in solving shared problems.

intergovernmental organizations (IGOs) Formal political bodies, representing two or more national governments, that permit their members to pursue goals beyond their individual reach and to solve shared problems.

intermestic policy The merger of international and domestic policy concerns, such as trade and the environment.

internal balancing The strengthening of military forces and other domestic measures used by relatively weak states to counter the ambitions and influence of a dominant power.

international political economy The domain of political economy in which governments seek to manage economic activity beyond their borders in ways that advance their policy goals and principles.

international trust A perception among some political leaders that other governments customarily behave in accordance with commonly accepted rules, norms, and laws of world politics.

iron curtain A term coined by British prime minister Winston Churchill in 1946 to describe the metaphorical line separating communist countries under Soviet control from the capitalist countries of Western Europe supported by the United States. Remained intact throughout the Cold War.

iron triangle The alliance of influential interest groups, congressional committees, and corresponding executive branch agencies to carry out policies of mutual concern to the exclusion of other policy actors or outside interests.

issue networks A model of decision making that involves more actors and is more open to competing viewpoints than the iron triangle model. Brings together interested governmental and private actors with shared expertise in a given area of public policy.

Jackson-Vanik Amendment A legislative measure approved in 1974 that prevented presidents from granting most-favored-nation trade status to foreign countries that restricted the emigration of their citizens.

jihadists Religious extremists in some Islamic societies who seek to attain religious goals through military means, including suicide bombings and other acts of terrorism.

judicial noninterference The judicial branch's reluctance to intervene in conflicts between the executive and legislative branches due to its traditional view of these interbranch conflicts as "political" in nature.

just-war doctrine A code of conduct originating in the Middle Ages that established moral and ethical standards on the use of military force.

Kellogg-Briand Pact A 1928 agreement among fifteen countries, including the United States, that condemned "recourse to war for the solution of international controversies [and] as an instrument of national policy."

Kyoto Protocol An intergovernmental agreement approved in 1997 that called on signatories to reduce the greenhouse gas emissions linked to global warming. Not approved by the United States.

latent public opinion Ingrained societal values and beliefs that are dormant until they are "activated" by the emergence of specific related issues on the policy agenda or in public debates.

legal internationalists Analysts of world politics who view international law rather than state sovereignty as the appropriate basis for global order and seek policy goals that extend beyond the interests of individual states.

legal nationalists Analysts of world politics who base their policy prescriptions on the sovereign authority of nation-states and their primary responsibility to pursue national interests and those of their citizens.

lend-lease program A program devised by the United States during World War II to provide military assets to Great Britain in exchange for U.S. access to British military bases.

levels of analysis The systemic, societal, governmental, and individual factors that shape foreign policy decisions and outcomes.

liberal internationalism A key aspect of President Jimmy Carter's foreign policy that called for U.S. global involvement consistent with the country's moral principles and political ideals.

liberalism A political theory that, when applied to foreign policy, emphasizes the learning of past lessons, the promotion of democratic political reforms, and the creation of multilateral institutions and laws, among other measures.

linkage strategy The Nixon administration's policy toward the Soviet Union that tied U.S. economic concessions to improved Soviet behavior on human rights and key foreign policy issues.

living-room war A term that originated during the Vietnam War to describe a U.S. military conflict brought to American homes graphically and daily through extensive television coverage.

lobbying A tactic of appealing directly to government officials for support of policy preferences. Commonly employed by interest groups.

logrolling The practice of "trading" legislative votes in which a member of Congress supports one measure with the expectation of garnering support from other legislators for a separate measure.

management style The working relationship a president establishes among his subordinates that reflects the president's worldview and personality.

manifest destiny A belief popular in the early history of the United States that the nation had God's blessing to expand and assume political control of a wider population.

Marshall Plan Named after President Harry Truman's secretary of state, George Marshall, a U.S. foreign policy initiative approved in 1947 that provided U.S. allies with economic aid to hasten their recovery after World War II.

mass public The large segment of the U.S. population that is neither well informed nor strongly interested in most foreign policy issues and thus has little direct impact on the policy process.

massive retaliation A security strategy based on the promise of the nuclear annihilation of the sponsor of an attack on the vital interests of the state that adopts the strategy.

mercantilism An economic model whose primary aim is to enhance the wealth of national firms and the government, often at the expense of foreign competitors, rival states, and a market-driven global economy.

Mexico City policy A policy first approved by the Reagan administration prohibiting U.S. economic assistance to foreign family-planning agencies that offer abortion counseling or services.

migration The mass movement of populations across national borders, either legally or illegally, that may alter demands on state resources and political arrangements on both sides of the border.

militant internationalism A form of activism in foreign policy that emphasizes coercive measures, including the use of force, over diplomacy and other peaceful means of statecraft.

military alliances Formal collaborations between two or more countries on security matters of mutual concern.

military-industrial complex An alignment of U.S. defense and private economic interests identified by President Dwight Eisenhower in 1961 as a potential threat to the nation's democracy and security.

military transformation A shift in U.S. defense policy, introduced by Defense Secretary Donald Rumsfeld in 2001, away from "heavy" conventional forces toward more lethal and precise weapons systems, sophisticated communications networks, and mobile armed forces.

mission creep The tendency of armed forces in limited military deployments to take on new tasks and open-ended commitments.

Monroe Doctrine Proclamation by President James Monroe in 1823 that politically separated the United States from Europe and declared future colonization in the Western Hemisphere a threat to U.S. national security.

most-favored-nation trading status The provision of equal market access and terms of trade to all states participating in the General Agreement on Tariffs and Trade (GATT) system.

multinational corporations (MNCs) Profit-seeking firms with operations, subsidiaries, and markets in more than one country. The largest and arguably most politically powerful type of nongovernmental organization.

multipolar balance of power A condition in world politics in which three or more countries maintain global predominance in terms of military, economic, and other forms of power.

mutual assured destruction (MAD) A nuclear stalemate that occurs when two nuclear-equipped adversaries credibly promise massive retaliation against each other in the event of an attack.

nation building The process by which an external government, intergovernmental organization, or nongovernmental organization attempts to create the conditions necessary for a nation to gain internal cohesion and solidarity.

national interest A self-justifying rationale for foreign policy actions that presumes an inherent "interest" maintained by the state that overrides the parochial interests of government bureaucracies or societal groups.

national security The freedom a nation-state enjoys from threats to its sovereignty, territory, and political autonomy.

national security adviser Technically known as the special assistant for national security affairs. A top aide who consults the president on a regular basis and coordinates the input of other foreign policy advisers.

national security state A political system in which the institutions of national defense overshadow the nonmilitary agencies of the government.

national style The expression of cultural influences that have historically shaped a country's identity and approach to international relations.

negative-sum game According to game theory, a context of diplomatic bargaining in which all parties are likely to suffer tangible, but uneven, overall losses of resources or other perceived assets.

Nelson-Bingham Amendment Legislative measure approved in 1974 authorizing Congress to review foreign arms sales of more than $25 million and to reject such sales through a concurrent resolution of both chambers.

neoconservatism A school of thought prominent in the George W. Bush administration that called for the regular, overwhelming, and potentially unilateral use of U.S. military force to create a world order that reflected the nation's normative values and replicated its systems of political economy.

neoliberal institutionalism A view of international cooperation that emphasizes reciprocal gestures of trust and goodwill, leading to a pattern of rewards on both sides that discourages future acts of coercion or aggression.

neorealism A variant of realist theory focusing on the anarchic nature of the international system as the ultimate and inevitable cause of interstate conflicts.

New Look President Dwight Eisenhower's shift in security strategy that enlarged the role of nuclear weapons and created new military alliances to contain the Soviet Union and China.

new media The loosely knit and interactive constellation of digital media—including blogs, chat rooms, and social media outlets—that engage news consumers alongside traditional print sources, radio stations, and television networks.

new unilateralism A shift in U.S. foreign policy in the late 1990s characterized by a hostile stance toward multilateral agreements and intergovernmental bodies, particularly the United Nations and its agencies.

new world order President George H. W. Bush's characterization of the emerging post–Cold War international system, emphasizing democratization, economic globalization, and multilateral cooperation.

nontariff barriers An array of trade measures, including industrial subsidies and favorable regulations, that heighten a country's competitive advantages in world markets while ostensibly respecting the rules of "free trade."

norms Widely agreed-upon normative principles and standards of appropriate conduct in political life, including foreign policy. A central element of liberal theory.

nuclear deterrence The prevention of hostilities through the threat of using nuclear weapons.

Open Door policy A policy adopted by the U.S. government in 1899 that called for free trade access to China and discouraged other trading states from dividing China into spheres of influence.

Operation Desert Storm The name of the 1991 U.S.-led counteroffensive against Iraq to eject its forces from Kuwait.

Operation Iraqi Freedom The U.S. invasion and subsequent occupation of Iraq in March 2003 ordered by President George W. Bush, whose claims that Iraq possessed weapons of mass destruction later proved unfounded.

operational code An individual's integrated set of conceptions about political life that informs his or her calculations of appropriate and effective policy.

organizational culture The set of shared values, goals, and functional priorities of the members of a government agency.

organizational process A model of decision making characterized by standard operating procedures and fragmented centers of authority that hinders unified, consistent, and effective government policies.

oversight Congress's ability, enhanced in the 1970s and 1980s, to monitor the president's conduct of foreign policy.

parachute journalism A pattern of news coverage in which reporters descend on a trouble spot and then move on, never gaining a deep understanding of the problems in the area that would have given their reporting greater substance.

particularistic groups Nongovernmental organizations seeking to influence U.S. foreign policy that serve a limited number of individuals with stakes in the groups' missions. An alternative to cosmopolitan groups.

passing the buck A tendency of Congress to defer to the president in foreign policy given that the White House, not Congress, will likely receive credit for major breakthroughs as well as blame for failures.

path dependency A pattern by which past structural choices, with their underlying values and goals, push future policies in particular directions.

peaceful coercion A tactic employed by a superior military power of exercising influence across national borders and gaining foreign policy preferences without the use of violence.

Pentagon Papers The detailed reports published in 1971 by the *New York Times* on the Nixon administration's efforts to conceal its military activities in Southeast Asia. Publication of these reports, which Nixon tried to block, was affirmed by the U.S. Supreme Court on constitutional grounds.

perestroika Political reforms adopted by Soviet president Mikhail Gorbachev in the late 1980s that called for restructuring the Soviet economy to spur innovation and efficiency.

political action committees (PACs) The electoral arms of organized groups that are responsible for fund-raising and distributing money to promote the election of desired candidates.

political alienation The sense of powerlessness among low-income citizens, minority groups, and others with little access to the U.S. foreign policy process or other areas of public affairs.

political economy An arena of public life, located at the crossroads of states and markets, in which governments seek to organize domestic economic activity in ways that advance their policy goals and principles.

political psychology A subfield of both political science and psychology that explores the effects of cognition, perceptions, personality, group dynamics, and other individual-level factors on political behavior.

positive sum game According to game theory, a context of diplomatic bargaining in which all parties may benefit from cooperation (as often happens in environmental issues).

Powell Doctrine Policy articulated in the early 1990s by Gen. Colin Powell when he was chairman of the Joint Chiefs of Staff. Calls for the United States to prevail decisively in military conflicts and to have a clear exit strategy.

preemptive war A military attack initiated by one country whose leaders believe an attack from another country is imminent.

prerogative powers A president's freedom to make independent and binding judgments, extending beyond national emergencies to include day-to-day decisions, that do not require the approval of Congress or the courts.

presidential control model A model of policy making that views presidents as caretakers of the national interest who can rise above domestic politics, particularly when U.S. security interests are at stake.

press leaks The widespread and private transfer of sensitive information regarding government policy from official sources to the news media, often in hopes that the released information will change policies.

preventive war A military attack initiated by one country whose leaders believe an emerging challenger presents a long-term threat, thereby eliminating the threat before it materializes.

primacy A country's predominant stature in the hierarchy of global power.

principled beliefs In contrast to causal beliefs, structured perceptions toward political problems that are informed primarily by such normative principles as liberty, justice, and equality.

procedural democracy The aspects of democratic rule that concern formal rules and structures that are designed to ensure representative governance.

procedural innovations Structural and institutional reforms that enhance Congress's impact on the policy-making process. Often of greater political value and easier to pass than substantive legislation.

propaganda False or misleading public information designed to enhance the stature of the originating government or its policies.

prospect theory An alternative to rational-choice theory, a model of decision making that emphasizes uncertainty and varying perceptions among policy makers regarding the relative costs and benefits of different policy choices.

protectionism   A trade policy that promotes the interests of domestic producers by restricting foreign competitors' access to home markets through tariffs and other barriers to entry.

public choice theory   A model of public policy arguing that competitive private firms supply goods and services more efficiently than government agencies.

public diplomacy   Efforts by the U.S. government, often through the mobilization of private citizens and groups, to appeal directly to foreign citizens and strengthen international support for the United States.

public relations presidency   A governing style in which the U.S. president is guided primarily by public opinion in making policy decisions.

rally around the flag effect   The sharp increase in a president's public approval rating that occurs when the nation faces a military crisis. Generally attributed to a patriotic sense among citizens that national unity must be maintained in times of crisis.

rational actors   Foreign policy makers who, in the view of realist theory, weigh their options based on common understandings of key problems and clear calculations of the costs and benefits of possible solutions.

rational choice   A behavioral approach to public policy that reduces decision making to objective calculations of costs and benefits.

raw intelligence   Unprocessed information about foreign governments and developments abroad collected by intelligence agents from various sources and later shared with policy makers after it has been processed.

realism   A pessimistic theory of world politics that emphasizes the irreversible flaws in human nature and the resulting conflicts that occur at all levels of societal interaction, including the relations among states in an anarchic and inherently threatening environment.

recess appointment   The ability of a president to make political appointments without the advice and consent of Congress when the legislative body is not in session, as in George W. Bush's controversial August 2005 appointment of John Bolton as U.S. ambassador to the United Nations.

regimes   Areas of interstate cooperation in foreign policy, such as arms control, in which decision makers enjoy positive-sum gains by adopting common norms, objectives, and institutionalized means of problem solving.

regional integration   The process by which close economic and political cooperation among states in a particular region offers a remedy for chronic military conflicts. Most often applied to the evolution of the European Union.

revolution in military affairs   A fundamental shift in the U.S. military's structure and strategic doctrine as the result of advances in technology in the United States and overseas.

Rome Statute   An intergovernmental agreement approved in 1998 in which signatories identified a variety of crimes—genocide, crimes against humanity, war crimes, and foreign aggression—that would fall under the jurisdiction of the proposed International Criminal Court.

rooftop journalism   Style of war reporting in which journalists provide accounts of military conflicts from nearby vantage points, often the tops of buildings. Became a staple of televised war coverage during the 1991 Persian Gulf War.

Roosevelt Corollary President Theodore Roosevelt's 1904 expansion of the Monroe Doctrine proclaiming that the United States had authority to act as an "international police power" outside its borders in order to maintain stability in the Western Hemisphere.

saber rattling A tactic used by foreign policy makers to gain concessions from rival states by escalating tensions through threats of imminent military attack.

security community A region of the world in which governments form close political, economic, and military ties to such an extent that war among them becomes unthinkable. Often associated with the European Union.

security dilemma The destabilizing effect of military expansion by one state, even for defensive purposes, as other states respond by expanding their armed forces.

selective exposure The tendency of news consumers to rely on sources of information that conform to their preexisting values and opinions, a practice that tends to reinforce rather than inform public opinion.

selective perception The process by which people tend to seek out information that reinforces their worldviews while ignoring or dismissing contradictory information.

shaming A tactic by which critics of governments, corporations, and other political actors raise moral or ethical doubts about the actions of these entities in the hope of heightening public pressure for policy reform.

signal intelligence (SIGINT) Information gathered by U.S. and other intelligence agencies through the interception of foreign radio broadcasts, telephone conversations, e-mail messages, and other electronic transmissions.

situational factors The objective details of a given problem facing Congress and the calculated costs and benefits of proposed legislative solutions.

smart sanctions Economic penalties designed to punish government elites rather than the most vulnerable citizens in the target state.

Smoot-Hawley Tariff Act Congressional measure passed in 1930 and signed by President Herbert Hoover that dramatically increased tariffs on goods coming into the United States. A central factor in the onset of the Great Depression.

social movement The mobilization of broad-based private groups, usually around shared concerns or grievances related to public policy on a specific issue and a desire to alter the policy through mass pressure.

socialism A political economy model that seeks to ensure economic equality through social welfare programs and government ownership of vital enterprises while also allowing citizens to own private property and operate firms.

soft news The presentation of public issues, such as political scandals, foreign policy crises, and social problems, in media venues designed to entertain rather than inform, often with considerable impact on public opinion.

soft power The attractiveness of a nation's political and cultural values to other states and societies that enhances the nation's ability to gain support from other governments for its policy goals.

sovereignty The highest level of political authority maintained by secular nation-states. Affirmed in the 1648 Treaty of Westphalia, which rejected political control by religious authorities and the divine right of kings.

sovereignty gap An area of world politics that is beyond the formal authority of individual states but still demands action from them on a day-to-day basis.

spectrum of armed conflict The variety of real and potential military challenges a country confronts in which the chance that each type of conflict will occur is inversely proportionate to its destructiveness.

spin control Action by government officials to shape news coverage in ways that show them in the best possible light.

standard operating procedures (SOPs) Consistent, routine measures for addressing commonly encountered problems in public policy. Stresses continuity over change and a high level of internal order.

state building The process by which an external government, intergovernmental organization, or nongovernmental organization attempts to create the conditions necessary for a state to establish a stable and democratic government.

state-society relations The interaction of government and private actors in matters of public policy. Often featuring tensions or mutual animosity in the case of U.S. security policy.

state terrorism Acts of terrorism committed by sovereign governments, against either their own people or people in other states.

stewardship theory A view of the U.S. presidency advanced by Theodore Roosevelt that provided the head of state, as the "steward" of the nation, broad discretion to act in foreign policy without regard for domestic opposition.

strategic communications Officially sanctioned messages originating from the U.S. government and disseminated through various channels to foreign governments, news outlets, and carefully selected interest groups in order to advance U.S. foreign policy goals.

strategic culture Widely shared normative beliefs, attitudes, and policy preferences as they pertain to a country's foreign relations.

Strategic Defense Initiative (SDI) President Ronald Reagan's 1983 plan to use space-based interceptors to destroy long-range nuclear weapons in midflight. Also known as "Star Wars."

strategic detachment An early grand strategy adopted by the United States based on the nation's self-reliance and avoidance of binding commitments to other countries.

strategic environment The context in which security policy is devised. Reflects trends in global and regional balances of power and the degree to which a state considers other powerful nations and mobilized private groups to be friends or foes.

strategic factors Political and electoral considerations weighed by legislators along with the substantive merits of bills coming up for a vote.

structural arrangements The governing bodies and legal system within which policy making takes place and that shape a grand strategy.

structural realism Also known as neorealism, a theory of international relations that emphasizes global anarchy, persistent fears and distrust, and a balance of power among states as the most reliable guarantor of world peace.

structural weaknesses Problems related to the size, complexity, and partisan composition of Congress that hinder its ability to act quickly and decisively on foreign policy issues.

substantive democracy The informal aspects of democratic rule that, even in the formal context of legal regulations and checks and balances, may diverge from representative governance.

substantive legislation Congressional measures that focus on specific issues, such as economic sanctions against South Africa in the 1980s, rather than on procedural innovations, such as enhanced oversight of the president, affecting legislative powers.

suicide terrorism A tactic by which terrorists, carrying explosive devices, detonate these explosives in populated areas in order to advance their policy goals, at the cost of their own lives.

surge strategy A military strategy adopted in 2007 by the U.S. Defense Department in which more than 20,000 additional troops were deployed to Iraq to suppress domestic violence and improve the prospects for subsequent withdrawals of U.S. forces from the country.

sustained primacy A grand strategy adopted by the United States after World War II based on preservation of the nation's predominance in the interstate system. Adopted explicitly by the George W. Bush administration in 2002.

tactics In the context of security strategy, the translation of proclaimed political ends into military means.

terrorism A tactic of gaining the upper hand in a political struggle through the use, by states or private actors, of political violence designed to raise mass fears.

trade promotion authority Formerly known as "fast-track" authority, a measure that strengthens the executive branch's ability to conclude trade agreements with other governments by restricting the time allotted for the consideration of such agreements in Congress.

tragedy of the commons A situation in which a group of people stands to lose a common resource because of overuse unless some limiting measures are taken. A "tragedy" because of the many constraints on undertaking collective action and the stark consequences of inaction.

transnational advocacy networks Large, well-organized coalitions of groups from two or more countries that apply political pressure on several governments at once to achieve their policy preferences.

transnational civil society Societal forces that extend beyond the political boundaries of a nation-state, including interest groups, public opinion, the news media, and intergovernmental organizations.

transnational interdependence The mutual reliance between two or more countries that stems from shared problems and interests and results in closer cooperation.

Treaty of Westphalia An agreement signed in 1648 ending the Thirty Years' War that helped establish and codify the nation-state system that exists today.

Truman Doctrine President Harry Truman's pledge to provide military aid to Greece and Turkey to help overcome internal communist revolts and, more broadly, to support "free peoples who are resisting attempted subjugation by armed minorities or by outside pressures."

trustee model One of two general models of political representation. Based on a political leader's presumed superior judgment. Provides for greater freedom of thought and autonomous decision making by elected officials than the delegate model.

two-level game A situation in which foreign policy makers simultaneously negotiate with their foreign counterparts and domestic actors (public and private) who have a stake in the policy process.

two presidencies A model of U.S. government developed by political scientist Aaron Wildavsky that describes the president as constrained on domestic issues while reigning supreme in foreign affairs.

unified government A partisan alignment that occurs when the executive and legislative branches of government are controlled by the same political party.

unilateral powers Constitutional authority that permits considerable freedom of action by the president in foreign policy, including issuing executive orders, approving executive agreements, commanding armed forces, and hiring top advisers without congressional approval.

unilateralism The pursuit of foreign policy objectives without the collaboration or assistance of other governments.

unipolar balance of power A global power structure in which one nation-state maintains a predominant share of the economic, military, and other resources needed to advance its interests in the interstate system.

unitary actors A model of national decision making that assumes that foreign policy makers act in a united fashion to make decisions in the name of the "national interest." A central tenet of realist theory.

USA PATRIOT Act Sweeping legislation passed after the September 11 attacks that increased the federal government's ability to investigate suspected terrorists in the United States. An acronym for "Uniting and Strengthening America by Providing Appropriate Tools Required to Intercept and Obstruct Terrorism."

Vietnam syndrome National self-doubts in the United States in the late 1960s and 1970s as the nation's involvement and defeat in the Vietnam War led to a weakened sense of U.S. primacy and moral superiority.

vindicators Advocates of a school of thought contending that U.S. leaders should actively engage, through diplomatic efforts as well as the use of military force, in a global effort to combat injustice and aggression.

War Powers Resolution A legislative measure approved by Congress in 1973 requiring presidents to inform Congress about imminent U.S. military deployments and authorizing Congress to order the troops home after sixty days if a majority of legislators oppose the deployments. Rarely invoked and routinely dismissed by presidents as unconstitutional.

wars of choice Military conflicts concerning nonvital national interests.

wars of necessity Military conflicts resulting from direct challenges to a nation's vital interests.

Washington consensus A shared understanding among major industrialized countries on the development strategies of smaller economies emphasizing the developing nations' need to promote private enterprise and open markets while restricting state intervention.

Weinberger Doctrine Policy developed in the 1980s by Caspar Weinberger, secretary of defense under Ronald Reagan, requiring that U.S. military interventions be thoroughly planned and the costs and benefits be calculated before offensive action is taken.

zero-sum game According to game theory, a context of diplomatic bargaining in which parties expect an outcome in which the gains of one side will be balanced proportionately by the losses of the other.

zone of twilight A conception of U.S. foreign policy often adopted by the courts that emphasizes the lack of explicit powers granted to the executive and legislative branches and that sees interbranch conflict as largely "political."

References

Abramson, Mark A., and Paul R. Lawrence, eds. 2001. *Transforming Organizations.* Lanham, Md.: Rowman and Littlefield.

Adams, Thomas. 1999. "The New Mercenaries and the Privatization of Conflict." *Parameters* 29 (summer): 103–116.

Addis, Adeno. 2003. "Economic Sanctions and the Problem of Evil." *Human Rights Quarterly* 25 (August): 573–623.

Adler, David Gray. 1996a. "Court, Constitution, and Foreign Affairs." In *The Constitution and the Conduct of American Foreign Policy,* ed. David Gray Adler and Larry N. George, 19–56. Lawrence: University Press of Kansas.

———. 1996b. "The President's Recognition Power." In *The Constitution and the Conduct of American Foreign Policy,* ed. David Gray Adler and Larry N. George, 133–157. Lawrence: University Press of Kansas.

Allan, Stuart. 2006. *Online News.* New York: Open University Press.

Allen, Mike. 2008. "Biden to Limit Role of Vice President." *Politico,* December 6. www.politico.com/news/stories/1208/16261.html.

Allen, Mike, and Romesh Ratnesar. 2006. "The End of Cowboy Diplomacy." *Time,* July 9.

Allison, Graham T. 1971. *Essence of Decision: Explaining the Cuban Missile Crisis.* Boston: Little, Brown.

Allison, Graham T., and Philip Zelikow. 1999. *Essence of Decision: Explaining the Cuban Missile Crisis,* 2nd ed. New York: Longman.

Almond, Gabriel. 1950. *The American People and Foreign Policy.* New York: Harcourt, Brace.

Alterman, Eric. 1997. "The CIA's Fifty Candles." *Nation,* October 6, 5–6.

———. 2006. "Another 9/11? Never Mind . . ." *Nation,* January 2.

Ambrose, Stephen E. 1988. *Rise to Globalism: American Foreign Policy since 1938,* 5th rev. ed. New York: Penguin Books.

Ambrosio, Thomas, ed. 2002. *Ethnic Identity Groups and U.S. Foreign Policy.* Westport, Conn.: Praeger.

American Council of Trustees and Alumni. 2000. "Losing America's Memory: Historical Illiteracy in the 21st Century." February 21. www.goacta.org/publications/reports.html.

Anderson, Fred, and Andrew Cayton. 2005. *The Dominion of War: Empire and Liberty in North America, 1500–2000.* New York: Viking.

Andrew, Christopher. 1995. *For the President's Eyes Only: Secret Intelligence and the American Presidency from Washington to Bush*. New York: HarperCollins.

Applebaum, Anne. 2005. "In Search of Pro-Americanism." *Foreign Policy* 149 (July–August): 32–40.

Arms Control Association. 2006. *The 2006 Biological Weapons Convention Review Conference: Articles and Interviews on Tackling the Threats Posed by Biological Weapons*. November. Washington, D.C.: Arms Control Association.

Armstrong, Jerome, and Markos M. Zuniga. 2006. *Crashing the Gate: Netroots, Grassroots, and the Rise of People-Powered Politics*. White River Junction, Vt.: Chelsea Green.

Arquilla, John, David Ronfeldt, and Michele Zanini. 1999. "Networks, Netwar, and Information-Age Terrorism." In *Countering the New Terrorism*, ed. Ian O. Lesser, Bruce Hoffman, John Arquilla, David Ronfeldt, and Michele Zanini, 39–84. Santa Monica, Calif.: RAND.

Art, Robert J. 1973. "Bureaucratic Politics and American Foreign Policy: A Critique." *Policy Sciences* 4 (December): 467–490.

———. 1996. "Why Western Europe Needs the United States and NATO." *Political Science Quarterly* 111 (spring): 1–39.

———. 2003. *A Grand Strategy for America*. Ithaca: Cornell University Press.

Art, Robert J., and Kenneth N. Waltz, eds. 2004. *The Use of Force: Military Power and International Politics*, 6th ed. Lanham, Md.: Rowman and Littlefield.

Ash, Timothy Garton. 2002. "The Peril of Too Much Power." *New York Times*, April 9, A25.

Ashcroft, John. 2001. "DOJ Oversight: Preserving Our Freedoms while Defending against Terrorism." Statement to the Senate Judiciary Committee. December 6. www.senate.gov/%7Ejudiciary/print_testimony.cfm?id=121&wit_id=42.

Asmus, Ronald D. 2002. *Opening NATO's Door: How the Alliance Remade Itself for a New Era*. New York: Columbia University Press.

Atwood, J. Brian, M. Peter McPherson, and Andrew Natsios. 2008. "Arrested Development: Making Foreign Aid a More Effective Tool." *Foreign Affairs* 87 (November–December): 123–132.

Auster, Bruce B., and David E. Kaplan. 1998. "What's Really Gone Wrong with the CIA?" *U.S. News and World Report*, June 1, 27.

Austin, D. Andrew, and Mindy R. Levit. 2010. "The Debt Limit: History and Recent Increases." Congressional Research Service, Washington, D.C., January 28.

Axelrod, Robert M. 1984. *The Evolution of Cooperation*. New York: Basic Books.

Bailey, Thomas A. 1948. *The Man in the Street: The Impact of American Public Opinion on Foreign Policy*. New York: Macmillan.

Baker, James A., III, with Thomas M. DeFrank. 1995. *The Politics of Diplomacy: Revolution, War, and Peace, 1989–1992*. New York: Putnam.

Baker, William D., and John R. Oneal. 2001. "Patriotism or Opinion Leadership? The Nature and Origins of the 'Rally around the Flag' Effect." *Journal of Conflict Resolution* 45 (October): 661–687.

Baldwin, David A. 1966. *Foreign Aid and American Foreign Policy*. New York: Praeger.

———. 1985. *Economic Statecraft*. Princeton: Princeton University Press.

———. 1999/2000. "The Sanctions Debate and the Logic of Choice." *International Security* 24 (winter): 80–107.

Bamberger, Robert. 2003. "Energy Policy: Historical Overview, Conceptual Framework, and Continuing Issues." CRS Report for Congress. Congressional Research Service, Washington, D.C., January 30.

Barber, James D. 1992. *The Presidential Character: Predicting Performance in the White House,* 4th ed. Englewood Cliffs, N.J.: Prentice Hall.

Bardes, Barbara. 1997. "Public Opinion and Foreign Policy: How Does the Public Think about America's Role in the World?" In *Understanding Public Opinion,* ed. Barbara Norrander and Clyde Wilcox, 150–169. Washington, D.C.: CQ Press.

Barnett, Michael, and Martha Finnemore. 2004. *Rules for the World: International Organizations in Global Politics.* Ithaca: Cornell University Press.

Barnett, Roger W. 2003. *Asymmetrical Warfare: Today's Challenge to U.S. Military Power.* Washington, D.C.: Brassey's.

Barnett, Thomas P. M. 2009. *Great Powers: America and the World after Bush.* New York: Putnam.

Barone, Michael, and Grant Ujifusa. 1999. *The Almanac of American Politics, 2000.* Washington, D.C.: National Journal Group.

Bartels, Larry M. 1991. "Constituency Opinion and Congressional Policy Making: The Reagan Defense Buildup." *American Political Science Review* 85 (June): 457–474.

Baum, Dan. 2003. "Nation Builders for Hire." *New York Times Magazine,* June 22, 32–37.

Baum, Matthew A. 2002. "The Constituent Foundations of the Rally-Round-the-Flag Phenomenon." *International Studies Quarterly* 46 (June): 263–298.

———. 2003. *Soft News Goes to War: Public Opinion and American Foreign Policy in the New Media Age.* Princeton: Princeton University Press.

Baumgartner, Jody, and Jonathan S. Morris. 2006. "The *Daily Show* Effect: Candidate Evaluations, Efficacy, and American Youth." *American Politics Research* 34 (3): 341–367.

Baumgartner, Jody C., Peter L. Francia, and Jonathan S. Morris. 2008. "A Clash of Civilizations? The Influence of Religion on Public Opinion of U.S. Foreign Policy in the Middle East." *Political Research Quarterly* 61 (2): 171–179.

Bax, Frank R. 1977. "The Legislative-Executive Relationship in Foreign Policy: New Partnership or New Competition?" *Orbis* 20 (winter): 881–904.

Baym, Geoffrey. 2005. "*The Daily Show*: Discursive Integration and the Reinvention of Political Journalism." *Political Communication* 22: 259–276.

BBC. 2007. *World View of U.S. Role Goes from Bad to Worse.* London: BBC.

Beckmann, Matthew N., and Joseph Godfrey. 2007. "The Policy Opportunities of Presidential Honeymoons." *Political Research Quarterly* 60 (June): 250–262.

Beehner, Lionel. 2006. "Reviewing the 2006 Quadrennial Defense Review." Council on Foreign Relations, New York, February 7.

Belasco, Amy. 2007. "The Cost of Iraq, Afghanistan, and Other Global War on Terror Operations since 9/11." Congressional Research Service, Washington, D.C., March 14.

Bell, Daniel A., and Joseph H. Carens. 2004. "The Ethical Dilemmas of International Human Rights and Humanitarian NGOs: Reflections on a Dialogue between Practitioners and Theorists." *Human Rights Quarterly* 26 (May): 300–329.

Below, Amy. 2008. "U.S. Presidential Decisions on Ozone Depletion and Climate Change: A Foreign Policy Analysis." *Foreign Policy Analysis* 4 (January): 1–20.

Bendor, Jonathan, and Thomas H. Hammond. 1992. "Rethinking Allison's Models." *American Political Science Review* 86 (June): 301–322.

Benjamin, Daniel, and Steven Simon. 2002. *The Age of Sacred Terror.* New York: Random House.

Bennett, John C. 1966. *Foreign Policy in Christian Perspective.* New York: Scribner's.

Bennett, W. Lance, and David L. Paletz, eds. 1994. *Taken by Storm: The Media, Public Opinion, and U.S. Foreign Policy in the Gulf War.* Chicago: University of Chicago Press.

Bergen, Peter, and Katherine Tiedemann. 2009. "The Drone War." *The New Republic,* June 3. www.tnr.com/article/the-drone-war.

Bernstein, Nina. 2010. "Officials Hid Truth of Immigrant Deaths in Jail." *New York Times,* January 10. www.nytimes.com/2010/01/10/us/10detain.html.

Berrigan, Frida. 2006. "United States Rides Weapons Bonanza Wave." *Foreign Policy in Focus,* November 16. www.fpif.org/fpiftxt/3715.

Berrigan, Frida, and William D. Hartung. 2005. *U.S. Weapons at War 2005: Promoting Freedom or Fueling Conflict?* Washington, D.C.: World Policy Institute, June.

Berrios, Ruben. 2000. *Contracting for Development: The Role of For-Profit Contractors in U.S. Foreign Development Assistance.* Westport, Conn.: Praeger.

Best, James R. 1992. "Who Talked with President Kennedy? An Interaction Analysis." *Presidential Studies Quarterly* 22 (spring): 351–369.

Best, Richard A., Jr. 2009. "Intelligence Issues for Congress." Congressional Research Service, Washington, D.C., September 18.

Best, Richard A., Jr., and Elizabeth Bazan. 2006. "Intelligence Spending: Public Disclosure Issues." Congressional Research Service, Washington, D.C., September 25.

Best, Samuel J., Brian Chmielewski, and Brian S. Krueger. 2005. "Selective Exposure to Online Foreign News During the Conflict with Iraq." *International Journal of Press/ Politics* 10 (4): 52–70.

Betts, Richard K. 2002. *Conflict after the Cold War: Arguments on Causes of War and Peace,* 2nd ed. New York: Longman.

———. 2007. "A Disciplined Defense: How to Regain Strategic Solvency." *Foreign Affairs* 86 (November–December): 67–80.

Biglaiser, Glen, and Karl DeRouen Jr. 2009. "The Interdependence of U.S. Troop Deployments and Trade in the Developing World." *Foreign Policy Analysis* 5 (July): 247–263.

Binder, Sarah A. 1996. "The Disappearing Political Center: Congress and the Incredible Shrinking Middle." *Brookings Review* 14 (fall): 36–39.

———. 2003. *Stalemate: Causes and Consequences of Legislative Gridlock.* Washington, D.C.: Brookings.

Blacker, Coit D. 1994. "A Typology of Post–Cold War Conflicts." In *U.S. Intervention Policy for the Post–Cold War World: New Challenges and Responses,* ed. Arnold Kanter and Linton Brooks, 42–63. New York: Norton.

Blanchard, Jean-Marc, and Norrin M. Ripsman. 2008. "A Political Theory of Economic Statecraft." *Foreign Policy Analysis* 4 (October): 371–398.

Blechman, Barry M., and Tamara C. Wittes. 1999. "Defining Moment: The Threat and Use of Force in American Foreign Policy." *Political Science Quarterly* 114 (1): 1–30.

Blinder, Scott B. 2007. "Going Public, Going to Baghdad: Presidential Agenda-Setting and the Electoral Connection in Congress." In *The Polarized Presidency of George W. Bush,* ed. George C. Edwards III and Desmond S. King, 325–350. New York: Oxford University Press.

Blustein, Paul. 2001. *The Chastening: Inside the Crisis that Rocked the Global Financial System and Humbled the IMF.* New York: Public Affairs.

Bobrow, Davis B. 2008. "Anti-Americanism and International Security: Indications in International Public Opinion." In *The Political Consequences of Anti-Americanism,* ed. Richard Higgott and Ivona Malbasic, 107–126. New York: Routledge.

Bond, Michael. 2000. "The Backlash against NGOs." *Prospect* (April). www.global policy.org/ngos/backlash.htm.

Boot, Max. 2002. *The Savage Wars of Peace: Small Wars and the Rise of American Power.* New York: Basic Books.

Bowser, Benjamin P. 2003. "A Meaning of 9/11: Failure in Race Relations at Home Has Led to a Failed U.S. Foreign Policy Overseas." *SAGE Race Relations Abstracts* 28 (3/4): 19–24.

Brace, Paul, and Barbara Hinckley. 1993. *Follow the Leader: Opinion Polls and the Modern Presidents.* New York: Basic Books.

Brainard, Lael, ed. 2007. *Security by Other Means: Foreign Assistance, Global Poverty, and American Leadership.* Washington, D.C.: Brookings.

Brands, H. W. 1998. *What America Owes the World: The Struggle for the Soul of Foreign Policy.* New York: Cambridge University Press.

Brehm, John, and Scott Gates. 1997. *Working, Shirking, and Sabotage: Bureaucratic Responses to a Democratic Public.* Ann Arbor: University of Michigan Press.

Brenner, Carl N. 1999. "Modeling the President's Security Agenda." *Congress and the Presidency* 26 (fall): 171–191.

Brewer, Paul R., Kimberly Gross, Sean Aday, and Lars Willnat. 2004. "International Trust and Public Opinion about World Affairs." *American Journal of Political Science* 48 (1): 93–109.

Brinkley, Douglas. 1997. "Democratic Enlargement: The Clinton Doctrine." *Foreign Policy* 106 (spring): 110–127.

British Petroleum. 2009. "Statistical Review of World Energy 2009." www.bp.com.

Broder, John M. 2010. "Environmental Advocates Are Cooling on Obama." *New York Times*, February 18. www.nytimes.com/2010/02/18/science/earth/18enviros.html.

Brodie, Bernard, ed. 1946. *The Absolute Weapon: Atomic Power and World Order.* New York: Harcourt, Brace.

Brooks, Stephen G., and William C. Wohlforth. 2008. *World Out of Balance: International Relations and the Challenge of American Primacy.* Princeton: Princeton University Press.

Brown, Cynthia, ed. 2003. *Lost Liberties: Ashcroft and the Assault on Personal Freedom.* New York: New Press.

Brunk, Darren C. 2008. "Curing the Somalia Syndrome: Analogy, Foreign Policy Decision Making, and the Rwandan Genocide." *Foreign Policy Analysis* 4 (July): 301–320.

Brunn, Stanley D., ed. 2006. *Wal-Mart World: The World's Biggest Corporation in the Global Economy.* New York: Routledge.

Brzezinski, Zbigniew. 1997. *The Grand Chessboard: American Primacy and Its Geostrategic Imperatives.* New York: Basic Books.

———. 2010. "From Hope to Audacity." *Foreign Affairs* 89 (January–February): 16–30.

Buchanan, James M. 1977. "Why Does Government Grow?" In *Budgets and Bureaucrats: The Sources of Government Growth,* ed. Thomas Bocherding. Durham: Duke University Press.

Buckley, Kevin. 1991. *Panama: The Whole Story.* New York: Simon and Schuster.

Bueno de Mesquita, Bruce. 2006. *Principles of International Politics: People's Power, Preferences, and Perceptions,* 3rd ed. Washington, D.C.: CQ Press.

———. 2009. *Principles of International Politics,* 4th ed. Washington, D.C.: CQ Press.

Bumiller, Elizabeth. 2003. "Evangelicals Sway White House on Human Rights Issues Abroad." *New York Times,* October 26, 1A.

Burgin, Eileen. 1993. "The Influence of Constituents: Congressional Decision-Making on Issues of Foreign and Domestic Policy." In *Congress Resurgent: Foreign and Defense Policy on Capitol Hill,* ed. Randall B. Ripley and James M. Lindsay, 67–88. Ann Arbor: University of Michigan Press.

Burkhalter, Holly. 2004. "The Politics of AIDS: Engaging Conservative Activists." *Foreign Affairs* 83 (January–February): 8–14.

BurrellesLuce. 2009. "Top Media Outlets: Newspapers, Blogs, Consumer Magazines, and Social Networks." http://insightentry.burrellesluce.com/top100/2009_top_100list.pdf.

Burton, Daniel F., Jr. 1997. "The Brave New Wired World." *Foreign Policy* 106 (spring): 22–37.

Buzan, Barry. 1991. "New Patterns of Global Security in the Twenty-First Century." *International Affairs* 67 (July): 431–451.

———. 2008. *A Leader without Followers? The United States in World Politics after Bush.* London: Global Policy Institute.

Calhoun, Craig, Frederick Cooper, and Kevin W. Moore, eds. 2006. *Lessons of Empire: Imperial Histories and American Power.* New York: New Press.

Caprioli, Mary. 2000. "Gendered Conflict." *Journal of Peace Research* 37 (1): 51–68.

Carothers, Thomas. 1999. *Aiding Democracy Abroad: The Learning Curve.* Washington, D.C.: Carnegie Endowment for International Peace.

Carroll, James. 2006. *The Pentagon and the Disastrous Rise of American Power.* Boston: Houghton Mifflin.

Carter, Ralph G. 1989. "Senate Defense Budgeting, 1981–1988: The Impacts of Ideology, Party, and Constituency Benefit on the Decision to Support the President." *American Politics Quarterly* 17 (July): 332–347.

Carter, Ralph G., and James M. Scott. 2009. *Choosing to Lead: Understanding Congressional Foreign Policy Entrepreneurs.* Durham: Duke University Press.

Caruson, Kiki, and Victoria A. Farrar-Myers. 2007. "Promoting the President's Foreign Policy Agenda: Presidential Use of Executive Agreements as Policy Vehicles." *Political Research Quarterly* 60 (December): 631–644.

Cashman, Greg, and Leonard C. Robinson. 2007. *An Introduction to the Causes of War: Patterns of Interstate Conflict from World War I to Iraq.* Lanham, Md.: Rowman and Littlefield.

Cauley, Leslie. 2006. "NSA Has Massive Database of Americans' Phone Calls." *USA Today,* May 11.

Center for Defense Information. 2003a. "Last of the Big Time Spenders: U.S. Military Budget Still the World's Largest, and Growing." www.cdi.org/program/issue/index.cfm?ProgramID=15& issueid=34.

———. 2003b. "Ten Largest U.S. Military Contractors, Fiscal Year 2002." www.cdi.org/news/mrp/contractors.pdf.

———. 2007. "Arms Trade." http://cdi.org/program/index.cfm?programid=73.

Central Intelligence Agency. 2004. "Special Review: Counterterrorism, Detention, and Interrogation Activities (September 2001–October 2003)." Office of Inspector General, May 7.

Centre for the Study of Political Change. 2006. "European Elites Survey: Key Findings of the Survey of Members of the European Parliament and Top European Commission Officials." www.gips.unisi.it/circap/ees_overview.

Chait, Jonathan. 2002. "Defense Secretary: The Peculiar Duplicity of Ari Fleischer." *New Republic,* June 10, 20–23.

Chan, Steve. 2008. "Soft Deterrence, Passive Resistance: American Lenses, Chinese Lessons." In *Hegemony Constrained: Evasion, Modification, and Resistance to American Foreign Policy,* ed. Davis Bobrow, 62–80. Pittsburgh: University of Pittsburgh Press.

Chanlett-Avery, Emma. 2009. "The Changing U.S.-Japan Alliance: Implications for U.S. Interests." Congressional Research Service, Washington, D.C., July 23.

Checkel, Jeffrey. 2008. "Constructivism and Foreign Policy." In *Foreign Policy: Theories, Actors, Cases,* ed. Steve Smith, Amelia Hadfield, and Tim Dunne, 71–82. New York: Oxford University Press.

Chicago Council on Foreign Relations, Program on International Policy Attitudes. 2004. "The Hall of Mirrors: Perceptions and Misperceptions in the Congressional Foreign Policy Process." October 1. www.pipa.org/onlinereports/fp_makingprocess/hallofmirrors_ocr04/hallofmirrors_oct04_rpt.pdf.

Chicago Council on Global Affairs. 2009. "Anxious Americans Seek a New Direction in United States Foreign Policy." www.thechicagocouncil.org.

Chomsky, Noam. 2003. *Hegemony or Survival: America's Quest for Global Dominance.* New York: Metropolitan Books.

Chong, Dennis, and James N. Druckman. 2007. "Framing Theory." *Annual Review of Political Science* 10: 103–126.

Christensen, Eben J., and Steven B. Redd. 2006. "Bureaucrats versus the Ballot Box in Foreign Policy Decision Making." *Journal of Conflict Resolution* 48 (February): 69–90.

Christensen, Jon. 2004. "Asking Do-Gooders to Prove They Do Good." *New York Times,* January 3.

Cincotta, Richard P., and Barbara B. Crane. 2001. "The Mexico City Policy and U.S. Family Planning Assistance." *Science,* October 19, 525–526.

Clark, Wesley K. 2001. *Waging Modern War: Bosnia, Kosovo, and the Future of Combat.* New York: Public Affairs.

Clifford, Mark L., and Pete Engardio. 2000. *Meltdown: Asia's Boom, Bust, and Beyond.* Paramus, N.J.: Prentice Hall.

Clinton, Hillary Rodham. 2009. "Remarks at Planned Parenthood Federation of America Awards Gala." March 27. www.state.gov/secretary/rm/2009a/03/120968.htm.

Cohen, Jeffrey E. 2009. *The Presidency in the Era of 24-Hour News.* Princeton: Princeton University Press.

Cohen, Joel E. 2003. "The Future of Population." In *What the Future Holds: Insights from Social Science,* ed. Richard N. Cooper and Richard Layard, 29–75. Cambridge: MIT Press.

Cohen, Michael A. 2009. "Arms for the World: How the U.S. Military Shapes American Foreign Policy." *Dissent* 56 (fall): 69–74.

Cohen, Richard E., and Peter Bell. 2005. "Congressional Insiders Poll." *National Journal,* March 5.

Cohen, Saul B. 2003. *Geopolitics of the World System.* Lanham, Md.: Rowman and Littlefield.

Cohen, Stephen D., Robert A. Blecker, and Peter D. Whitney. 2003. *Fundamentals of U.S. Foreign Trade Policy,* 2nd ed. Boulder, Colo.: Westview Press.

Coll, Steve. 2004. *Ghost Wars: The Secret History of the CIA, Afghanistan, and bin Laden, from the Soviet Invasion to September 10, 2001.* New York: Penguin Books.

———. 2010. "Threats." *New Yorker,* January 18, 19–20.

Collins, Stephen D. 2009. "Can America Finance Freedom? Assessing U.S. Democracy Promotion via Economic Statecraft." *Foreign Policy Analysis* 5 (October): 367–389.

Combs, Cindy C. 2003. *Terrorism in the 21st Century,* 3rd ed. Upper Saddle River, N.J.: Prentice Hall.

Compaine, Benjamin M., and Douglas Gomery. 2000. *Who Owns the Media? Competition and Concentration in the Mass Media Industry,* 3rd ed. Mahwah, N.J.: Lawrence Erlbaum Associates.

Congressional Budget Office. 2007. *The Budget and Economic Outlook: Fiscal Years 2008–2017.* Washington, D.C.: Congress of the United States, January.

———. 2009. *The Budget and Economic Outlook: Fiscal Years 2009–2019.* Washington, D.C.: Congress of the United States, January. www.cbo.gov/ftpdocs/99xx/doc9957/01-07-Outlook.pdf.

Congressional Research Service. 2001. "Treaties and Other International Agreements: The Role of the U.S. Senate." Congressional Research Service, Washington, D.C.

Converse, Philip. 1964. "The Nature of Belief Systems in Mass Publics." In *Ideology and Discontent,* ed. David Apter, 206–261. New York: Free Press.

Cooper, Andrew F. 2008. *Celebrity Diplomacy*. Boulder, Colo.: Paradigm.

Cortright, David, and George A. Lopez, eds. 2002. *Smart Sanctions: Targeting Economic Statecraft*. Lanham, Md.: Rowman and Littlefield.

Corwin, Edward S. 1957. *The President: Office and Powers, 1787–1957; History and Analysis of Practice and Opinion*, 4th ed. New York: New York University Press.

Council on American-Islamic Relations. 2006. "American Public Opinion about Islam and Muslims." www.cair.com/cairsurveyanalysis.pdf.

Council on Foreign Affairs. 2005. "How Americans View U.S. Foreign Policy: Editor's Note." August 3. www.foreignaffairs.org/public_agenda/2005.

Council on Foreign Relations. 2009. *Public Opinion on Global Issues*, chap. 9. November. www.cfr.org/public_opinion.

Cowan, Geoffrey, and Nicholas J. Cull, eds. 2008. *Public Diplomacy in a Changing World*. Special issue of *The Annals of the American Academy of Political and Social Science* 616 (March): 6–8.

Cox, Dan G., and Cooper A. Drury. 2006. "Democratic Sanctions: Connecting the Democratic Peace and Economic Sanctions." *Journal of Peace Research* 43 (November): 709–722.

Coyle, Philip E. 2006. "Missile Defense: An Expensive Bluff?" *Defense Monitor* (July–August): 1–2.

Crabb, Cecil V., and Pat M. Holt. 1992. *Invitation to Struggle: Congress, the President, and Foreign Policy*. Washington, D.C.: CQ Press.

Crabb, Cecil V., Jr., and Kevin V. Mulcahy. 1995. "George Bush's Management Style and Operation Desert Storm." *Presidential Studies Quarterly* 25 (spring): 251–265.

Crichlow, Scott. 2005. "Psychological Influences on the Policy Choices of Secretaries of State and Foreign Ministers." *Cooperation and Conflict* 40 (2): 179–205.

Cronin, Patrick, and Benjamin O. Fordham. 1999. "Timeless Principles or Today's Fashion? Testing the Stability of the Linkage between Ideology and Foreign Policy in the Senate." *Journal of Politics* 61 (November): 967–998.

Crowley, Michael. 2004. "Playing Defense: Bush's Disastrous Homeland Security Department." *New Republic*, March 16, 17–21.

Cumming, Alfred. 2006. "Covert Action: Legislative Background and Possible Policy Questions." Congressional Research Service, Washington, D.C., November 2.

Daalder, Ivo H. 1991. *The Nature and Practice of Flexible Response: NATO Strategy and Theater Nuclear Forces since 1967*. New York: Columbia University Press.

Daalder, Ivo H., and I. M. Destler. 2000. *A New NSC for a New Administration*. Policy Brief 68. Washington, D.C.: Brookings.

Daalder, Ivo H., and James M. Lindsay, eds. 2003. *America Unbound: The Bush Revolution in Foreign Policy*. Washington, D.C.: Brookings.

Daalder, Ivo H., and Jan Lodal. 2008. "The Logic of Zero." *Foreign Affairs* 87 (November–December): 80–95.

Daalder, Ivo H., and Michael E. O'Hanlon. 2000. *Winning Ugly: NATO's War to Save Kosovo*. Washington, D.C.: Brookings.

Dadge, David. 2004. *Casualty of War: The Bush Administration's Assault on a Free Press*. Amherst, N.Y.: Prometheus Press.

Dale, Catherine, Nina Serafino, and Pat Towell. 2008. "Organizing the U.S. Government for National Security: Overview of the Interagency Debates." Congressional Research Service, Washington, D.C., April 18.

Dallek, Robert. 1989. *The American Style of Foreign Policy: Cultural Politics and Foreign Affairs*. New York: Oxford University Press.

Davidson, Roger H., and Walter J. Oleszek, eds. 2004. *Congress and Its Members*, 9th ed. Washington, D.C.: CQ Press.

———. 2006. *Congress and Its Members,* 10th ed. Washington, D.C.: CQ Press.

de Wijk, Rob. 2002. "The Limits of Military Power." *Washington Quarterly* 25 (winter): 75–92.

DeConde, Alexander. 1992. *Ethnicity, Race, and American Foreign Policy.* Boston: Northeastern University Press.

Deering, Christopher J. 1993. "Decision Making in the Armed Services Committees." In *Congress Resurgent: Foreign and Defense Policy on Capitol Hill,* ed. Randall B. Ripley and James M. Lindsay, 155–182. Ann Arbor: University of Michigan Press.

———. 1996. "Congress, the President, and Automatic Government: The Case of Military Base Closures." In *Rivals for Power: Presidential-Congressional Relations,* ed. James A. Thurber, 153–169. Washington, D.C.: CQ Press.

Deering, Christopher J., and Steven S. Smith. 1997. *Committees in Congress,* 3rd ed. Washington, D.C.: CQ Press.

Defense Science Board. 2004. *Report of the Defense Science Board Task Force on Strategic Communications.* Washington, D.C.: Defense Science Board.

Dershowitz, Alan. 2006. "Debunking the Newest—and Oldest—Jewish Conspiracy: A Reply to the Mearsheimer-Walt Working Paper." Harvard Law School, Cambridge. April. www.ksg.harvard.edu/research/working_papers/dershowitzreply.pdf.

Destler, I. M. 1994. "A Government Divided: The Security Complex and the Economic Complex." In *The New Politics of American Foreign Policy,* ed. David A. Deese, 132–147. New York: St. Martin's Press.

———. 1995. *American Trade Politics: System under Stress,* 3rd ed. Washington, D.C.: Institute for International Economics.

———. 2001a. "Congress and Foreign Policy at Century's End: Requiem or Cooperation?" In *Congress Reconsidered,* 7th ed., ed. Lawrence C. Dodd and Bruce I. Oppenheimer, 315–333. Washington, D.C.: CQ Press.

———. 2001b. "The Reasonable Public and the Polarized Policy Process." In *The Real and the Ideal: Essays in International Relations in Honor of Richard H. Ullman,* ed. Anthony Lake and David Ochmanek, 75–90. Lanham, Md.: Rowman and Littlefield.

Destler, I. M., Leslie H. Gelb, and Anthony Lake. 1984. *Our Own Worst Enemy: The Unmaking of American Foreign Policy.* New York: Touchstone.

Deutsch, Karl W., S. A. Burrell, R. A. Kann, M. Lee Jr., M. Lichterman, R. E. Lindgern, F. L. Loewenheim, and R. W. Van Wagenen. 1957. *Political Community and the North Atlantic Area: International Organization in the Light of Historical Experience.* Princeton: Princeton University Press.

Diamond, John. 2008. *The CIA and the Culture of Failure.* Stanford: Stanford University Press.

Dizard, Wilson, Jr. 2001. *Digital Diplomacy: U.S. Foreign Policy in the Information Age.* Westport, Conn.: Praeger.

Dolan, Chris J., and Jerel A. Rosati. 2006. "U.S. Foreign Economic Policy and the Significance of the National Economic Council." *International Studies Perspectives* 7 (2): 102–123.

Donnelly, Thomas. 2006. "Countering Aggressive Rising Powers: A Clash of Strategic Cultures." *Orbis* 50 (summer): 413–428.

Dorman, S., ed. 2003. *Inside a U.S. Embassy: How the Foreign Service Works for America.* Washington, D.C.: American Foreign Service Association.

Dower, John. 1986. *War without Mercy: Race and Power in the Pacific War.* New York: Pantheon.

Doyle, Charles. 2006. "Federal Habeas Corpus: An Abridged Sketch." Congressional Research Service, Washington, D.C., April 28.

Doyle, Michael W. 1986a. *Empires.* Ithaca: Cornell University Press.

———. 1986b. "Liberalism and World Politics." *American Political Science Review* 80 (December): 1151–1169.

———. 2008. "Liberalism and Foreign Policy." In *Foreign Policy: Theories, Actors, Cases*, ed. Steve Smith, Amelia Hadfield, and Tim Dunne, 49–70. New York: Oxford University Press.

Doyle, Michael W., and Nicholas Sambanis. 2006. *Making War and Building Peace: United Nations Peace Operations*. Princeton: Princeton University Press.

Drezner, Daniel W. 2000. "Ideas, Bureaucratic Politics, and the Crafting of Foreign Policy." *American Journal of Political Science* 44 (October): 733–749.

———. 2003. "The Hidden Hand of Economic Coercion." *International Organization* 57 (summer): 643–659.

Drum, Kevin. 2010. "Capital City." *Mother Jones* (January–February). http://mother-jones.com/politics/2010/01/wall-street-big-finance-lobbyists.

Dryden, Steve. 1995. *Trade Warriors: USTR and the American Crusade for Free Trade*. New York: Oxford University Press.

Duffy, Helen. 2005. *The "War on Terror" and the Framework of International Law*. New York: Cambridge University Press.

Dumbrell, John. 2002. "Was There a Clinton Doctrine? President Clinton's Foreign Policy Reconsidered." *Diplomacy and Statecraft* 13 (June): 43–56.

Dunn, David Hastings. 2006a. "A Doctrine Worthy of the Name? George W. Bush and the Limits of Pre-Emption, Pre-Eminence, and Unilateralism." *Diplomacy and Statecraft* 17 (March): 1–29.

———. 2006b. "Quacking Like a Duck? Bush II and Presidential Power in the Second Term." *International Affairs* 82 (1): 95–120.

Earle, Edward Mead, ed. 1937. *The Federalist*. Washington, D.C.: National Home Library.

Easterly, William R. 2006. *The White Man's Burden: Why the West's Efforts to Aid the Rest Have Done So Much Ill and So Little Good*. New York: Penguin Books.

Economist. 2002. "From Uncle Ben's to Uncle Sam." February 21. www.economist.com/business/printer-friendly.crf?story_ID=998594.

———. 2006. "The New Titans." September 16, 3–8.

Eichenberg, Richard C. 2005. "Victory Has Many Friends: U.S. Public Opinion and the Use of Military Force, 1981–2005." *International Security* 30 (summer): 140–177.

Eichengreen, Barry. 2002. "The Globalization Wars." *Foreign Affairs* 81 (July–August): 157–164.

Eisensee, Thomas, and David Strömberg. 2007. "News Droughts, News Floods, and U.S. Disaster Relief." *Quarterly Journal of Economics* 122 (2): 693–728.

Engelbrecht, H. C. 1934. *Merchants of Death: A Study of the International Armament Industry*. New York: Dodd, Mead.

Entman, Robert M. 2004. *Projections of Power: Framing News, Public Opinion, and U.S. Foreign Policy*. Chicago: University of Chicago Press.

Esposito, John L. 2002. *Unholy War: Terror in the Name of Islam*. New York: Oxford University Press.

Etheridge, Lloyd. 1978. "Personality Effects on American Foreign Policy, 1898–1968: A Test of Interpersonal Generalization Theory." *American Political Science Review* 72 (June): 434–451.

Euromonitor International. 2007. *World Economic Factbook*, 15th ed. London: Euromonitor International.

Evans, Michael. 2004. "Of Smoking Guns and Mushroom Clouds: Explaining the Bush Doctrine and the Rise of Military Pre-Emption." *Australian Army Journal* 1 (2): 17.

Fallows, James M. 1997. *Breaking the News: How the Media Undermine American Democracy.* New York: Vintage.

Farnham, Barbara. 2004. "Impact of Political Context on Foreign Policy Decision-Making." *Political Psychology* 25 (June): 441–463.

Feaver, Peter D., and Christopher Gelpi. 2004. *Choosing Your Battles: American Civil-Military Relations and the Use of Force.* Princeton: Princeton University Press.

Federation of American Scientists. 2007. "Arms Sales Monitoring Project." Washington, D.C. http://fas.org/asmp.

———. 2009. "Arms Sales Monitoring Project." Washington, D.C. http://fas.org/programs/ssp/asmp/index.html.

Feldman, Noah. 2008. "When Judges Make Foreign Policy." *New York Times Magazine,* September 28, 50.

Ferguson, Niall. 2004. *Colossus: The Rise and Fall of the American Empire.* New York: Penguin Books.

Fineman, Howard. 2003. "Bush and God: A Higher Calling." *Newsweek,* March 10, 22–30.

Finnemore, Martha. 2003. *The Purpose of Intervention: Changing Beliefs about the Use of Force.* Ithaca: Cornell University Press.

Fiorina, Morris. 1989. *Congress: Keystone of the Washington Establishment,* 2nd ed. New Haven: Yale University Press.

Fisher, Louis. 2004. "The Way We Go to War: The Iraq Resolution." In *Considering the Bush Presidency,* ed. Gary L. Gregg II and Mark J. Rozell, 107–124. New York: Oxford University Press.

———. 2007. "The Scope of Inherent Powers." In *The Polarized Presidency of George W. Bush,* ed. George C. Edwards III and Desmond S. King, 31–64. New York: Oxford University Press.

Fleisher, Richard, Jon R. Bond, and B. Dan Wood. 2008. "Which Presidents Are Uncommonly Successful in Congress?" In *Presidential Leadership: The Vortex of Power,* ed. Bert A. Rockman and Richard W. Waterman, 191–214. New York: Oxford University Press.

Ford, Jess T. 2009. "Department of State: Persistent Staffing and Foreign Language Gaps Compromise Diplomatic Readiness." U.S. Government Accountability Office, Washington, D.C., September 24.

Fordham, Benjamin O., and Timothy McKeown. 2003. "Selection and Influence: Interest Groups and Congressional Voting on Trade Policy." *International Organization* 57 (summer): 519–549.

Fordham, Benjamin O., and Thomas C. Walker. 2005. "Kantian Liberalism, Regime Type, and Military Resource Allocation: Do Democracies Spend Less?" *International Studies Quarterly* 49 (1): 141–157.

Forest, James J. F., ed. 2009. *Influence Warfare.* Westport, Conn.: Praeger.

Forest, James J. F., and Matthew V. Sousa. 2006. *Oil and Terrorism in the New Gulf: Framing U.S. Energy and Security Policies for the Gulf of Guinea.* Lanham, Md.: Lexington Books.

Forsythe, David P. 1995. "Human Rights and U.S. Foreign Policy: Two Levels, Two Worlds." *Political Studies* 43 (4): 111–130.

Franck, Thomas M., and Edward Weisband. 1979. *Foreign Policy by Congress.* New York: Oxford University Press.

Freedman, Lawrence. 2003. *The Evolution of Nuclear Strategy,* 3rd ed. New York: Palgrave Macmillan.

Freedom House. Various years. *Freedom in the World.* New York: Freedom House.

———. 2010. *Freedom in the World 2010.* Lanham, Md.: Rowman and Littlefield.

Friedberg, Aaron. 2005. "The Future of U.S.-China Relations: Is Conflict Inevitable?" *International Security* 30 (fall): 7–45.

Froomkin, Dan. 2006. "It's a Civil War, Stupid." *Washington Post,* November 27.

Fry, Earl H. 1998. *The Expanding Role of State and Local Governments in U.S. Foreign Affairs.* New York: Council on Foreign Relations.

Fukuyama, Francis. 1989. "The End of History?" *National Interest* 16 (summer): 3–18.

———. 2004. *State-Building: Governance and World Order in the 21st Century.* Ithaca: Cornell University Press.

Gaddis, John L. 2005. *Surprise, Security, and the American Experience.* Cambridge: Harvard University Press.

Galdi, Theodor W. 1995. "Revolution in Military Affairs? Competing Concepts, Organizational Responses, Outstanding Issues." Congressional Research Service, Washington, D.C., December 11.

GAO (General Accounting Office). 2003. "Energy Task Force: Process Used to Develop the National Energy Policy." GAO, Washington, D.C.

GAO (Government Accountability Office). 2007. "Securing, Stabilizing, and Rebuilding Iraq: Key Issues for Congressional Oversight." GAO, Washington, D.C., January. www.gao.gov/new.items/d07308sp.pdf.

Gardner, Richard N. 1980. *Sterling-Dollar Diplomacy in Current Perspectives: The Origins and Prospects of Our International Economic Order,* exp. ed. New York: Columbia University Press.

Garrison, Jean. 1999. *Games Advisers Play: Foreign Policy in the Nixon and Carter Administrations.* College Station: Texas A&M University Press.

Gates, Robert M. 1996. *From the Shadows: The Ultimate Insider's Story of Five Presidents and How They Won the Cold War.* New York: Simon and Schuster.

———. 2009. "A Balanced Strategy: Reprogramming the Pentagon for a New Age." *Foreign Affairs* 88 (January–February): 28–40.

Gelpi, Christopher, Peter D. Feaver, and Jason Reifler. 2005/2006. "Success Matters: Casualty Sensitivity and the War in Iraq." *International Security* 30 (winter): 7–46.

George, Alexander L. 1974. *Deterrence in American Foreign Policy: Theory and Practice.* New York: Columbia University Press.

———. 1980. *Presidential Decision-Making in Foreign Policy: The Effective Use of Information and Advice.* Boulder, Colo.: Westview Press.

———. 1989. "The 'Operational Code': A Neglected Approach to the Study of Political Leaders and Decision Making." In *American Foreign Policy: Theoretical Essays,* ed. G. John Ikenberry, 483–506. New York: HarperCollins.

———. 2000. "The Role of Force in Diplomacy: A Continuing Dilemma for U.S. Foreign Policy." In *The Use of Force after the Cold War,* ed. H. W. Brands, 59–92. College Station: Texas A&M University Press.

George, Alexander L., and Juliette L. George. 1956. *Woodrow Wilson and Colonel House: A Personality Study.* New York: J. Day Co.

Gereffi, Gary, Ronie Garcia-Johnson, and Erika Sasser. 2001. "The NGO-Industrial Complex." *Foreign Policy* 125 (July–August): 56–65.

Ghanem, Salma. 1997. "Filling in the Tapestry: The Second Level of Agenda Setting." In *Communication and Democracy: Exploring the Intellectual Frontiers in Agenda-Setting Theory,* ed. Maxwell E. McCombs, Donald L. Shaw, and David Weaver, 3–14. Mahwah, N.J.: Lawrence Erlbaum Associates.

Gibson, Martha L. 2000. *Conflict and Consensus in American Trade Policy.* Washington, D.C.: Georgetown University Press.

Gilmore Commission. 2003. "Forging America's New Normalcy: Securing Our Homeland, Protecting Our Liberty." www.rand.org/nsrd/terrpanel.

Gilpin, Robert. 1981. *War and Change in World Politics.* New York: Cambridge University Press.

———. 1986. "The Richness of the Tradition of Political Realism." In *Neorealism and Its Critics,* ed. Robert O. Keohane, 301–321. New York: Columbia University Press.

———. 1987. *The Political Economy of International Relations.* Princeton: Princeton University Press.

Ginsberg, Benjamin. 1986. *The Captive Public.* New York: Basic Books.

Glad, Betty. 1983. "Black-and-White Thinking: Ronald Reagan's Approach to Foreign Policy." *Political Psychology* 4 (March): 33–76.

Glad, Betty, and Chris J. Dolan, eds. 2004. *Striking First: The Preventive War Doctrine and the Reshaping of U.S. Foreign Policy.* New York: Palgrave Macmillan.

Glaser, Daryl. 2006. "Does Hypocrisy Matter? The Case of U.S. Foreign Policy." *Review of International Studies* 32: 251–268.

Glasser, Susan B., and Michael Grunwald. 2005. "Department's Mission Was Undermined from Start." *Washington Post,* December 22, A01.

Global Security. 2010. "U.S.-Mexico Border Fence/Great Wall of Mexico Secure Fence." www.globalsecurity.org/security/systems/mexico-wall.htm.

Golan, Guy G. 2010. "Determinants of International News Coverage." In *International Media Communications in a Global Age,* ed. Guy Golan, Thomas J. Johnson, and Wayne Wanta, 125–144. New York: Routledge.

Golan, Guy G., and Wayne Wanta. 2001. "Second-level Agenda Setting in the New Hampshire Primary." *Journalism and Mass Communication Quarterly* 78 (summer): 247–259.

Goldberg, D. H. 1990. *Foreign Policy and Ethnic Interest Groups: American and Canadian Jews Lobby for Israel.* New York: Greenwood Press.

Goldstein, Joshua. 2001. *War and Gender: How Gender Shapes the War System and Vice-Versa.* New York: Cambridge University Press.

Goldstein, Judith, and Robert Keohane. 1993. *Ideas and Foreign Policy: Beliefs, Institutions, and Political Change.* Ithaca: Cornell University Press.

Goodman, Melvin A. 2008. *Failure of Intelligence: The Decline and Fall of the CIA.* Lanham, Md.: Rowman and Littlefield.

Goodwin, Jacob. 1985. *Brotherhood of Arms: General Dynamics and the Business of Defending America.* New York: Times Books.

Gordon, Michael R., and Bernard E. Trainor. 2006. *Cobra II: The Inside Story of the Invasion and Occupation of Iraq.* New York: Pantheon.

Gourevitch, Peter. 2002. "Domestic Politics and International Relations." In *Handbook of International Relations,* ed. Walter Carlsnaes, Thomas Risse, and Beth A. Simmons, 309–328. Thousand Oaks, Calif.: Sage.

Graber, Doris A. 2006. *Mass Media and American Politics,* 7th ed. Washington, D.C.: CQ Press.

Graebner, Norman A., ed. 1964. *Ideas and Diplomacy: Readings in the Intellectual Tradition of American Foreign Policy.* New York: Oxford University Press.

Graham, Sarah E., and John R. Kelley. 2009. "U.S. Engagement in East Asia: A Case of Two-Track Diplomacy." *Orbis* 53 (winter): 80–98.

Gray, Christine. 2004. *International Law and the Use of Force,* 2nd ed. New York: Oxford University Press.

Gray, Colin S. 1999. *Modern Strategy.* New York: Oxford University Press.

———. 2002. "Thinking Asymmetrically in Times of Terror." *Parameters* 32 (spring): 5–14.

Greco, Emily S. 2008. "Global Cooperation: The Candidates Speak." *Foreign Policy in Focus,* March 26. www.fpif.org/articles/global_cooperation_the_candidates_speak.

Greenberger, Robert S. 1995/1996. "Dateline Capitol Hill: The New Majority's Foreign Policy." *Foreign Policy* 101 (winter): 159–169.

Gregg, Gary L., II. 2004. "Dignified Authenticity: George W. Bush and the Symbolic Presidency." In *Considering the Bush Presidency,* ed. Gary L. Gregg II and Mark J. Rozell, 88–106. New York: Oxford University Press.

Gregory, William H. 1989. *The Defense Procurement Mess.* Lexington, Mass.: Lexington Books.

Grimmett, Richard F. 2001. "The War Powers Resolution after 28 Years." Congressional Research Service, Washington, D.C., November 15.

———. 2004. "Instances of Use of United States Armed Forces Abroad, 1798–2004." Congressional Research Service, Washington, D.C., October 5.

———. 2006. "Conventional Arms Transfers to Developing Nations, 1998–2005." Congressional Research Service, Washington, D.C., October 23.

———. 2009. "Conventional Arms Transfers to Developing Nations." Congressional Research Service, Washington, D.C., September 4. http://fpc.state.gov/documents/organization/129342.pdf.

———. 2010. "Instances of Use of United States Armed Forces Abroad, 1798–2009." Congressional Research Service, Washington D.C., January 27.

Grunwald, Henry A. 1993. "The Post–Cold War Press." *Foreign Affairs* 72 (summer): 12–16.

Grunwald, Michael, and Juliet Eilperin. 2005. "Energy Bill Raises Fears about Pollution, Fraud." *Washington Post,* July 30, 1A.

Gulbrandsen, Lars H., and Steinar Andresen. 2004. "NGO Influence in the Implementation of the Kyoto Protocol: Compliance, Flexibility Mechanisms, and Sinks." *Global Environmental Politics* 4 (November).

Haass, Richard N., ed. 1998. *Economic Sanctions and American Diplomacy.* New York: Council on Foreign Relations.

Hallin, Daniel C., and Todd Gitlin. 1994. "The Gulf War as Popular Culture and Television Drama." In *Taken by Storm: The Media, Public Opinion, and U.S. Foreign Policy in the Gulf War,* ed. W. Lance Bennett and David L. Paletz, 149–163. Chicago: University of Chicago Press.

Halperin, Morton H. 1963. *Limited War in a Nuclear Age.* New York: Wiley.

Hamilton, John M., and Eric Jenner. 2004. "Redefining Foreign Correspondence." *Journalism* 5 (3): 301–321.

Hamilton, Lee. 2009. *Strengthening Congress.* Bloomington: Indiana University Press.

Hammond, Paul. 1960. "The National Security Council as a Device for Interdepartmental Coordination: An Interpretation and Appraisal." In *American Political Science Review* 54 (December): 899–910.

Haney, Patrick J. 1997. *Organizing for Foreign Policy Crises: Presidents, Advisers, and the Management of Decision Making.* Ann Arbor: University of Michigan Press.

———. 2005. "Foreign-Policy Advising: Models and Mysteries from the Bush Administration." *Presidential Studies Quarterly* 35 (June): 289–302.

Haney, Patrick J., and Walt Vanderbush. 1999. "The Role of Ethnic Interest Groups in U.S. Foreign Policy: The Case of the Cuban American National Foundation." *International Studies Quarterly* 43 (June): 341–361.

Hansen, Victor M., and Lawrence Friedman. 2009. *The Case for Congress: Separation of Powers and the War on Terror.* Burlington, Vt.: Ashgate.

Hart, Jeffrey A. 1992. *Rival Capitalists: International Competitiveness in the United States, Japan, and Western Europe.* Ithaca: Cornell University Press.

Hart, John. 1987. *The Presidential Branch.* New York: Pergamon Press.

Hart, Paul 't. 1994. *Groupthink in Government.* Baltimore: Johns Hopkins University Press.

Hart, Paul 't., Eric Stern, and Bengt Sundelius, eds. 1997. *Beyond Groupthink: Political Group Dynamics and Foreign Policymaking.* Ann Arbor: University of Michigan Press.

Haslam, Jonathan. 2002. *No Virtue Like Necessity: Realist Thought in International Relations since Machiavelli.* New Haven: Yale University Press.

Hayden, Patrick, and Chamsy el-Ojeili, eds. 2005. *Confronting Globalization: Humanity, Justice, and the Renewal of Politics.* New York: Palgrave Macmillan.

Hays, Peter L., Brenda J. Vallance, and Alan R. Van Tassel, eds. 1996. *American Defense Policy,* 7th ed. Baltimore: Johns Hopkins University Press.

Heclo, Hugh. 1978. "Issue Networks and the Executive Establishment." In *The New American Political System,* ed. Anthony King, 87–124. Washington, D.C.: American Enterprise Institute.

Heilbroner, Robert L. 1999. *The Worldly Philosophers: The Lives, Times, and Ideas of the Great Economic Thinkers,* 7th rev. ed. New York: Simon and Schuster.

Heine-Ellison, Sofia. 2001. "The Impact and Effectiveness of Multilateral Economic Sanctions: A Comparative Study." *International Journal of Human Rights* 5 (spring): 81–113.

Henehan, Marie T. 2000. *Foreign Policy and Congress: An International Relations Perspective.* Ann Arbor: University of Michigan Press.

Henkin, Louis. 1996. *Foreign Affairs and the Constitution,* 2nd ed. New York: Oxford University Press.

Herman, Edward, and Noam Chomsky. 1988. *Manufacturing Consent: The Political Economy of the Mass Media.* New York: Pantheon.

Hermann, Margaret G. 1984. "Personality and Foreign Policy Decision Making: A Study of 53 Heads of Government." In *Foreign Policy Decision Making: Perception, Cognition, and Artificial Intelligence,* ed. Donald A. Sylvan and Steve Chan, 53–80. New York: Praeger.

———. 1993. "Leaders and Foreign Policy Decision-Making." In *Diplomacy, Force, and Leadership: Essays in Honor of Alexander George,* ed. Dan Caldwell and Timothy J. McKeown, 77–94. Boulder, Colo.: Westview Press.

Hermann, Margaret G., and Thomas Preston. 1999. "Presidents, Leadership Style, and the Advisory Process." In *The Domestic Sources of American Foreign Policy,* 3rd ed., ed. Eugene Wittkopf and James M. McCormick, 351–367. Lanham, Md.: Rowman and Littlefield.

Herrling, Sheila, and Steve Radelet. 2005. "The MCC between a Rock and a Hard Place: More Countries, Less Money and the Transformational Challenge." Washington, D.C.: Center for Global Development, October 26.

Herrmann, Richard K. 1984. "Perceptions and Foreign Policy Analysis." In *Foreign Policy Decision Making: Perception, Cognition, and Artificial Intelligence,* ed. Donald A. Sylvan and Steve Chan, 25–52. New York: Praeger.

Hersh, Seymour M. 2004. "Torture at Abu Ghraib." *New Yorker,* May 10. www.newyorker.com/printable/?fact/040510fa_fact.

Hersman, Rebecca. 2000. *Friends and Foes: How Congress and the President Really Make Foreign Policy.* Washington, D.C.: Brookings.

Hertzke, Allen D. 2004. *Freeing God's Children: The Unlikely Alliance for Global Human Rights.* Lanham, Md.: Rowman and Littlefield.

Hess, Stephen, and James P. Pfiffner. 2002. *Organizing the Presidency.* Washington, D.C.: Brookings.

Hetherington, Marc J. 1998. "The Political Relevance of Political Trust." *American Political Science Review* 92 (December): 791–808.

Hildreth, Steven A. 2005. "Missile Defense: The Current Debate." Congressional Research Service, Washington, D.C., July 19.

Hill, Christopher. 2003. *The Changing Politics of Foreign Policy.* New York: Palgrave Macmillan.

Hill, Steven. 2009. "Obama the Impotent." *The Guardian* (London), September 26, 44. www.guardian.co.uk/commentisfree/cifamerica/2009/sep/22/obama-un-climate-change-europe.

Hilsman, Roger. 2000. "After the Cold War: The Need for Intelligence." In *National Insecurity: U.S. Intelligence after the Cold War,* ed. Craig Eisendrath, 8–22. Philadelphia: Temple University Press.

Hinckley, Barbara. 1994. *Less than Meets the Eye: Foreign Policy Making and the Myth of the Assertive Congress.* Chicago: University of Chicago Press.

Hirata, Keiko. 2002. "Wither the Developmental State? The Growing Role of NGOs in Japanese Policymaking." *Journal of Comparative Policy Analysis: Research and Practice* 4: 165–188.

Hirsh, Michael. 2003. *At War with Ourselves: Why America Is Squandering Its Chance to Build a Better World.* New York: Oxford University Press.

Hixson, Walter L. 2008. *The Myth of American Diplomacy: National Identity and U.S. Foreign Policy.* New Haven: Yale University Press.

Hodgson, Godfrey. 2009. *The Myth of American Exceptionalism.* New Haven: Yale University Press.

Hoff, Joan. 2008. *A Faustian Foreign Policy from Woodrow Wilson to George W. Bush: Dreams of Perfectibility.* New York: Cambridge University Press.

Hoffman, Bruce. 1998. *Inside Terrorism.* New York: Columbia University Press.

Hoffman, Frank G. 2006. "Complex Irregular Warfare: The Next Revolution in Military Affairs." *Orbis* 50 (3): 395–411.

Hofman, Ross, and Paul Levack, eds. 1949. *Burke's Politics.* New York: Knopf.

Holmes, Jack. 1985. *The Mood/Interest Theory of American Foreign Policy.* Lexington: University of Kentucky Press.

Holsti, Ole R. 1962. "The Belief System and National Images: A Case Study." *Journal of Conflict Resolution* 6 (September): 244–252.

———. 1984. "Theories of Crisis Decision Making." In *International Conflict and Conflict Management: Readings in World Politics*, ed. R. Matthews, A. Rubinoff, and J. Gross Stein, 65–83. New York: Prentice-Hall.

———. 1992. "Public Opinion and Foreign Policy: Challenges to the Almond-Lippmann Consensus." *International Studies Quarterly* 36 (December): 439–466.

———. 1996. *Public Opinion and American Foreign Policy.* Ann Arbor: University of Michigan Press.

Holsti, Ole R., and James M. Rosenau. 1979. "Vietnam, Consensus, and the Belief Systems of American Leaders." *World Politics* 32 (October): 1–56.

Hook, Steven W. 1995. *National Interest and Foreign Aid.* Boulder, Colo.: Lynne Rienner.

———. 1998. "Building Democracy through Foreign Aid: The Limitations of United States Political Conditionalities, 1992–1996." *Democratization* 5 (autumn): 156–180.

———. 2003. "Domestic Obstacles to International Affairs: The State Department under Fire." *PS: Political Science and Politics* 36 (January): 23–29.

———. 2008. "Ideas and Change in U.S. Foreign Aid: Inventing the Millennium Challenge Corporation." *Foreign Policy Analysis* 4 (April): 147–167.

Hook, Steven W., and Franklin Barr Lebo. 2008. "Sino-American Trade Relations: Privatizing Foreign Policy." In *Contemporary Cases in U.S. Foreign Policy: From Terrorism to Trade,* 3rd ed., ed. Ralph G. Carter, 305–333. Washington, D.C.: CQ Press.

———. 2010. "Development/Poverty Issues and Foreign Policy Analysis." In *The International Studies Encyclopedia,* ed. Robert A. Denemark. Malden, Mass.: Blackwell.

Hook, Steven W., and Xiaoyu Pu. 2006. "Framing Sino-American Relations under Stress: A Reexamination of News Coverage of the 2001 Spy Plane Crisis." *Asian Affairs: An American Review* 33 (fall): 167–183.

Hook, Steven W., and David Rothstein. 2005. "New Rationales and Old Concerns about U.S. Arms Exports." In *Guns and Butter: The Political Economy of International Security,* ed. Peter Dombrowski, 153–178. Boulder, Colo.: Lynne Rienner.

Hook, Steven W., and John Spanier. 2004. *American Foreign Policy since World War II,* 16th ed. Washington, D.C.: CQ Press.

———. 2010. *American Foreign Policy since World War II,* 18th ed. Washington, D.C.: CQ Press.

Houghton, David Patrick. 2007. "Reinvigorating the Study of Foreign Policy Decision Making: Toward a Constructivist Approach." *Foreign Policy Analysis* 3 (January): 24–45.

Howell, William G. 2003. *Power without Persuasion: The Politics of Direct Presidential Action.* Princeton: Princeton University Press.

———. 2005. "Unilateral Powers: A Brief Overview." *Presidential Studies Quarterly* 35 (September): 417–439.

Howell, William G., and Douglas Kriner. 2008. "Power without Persuasion: Identifying Executive Influence." In *Presidential Leadership: The Vortex of Power*, ed. Bert A. Rockman and Richard W. Waterman, 105–144. New York: Oxford University Press.

Howell, William G., and Jon C. Pevehouse. 2005. "Presidents, Congress, and the Use of Force." *International Organization* 59 (winter): 209–232.

Hulnick, Arthur S. 1999. *Fixing the Spy Machine: Preparing American Intelligence for the Twenty-First Century.* Westport, Conn.: Praeger.

Hunt, Michael. 1987. *Ideology and U.S. Foreign Policy.* New Haven: Yale University Press.

Huntington, Samuel P. 1957. *The Soldier and the State: The Theory and Politics of Civil-Military Relations.* Cambridge, Mass.: Belknap Press.

———. 1961. *The Common Defense: Strategic Programs in National Politics.* New York: Columbia University Press.

———. 1970/1971. "Foreign Aid for What and for Whom." *Foreign Policy* 1 (winter): 161–189.

———. 1981. *American Politics: The Promise of Disharmony.* Cambridge: Harvard University Press.

———. 1982. "American Ideals versus American Institutions." *Political Science Quarterly* 97 (spring): 1–37.

———. 2004. "The Hispanic Challenge." *Foreign Policy* 141 (March–April): 30–45.

Huus, Kari. 2003. "U.S. Takes Hard Line on Greenpeace: Bush Critics Say Use of Obscure Law Smacks of Retribution." November 14. www.msnbc.msn.com.

Ifill, Gwen. 1993. "The Economic Czar behind the Economic Czars." *New York Times,* March 7, A22.

Ignatieff, Michael. 2005. "Introduction: American Exceptionalism and Human Rights." In *American Exceptionalism and Human Rights,* ed. Michael Ignatieff, 1–26. Princeton: Princeton University Press.

Ikenberry, G. John. 2001. *After Victory: Institutions, Strategic Restraint, and the Rebuilding of Order after Major Wars.* Princeton: Princeton University Press.

———. 2004. "The End of the Neo-Conservative Moment." *Survival* 46 (March): 7–22.

———. 2009. "Woodrow Wilson, the Bush Administration, and the Future of Liberal Internationalism." In *The Crisis of American Foreign Policy*, ed. G. John Ikenberry, Thomas J. Knock, Anne-Marie Slaughter, and Tony Smith, 1–24. Princeton: Princeton University Press.

Ikenberry, G. John, and Charles A. Kupchan. 2004. "Liberal Realism: The Foundations of a Democratic Foreign Policy." *National Interest* (fall).

Ikenberry, G. John, David A. Lake, and Michael Mastanduno, eds. 1988. *The State and American Foreign Economic Policy.* Ithaca: Cornell University Press.

Ikenberry, G. John, Michael Mastanduno, and William C. Wohlforth. 2009. "Unipolarity, State Behavior, and Systemic Consequences." *World Politics* 61 (January): 1–27.

Inderfurth Karl F., and Loch K. Johnson. 2004. *Fateful Decisions: Inside the National Security Council.* New York: Oxford University Press.

Inglehart, Ronald, Miguel Basañez, and Alejandro Moreno. 1998. *Human Values and Beliefs: A Cross-Cultural Sourcebook.* Ann Arbor: University of Michigan Press.

International Committee of the Red Cross (ICRC). 2004. *Guantanamo Bay: Overview of the ICRC's Work for Internees.* Geneva: ICRC. www.icrc.org.

International Monetary Fund. 2010a. *Factsheet: Debt Relief under the Heavily Indebted Poor Countries (HIPC) Initiative,* February 18. www.imf.org/external/np/exr/facts/hipc.htm.

———. 2010b. "World Economic Outlook Database" (May 20, 2010). www.imf.org/external/pubs/ft/weo/2010/01/weodata/index.aspx.

International Monetary Fund and International Development Association. 2004. "The Impact of Debt Reduction under the Hawaii PC Initiative on External Debt Service and Social Expenditures." www.worldbank.org/hipc/hipc-review/impact_of_debt_reduction.pdf.

IPCC (Intergovernmental Panel on Climate Change). 2007. *Climate Change 2007: The Physical Science Basis.* Paris: IPCC.

Iraq Study Group. 2006. *The Iraq Study Group Report.* New York: Vintage Press.

Irons, Peter. 2005. *War Powers: How the Imperial Presidency Hijacked the Constitution.* New York: Metropolitan Books.

Isenberg, David. 1997. *Soldiers of Fortune, Ltd.: A Profile of Today's Private Sector Corporate Mercenary Firms.* Washington, D.C.: Center for Defense Information.

Iyengar, Shanto. 1991. *Is Anyone Responsible? How Television Frames Political News.* Chicago: University of Chicago Press.

Iyengar, Shanto, and Richard Morin. 2006. "Mind the Gap: Differences in Public Knowledge about Domestic and Overseas Events." *Washington Post,* July 5.

Iyengar, Shanto, and Adam Simon. 1994. "News Coverage of the Gulf Crisis and Public Opinion: A Study of Agenda-Setting, Priming, and Framing." In *Taken by Storm: The Media, Public Opinion, and U.S. Foreign Policy in the Gulf War,* ed. Lance W. Bennett and David L. Paletz. Chicago: University of Chicago Press.

Jackson, Brian A., ed. 2009. *The Challenge of Domestic Intelligence in a Free Society.* Santa Monica, Calif.: RAND.

Jacobs, Lawrence R., and Benjamin I. Page. 2005. "Who Influences U.S. Foreign Policy?" *American Political Science Review* 99 (1): 107–123.

Jacobs, Lawrence R., and Robert Y. Shapiro. 1995. "The Rise of Presidential Polling: The Nixon White House in Historical Perspective." *Public Opinion Quarterly* 59 (summer): 163–195.

Jacobson, Gary C. 1987. "Running Scared: Elections and Congressional Politics in the 1980s." In *Congress: Structure and Policy,* ed. Mathew McCubbins and Terry Sullivan, 34–81. New York: Cambridge University Press.

———. 2000. "Party Polarization in National Politics: The Electoral Connection." In *Polarized Politics: Congress and the President in a Partisan Era,* ed. Jon R. Bond and Richard Fleisher, 9–30. Washington, D.C.: CQ Press.

Jagger, Suzy. 2008. "Vladimir Putin Blames America for World Economic Crisis." *Times-Online,* October 2. http://business.timesonline.co.uk/tol/business/markets/russia/article4863967.ece.

Janis, Irving L. 1982. *Groupthink: Psychological Studies of Policy Decisions and Fiascoes*, 2nd rev. ed. Boston: Houghton Mifflin.

Jehl, Douglas. 2003. "On Rules for Environment, Bush Sees a Balance, Critics a Threat." *New York Times*, February 23, 1A.

———. 2005. "In Cheney's New Chief, a Bureaucratic Master." *New York Times*, November 2, A22.

Jentleson, Bruce W. 1992. "The Pretty Prudent Public: Post Post–Vietnam American Opinion on the Use of Military Force." *International Studies Quarterly* 36 (March): 49–73.

Jervis, Robert. 1976. *Perception and Misperception in International Politics*. Princeton: Princeton University Press.

———. 2003. "Understanding the Bush Doctrine." *Political Science Quarterly* 118 (September): 365–388.

Jess, Kevin. 2009. "IMF: Total Cost of Financial Crisis at $11.9 Trillion." *Digital Journal*, August 9. www.digitaljournal.com/article/277282.

Johnson, Chalmers. 2000. *Blowback: The Costs and Consequences of American Empire*. New York: Metropolitan Books.

———. 2004. *The Sorrows of Empire: Militarism, Secrecy, and the End of the Republic*. New York: Metropolitan Books.

Johnson, James T. 1981. *Just War Tradition and the Restraint of War*. Princeton: Princeton University Press.

Johnson, Richard T. 1974. *Managing the White House*. New York: Harper and Row.

Johnson, Robert D. 2001. "Congress and the Cold War." *Journal of Cold War Studies* 3 (spring): 76–100.

Joint Chiefs of Staff. 2002. *National Military Strategy*. Washington, D.C.: Department of Defense.

Jones, Alex S. 2009. *Losing the News*. New York: Oxford University Press.

Jones, Dorothy. 2002. *Toward a Just World: The Critical Years in the Search for International Justice*. Chicago: University of Chicago Press.

Jones, Gordon S., and John A. Marini, eds. 1988. *The Imperial Congress: Crisis in the Separation of Powers*. New York: Pharos Books.

Jones, Howard. 2002. *Crucible of Power: A History of American Foreign Relations to 1913*. Wilmington, Del.: SR Books.

Jones, Seth. 2008. "The Rise of Afghanistan's Insurgency." *International Security* 32 (spring): 7–40.

Jordan, Amos A., William J. Taylor Jr., and Michael J. Mazarr. 1999. *American National Security*, 5th ed. Baltimore: Johns Hopkins University Press.

Joskow, Paul L. 2002. "United States Energy Policy during the 1990s." *Current History* 101 (March): 105–125.

Kaarbo, Juliet. 1998. "Power Politics in Foreign Policy: The Influence of Bureaucratic Minorities." *European Journal of International Relations* 4 (spring): 67–97.

Kagan, Robert. 2006. *Dangerous Nation: America's Foreign Policy from Its Earliest Days to the Dawn of the Twentieth Century*. New York: Vintage.

Kant, Immanuel. [1795] 1914. *Eternal Peace and Other International Essays*. Boston: World Peace Foundation.

Karnow, Stanley. 1983. *Vietnam: A History*. New York: Viking.

Karns, Margaret P., and Karen A. Mingst. 2004. *International Organizations: The Politics and Processes of Global Governance*. Boulder, Colo.: Lynne Rienner.

Kastner, Scott L., and Douglas B. Grob. 2009. "Legislative Foundations of U.S.–Taiwan Relations: A New Look at the Congressional Taiwan Caucus." *Foreign Policy Analysis* 5 (January): 57–72.

Katovsky, Bill, and Timothy Carlson, eds. 2003. *Embedded: The Media at War in Iraq.* Guilford, Conn.: Lyons Press.

Kattenburg, Paul M. 1980. *The Vietnam Trauma in American Foreign Policy, 1945–1975.* New Brunswick, N.J.: Transaction Books.

Katzenstein, Peter J. 1996. *The Culture of National Security: Norms and Identity in World Politics.* New York: Columbia University Press.

Katzenstein, Peter J., and Robert O. Keohane, eds. 2007. *Anti-Americanisms in World Politics.* Ithaca: Cornell University Press.

Katzman, Kenneth. 2003. "Afghanistan: Current Issues and U.S. Policy." Congressional Research Service, Washington, D.C., August 1.

Kaufmann, Chaim. 2004. "Threat Inflation and the Failure of the Marketplace of Ideas: The Selling of the Iraq War." *International Security* 29 (summer): 5–48.

Keck, Margaret E., and Kathryn Sikkink. 1998. *Activists beyond Borders: Advocacy Networks in International Politics.* Ithaca: Cornell University Press.

Kegley, Charles W., Jr., and Eugene R. Wittkopf. 2004. *World Politics: Trend and Transformation,* 9th ed. Belmont, Calif.: Thomson/Wadsworth.

Kelley, Matt. 2006. "Wars Wearing Down Military Gear at Cost of about $2 Billion a Month." *USA Today,* November 29.

Kengor, Paul. 2004. "Cheney and Vice Presidential Power." In *Considering the Bush Presidency,* ed. Gary L. Gregg II and Mark J. Rozell, 177–200. New York: Oxford University Press.

Kennan, George F. 1951. *American Diplomacy, 1900–1950.* Chicago: University of Chicago Press.

———. 1996. *At a Century's End: Reflections 1982–1995.* New York: Norton.

———. 1997. "Diplomacy without Diplomats?" *Foreign Affairs* 76 (September–October): 198–212.

Kennedy, Craig, and Marshall M. Bouton. 2002. "The Real Trans-Atlantic Gap." *Foreign Policy* 133 (November–December): 66–74.

Kennedy, Paul. 1987. *The Rise and Fall of the Great Powers: Economic Change and Military Conflict from 1500 to 2000.* New York: Random House.

———. 2003. "The Perils of Empire: This Looks Like America's Moment. History Should Give Us Pause." *Washington Post,* April 20, B1.

Keohane, Robert O. 1989. "International Relations Theory: Contributions of a Feminist Standpoint." *Millennium* 18 (2): 245–253.

Keohane, Robert O., and Joseph S. Nye Jr. 2001. *Power and Interdependence,* 3rd ed. New York: Longman.

Kessler, Glenn, and Michael D. Shear. 2009. "Human Rights Activists Troubled by Administration's Approach." *Washington Post,* May 5. www.washingtonpost.com/wp-dyn/content/article/2009/05/04/AR2009050403450.html.

Key, V. O. 1961. *Public Opinion and American Democracy.* New York: Knopf.

Khong, Yuen F. 1992. *Analogies at War: Korea, Munich, Dien Bien Phu, and the Vietnam Decisions of 1965.* Princeton: Princeton University Press.

Kiefer, Peter. 2006. "Vatican Decries Fence Planned for U.S. Border." *New York Times,* November 15, 10.

Kinder, Donald R., and Lynn M. Sanders. 1996. *Divided by Color: Racial Politics and Democratic Ideals.* Chicago: University of Chicago Press.

Kingdon, John W. 1981. *Congressmen's Voting Decisions.* New York: Harper and Row.

Kirshner, Orin. 2005. "Triumph of Globalism: American Trade Politics." *Political Science Quarterly* 120 (3): 479–503.

Kissinger, Henry. 1957. *Nuclear Weapons and Foreign Policy.* New York: Harper.

Klare, Michael T. 2002. "Global Petro-Politics: The Foreign Policy Implications of the Bush Administration's Energy Plan." *Current History* 101 (March): 99–104.

———. 2004. *Blood and Oil: The Dangers and Consequences of America's Petroleum Dependency*. New York: Metropolitan Books.

Klein, Joe. 2009. "The State of Hillary: A Mixed Record on the Job." *Time*, November 5.

Klingberg, Frank L. 1952. "The Historical Alternation of Moods in American Foreign Policy." *World Politics* 4 (January): 239–273.

———. 1983. *Cyclical Trends in American Foreign Policy Moods: The Unfolding of America's World Role*. New York: University Press of America.

Knecht, Thomas. 2009. "A Pragmatic Response to an Unexpected Constraint: Problem Representation in a Complex Humanitarian Emergency." *Foreign Policy Analysis* 5 (April): 135–168.

Knutsen, Torbjörn L. 1992. *A History of International Relations Theory*. New York: Manchester University Press.

Koh, Harold Hongiu. 2005. "America's Jekyll-and-Hyde Exceptionalism." In *American Exceptionalism and Human Rights*, ed. Michael Ignatieff, 111–143. Princeton: Princeton University Press.

Kohut, Andrew, and Bruce Stokes. 2006. *America against the World: How We Are Different and Why We Are Disliked*. New York: Times Books.

Kolko, Gabriel. 2003. "Iraq, the United States, and the End of the European Coalition." *Journal of Contemporary Asia* 33 (3): 291–298.

Kopp, Harry W., and Charles A. Gillespie. 2008. *Career Diplomacy: Life and Work in the U.S. Foreign Service*. Washington, D.C.: Georgetown University Press.

Korey, William. 1999. "Human Rights NGOs: The Power of Persuasion." *Ethics and International Affairs* 13 (winter): 151–174.

Kostadinova, Tatiana. 2000. "East European Public Support for NATO Membership: Fears and Aspirations." *Journal of Peace Research* 37 (March): 235–249.

Krasner, Stephen D. 1972. "Are Bureaucracies Important? (Or Allison Wonderland)." *Foreign Policy* 7 (summer): 159–179.

———. 1978. *Defending the National Interest: Raw Materials Investments and U.S. Foreign Policy*. Princeton: Princeton University Press.

Kratochwil, Friedrich. 1989. *Rules, Norms, and Decisions: On the Conditions of Practical and Legal Reasoning in International Relations and Domestic Affairs*. New York: Cambridge University Press.

Krepon, Michael. 2003. *Cooperative Threat Reduction, Missile Defense, and the Nuclear Future*. New York: Palgrave.

Kriesberg, Martin. 1949. "Dark Areas of Ignorance." In *Public Opinion and Foreign Policy*, ed. Lester Markel, 49–64. New York: Harper.

Kris, Ernst, and Nathan Leites. 1947. "Trends in Twentieth Century Propaganda." In *Psychoanalysis and the Social Sciences*, ed. Géza Rheim, 393–409. New York: International University Press.

Krueger, Anne O. 1996. "Conclusions." In *The Political Economy of American Trade Policy*, ed. Anne O. Krueger, 423–443. Chicago: University of Chicago Press.

Krugman, Paul. 2009. "How Did Economists Get It So Wrong?" *New York Times Magazine*, September 6, 36–43.

Krutz, Glen S., and Jeffrey S. Peake. 2009. *Treaty Politics and the Rise of Executive Agreements: International Commitments in a System of Shared Powers*. Ann Arbor: University of Michigan Press.

Kukla, Jon. 2003. *A Wilderness So Immense: The Louisiana Purchase and the Destiny of America*. New York: Knopf.

Kull, Steven. 2004. "Americans on Climate Change." PIPA/Knowledge Networks Study. Program on International Policy Attitudes, College Park, Md., June 25.

Kull, Steven, and I. M. Destler. 1999. *Misreading the Public: The Myth of a New Isolationism.* Washington, D.C.: Brookings.

Kull, Steven, and Clay Ramsay. 2001. "The Myth of the Reactive Public: American Public Attitudes on Military Fatalities in the Post–Cold War Period." In *Public Opinion and the International Use of Force,* ed. Philip Everts and Pierangelo Isernia, 205–228. New York: Routledge.

Kull, Steven, Clay Ramsay, and Evan Lewis. 2003/2004. "Misperceptions, the Media, and the Iraq War." *Political Science Quarterly* 118 (winter): 569–598.

Kull, Steven, Clay Ramsay, Stephen Weber, and Evan Lewis. 2009. "America's Global Image in the Obama Era." July 7. www.worldpublicopinion.org/pipa/pdf/jul09/WPO_USObama_Jul09_packet.pdf.

Kupchan, Charles A., and Peter L. Trubowitz. 2007. "Dead Center: The Demise of Liberal Internationalism in the United States." *International Security* 32 (fall): 7–44.

Kurtz, Howard. 1998. *Spin Cycle: How the White House and the Media Manipulate the News.* New York: Simon and Schuster.

Kux, Dennis. 1998. "Pakistan." In *Economic Sanctions and American Diplomacy,* ed. Richard N. Haass, 157–176. New York: Council on Foreign Relations.

Lacy, Dean, and Emerson M. S. Niou. 2004. "A Theory of Economic Sanctions and Issue Linkage: The Roles of Preferences, Information, and Threats." *Journal of Politics* 66 (February): 25–42.

LaFeber, Walter. 1963. *The New Empire: An Interpretation of American Expansion, 1860–1898.* Ithaca: Cornell University Press.

———. 1989. *The American Age.* New York: Norton.

———. 2002. "The Bush Doctrine." *Diplomatic History* 26 (fall): 543–558.

———. 2004. *America, Russia, and the Cold War, 1945–2002,* 9th ed. Boston: McGraw-Hill.

Lake, Anthony. 1993. "From Containment to Enlargement." *U.S. Department of State Dispatch* 4 (39): 658–665.

Lake, Daniel R. 2009. "The Limits of Coercive Air Power: NATO's 'Victory' in Kosovo Revisited." *International Security* 34 (August): 83–122.

Lal, Deepak. 2006. *Reviving the Invisible Hand: The Case for Classical Liberalism in the Twenty-First Century.* Princeton: Princeton University Press.

Lancaster, Carol. 2007. *Foreign Aid: Diplomacy, Development, Domestic Politics.* Chicago: University of Chicago Press.

Lancaster, Carol, and Ann Van Dusen. 2005. *Organizing U.S. Foreign Aid: Confronting the Challenges of the Twenty-First Century.* Washington, D.C.: Brookings.

Lanoszka, Anna. 2009. *The World Trade Organization: Changing Dynamics in the Global Political Economy.* Boulder, Colo.: Lynne Rienner.

Lantis, Jeffrey S. 2009. *The Life and Death of International Treaties: Double-Edged Diplomacy and the Politics of Ratification in Comparative Perspective.* New York: Oxford University Press.

Laqueur, Walter. 1999. *The New Terrorism: Fanaticism and the Arms of Mass Destruction.* New York: Oxford University Press.

Larson, Deborah W. 1985. *Origins of Containment: A Psychological Explanation.* Princeton: Princeton University Press.

Larson, Eric V. 1996. *Casualties and Consensus: The Historical Role of Casualties in Domestic Support for U.S. Military Operations.* Santa Monica, Calif.: RAND.

Larson, Eric V., et al. 2009. *Foundations of Effective Influence Operations.* Santa Monica, Calif.: RAND.

Laurance, William F., Ana K. M. Albernaz, and Carlos Da Costa. 2001. "Is Deforestation Accelerating in the Brazilian Amazon?" *Environmental Conservation* 28 (4): 305–311.

Layne, Christopher. 2006. *The Peace of Illusions: American Grand Strategy from 1940 to the Present.* Ithaca: Cornell University Press.

Lebow, Richard Ned. 1981. *Between Peace and War: The Nature of International Crisis.* Baltimore: Johns Hopkins University Press.

Lee, Taeku. 2002. "The Sovereign Status of Survey Data." In *Navigating Public Opinion,* ed. Jeff Manza, Fay L. Cook, and Benjamin I. Page, 290–312. New York: Oxford University Press.

Leffler, Melvyn P. 1992. *A Preponderance of Power: National Security, the Truman Administration, and the Cold War.* Stanford: Stanford University Press.

Leffler, Melvyn P., and Jeffrey W. Legro, eds. 2008. *To Lead the World: American Strategy after the Bush Doctrine.* New York: Oxford University Press.

Leguey-Feilleux, Jean-Robert. 2009. *The Dynamics of Diplomacy.* Boulder, Colo.: Lynne Rienner.

Lehman, Ingrid. 2005. "Exploring the Transatlantic Media Divide over Iraq." *Harvard International Journal of Press/Politics* 10: 63–89.

Lektzian, David, and Mark Souva. 2003. "The Economic Peace between Democracies: Economic Sanctions and Domestic Institutions." *Journal of Peace Research* 40 (November): 641–660.

Lektzian, David J., and Christopher M. Sprecher. 2007. "Sanctions, Signals, and Militarized Conflict." *American Journal of Political Science* 51 (April): 415–431.

LeLoup, Lance T., and Steven A. Shull. 2003. *The President and Congress: Collaboration and Combat in National Policymaking.* New York: Longman.

Lemann, Nicholas. 2001. "The Quiet Man: Dick Cheney's Discreet Rise to Unprecedented Power." *New Yorker,* May 7, 56–71.

———. 2002. "The Next World Order: The Bush Administration May Have a Brand-New Doctrine of Power." *New Yorker,* April 1, 42–48.

Leone, Richard C., and Greg Anrig Jr., eds. 2003. *The War on Our Freedoms: Civil Liberties in an Age of Terrorism.* New York: Public Affairs.

Lesser, Ian O., Bruce Hoffman, John Arquilla, David Ronfeldt, and Michele Zanini, eds. 1999. *Countering the New Terrorism.* Santa Monica, Calif.: RAND.

Levy, Jack. 1987. "Declining Power and the Preventive Motivation for War." *World Politics* 40 (October): 82–107.

———. 1989. "The Diversionary Theory of War: A Critique." In *Handbook of War Studies,* ed. Manus Midlarsky, 259–288. London: Unwin Hyman.

———. 1997. "Prospect Theory, Rational Choice, and International Relations." *International Studies Quarterly* 41 (March): 87–112.

Lewis, David A., and Roger P. Rose. 2002. "The President, the Press, and the War-Making Power: An Analysis of Media Coverage Prior to the Persian Gulf War." *Presidential Studies Quarterly* 32 (September): 559–571.

Lewis, David E. 2008. "The Evolution of the Institutional Presidency: Presidential Choices, Institutional Change, and Staff Performance." In *Presidential Leadership: The Vortex of Power,* ed. Bert A. Rockman and Richard W. Waterman, 237–259. New York: Oxford University Press.

Liang-Fenton, Debra, ed. 2004. *Implementing U.S. Human Rights Policy.* Washington, D.C.: United States Institute of Peace.

Lichtblau, Eric. 2003. "U.S. Uses Terror Law to Pursue Crimes from Drugs to Swindling." *New York Times,* September 28, A1.

Liddell Hart, B. H. 1967. *Strategy,* 2nd rev. ed. New York: Praeger.

Lieber, Keir A., and Gerard Alexander. 2005. "Waiting for Balancing: Why the World Is Not Pushing Back." *International Security* 30 (1): 109–139.

Lieber, Keir A., and Daryl G. Press. 2006. "The End of MAD? The Nuclear Dimension of U.S. Primacy." *International Security* 30 (4): 7–44.

Lieberman, Robert C. 2009. "The 'Israel Lobby' and American Politics." *Perspectives on Politics* 7 (June): 235–257.

Lindsay, James M. 1994. "Congress, Foreign Policy, and the New Institutionalism." *International Studies Quarterly* 38 (June): 281–304.

———. 2003. "Deference and Defiance: The Shifting Rhythms of Executive-Legislative Relations in Foreign Policy." *Presidential Studies Quarterly* 33 (September): 530–546.

Lindsey, Charlotte. 2000. "Women and War." *International Review of the Red Cross* 839: 561–579.

Lippmann, Walter. 1922. *Public Opinion*. New York: Macmillan.

———. 1947. *The Cold War: A Study in U.S. Foreign Policy*. New York: Harper.

———. 1955. *Essays in the Public Philosophy*. Boston: Little, Brown.

Lipset, Seymour Martin. 1966. "The President, the Polls, and Vietnam." *Trans-Action* 3 (6): 20–22.

Lohr, Steve. 2000. "Welcome to the Internet, the First Global Colony." January 9. www.crab.rutgers.edu/~goertzel/globalcolony.htm.

Lopez, George A., and David Cortright. 2004. "Containing Iraq: Sanctions Worked." *Foreign Affairs* (July–August): 90–102.

Lowenthal, Mark M. 2009. *Intelligence: From Secrets to Policy*, 4th ed. Washington, D.C.: CQ Press.

MacGregor, Douglas A. 2003. *Transformation under Fire: Revolutionizing How America Fights*. Westport, Conn.: Praeger.

Machiavelli, Niccolò. [1532] 1985. *The Prince*, trans. Harvey C. Mansfield Jr. Chicago: University of Chicago Press.

Mackinder, Halford J. 1942. *Democratic Ideals and Reality*. New York: Norton.

Macmillan, John. 2004. "Liberalism and the Democratic Peace." *Review of International Studies* 30 (2): 179–200.

Magazine Publishers of America. 2002. "Fact Sheet: Average Circulation for Top 100 ABC Magazines 2001." www.magazine.org.

Mahan, Alfred Thayer. 1897. *The Interest of America in Sea Power*. Boston: Little, Brown.

Major, Solomon, and Anthony J. McGann. 2005. "Caught in the Crossfire: 'Innocent Bystanders' as Optimal Targets of Economic Sanctions." *Journal of Conflict Resolution* 49 (June): 337–359.

Mandelbaum, Michael. 1983. "Vietnam: The Television War." *Parameters* 13 (March): 89–97.

Mann, James. 2004. *Rise of the Vulcans: The History of Bush's War Cabinet*. New York: Viking.

Mannheim, Karl. 1952. *Essays in the Sociology of Knowledge*. New York: Routledge and Kegan Paul.

Manning, Bayless. 1977. "The Congress, the Executive, and Intermestic Affairs: Three Proposals." *Foreign Affairs* 55 (January): 306–324.

Maren, Michael. 1997. *The Road to Hell: The Ravaging Effects of Foreign Aid and International Charity*. New York: Free Press.

Margolis, Michael, and David Resnick. 2000. *Politics as Usual: The Cyberspace "Revolution."* Thousand Oaks, Calif.: Sage.

Margulies, Joseph. 2006. *Guantanamo and the Abuse of Presidential Power*. New York: Simon and Schuster.

Marinov, Nikolay. 2005. "Do Economic Sanctions Destabilize Country Leaders?" *American Journal of Political Science* 49 (July): 564–576.

Marra, Robin F., and Charles W. Ostrom Jr. 1989. "Explaining Seat Changes in the U.S. House of Representatives, 1950–1986." *American Journal of Political Science* 33 (August): 541–569.

Martin, William. 1999. "The Christian Right and American Foreign Policy." *Foreign Policy* (spring): 66–80.

Mathews, Jessica T. 1997. "Power Shift." *Foreign Affairs* 76 (January–February): 50–66.

May, Christopher, ed. 2006. *Global Corporate Power.* Boulder, Colo.: Lynne Rienner.

Mayer, Jane. 2004. "Contract Sport: What Did the Vice-President Do for Halliburton?" *New Yorker*, February 16 and 23, 80–91.

———. 2008. *The Dark Side: The Inside Story of How the War on Terror Turned into a War on American Ideals.* New York: Doubleday.

———. 2009. "The Predator War: What Are the Risks of the CIA's Covert Drone Program?" *New Yorker*, October 26. www.newyorker.com/reporting/2009/10/26/091026fa_fact_mayer.

Mayer, William G. 1992. *The Changing American Mind: How and Why American Public Opinion Changed between 1960 and 1988.* Ann Arbor: University of Michigan Press.

Mayerfield, Jamie. 2003. "Who Shall Be Judge? The United States, the International Criminal Court, and the Global Enforcement of Human Rights." *Human Rights Quarterly* 25 (February): 93–129.

Mayhew, David R. 1974. *Congress: The Electoral Connection.* New Haven: Yale University Press.

McCain, John. 2004. "Remarks to the Republican National Convention." *Washington Post*, August 30.

McCartney, Paul T. 2004. "American Nationalism and U.S. Foreign Policy from September 11 to the Iraq War." *Political Science Quarterly* 119 (fall): 399–423.

McCombs, M. E., and D. L. Shaw. 1972. "The Agenda-Setting Function of Mass Media." *Public Opinion Quarterly* 36 (summer): 176–187.

McConnell, Grant. 1966. *Private Power and American Democracy.* New York: Knopf.

McCormick, James M., and Neil J. Mitchell. 2007. "Commitments, Transnational Interests, and Congress: Who Joins the Congressional Human Rights Caucus?" *Political Research Quarterly* 60 (December): 579–592.

McCormick, James M., and Eugene R. Wittkopf. 1998. "Congress, the President, and the End of the Cold War: Has Anything Changed?" *Journal of Conflict Resolution* 42 (August): 440–467.

McCormick, James M., Eugene R. Wittkopf, and David M. Danna. 1997. "Politics and Bipartisanship at the Water's Edge: A Note on Bush and Clinton." *Polity* 30 (fall): 133–149.

McCormick, Thomas J. 1995. *America's Half Century: United States Foreign Policy in the Cold War and After,* 2nd ed. Baltimore: Johns Hopkins University Press.

McCubbins, Mathew, Roger Noll, and Barry R. Weingast. 1987. "Administrative Procedures as Instruments of Political Control." *Journal of Law, Economics, and Organization* 3 (fall): 243–277.

McDermott, Rose. 1998. *Risk-Taking in International Politics: Prospect Theory in American Foreign Policy.* Ann Arbor: University of Michigan Press.

———. 2004. *Political Psychology in International Relations.* Ann Arbor: University of Michigan Press.

McDougall, Walter A. 1997. *Promised Land, Crusader State: The American Encounter with the World since 1776.* Boston: Houghton Mifflin.

McGann, James G., and Mary Johnstone. 2005. "The Power Shift and the NGO Credibility Crisis." *Brown Journal of World Affairs* (winter/spring).

McGee, Robert W. 2003. "The Ethics of Economic Sanctions." *Economic Affairs* 23 (December): 41–45.

McMillan, Samuel L. 2008. "Subnational Foreign Policy Actors: How and Why Governors Participate in U.S. Foreign Policy." *Foreign Policy Analysis* 4 (July): 227–253.

McNamara, Robert S. 1995. *In Retrospect: The Tragedies and Lessons of Vietnam.* New York: Times Books.

Mearsheimer, John J. 2001. *The Tragedy of Great Power Politics.* New York: Norton.

Mearsheimer, John J., and Stephen M. Walt. 2003. "An Unnecessary War." *Foreign Policy* 134 (January–February): 51–59.

———. 2006. "The Israel Lobby and U.S. Foreign Policy." Faculty Research Working Papers Series. Harvard University, Cambridge, Mass.

Merrill, Dennis, and Thomas G. Paterson, eds. 2000. *Major Problems in American Foreign Relations,* 5th ed. Boston: Houghton Mifflin.

Mertus, Julie. 2003. "The New U.S. Human Rights Policy: A Radical Departure." *International Studies Perspectives* 4 (November): 371–384.

Meyer, David S., and Catherine Corrigall-Brown. 2005. "Coalitions and Political Context: U.S. Movements against Wars in Iraq." *Mobilization* 10 (October): 327–344.

Milbank, Dana. 2003. "Curtains Ordered for Media Coverage of Returning Coffins." *Washington Post,* October 21, A23.

Miller, Mark Crispin. 2002. "What's Wrong with This Picture?" *Nation,* January 7.

Mills, C. Wright. 1956. *The Power Elite.* New York: Oxford University Press.

Mingst, Karen A. 2004. *Essentials of International Relations,* 3rd ed. New York: Norton.

Mintz, Alex, and Karl DeRouen Jr. 2010. *Understanding Foreign Policy Decision Making.* New York: Cambridge University Press.

Mitchell, David, and Tansa George Massoud. 2009. "Anatomy of Failure: Bush's Decision-Making Process and the Iraq War." *Foreign Policy Analysis* 5 (July): 265–286.

Moe, Terry M. 1989. "The Politics of Bureaucratic Structure." In *Can the Government Govern?* ed. John E. Chubb and Paul E. Peterson, 267–330. Washington, D.C.: Brookings.

Moghadam, Assaf. 2008/2009. "Motives for Martyrdom: Al-Qaeda, Salafi Jihad, and the Spread of Suicide Attacks." *International Security* 33 (winter): 46–78.

Monten, Jonathan. 2005. "The Roots of the Bush Doctrine." *International Security* 29 (spring): 112–156.

Montgomery, John D. 1962. *The Politics of Foreign Aid: American Experience in Southeast Asia.* New York: Council on Foreign Relations by Praeger.

Mooney, Chris. 2004. "The Editorial Pages and the Case for War: Did Our Leading Newspapers Set Too Low a Bar for a Preemptive Attack?" *Columbia Journalism Review* 42 (March–April): 28–34.

Moore, James, and Wayne Slater. 2003. *Bush's Brain: How Karl Rove Made George W. Bush Presidential.* New York: Wiley.

Moore, Robin. 2003. *The Hunt for bin Laden: Task Force Dagger.* New York: Random House.

Moravcsik, Andrew. 2005. "The Paradox of U.S. Human Rights Policy." In *American Exceptionalism and Human Rights,* ed. Michael Ignatieff, 147–197. Princeton: Princeton University Press.

Morgenthau, Hans J. 1967. *Politics among Nations: The Struggle for Power and Peace,* 4th ed. New York: Knopf.

Morris, Edmund. 2001. *The Rise of Theodore Roosevelt.* New York: Modern Library.

Morris, Richard. 1966. *Great Presidential Decisions.* Greenwich, Conn.: Fawcett.

Morrison, Wayne M. 2009. "China's Economic Conditions." Congressional Research Service, Washington, D.C., December 11.

Mowle, Thomas S. 2003. "Worldviews in Foreign Policy: Realism, Liberalism, and External Conflict." *Political Psychology* 24 (September): 561–592.

Mueller, John. 1970. "Presidential Popularity from Truman to Johnson." *American Political Science Review* 64 (March): 18–33.

———. 1973. *War, Presidents, and Public Opinion.* New York: Wiley.

———. 1989. *Retreat from Doomsday: The Obsolescence of Major War.* New York: Basic Books.

———. 1994. *Public Opinion in the Gulf War.* Chicago: University of Chicago Press.

———. 2006. "Is There Still a Terrorist Threat? The Myth of the Omnipresent Enemy." *Foreign Affairs* (September–October): 234–245.

Muravchik, Joshua. 1991. *Exporting Democracy: Fulfilling America's Destiny.* Washington, D.C.: American Enterprise Institute.

Murtha, John P. 2005. "Press Release on Congressman John P. Murtha's speech on the 'War in Iraq.' " November 17. www.house.gov/list/press/pa12_murtha/pr051117iraq.html.

Musharraf, Pervez. 2006. *In the Line of Fire.* New York: Free Press.

Mutz, Diana. 2006. *Hearing the Other Side: Deliberative versus Participatory Democracy.* Cambridge: Cambridge University Press.

Nabers, Dirk. 2009. "Filling the Void of Meaning: Identity Construction in U.S. Foreign Policy after September 11, 2001." *Foreign Policy Analysis* 5 (April): 191–214.

Nakaya, Andrea C. 2005. *Homeland Security.* San Diego: Greenhaven Press.

Nanto, Dick K., and Thomas Lum. 2006. "U.S. International Trade: Data and Forecasts." Congressional Research Service, Washington, D.C., May 23.

National Commission on Terrorist Attacks upon the United States. 2004. "The 9/11 Commission Report." www.9-11commission.gov.

National Counterterrorism Center (NCTC). 2009. *2008 Report on Terrorism.* April 30. Mclean, Va.: NCTC.

National Geographic. 2006. "National Geographic–Roper Public Affairs 2006 Geographic Literacy Study." May. www.nationalgeographic.com/roper2006/findings.html.

National Intelligence Council. 2006. "Declassified Key Judgments of the National Intelligence Estimate, 'Trends in Global Terrorism: Implications for the United States.' " Office of the Director of National Intelligence, Washington, D.C., September 26.

National Security Archive. 2006. "New State Department Releases on the 'Future of Iraq' Project." September 1. www.gwu.edu/~nsarchiv/NSAEBB/NSAEBB198/index.htm.

National Security Council. 2005. "National Strategy for Victory in Iraq." White House, Washington, D.C., November.

Natsios, Andrew S. 2001. "Faith-Based NGOs and U.S. Foreign Policy." In *The Influence of Faith: Religious Groups and U.S. Foreign Policy,* ed. Elliot Abrams, 175–202. Lanham, Md.: Rowman and Littlefield.

Neack, Laura. 2008. *The New Foreign Policy: Power Seeking in a Globalized Era,* 2nd ed. Lanham, Md.: Rowman and Littlefield.

Neilsen Media Research. 2009. "Basic Cable Network Ranking for 2009." www.docstoc.com/docs/20726492/2009-Cable-Network-Ranker/.

Nelson, Douglas R. 1996. "The Political Economy of U.S. Automobile Protection." In *The Political Economy of American Trade Policy,* ed. Anne O. Krueger, 133–190. Chicago: University of Chicago Press.

Nelson, Michael. 2004. "George W. Bush and Congress: The Electoral Connection." In *Considering the Bush Presidency,* ed. Gary L. Gregg II and Mark J. Rozell, 141–160. New York: Oxford University Press.

Netcraft. 2009. "April 2009 Web Server Survey." Bath, England. http://news.netcraft .com/archives/2009/04/06/april_2009_web_server_survey.html.

Neuman, W. Russell. 1986. *The Paradox of Mass Politics*. Cambridge: Harvard University Press.

Neustadt, Richard E. 1960. *Presidential Power*. New York: Wiley.

Newhouse, John. 2009. "Diplomacy, Inc." *Foreign Affairs* 88 (May–June): 73–92.

New York Times. 1971. *The Pentagon Papers*. New York: Bantam Books.

———. 1992. "Excerpts from Pentagon's Plan: Prevent the Re-Emergence of a New Rival." March 8, A14.

———. 2004. "Testimony of Condoleezza Rice Before 9/11 Commission." April 8.

———. 2009. "Detention Reform." August 7. www.nytimes.com/2009/08/07/opinion/07fri2 .html.

Nincic, Miroslav. 1988. "The United States, the Soviet Union, and the Politics of Opposites." *World Politics* 40 (July): 452–475.

———. 1990. "U.S.-Soviet Policy and the Electoral Connection." *World Politics* 42 (April): 370–396.

Nincic, Miroslav, and Donna J. Nincic. 2002. "Race, Gender, and War." *Journal of Peace Research* 39 (5): 547–568.

9/11 Public Discourse Project. 2005a. "Final Report on 9/11 Commission Recommendations." December 5. www.9-11pdp.org.

———. 2005b. "Report on the Status of 9/11 Commission Recommendations. Part II: Reforming the Institutions of Government." October 20. www.9-11pdp.org.

Norris, Pippa, Montague Kern, and Marion Just, eds. 2003. *Framing Terrorism: The News Media, the Government, and the Public*. New York: Routledge.

Nuruzzaman, Mohammed. 2006. "Beyond the Realist Theories: 'Neo-Conservative Realism' and the American Invasion of Iraq." *International Studies Perspectives* 7 (3): 239–253.

Nye, Joseph S., Jr. 2002. *The Paradox of American Power: Why the World's Only Superpower Can't Go It Alone*. New York: Oxford University Press.

———. 2004. *Soft Power: The Means to Success in World Politics*. New York: Public Affairs.

Obey, David, and Carol Lancaster. 1988. "Funding Foreign Aid." *Foreign Policy* 71 (summer): 141–156.

Ochs, Alexander, and Detlef F. Sprinz. 2008. "Europa Riding the Hegemon? Transatlantic Climate Policy." In *Hegemony Constrained: Evasion, Modification, and Resistance to American Foreign Policy*, ed. Davis Bobrow, 144–166. Pittsburgh: University of Pittsburgh Press.

O'Connor, John. 2006. "Sanford in Iraq, Kuwait." *The State,* June 22, B3.

OECD (Organisation for Economic Co-operation and Development). 2006. *Recent Trends in Foreign Direct Investment in OECD Countries*. Paris: OECD.

———. 2009. "Investment News" (June). www.oecd.org/dataoecd/18/28/40887916.pdf.

———. 2010. *Statistical Annex of the 2010 Development Co-operation Report*. Paris: OECD (Paris: OECD, 2010).

O'Halloran, Sharyn. 1993. "Congress and Foreign Trade Policy." In *Congress Resurgent: Foreign and Defense Policy on Capitol Hill,* ed. Randall B. Ripley and James M. Lindsay, 283–304. Ann Arbor: University of Michigan Press.

O'Hanlon, Michael E. 2002. *Defense Policy Choices for the Bush Administration,* 2nd ed. Washington, D.C.: Brookings.

———. 2009. *Budgeting for Hard Power: Defense and Security Spending under Barack Obama*. Washington, D.C.: Brookings.

O'Hanlon, Michael E., Peter R. Orszag, Ivo H. Daalder, I. M. Destler, David Gunter, Robert E. Litan, and James Steinberg. 2002. *Protecting the American Homeland: One Year On.* Washington, D.C.: Brookings.

O'Leary, Michael K. 1967. *The Politics of American Foreign Aid.* New York: Atherton Press.

Olson, Mancur. 1982. *The Rise and Decline of Nations.* New Haven: Yale University Press.

Onuf, Nicholas G. 1989. *World of Our Making: Rules and Rule in Social Theory and International Relations.* Columbia: University of South Carolina Press.

Ornstein, Norman J., and Thomas E. Mann. 2006. "When Congress Checks Out." *Foreign Affairs* 85 (November–December): 67–82.

Ornstein, Norman J., Thomas E. Mann, and Michael J. Malbin. 2002. *Vital Statistics on Congress, 2001–2002.* Washington, D.C.: American Enterprise Institute.

Osgood, Robert E. 1957. *Limited War.* Chicago: University of Chicago Press.

Overby, L. Marvin. 1991. "Assessing Constituency Influence: Congressional Voting on the Nuclear Freeze, 1982–1983." *Legislative Studies Quarterly* 16 (May): 297–312.

Overseas Presence Advisory Panel. 1999. *America's Overseas Presence in the 21st Century.* Washington, D.C.: Government Printing Office.

Oye, Kenneth, ed. 1986. *Cooperation under Anarchy.* Princeton: Princeton University Press.

Paarlberg, Robert L. 2004. "Knowledge as Power: Science, Military Dominance, and U.S. Security." *International Security* 29 (summer): 122–151.

Packenham, Robert A. 1973. *Liberal America and the Third World.* Princeton: Princeton University Press.

Page, Benjamin I. 1996. *Who Deliberates? Mass Media in Modern Democracy.* Chicago: University of Chicago Press.

Page, Benjamin I., and Jason Barabas. 2000. "Foreign Policy Gaps between Citizens and Leaders." *International Studies Quarterly* 44 (September): 339–364.

Page, Benjamin, I., and Marshall M. Bouton. 2006. *The Foreign Policy Disconnect.* Chicago: University of Chicago Press.

Page, Benjamin I., and Robert Y. Shapiro. 1992. *The Rational Public: Fifty Years of Trends in Americans' Policy Preferences.* Chicago: University of Chicago Press.

Palmisano, Samuel J. 2006. "The Globally Integrated Enterprise." *Foreign Affairs* 85 (May/June): 127–136.

Pape, Robert. 1997. "Why Economic Sanctions Don't Work." *International Security* 22 (summer): 90–136.

———. 2005. *Dying to Win: The Strategic Logic of Suicide Terrorism.* New York: Random House.

Parenti, Christian. 2003. *The Soft Cage: Surveillance in America from Slavery to the War on Terror.* New York: Basic Books.

Parenti, Michael. 1993. *Inventing Reality: The Politics of News Media,* 2nd ed. New York: St. Martin's Press.

Passel, Jeffrey S. 2006. "The Size and Characteristics of the Unauthorized Migrant Population in the U.S." Pew Hispanic Center, Washington, D.C.

Paterson, Thomas G., J. Garry Clifford, and Kenneth J. Hagan. 2000. *American Foreign Relations: A History since 1895,* vol. 2, 5th ed. Boston: Houghton Mifflin.

PBS (Public Broadcasting System). 2003. *NOW with Bill Moyers.* Transcript: Bill Moyers Interviews Jon Stewart. www.pbs.org/now/transcript/transcript_stewart.html.

Peake, Jeffrey S. 2002. "Coalition Building and Overcoming Legislative Gridlock in Foreign Policy." *Presidential Studies Quarterly* 32 (March): 67–83.

Peffley, Mark, and Jon Hurwitz. 1992. "International Events and Foreign Policy Beliefs: Public Response to Changing Soviet-American Relations." *American Journal of Political Science* 36 (May): 431–461.

Perl, Raphael. 2006. "Trends in Terrorism: 2006." Congressional Research Service, Washington, D.C., July 21.

Peterson, Mark A. 2004. "Bush and Interest Groups: A Government of Chums." In *The George W. Bush Presidency: Appraisals and Prospects,* ed. Colin Campbell and Bert A. Rockman, 226–264. Washington, D.C.: CQ Press.

Pew Global Attitudes Project. 2005. "American Character Gets Mixed Reviews: U.S. Image Up Slightly, but Still Negative." June 23. http://pewglobal.org/reports/pdf/247.pdf.

Pew Research Center for the People and the Press. 2004. "News Audience Increasingly Politicized." June 8.

———. 2005. "Opinion Leaders Turn Cautious, Public Looks Homeward." November 17.

———. 2006a. "Iran a Growing Danger, Bush Gaining on Spy Issue." February 7. http://people-press.org/reports/pdf/269.pdf.

———. 2006b. "Online Papers Modestly Boost Newspaper Readership: Maturing Internet News Audience Broader than Deep." July 30. http://people-press.org/reports/display.php3?ReportID=282.

———. 2006c. "Many Americans Uneasy with Mix of Religion and Politics." August 24. www.people-press.org.

———. 2007. "War Support Slips, Fewer Expect a Successful Outcome." February 15. http://people-press.org/reports/pdf/304.pdf.

———. 2008. "Key News Audiences Now Blend Online and Traditional Sources." August 17. http://people-press.org/reports/pdf/444.pdf.

Pfiffner, James P. 2005. "Presidential Decision Making: Rationality, Advisory Systems, and Personality." *Presidential Studies Quarterly* 35 (June): 217–228.

Phillips, Kevin P. 2006. *American Theocracy: The Peril of Politics of Radical Religion, Oil, and Borrowed Money in the 21st Century.* New York: Viking.

Pillar, Paul R. 2001. *Terrorism and U.S. Foreign Policy.* Washington, D.C.: Brookings.

Pitkin, Hanna F. 1967. *The Concept of Representation.* Berkeley: University of California Press.

Polsby, Nelson W. 1990. "Congress, National Security, and the Rise of the 'Presidential Branch.' " In *The Constitution and National Security: A Bicentennial View,* ed. Howard E. Shuman and Walter R. Thomas, 201–210. Washington, D.C.: National Defense University Press.

Pomper, Miles. 1998. "The New Faces of Foreign Policy." *CQ Weekly,* November 28, 3203–3208.

Porretto, John. 2007. "Exxon Posts Record Corporate Profit." Associated Press, Houston, February 1.

Posen, Barry R. 2001/2002. "The Struggle against Terrorism: Grand Strategy, Strategy, and Tactics." *International Security* 26 (winter): 39–55.

———. 2003. "Command of the Commons: The Military Foundation of U.S. Hegemony." *International Security* 28 (summer): 5–46.

Posen, Barry R., and Andrew Ross. 1996/1997. "Competing Visions for U.S. Grand Strategy." *International Security* 21 (winter): 5–53.

Posner, Eric A., and Adrian Vermeule. 2007. *Terror in the Balance: Security, Liberty, and the Courts.* New York: Oxford University Press.

Powell, Colin. 1992. "Why Generals Get Nervous." *New York Times,* October 8, A35.

———. 1992/1993. "U.S. Forces: Challenges Ahead." *Foreign Affairs* 71 (winter): 32–45.

Powell, Colin, with Joseph E. Persico. 1995. *My American Journey.* New York: Random House.

Powell, Jody. 1984. *The Other Side of the Story*. New York: Morrow.

Powlick, Philip J., and Andrew Z. Katz. 1998. "Defining the Public Opinion/Foreign Policy Nexus." *Mershon International Studies Review* 42 (May): 29–61.

Prados, John. 1996. *Presidents' Secret Wars: CIA and Pentagon Covert Operations from World War II through the Persian Gulf War*, rev. ed. Chicago: I. R. Dee.

Pratt, Julius. 1927. "The Origin of Manifest Destiny." *American Historical Review* 32 (July): 795–798.

Presidential Committee on Administrative Management. 1937. *Administrative Management in the Government of the United States*. Washington, D.C.: Government Printing Office.

Pressman, Jeremy. 2009. "Power without Influence: The Bush Administration's Foreign Policy Failure in the Middle East." *International Security* 33 (spring): 149–179.

Prestowitz, Clyde V. 2003. *Rogue Nation: American Unilateralism and the Failure of Good Intentions*. New York: Basic Books.

Priest, Dana. 2005. "CIA Holds Terror Suspects in Secret Prisons." *Washington Post*, November 2, A1.

Priest, Dana, and Robin Wright. 2005. "Cheney Fights for Detainee Policy." *Washington Post*, November 7, A01.

Prior, Markus. 2005. "News v. Entertainment: How Increasing Media Choice Widens Gaps in Political Knowledge and Turnout." *American Journal of Political Science* 49 (July): 577–592.

Program on International Policy Attitudes. 2005. "In 20 of 23 Countries Polled Citizens Want Europe to Be More Influential than U.S." April 6. www.worldpublicopinion.org.

Project for Excellence in Journalism. 2006. *The State of the News Media: An Annual Report on American Journalism*. Washington, D.C.: Pew Research Center.

———. 2009. *The New Washington Press Corps: A Special Report*. July 16. www.journalism.org/print/14678.

Public Agenda. 2005. "Americans Perplexed and Anxious about Relations with Muslim World." August 3. www.publicopinion.org.

———. 2006. "Public Agenda Confidence in U.S. Foreign Policy Index: Americans Wary of Creating Democracies Abroad." March 30. www.publicagenda.org.

Putnam, Robert P. 1988. "Diplomacy and Domestic Politics: The Logic of Two-Level Games." *International Organization* 42 (summer): 427–460.

———. 2000. *Bowling Alone: The Collapse and Revival of American Community*. New York: Simon and Schuster.

Radelet, Steve. 2008. *Modernizing Foreign Assistance for the 21st Century: An Agenda for the Next U.S. President*. Washington, D.C.: Center for Global Development. www.cgdev.org/content/publications/detail/15561.

Randall, Stephen J. 2005. *United States Foreign Oil Policy since World War I*. Montreal and Kingston: McGill-Queen's University Press.

Rarick, Charles A. 2006. "Destroying a Country in Order to Save It: The Folly of Economic Sanctions against Myanmar." *Economic Affairs* 26 (June): 60–63.

Rarick, Charles A., and M. Duchatelet. 2008. "An Ethical Assessment of the Use of Economic Sanctions as a Tool of Foreign Policy." *Journal of the Institute of Economic Affairs* (June): 49–52.

Rasler, Karen, and William R. Thompson. 2005. *Puzzles of the Democratic Peace*. New York: Palgrave Macmillan.

Ray, James Lee. 1995. *Democracy and International Conflict: An Evaluation of the Democratic Peace Proposition*. Columbia: University of South Carolina Press.

Redd, Steven B. 2005. "The Influence of Advisers and Decision Strategies on Foreign Policy Choices: President Clinton's Decision to Use Force in Kosovo." *International Studies Perspectives* 6 (1): 129–150.

Reiter, Dan. 1995. "Exploding the Powder Keg Myth: Preemptive Wars Almost Never Happen." *International Security* 20 (fall): 5–34.

Renshon, Jonathan. 2008. "Stability and Change in Belief Systems: The Operational Code of George W. Bush." *Journal of Conflict Resolution* 52 (December): 820–849.

Renshon, Jonathan, and Stanley A. Renshon. 2008. "The Theory and Practice of Foreign Policy Decision Making." *Political Psychology* 29 (August): 509–536.

Renshon, Stanley. 1996. *High Hopes: The Clinton Presidency and the Politics of Ambition.* New York: New York University Press.

Renshon, Stanley, and Deborah W. Larson, eds. 2003. *Good Judgment in Foreign Policy: Theory and Application.* Lanham, Md.: Rowman and Littlefield.

Rice, Condoleezza. 2004. "Testimony of Condoleezza Rice before 9/11 Commission." *New York Times,* April 8, A6.

Rich, Andrew. 2004. *Think Tanks, Public Policy, and the Politics of Expertise.* New York: Cambridge University Press.

Richelson, Jeffrey T. 1985. *The U.S. Intelligence Community.* Cambridge: Ballinger.

———. 2008. *The U.S. Intelligence Community,* 5th ed. Boulder, Colo.: Westview Press.

Ricks, Thomas E. 2006. *Fiasco: The American Military Adventure in Iraq.* New York: Penguin Press.

Rieff, David. 2003a. "Blueprint for a Mess: How the Bush Administration's Prewar Planners Bungled Postwar Iraq." *New York Times Magazine,* November 2, 28–78.

———. 2003b. "Were Sanctions Right?" *New York Times Magazine,* July 27, 41–46.

Rielly, John E. 1999. "Americans and the World: A Survey at Century's End." *Foreign Policy* 114 (spring): 97–114.

———, ed. 2003. *American Public Opinion and U.S. Foreign Policy 2002.* Chicago: Chicago Council on Foreign Relations.

Risen, James, and Mark Mazzetti. 2009. "Blackwater Guards Tied to Secret CIA Raids." *New York Times,* December 11, A1.

Risse-Kappen, Thomas. 1995. *Bringing Transnational Relations Back In: Non-State Actors, Domestic Structures, and International Institutions.* New York: Cambridge University Press.

———. 1996. "Collective Identity in a Democratic Community: The Case of NATO." In *The Culture of National Security: Norms and Identity in World Politics,* ed. Peter J. Katzenstein, 357–399. New York: Columbia University Press.

Rivers, Douglas, and Nancy Rose. 1985. "Passing the President's Program." *American Journal of Political Science* 29 (May): 183–196.

Roberts, Dexter, and Pete Engardio. 2006. "Secrets, Lies, and Sweatshops." *Business Week,* November 27, 50–58.

Robinson, Donald L. 1996. "Presidential Prerogative and the Spirit of American Constitutionalism." In *The Constitution and the Conduct of American Foreign Policy,* ed. David Gray Adler and Larry N. George, 114–132. Lawrence: University Press of Kansas.

Robinson, Piers. 2001. "Operation Restore Hope and the Illusion of a News Media Driven Intervention." *Political Studies* 49 (December): 941–956.

Robinson, Simon. 2005. "The Farm Fight." *Time,* November 20.

Rockman, Bert A. 1981. "America's Department of State: Irregular and Regular Syndromes of Policy Making." *American Political Science Review* 75 (December): 911–927.

———. 1997. "The Presidency and Bureaucratic Change after the Cold War." In *U.S. Foreign Policy after the Cold War,* ed. Randall B. Ripley and James M. Lindsay, 21–41. Pittsburgh: University of Pittsburgh Press.

Rodman, Peter W. 2009. *Presidential Command: Power, Leadership, and the Making of Foreign Policy from Richard Nixon to George W. Bush.* New York: Knopf.

Rogers, Elizabeth S. 1993. "The Conflicting Roles of American Ethnic and Business Interests in the U.S. Economic Sanctions Policy: The Case of South Africa." In *The Limits of State Autonomy*, ed. David Skidmore and Valerie M. Hudson, 185–204. Boulder, Colo.: Westview Press.

Rogoff, Kenneth. 2003. "The IMF Strikes Back." *Foreign Policy* 134 (January–February): 38–46.

Rohde, David W. 1994. "Partisanship, Leadership, and Congressional Assertiveness in Foreign and Defense Policy." In *The New Politics of American Foreign Policy,* ed. David E. Deese, 76–101. New York: St. Martin's Press.

Rohter, Larry. 1993. "The Supreme Court: Rights Groups Fault Decisions, as Do Haitians." *New York Times*, June 22, A18.

Rosati, Jerel. 1987. *The Carter Administration's Quest for Global Community*. Columbia: University of South Carolina Press.

Rosato, Sebastian. 2003. "The Flawed Logic of Democratic Peace Theory." *American Political Science Review* 97 (November): 603–620.

Rosecrance, Richard, and Arthur A. Stein, eds. 1993. *The Domestic Bases of Grand Strategy*. Ithaca: Cornell University Press.

Rosenau, James N. 1961. *Public Opinion and Foreign Policy: An Operational Formulation*. New York: Random House.

Rosenson, Beth A., Elizabeth A. Oldmixon, and Kenneth D. Wald. 2009. "U.S. Senators' Support for Israel Examined through Sponsorship/Cosponsorship Decisions, 1993–2002." *Foreign Policy Analysis* 5 (January): 73–91.

Roskin, Michael. 1974. "From Pearl Harbor to Vietnam: Shifting Generational Paradigms and Foreign Policy." *Political Science Quarterly* 89 (fall): 563–588.

Rosner, Jeremy D. 1995. *The New Tug-of-War: Congress, the Executive, and National Security*. Washington, D.C.: Carnegie Endowment for International Peace.

Rossiter, Clinton, ed. 1999. *The Federalist Papers*. New York: Mentor.

Roth, Kenneth. 2004. "The Law of War in the War on Terror." *Foreign Affairs* 83 (January–February): 2–7.

Rothgeb, John M., Jr. 2001. *U.S. Trade Policy: Balancing Economic Dreams and Political Realities*. Washington, D.C.: CQ Press.

Rothkopf, David. 2009a. "It's 3 a.m. Do You Know Where Hillary Clinton Is?" *Washington Post*, August 23.

———. 2009b. "The Missing General and the Phantom Army." ForeignPolicy.com. September 12. http://rothkopf.foreignpolicy.com/Obama.

Rubin, Barry. 1985. *Secrets of State: The State Department and the Struggle over U.S. Foreign Policy*. New York: Oxford University Press.

Russett, Bruce. 1993. *Grasping the Democratic Peace: Principles for a Post–Cold War World*. Princeton: Princeton University Press.

Rutherford, Kenneth R. 2000. "The Evolving Arms Control Agenda: Implications of the Role of NGOs in Banning Antipersonnel Landmines." *World Politics* 53 (October): 74–114.

Sagan, Carl. 1983/1984. "Nuclear War and Climatic Catastrophe: Some Policy Implications." *Foreign Affairs* 62 (winter): 257–292.

Sanger, David E. 2007. "Outside Pressure Broke Korean Deadlock." *New York Times*, February 14, A1.

Savage, Charlie. 2006. "Bush Could Bypass New Torture Ban." *Boston Globe*, January 4.

———. 2009. "Obama's Embrace of a Bush Tactic Riles Congress." *New York Times*, August 9.

Sayen, John. 2008. "Introduction and Historic Overview: The Overburden of America's Outdated Defenses." In *America's Defense Meltdown: Pentagon Reform for President Obama and the New Congress,* ed. John Sayen, 1–25. Stanford: Stanford Security Studies.

Schafer, Mark, and Scott Crichlow. 2002. "The Process-Outcome Connection in Foreign Policy Decision Making: A Quantitative Study Building on Groupthink." *International Studies Quarterly* 46 (March): 45–68.

———. 2010. *Groupthink versus High-Quality Decision Making in International Relations*. New York: Columbia University Press.

Schafer, Mark, and Stephen G. Walker, eds. 2006. *Beliefs and Leadership in World Politics: Methods and Applications of Operational Code Analysis*. New York: Palgrave Macmillan.

Scharnberg, Kirsten. 2007. "Governors Say War Has Gutted Guard: States Fear Lack of Disaster Response." *Chicago Tribune*, May 13, 1A.

Schattschneider, E. E. 1960. *The Semisovereign People: A Realist's View of Democracy in America*. New York: Holt, Rinehart and Winston.

Schelling, Thomas. 1960. *The Strategy of Conflict*. Cambridge: Harvard University Press.

Schlesinger, Arthur M., Jr. 1973. *The Imperial Presidency*. Boston: Houghton Mifflin.

———. 1978. "Human Rights and the American Tradition." *Foreign Affairs* 57 (May–June): 503–526.

Schmidt, Siegmar. 2008. "The Reluctant Ally: German Domestic Politics and the War against Saddam Hussein." In *Hegemony Constrained: Evasion, Modification, and Resistance to American Foreign Policy*, ed. Davis Bobrow, 62–80. Pittsburgh: University of Pittsburgh Press.

Schmitt, Eric. 1999. "Senate Kills Test Ban Treaty." *New York Times,* October 14, A1.

———. 2006. "Clash Foreseen between C.I.A. and Pentagon." *New York Times,* May 10, A1.

Schmitt, Michael N., and Peter J. Richards. 2000. "Into Uncharted Waters: The International Criminal Court." *NWC Review* 53 (winter): 93–136.

Schulman, Mark, and Tara Regan. 2006. "Post 9-11: Americans See Long Road Ahead in War on Terrorism." September 5. www.srbi.com/time_poll_arc31.html.

Schulzinger, Robert D. 1994. *American Diplomacy in the Twentieth Century,* 3rd ed. New York: Oxford University Press.

Schwartz, Herman M. 2009. *Subprime Nation: American Power, Global Capital, and the Housing Bubble*. Ithaca: Cornell University Press.

Scott, James M. 1996. "Reagan's Doctrine? The Formulation of an American Foreign Policy Strategy." *Presidential Studies Quarterly* 26 (fall): 1047–1061.

Scott, James M., and Ralph G. Carter. 2002. "Acting on the Hill: Congressional Assertiveness in U.S. Foreign Policy." *Congress and the Presidency* 29 (autumn): 151–169.

Seib, Philip. 1997. *Headline Diplomacy: How News Coverage Affects Foreign Policy*. Westport, Conn.: Praeger.

Seidman, Harold R. 1986. *Politics, Position, and Power: From the Positive to the Regulatory State*. New York: Oxford University Press.

Shane, Scott. 2005a. "Behind Power, One Principle as Bush Pushes Prerogatives." *New York Times,* December 17, A1.

———. 2005b. "Official Reveals Budget for U.S. Intelligence." *New York Times,* November 8, A18.

———. 2009. "Waterboarding Used 266 Times on 2 Suspects." *New York Times,* April 20. www.nytimes.com/2009/04/20/world/20detain.html?_r=1&pagewanted=print.

Shannon, Vaughn P., and Jonathan W. Keller. 2007. "Leadership Style and International Norm Violation: The Case of the Iraq War." *Foreign Policy Analysis* 3 (January): 79–104.

Shapiro, Robert Y., and Lawrence R. Jacobs. 2002. "Public Opinion, Foreign Policy, and Democracy: How Presidents Use Public Opinion." In *Navigating Public Opinion*, ed.

Jeff Manza, Fay L. Cook, and Benjamin I. Page, 184–200. New York: Oxford University Press.

Sharp, Jeremy M. 2006. "U.S. Foreign Assistance to the Middle East: Historical Background, Recent Trends, and the FY2007 Request." Congressional Research Service, Washington, D.C., December 21.

Shearer, David. 1998. "Private Armies and Military Intervention." *Adelphi Papers* 316. London: International Institute for Strategic Studies.

Shepsle, Kenneth A. 1979. "Institutional Arrangements and Equilibrium in Multidimensional Voting Models." *American Journal of Political Science* 23 (February): 27–59.

Shoch, James. 2001. *Trading Blows: Party Competition and U.S. Trade Policy in a Globalizing Era.* Chapel Hill: University of North Carolina Press.

Shultz, Richard H., and Andrea J. Dew. 2006. *Insurgents, Terrorists, and Militias.* New York: Columbia University Press.

Shuman, Michael H. 1992. "Dateline Main Street: Courts v. Local Foreign Policies." *Foreign Policy* 86 (spring): 158–177.

Sicker, Martin. 2002. *The Geopolitics of Security in the Americas: Hemispheric Denial from Monroe to Clinton.* Westport, Conn.: Praeger.

Sikkink, Kathryn. 2004. *Mixed Signals: U.S. Human Rights Policy and Latin America.* Ithaca: Cornell University Press.

Silverstein, Gordon. 1997. *Imbalance of Powers: Constitutional Interpretation and the Making of American Foreign Policy.* New York: Oxford University Press.

Simmons, P. J. 1998. "Learning to Live with NGOs." *Foreign Policy* 112 (fall): 82–96.

Simon, Herbert. 1957. *Administrative Behavior.* New York: Macmillan.

Singer, Peter W. 2003. *Corporate Warriors: The Rise of the Privatized Military Industry.* Ithaca: Cornell University Press.

———. 2009. *Wired for War: The Robotics Revolution and Conflict in the Twenty-First Century.* New York: Penguin.

SIPRI (Stockholm International Peace Research Institute). 2006. *SIPRI Yearbook 2006: World Armaments, Disarmament, and International Security.* New York: Oxford University Press.

———. 2009. *Military Expenditure Data, 1999–2008.* www.sipri.org/yearbook/2009/05/05A.

Sjöstedt, Roxanna. 2007. "Norms, Identity, and Securitization under Harry S. Truman and George W. Bush." *Foreign Policy Analysis* 3 (July): 233–254.

Skidmore, David. 2005. "Understanding the Unilateralist Turn in U.S. Foreign Policy." *Foreign Policy Analysis* 1 (2): 207–228.

Slaughter, Anne-Marie. 2004. *A New World Order.* Princeton: Princeton University Press.

Small Arms Survey. 2007. "Frequently Asked Questions." www.smallarmssurvey.org.

Smist, Frank J. 1990. *Congress Oversees the United States Intelligence Community, 1947–1989.* Knoxville: University of Tennessee Press.

Smith, Adam. [1776] 2000. *Inquiry into the Nature and Causes of the Wealth of Nations.* New York: Modern Library.

Smith, Hedrick. 1988. *The Power Game.* New York: Random House.

Smith, James A. 1991. *The Idea Brokers: Think Tanks and the Rise of the New Policy Elite.* New York: Free Press.

Smith, Rupert (General). 2005. *The Utility of Force: The Art of War in the Modern World.* London: Allen Lane.

Smith, Tony. 1994. *America's Mission: The United States and the Worldwide Struggle for Democracy in the Twentieth Century.* Princeton: Princeton University Press.

———. 2007. *A Pact with the Devil: Washington's Bid for World Supremacy and the Betrayal of the American Promise.* New York: Routledge.

Snow, Donald M. 2004. *National Security for a New Era: Globalization and Geopolitics.* New York: Pearson Longman.

Snyder, Glenn H. 1961. *Deterrence and Defense: Toward a Theory of National Security.* Princeton: Princeton University Press.

Snyder, Jack. 2003. "Imperial Temptations." *National Interest* 71 (spring): 29–40.

Snyder, Richard C., Henry W. Bruck, and Burton Sapin. 2002. *Foreign Policy Decision Making: An Approach to the Study of International Politics,* 2nd rev. ed. New York: Palgrave Macmillan.

Sobel, Richard. 2001. *The Impact of Public Opinion on U.S. Foreign Policy since Vietnam.* New York: Oxford University Press.

Spinner, Jackie. 2004. "Halliburton Reviews Food Service Bill." *Washington Post,* February 3, A2.

Spykman, Nicholas J. 1942. *America's Strategy in World Politics: The United States and the Balance of Power.* New York: Harcourt, Brace.

Squeo, Anne Marie. 2002. "Dollars for the Defense: Military Contractors Are Likely to Get a Big Boost from the War on Terrorism." *Wall Street Journal Europe,* October 18–20, R4.

Stanley, Harold W., and Richard G. Niemi. 2006. *Vital Statistics on American Politics, 2005–2006.* Washington, D.C.: CQ Press.

Stanton, John J. 2002. "Terror in Cyberspace: Terrorists Will Exploit and Widen the Gap between Governing Structures and the Public." *American Behavioral Scientist* 45 (February): 1017–1032.

Steele, Ian K. 1994. *Warpaths: Invasions of North America.* New York: Oxford University Press.

Steger, Manfred B., ed. 2010. *Globalization: The Greatest Hits.* Boulder, Colo.: Paradigm.

Steil, Benn, and Robert E. Litan. 2006. *Financial Statecraft: The Role of Financial Markets in American Foreign Policy.* New Haven: Yale University Press.

Stein, Arthur A. 1990. *Why Nations Cooperate.* Ithaca: Cornell University Press.

———. 1993. "Domestic Constraints, Extended Deterrence, and the Incoherence of Grand Strategy: The United States, 1938–1950." In *The Domestic Bases of Grand Strategy,* ed. Richard Rosecrance and Arthur A. Stein, 96–123. Ithaca: Cornell University Press.

Stein, Jeff. 2006. "Can You Tell a Sunni from a Shiite?" *New York Times,* October 17, A21.

Stephanopoulos, George. 1999. *All Too Human: A Political Education.* Boston: Little, Brown.

Stern, Jessica. 1999. *The Ultimate Terrorists.* Cambridge: Harvard University Press.

Stewart, Jon, Ben Karlin, and David Javerbaum. 2004. *America (The Book): A Citizen's Guide to Democracy Inaction.* New York: Warner Books.

Stiglitz, Joseph E. 2002. *Globalization and Its Discontents.* New York: Norton.

Stimson, James A. 1991. *Public Opinion in America: Moods, Cycles, and Swings.* Boulder, Colo.: Westview Press.

Stoessinger, John. 1985. *Crusaders and Pragmatists: Movers of Modern American Foreign Policy.* New York: Norton.

Stoll, Richard J. 1984. "The Guns of November: Presidential Reelections and the Use of Force, 1947–1982." *Journal of Conflict Resolution* 28 (June): 231–246.

Stop Big Media. 2007. "Who Owns the Media?" www.stopbigmedia.com/chart.php.

Stout, David. 2006. "Bush, Signing Bill for Border Fence, Urges Wider Overhaul." *New York Times,* October 27, 16.

Strobel, Warren P. 1997. *Late-Breaking Foreign Policy: The News Media's Influence on Peace Operations.* Washington, D.C.: U.S. Institute of Peace Press.

Stroud, Natalie J. 2008. "Media Use and Political Predispositions: Revisiting the Concept of Selective Exposure." *Political Behavior* 30 (September): 341–366.

Stuart, Douglas T. 2003. "Ministry of Fear: The 1947 National Security Act in the Historical and Institutional Context." *International Studies Perspectives* 4 (August): 293–313.

———. 2008. *Creating the National Security State: A History of the Law that Transformed America*. Princeton: Princeton University Press.

Sullivan, Andrew. 2008. "Why I Blog." *Atlantic Monthly* (November): 106–113.

Suskind, Ron. 2006. *The One-Percent Doctrine: Deep Inside America's Pursuit of Its Enemies since 9/11*. New York: Simon and Schuster.

Sutcliffe, Kathleen. 2006. "The Growing Nuclear Club." *Backgrounder,* November 17. Council on Foreign Relations, New York. www.cfr.org/publication/12050/#2.

Sweig, Julia E. 2006. *Friendly Fire: Losing Friends and Making Enemies in the Anti-American Century*. New York: Public Affairs.

Sylvan, Donald A., and Stuart J. Thorson. 1992. "Ontologies, Problem Representation, and the Cuban Missile Crisis." *Journal of Conflict Resolution* 36: 709–732.

Sylvan, Donald A., and James F. Voss, eds. 1998. *Problem Representation in Foreign Policy Decision Making*. New York: Cambridge University Press.

Taliafarro, Jeffrey W. 2000/2001. "Security-Seeking under Anarchy: Defensive Realism Reconsidered." *International Security* 25 (winter): 152–186.

Tarnoff, Curt. 2007. "Millennium Challenge Account." Congressional Research Service, Washington, D.C., January 3.

Tedesco, John C. 2001. "Issue and Strategy Agenda-Setting in the 2000 Presidential Primaries." *American Behavioral Scientist* 44 (August): 2048–2067.

Thomas, Gary. 2006. "Terror Spurs U.S. Intelligence Reform." *VOA News,* October 11. www.voanews.com/english/archive/2006-10/Terror2006-10-11-voa47.cfm.

Thompson, Cheryl W., and William Booth. 2009. "Obama Vows to Focus on Borders, but Immigration Action Won't Come until 2010." *Washington Post,* August 11. www.washingtonpost.com/wp-dyn/content/article/2009/08/10/AR2009081001797.html.

Thumma, Scott, and Warren Bird. 2009. "Not Who You Think They Are: A Profile of the People Who Attend America's Megachurches." Hartford Institute for Religious Research. June. http://hirr.hartsem.edu/megachurch/megachurch_attender_report.htm.

Tickner, Ann. 1992. *Gender in International Relations: Feminist Perspectives on Achieving International Security*. Ithaca: Cornell University Press.

Tocqueville, Alexis de. [1835] 1988. *Democracy in America,* ed. J. P. Mayer. New York: Perennial Library.

Todorov, Alexander, and Anesu N. Mandisodza. 2004. "Public Opinion on Foreign Policy: The Multilateral Public that Perceives Itself as Unilateral." *Public Opinion Quarterly* 68 (fall): 323–348.

Tornquist-Chesnier, Marie. 2004. "NGOs and International Law." *Journal of Human Rights* 3 (June): 253–263.

Tostensen, Arne, and Beate Bull. 2002. "Are Smart Sanctions Feasible?" *World Politics* 54 (April): 373–403.

Tower Commission. 1987. *The Tower Commission Report*. New York: Bantam/Times Books.

Treverton, Gregory F. 2009. *Intelligence for an Age of Terror*. New York: Cambridge University Press.

Trubowitz, Peter. 1992. "Sectionalism and American Foreign Policy: The Political Geography of Consensus and Conflict." *International Studies Quarterly* 36 (March): 173–190.

Truman, David B. 1951. *The Governmental Process: Political Interests and Public Opinion*. New York: Knopf.

Tuchman, Barbara W. 1962. *The Guns of August*. New York: Macmillan.

Tunç, Hakan. 2009. "Preemption in the Bush Doctrine: A Reappraisal." *Foreign Policy Analysis* 5 (January): 1–16.

Turchin, Peter. 2003. *Historical Dynamics: Why States Rise and Fall.* Princeton: Princeton University Press.

Turnbull, Lornet, and Janet I. Tu. 2005. "Minutemen Watch U.S.-Canada Border." *Seattle Times,* October 4.

Turner, Frederick Jackson. 1920. *The Frontier in American History.* New York: Holt.

Twight, Charlotte. 1989. "Institutional Underpinnings of Parochialism: The Case of Military Base Closures." *Cato Journal* 9 (spring/summer): 73–105.

Tyson, Ann S. 2007. "Iraq Troop Boost Erodes Readiness, General Says." *New York Times,* February 16, A13.

United Nations. 2005. *World Population Prospects: The 2004 Revision.* New York: United Nations Population Division.

United Nations Economic and Social Council. 2006. "Situation of Detainees at Guantánamo Bay." Report No. E/CN.4/2006/120, Commission on Human Rights, February 15. New York: United Nations.

United Nations Framework Convention on Climate Change. 2010. "Kyoto Protocol: Status of Ratification." http://unfccc.int/kyoto_protocol/status_of_ratification/items/2613 .php.

USAID (U.S. Agency for International Development). 1992. *Why Foreign Aid? The Benefit of Foreign Assistance to the United States.* Bureau for Legislative Affairs. Washington, D.C.: USAID.

———. 2004. *U.S. Foreign Aid: Meeting the Challenges of the Twenty-First Century.* Washington, D.C.: USAID.

U.S. Census Bureau. 2004. *The Foreign-Born Population in the United States: 2003.* Washington, D.C.: Department of Commerce.

———. 2010. *Foreign Trade Statistics.* Bureau of Economic Analysis. www.census.gov/foreign-trade/statistics.

U.S. Commission on National Security/21st Century. 2001. "Roadmap for National Security: Imperatives for Change." www.nssg.gov/Reports.html.

U.S. Congress. 2001. *Authorization for Use of Military Force.* Public Law 107-40, 197th Cong., 2nd sess. (September 18).

U.S. Defense Security Cooperation Agency. 2007. "Frequently Asked Questions." www .dsca.osd.mil/pressreleases/faq.htm.

———. 2009. *DSCA Facts Book.* www.dsca.mil/programs/biz-ops/factsbook/default.htm.

U.S. Department of the Army. 2006. "Human Intelligence Collector Operations" (Sec. FM2-22-3). www.army.mil/institution/armypublicaffairs/pdf/fm2-22-3.pdf.

U.S. Department of Commerce. 2004. *Statistical Abstract of the United States.* www .census.gov/compendia/statab/.

———. 2006. "U.S. International Trade in Goods and Services." Bureau of Economic Analysis, Washington, D.C., June 9.

U.S. Department of Defense. 2003. *Base Structure Report: Fiscal Year 2003 Baseline.* Washington, D.C.: Department of Defense. www.defenselink.mil/pubs/almanac/almanac/Graphics/BSR_03.pdf.

———. 2004. "Procurement Statistics: Directorate for Information Operations and Reports." http://web1.whs.osd.mil/peidhome/procstat/procstat.htm.

———. 2006. *Joint Operations Planning.* Washington, D.C.: Department of Defense.

———. 2008. *National Defense Strategy.* June. www.defense.gov/news/2008%20 National%20Defense%20Strategy.pdf.

———. 2009. *Base Structure Report: Fiscal Year 2009 Baseline.* Washington, D.C.: Department of Defense. www.defense.gov/pubs/pdfs/2009baseline.pdf.

———. 2010. *Nuclear Posture Review Report.* April. www.defense.gov/npr/docs/2010%20 Nuclear%20Posture%20Review%20Report.pdf.

U.S. Department of Education. 2002. *The Nation's Report Card, 2001.* Washington, D.C.: Office of Educational Research and Improvement.

U.S. Department of Energy. 2004. "Annual Energy Outlook 2004 with Projections to 2025." www.eia.doe.gov/oiaf/aeo/pdf/appa.pdf.

———. 2006. *International Energy Outlook 2006.* Washington, D.C.: Energy Information Administration.

U.S. Department of Homeland Security. 2006. *2005 Yearbook of Immigration Statistics.* Washington, D.C.: Department of Homeland Security.

U.S. Department of Labor. 2004. Bureau of Labor Statistics. "Union Members Summary." January 21. www.bls.gov/news.release/union2.nr0.htm.

U.S. Department of State. 1981. Bureau of Public Affairs. *A Short History of the U.S. Department of State, 1781–1981.* Washington, D.C.: Government Printing Office.

———. 2006a. "Country Reports on Terrorism 2005." Washington, D.C.: Office of the Coordinator for Counterterrorism.

———. 2006b. "International Military Education and Training Account Summaries." www.state.gov/t/pm/ppa/sat/c14562.htm.

U.S. Embassy in Mexico. 2004. "Sections in the U.S. Embassy." http://mexico.usembassy .gov/eembdir.html.

U.S. Energy Information Administration. 2008. *International Energy Annual 2006* (August). www.eia.doe.gov/emeu/iea/overview.html.

———. 2009. "How Dependent Are We on Foreign Oil?" December 10. http://tonto.eia .doe.gov/energy_in_brief/foreign_oil_dependence.cfm.

U.S. Environmental Protection Agency. 2009. "Endangerment and Cause or Contribute Findings for Greenhouse Gases under Section 202(a) of the Clean Air Act." December 7. www.epa.gov/climatechange/endangerment.html.

U.S. Federal Election Commission. 2004. "Campaign Finance Reports and Data." www .fec.gov/finance_reports.html.

U.S. Office of Management and Budget. 2002. *Budget of the United States Government: Historical Tables.* Washington, D.C.: Government Printing Office.

———. 2007. *Budget of the United States Government: Historical Tables.* Washington, D.C.: Government Printing Office.

———. 2009. *Budget of the United States Government: Historical Tables.* Washington, D.C.: Government Printing Office.

U.S. Office of Science and Technology Policy. 2006. "U.S. National Space Policy." October 6. www.ostp.gov/html/US%20National%20Space%20Policy.pdf.

U.S. Public Interest Research Group. 2002. "U.S. Lags Behind in Development of Renewable Energy." March 12. http://uspirg.org/uspirg.asp?id2=5958&id3=USPIRG&.

U.S. Senate. 1976. Select Committee to Study Governmental Operations with Respect to Intelligence Activities of the United States. *Final Report.* 94th Cong., 2nd sess., April 26.

———. 2004. Select Committee on Intelligence. *Report on the U.S. Intelligence Community's Prewar Intelligence Assessments on Iraq.* 108th Cong., 2nd sess., July 7.

Uslaner, Eric M. 2002. "Cracks in the Armor? Interest Groups and Foreign Policy." In *Interest Group Politics,* 6th ed., ed. Allan J. Cigler and Burdett A. Loomis, 355–377. Washington, D.C.: CQ Press.

Van Alstyne, Richard W. 1965. *Empire and Independence: The International History of the American Revolution.* New York: Wiley.

Van Belle, Douglas A. 2003. "Bureaucratic Responsiveness to the News Media: Comparing the Influence of *The New York Times* and Network Television News Coverage on U.S. Foreign Aid Allocations." *Political Communications* 20: 263–285.

Van Belle, Douglas A., and Steven W. Hook. 2000. "Greasing the Squeaky Wheel: News Media Coverage and U.S. Development Aid, 1977–1992." *International Interactions* 26 (July–September): 321–346.

Vanderbush, Walt. 2009. "Exiles and the Marketing of U.S. Policy toward Cuba and Iraq." *Foreign Policy Analysis* 5 (July): 287–306.

Verba, Sidney. 1961. "Assumptions of Rationality and Non-Rationality in Models of the International System." In *The International System,* ed. Klaus Knorr and Sidney Verba, 93–117. Princeton: Princeton University Press.

Vertzberger, Yaacov. 1990. *The World in Their Minds: Information Processing, Cognition, and Perception in Foreign Policy Decisionmaking.* Stanford: Stanford University Press.

Veseth, Michael. 2010. *Globaloney 2.0: The Crash of 2008 and the Future of Globalization.* Lanham, Md.: Rowman and Littlefield.

von Clausewitz, Carl. [1832] 1982. *On War.* New York: Penguin Books.

von Hippel, Karin. 2000. "Democracy by Force: A Renewed Commitment to Nation Building." *Washington Quarterly* 23 (winter): 95–112.

Walcott, Charles E., and Karen M. Hult. 2004. "The Bush Staff and Cabinet System." In *Considering the Bush Presidency,* ed. Gary L. Gregg II and Mark J. Rozell, 52–68. New York: Oxford University Press.

Wald, Kenneth, and Clyde Wilcox. 2006. "Getting Religion: Has Political Science Rediscovered the Faith Factor?" *American Political Science Review* 100 (November): 523–537.

Waldron, Beth. 2003. "All Politics Should *Not* Be Local." *Christian Science Monitor,* May 22, 11.

Walker, Stephen G. 1977. "The Interface between Beliefs and Behavior: Henry Kissinger's Operational Code and the Vietnam War." *Journal of Conflict Resolution* 21 (March): 129–168.

Walker, Stephen G., Mark Schafer, and Michael D. Young. 2003. "William Jefferson Clinton: Operational Code Beliefs and Object Appraisal." In *The Psychological Assessment of Political Leaders,* ed. Jerrold M. Post. Ann Arbor: University of Michigan Press.

Walt, Stephen M. 1987. *The Origin of Alliances.* Ithaca: Cornell University Press.

———. 2005. *Taming American Power: The Global Response to U.S. Primacy.* New York: Norton.

Walton, C. Dale. 2007. *Geopolitics and the Great Powers in the Twenty-First Century: Multipolarity and the Revolution in Strategic Perspective.* New York: Routledge.

Walton, Don. 2006. "Hagel: Begin Iraq Withdrawal within 6 Months." *Lincoln Journal Star,* August 3, 1A.

Waltz, Kenneth N. 1979. *Theory of International Politics.* Reading, Mass.: Addison-Wesley.

———. 1997. "Evaluating Theories." *American Political Science Review* 91 (December): 913–917.

Walzer, Michael. 1977. *Just and Unjust Wars: A Moral Argument with Historical Illustrations,* 2nd ed. New York: Basic Books.

Wanta, Wayne, Guy Golan, and Cheolhan Lee. 2004. "Agenda Setting and International News: Media Influence on Public Perceptions of Foreign Nations." *J&MC Quarterly* 81 (summer): 364–377.

Wardlaw, Grant. 1989. *Political Terrorism: Theory, Tactics, and Counter-Measures,* 2nd rev. ed. New York: Cambridge University Press.

Warshaw, Shirley A. 1996. *Powersharing: White House-Cabinet Relations in the Modern Presidency.* Albany: State University of New York Press.

Wawro, Gregory. 2000. *Legislative Entrepreneurship in the U.S. House of Representatives.* Ann Arbor: University of Michigan Press.

Weber, Max. 1946. *From Max Weber: Essays in Sociology.* New York: Oxford University Press.

Weiner, Tim. 1996. "Military Chiefs Trying to Gain Extra Billions." *New York Times,* April 10, A10.

Weingast, Barry R. 1984. "The Congressional-Bureaucratic System: A Principal-Agent Perspective with Applications to the SEC." *Public Choice* 44 (1): 147–191.

Weinstein, Michael M., and Steve Charnovitz. 2001. "The Greening of the WTO." *Foreign Affairs* 80 (November–December): 147–156.

Weisburd, A. Mark. 1997. *The Use of Force: The Practice of States since World War II.* University Park: Pennsylvania State University Press.

Weiss, Thomas G. 2009. "What Happened to the Idea of World Government?" *International Studies Quarterly* 53 (June): 253–271.

Weissbrodt, David. 1984. "The Contribution of International Nongovernmental Organizations to the Protection of Human Rights." In *Human Rights in International Law: Legal and Policy Issues,* ed. Theodor Meron, 403–448. Oxford: Clarendon Press.

Weissman, Stephen R. 1995. *A Culture of Deference: Congress's Failure of Leadership in Foreign Policy.* New York: Basic Books.

Welch, Claude E., Jr. 2001. "Conclusion." In *NGOs and Human Rights: Promise and Performance,* ed. Claude E. Welch Jr., 261–280. Philadelphia: University of Pennsylvania Press.

Welch, David A. 1992. "The Organizational Process and Bureaucratic Politics Paradigms: Retrospect and Prospect." *International Security* 17 (fall): 112–146.

Weldes, Jutta. 1999. *Constructing National Interests: The United States and the Cuban Missile Crisis.* Minneapolis: University of Minnesota Press.

Wendt, Alexander. 1992. "Anarchy Is What States Make of It: The Social Construction of World Politics." *International Organization* 46 (spring): 391–425.

———. 1999. *Social Theory of International Politics.* New York: Cambridge University Press.

West, Bing. 2009. "Reflections on the Iraq War: Implications for U.S. Foreign Policy." *Orbis* 53 (January): 54–64.

White House. 2001a. "Detention, Treatment, and Trial of Certain Non-Citizens in the War against Terrorism." Press release, November 13, 2001. www.whitehouse.gov.

———. 2001b. "The President's Daily Briefing." August 6. www.washingtonpost.com/wp-dyn/articles/A2285–2004Apr10.html.

———. 2001c. "Reliable, Affordable, and Environmentally Sound Energy for America's Future: Report of the National Energy Policy Development Group." Washington, D.C.

———. 2002. "The National Security Strategy of the United States of America." September. www.whitehouse.gov/nsc/nss.pdf.

———. 2009. "Remarks by the President to the United Nations General Assembly." September 23. www.whitehouse.gov/the_press_office/remarks-by-the-president-to-the-united-nations-general-assembly/.

Wiarda, Howard J. 2000. "Beyond the Pale: The Bureaucratic Politics of United States Policy in Mexico." *World Affairs* 162 (spring): 174–190.

Wildavsky, Aaron. 1966. "The Two Presidencies." *Trans-Action* 4 (December): 7–14.

Wildavsky, Aaron, and Naomi Caiden. 1997. *The New Politics of the Budgetary Process,* 3rd ed. New York: Longman.

Wilkerson, Lawrence B. 2005. "The White House Cabal." *Los Angeles Times,* October 25, B11.

Willett, Thomas D. 2001. "Understanding the IMF Debate." *Independent Review* 5 (spring): 593–610.

Williams, Michael C. 2005. "What Is the National Interest? The Neoconservative Challenge in I.R. Theory." *European Journal of International Relations* 11 (3): 307–337.

Williams, William A. 1959. *The Tragedy of American Diplomacy.* Cleveland: World Publishing.

Williamson, John. 1990. *Latin American Adjustment: How Much Has Happened?* Washington, D.C.: Institute for International Economics.

Wilson, James Q. 1989. *Bureaucracy: What Government Agencies Do and Why They Do It.* New York: Basic Books.

Wilson, Joseph C. 2004. *The Politics of Truth: Inside the Lies that Led to War and Betrayed My Wife's CIA Identity: A Diplomat's Memoir.* New York: Carroll and Graf.

Wilson, Woodrow. 1927. "Speech at the Coliseum, St. Louis, Missouri." In *War and Peace: Presidential Messages, Addresses, and Public Papers, 1917–1924,* vol. 1. New York: Harper and Brothers.

Wittes, Benjamin. 2008. *Law and the Long War.* New York: Penguin.

Wittkopf, Eugene R. 1990. *Faces of Internationalism: Public Opinion and U.S. Foreign Policy.* Durham: Duke University Press.

Wohlforth, William C. 2008. "Realism and Foreign Policy." In *Foreign Policy: Theories, Actors, Cases,* ed. Steve Smith, Amelia Hadfield, and Tim Dunne, 31–48. New York: Oxford University Press.

Wohlstetter, Albert. 1959. "The Delicate Balance of Terror." *Foreign Affairs* 37 (January): 211–234.

Wolfers, Arnold. 1962. *Discord and Collaboration: Essays on International Politics.* Baltimore: Johns Hopkins University Press.

Wood, B. Dan. 2009. "Presidential Saber Rattling and the Economy." *American Journal of Political Science* 53 (July): 695–709.

Woods, Ngaire. 2000. "The Challenges of Multilateralism and Governance." In *The World Bank: Structure and Policies,* ed. Chris Gilbert and David Vines, 132–158. New York: Cambridge University Press.

———. 2006. *The Globalizers: The IMF, the World Bank, and Their Borrowers.* Ithaca: Cornell University Press.

Woodward, Bob. 2002. *Bush at War.* New York: Simon and Schuster.

———. 2004. *Plan of Attack.* New York: Simon and Schuster.

———. 2006. *State of Denial.* New York: Simon and Schuster.

———. 2008. *The War Within: A Secret White House History, 2006–2008.* New York: Simon and Schuster.

World Bank. 1998. *Assessing Aid: What Works, What Doesn't, and Why.* New York: Oxford University Press.

———. 2004a. "Debt Initiative for Heavily Indebted Poor Countries." www.world bank.org/hipc.

———. 2004b. *World Development Indicators.* New York: Oxford University Press.

———. 2006. *World Development Indicators.* New York: Oxford University Press.

———. 2007. *World Development Report 2008.* Washington, D.C.: World Bank Publications.

———. 2009. *World Development Indicators.* Washington, D.C.: World Bank Publications. http://siteresources.worldbank.org/datastatistics/resources/gdp.pdf.

World Commission on Environment and Development. 1987. *Our Common Future.* New York: Oxford University Press.

World Public Opinion. 2006. "World Public Says Iraq War Has Increased Global Terrorist Threat." Program on International Policy Attitudes, Washington, D.C., December 1. www.worldpublicopinion.org/pipa/articles/home_page/172.php?nid=&id=&pnt=172&lb=hmpg1.

———. 2008. "American Public Says Government Leaders Should Pay Attention to Polls." March 21. www.worldpublicopinion.org/pipa/articles/governance_bt/461.php.

———. 2009. "Obama Rockets to Top of Poll on Global Leaders." June 29. www.world-publicopinion.org/pipa/articles/views_on_countriesregions_bt/618.php.

WTO (World Trade Organization). 2006. "Country Profiles: United States." http://stat.wto.org/CountryProfiles/US_e.htm.

———. 2009. "Statistics Database." www.wto.org/english/res_e/statis_e/statis_e.htm.

Wu, H. Denis. 2000. "Systemic Determinants of International News Coverage: A Comparison of 38 Countries." *Journal of Communication* 50 (2): 110–130.

Yankelovich, Daniel. 2005. "Poll Positions: What Americans Really Think about U.S. Foreign Policy." *Foreign Affairs* 84 (September–October): 2–16.

———. 2006. "The Tipping Points." *Foreign Affairs* 85 (May–June): 115–125.

Yergin, Daniel. 1977. *Shattered Peace: The Origins of the Cold War.* New York: Penguin Books.

———. 1991. *The Prize: The Epic Quest for Oil, Money, and Power.* New York: Simon and Schuster.

Yetiv, Steve A. 2004a. *Crude Awakenings: Global Oil Security and American Foreign Policy.* Ithaca: Cornell University Press.

———. 2004b. *Explaining Foreign Policy: U.S. Decision Making and the Persian Gulf War.* Baltimore: Johns Hopkins University Press.

Yoo, John. 2006. *War by Other Means: An Insider's Account of the War on Terror.* New York: Atlantic Monthly Press.

Yost, David S. 1998. *NATO Transformed: The Alliance's New Roles in International Security.* Washington, D.C.: U.S. Institute of Peace Press.

Zakaria, Fareed. 1997. "The Rise of Illiberal Democracy." *Foreign Affairs* 76 (November–December): 22–43.

———. 2008. *The Post-American World.* New York: Norton.

Zaller, John R. 1992. *The Nature and Origins of Mass Opinion.* New York: Cambridge University Press.

Zaller, John R., and Dennis Chiu. 1996. "Government's Little Helper: U.S. Press Coverage of Foreign Policy Crises, 1945–1991." *Political Communication* 13 (4): 385–405.

Zegart, Amy B. 1999. *Flawed by Design: The Evolution of the CIA, JCS, and NSC.* Stanford: Stanford University Press.

———. 2005. "September 11 and the Adaptation Failure of U.S. Intelligence Agencies." *International Security* 29 (spring): 78–111.

———. 2009. *Spying Blind: The CIA, the FBI, and the Origins of 9/11.* Princeton: Princeton University Press.

Zinn, Howard. 1968. *Disobedience and Democracy: Nine Fallacies on Law and Order.* New York: Random House/Vintage.

Map Credits

All maps (see color map section at the front of the book) by International Mapping Associates, adapted from, or based on data from, the following sources:

Map 1 Nineteenth-Century European Empires and U.S. Continental Expansion

Thomas M. Magstadt, *An Empire If You Can Keep It: Power and Principle in American Foreign Policy* (Washington, D.C.: CQ Press, 2004), xviii, xix.

Map 2 Cold War Division of Europe

Bruce Bueno de Mesquita, *Principles of International Politics: People's Power, Preferences, and Perceptions,* 2nd ed. (Washington, D.C.: CQ Press, 2003), 197; Steven W. Hook and John Spanier, *American Foreign Policy Since World War II,* 18th ed. (Washington, D.C.: CQ Press, 2010), 30.

Map 3 Cold War Alliances with the United States

Organization of American States, www.oas.org; North Atlantic Treaty Organisation, www.nato.int; Steven W. Hook and John Spanier, *American Foreign Policy Since World War II,* 18th ed. (Washington, D.C.: CQ Press, 2010), 71.

Map 4 Post–Cold War U.S. Military Operations

Richard F. Grimmett, *Instances of Use of United States Armed Forces Abroad, 1798–2009,* CRS Report RL 32170 (Washington, D.C.: Congressional Research Service, January 27, 2010).

Map 5 Major Ongoing Conflicts in the Middle East and South Asia

Various primary and secondary sources.

Map 7 Department of Defense Regional Commands

U.S. Department of Defense, www.defenselink.mil/specials/unifiedcommand.

Map 8 NATO Expansion

Various primary and secondary sources, including North Atlantic Treaty Organization, "Enlargement," www.nato.int/issues/enlargement/index.html.

Map 9 Nuclear Threats and U.S. Defense Installations

"Department of Defense Base Structure Report: Fiscal Year 2009 Baseline (A Summary of DoD's Real Property Inventory)" (Washington, D.C.: Office of the Deputy Under Secretary of Defense, Installations and Environment), www.defense.gov/pubs/pdfs/2009Baseline.pdf.

Map 10 U.S. Foreign Economic Relations

U.S. Department of the Treasury, Office of Foreign Assets Control, www.ustreas.gov/offices/enforcement/ofac/programs; U.S. Department of Commerce, Census Bureau, *Foreign Trade Statistics,* www.census.gov/foreign-trade/statistics/index.html; Organisation for Economic Co-operation and Development, *Statistical Annex of the 2010 Development Co-operation Report* (Paris: OECD, 2010), www.oecd.org/document/9/0,3343,en_2649_34447_1893129_1_1_1_1,00.html.

Map 11 Freedom in the World, 2009

"Freedom in the World, 2010: The Annual Survey of Political Rights and Civil Liberties" (Washington, D.C.: Freedom House, 2010), www.freedomhouse.org/template.cfm?page=505.

Photo Credits

Author Citations Index

Note: tables, figures, and notes are indicated by *t, f,* and *n,* respectively.

Subject Index

Note: tables, figures, photos, and notes are indicated by *t, f, p,* and *n,* respectively.